WEB TECHNOLOGIES
A Computer Science Perspective

Jeffrey C. Jackson

Duquesne University

PEARSON

Prentice
Hall

Upper Saddle River, New Jersey 07458

Library of Congress Cataloging-in-Publication Data

Jackson, Jeffrey C.
    Web technologies : a computer science perspective / Jeffrey C. Jackson.
        p. cm.
    Includes bibliographical references and index.
    ISBN 0-13-185603-0
    1. Web services. 2. World wide web. 3. Internet programming. I. Title.
    TK5105.88813.J33 2006
    006.7′6—dc22

                                                                2006019529

Vice President and Editorial Director,
    ECS: *Marcia J. Horton*
Executive Editor: *Tracy Dunkelberger*
Associate Editor: *Carole Snyder*
Editorial Assistant: *Christianna Lee*
Executive Managing Editor: *Vince O'Brien*
Managing Editor: *Camille Trentacoste*
Production Editor: *Shelley L. Creager*
Director of Creative Services: *Paul Belfanti*

Creative Director: *Juan Lopez*
Art Director and Cover Manager: *Jayne Conte*
Managing Editor, AV Management and
    Production: *Patricia Burns*
Art Editor: *Gregory Dulles*
Manufacturing Manager, ESM: *Alexis Heydt-Long*
Manufacturing Buyer: *Lisa McDowell*
Executive Marketing Manager: *Robin O'Brien*
Marketing Assistant: *Mack Patterson*

© 2007 Pearson Education, Inc.
Pearson Prentice Hall
Pearson Education,Inc.
Upper Saddle River, NJ 07458

Pearson Prentice Hall™ is a trademark of Pearson Education, Inc.
All other tradmarks or product names are the property of their respective owners.

The author and publisher of this book have used their best efforts in preparing this book. These efforts include the development, research, and testing of the theories and programs to determine their effectiveness. The author and publisher make no warranty of any kind, expressed or implied, with regard to these programs or the documentation contained in this book. The author and publisher shall not be liable in any event for incidental or consequential damages in connection with, or arising out of, the furnishing, performance, or use of these programs.

Printed in the United States of America
10 9 8 7 6 5 4 3 2 1

ISBN 0-13-185603-0

Pearson Education Ltd., *London*
Pearson Education Australia Pty. Ltd., *Sydney*
Pearson Education Singapore, Pte. Ltd.
Pearson Education North Asia Ltd., *Hong Kong*
Pearson Education Canada, Inc., *Toronto*

Pearson Educación de Mexico, S.A. de C.V.
Pearson Education—Japan, *Tokyo*
Pearson Education Malaysia, Pte. Ltd.
Pearson Education, Inc., *Upper Saddle River,
    New Jersey*

Contents

Preface

PURPOSE AND SCOPE

This textbook is designed to provide a careful introduction to key technologies that have been developed as part of the birth and maturation of the World Wide Web. My goal is for students using this book to understand the Web at a fundamental level, much as students who learn assembly language understand computers at such a level. This level of understanding should provide a solid foundation on which to build as students subsequently learn about higher-level web development tools based on the technologies covered here. It should also prepare them well for further study of web technologies, both those that exist today and those that will be developed in the future.

The textbook is designed primarily for use in computer science (CS) courses, but other uses are mentioned later. I assume that the reader has a background roughly equivalent to the first three semesters of an undergraduate CS major. For instance, I expect well-developed skills in at least one programming language, familiarity with Java or the background and ability to learn it quickly from other sources (no Java knowledge is required until the last half of the book), and facility with basic data structures, especially trees.

I have chosen topics so as to treat the subject with reasonable breadth while also allowing for significant depth. With respect to breadth, the textbook focuses on technologies that are unlikely to receive detailed treatment in nonweb CS courses. Conversely, this book covers only lightly a number of topics that, while related to the Web, are not web technologies *per se* and are likely to be covered in other CS courses. For instance, while an appendix describes how to connect a Java-based web application to a database management system (DBMS), the book does not attempt to present SQL or database concepts. Other web-related CS topics that are covered narrowly—that is, primarily as they relate directly to web technologies—include computer networks, software engineering, and security. Finally, because of the emphasis on foundational technologies that are fundamentally web-related, higher-level development tools (such as Macromedia® Dreamweaver® software) and content presentation tools (such as Macromedia® Flash® software) are not covered.

Another scope consideration arises from the fact that, especially when it comes to server-side software, several web technologies provide similar capabilities, forming a technology class. For example, the ASP.NET, ColdFusion®, JSP™, and PHP technologies all occupy the same server-side software niche, and each is currently in widespread use. Even if time and space allowed all of these technologies to be covered in some depth, I suspect that most students would tire of seeing similar concepts dressed in several different sets of clothes. So I have chosen instead to cover one member of each class in some detail and also to provide a high-level comparison of the example technology with other widely used members of the class. It seems reasonable to expect that a student who understands one technology well will be able to quickly adapt to conceptually related technologies as the need arises in the future.

Along these same lines, for each technology class covered I have chosen to use a Java-based representative as the example for the class. Several factors were significant in this choice. The Java-based technologies covered in this textbook are available for free download and run on all major operating systems. Also, it seems that most CS students today know Java or a closely related language, so using Java-based software should maximize the time that these students can spend learning web technologies themselves as opposed to learning programming languages. Finally, the significant use of Java-based web technologies in support of many major Web sites would seem to imply that knowledge of these technologies may be directly beneficial to many students when they join real-world development environments.

By limiting its scope as described, my hope is that this book will provide readers with a depth of understanding of foundational web technologies and concepts that will enable them to develop high-quality web applications and avoid many of the common mistakes made by less-knowledgeable web developers. Furthermore, my expectation is that students using this book will be able to quickly learn and adapt to new web technologies as they emerge in the future. I also hope that many of them will be well prepared for further research on core web technologies and to eventually contribute to the development of new technologies. In fact, one of my goals is to provide enough background so that anyone who has read this book should be able to subsequently read and understand (with a reasonable amount of effort) the primary reference sources for the standards and technologies covered. From an instructional point of view, this depth of coverage also allows the instructor to assign some challenging and interesting homework and projects.

While the textbook adopts a CS perspective, many courses taught outside CS departments (for example, in information systems/technologies programs) cover similar topics and may benefit from using this book as either a primary or a reference text. Furthermore, I believe that the book may also be helpful to web development professionals who have not had much formal training in web technologies. In fact, I initially taught myself about the Web on the job at a dot-com, and this book to some extent represents "what I wish I'd known."

FEATURES

Some of the features of the textbook are:

- Detailed coverage of a wide spectrum of web technologies, including:
  Hypertext Transport Protocol (HTTP)
  Extensible HyperText Markup Language (XHTML)
  Cascading Style Sheets (CSS)
  JavaScript^{TM} language
  Document Object Model (DOM)
  Java servlets
  Extensible Markup Language (XML)
  XML namespaces
  Simple API for XML (SAX)
  XML Path Language (XPath)
  Extensible Stylesheet Language Transformations (XSLT)
  Asynchronous JavaScript and XML (Ajax)

JavaServer Pages™ (JSP) technology, including JavaBeans™ object usage
SOAP
Web Services Definition Language (WSDL)
XML Schema
Java API for XML Remote Procedure Call (JAX-RPC)
- Brief overviews of related technologies, including:
Common Gateway Interface (CGI)
Active Server Pages (ASP) and ASP.NET
PHP
ColdFusion technology
- Focus on standards, both formal and de facto.
- Detailed coverage of common features in web servers and browsers, using Apache Tomcat and Mozilla™ software as representative examples.
- Use of student-accessible software, so lab setup may not be necessary:
Software discussed and used in examples is available for free download and runs on multiple platforms.
Detailed instructions are provided for obtaining, installing, and operating all software.
- Detailed instructions for running server-side software using either the file system or a database management system for persistent storage.
- Ongoing "My Own Blog" case study that illustrates how various technologies can be employed together to build a simple blogging application.
- Extensive use of examples. Virtually every concept covered is illustrated by a concrete example. Examples are often short, providing an uncluttered demonstration of the concept. Larger examples are also given to illustrate interactions and provide context and motivation.
- Three types of end-of-chapter problems:
Exercises: short-answer problems that test students' understanding of content (and, in some cases, their analytical skills).
Research and exploration: problems that either direct students to reference materials to learn more about selected topics or ask them to perform various experiments, giving them hands-on experience with topics covered.
Projects: generally multipart problems that provide instructors with options, from having students add a small function to code provided by the instructor to writing a fairly extensive application (which may be suitable for assignment to a team of students).
- Comprehensive bibliography of authoritative reference materials, all of which are freely available on the Web. (Bibliographic references appear in square brackets, e.g., [IANA-PORTS].)
- Historical perspective sections, providing context for several key web technologies.

TEXTBOOK PLAN AND COURSE SEQUENCES

The first three chapters are about nonprogramming technologies that are fundamental to understanding communication between web browsers and servers as well as how information is displayed by browsers. The next two chapters cover software development on the client (browser) side. The final four chapters focus on server-side software development.

The progression is a natural one, but the material is covered in a way that allows significant flexibility in the order of coverage. Chapters 1 and 2 should normally be covered first. The next chapter covered could be either Chapter 3 (some of which is a prerequisite for Chapter 5), Chapter 4 (which is a prerequisite for Chapter 5) or Chapter 6 (which is a prerequisite for the final three chapters). The material on Ajax (Section 7.4) and DOM-based XML processing (Section 7.5) depends on Chapter 5 (and therefore on Chapter 4), but otherwise the material in the final four chapters might be taught before Chapters 3 through 5. I suggest teaching the final four chapters in order, as each chapter depends on the preceding one to some extent.

Each chapter is arranged so that the later sections tend to be those that can be covered briefly or even skipped entirely on a first pass through the material. Similarly, within the longer sections it is generally the case that earlier information is more critical than that found later in the section. My own approach, which seemed to work well when classroom-testing early versions of this textbook, was to allocate a fixed length of time to each chapter (slightly more than one week for each of the first two chapters, one and one-half to two weeks for each of the remaining chapters), start at the beginning of the chapter, and cover as much material as the students could reasonably handle within that time. An alternative would be to allocate as much time as needed for full coverage of selected chapters while skimming material in other chapters. The chapter dependencies mentioned in the preceding paragraph should provide guidance if this approach is adopted; for example, based on these dependences, Chapter 3 might make a good candidate for abbreviated coverage.

Source Files

Source files for most of the examples described in this book are available online at `http://www.prenhall.com/jackson`.

Acknowledgments

This book grew from notes I prepared for a course I taught in the spring of 2002. Several students in that course, especially Brian Blackburn, Matt Hershberger, Alex Mezhinsky, Jon Stanich, and Amy Ulinski, encouraged me to turn those notes into a textbook. If I had known then how much work this would entail, I doubt that I would have started! But I am certain that I would not have begun without their encouraging words. Matt's work with me during a subsequent independent study was also a tremendous help. I also appreciate the comments from a number of students on a preliminary version of this textbook, especially Matt Caporali, Dan Dressler, Bobbie Johnson, and Steve Schwab. Dave Eland, a former professor and colleague without whom I would almost certainly not be a computer scientist, also provided useful feedback on an early manuscript.

I learned a great deal about developing software for the Web while working off and on for Essential Surfing Gear, Inc. from 1996 through 2000. I'm grateful to Merrick Furst for providing both that opportunity and the freedom to research a variety of web technologies, and I thank all of my former colleagues for making esgear such a stimulating and fun place to work. I also appreciate my "day job" employer, Duquesne University, and my former department chairman, Tom Keagy, for being supportive of my work with esgear, first as a consultant and ultimately full time during a leave of absence from Duquesne. In addition, I greatly appreciate the later sabbatical from Duquesne that allowed me to write the bulk of this book.

Jan Luehe of Sun Microsystems provided the fix given in Appendix A for running a secure server under JWSDP 1.3. Jan also helped to secure the agreement of the JWSDP product team to keep JWSDP 1.3 available for download so that readers of this book should be able to run the examples provided for the foreseeable future.

Several folks at Prentice Hall of course deserve mention. Acquisition editors Kate Hargett and Tracy Dunkelberger along with their assistants Mike Giacobbe and Christianna Lee were extremely helpful in getting the project started and providing reviewer feedback. Carole Snyder guided my work on supplemental materials and also helped keep me in the loop with respect to where the book was in the development process. Marcia Horton was very patient in working out contract details with me, and Barrie Reinhold did a masterful job producing marketing materials. The production staffs, headed by Camille Trentacoste at Prentice Hall and Shelley Creager at Techbooks, were professional and supportive. Thanks especially to copy editor Joseph Fineman for making me sound like a better writer than I am.

My immediate family—Cindy, Rebecca, Peter, Emily, and Benjamin—have all been wonderfully understanding and supportive. Benjamin was especially helpful, providing some of the graphics. Many other extended-family members and friends have also provided encouragement. I hope that those whose names don't appear here will know that I do appreciate what they've done.

the United States and/or other countries. Screen shots of Microsoft products reprinted by permission from Microsoft Corporation.

Mosaic^{TM} and NCSA Mosaic^{TM} are proprietary trademarks of the University of Illinois.

MySQL$^®$ is a registered trademark of MySQL AB in the United States, the European Union and other countries.

Netscape$^®$ and Netscape Navigator$^®$ are registered trademarks of Netscape Communications Corporation in the United States and other countries. LiveWire^{TM} is also a trademark of Netscape Communications Corporation, which may be registered in other countries.

OMG^{TM} and OMG Interface Definition Language (IDL)^{TM} are either registered trademarks or trademarks of Object Management Group, Inc. in the United States and/or other countries.

Opera^{TM} is a trademark of Opera Software ASA.

Sun^{TM}, J2EE^{TM}, J2SE^{TM}, Java^{TM}, JavaBeans^{TM}, Javadoc^{TM}, JavaScript^{TM}, JavaServer Pages^{TM}, JDBC^{TM}, JDK^{TM}, JSP^{TM}, NetBeans^{TM}, SOAP with Attachments API for Java^{TM}, and Sun Java^{TM} are trademarks or registered trademarks of Sun Microsystems, Inc. in the U.S. or other countries.

Times New Roman$^®$ is a trademark of The Monotype Corporation registered in the U.S. Patent and Trademark Office and may be registered in certain other jurisdictions.

Unicode is a registered trademark of Unicode, Inc.

UNIX$^®$ is a registered trademark in the United States and other countries, licensed exclusively through X/Open Company Ltd.

W3C$^®$ is a trademark (registered in numerous countries) and P3P$^®$ is a registered trademark of the World Wide Web Consortium; marks of W3C are registered and held by its host institutions MIT, ERCIM, and Keio.

WS-I and Web Services-Interoperability Organization are trademarks of the Web Services-Interoperability Organization in the United States and other countries.

All other trademarks are property of their respective owners.

CHAPTER 1

Web Essentials
Clients, Servers, and Communication

The essential elements of the World Wide Web are the web browsers used to surf the Web, the server systems used to supply information to these browsers, and the computer networks supporting browser-server communication. This chapter will provide an overview of all of these elements. We'll begin by considering communication, with a focus on the Internet and some of its key communication protocols, especially the Hypertext Transport Protocol used for the bulk of web communication. The chapter also reviews features common to modern web browsers and introduces web servers, the software applications that provide web pages to browsers.

1.1 The Internet

"So, you're into computers. Maybe you can answer a question I've had for a while: I hear people talk about the Internet, and I'm not sure exactly what it is, or where it came from. Can you tell me?"

You may have already been asked a question like this. If not, if you work with computers long enough, you'll probably hear it at least once in your career, and more likely several times. At this point in your career, you may even be curious about the Internet yourself: you use it a lot, but what exactly is it?

The Internet traces its roots to a project of the U.S. Department of Defense's then-named Advanced Research Projects Agency, or ARPA. The ARPANET project was intended to support DoD research on computer networking. As this project began in the late 1960s, there had been only a few small experimental networks providing communication between geographically dispersed computers from different manufacturers running different operating systems. The purpose of ARPANET was to create a larger such network, both in order to electronically connect DoD-sponsored researchers and in order to experiment with and develop tools for heterogeneous computer networking.

The ARPANET computer network was launched in 1969 and by year's end consisted of four computers at four sites running four different operating systems. ARPANET grew steadily, but because it was restricted to DoD-funded organizations and was a research project, it was never large. By 1983, when many ARPANET nodes were split off to form a separate network called MILNET, there were only 113 nodes in the entire network, and these were primarily at universities and other organizations involved in DoD-sponsored research.

Despite the relatively small number of machines actually on the ARPANET, the benefits of networking were becoming known to a wide audience. For example, e-mail was available on ARPANET beginning in 1972, and it soon became an extremely popular application for those who had ARPANET access. It wasn't long before other networks were being built, both internationally and regionally within the United States. The regional U.S. networks were often cooperative efforts between universities. As one example, SURAnet (Southeastern University Research Association Network) was organized by the University of Maryland beginning in 1982 and eventually included essentially all of the major universities and research institutions in the southeastern United States. Another of these networks, CSNET (Computer Science Network), was partially funded by the U.S. National Science Foundation (NSF) to aid scientists at universities without ARPANET access, laying the groundwork for future network developments that we'll say more about in a moment.

While these other networks were springing up, the ARPANET project continued to fund research on networking. Several of the most widely used Internet protocols—including the File Transfer Protocol (FTP) and Simple Mail Transfer Protocol (SMTP), which underlie many of the Internet's file transfer and e-mail operations, respectively—were initially developed under ARPANET. But perhaps most crucial to the emergence of the Internet as we know it was the development of the TCP/IP (Transmission Control Protocol/Internet Protocol) communication protocol. TCP/IP was designed to be used for host-to-host communication both within *local area networks* (that is, networks of computers that are typically in close proximity to one another, such as within a building) and between networks. ARPANET switched from using an earlier protocol to TCP/IP during 1982. At around the same time, an ARPA Internet was created, allowing computers on some outside networks such as CSNET to communicate via TCP/IP with computers on the ARPANET.

A "connection" from CSNET to the ARPA Internet often meant that a modem connection was made from one computer to another for the purpose of sending along an e-mail message. This form of communication was asynchronous. That is, the e-mail might be delayed some time before it was actually delivered, which precluded interactive communication of any type. Furthermore, each institution connecting to CSNET was largely on its own in determining how it was going to connect to the network. At first, many institutions connected through the so-called PhoneNet (modem) approach for passing e-mail messages. This generally involved long distance calls, and the expense of these calls could be a problem. Other options, such as leasing telephone lines for dedicated use, could be even more expensive. It was obvious to everyone that the CSNET institutions were still not enjoying all the potential benefits of the ARPA Internet.

Beginning in 1985, the NSF began work on a new network based on TCP/IP, called NSFNET. One of the primary goals of this network was to connect the NSF's new regional supercomputing centers. But it was also decided that regional networks should be able to connect to NSFNET, so that the NSFNET would provide a *backbone* through which other networks could interconnect synchronously. Figure 1.1 shows the geographic distribution of the six supercomputer centers connected by the early NSFNET backbone. Regional networks connecting to the backbone included SURAnet as well as NYSERNet (with primary connections through the Ithaca center), JvNCnet (with primary connection through the Princeton center) and SDSCnet (with primary connection through the San Diego center). In addition, many universities and other organizations connected to the NSFNET backbone either directly or through agreements with other institutions that had NSFNET access, either directly or indirectly.

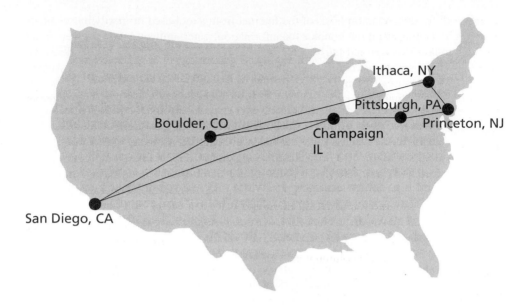

FIGURE 1.1 Geographic distribution of and connections between nodes on the early NSFNET backbone.

The original backbone operated at only 56 kbit/s, the maximum speed of a home dial-up line today. But at the time the primary network traffic was still textual, so this was a reasonable starting point. Once operational, the number of machines connected to NSFNET grew quickly, in part because the NSF directly or indirectly provided significant support—both technically and with monetary grants—to educational and research organizations that wished to connect. The backbone rate was upgraded to 1.5 Mbit/s (T1) in 1988 and then to 45 Mbit/s (T3) in 1991. Furthermore, the backbone was expanded to directly include several research networks in addition to the supercomputer centers, making it that much easier for sites near these research networks to connect to the NSFNET. In 1988, networks in Canada and France were connected to NSFNET; in each succeeding year for the remaining seven years of NSFNET's existence, networks from 10 or so new countries were added per year.

NSFNET quickly supplanted ARPANET, which was officially decommissioned in 1990. At this point, NSFNET was at the center of the *Internet*, that is, the collection of computer networks connected via the public backbone and communicating across networks using TCP/IP. This same year, commercial Internet dial-up access was first offered. But the NSFNET terms of usage stipulated that purely commercial traffic was not to be carried over the backbone: the purpose of the Internet was still, in the eyes of the NSF, research and education.

Increasingly, though, it became clear that there could be significant benefits to allowing commercial traffic on the Internet as well. One of the arguments for allowing commercial traffic was economic: commercial traffic would increase network usage, leading to reduced unit costs through economies of scale. This in turn would provide a less expensive network for research and educational purposes. Whatever the motivation, the restriction on commercial traffic was rescinded in 1991, spurring further growth of the Internet and laying the groundwork for the metamorphosis of the Internet from a tool used primarily by scientists at research institutions to the conduit for information, entertainment, and commerce that we know today. This also led fairly quickly to the NSF being able to leave its role as the operator of the Internet backbone in the United States. Those responsibilities were assumed by private telecommunication firms in 1995. These firms are paid by other firms, such as some of the larger Internet service providers (ISPs), who connect directly with the Internet backbone. These ISPs, in turn, are paid by their users, which may include smaller ISPs as well as end users.

In summary, the Internet is the collection of computers that can communicate with one another using TCP/IP over an open, global communications network. Before describing how the World Wide Web is related to the Internet, we'll take a closer look at several of the key Internet protocols. This will be helpful in understanding the place of the Web within the wider Internet.

1.2   Basic Internet Protocols

Before covering specific protocols, it may be helpful to explain exactly what the term "protocol" means in the context of networked communication. A computer *communication protocol* is a detailed specification of how communication between two computers will be carried out in order to serve some purpose. For example, as we will learn, the Internet Protocol specifies both the high-level behavior of software implementing the protocol and the low-level details such as the specific fields of information that will be contained in a communication message, the order in which these fields will appear, the number of bits in each field, and how these bits should be interpreted. We are primarily interested in a high-level view of general-purpose Internet protocols in this section; we'll look at a key Web protocol, HTTP, in more detail in the next section.

1.2.1   TCP/IP

Since TCP/IP is fundamental to the definition of the Internet, it's natural to begin our study of Internet protocols with these protocols. Yes, I said protocols (plural), because although so far I have treated TCP/IP as if it were a single protocol, TCP and IP are actually two different protocols. The reason that they are often treated as one is that the bulk of the services we associate with the Internet—e-mail, Web browsing, file downloads, accessing remote databases—are built on top of both the TCP and IP protocols. But in reality, only one of these protocols—IP, the Internet Protocol—is fundamental to the definition of the Internet. So we'll begin our study of Internet protocols with IP.

A key element of IP is the *IP address*, which is simply a 32-bit number. At any given moment, each device on the Internet has one or more IP addresses associated with it (although the device associated with a given address may change over time). IP addresses are normally written as a sequence of four decimal numbers separated by periods (called "dots"), as in 192.0.34.166. Each decimal number represents one byte of the IP address.

The function of IP software is to transfer data from one computer (the *source*) to another computer (the *destination*). When an application on the source computer wants to send information to a destination, the application calls IP software on the source machine and provides it with data to be transferred along with an IP address for each of the source and destination computers. The IP software running on the source creates a *packet*, which is a sequence of bits representing the data to be transferred along with the source and destination IP addresses and some other header information, such as the length of the data. If the destination computer is on the same local network as the source, then the IP software will send the packet to the destination directly via this network. If the destination is on another network, the IP software will send the packet to a *gateway*, which is a device that is connected to the source computer's network as well as to at least one other network. The gateway will select a computer on one of the other networks to which it is attached and send the packet on to that computer. This process will continue, with the packet going through perhaps a dozen or more *hops*, until the packet reaches the destination computer. IP software on that computer will receive the packet and pass its data up to an application that is waiting for the data.

For example, returning to the Internet as it existed in the mid-1980s, suppose that a computer in the SURAnet network (say, at the University of Delaware) was a packet source and that a computer in a network directly connected to the NSFNET backbone at San Diego (say, at the San Diego Supercomputer Center) was the destination. The IP packet would first go through the Delaware local computer network to a gateway device connecting the Delaware network to SURAnet. The gateway device would then send the packet on to another SURAnet gateway device (how this gateway is chosen is discussed later in this subsection) until it reached a gateway on the NSFNET backbone at Ithaca (the primary SURAnet connection to the NSFNET backbone). As there was no direct connection from Ithaca to San Diego in the NSFNET at the time (Figure 1.1), the packet would need to go through at least one other gateway on the NSFNET backbone before reaching the San Diego node. From there, it would be passed to the San Diego Supercomputer Center local network, and from there on to the destination machine.

The sequence of computers that a packet travels through from source to destination is known as its *route*. How does each computer choose the next computer in the route for a packet? A separate protocol (the current standard is BGP-4, the Border Gateway Protocol) is used to pass network connectivity information between gateways so that each can choose a good next hop for each packet it receives.

IP software also adds some error detection information (a *checksum*) to each packet it creates, so that if a packet is corrupted during transmission, this can usually be detected by the recipient. The IP standard calls for IP software to simply discard any corrupted packets. Thus, IP-based communication is unreliable: packets can be lost. Obviously, IP alone is not a particularly good form of communication for many Internet applications.

TCP, the Transmission Control Protocol, is a higher-level protocol that extends IP to provide additional functionality, including reliable communication based on the concept of a *connection*. A connection is established between TCP software running on two machines by one of the machines (let's call it A) sending a connection-request message via IP to the other (B). That is, the IP message contains a message conforming to the TCP protocol and representing a TCP connection request. If the connection is accepted by B, then B returns a message to A requesting a connection in the other direction. If A responds affirmatively, then the connection is established. Notice that this means that A and B can both send messages to one another at the same time; this is known as *full duplex* communication. When A and

B are both done sending messages to one another (or at least done for the time being), a similar set of three messages is used to close the connection.

Once a connection has been established, TCP provides reliable data transmission by demanding an *acknowledgment* for each packet it sends via IP. Essentially, the software sets a timer after sending each packet. The TCP software on the receiving side sends a packet containing an acknowledgment for every TCP-based packet it receives that passes the checksum test. If the TCP software sending a packet does not receive an acknowledgment packet before its timer expires, then it resends the packet and restarts the timer.

Another important feature that TCP adds to IP is the concept of a *port*. The port concept allows TCP to be used to communicate with many different applications on a machine. For example, a machine connected to the Internet may run a mail server for users on its local network, a file download server, and also a server that allows users to log in to the machine and execute commands from remote locations. As illustrated in Figure 1.2 (which ignores connections and acknowledgments for simplicity), such a server application will make a call to the TCP software on its system to request that any incoming TCP connection requests that specify a certain port number as part of the TCP/IP message be sent to the application. For example, a mail server conforming with SMTP will typically ask TCP to listen for requests to port 25. If at a later time an IP message is received by the machine running the mail server application and that IP message contains a TCP message with port

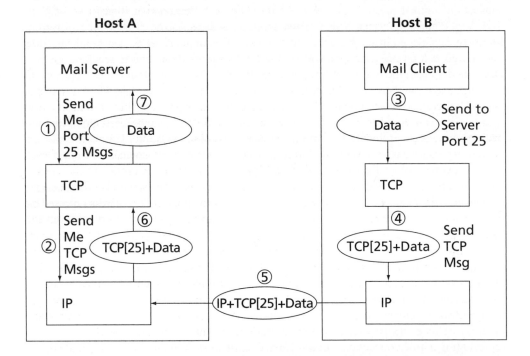

FIGURE 1.2 Simplified view of communication using TCP/IP. Boxes represent software applications on the respective host machines, ovals represent data transmitted between applications, and circled numbers denote the time order of operations. "TCP[25]" represents a TCP header containing 25 as the port number.

25 indicated in its header, then the data contained within the TCP message will be returned to the mail server application. Such an IP message could be generated by a mail client calling on TCP software on another system, as illustrated on the right side of the figure.

Though the connection between port numbers and applications is managed individually by every machine on the Internet, certain broadly useful applications (such as e-mail over SMTP) have had port numbers assigned to them by the Internet Assigned Numbers Authority (IANA) [IANA-PORTS]. These port numbers, in the range 0–1023, can usually be requested only by applications that are run by the system at boot-up or that are run by a user with administrative permissions on the system. Other possible port numbers, from 1024 to 65535, can generally be used by the first application on a system that requests the port.

TCP and IP provide many other functions, such as splitting long messages into shorter ones for transport over the Internet and transparently reassembling them on the receiving side. But this brief overview of TCP/IP covers the essential concepts for our purposes.

1.2.2 UDP, DNS, and Domain Names

UDP (User Datagram Protocol) is an alternative protocol to TCP that also builds on IP. The main feature that UDP adds to IP is the port concept that we have just seen in TCP. However, it does not provide the two-way connection or guaranteed delivery of TCP. Its advantage over TCP is speed for simple tasks. For example, if all you want to do is send a short message to another computer, you're expecting a single short response message, and you can handle resending if you don't receive the response within a reasonable amount of time, then UDP is probably a good alternative to TCP.

One Internet application that is often run using UDP rather than TCP is the Domain Name Service (DNS). While every device on the Internet has an IP address such as 192.0.34.166, humans generally find it easier to refer to machines by names, such as www.example.org. DNS provides a mechanism for mapping back and forth between IP addresses and host names. Basically, there are a number of DNS servers on the Internet, each listening through UDP software to a port (port 53 if the server is following the current IANA assignment). When a computer on the Internet needs DNS services—for example, to convert a host name such as www.example.org to a corresponding IP address—it uses the UDP software running on its system to send a UDP message to one of these DNS servers, requesting the IP address. If all goes well, this server will then send back a UDP message containing the IP address. Recall that it took three messages just to get a TCP connection set up, so the UDP approach is much more efficient for sporadic DNS queries. (UDP is sometimes referred to as a lightweight communication protocol and TCP as a heavyweight protocol, at least in comparison with UDP. In general, the terms *lightweight* and *heavyweight* in computer science are used to describe alternative software solutions to some problem, with the lightweight solution having less functionality but also less overhead.)

Internet host names consist of a sequence of *labels* separated by dots. The final label in a host name is a *top-level domain*. There are two standard types of top-level domain: generic (such as .com, .edu, .org, and .biz) and country-code (such as .de, .il, and .mx). The top-level domain names are assigned by the Internet Corporation for Assigned Names and

Numbers (ICANN), a private nonprofit organization formed to take over technical Internet functions that were originally funded by the U.S. government.

Each top-level domain is divided into subdomains (second-level domains), which may in turn be further divided, and so on. The assignment of second-level domains within each top-level domain is performed (for a fee) by a *registry operator* selected by ICANN. The owner of a second-level domain can then further divide that domain into subdomains, and so on. Ultimately, the subdomains of a domain are individual computers. Such a subdomain, consisting of a local host name followed by a domain name (typically consisting of at least two labels) is sometimes called a *fully qualified domain name* for the computer. For example, www.example.org is a fully qualified domain name for a host with local name www that belongs to the example second-level domain of the org top-level domain.

Some user-level tools are available that allow you to query the Internet DNS. For example, on most systems the nslookup command can be typed at a command prompt (see *Appendix A* for instructions on obtaining a command prompt on some systems) in order to find the IP address given a fully qualified domain name or vice versa. Typical usage of nslookup is illustrated by the following (user input is italicized):

```
C:\>nslookup www.example.org
Server: slave9.dns.stargate.net
Address: 209.166.161.121

Name: www.example.org
Address: 192.0.34.166

C:\>nslookup 192.0.34.166
Server: slave9.dns.stargate.net
Address: 209.166.161.121

Name: www.example.com
Address: 192.0.34.166
```

The first two lines following the command line identify the qualified name and IP address of the DNS server that is providing the domain name information that follows. Also notice that a single IP address can be associated with multiple domain names. In this example, both www.example.org and www.example.com are associated with the IP address 192.0.34.166. A lookup that specifies an IP address, such as the second lookup in the example, is sometimes referred to as a *reverse lookup*. As shown, even if multiple qualified names are associated with an IP address, only one of the names will be returned by a reverse lookup. This is known as the *canonical name* for the host; all other names are considered *aliases*. The reverse lookup in the example indicates that www.example.com is the canonical name for the host with IP address 192.0.34.166.

1.2.3 Higher-Level Protocols

The following analogy may help to relate the computer networking concepts described in Sections 1.2.1 and 1.2.2 with something more familiar: the telephone network. The Internet is like the physical telephone network: it provides the basic communications infrastructure. UDP is like calling a number and leaving a message rather than actually speaking with the intended recipient. DNS is the Internet version of directory assistance, associating names with numbers. TCP is roughly equivalent to placing a phone call and having the other party answer: you now have a connection and are able to communicate back and forth.

However, in the cases of both TCP and a phone call, different protocols can be used to communicate once a connection has been established. For example, when making a telephone call, the parties must agree on the language(s) that will be used to communicate. Beyond that, there are also conventions that are followed to decide which party will speak first, how the parties will take turns speaking, and so on. Furthermore, different conventions may be used in different contexts: I answer the phone differently at home ("Hello") than I do at work ("Mathematics and Computer Science Department, this is Jeff Jackson"), for example.

Similarly, a variety of *higher-level protocols* are used to communicate once a TCP connection has been established. SMTP and FTP, mentioned earlier, are two examples of widely used higher-level protocols that are used to communicate over TCP connections. SMTP supports transfer of e-mail between different e-mail servers, while FTP is used for transferring files between machines. Another higher-level TCP protocol, Telnet, is used to execute commands typed into one computer on a remote computer. As we will see, Telnet can also be used to communicate directly (via keyboard entries) with some TCP-based applications. As described earlier, which protocol will be used to communicate over a TCP connection is normally determined by the port number used to establish the connection.

The primary TCP-based protocol used for communication between web servers and browsers is called the Hypertext Transport Protocol (HTTP). In some sense, just as IP is a key component in the definition of the Internet, HTTP is a key component in the definition of the World Wide Web. So, before getting into details of HTTP, let's briefly consider what the Web is, and in particular how HTTP figures in its definition.

1.3   The World Wide Web

Public sharing of information has been a part of the Internet since its early days. For example, the Usenet newsgroup service began in 1979 and provided a means of "posting" information that could be read by users on other systems with the appropriate software (the Google Groups™ Usenet discussion forum at `http://www.google.com` provides one of several modern interfaces to Usenet). Large files were (and still are) often shared by running an FTP server application that allowed any user to transfer the files from their origin machine to the user's machine. The first Internet chat software in widespread use, Internet Relay Chat (IRC), provided both public and private chat facilities.

However, as the amount of information publicly available on the Internet grew, the need to locate information also grew. Various technologies for supporting information management and search on the Internet were developed. Some of the more popular information management technologies in the early 1990s were Gopher information servers, which provided a simple hierarchical view of documents; the Wide Area Information System

(WAIS) system for indexing and retrieving information; and the ARCHIE tool for searching online information archives accessible via FTP.

The World Wide Web also was developed in the early 1990s (we'll learn more about its development in the next chapter), and for a while was just one among several Internet information management technologies. To understand why the Web supplanted the other technologies, it will be helpful to know a bit about the mechanics of the Web and other Internet information management technologies. All of these technologies consist of (at least) two types of software: server and client. An Internet-connected computer that wishes to provide information to other Internet systems must run *server* software, and a system that wishes to access the information provided by servers must run *client* software (for the Web, the client software is normally a web browser). The server and client applications communicate over the Internet by following a communication protocol built on top of TCP/IP.

The protocol used by the Web, as just noted, is the Hypertext Transport Protocol, HTTP. As we will learn in the next section, this is a rather generic protocol that for the most part supports a client requesting a document from a server and the server returning the requested document. This generic nature of HTTP gives it the advantage of somewhat more flexibility than is present in the protocols used by WAIS and Gopher.

Perhaps a bigger advantage for the Web is the type of information communicated. Most web pages are written using the Hypertext Markup Language, HTML, which along with HTTP is a fundamental web technology. HTML pages can contain the familiar web links (technically called *hyperlinks*) to other documents on the Web. While certain Gopher pages could also contain links, normal Gopher documents were plain text. WAIS and ARCHIE provided no direct support for links. In addition to hyperlinks, modern versions of HTML also provide extensive page layout facilities, including support for inline graphics, which (as you might guess) has added significantly to the commercial appeal of the Web.

The World Wide Web, then, can be defined in much the same way as the Internet. While the Internet can be thought of as the collection of machines that are globally connected via IP, the World Wide Web can be informally defined as the collection of machines (web servers) on the Internet that provide information via HTTP, and particularly those that provide HTML documents.

Given this overview, we'll now spend some time looking closely at HTTP.

1.3.1 Hypertext Transport Protocol

HTTP is a form of communication protocol, in particular a detailed specification of how web clients and servers should communicate. The basic structure of HTTP communication follows what is known as a *request–response* model. Specifically, the protocol dictates that an HTTP interaction is initiated by a client sending a request message to the server; the server is then expected to generate a response message. The format of the request and response messages is dictated by HTTP. HTTP does not dictate the network protocol to be used to send these messages, but does expect that the request and response are both sent within a TCP-style connection between the client and the server. So most HTTP implementations send these messages using TCP.

Let's relate this to what happens when you browse the Web. Figure 1.3 shows a browser window in which I typed `http://www.example.org` in the Location bar (note that this is technically not a web site address and therefore might not be operational by the time you read this). When I pressed the Enter key after typing this address, the browser created a message conforming to the HTTP protocol, used DNS to obtain an IP address for `www.example.org`, created a TCP connection with the machine at the IP address obtained, sent the HTTP message over this TCP connection, and received back a message containing the information that is shown displayed in the *client area* of the browser (the portion of the browser containing the information received from the web server).

A nice feature of HTTP is that these request and response messages often consist entirely of plain text in a fairly readable form. An HTTP request message consists of a start line followed by a message header and optionally a message body. The start line always consists of printable ASCII characters, and the header normally does as well. What's more, the HTTP response (or at least most of it) is often also a stream of printable characters. So, to see an example of HTTP in action, let's connect to the same web server shown in Figure 1.3 using Telnet. This can be done on most modern systems by entering `telnet` at a command prompt. Specifically, we will Telnet to port 80, the IANA standard port for HTTP web servers, type in an HTTP request message corresponding to the Internet address entered into the browser before, and view the response (the request consists of the three lines beginning with the GET and ending with a blank line, and user input is again italicized):

```
$ telnet www.example.org 80
Trying 192.0.34.166...
Connected to www.example.com (192.0.34.166).
Escape character is '^]'.
GET / HTTP/1.1
Host: www.example.org

HTTP/1.1 200 OK
Date: Thu, 09 Oct 2003 20:30:49 GMT
```

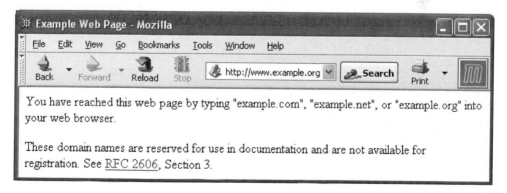

FIGURE 1.3 Web browser displaying information received in an HTTP response message received after the browser sent an HTTP request message to a web server. The content shown is subject to copyright and used by permission of the Internet Assigned Numbers Authority (IANA).

```
Server: Apache/1.3.27 (Unix)  (Red-Hat/Linux)
Last-Modified: Wed, 08 Jan 2003 23:11:55 GMT
ETag: "3f80f-1b6-3e1cb03b"
Accept-Ranges: bytes
Content-Length: 438
Connection: close
Content-Type: text/html

<HTML>
<HEAD>
<TITLE>Example Web Page</TITLE>
</HEAD>
<body>
<p>You have reached this web page by typing &quot;example.com&quot;,
  &quot;example.net&quot;,
  or &quot;example.org&quot; into your web browser.</p>
<p>These domain names are reserved for use in documentation and are
  not available for registration. See
  <a href="http://www.rfc-editor.org/rfc/rfc2606.txt">RFC 2606</a>,
  Section 3.</p>
</BODY>
</HTML>
```

The response message in this case begins with the line

```
HTTP/1.1 200 OK
```

which is known as the *status line* of the response, and continues to the end of the example. The portion of the response between the status line and the first blank line following it is the header of the response. The part following this blank line—from <HTML> down—is the body of the response and is written using the HTML language, which will be discussed in the next chapter. For now, just notice that this body contains the information displayed by the browser.

Now that we have an idea of HTTP's basic structure, we'll look at some details of request and response messages.

1.4 HTTP Request Message

1.4.1 Overall Structure

Every HTTP request message has the same basic structure:

    Start line
    Header field(s) (one or more)
    Blank line
    Message body (optional)

The start line in the example request in Section 1.3.1 was

```
GET / HTTP/1.1
```

Every start line consists of three parts, with a single space used to separate adjacent parts:

1. Request method
2. Request-URI portion of web address
3. HTTP version

We'll cover each of these parts of the start line—in reverse order—in the next several subsections, then move on to the header fields and body.

1.4.2   HTTP Version

The initial version of HTTP was referred to as HTTP/0.9, and the first Internet RFC (Request for Comments; see the References section (Section 1.9) for more on RFCs) regarding HTTP described HTTP/1.0. In 1997, HTTP/1.1 was formally defined, and is currently an Internet Draft Standard [RFC-2616]. Essentially all operational browsers and servers support HTTP/1.1, including the server that generated the example in Section 1.3.1 (as indicated by the HTTP version portion of the status line). We will therefore focus on HTTP/1.1 in this chapter. If a new version of HTTP is developed in the future, the new standard defining this version will specify a new value for the version portion of the start line (assuming that the new standard has the same start line). The version string for HTTP/1.1 must appear in the start line exactly as shown, with all capital letters and no embedded white space.

1.4.3   Request-URI

The second part of the start line is known as the *Request-URI*. The concatenation of the string http://, the value of the Host header field (www.example.org, in this example), and the Request-URI (/ in this example) forms a string known as a *Uniform Resource Identifier* (URI). A URI is an identifier that is intended to be associated with a particular resource (such as a web page or graphics image) on the World Wide Web. Every URI consists of two parts: the *scheme*, which appears before the colon (:), and another part that depends on the scheme. Web addresses, for the most part, use the http scheme (the scheme name in URIs is case insensitive, but is generally written in lowercase letters). In this scheme, the URI represents the location of a resource on the Web. A URI of this type is said to be a *Uniform Resource Locator* (URL). Therefore, URIs using the http scheme are both URIs and URLs. Some other URI schemes that mark the URI as a URL are shown in Table 1.1. A complete list of the currently registered URI schemes along with references to details on each scheme can be found at [IANA-SCHEMES].

In addition to the URL type of URI, there is one other type, called a *Uniform Resource Name* (URN). While not as common as URLs, URNs are sometimes used in web development (see Section 8.6 for an example). A URN is designed to be a unique name for a resource rather than specifying a location at which to find the resource. For example, an edition of *War and Peace* has an ISBN (International Standard Book Number) of 0-1404-4417-3 associated with it, and this is the only book worldwide with this number.

TABLE 1.1 Some Non-http URL Schemes

Scheme Name	Example URL	Type of Resource
ftp	`ftp://ftp.example.org/pub/afile.txt`	File located on FTP server
telnet	`telnet://host.example.org/`	Telnet server
mailto	`mailto:someone@example.org`	Mailbox
https	`https://secure.example.org/sec.txt`	Resource on web server supporting encrypted communication
file	`file:///C:/temp/localFile.txt`	File accessible from machine processing this URL

So it makes sense to associate information regarding this book, such as bibliographic data, with its ISBN. In fact, this book has an associated URN, which can be written as follows:

```
urn:ISBN:0-1404-4417-3
```

The URI for a URN always consists of three colon-separated parts, as illustrated here. The first part is the scheme name, which is always urn for a URN-type URI. The second part is the *namespace identifier*, which in this example is ISBN. Other currently registered URN namespace identifiers along with pointers to documentation for each are listed at [IANA-URNS]. The third part is the *namespace-specific string*. The exact format and meaning of this string varies with the namespace. In this example it represents the ISBN of a book and has a format defined by the documentation linked to at [IANA-URNS].

We will have more to say about URLs, particularly those with an http scheme, in Section 1.6. For now, we will complete our coverage of the HTTP request start line by examining the first part, the request method.

1.4.4   Request Method

The standard HTTP methods and a brief description of each are shown in Table 1.2. The method part of the start line of an HTTP request must be written entirely in uppercase letters, as shown in the table. In addition to the methods shown, the HTTP/1.1 standard defines a CONNECT method, which can be used to create certain types of secure connections. However, its use is beyond our scope and therefore will not be discussed further here.

The primary HTTP method is GET. This is the method used when you type a URL into the Location bar of your browser. It is also the method that is used by default when you click on a link in a document displayed in your browser and when the browser downloads images for display within an HTML document. The POST method is typically used to send information collected from a form displayed within a browser, such as an order-entry form, back to the web server. The other methods are not frequently used by web developers, and we will therefore not discuss them further here.

TABLE 1.2 Standard HTTP/1.1 Methods

Method	Requests server to . . .
GET	return the resource specified by the Request-URI as the body of a response message.
POST	pass the body of this request message on as data to be processed by the resource specified by the Request-URI.
HEAD	return the same HTTP header fields that would be returned if a GET method were used, but not return the message body that would be returned to a GET (this provides information about a resource without the communication overhead of transmitting the body of the response, which may be quite large).
OPTIONS	return (in Allow header field) a list of HTTP methods that may be used to access the resource specified by the Request-URI.
PUT	store the body of this message on the server and assign the specified Request-URI to the data stored so that future GET request messages containing this Request-URI will receive this data in their response messages.
DELETE	respond to future HTTP request messages that contain the specified Request-URI with a response indicating that there is no resource associated with this Request-URI.
TRACE	return a copy of the complete HTTP request message, including start line, header fields, and body, received by the server. Used primarily for test purposes.

1.4.5 Header Fields and MIME Types

We have already learned that the Host header field is used when forming the URI associated with an HTTP request. The Host header field is required in every HTTP/1.1 request message. HTTP/1.1 also defines a number of other header fields, several of which are commonly used by modern browsers. Each header field begins with a *field name*, such as Host, followed by a colon and then a *field value*. White space is allowed to precede or follow the field value, but such white space is not considered part of the value itself. The following slightly modified example of an actual HTTP request sent by a browser consists of a start line, 10 header fields, and a short message body:

```
POST /servlet/EchoHttpRequest HTTP/1.1
host: www.example.org:56789
user-agent: Mozilla/5.0 (Windows; U; Windows NT 5.1; en-US; rv:1.4)
  Gecko/20030624
accept: text/xml,application/xml,application/xhtml+xml,
  text/html;q=0.9,text/plain;q=0.8,video/x-mng,image/png,image/jpeg,
  image/gif;q=0.2,*/*;q=0.1
accept-language: en-us,en;q=0.5
accept-encoding: gzip,deflate
accept-charset: ISO-8859-1,utf-8;q=0.7,*;q=0.7
connection: keep-alive
keep-alive: 300
content-type: application/x-www-form-urlencoded
content-length: 13

doit=Click+me
```

Before describing each of the header fields, it will be helpful to understand some common header field features. First, header names are not case sensitive, although I will throughout this text refer to header field names following the capitalization used by the HTTP/1.1 reference [RFC-2616]. So, while the browser used "host" to name the first header field, I will refer to this as the "Host" header field. Second, a header field value may wrap onto several lines by preceding each continuation line with one or more spaces or tabs, as shown for the User-Agent and Accept fields of the preceding example. This also means that a header field name must begin at the first character of a line, with no preceding white space.

A third common feature is the use of so-called MIME types in several header field values. *MIME* is an acronym standing for Multipurpose Internet Mail Extensions, and refers to a standard that can be used to pass a variety of types of information, including graphics and applications, through e-mail as well as through other Internet message protocols. In particular, as defined in the MIME Internet Draft Standard [RFC-2045], the content of a MIME message is specified using a two-part, case-insensitive string which, in web applications, is known as the *content type* of the message. Two examples of standard MIME content-type strings are text/html and image/jpeg. The substring preceding the slash in these strings is the *top-level type*, and is normally one of a small number of standard types shown in Table 1.3. The substring following the slash, called the *subtype*, specifies the particular type of content relative to the top-level type. A complete list of current registered top-level types and subtypes can be found at [IANA-MIME]. In addition, *private* (unregistered) MIME top-level types and subtypes may be used. A private type or subtype is indicated by an "x-" (or "X-") prefix. Table 1.4 lists some common MIME types.

Yet another common feature of header fields is that many header field values use so-called *quality values* to indicate preferences. A quality value is specified by a string of

TABLE 1.3 Standard Top-level MIME Content Types

Top-level Content Type	Document Content
application	Data that does not fit within another content type and that is intended to be processed by application software, or that is itself an executable binary.
audio	Audio data. Subtype defines audio format.
image	Image data, typically static. Subtype defines image format. Requires appropriate software and hardware in order to be displayed.
message	Another document that represents a MIME-style message. For example, following an HTTP TRACE request message to a server, the server sends a response with a body that is a copy of the HTTP request. The value of the Content-Type header field in the response is message/http.
model	Structured data, generally numeric, representing physical or behavioral models.
multipart	Multiple entities, each with its own header and body.
text	Displayable as text. That is, a human can read this document without the need for special software, although it may be easier to read with the assistance of other software.
video	Animated images, possibly with synchronized sound.

TABLE 1.4 Some Common MIME Content Types

MIME Type	Description
text/html	HTML document
image/gif	Image represented using Graphics Interchange Format (GIF)
image/jpeg	Image represented using Joint Picture Expert Group (JPEG) format
text/plain	Human-readable text with no embedded formatting information
application/octet-stream	Arbitrary binary data (may be executable)
application/x-www-form-urlencoded	Data sent from a web form to a web server for processing

the form ;q=*num*, where *num* is a decimal number between 0 and 1, with a higher number representing greater preference. Each quality value applies to all of the comma-separated field values preceding it back to the next earlier quality value. So, for example, according to the Accept header field (explained in Section 1.5) the browser in this example prefers text/xml (quality value 0.9) over image/jpeg (quality value 0.2). A final common header field feature is the use of the * character in a header field value as a wildcard character. For instance, the string */* in the Accept header field value represents all possible MIME types.

Each of the header fields shown in the example, along with the Referer field (yes, this misspelling of "referrer" is the name of the field in the HTTP/1.1 standard), are briefly described in Table 1.5. The field values for Accept-Charset are discussed in detail in Section 1.5.4. Full details on all of these header fields, along with descriptions of the many other header fields defined in HTTP/1.1 plus an explanation of how you can define your own header fields, are contained in [RFC-2616].

1.5   HTTP Response Message

As we have seen earlier, an HTTP response message consists of a status line, header fields, and the body of the response, in the following format:

> Status line
> Header field(s) (one or more)
> Blank line
> Message body (optional)

In this section, we'll begin by describing the status line and then move on to an overview of some of the response header fields and related topics. The message body, if present, is often an HTML document; HTML is covered in the next chapter.

1.5.1   Response Status Line

The example status line shown earlier was

```
HTTP/1.1 200 OK
```

TABLE 1.5 Some Common HTTP/1.1 Request Header Fields

Field Name	Use
Host	Specify *authority* portion of URL (host plus port number; see Section 1.6.2). Used to support *virtual hosting* (running separate web servers for multiple fully qualified domain names sharing a single IP address).
User-Agent	A string identifying the browser or other software that is sending the request.
Accept	MIME types of documents that are acceptable as the body of the response, possibly with indication of preference ranking. If the server can return a document according to one of several formats, it should use a format that has the highest possible preference rating in this header.
Accept-Language	Specifies preferred language(s) for the response body. A server may have several translations of a document, and among these should return the one that has the highest preference rating in this header field. For complete information on registered language tags, see [RFC-3066] and [ISO-639-2].
Accept-Encoding	Specifies preferred encoding(s) for the response body. For example, if a server wishes to send a compressed document (to reduce transmission time), it may only use one of the types of compression specified in this header field.
Accept-Charset	Allows the client to express preferences to a server that can return a document using various character sets (see Section 1.5.4).
Connection	Indicates whether or not the client would like the TCP connection kept open after the response is sent. Typical values are `keep-alive` if connection should be kept open (the default behavior for servers/clients compatible with HTTP/1.1), and `close` if not.
Keep-Alive	Number of seconds TCP connection should be kept open.
Content-Type	The MIME type of the document contained in the message body, if one is present. If this field is present in a request message, it normally has the value shown in the example, application/x-www-form-urlencoded.
Content-Length	Number of bytes of data in the message body, if one is present.
Referer	The URI of the resource from which the browser obtained the Request-URI value for this HTTP request. For example, if the user clicks on a hyperlink in a web page, causing an HTTP request to be sent to a server, the URI of the web page containing the hyperlink will be sent in the Referer field of the request. This field is not present if the HTTP request was generated by the user entering a URI in the browser's Location bar.

Like the start line of a request message, the status line consists of three fields: the HTTP version used by the server software when formatting the response; a numeric *status code* indicating the type of response; and a text string (the *reason phrase*) that presents the information represented by the numeric status code in human-readable form. In this example, the status code is 200 and the reason phrase is OK. This particular status code indicates that no errors were detected by the server. The body of a response having this status code should contain the resource requested by the client.

All status codes are three-digit decimal numbers. The first digit represents the general class of status code. The five classes of HTTP/1.1 status codes are given in Table 1.6. The last two digits of a status code define the specific status within the specified class. A few of the more common status codes are shown in Table 1.7. The HTTP standard recommends

TABLE 1.6 HTTP/1.1 Status Code Classes (First Digit of Status Code)

Digit	Class	Standard Use
1	Informational	Provides information to client before request processing has been completed.
2	Success	Request has been successfully processed.
3	Redirection	Client needs to use a different resource to fulfill request.
4	Client Error	Client's request is not valid.
5	Server Error	An error occurred during server processing of a valid client request.

reason phrases for all status codes, but a server may use alternative but equivalent phrases. All status codes and recommended reason phrases are contained in [RFC-2616].

1.5.2   Response Header Fields

Some of the header fields used in HTTP request messages, including Connection, Content-Type, and Content-Length, are also valid in response messages. The Content-Type of a response can be any one of the MIME type values specified by the Accept header field of the corresponding request. Some other common response header fields are shown in Table 1.8.

TABLE 1.7 Some Common HTTP/1.1 Status Codes

Status Code	Recommended Reason Phrase	Usual Meaning
200	OK	Request processed normally.
301	Moved Permanently	URI for the requested resource has changed. All future requests should be made to URI contained in the Location header field of the response. Most browsers will automatically send a second request to the new URI and display the second response.
307	Temporary Redirect	URI for the requested resource has changed at least temporarily. This request should be fulfilled by making a second request to URI contained in the Location header field of the response. Most browsers will automatically send a second request to the new URI and display the second response.
401	Unauthorized	The resource is password protected, and the user has not yet supplied a valid password.
403	Forbidden	The resource is present on the server but is read protected (often an error on the part of the server administrator, but may be intentional).
404	Not Found	No resource corresponding to the given Request-URI was found at this server.
500	Internal Server Error	Server software detected an internal failure.

TABLE 1.8 Some Common HTTP/1.1 Response Header Fields

Field Name	Use
Date	Time at which response was generated. Used for cache control (see Section 1.5.3). This field must be supplied by the server.
Server	Information identifying the server software generating this response.
Last-Modified	Time at which the resource returned by this request was last modified. Can be used to determine whether cached copy of a resource is valid or not (see Section 1.5.3).
Expires	Time after which the client should check with the server before retrieving the returned resource from the client's cache (see Section 1.5.3).
ETag	A hash code of the resource returned. If the resource remains unchanged on subsequent requests, then the ETag value will also remain unchanged; otherwise, the ETag value will change. Used for cache control (see Section 1.5.3).
Accept-Ranges	Clients can request that only a portion (*range*) of a resource be returned by using the Range header field. This might be used if the resource is, say, a large PDF file and only a single page is currently needed. Accept-Ranges specifies the units that may be used by the client in a range request, or none if range requests are not accepted by this server for this resource.
Location	Used in responses with redirect status code to specify new URI for the requested resource.

1.5.3 Cache Control

Several of the response header fields described in Table 1.8 are used in conjunction with cache control. In computer systems, a *cache* is a repository for copies of information that originates elsewhere. A copy of information is placed in a cache in order to improve system performance. For example, most personal computer systems use a small, high-speed memory cache to hold copies of some of the data contained in RAM memory, which is slower than cache memory.

Most web browsers automatically cache on the client machine many of the resources that they request from servers via HTTP. For example, if an image such as a button icon is included in a web page, a copy of the image obtained from the server will typically be cached in the client's file system. Then if another page at the same site uses the same image, the image can be retrieved from the client file system rather than sending another HTTP request to the server and waiting for the server's response containing the image. HTTP caching, when successful, generally leads to quicker display by the browser, reduced network communication, and reduced load on the web server.

However, there is a key drawback to using a cache: information in a cache can become *invalid*. For example, if the button image in the preceding example is modified on the server, but a client accesses its cached copy of the older version of the image, then the client will display an invalid version of the image. This problem can be avoided in several ways.

One approach to guaranteeing that a cached copy of a resource is valid is for the client to ask the server whether or not the client's copy is valid. This can be done with relatively little communication by sending an HTTP request for the resource using the HEAD method, which returns only the status line and header portion of the response. If the response message contains a Last-Modified time, and this time precedes the value of the Date header field returned with the cached resource, then the cached copy is still valid and can be used. Otherwise, the cached copy is invalid and the browser should send a normal GET request for the resource.

A somewhat simpler approach can be used if the server returns an ETag with the resource. The client can then simply compare the ETag returned by a HEAD request with the ETag stored with the cached resource. If the ETag values match, then the cached copy is valid; otherwise, it is not. This approach avoids the complexity of comparing two dates to determine which is larger.

Finally, if the server can determine in advance the earliest time at which a resource will change, the server can return that time in an Expires header. In this case, as long as the Expires time has not been reached, the client may use the cached copy of the resource without the need to validate with the server. If an Expires time is not included in a response, a browser may use a heuristic algorithm to choose an expiration time and then behave as if this time had been passed to it in an Expires header. This behavior can be prevented by sending an Expires time that precedes the Date value (a value of 0 is commonly used for this purpose). If this is done, then an HTTP/1.1-compliant browser will validate before each access to the resource.

The HTTP/1.1 specification provides a variety of other header fields related to caching; see [RFC-2616] for full details.

1.5.4   Character Sets

Finally, a word about how characters are represented in web documents. As you know, characters are represented by integer values within a computer. A *character set* defines the mapping between these integers, or *code points*, and characters. For example, US-ASCII [RFC-1345] is the character set used to represent the characters used in HTTP header field names, and is also used in key portions of many other Internet protocols. Each US-ASCII character can be represented by a 7-bit integer, which is convenient in part because the messages transmitted by the Internet Protocol are viewed as streams of 8-bit bytes, and therefore each character can be represented by a single byte.

However, many characters in common use in modern languages are not contained in the US-ASCII character set. Over the years, a wide variety of other character sets have been defined for use with languages other than U.S. English and also for representing characters that are not associated with human language representation, such as mathematical and graphical symbols.

For web pages, which are meant to be viewed throughout the world, it is vital that a single worldwide character set be used. So, as in the Java™ programming language, the underlying character set used internally by web browsers is defined by the Unicode™ Standard [UNICODE]. The Unicode Standard is an attempt to provide a single character set that encompasses every human language representation as well as all other commonly used symbols. The Unicode Standard's Basic Multilingual Plane (BMP), which covers most of the commonly used characters in every modern language, uses 16-bit character codes, and the full character code space of the Unicode Standard extends to 21-bit integers.

Of course, if the resource requested by a client is written using the US-ASCII character set, then sending 21 (or more) bits per character from the server to the client would take roughly three times as long as sending the ASCII characters. Therefore, most browsers, for purposes of efficiency and compatibility, accept a variety of character sets in addition to those in Unicode. See [IANA-CHARSETS] for a complete (long) list of character sets currently registered for use over the Internet.

More generally, in addition to a variety of character sets, most browsers also accept certain character encodings. A *character encoding* is a bit string that must be decoded into a code-point integer that is then mapped to a character according to the definition provided by some character set. A character encoding often represents characters using variable-length bit strings, with common characters represented using shorter strings and less-common characters using longer strings. For example, UTF-8 and UTF-16 are encodings of the character set in Unicode that use variable numbers of 8- and 16-bit values to encode all possible Unicode Standard characters. (Don't confuse character encoding with the message encoding concept mentioned earlier. Message encoding typically involves applying a general-purpose compression algorithm to the body of a message, regardless of the character encoding used.)

The Accept-Charset header field is used by a client to tell a server the character sets and character encodings that it will accept as well as its preferred character sets or encodings, if more than one is available for the requested document. In our earlier example, the header field

```
accept-charset: ISO-8859-1,utf-8;q=0.7,*;q=0.7
```

said that the client would prefer to receive documents using the ISO-8859-1 character set or the UTF-8 encoding of the characters in Unicode, but that it would also accept any other valid Internet character set/encoding. (ISO-8859-1 is an 8-bit superset of US-ASCII that contains many characters found in Latin-based languages but not in English. ISO-8859-1 and UTF-8 are preferred even though they have the same quality value as * because specific field values are given preference over the * wildcard.)

A web server can inform a client about the character set/encoding used in a returned document by adding a `charset` parameter to the value of the Content-Type header field. For example, the following Content-Type header field in an HTTP response would indicate that the body of the message is an HTML document written using the UTF-8 character encoding:

```
Content-Type: text/html; charset=UTF-8
```

The US-ASCII character set is a subset of both the ISO-8859-1 character set and the UTF-8 character encodings, so the `charset` parameter is set to one of these two values for many US-ASCII documents in order to ensure international compatibility. We will learn other ways to indicate the character set/encoding for a document in later chapters.

Now that we have covered HTTP in some detail, we're ready to look at the primary software applications that communicate using HTTP: web clients and servers. We'll begin with the more familiar client software before moving on to web servers.

1.6 Web Clients

A *web client* is software that accesses a web server by sending an HTTP request message and processing the resulting HTTP response. Web browsers running on desktop or laptop computers are the most common form of web client software, but there are many other forms of client software, including text-only browsers, browsers running on cell phones, and browsers that speak a page (over the phone, for example) rather than displaying the page. In general, any web client that is designed to directly support user access to web servers is known as a *user agent*. Furthermore, some web clients are not designed to be used directly by humans at all. For example, software *robots* are often used to automatically crawl the Web and download information for use by search engines (and, unfortunately, e-mail spammers).

We will focus here on traditional browsers, since they are the most widely used web client software and have features that are generally a superset of those found in other clients. A brief history of these browsers will provide some useful background.

Early web browsers generally either were text-based or ran on specialized platforms, such as computers from Sun Microsystems or the now-defunct NeXT Systems. The Mosaic™ browser, developed at the National Center for Supercomputer Applications (NCSA) in 1993, was the starting point for bringing graphical web browsing to the general public. The developers of Mosaic founded Netscape Communications Corporation, which dedicated a large team to developing and marketing a series of Netscape Navigator® browsers based on Mosaic. Microsoft soon followed with the Microsoft® Internet Explorer (IE) browser, which was originally based on Mosaic.

For a time, a "browser war" was waged between Netscape and Microsoft, with each company trying to add features and performance to its browser in order to increase its market share. Netscape soon found itself at a disadvantage, however, as Microsoft began bundling IE with its popular Windows® operating system. The war soon ended, and Microsoft was victorious. Netscape, acquired by America Online (at the time primarily an Internet service provider), chose to make its source code public and launched the Mozilla project as an open-source approach to developing new core functionality for the Netscape® browser. In particular, Netscape browser releases starting with version 6.0 have been based on software developed as part of the Mozilla project.

At the time of this writing, IE is by far the most widely used browser in the world. However, the Mozilla™ and Firefox™ browsers from the Mozilla Foundation are increasingly popular, and other browsers, including the Opera™ and Safari™ browsers, also have significant user communities.

Despite this diversity, all of the major modern browsers support a common set of basic user features and provide similar support for HTTP communication. A number of common browser features are discussed in the remainder of this section. For concreteness, I will also explain how to access the features described using one particular browser, Mozilla 1.4, and will also use the Mozilla browser for most examples in later chapters. A primary reason for choosing to use Mozilla as a concrete browser example is that it runs on Linux®, Windows, and Macintosh® systems. Also, the fact that it is open source means that if you're curious about details of how a feature operates, you have access to the source code itself. In addition to having essentially all of the features found in IE, Mozilla has some nice tools for software developers that are not found in basic IE distributions. Finally, as we will learn in later chapters, Mozilla browsers are designed to comply with HTML and other Internet standards, while IE is (at this time, at least) less standards compliant. Instructions for downloading and installing Mozilla 1.4 are found in Appendix A.

1.6.1   Basic Browser Functions

The window of a typical modern browser is split into several rectangular regions, most of which are known as *bars*. Figure 1.4 shows five standard regions in a Mozilla 1.4 window. The primary region is the *client area*, which displays a document. For many documents, the *title bar* displays a title assigned by the document author to the document currently displayed within the client area. The title bar also displays the browser name as well as standard window-management controls. The *menu bar* contains a set of dropdown menus, much like most other applications that incorporate a graphical user interface (GUI). We'll take a closer look at the Mozilla menus in Section 1.6.3. The browser's *Navigation toolbar* contains standard push-button controls that allow the user to return to a previously viewed web page (Back), reverse the effect of pressing Back (Forward), ask the server for an updated version of the page currently viewed (Reload), halt page downloading currently in progress (Stop), and print the client area of the window (Print). Clicking the small down-arrow to the right of some buttons produces a menu allowing users to override the default behavior of the associated button. For example, clicking the arrow to the right of Back produces a menu of titles of a number of documents that have been recently viewed, any of which can be loaded into the client area by selecting its title from the menu. The Navigation toolbar also contains a text box, known as the *Location bar*, where a user can enter a URL and press the Enter key in order to request the browser to display the document located at the specified URL. Clicking the Search button instead of pressing Enter causes the information entered in the text box to be sent to a search engine. Clicking the down-arrow at the right side of the Location bar produces a dropdown menu of recently visited URLs that can be visited again with a single click. Finally, the *status bar* displays messages and icons related to the

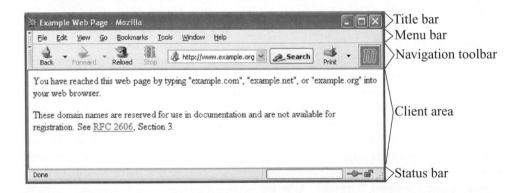

status of the browser. For example, the two icons in the right portion of the status bar in Figure 1.4 show that the browser is online (left icon) and that the browser is communicating with the server over an insecure communication channel. The messages displayed in the left portion of the status bar are normally information about the communication between client and server (Table 1.9).

A primary task of any browser is to make HTTP requests on behalf of the browser user. If a user types an `http`-scheme URL in Mozilla's Location bar, for example, the browser must perform a number of tasks:

1. Reformat the URL entered as a valid HTTP request message.
2. If the server is specified using a host name (rather than an IP address), use DNS to convert this name to the appropriate IP address.
3. Establish a TCP connection using the IP address of the specified web server.
4. Send the HTTP request over the TCP connection and wait for the server's response.
5. Display the document contained in the response. If the document is not a plain-text document but instead is written in a language such as HTML, this involves *rendering* the document: positioning text and graphics appropriately within the browser window, creating table borders, using appropriate fonts and colors, etc.

Before discussing various features of browsers that can be controlled by users, it will be helpful to have a more complete understanding of URLs.

1.6.2 URLs

An `http`-scheme URL consists of a number of pieces. In order to show the main possibilities, let's consider the following example URL:

```
http://www.example.org:56789/a/b/c.txt?t=win&s=chess#para5
```

The portion of an `http` URL following the `://` string and before the next slash (`/`) (or through the completion of the URL, if there is no trailing slash) is known as the *authority* of the URL. It consists of either a fully qualified domain name (or other name that can be resolved to an IP address, such as an unqualified name of a machine on the local network) or an IP

TABLE 1.9 Some Mozilla Status Messages

Status Message	Meaning
Resolving host www.example.org . . .	Requested IP address from DNS; waiting for response.
Connecting to www.example.org . . .	Creating TCP connection to server.
Waiting for www.example.org . . .	Sent HTTP request to server; waiting for HTTP response.
Transferring data from www.example.org . . .	HTTP response has begun, but has not completed.
Done	HTTP response has been received, although further processing may be needed before the document will be displayed.

address of an Internet web server, optionally followed by a colon (:) and a port number. As indicated earlier, if the port number is omitted, then a TCP connection to port 80 is implied. In this example, the authority is `www.example.org:56789` and consists of the fully qualified domain name `www.example.org` followed by the port number 56789.

The portion from the slash following the authority through the question mark (?) (or through the end of the URL, if there is no question mark) is called the *path* of the URL. The leading slash is part of the path, but the question mark is not. So the path in the example URL just given is `/a/b/c.txt`. The fact that this looks a great deal like a Linux file reference to a file named `c.txt` located within the `b` subdirectory of the `a` directory of the root (/) of the file system is not entirely a coincidence. In many cases, the path portion of a URL is in fact concatenated by the server with a base file path in order to form an actual file path on the server's system. We'll learn more about how servers use URL paths later in this chapter as well as in later chapters.

Following the path there may be a question mark followed by information up to a number sign (#). The information between but not including the question mark and number sign is the *query* portion of the URL, and in general a string of the form shown is known as a *query string*. The query portion of the example URL is `t=win&s=chess`. Originally, the query portion of a URL was intended to pass search terms to a web server. So in this example, it might be that the user is seeking a resource with a title containing the string "win" that is related to the subject "chess." As we will learn in later chapters, while query strings are still sometimes used to represent search terms, they are also used for a variety of other purposes in modern web systems. We will also learn that query strings may appear in the body of POST requests, as well as how to encode special characters in the query strings sent to web servers.

A browser forms the Request-URI portion of an HTTP request from a URL by concatenating the path and query portions of the URL with an intervening question mark. Thus, the Request-URI for the example URL would be

```
/a/b/c.txt?t=win&s=chess
```

Syntactically, the query portion of a URL can only be present if the path portion is present. If both the path and query are missing from a URL, then the Request-URI must be set to /, which is known as the *root* path. This is why we used a / as the Request-URI in the example of Section 1.3.1.

The final optional part of an `http`-scheme URL—the portion following but not including the number sign—is known as the *fragment* of the URL, and the string contained in the fragment is known as a *fragment identifier*. Fragment identifiers are used by browsers to scroll HTML documents; details are given in the next chapter, which covers HTML.

Summarizing, if a user types a URL such as the one considered into a browser's Location bar and presses Enter, the browser will generate an HTTP request message as follows. The request start line will begin with GET. The path and query portions of the URL will be used as the second, Request-URI portion of the start line. Assuming the browser is HTTP/1.1 compliant, the final portion of the start line will be the string `HTTP/1.1` (this string must be uppercase). The request will also contain a Host header field having as its value the authority portion of the URL. The fragment portion of the URL is not sent to the web server, but is instead used by the browser to modify the way in which it displays any HTML document sent to the browser in the HTTP response returned as a result of this request. Other header fields will also generally be included, as described earlier.

So, given the example URL, the browser would send a request containing the lines (spacing and some capitalization might vary from that shown):

```
GET /a/b/c.txt?t=win&s=chess HTTP/1.1
...
Host: www.example.org:56789
...
```

1.6.3   User-Controllable Features

Graphical browsers also provide many user-controllable features, including:

- *Save:* Most documents can be saved by the user to the client machine's file system. If the document is an HTML page that contains other documents, such as images, then the browser will attempt to save all of these documents locally so that the entire page can be displayed from the local file system. A user saves a document in Mozilla under the **File|Save Page As** menu.
- *Find in page:* Standard documents (text and HTML) can be searched with a function that is similar to that provided by most word processors. In Mozilla, the find function is accessed under the **Edit|Find in This Page** menu. (Mozilla also provides a "find as you type" feature under Edit that is similar to the incremental search in Emacs, for users familiar with that paradigm.)
- *Automatic form filling:* The browser can "remember" information entered on certain forms, such as billing address, phone numbers, etc. When another form is visited at a later date, the browser can automatically fill in previously saved data. The **Edit|Save Form Info** and **Edit|Fill in Form** menu options can be used to save and retrieve form information in Mozilla. The **Tools|Form Manager** menu can be used to manage saved form information.
- *Preferences:* Users can customize browser functionality in a wide variety of ways. In Mozilla, a window presenting preference options is obtained by selecting **Edit| Preferences** (Figure 1.5). The Appearance, Navigator, and Advanced categories (left subwindow) and their subcategories are used to customize Mozilla. Some preference settings directly related to the HTTP topics covered earlier are:
  - *Accept-Language:* The non-* values sent by the browser for this HTTP request header field can be set under the **Navigator|Languages** category, **Languages for Web Pages** box.
  - *Default character set/encoding:* The character set/encoding to be assumed for documents that do not specify one is also set under **Navigator|Languages** in the **Character Coding** box.
  - *Cache properties:* The amount of local storage allocated to the cache and the conditions controlling when a cached file will be validated are set under **Advanced| Cache** in the **Set Cache Options** box.

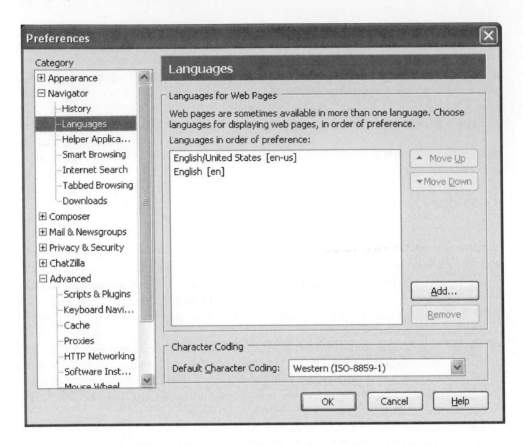

FIGURE 1.5 Preferences window with Languages category selected.

- *HTTP settings:* The version of HTTP used and whether or not the client will keep connections alive is set under **Advanced|HTTP Networking** in the **Direct Connection Options** box.
- *Style definition:* The user can define certain aspects affecting how the browser renders HTML pages, such as font sizes, background and foreground colors, etc. In Mozilla, the font size can be modified using **View|Text Zoom**. If a page offers alternative styles, they can be selected using the **View|Use Style** menu as discussed in Chapter 3, where methods for changing default browser style settings are also described.
- *Document meta-information:* Interested users can view information about the displayed document, such as the document's MIME type, character encoding, size, and, if the document was written using HTML, the raw HTML source from which the rendering in the client area was produced. In Mozilla, **View|Page Source** is used to view raw HTML, and **View|Page Info** to view other so-called *meta-information*, that is, information about the document rather than information contained in the document itself.
- *Themes:* The look of one or more of the browser bars, particularly the navigation bar, can be modified by applying a certain theme (sometimes called a "skin"). In Mozilla, the

browser scheme can be modified using **View|Apply Theme**. Additional themes can be obtained from **View|Apply Theme|Get New Themes**.

- *History:* The browser will automatically maintain a list of all pages visited within the last several days. Users can use the history list to easily return to any recently visited page. In Mozilla, the history list can be reached by selecting **Go|History**.
- *Bookmarks ("favorites" in Internet Explorer):* Users can explicitly *bookmark* a web page, that is, save the URL for that page for an indefinite length of time. At any later time, the browser's bookmark facility can be used to easily return to any bookmarked page. Options under the **Bookmarks** menu in Mozilla allow users to bookmark a page, return to a bookmarked page, and edit the bookmark list.

1.6.4   Additional Functionality

In addition to the facilities for end users described in the preceding subsection, browsers perform a number of other functions, including:

- *Automatic URL completion:* If the user has entered a URL in the Location bar and begins to type it again (within the next several days), the URL will be completed automatically by the browser.
- *Script execution:* In addition to displaying documents, browsers can run programs (scripts). These programs can perform a variety of tasks, from validating data entered on a form before sending it to a web server to creating various dynamic effects on web pages, such as drop-down menus.
- *Event handling:* When the user performs an action, such as clicking on a link or a button in a web page, the browser treats this as the occurrence of an *event*. Browsers recognize a number of different types of events, including mouse button clicks, mouse movement, and even events not directly under user control such as the completion of the browser's rendering of a document. A browser can perform a variety of actions in response to an event—loading a document from a URL, clearing a form, or calling a script function defined by the document author, for example.
- *Management of form GUI:* If a web page contains a form with fill-in fields, the browser must allow the user to perform standard text-editing functions within these fields. It also needs to automatically provide certain graphical feedback, such as changing a button image when it is pressed or providing a text cursor in a text field that will receive keyboard input.
- *Secure communication:* When the user sends sensitive information, such as a credit card number, to a web server, the browser can encode this information in a way the prevents any machines along the IP route from the client to the server from obtaining the information.
- *Plug-in execution:* While the browser itself normally understands only a limited number of MIME types, most browsers support some form of *plug-in* protocol that allows the browser's capabilities to be supplemented by other software. If a browser has a plug-in for displaying, say, a document conforming to the application/pdf MIME type, then when the browser receives such a document it will pass it—via the plug-in protocol—to the appropriate plug-in for display. Some plug-ins may display the document within the

browser's client area, while others may display in a separate window that is controlled by the plug-in itself. Plug-ins are often installed automatically, after user permission is obtained, when an unsupported MIME type is encountered. To see a list of plug-ins installed in your copy of Mozilla, select **Help|About Plug-ins**.

Some other standard browser features, such as a facility for managing so-called *cookies*, are described in later chapters. In addition to standard browser features, Mozilla also provides a number of tools specifically designed for use by software developers, such as a script console and debugging tools. Some of these tools will also be described in later chapters.

This completes our coverage of web browsers. It's now time to move to the software running on the other end of the HTTP communications pipeline: web servers.

1.7   Web Servers

In this section, we'll cover basic functionality found in most web servers as well as some specific instructions for accessing and modifying the parameters for one particular web server, Tomcat 5.0. We'll also briefly look at how web servers support secure communication with browsers.

1.7.1   Server Features

The primary feature of every web server is to accept HTTP requests from web clients and return an appropriate resource (if available) in the HTTP response. Even this basic functionality involves a number of steps (the quoted terms used in this list are defined in subsequent paragraphs):

1. The server calls on TCP software and waits for connection requests to one or more ports.
2. When a connection request is received, the server dedicates a "subtask" to handling this connection.
3. The subtask establishes the TCP connection and receives an HTTP request.
4. The subtask examines the Host header field of the request to determine which "virtual host" should receive this request and invokes software for this host.
5. The virtual host software maps the Request-URI field of the HTTP request start line to a resource on the server.
6. If the resource is a file, the host software determines the MIME type of the file (usually by a mapping from the file-name extension portion of the Request-URI), and creates an HTTP response that contains the file in the body of the response message.
7. If the resource is a program, the host software runs the program, providing it with information from the request and returning the output from the program as the body of an HTTP response message.
8. The server normally logs information about the request and response—such as the IP address of the requester and the status code of the response—in a plain-text file.

9. If the TCP connection is kept alive, the server subtask continues to monitor the connection until a certain length of time has elapsed, the client sends another request, or the client initiates a connection close.

A few definitions will be helpful before proceeding to more detailed coverage of web server features. First, all modern servers can concurrently process multiple requests. It is as if multiple copies of the server were running simultaneously, each devoted to handling the requests received over a single TCP connection. The specifics of how this concurrency is actually implemented on a system may depend on many factors, including the number of processors available in the system, the programming language used, and programmer choices. We will learn more about concurrent server processing in Chapter. 6. For now, I will simply use the term *subtask* to refer to the concept of a single "copy" of the server software handling a single client connection.

Another term that may need some explanation is *virtual host*. As noted earlier, every HTTP request must include a Host header field. The reason for this requirement is that multiple host names may all be mapped by the Internet DNS system to a single IP address. For example, a single server machine within a college may host web sites for multiple departments. Each web site would be assigned its own fully qualified domain name, such as `www.cs.example.edu`, `www.physics.example.edu`, and so on. But DNS would be configured to map all of these domain names to a single IP address. When an HTTP request is received by the web server at this address, it can determine which *virtual* host is being requested by examining the Host header. Separately configured software can then be used to handle the requests for each virtual host.

Finally, as noted in point 7, the documents returned by web servers are often produced by executing software at the time of the HTTP request rather than being generated beforehand and stored in the server's file system for later retrieval. One significant difference between web servers concerns the support that each has for executing software written in various traditional programming languages as well as in scripting languages. We'll touch on some of these differences in the next subsection, which briefly surveys the history of web server development.

1.7.2 Server History

Just as the NCSA Mosaic™ browser was the starting point for subsequent browser development efforts by Netscape and Microsoft, NCSA's *httpd* web server was also a starting point for server development. httpd was used on a large fraction of the early web servers, but the NCSA discontinued development of the server in the mid-1990s. When this happened, several individuals who were running httpd at their sites joined forces and began developing their own updates to the open-source httpd software. Their updates were called "patches," and this led to calling their work "a patchy server," which soon became known as "the Apache server." They made the first public release of their free, open-source server in April 1995, and within a year Apache was the most widely used server on the Web. It has held that distinction to this day, although many large corporate and government sites tend to use commercial server software instead.

As with web browsers, Microsoft began development of web servers well after others had begun, but quickly caught up. Microsoft's Internet Information Server (IIS) provides essentially all of the features found in Apache, although IIS does have the drawback of running only on Windows systems, while Apache runs on Windows, Linux, and Macintosh systems. IIS and Apache are, at the time of this writing, by far the most widely used servers on the market.

Both servers can be configured to run a variety of types of programs, although certain programming languages tend to be used more frequently on one system than the other. For example, many IIS servers run programs written in VBScript (a derivative of Visual Basic), while a typical Apache server might run programs written in either Perl or the PHP scripting language (PHP stands for "PHP Hypertext Processor"; yes, the definition is infinitely recursive). A number of IIS and Apache servers also run Java programs. When running a Java program, both Apache and IIS servers are usually configured to run the program by using separate software called a *servlet container*. The servlet container provides the Java Virtual Machine that runs the Java program (known as a *servlet*), and also provides communication between the servlet and the Apache or IIS web server.

Tomcat is a popular, free, and open-source servlet container developed and maintained by the Apache Software Foundation, the same organization that is continuing development of the Apache web server. In addition to running as a servlet container called on by web servers, Tomcat can also be run as a standalone web server that communicates directly with web clients. Furthermore, the standalone Tomcat server can serve documents stored in the server machine's file system and run programs written in non-Java languages.

To provide a concrete illustration of server configuration, we will next cover configuration of a Tomcat 5.0 server in some detail (this is the server you will have if you follow the instructions for installing JWSDP in Appendix A). The Tomcat material presented here is not meant to be a comprehensive reference, but is primarily intended to introduce you to some key terms and concepts that are encountered when setting up any web server, not just Tomcat. Since we will be using Java servlets and related technologies to illustrate server-side programming in later chapters, it is natural for us to focus on Tomcat rather than non-Java servers in this chapter. If you understand Tomcat configuration well, configuring a basic IIS or Apache server should not be particularly difficult.

1.7.3 Server Configuration and Tuning

Modern servers have a large number of configuration parameters. In this section, we will cover many of the key configuration items found in Tomcat. Similar features, along with some not found in Tomcat, are included in the Apache and IIS servers.

Broadly speaking, server configuration can be broken into two areas: external communication and internal processing. In Tomcat, this corresponds to two separate Java packages: Coyote, which provides the HTTP/1.1 communication, and Catalina, which is the actual servlet container. Some of the Coyote parameters, affecting external communication, include the following:

- IP addresses and TCP ports that may be used to connect to this server.
- Number of subtasks (called *threads* in Java) that will be created when the server is initialized. This many TCP connections can be established simultaneously with minimal overhead.

- Maximum number of threads that will be allowed to exist simultaneously. If this is larger than the previous value, then the number of threads maintained by the server may change, either up or down, over time.
- Maximum number of TCP connection requests that will be queued if the server is already running its maximum number of threads. Connection requests received if the queue is full will be refused.
- Length of time the server will wait after serving an HTTP request over a TCP connection before closing the connection if another request is not received.

The settings of these parameters can have a significant influence on the performance of a server; changing the values of these and similar parameters in order to optimize performance is often referred to as *tuning* the server. As with all optimization problems, there are various trade-offs involved in attempting to tune a server. For example, increasing the maximum number of simultaneous threads that may execute increases memory requirements and thread-management overhead, and may lead to slower responses to individual requests, due to sharing CPU cycles among the large number of threads. On the other hand, lower values for this parameter may lead to some clients having their connection requests refused, which may lead some users to believe that the site is down. Tuning is therefore often performed by trial and error: if a server seems to be running poorly by some measure, the server administrator may try to vary one or more of these parameters and observe the impact, retaining parameter values that seem to help. *Load generation* or *stress test* tools can be used to simulate requests to a web server, and can therefore be helpful for experimenting with tuning parameters based on anticipated traffic patterns even before a web site "goes live." A fuller discussion of server tuning is beyond the scope of this book.

The internal Catalina portion of Tomcat also has a number of parameter settings that affect functionality. These settings can determine:

- Which client machines may send HTTP requests to the server.
- Which virtual hosts are listening for TCP connections on a given port.
- What logging will be performed.
- How the path portion of Request-URIs will be mapped to the server's file system or other resources.
- Whether or not the server's resources will be password protected.
- Whether or not resources will be cached in the server's memory.

The Tomcat 5.0 server you have installed if you followed the instructions in Appendix A has a web interface for setting most of these parameters. If your server is installed at the default port 8080 and you open a browser on the machine running the server, then browsing to the URL

```
http://localhost:8080
```

(more on `localhost` in Section 1.7.4) and clicking the Server Administration link (you may need to scroll down to find this link) should cause a log-in page to be displayed. Otherwise, if the server is not on the machine you are browsing from, or if your browser is not at port

8080, modify the URL to contain the correct host and/or port number. You were asked for a user name and password when you installed Tomcat; enter them on this log-in page. You should then see a page such as the one in Figure 1.6.

Because your copy of Tomcat was included in the Java Web Services Developer Pack (JWSDP), there is already a JWSDP Service entry in the list on the left side of the browser window. Each Service in Tomcat is almost its own web server, except that a Service cannot be individually stopped and started (only the underlying server can be stopped and started, as described in Appendix A). We will only cover here how to change parameters of the JWSDP Service; the procedures for creating a new Service are similar.

First, click on the handle icon next to the JWSDP Service entry in order to reveal its associated server components (Figure 1.7). This Service has five components: one each of Connector, Host, Logger, Realm, and Valve. A Connector is a Coyote component that handles HTTP communications directed to a particular port. Clicking on the Connector item in the JWSDP Service list will produce a window such as the one shown in Figure 1.8. The panel on the right in this figure is typical of the panels displayed for creating and editing Tomcat components. At the top of the panel is a dropdown menu of possible actions that can be performed for this component, such as creating subcomponents or deleting a component (there are no actions for this particular component). Below this menu is a Save button that must be clicked after entering data in the fields further below in order to save this data. This temporarily saves the data from these fields in memory, but any changes made are not saved permanently to disk until the Commit Changes button at the top of the window is clicked. Furthermore, the server will, in general, ignore the committed changes until it is restarted.

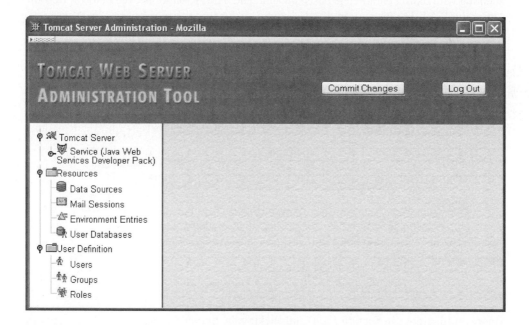

FIGURE 1.6 Tomcat administration tool entry page. The content of this screen shot is reproduced by permission of the Apache Software Foundation.

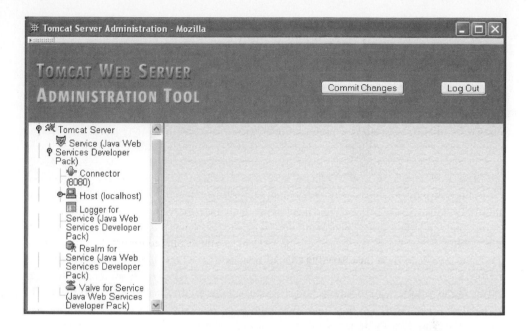

FIGURE 1.7 List of Service components produced by clicking on Service "handle" icon. The content of this screen shot is reproduced by permission of the Apache Software Foundation.

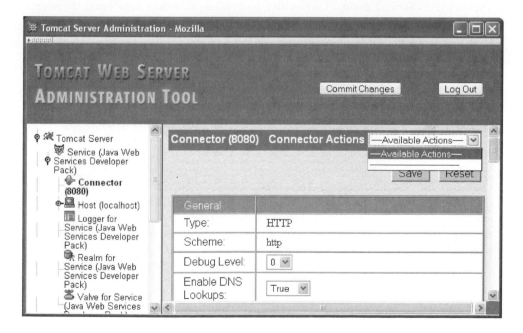

FIGURE 1.8 Connector edit page. The content of this screen shot is reproduced by permission of the Apache Software Foundation.

Some of the data fields in a panel, such as Edit Connector, have fixed values, while others can be edited (if we were creating a Connector, all fields would be editable). Some of the key fields for the Connector component type are listed in Table 1.10. Notice that the Port Number field value (8080 in this example) is used as the name of the Connector in the Service list. This is because the Port Number value for this Connector will be unique to this Connector, since each IP port can "belong" to, at most, one application on a system. On the other hand, multiple Connectors can be associated with a single Service, so a Service can potentially be accessed through multiple ports.

1.7.4   Defining Virtual Hosts

The Host component (Figure 1.9) is used to define a virtual host. Some of the key fields are described in Table 1.11. The virtual host name should normally be a fully qualified domain name that would be used by visitors to your web site, although the Host supplied as part of the JWSDP Service is given the unqualified name localhost. This is a special name that the DNS system treats as a reference to a special IP address, 127.0.0.1. If an IP message is sent to this address, the IP software causes the message to loop back to itself for receipt. In short, browsing to a URL with domain name localhost causes the browser to send the HTTP request to a web server on the machine running the browser. So it would seem that this virtual host should only be accessible if the browser runs on the server machine. However, clicking on the JWSDP Service link in the left panel reveals (in the right panel) that the value of the Default Hostname field for this Service is localhost. This means that if a user browses to this Service using a URL with a host name other than localhost, the request will be passed to the localhost virtual host. In essence, this Host component will respond to any HTTP request sent to the Service's Connector (at port 8080), regardless of the value of the request's Host header field.

TABLE 1.10 Some of the Fields for the Connector Component

Field Name	Description
Accept Count	Length of the TCP connection wait queue.
Connection Timeout	Server will close connection if it is idle for this many milliseconds.
IP Address	Blank indicates that this Connector will accept TCP connections directed to any IP address associated with this machine. Specifying an address restricts connections to requests for that address.
Port Number	Port number on which this Connection will listen for TCP connection requests.
Min Spare Threads	Initial number of threads that will be allocated to process TCP connections associated with this Connector. Once connections are established with the Connector, the server will maintain at least this many *idle* processing threads, that is, threads waiting for new connections but otherwise unused.
Max Threads	Maximum number of threads that will be allocated to process TCP connections associated with this Connector.
Max Spare Threads	Maximum number of idle threads allowed to exist at any one time. The server will begin stopping threads if the number of idle threads exceeds this value.

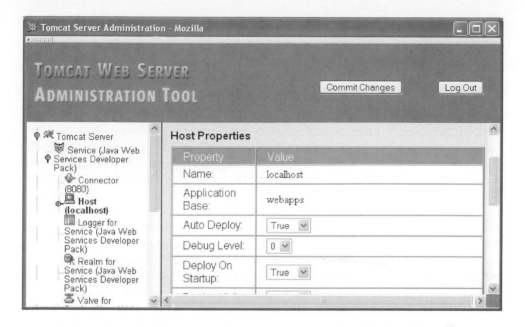

FIGURE 1.9 Host component panel for the JWSDP Service. The content of this screen shot is reproduced by permission of the Apache Software Foundation.

Now let's assume an additional Host component with name, say, www.example.org was added to this Service (through the Tomcat Administration Tool by clicking on the Service in the left panel of the web page and then selecting the Create New Host item from the Service Actions menu in the right panel). Then this new virtual host would handle requests containing a Host header field with value www.example.org, while all requests with any other Host value would continue to be handled by the default localhost virtual host.

Several of the fields listed in Table 1.11 are associated with web applications. A *web application* is a collection of files and programs that work together to provide a particular function to web users. For example, a Web site might run two web applications: one for

TABLE 1.11 Key Fields for Host Component

Field Name	Description
Name	Usually the fully qualified domain name (or localhost) that clients will use to access this virtual host.
Application Base	Directory containing *web applications* for this virtual host (see text).
Deploy on Startup	Boolean value indicating whether or not web applications should be automatically initialized when the server starts.
Auto Deploy	Boolean value indicating whether or not web applications added to the Application Base while the server is running should be automatically initialized.

use by administrators of the site that provides maintenance functionality, and another for use by external clients that provides customer functionality. In Tomcat, a web application is represented by a Context component. Clicking on a Host handle icon will reveal the list of Contexts provided with that virtual host. If you open the localhost Host, you will find that it has several contexts predefined (Figure 1.10).

Each Host and Context is associated with a directory in the server's file system. The directory associated with a Host is specified by the value of the Application Base field. If this value is a *relative pathname*—a pathname that does not begin with a / in Linux or with a drive specification such as C:\ in Windows—then it is taken as relative to the directory in which JWSDP 1.3 (and therefore Tomcat 5.0) was installed. For example, on my Linux machine I installed JWSDP 1.3 at /usr/java/jwsdp-1.3, so the relative pathname webapps given in Figure 1.9 corresponds on my machine to the directory /usr/java/jwsdp-1.3/webapps. [I will normally use forward slash (/) as the separator in file paths; change this to backslash (\) if you are using Windows.] This is known as the *absolute pathname* for the directory, and could have been specified instead of the relative pathname. Using a relative pathname for the Application Base value is generally recommended, since this allows your JWSDP 1.3 installation to be moved to another location within the server file system without the need to change the Application Base value.

The directory associated with a Context is specified by the value of the Document Base field (Figure 1.10). The figure shows an absolute pathname value (on a Windows system), but again the pathname can be relative instead. However, if a relative pathname is specified, it will be relative to the Application Base, not relative to the JWSDP 1.3 installation directory. So, assuming that the Application Base is at C:\jwsdp-1.3\webapps, the Document Base in Figure 1.10 could have been specified as simply ROOT. If you create a Context (by selecting Create New Context from the Host Action menu for a Host), be sure to create the directory that will be specified in the Document Base field before clicking the Save button for the Context.

As we will discuss in some detail in Chapter 8, a Context associates certain URLs with the specified Document Base. Figure 1.10, for example, shows that the root URL path (/) is associated with a directory named ROOT. And, in fact, if you examine the webapps/ROOT directory of your JWSDP 1.3 installation, you will find a file THIRDPARTYLICENSEREADME.html that contains the text (and some other information, discussed in the next chapter) that is displayed when you navigate to http://localhost:8080/THIRDPARTYLICENSEREADME.html (or the equivalent URL for your server). Similarly, if you navigate to http://localhost:8080/, you will see the contents of the webapps/ROOT/index.html file. This is because the server by default displays certain "welcome" files (such as index.html) if you do not explicitly specify a file name at the end of the path portion of the URL used to visit the server. What's more, navigating to http://localhost:8080/servlets-examples will display the contents of the webapps/servlets-examples/index.html file, because (as you can verify by clicking on the /servlets-examples Context object) the Document Base for URLs with paths beginning with /servlets-examples is the webapps/servlets-examples subdirectory of your JWSDP 1.3 installation. Note that the URL path for the Context object is specified using the Path field of the edit page.

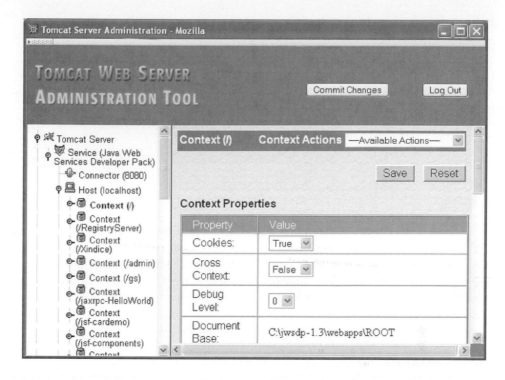

FIGURE 1.10 Context edit page. The content of this screen shot is reproduced by permission of the Apache Software Foundation.

This brief introduction to virtual host concepts is intended to provide you with enough information to be able to set up your own virtual host that will serve simple text files. Again, we will have much more to say about associating URLs with server resources in later chapters. For now, we will move on to some other server capabilities.

1.7.5 Logging

Web server *logs* record information about server activity. The primary web server log recording normal activity is an *access log*, a file that records information about every HTTP request processed by the server. A web server may also produce one or more *message logs* containing a variety of debugging and other information generated by web applications as well as possibly by the web server itself. Finally, information written to the standard output and error streams by the web server or applications may also be logged. We will cover Tomcat's handling of these types of logs as well as some general logging concepts in this subsection.

Access logging in Tomcat is performed by adding a Valve component to a Service. For example, Figure 1.7 shows that the JWSDP Service includes a Valve, and if you click on it, you will find that it is of type AccessLogValve (some other types of Valves are discussed in the next subsection). The primary fields for an AccessLogValve are shown in Table 1.12.

TABLE 1.12 Key Fields for Valve Component of Type AccessLogValve

Field Name	Description
Directory	Directory (relative to Tomcat installation directory or absolute) where log file will be written
Pattern	Information to be written to the log (see text)
Prefix	String that will be used to begin log file name
Resolve Hosts	Whether IP addresses (`False` value) or host names (`True` value) should be written to the log file
Rotatable	Whether or not date should be added to file name and file should be automatically rotated each day
Suffix	String that will be used to end log file name

The combination of values for the Directory, Prefix, Rotatable, and Suffix fields determine the file system path to the access log. The JWSDP Service settings for the values of these Valve fields cause the access log for this Service to be written to the `logs` directory under the JWSDP 1.3 installation directory in a file that starts with the string `access_log.` and ends with the string `.txt`. In between these strings, because Rotatable is given the value `True`, Tomcat inserts the current date, in YYYY-MM-DD (year-month-day) format. So an example JWSDP access log name might be `access_log.2005-07-20.txt`. If you have started and browser to your Tomcat server, you should see one or more files of this form in the `logs` directory under your JWSDP 1.3 installation directory.

The Tomcat server writes one line of information per HTTP request processed to the access log, with the information to be output and its format specified by the Pattern field. The Pattern for the JWSDP Service access log Valve is

```
%h %l %u %t "%r" %s %b
```

This corresponds to what is often called the *common* access log format (in fact, the word `common` can be specified as the value of the Pattern field to specify this log format). The following is an example access log line in common format (this example is split into two lines for readability):

```
www.example.org - admin [20/Jul/2005:08:03:22 -0500]
"GET /admin/frameset.jsp HTTP/1.1" 200 920
```

The following information is contained in this log entry:

- Host name (or IP address; see Table 1.12) of client machine making the request
- User name used to log in, if server password protection is enabled (user "admin" logged in here)
- Date and time of response, plus the time zone (offset from GMT) of the time
- Start line of HTTP request (quoted)
- HTTP status code of response (200 in this example)
- Number of bytes sent in body of response

The Tomcat 5.0 server always returns the hyphen character (-) as the value of the %l pattern.

An advantage of using this log format is that a variety of *log analyzers* have been developed that can read logs in this (and some other) formats and produce reports on various aspects of a site's usage. For example, a log analyzer might report on the number of accesses per day, the percentage of requests that received error status codes, or a breakdown of accesses by domain. Such information can be useful for server tuning, locating software problems, or modifying site content to better target a desired audience. Analog (http://www.analog.cx) is one popular free log analyzer available at the time of this writing.

Another standard log format can be obtained by specifying the value combined for the Pattern. The combined format is the same as the common format but also has the Referer and User-Agent HTTP header field values appended. Custom log formats can also be created; see the section on the Valve component in the Tomcat 5 Server Configuration Reference [APACHE-TOMCAT-5-CONFIG] for details.

The Tomcat Logger component can be used to create a message log for a Service such as the JWSDP service (see Figure 1.7). A message log records informational, debugging, and error messages passed to logging methods by either servlets or Tomcat itself. Some of the key fields for File Loggers (the standard type of message log) are described in Table 1.13.

The JWSDP service sets the values of these fields so that the message log produced is written to the logs directory under the JWSDP 1.3 installation directory in a file that starts with the string jwsdp_log. followed by the date (this is not an option for message logs in Tomcat) and ends with the string .txt. If you look at the contents of one of these files, you will see lines such as

```
2005-08-02 07:38:54 createObjectName with StandardEngine[Catalina]
```

Because the JWSDP service has its Timestamp property set to true, the beginning of each message log entry begins with a *timestamp*, that is, with the date and time at which the entry was written to the log. Timestamps can be useful, particularly when trying to debug an application. One thing to be aware of when using timestamps is that some applications may write timestamps in universal (GMT) time, whereas others, including Tomcat, use local time.

Loggers can be associated with different levels of the Tomcat object hierarchy: with a Service (such as JWSDP, the example just given); with a Host within a Service (such as localhost); and even with a Context, or web application, within a Host (such as admin,

TABLE 1.13 Key Fields for Logger Component of Type File Logger

Field Name	Description
Directory	Directory (relative to Tomcat installation directory or absolute) where log file will be written
Prefix	String that will be used to begin log file name
Suffix	String that will be used to end log file name
Timestamp	Whether or not date and time should be added to beginning of each message written to the log file

the web application that implements the Tomcat administration tool). For example, if you examine the `admin` Context under the `localhost` Host using the Tomcat administration tool, you will see that this Context has its own Logger that produces files beginning with `localhost_admin_log.`, also within the `logs` directory. Messages sent to logging methods by servlets within the `admin` web application will go to this message log file rather than to the JWSDP Service's logger. In general, logging methods will search for a Logger beginning in the Context, then the Host, and finally the Service, sending the log message to the first Logger found. Access logs in Tomcat can also be associated with different levels of the server object hierarchy, although typically there is only one access log per service.

Finally, Tomcat itself or servlets it runs may write directly to the Java standard output and error streams `System.out` and `System.err`. The JWSDP 1.3 installation of Tomcat redirects both of these streams to a file named `launcher.server.log` in the `logs` subdirectory of the JWSDP 1.3 installation directory. Thus, if you write an application that prints an exception stack trace, this is likely where you will find it.

1.7.6 Access Control

Tomcat can provide automatic password protection for resources that it serves. At its heart, this is a two-stage process. First, a database of user names is created. Each user name is assigned a password and a list of *roles*. Think of a role as a user's functional relationship to a web application: administrator, developer, end user, etc. Some users may be assigned to multiple roles. The second stage is to tell Tomcat that certain resources can only be accessed by users who belong to certain roles and who have authenticated themselves as belonging to one of these roles by logging in with an appropriate user name and password. For example, the Tomcat administration tool application (`admin` Context) can only be accessed by users who have logged in and who belong to the admin role.

The second stage of this process—associating resources with required roles—is normally performed by web application developers, as described in Section 8.3.3. The first stage—defining one or more user databases—can be performed by web system administrators, application developers, or both. The JWSDP Service contains an example of a database defined at the Service level through the use of a Realm component, which associates a user database with a Service (Figure 1.11). This particular type of Realm indicates that a Tomcat Resource—an object representing a file or other static resource on the server—will be used to store the user database. The Realm's Resource Name field contains the name of the Resource, which in this case is UserDatabase. If you click on the User Databases link in the Resources list in the left panel of your Tomcat administration tool window and then click on the UserDatabase link in the User Databases panel, you will see that this Resource is associated with a file located at `conf/tomcat-users.xml` (this is relative to the Tomcat installation directory). The administration tool also automatically loads the contents of this file under the User Definition folder in the left panel. Clicking on the Users link under this folder shows that there is one user name in this user database: the user name that you chose for the Tomcat administrator when you installed Tomcat. Finally, clicking on this user name in the right panel shows the roles to which a user logged in with this user name belongs: admin and manager.

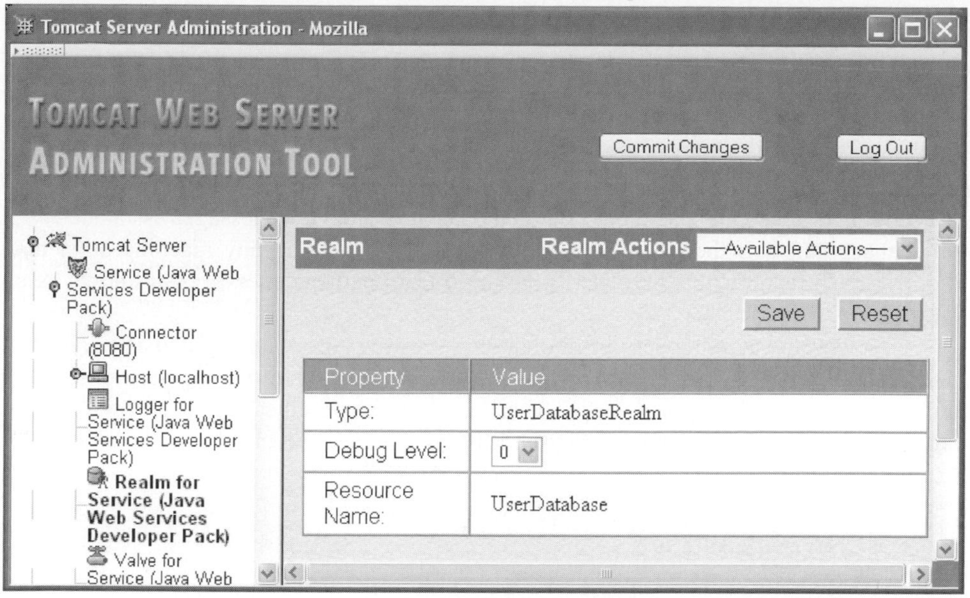

FIGURE 1.11 Realm component panel for the JWSDP Service. The content of this screen shot is reproduced by permission of the Apache Software Foundation.

As mentioned, the admin role is the role required to run the Tomcat administration tool. So, if you wanted to allow another user to run this tool (and other web applications accessible in the admin role), you would simply create that user by selecting Create New User from the Actions dropdown menu of the Users panel and be sure to check the admin role for that user.

A coarser-grained access control can be provided by using Valve objects of type RemoteHostValve and RemoteAddressValve. Both are used to specify client machines that should be rejected if they request a connection to the server. They differ only in whether client machine host names or IP addresses are specified. Each type of Valve has two possible lists of clients: an Allow list and a Deny list. If one or more host names (comma-separated) is entered in the Allow list, then only these hosts can access the server. You can use the * wildcard in place of any label within a host name. So, for example, to allow access only from machines in the example.org and example.net domains, you would enter in the Allow list

```
*.example.org,*.example.net
```

In addition, whether or not any names are entered in the Allow list, any hosts (possibly wildcarded) entered in the Deny list will be prevented from accessing the server. So, to exclude a single machine from the example.org domain while allowing all of the others, we might enter in the Deny list something like

```
baduser.example.org
```

1.7.7   Secure Servers

Normally, the HTTP request and response messages are sent as simple text files. Because these messages are carried by TCP/IP, each message may travel through a number of machines before reaching its destination. It is possible that some machine along the route will extract information from the IP messages it forwards for nefarious purposes. Furthermore, it is often possible for other machines sharing a local network with the sending or receiving machine to snoop the network and view messages associated with other machines as if they were sent to the snooper. In general, any machine other than the sender or receiver that extracts information from network messages is known as an *eavesdropper*.

To prevent eavesdroppers from obtaining sensitive information, such as credit card numbers, all such sensitive information should be *encrypted* before being transmitted over any public communication network. The standard means of indicating to a browser that it should encrypt an HTTP request is to use the `https` scheme on the URL for the request. For example, entering the URL

```
https://www.example.org
```

in Mozilla's Location bar will cause the browser to attempt to send an encrypted HTTP GET request to `www.example.org`.

Various protocols have been used to support encryption of HTTP messages. Many browsers and servers support one or more versions of the Secure Socket Layer (SSL) protocol as well as the newer Transport Layer Security (TLS) protocol, which is based on SSL 3.0. The following description of HTTP encryption is derived from the TLS 1.0 specification [RFC-2246], but the same general ideas apply to the earlier SSL protocols as well.

A client browser that wishes to communicate securely with a server begins by initiating (over TCP/IP) a *TLS Handshake* with the server. During the Handshake process, the server and client agree on various parameters that will be used to encrypt messages sent between them. The server also sends a *certificate* to the client. The certificate enables the client to be sure that the machine it is communicating with is the one the client intends (as specified by the host name in the URL the browser is requesting). Certificates are necessary to avoid so-called *man-in-the-middle attacks*, in which some machine intercepts a message intended for another machine (the target), prevents the message from further forwarding, and returns an HTTP reply to the sender pretending to be from the target. Such an interception could occur at a rogue Internet bridge device on the route between client and server, or through unauthorized alteration of the DNS system, for example.

At the conclusion of the TLS Handshake, the client uses the cryptographic parameter information obtained to encrypt its HTTP request message before sending it to the server over TCP/IP. The server's TLS software decrypts this request before any other server processing is performed. The server similarly encrypts its response before sending it to the client, and the client immediately decrypts the received message. Therefore, other HTTP-processing software running on the client and server are, for the most part, unaffected by the encryption process.

One small point involves the port used for the TCP/IP communication of TLS data. Since the TLS protocol begins with a TLS Handshake, and not with an HTTP request start line, different communication ports are used for the two types of communication. Whereas the default port for HTTP communication is 80, the default for TLS/SSL is 443. This port can be overridden just as the HTTP port can be overridden, by explicitly adding a port number after the host name in an `https`-scheme URL. So, for example, to access the root of a secure server on localhost at port 8443, you would use the URL

```
https://localhost:8443/
```

Tomcat supports the TLS 1.0 and earlier protocols. To enable the secure server Tomcat features, you must do two things:

1. Obtain and install a certificate.
2. Configure the server to listen for TLS connections on some port.

For test purposes, you can generate your own "self-signed" certificates using the `keytool` program distributed with Sun Java™ JDK™ development software. This program is located in the same directory as the `javac` and `java` programs. Assuming that this directory is included in your PATH environment variable, you can begin to create a self-signed certificate suitable for use with Tomcat 5.0 by entering the following at a command prompt:

```
keytool -genkey -alias tomcat -keyalg RSA
```

This says that you want to generate a self-signed certificate that can be referenced by the name `tomcat` and that the encryption/decryption keys generated for use with this certificate should be compatible with the RSA encryption/decryption algorithm (which is the algorithm Tomcat uses). You will be prompted to enter several pieces of information. Since this certificate is self-signed and will be used for test purposes only, for the most part, it does not matter what you enter. However, I suggest entering the fully qualified domain name of your machine when asked to enter your first and last name, as this will prevent a warning later when you try to use the certificate. Also, I suggest using the password `changeit` when asked, which will allow you to use defaults when you configure the server to use this certificate (but use this password for testing purposes only).

Configuring the server to listen for TLS connections simply involves adding a second Connector to a Service (by selecting Create New Connector from the Service's Action drop-down menu). The Type field of the new Connector must be set to HTTPS. On the resulting Connector panel, make sure that the Secure field is set to `True` (since this is a secure connection), and fill in the port number (say 8443) to be used for this connection. Other fields can retain their default values if you run `keytool` with its defaults. After Saving and Committing the changes made in order to create your new Connector, stop your server. If you have not already performed the JWSDP 1.3 postinstallation tasks described in the appendix (Section A.4.2), do so at this time. Now restart your Tomcat server, close and reopen your browser, and then browse to `https://localhost:8443` (modify this as appropriate for the host name and port number for your secure server). If you created a self-signed certificate, you should see a message asking you whether or not you wish to accept the certificate. After accepting it, you should see the default JWSDP web page produced by your server. Note that a small padlock icon at the bottom of your browser window is shown locked, indicating that the page is being viewed securely.

Since there is no independent validation of self-signed certificates, anyone can generate a self-signed certificate for your machine. This is why browsers will typically display a warning message if a self-signed certificate is presented by a server: while it is syntactically a certificate, it does not prevent a man-in-the-middle attack, because an attacker could easily have generated the certificate. In order for your server to provide transparent secure communication using certificates that browsers will trust automatically, you must have your certificate verified and then digitally "signed" (for a fee) by a certificate authority, such as VeriSign. Details are provided in the SSL section of the Tomcat User Guide [APACHE-TOMCAT-5-UG].

1.8 · Case Study

To provide some context for the various technologies we will be covering, an ongoing case study will be part of most chapters. Specifically, we'll create a simple tool for writing and reading a web log (*blog*). One user, the *blogger*, will be able to add text entries to the blog. The most recent entry will appear at the beginning of a web page, followed by the next most recent, and so on for all entries made during the current month. Links elsewhere on the page will provide access to entries made in earlier months (Figure 1.12). Other capabilities will be described in later chapters.

Although we're not ready to start developing any software for this application, we can make some decisions related to the material covered in this chapter:

- Which browsers will we support?
- Which web server(s) will we use?
- How extensive will our security measures be?

At the time of this writing, if our application runs well with IE6 and Mozilla-like browsers, then we will have covered a large percentage of browsers in use, so we will test our application against Mozilla 1.4 and IE6. We will use the Tomcat server distributed with JWSDP 1.3 because it is freely available, runs on multiple platforms, is simple to configure (compared with running, say, both Apache and Tomcat), is sufficiently fast for our needs, and supports the technologies that we will be covering in later chapters.

The question of security is somewhat more difficult. The key security task for the case study application is to prevent everyone but the blogger from adding entries to the blog. A preceding task—one that is beyond the scope of this textbook—is to make sure that the machine running the web server is itself secure from unauthorized access. Obviously, if someone can gain administrative privileges on the server machine, then no amount of work we put into securing the application itself will make it truly secure.

Assuming a secure server machine, the weakest level of security would be to have a "secret" URL that the blogger visits in order to add an entry to the blog. This approach is open to several attacks, one of which is to simply try a variety of reasonable URLs. For

FIGURE 1.12 Example blog page with entries on left and links on right.

example, if the blog can be read by visiting the URL http://www.example.com/blog/read, we might guess that the "secret" URL is http://www.example.com/blog/add. Somewhat more security can be achieved by requiring the blogger to log in before adding an entry. A weakness with this approach, as pointed out in the preceding section, is that an eavesdropper might be able to learn the log-in information (eavesdropping might also be used to learn a "secret" URL). This weakness can be overcome by using a secure server and visiting only https-scheme URLs when logging in and adding entries to the blog. Even this level of security can be defeated if the log-in information can be guessed, so for even more security we would force all passwords to conform with certain conventions (e.g., consist of at least eight characters including both a lowercase and an uppercase letter plus at least one digit).

The application we develop will require that the blogger log in before adding an entry, but we won't require a secure server or password conventions. This is probably an appropriate level of security for this application: we want to discourage people from impersonating the blogger, but the damage if someone does is probably not so great that it requires the additional development effort (and potential problems for users) of additional security measures.

1.9   References

Unlike most topics in this textbook, there is no one definitive reference for the history of the Internet. The brief history presented here was culled from a number of sources. A good starting point for further reading is the Internet Society's list of links to online Internet histories (`http://www.isoc.org/internet/history/`). One of the more comprehensive histories is Hobbes' Internet Timeline (`http://www.zakon.org/robert/internet/timeline/`). An outstanding Internet history through 1992 is available at the Computer History Museum (`http://www.computerhistory.org/exhibits/internet_history/`). Finally, a good starting point for early World Wide Web history is the World Wide Web Consortium's "A Little History of the World Wide Web" at `http://www.w3.org/History.html`.

A particularly nice feature of the Internet is that from the earliest days of ARPANET, electronic communication has been used to support technical discussions about and documentation of network standards. Much of this documentation is in the form of RFCs (requests for comment), which are basically numbered memos written by and to the Internet technical community. The RFC collection is maintained by an organization known, appropriately enough, as the RFC Editor (`http://rfc-editor.org`).

Most of the key standards for the Internet are documented via one or more RFCs. An organization known as the Internet Engineering Steering Group (IESG) is responsible for deciding which RFCs become standards. A list of the RFCs describing all current Internet standards is maintained at `http://www.rfc-editor.org/rfcxx00.html`, and periodic snapshots of this information are published in document form [STD-1]. Section 1 of this document gives an overview of the standards process.

RFCs themselves are never changed once published. However, the RFC Editor does maintain an errata list at `http://www.rfc-editor.org/errata.html`. Furthermore, it is not uncommon for later RFCs to update or even obsolete earlier RFCs. Searching for an RFC number using the RFC Editor's RFC-Search function will provide a list of RFCs that update or obsolete the given RFC.

Many of the RFCs and STDs (Internet standards) on which the information in this chapter is based are given in Table 1.14 for easy reference. The Bibliography provides the title and a URL for each STD (or RFC if no STD is available).

Most of the end-user reference material for the Mozilla browser is contained in its built-in help files. The home page for web developers who are writing software to be run by Mozilla is currently at `http://www.mozilla.org/docs/web-developer/`. This is, to some extent, a list of links to documentation for various standards, since Mozilla is one of the

TABLE 1.14 RFCs Related to Topics in this Chapter

Topic	RFCs
IP	STD 5/RFC 791
TCP	STD 7/RFC 793
UDP	STD 6/RFC 768
DNS	STD 13/RFCs 1034, 1035
HTTP 1.1	RFC 2616
URI/URL	STD 66/RFC 3986
URN	RFC 2141
https	RFC 2818
MIME	RFCs 2045–2047, 2049, 2077, 4288, 4289
UTF-8	STD 63/RFC 3629
TLS	RFC 2246

more standards-compliant browsers available at this time. References to these standards will be presented in later chapters as we learn about the related technologies.

The various components of Tomcat 5 servers—Service, Connector, Host, etc.—are documented in the Tomcat 5 Server Configuration Reference [APACHE-TOMCAT-5-CONFIG]. Appendix A of the Java Web Services Tutorial [SUN-JWS-TUTORIAL-1.3] provides a full description of the Tomcat web server administration tool covered briefly in Section. 1.7.3. The Tomcat 5 User Guide [APACHE-TOMCAT-5-UG] provides an overview of many Tomcat concepts, including SSL in Chapter. 12. SSL is also covered in Chapter 24 of the JWSDP Tutorial [SUN-JWS-TUTORIAL-1.3].

Exercises

1.1. Using `nslookup` (or some other mechanism), determine IP addresses for three Internet hosts assigned by your instructor.

1.2. Send HTTP requests using `telnet` (or some other mechanism) in order to determine the Server header field value for three Internet hosts assigned by your instructor. You may want to include the header field "Connection: close" in your requests in order to tell the server to immediately close the TCP connection rather than keeping it open (most servers will otherwise keep the connection open for a minute or so, tying up your command prompt). Also note that some systems may not echo the characters you type while executing `telnet`. (Hint: Don't forget that HTTP requests end with a blank line.)

1.3. For three Internet hosts assigned by your instructor, list the names of the header fields that each host returns in response to a HEAD request for the root document (Request-URI of /). As in the previous question, you may want to use the "Connection: close" header in your requests.

1.4. For each host assigned by your instructor, give a list of the HTTP methods allowed by the host. (Hint: You may want to try using an OPTIONS HTTP request, although not all web servers support this method.)

1.5. Given the header field

```
accept: text/xml,application/xml,application/xhtml+xml,
    text/html;q=0.9,text/plain;q=0.8,video/x-mng,image/png,
    image/jpeg,image/gif;q=0.2,*/*;q=0.1
```

place the following MIME types in order from high to low preference: `image/png`, `application/pdf`, `text/plain`, `application/xhtml+xml`.

1.6. Explain how a web site could learn something about your browsing habits outside its site from an HTTP request sent to the site by your browser. Assume that the request has only the headers listed in Table 1.5.

1.7. In Java J2SE™ version 1.5, characters are represented using the UTF-16 encoding. Specifically, each `char` value consists of 16 bits representing a UTF-16 *character code unit*. Every character in the Unicode Standard can be represented by either one or two UTF-16 code units, with virtually all characters in widespread use requiring only a single code unit. Give an argument for and one against this design for representing characters in Java versus using 8-bit `char`'s and the UTF-8 encoding.

1.8. Can a web browser load an HTML document from a web server running on a different host if DNS is not operational? Explain.

1.9. Give a complete minimal HTTP GET request corresponding to the URL

```
http://www.ThisIsATest.net:2012/hmm/oh/well?isThis=right#now
```

1.10. Modify your browser preferences to specify a language other than the one that you normally use as your preferred language (for example, if you normally use English, you might specify German as your preferred language). Then browse to `www.google.com` or another web site that returns different documents based on the setting of the Accept-Language HTTP request header field. Print the web page to verify that you successfully modified your language preference.

1.11. The Host field of an HTTP request can contain a port number as well as a host name. Based on the discussion in Section 1.7.1, explain how a web server can determine the port number of the request even if it is not included in the Host field, as long as the HTTP request is transmitted via TCP.

The following questions assume that you have installed JWSDP 1.3 or otherwise set up a Tomcat web server.

1.12. What is the connection timeout (in seconds) for the 8080 Connector to the JWSDP Service of your server?

1.13. Change the connection timeout of your 8080 Connector to 10 seconds, and test your change (for example, by using Telnet to connect to the server and then verifying that the server closes the connection in 10 seconds). Submit the host name and port number of your server to your instructor so that the change can be independently verified.

1.14. Add a virtual host named `www.example.org` to the JWSDP Service of your Tomcat server with Application Base `virtualhost`. Then create a Context within this virtual host with Document Base docs and Path /. (Hint: Don't forget to create the directory before saving the Context object.) After committing your changes, create a short text file named `test.txt` in your docs directory (you should have no other files in this directory). Finally, test that you have created your virtual host properly by using Telnet to visit it using the Request-URI `/test.txt` and an appropriate value for the Host field. You should see the contents of your `test.txt` file. Submit the host name and port number of your server to your instructor so that your work can be verified.

1.15. Explain why in the previous question you needed to use Telnet rather than standard browser navigation in order to test that the virtual host was set up properly.

1.16. Heuristic estimation of cache expiration.

    (a) Determine whether or not your Tomcat server returns an Expires header field when the root (/) document is requested. If it does return this header field, give the value returned. Repeat for the Last-Modified header field.

    (b) Assuming that you are using Mozilla 1.4 as your browser, select the **View|Page Info** menu item. In the pop-up window under the **General** tab, what are the values of the Modified and Expires fields?

    (c) The HTTP/1.1 specification (RFC 2616) says that if an Expires header field (or similar information) is not provided by a web server in its response to a request for a resource, then browsers may use a heuristic to determine how long to wait before validating a cached copy of the resource. It also says that if the server provides a Last-Modified time, then this waiting period should be no more than a certain percentage of the difference between the current time and the Last-Modified time. Based on the information gathered in the first two parts of this question, give a reasonable explanation for how the browser produced the Modified and Expires field values displayed in the **View|Page Info** pop-up window. [Hint: Note that time values in header fields are often given in Greenwich Mean Time (GMT), while the browser generally displays local times.] In particular, estimate the percentage the browser might be using in any heuristic it employs to compute the displayed Expires value.

1.17. This question explores the interaction between browsers and cache. First, open Mozilla 1.4 and select the **Edit | Preferences** menu item. In the Preferences window that appears, click on the + to the left of **Advanced** in the Category panel, and select **Cache** under **Advanced**. In the Cache panel make sure that, under "Compare the page in the cache to the page on the network," "When the page is out of date" has been selected. If not, select this button, click OK, and then close and reopen your browser. Next, locate the access log for your server in the server's local file system. View the last three or so lines of this log. Next, make sure that your Tomcat server is running, and navigate your Mozilla 1.4 browser to `http://localhost:8080/`. You should see a JWSDP 1.3 welcome page. Now answer the following questions:

(a) Reexamine the final three or so lines of the server access log. Have they changed? (Yes or no is sufficient for this question.)

(b) Scroll down to the bottom of the web page; then click your mouse in the Location bar of your browser and press the Enter key on the keyboard. This causes your browser to navigate to the `http://localhost:8080/` URL again, as indicated by the fact that the top of the web page is again shown in the browser. Now again reexamine the final three or so lines of the server access log. Have they changed? Explain why this has (or has not) happened.

(c) Now click the browser's Reload button. Once again, reexamine the final three or so lines of the server access log. Have they changed? Again, explain.

1.18. Configure your Tomcat server to deny access to the `localhost` Host of the JWSDP Service from an IP address supplied by your instructor. What status code is returned by your server when it is accessed from a host that is denied access? What message does the Tomcat administration tool produce if you try to deny access to the IP address of the machine running the browser through which you are accessing the tool? Explain why this message is generated.

1.19. Create a self-signed certificate, and use it to set up secure access to the JWSDP Service running on your Tomcat web server. Send the host name and port number of your server to your instructor for verification.

Research and Exploration

1.20. Learn about your educational institution's network history by answering questions such as the following: In what year was your institution first connected to the Internet? What was the original connection type: PhoneNet or something else? What was the original connection speed? Was your institution a member of a regional or other specialized network, such as SURAnet or CSNET? Answer these questions for your institution currently.

1.21. Use the `tracert` (Windows) or `traceroute` (Linux) command to determine the number of hops from your machine to the Internet host(s) assigned by your instructor. Each command can be run by typing the command name followed by a host name. (Note: If you attempt to run `traceroute` on a Linux system and get the message "Command not found," try using the command `whereis traceroute` to locate it. Then prefix the command name with the directory where it is located.) Provide a copy of the output and briefly explain what it means.

1.22. The standard port number for HTTP is 80. What is the standard port number for an initial connection to an FTP server? For a DNS request? Name and give a standard port number for one IANA-registered UDP service and one TCP service not mentioned in this chapter.

1.23. List all of the generic Internet top-level domains.

1.24. Which country is associated with the top-level domain de? What is the top-level domain for Bolivia?

1.25. How could you determine whether or not a TCP service is running at port 13 of a given Internet host? Test this for the host(s) assigned by your instructor. What is the standard IANA-registered higher-level protocol associated with this port?

1.26. Refer to RFC 1436, and then write a short example Gopher directory (menu) file. How does the protocol used for communicating with Gopher servers differ from HTTP?

1.27. Give a mailto-scheme URL to send e-mail with subject Test Message to a user named Kim at host www.example.net.

1.28. What is one of the MIME types used to represent a sound file? What type of data is represented using the MIME type model/vrml?

1.29. Write an Accept-Language header indicating a preference for documents in English, then in French, and finally in German.

1.30. Compare the basic features of HTTP status codes with those of the FTP reply codes given by RFC 640. What is one way in which these codes are similar and one way in which they are different?

1.31. Refer to [IANA-CHARSETS] to find three alternative registered names for the US-ASCII character set. For which character set is latin1 an alias? Name a character set tailored to Danish.

1.32. Research and report on current browser usage statistics. In particular, give approximate percentages of users of Internet Explorer, Firefox, Safari, Opera, and other popular browsers. Cite your source(s). Why should you be aware of browser usage statistics when developing web documents?

1.33. Research and report on current web server usage statistics. In particular, give approximate usage percentages for Apache, IIS, and other popular servers. Cite your source(s).

1.34. A *robot* (also known as a *bot* or *spider* or *crawler*) is a program that accesses web documents automatically rather than in direct response to a user input. For example, the Google search engine uses a program called googlebot to automatically crawl the World Wide Web and build its searchable index of Web pages. An indexing robot such as googlebot begins by reading some Web document, then reading documents linked to by the initial document, and recursively continuing this process on previously unread documents. Some informal standards have been developed to allow Web site administrators and document authors to request robots not to read certain documents.

    (a) Read the first part of Section 4.1 of Appendix B of the HTML 4.01 Recommendation [W3C-HTML-4.01], and explain what you would do in order to request that robots not crawl the documents accessible from your Tomcat web server. (See http://www.robotstxt.org/wc/norobots.html for more information on the Robot Exclusion Standard.)

    (b) For one or more Web sites as directed by your instructor, list for each the robots (if any) that are explicitly excluded from crawling one or more of the files at that site.

Projects

1.35. Write a simple web browser. Specifically, write a Java program that meets one or more of the following requirements, as specified by your instructor:

(a) Input a URL from the user, and output the complete HTTP response produced by visiting this URL. This is relatively easy if you use the classes HttpURLConnection and URL in the java.net package of the Java API. For example, if url is a String variable containing a URL, then the code

```
HttpURLConnection connection =
  (HttpURLConnection)(new URL(url).openConnection());
connection.connect();
```

opens a TCP connection with the server specified in the url variable, sends an appropriate HTTP GET request over this connection, and receives back the HTTP response. The methods getHeaderFieldKey() and getHeaderField() can then be called on the connection variable in order to retrieve header field names and values, respectively (and even the status line, on many systems), while the getInputStream() method provides access to the body of the HTTP response. See the Java API [SUN-JAVA-API-1.4.2] for details on these and other methods of these classes.

(b) By default, when the connect() method of the HttpURLConnection class is called, if the initial response from the server is a redirect (first digit of status code is a 3), then the method automatically issues a request for the URL contained in the redirect response. This automatic redirection is applied to subsequent responses until a nonredirect response is finally received. The application calling the method only sees the final response. Modify the original program so that it overrides this default (using the setInstanceFollowRedirects() method of HttpURLConnection) before connecting with the server. Then modify your program so that, if it receives a redirection response, it outputs the URL to which it is redirected (and only that URL) and then sends a request to that URL. Note that you must create a separate HttpURLConnection instance for each request. Your program should repeat this process until a nonredirect response is received; this final response should be printed in its entirety. (Hint: In order to test this program, you'll need a URL that returns a redirect response. If your instructor does not supply such a URL, find any URL that ends with a / and visit the URL obtained by removing the trailing /. Many servers will respond to such a URL with a redirect status code.)

(c) In order to appreciate some of the HTTP protocol complexities handled by the HttpURLConnection class, write your program without using this class or the openConnection() method of URL. Instead, write your program using the java.net.Socket class. Creating an instance of this class using the Socket(String host, int port) constructor causes Java to open a TCP/IP connection between your program and the specified host at the specified port. You can then call the getOutputStream() method on this Socket instance in order to get a stream to which you can write an HTTP request message. Notice that you will need to extract some of the information needed for this request, such as the Request-URI and the port, from the URL input by the user. If values are not supplied by the URL, then your program must supply appropriate defaults. You will find that the URL Java API class has many methods that are useful for extracting the appropriate information. Be sure to *flush* the output stream after writing the request message to it: this moves the message you wrote from your system's memory to the actual TCP/IP connection. After flushing the output stream, you can call `getInputStream()` on your Socket instance to get a stream through which the server will send the HTTP response. If you include a "Connection: close" header field in your request, then you should be able to obtain the entire response by simply reading from the input stream until the end of the stream is reached (note that this stream contains the entire response, including the headers and the body, while the `HttpURLConnection`'s input stream provides only the body).

1.36. Write a simple web server. Specifically, write a Java program that meets one or more of the following requirements, as specified by your instructor:

(a) Write a server that listens for HTTP requests on port 8080 (or other port specified by your instructor) and accepts one request at a time. This is relatively easy using classes from the `java.net` package of the Java API. In particular, the first line of the code

```
ServerSocket mySocket = new ServerSocket(8080);
Socket yourSocket = mySocket.accept();
```

creates a socket on port 8080 of the machine running this code. The second line then causes the program to listen for a connection to this port. The program will not execute the line of code following the `accept()` call until a connection is made to the port. When the connection is made, `yourSocket` will provide communication with the connecting program. Specifically, the `getInputStream()` method on this object will return a stream that can be read to obtain the HTTP request being sent, and `getOutputStream()` will return a stream to which the server program can write its response. If a valid HTTP/1.1 request for the root (/) document is received, then send back a response with status code 200 (OK) and containing a short text document (such as "Success!"). Otherwise, send a response with status code 404 (Not Found) and a short text document giving further information (such as "Failure ..."). In either case, the response should contain at least the header fields Date, Content-Type (with value "text/plain"), and Content-Length. Don't forget to flush your output after you have written the entire response. You can then call `close()` on `yourSocket` followed by a call to `accept()` to await the next connection. Your server can continue iterating in this way until it is killed. Test your program by starting it (first make sure that no other program that uses port 8080, such as Tomcat, is running) and then browsing to `http://localhost:8080/` and `http://localhost:8080/fail`. Visiting the first URL should display your successful response; the second should fail. (Hint: Section 3.3.1 of the HTTP/1.1 specification [RFC-2616] requires that the Date header field value generated by a web server follow a particular format. You can produce a String `dateTime` representing the current date and time in the appropriate format using the code

```
import java.util.Date;
import java.util.Locale;
import java.util.TimeZone;
import java.text.SimpleDateFormat;
import java.text.DateFormatSymbols;
. . .
```

```
SimpleDateFormat formatter =
    new SimpleDateFormat("E, dd MMM yyyy HH:mm:ss zzz",
                         new DateFormatSymbols(Locale.US));
formatter.setTimeZone(TimeZone.getTimeZone("GMT"));
String dateTime = formatter.format(new Date());
```

(b) Modify the server program described in (a) so that if the Request-URI of an HTTP request corresponds to a file within the server's file system, the server will return that file. Otherwise, the server should return a 404 response as before. In particular, if the Request-URI is of the form /filename.ext and a file named filename.ext exists in the directory from which the server is being run, then this file should be returned in the response. You may assume for simplicity that every requested file is character-oriented (rather than the more general case of treating a file as a stream of bytes). The Date, Content-Type, and Content-Length header fields should all be set appropriately in the response. The static method getFileNameMap() of the java.net.URLConnection class can be used to get a java.net.FileNameMap, which in turn provides a method getContentTypeFor() that maps a filename to a corresponding MIME type based on its extension ext. The resulting MIME type is appropriate for use as the value of a Content-Type header field. Test your program by creating small text files named test.txt and test.xml in the directory from which your server runs and then browsing to these files using URLs such as http://localhost:8080/test.xml. The Type field of Mozilla's **View|Page Info** pop-up window will display the MIME type of the document.

(c) Modify your server to produce an access log in common log format. Output the IP address of the client rather than the host name, and output a hypen (-) for the user-name field. The date and time can be produced using the formatter

```
SimpleDateFormat formatter =
    new SimpleDateFormat("dd/MMM/yyyy:HH:mm:ss Z",
                         new DateFormatSymbols(Locale.US));
```

Write the log to a file named access.log. Be sure to flush the buffer after each output to the log file so that each access is immediately visible in the file.

CHAPTER 2

Markup Languages
XHTML 1.0

The previous chapter presented an overview of how computers communicate over the Internet, particularly as part of the World Wide Web. It also discussed the functions of web browsers and servers. While many types of information can be communicated between browsers and servers, most documents are written using the Hypertext Markup Language (HTML), which is a primary focus of this chapter.

Actually, HTML is not a single language, but the name for a family of related languages that have evolved over the years. We will cover one of the newer members of this family, XHTML 1.0. In order to fully understand XHTML, you'll need some familiarity with another language, the Extensible Markup Language (XML). So we will also cover enough XML to allow you to understand the formal definition of XHTML 1.0. XML is important in other contexts as well; additional XML details will be covered in later chapters, particularly Chapter 7.

We'll begin this chapter by looking at a simple HTML example. Next, you'll learn a bit about the history of HTML, why HTML standards are important, and why we will study XHTML 1.0 rather than some other version of HTML. After that, many of the basic features of XHTML 1.0 will be covered. Then XML and its relationship to XHTML will be presented. The blogging case study as well as some key online references for XHTML, XML, and browser handling of HTML are included at the end of the chapter.

When you have finished this chapter, you should be able to:

- Create standards-compliant static HTML documents using a variety of HTML elements.
- Know where to find the reference definitions of HTML and XML and be able to understand (at least most of) these definitions.
- Determine whether or not an XHTML document is syntactically correct by consulting an XML document type definition.
- Describe some of the history of HTML and the relationships between HTML, XML, and XHTML.
- Discuss pros and cons of following standards in web development.

2.1 An Introduction to HTML

Before saying any more about the Hypertext Markup Language, let's briefly look at a small example file to gain a more concrete understanding of HTML syntax and semantics. Figure 2.1 presents an HTML "Hello World!" document. Figure 2.2 shows how this document would appear if it were opened using the Mozilla browser as discussed in the previous chapter (the figure may not look much like a browser window, because toolbars and menus

```
<!DOCTYPE html
        PUBLIC "-//W3C//DTD XHTML 1.0 Strict//EN"
        "http://www.w3.org/TR/xhtml1/DTD/xhtml1-strict.dtd">
<html xmlns="http://www.w3.org/1999/xhtml">
  <head>
    <title>
      HelloWorld.html
    </title>
  </head>
  <body>
    <p>
      Hello World!
    </p>
  </body>
</html>
```

FIGURE 2.1 "Hello World!" HTML file.

have been suppressed). You can try this example and others in this chapter by downloading the examples from the Web site for this textbook (see the Preface for the address), navigating your browser to the examples for this chapter, and selecting the file indicated by the title of the browser window (HelloWorld.html in this example).

This document, like every HTML document, contains two types of information:

- The markup information, which is contained in *tags* consisting of angle bracket tag delimiters (< and >) plus the text contained between these delimiters.
- The *character data* of the document, which is everything outside of the markup tags and is generally information that is intended to be displayed by the browser. In this case, the character data consists of the two strings HelloWorld.html and Hello World! as well as some white space.

The first tag appearing in the "Hello World!" document (the tag beginning with <!DOCTYPE) is special markup information called the *document type declaration*. We'll have more to say about this declaration later. For now, it is enough to observe that a primary function of this tag is to identify the particular version of HTML used to write the remainder of the file. In this case, the file is written in the XHTML 1.0 Strict version. How this version relates to other versions of HTML is discussed in Section 2.2.2.

Everything in the "Hello World!" document following the document type declaration—the text from <html down—is called the *document instance*. Each of the tags

FIGURE 2.2 Appearance of "Hello World!" document when opened by a web browser.

in this example document instance is either a *start tag* or an *end tag*. Syntactically, within start tags a word—the *element name*—immediately follows the < of the tag, while in end tags the element name is preceded by a slash (/). As indicated by the indentation in this example, each start tag can be viewed as starting a nesting level that is closed by its corresponding end tag, much as an open curly brace ({) in C++ or Java begins a block that is closed by a corresponding closing curly brace (}). The markup tags therefore impose a tree structure on the document (the reader unfamiliar with the notion of "trees" in computer science should refer to any introductory textbook on data structures). The start tag and its corresponding end tag, along with all of the document between the tags, is called an *element* of the document. The portion between the tags (not including the tags themselves) is called the *content* of the element.

We have seen that the document type declaration indicates the version of HTML used in the file. Another piece of information contained in the document type declaration is the name of the *root element* of the document. The first word after the DOCTYPE keyword is the name of the root element. For HTML documents, the root element is always named, appropriately enough, html. The first tag in the document instance of an HTML file must be a start tag for the root element, and the root element can only occur once in the document. In order to strictly conform with the XHTML 1.0 standard, the html start tag must also contain the xmlns="..." string shown. That string is an example of an *attribute specification*, which consists of an *attribute name* (xmlns in this case) and an *attribute value* (the string within quotes). We'll have much more to say about attributes later.

Viewed as a tree, the elements of our example document are shown in Figure 2.3. In all XHTML 1.0 Strict documents, the root html element has two children: head and body. Any text contained in the head element does not appear directly in the primary window area (the *client area*) of the browser window. Instead, the head element is used for providing certain instructions to the browser, as we will see in later chapters. The only such instruction to the browser in this example is provided by the title element, which directs the browser to display the element content as the window title (displayed in the title bar at the very top of the browser window; see Fig. 2.2). Also, if you bookmark this page in Mozilla, the content of the title element will appear in the list of bookmarks.

The body element contains the information that is to be displayed in the client area of the browser. This document's body contains a single paragraph (p) element. Notice that only the content of this element is displayed; the p start and end tags are used to inform the browser about the content and are not displayed themselves. A p element in particular tells the browser that its content represents a single paragraph of text (and possibly other elements) and should be displayed accordingly.

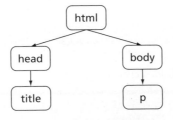

FIGURE 2.3 The element tree for "Hello World!"

Now that we've covered a few HTML basics, we will consider some of the history of HTML and its different versions.

2.2 HTML's History and Versions

HTML was initially defined by a single person, Tim Berners-Lee, in 1990. Berners-Lee was working at a European high-energy physics research center (CERN) when he began developing HTML, and the early language was designed with science and engineering interests in mind. Even after a few years of use and revision, the elements of the language could still be described in a short document [W3C-HTML-HIST]. Specifically, the elements in use as of November 1992 included the title and paragraph elements that we have already seen, along with elements for creating hyperlinks, headings, simple lists, glossaries, examples (text with monospace fonts and any white space retained), and address blocks (containing information about the document author, and typically italicized). There was also an element that could be included in a web document to indicate that the web server providing the document would accept search terms appended to the URL. That was all! There was no facility for producing tables or fill-in forms, much less for including images within a document.

2.2.1 The "War" Years

Around this time, Marc Andreessen and Eric Bina of the National Center for Supercomputer Applications (NCSA), a unit of the University of Illinois at Urbana-Champaign, were working on a graphical web browser designed for UNIX® systems as part of a larger project called Mosaic. By February 1993 they had publicly released a preliminary version of their browser. Figure 2.4 shows the screen shot example contained in Andreessen's short technical report announcing the project and public availability of preliminary software (a revised version of this report with later screen shots is available at [NCSA-MOSAIC]). By September of the same year an initial release of this browser, along with Windows and Macintosh versions, was made available. In addition to displaying images within documents, the NCSA Mosaic browser could play video clips as well as sounds. Its user-friendly interface, multimedia support, and implementation on widely available systems jump-started the transformation of the Web from a tool used primarily by a small number of researchers in engineering and the sciences to the ubiquitous entity that we know today.

Many of the key individuals involved in the early Mosaic development at NCSA left to begin the company that became Netscape Communications. This included Andreessen, who had worked on Mosaic as an undergraduate at UIUC and was now Netscape's chief executive officer. The company soon had hundreds of employees working on various aspects of web software development. Meanwhile, after an initial delay, Microsoft deployed a similarly large development team to work on its Internet Explorer browser, initiating what became known as the "browser wars" between Netscape and Microsoft. Innovation in web technology in general—and in the HTML definition in particular—proceeded at a furious pace. HTML therefore went quickly from being a language defined by Berners-Lee and others interested in producing a "clean" language to being a language defined by browser developers working under intense market pressures.

During the period from 1993 through 1997, HTML was being defined operationally by the elements that browser software developers chose to implement and the ways in which their browsers responded to these elements. In an attempt to gain competitive advantage,

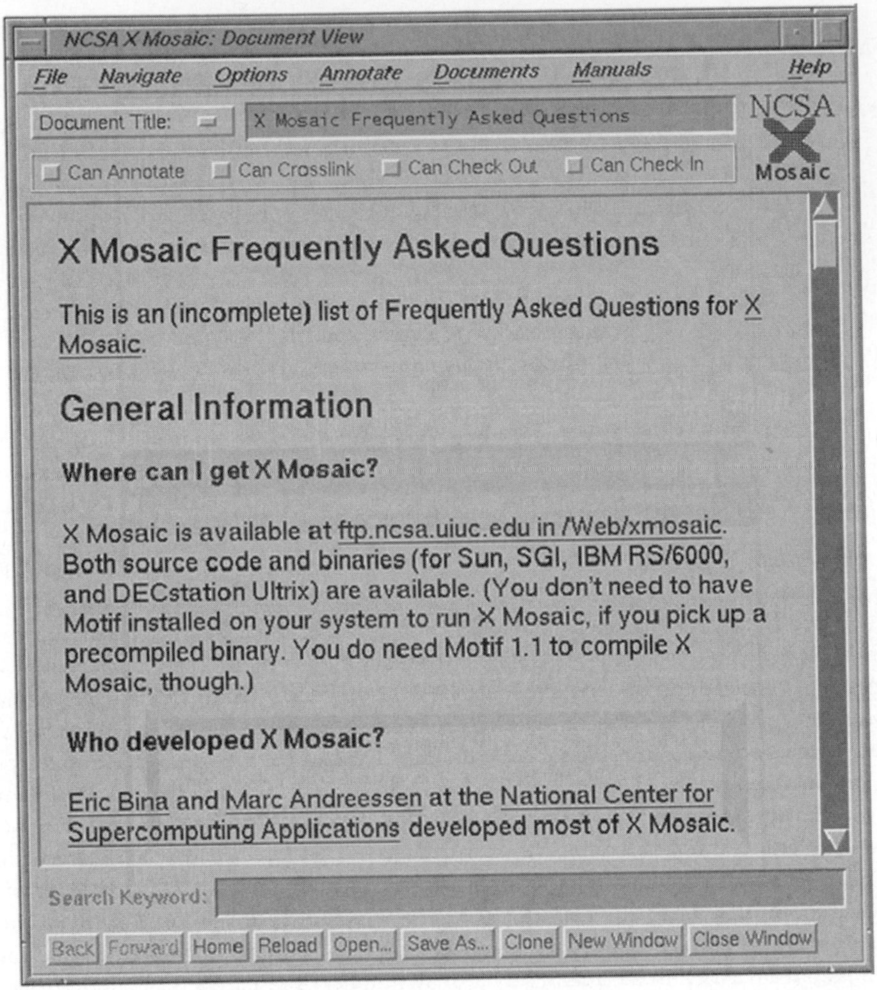

FIGURE 2.4 Screen shot of early Mosaic web browser. Courtesy of the National Center for Supercomputing Applications (NCSA) and the Board of Trustees of the University of Illinois.

each of the two major browser manufacturers sought to incorporate new features (often HTML elements) into its browser so that it could tout the benefits of its browser over the competitor's. This led to significant HTML differences, not only between the latest products of each manufacturer, but also between newer and older versions of browsers from the same manufacturer. On top of this, because of the rush to get products to market and the inherent complexities of software development, browsers often had quirks or even outright bugs that had to be considered when writing the HTML for a web page. Since there were generally many end users of each of these different browsers, developing a sophisticated web page that would look right to almost all web users often required writing carefully crafted HTML.

From a page writer's perspective, this situation proved onerous. Not only did you have to write pages that took into account idiosyncrasies of current and past browsers, but you also were faced with maintaining these pages as other changes were rapidly introduced. Nearly everyone involved in web development at this time was painfully aware of the need for standardization.

In October of 1994, Tim Berners-Lee launched the World Wide Web Consortium (W3C®), in part with the goal of producing standards for HTML as well as other web technologies. During the next several years, the W3C's efforts at standards development trailed well behind the de facto standards development being carried out by the browser manufacturers. For example, HTML version 2.0 became a standard over six months after a draft for version 3.0 had been published, and 3.0 was never formally adopted as a standard because of the rapid browser changes. Version 3.2 was adopted as a standard by the W3C in January of 1997, and by its own admission in the 3.2 specification document [W3C-HTML-3.2] aimed "to capture recommended practice as of early '96," so was still at least a year behind the browser manufacturers. Finally, the "browser wars" slowed and the standards community caught up. The W3C released its HTML 4 recommendation in December of 1997. The current version of this recommendation, HTML 4.01, is the standard that is more or less followed by many if not most HTML documents on the Web at the time of this writing.

2.2.2   The Clean-up Effort

Following the "war" years, the push for further change in HTML standards seems to have come from the standards community more than from browser developers. In particular, the W3C has been engaged in several efforts to clean up the definition of HTML in various ways. One of these directions has involved changing the way in which HTML is defined. Defining a language such as HTML (or any computer language, for that matter) involves two aspects: its syntax and its semantics. The *syntax* of a computer language defines which strings of characters represent a document that conforms to the language and which do not. For a programming language such as Java, a program that compiles is a syntactically correct document. The *semantics* of a language is a description of what the various elements of a syntactically correct document mean. For example, a syntactically correct assignment statement in Java has a certain meaning: a variable is associated with a value that can later be referenced by the variable's name. Similarly, the p element in HTML 4.01 also has a certain meaning: its content is to be displayed as a paragraph in the browser that is reading the document containing the p element.

Although precise formal methods for semantic definition have been developed and are sometimes used, the semantics of many languages is defined using natural-language descriptions such as the examples just given. In particular, the semantics of the elements and attributes in HTML 4.01 are defined using natural language [W3C-HTML-4.01]. On the other hand, the syntax for a computer language is almost always defined using some other language specially designed for the purpose of defining language syntax. A language used to describe the syntax of other languages is sometimes referred to as a *metalanguage*. The metalanguage commonly used to describe the syntax of programming languages such as Java is called Backus-Naur Form (BNF) notation. In fact, BNF notation could also be used to define the syntax for HTML. However, HTML and other similar markup languages are simpler than typical programming languages, and therefore specialized metalanguages can be used to describe them.

The metalanguage used to define the syntax for HTML 4.01 is SGML, the Standard Generalized Markup Language. As the "Generalized" part of its name implies, even this metalanguage is fairly general. This generality can complicate the *parsing* of an HTML document. Loosely speaking, parsing an HTML document involves inputting the document and creating an internal element tree (an *abstract syntax tree* or *parse tree*) representing the document, such as the tree in Figure 2.3. One example of a way in which SGML's generality increases the difficulty of parsing is its feature allowing certain tags to be omitted. For example, in HTML 4.01, the end tag of a p element can be omitted from a document. In fact, both start and end tags can be omitted for some elements, including the head and body elements. An HTML parser must therefore be able to correctly parse a document whether or not it contains tags that can be omitted. It is obviously more difficult to write a parser that allows for omitted tags than to write one that requires that all start and end tags be present.

In February 1998, the W3C introduced the Extensible Markup Language (XML), a restricted version of SGML. XML limits some of the generality of SGML while retaining enough power to define syntaxes for languages such as HTML. In fact, the syntaxes for several HTML versions have been defined using XML. A hypertext markup language whose syntax is defined using XML rather than SGML is called an XHTML language.

The first of the XHTML languages, XHTML 1.0, is semantically identical to HTML 4.01. Syntactically, XHTML 1.0 is also the same as HTML 4.01 except that XHTML restricts some of HTML's generality in a few small ways. In order to more precisely understand the nature of these restrictions, it will be helpful to define a few more terms. The *abstract syntax* of a language defines a language at the level of abstract syntax trees. For HTML and XHTML languages, this primarily involves defining what elements can be contained in the tree; what attributes can be associated with each element and what values these attributes can take on; and what children an element can have and the order in which the children must appear. The *concrete syntax* of a language defines how this tree structure is represented within the language. In the case of HTML and XHTML, this involves a variety of low-level details, such as what characters are used to delimit tags, how these characters can be escaped so that they do not have a tag-delimiting meaning, whether or not element names are case sensitive, how attribute values should be quoted, if at all, and so on.

Now that we have made this distinction between abstract and concrete syntax, we can be more precise about the difference between XHTML 1.0 and HTML 4.01: these languages are equivalent at the semantic and abstract syntactic levels. They differ *only* in terms of concrete syntax. The primary concrete syntactic restrictions on XHTML include the following:

- Omitted tags are not allowed.
- All element and attribute names must be lowercased (HTML 4.01 names are case insensitive).
- All attribute values must be quoted (not always necessary in HTML 4.01 documents).

As you can see, these restrictions are not too burdensome, and may actually be helpful to human as well as machine readers of an HTML document.

A primary advantage of following the XHTML 1.0 restrictions is that an XHTML 1.0 document is a particular form of XML document, and a wide variety of tools have been developed for processing XML documents. As a simple example, one XML tool can easily extract the content of the `title` element of an XHTML document; such a tool might be helpful in a larger application that produces a table of contents for a directory containing XHTML files. A number of XML tools and technologies are covered in Chapter 7. While there are also some SGML tools that can be used to process SGML-based documents such as those written in HTML 4.01, the SGML tools are few in comparison with the wide array of XML tools. In addition, since XML is a restricted version of SGML, these SGML tools can be applied to XHTML documents as well, if desired. Figure 2.5 summarizes the relationships between SGML, XML, HTML 4.01, and XHTML 1.0.

XHTML 1.0 and HTML 4.01 are both currently "recommendations" of the W3C, which means that "consensus has been reached among the Consortium Members that [each] specification is appropriate for widespread use." Another current recommendation is XHTML Basic 1.0, which is a subset of XHTML 1.0 designed for use with limited devices such as cell phones. Yet another recommendation is XHTML 1.1, which is identical to XHTML 1.0 in both semantics and syntax. The only difference between the XHTML 1.0 and 1.1 languages is grammatical. A *grammar* is the collection of rules (XML-based rules in the case of these languages) defining the syntax of a language. The difference between the XHTML 1.0 and 1.1 languages is that XHTML 1.1 is defined using a grammar that is more modular (and somewhat more complicated) than the grammar used to define XHTML 1.0.

Given this history as well as current development trends, I have chosen to follow the XHTML 1.0 standard in this textbook. With few exceptions, all modern browsers properly implement the elements of XHTML 1.0, so writing your documents according to this standard means that they should be highly portable. Also, if you understand the material covered in this chapter, you should not have much difficulty in switching to a different standard at a later time if necessary.

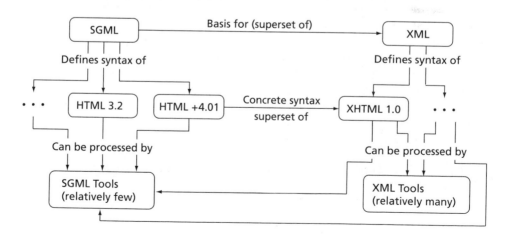

FIGURE 2.5 Relationships between SGML, XML, HTML, and XHTML.

The next section will focus on some of the concrete syntactic and semantic basics of XHTML 1.0. Following that, several sections will cover the semantics of a variety of elements; the same semantics apply to all of the other current HTML specifications as well. Then you'll learn how to read XHTML 1.0's XML grammar, which defines the abstract syntax of XHTML 1.0. The chapter will close with a brief discussion of tools for writing HTML documents and the case study. (Here and throughout the rest of this text, when I use the term "HTML" without qualification I will have in mind both XHTML and HTML documents.)

2.3 Basic XHTML Syntax and Semantics

2.3.1 Document Type Declaration

We have already seen that every XHTML document must begin with a document type declaration. Each HTML specification provides such a declaration that can be used at the beginning of documents intended to conform with the specification. However, there are three *flavors* of both the HTML 4.01 and XHTML 1.0 specifications, each with its own document type declaration. Each flavor includes a somewhat different set of elements and attributes. The three flavors are:

1. Strict: The W3C's ideal for HTML as of late 1997.
2. Transitional: A superset of Strict HTML that includes *deprecated* elements and attributes, that is, elements and attributes that should not be used if possible because they will likely be eliminated from HTML recommendations at some future time.
3. Frameset: A superset of the Transitional flavor that includes a feature allowing several subwindows (*frames*) to be displayed within a browser's client area. You've probably seen frames if, for example, you've viewed the Sun Java API specification (Fig. 2.6).

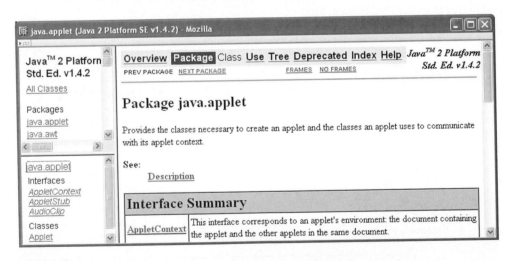

FIGURE 2.6 Example of a web page with three frames. (Browser content copyright © 2006 Sun Microsystems, Inc. All rights reserved. Reproduced by permission of Sun Microsystems Inc.)

Many documents on the Web today begin with a document type declaration for the HTML 4.01 Transitional flavor. However, almost all usage of deprecated elements and attributes included in the Transitional flavor can be replaced by using *style sheet* technology, which is supported by almost all browsers in use today (style sheets are covered in the next chapter). So there is little if any reason to use the Transitional HTML flavor any longer, and I will avoid it in this text. Instead, we will focus primarily on the Strict XHTML 1.0 flavor. The Frameset flavor is covered briefly in a later section, but—as we will see—there are also some good reasons to avoid its use except for certain specialized applications. The recommended XHTML 1.0 Strict, XHTML 1.0 Frameset, and HTML 4.01 Transitional document type declarations are:

```
<!DOCTYPE html
PUBLIC "-//W3C//DTD XHTML 1.0 Strict//EN"
"http://www.w3.org/TR/xhtml1/DTD/xhtml1-strict.dtd">

<!DOCTYPE html
PUBLIC "-//W3C//DTD XHTML 1.0 Frameset//EN"
"http://www.w3.org/TR/xhtml1/DTD/xhtml1-frameset.dtd">

<!DOCTYPE HTML
PUBLIC "-//W3C//DTD HTML 4.01 Transitional//EN"
"http://www.w3.org/TR/html4/loose.dtd">
```

The last of these is included for informational purposes, so that you can recognize it if it is included in a document.

2.3.2   White Space in Character Data

Recall that the character data of an HTML document is the information that lies outside the markup of the document, and to a large extent is the textual content of the web page produced by the document. With a few exceptions that are covered later, any XHTML white space characters (Table 2.1) within character data are treated by the browser as word separators, and the specific white space character(s) used to separate words, as well as the number of characters, is considered irrelevant. In a language such as English, the net effect of this treatment of white space is that the browser replaces any string of white space characters within character data by a single blank.

TABLE 2.1 XHTML (and XML) White Space Characters

Character	ASCII Code (Decimal)	Unicode Standard Value (Hex)
Carriage return	13	000D
Line feed	10	000A
Space	32	0020
Tab	9	0009

As an example of browser handling of white space in element content, consider the following HTML document, which changes the content of the p element of the original "Hello World!" example:

```
<!DOCTYPE html
        PUBLIC "-//W3C//DTD XHTML 1.0 Strict//EN"
        "http://www.w3.org/TR/xhtml1/DTD/xhtml1-strict.dtd">
<html xmlns="http://www.w3.org/1999/xhtml">
  <head>
    <title>
      HelloWorldWhiteSpace.html
    </title>
  </head>
  <body>
    <p>
      Hello World!

      This is my second HTML paragraph.
    </p>
  </body>
</html>
```

Figure 2.7 shows a browser window loaded with this HTML file. Notice that although the text within the p element is typed into the HTML document as two paragraphs (there is a blank line between two pieces of text), the browser displays all of the text as a single paragraph with a single space between the two sentences, and in fact even performs rewrapping of the paragraph (moves the last word to a second line in this example) so that the paragraph fits within the browser window.

A simple way to tell the browser that we want the text in this example to be displayed as two paragraphs is to use two p elements instead of one:

```
<p>
  Hello World!
</p>
<p>
  This is my second HTML paragraph.
</p>
```

An example of a browser loaded with such a document is shown in Figure 2.8.

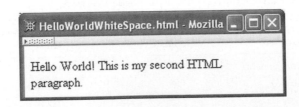

FIGURE 2.7 Browser collapses white space in modified "Hello World!"

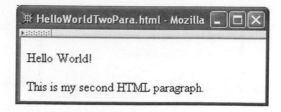

FIGURE 2.8 "Hello World!" with two p elements.

2.3.3   Unrecognized Elements and Attributes

A second feature of HTML that sometimes confuses beginning web authors is that browsers don't complain if a document contains element or attribute names that the browser does not recognize. This is different from what we're accustomed to when writing programs: if we mistype a keyword such as `while` in a Java program, the compiler will issue an error and the program will not run. But if we mistype an element name such as `p`, the browser will still attempt to display the entire web page. For attributes with unrecognized names, the browser acts as if the attribute is not present at all. For unrecognized element names, the browser displays the content of the element as if the markup were not present.

For example, let's say that we leave off the "e" in "title" in the the `title` start tag, as in the following example:

```
<!DOCTYPE html
        PUBLIC "-//W3C//DTD XHTML 1.0 Strict//EN"
        "http://www.w3.org/TR/xhtml1/DTD/xhtml1-strict.dtd">
<html xmlns="http://www.w3.org/1999/xhtml">
  <head>
    <titl>
      HelloWorldBadElt.html
    </title>
  </head>
  <body>
    <p>
      Hello World!
    </p>
  </body>
</html>
```

Mozilla displays this page as shown in Figure 2.9.

In this example, the browser treats the content of the `titl` element as if it were text typed directly within the `head` element. Text is not supposed to appear here, and the HTML standard does not specify how a browser should display such information. Mozilla chooses to display the text as if it were the initial content of the `body`, as shown in the figure. Notice that the title bar of the window does not display this text.

This handling of unrecognized names is important because it allows HTML to continue to evolve. For instance, if an XHTML 1.2 standard is someday released that contains a `sproing` element that causes character data within the content of the element to bounce up

FIGURE 2.9 Browser displaying HTML file with misspelled element name `titl`.

and down a bit when displayed, page authors can immediately begin including the `sproing` element in their documents. Browsers that don't recognize the `sproing` element will still display character data contained in this element; they just won't jiggle this data. (No, I am *not* suggesting that I want a `sproing` element in my next browser!)

One implication of HTML's handling of unrecognized tag names is that an HTML page may display correctly in a browser but still have typographical errors in its markup. For example, consider the following document body:

```
<p>
  Hello World!
</p>
<l>
  This is my second HTML paragraph.
</p>
```

The second paragraph mistakenly begins with an `l` tag. Since `l` is not a valid element name in HTML, this tag will be ignored. Yet Mozilla will still display this document as shown in Figure 2.8. This is because, for display purposes, Mozilla treats text that is contained directly in the `body` element as if it were the content of a `p` element. Although it displays properly, such a document could lead to other problems. For example, if this document were later processed by some other software—say a program that converts XHTML documents to plain text—it would likely produce an error.

To avoid such problems, it is a good idea to check the validity of the HTML in a document using means other than simply loading the document into a browser. An XHTML document is *valid* if it conforms with the XML grammar defining the syntax of the language. One simple way to perform validation checking is to use an *HTML validator*, such as the one available at the W3C [W3C-VAL]. This is a program that will analyze your document and not only catch typographical errors, but also help you to ensure that the HTML you generate conforms to the standards of the HTML version you are using.

2.3.4   Special Characters

Another troublesome aspect of HTML is that a few characters must be used carefully in HTML documents. For example, the less-than symbol (<) is the special symbol used to begin tags. You might reasonably assume that the less-than symbol would only be treated specially if it was followed by an element name such as `head` or `p`, but, as we have just seen in the previous subsection, this is not the case. Instead, a browser will almost always view a less-than as the beginning of a tag, regardless of what follows.

So how do we produce a document that displays a less-than symbol? Instead of typing the symbol itself into the document, we use a type of markup known as a *reference*. For example, < is a reference that represents the less-than symbol. A reference within an HTML document always begins with an ampersand (&) and ends with a semicolon (;). The form of the data between these characters determines the type of reference. A reference such as <, which uses a mnemonic name for the character referenced, is called an *entity reference*. Not all characters have entity references associated with them, but many do; some examples of entity references are contained in Table 2.2. This table also contains a second type of reference for each symbol, a *character reference*. In this case, a number sign (#) follows the ampersand beginning the reference and is followed by the Unicode Standard value of the character (prefixed with a lowercase x if hexadecimal is used, or with no prefix for decimal). A complete list of entity references defined for XHTML 1.0 can be found in Section A.2 of [W3C-XHTML-DTDS].

The bottom line is that you must use < (or < or < or <) to include a less-than sign as part of the content of a document. Similarly, you must use a reference for the ampersand (&), because it is the special character used to begin a reference. Also, there is one particular three-character string—]]>—that cannot be used as the content of an element; just to be on the safe side, it is therefore probably best to be in the habit of using a reference for the greater-than symbol as well. Finally, references can also be used to produce symbols that do not appear on your keyboard, such as the copyright symbol ©.

One other HTML entity reference that is frequently used is , the *nonbreaking space* character. The defined purpose of this character is to insert a space between two strings while also informing the browser that it should not perform word-wrapping between these strings. For example, a browser displaying the HTML source

```
<p>
keep together keep together keep together keep together
</p>
```

will never end a line with the word "keep," as illustrated by Figure 2.10.

Although the nonbreaking property of   is at times useful, the main reason that it is frequently used is that it is displayed as a space character but is not one of the four

TABLE 2.2 Example Entity and Character References

Character	Entity Reference	Character Reference (Decimal)
<	&lt;	&#60;
>	&gt;	&#62;
&	&amp;	&#38;
"	&quot;	&#34;
'	&apos;	&#39;
©	&copy;	&#169;
ñ	&ntilde;	&#241;
α	&alpha;	&#945;
∀	&forall;	&#8704;

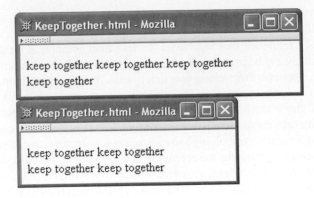

FIGURE 2.10 Two browser windows of different widths displaying an HTML file using the ` ` reference.

XHTML white space characters (Table 2.1). This means that we can force a browser to display multiple consecutive spaces, even though HTML specifies that consecutive white space characters must be collapsed to a single character. So, for example, if we want two spaces to follow a sentence-ending period, we can used HTML such as the following:

```
<p>
  Hey, you.  Yes.  I am talking to you.
</p>
```

which produces better-looking output than does the following:

```
<p>
  Hey, you.  Yes.  I am talking to you.
</p>
```

as shown in Figure 2.11.

2.3.5 Attributes

In our earlier "Hello World!" example Figure 2.1, we learned that the `html` element of any XHTML 1.0 document must contain an `xmlns` attribute specification. It turns out that every

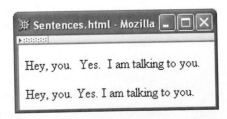

FIGURE 2.11 Sentences with (top) and without (bottom) the use of ` `.

HTML element has a set of associated attributes that can be specified for it. The values of an element's attributes typically influence how the element is displayed or how it behaves, or they may supply identifying information. For example, the xmlns attribute identifies the XML *namespace* for the document, which can be considered identifying information. We'll learn more about namespaces in Chapter 7, and we'll learn about several other common HTML attributes later in this chapter. For now, we'll just cover some syntactic aspects of attributes.

All XHTML attribute specifications have the form shown for xmlns: white space (Table 2.1) separates the attribute name from the element name in the start tag of the element; the attribute name is followed by an equals sign (=), optionally preceded and followed by white space; and the value of the attribute, enclosed in quotes, follows the equals sign. Either a pair of single quotes or a pair of double quotes may be used to quote the attribute value. The attribute value string may not contain the character used to quote the string, but it may contain the other quote character. So, for example, an attribute specification such as

```
value = "Ain't this grand!"
```

is legal, but

```
value = "He said, "She said", then sighed."
```

is not. However, references may appear within an attribute value, so

```
value = "He said, &quot;She said&quot;, then sighed."
```

is valid. The " references will be converted to double quotes when the document is parsed. Also note that, as in the case of element content, the less-than (<) and ampersand (&) symbols cannot be used to represent themselves within an attribute value but instead must be included using a reference. To be safe, you should probably use a reference for the greater-than symbol (>) as well.

Multiple attribute specifications can be included within a single tag by separating the specifications with white space. For example, it can be useful to certain applications, such as search engines and accessibility software, to identify the human language in which the character data of the document is written. A standard way to do this is to include lang and xml:lang attribute specifications in the html start tag. Both attributes are used so that the document will be compatible with software that understands HTML 4.01, which does not contain the xml:lang attribute (but which will ignore it due to the unrecognized-name feature described earlier), as well as with software that understands XML, which defines the xml:lang attribute for use across arbitrary XML-based languages, including XHTML. An html start tag containing attribute specifications for both of these attributes as well as xmlns is

```
<html xmlns="http://www.w3.org/1999/xhtml" lang="en" xml:lang="en">
```

This assigns the value en (English) to both of the language attributes. Multiple attribute specifications can appear in any order, so

```
<html xml:lang="en" xmlns="http://www.w3.org/1999/xhtml" lang="en">
```

is equivalent to the previous start tag.

Finally, it is good practice to observe certain restrictions on attribute values to ensure compatibility across different browsers. First, newline characters should not appear within an attribute value; in other words, an attribute value should appear on a single line. In fact, of the four white space characters, it is best to use only the space character within an attribute value. Furthermore, avoid including any leading or trailing white space, and also avoid having multiple adjacent white space characters within attribute values. If you follow these conventions, your attribute values will be *normalized*. Some browsers may normalize all attribute values whereas others may not, so normalizing the values yourself should ensure consistency across browsers.

Now that we've learned some of the foundational aspects of XHTML's semantics (the "meaning" assigned to white space and unrecognized elements and attributes) and concrete syntax, we're ready to move on to learning about a number of fundamental HTML elements and their semantics.

2.4 Some Fundamental HTML Elements

This section introduces a number of structurally simple HTML elements. While simple, these elements include some of the most fundamental, such as elements for creating hyperlinks and displaying images. We will use a single example to illustrate the elements described in this section. The body element of the HTML for this example is shown in Figure 2.12, and a browser displaying a rendering of this HTML is shown in Figure 2.13. Each of the new elements introduced in this example is described briefly in Sections 2.4.1–2.4.6.

2.4.1 Headings: h1 and Friends

h1 and h2 are examples of HTML *heading* elements. As shown in the example of Figure 2.13 and Figure 2.12, HTML markup such as

```
<h1>
  Some Common HTML Elements
</h1>
<h2>
  Simple formatting elements
</h2>
```

can be used to produce section headings for an HTML document. h1 represents a top-level heading, h2 a subheading, and so on. In all, six different levels (h1 through h6) are provided in HTML. The content of each heading element is shown on a separate line. Browsers will typically display each heading in a different type face, with h1 the largest and in bold while

```
<body>
  <h1>
    Some Common HTML Elements
  </h1>
  <h2>
    Simple formatting elements
  </h2>
  <pre>
Use pre (for "preformatted") to
  preserve white space and use
    monospace type.
    (But note that tags such as<br />still work!)
  </pre>
  <p>
    A horizontal <span style="font-style:italic">separating line</span>
    is produced using
    <tt><strong>hr</strong></tt>:
  </p>
  <hr />
  <h2>
    Other elements
  </h2>
  <!-- Notice that img must nest within a "block" element,
       such as p -->
  <p>
    <img
        src="http://www.w3.org/Icons/valid-xhtml10"
        alt="Valid XHTML 1.0!" height="31" width="88"
        style="float:right" />
    See
    <a href="http://www.w3.org/TR/html4/index/elements.html">the
      W3C HTML 4.01 Element Index</a>
    for a complete list of elements.
  </p>
</body>
```

FIGURE 2.12 Body of an HTML document containing some common elements.

h6 may look much like normal text. This default formatting can be overridden as described later in the chapter on style sheets.

Since the heading elements carry some semantic meaning (concerning section levels) as well as default formatting, it is generally considered poor practice to skip heading levels. For instance, an h1 element should be followed by an h1 or h2 element, not by a higher-numbered heading element.

2.4.2 Spacing: pre and br

The pre element is used to override a browser's normal white space processing. So, in the example, the HTML markup

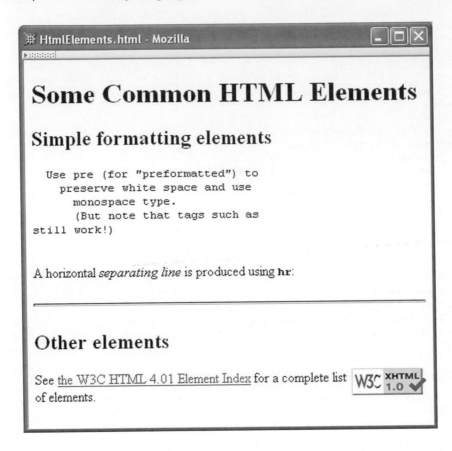

FIGURE 2.13 Browser rendering of some common HTML elements.

```
  <pre>
Use pre (for "preformatted") to
  preserve white space and use
    monospace type.
    (But note that tags such as<br />still work!)
  </pre>
```

produces output that looks almost identical to the HTML source. In fact, most browsers will not perform word wrapping on this text even if a line is too long to fit within the width of the browser window. Instead, the browser will provide a horizontal scroll bar that the user can manipulate to see all of the text. Also, most browsers will display the content of the pre element using a monospace font. This is particularly useful for displaying a Java program listing, for example.

However, a potential difficulty with using pre is that the content of a pre element is still considered to be HTML by the browser. This means, for example, that if a less-than symbol (<) appears in the content, it will be viewed as the beginning of a tag. This is why the text still work!) appears on a line by itself: the browser encounters the string

`<br />` and interprets it as markup, not as text. In fact, the `br` element in HTML represents a line break. It causes the browser to start a new line, much as a \n character causes a new line of output to begin when written by a C++ or Java program.

The `br` element is an example of an *empty element*. An empty element is one that is not allowed to contain content. That is, it is syntactically illegal to write HTML markup such as

```
<br>
   Content of the br element.
</br>
```

The `img` element (discussed in Section 2.4.5) is another example of an empty element. We will learn later in this chapter how to know for sure whether or not an element is defined to be empty by a given version of HTML. For now, it is important to know that such elements should be written as shown by these examples: follow the element name and any attribute name–value pairs by white space and the string `/>`. A tag ending with this string is known as an *empty-element tag*. Technically, there are other ways to write an empty XHTML element, such as without the white space preceding the / or as a start–end pair of tags. However, the syntax shown here should be more compatible with most current browsers and is therefore the form we will always use for XHTML.

2.4.3   Formatting Text Phrases: `span`, `strong`, `tt`, etc.

HTML provides a number of different means for performing the sorts of text-oriented tasks that we identify with word processing, such as boldfacing or changing the font or even the color of a word or phrase. One way to specify the style of words and phrases is by making the text the content of a `span` element and setting the value of the `style` attribute appropriately. For example,

```
<span style="font-style:italic">separating line</span>
```

will display `separating line` in italics, assuming an italic font is available on the display device. We'll learn much more about the `style` attribute in the next chapter.

The `span` element itself has no effect on the text. It is merely a *wrapper* that allows style and other attributes to be applied to portions of a document (see Section 2.4.8 for more on what can be contained within a `span` element).

The technique of wrapping text in a `span` with appropriate values for the `style` attribute can be used to perform a wide variety of text operations. However, there are shorter and simpler alternatives for some of the most common text operations. For example, text can be made boldface by making it the content of a `strong` element:

```
<strong>hr</strong>
```

Technically, this only marks the text "hr" as being something that has a certain semantic meaning, specifically, that it is text that should be "made strong." How this is actually displayed is not specified by the HTML standard, but in practice it is displayed in bold by

TABLE 2.3 HTML Font Style Elements

Element	Font Used for Content
b	Boldface
i	Italic
tt	Monospace ("teletype": fixed-width font)
big	Increased font size
small	Decreased font size

modern browsers. Another element, em, marks its content as something that should be given "emphasis," which in practice means that the content is displayed in italics in most browsers. However, such semantic elements also have meaning to other user agents. For example, a user agent based on a speech synthesizer might represent the strong element by increasing volume.

Yet another way to mark up text phrases is by using one of the *font style elements*. The (undeprecated) font style elements available in HTML 4.01 are shown in Table 2.3. These differ from the *phrase elements* such as strong and em in that they specify the actual typography to be used rather than associating semantics with text.

All of these font effects can be achieved using span with appropriate values of the style attribute, and in fact, even though these font style elements are part of the Strict standard, the W3C recommends that a style sheet approach (of which the style attribute is one example) be used rather than these elements. The phrase elements strong and em are similarly generally preferable to their font style counterparts b and i because they provide semantic information. The font style elements are discussed here mainly so that you will be familiar with them if you see them used—as they often are—on other web pages.

Finally, you may have noticed that we haven't mentioned underlining, another common word-processing feature. The reason is that most web users associate underlined text with hyperlinks. Therefore, it's generally a good idea to avoid using underlining for other purposes. However, if you must underline text, there is a style—text-decoration:underline—that can be used. Transitional HTML also includes a u element for this purpose.

2.4.4 Horizontal Rule: hr

The hr element adds a horizontal line to the document. This line appears below the preceding HTML content and above the content following the hr element.

Like the br element, hr is an empty element. The hr element defines several attributes that can be used to modify its style, but these have been deprecated in favor of the use of the style attribute, which again is covered in more detail in the next chapter.

2.4.5 Images: The img Element

The "image" element img is the primary means of including a graphic in a document, and is illustrated in our example by

```
<img
    src="http://www.w3.org/Icons/valid-xhtml10"
    alt="Valid XHTML 1.0!" height="31" width="88"
    style="float:right" />
```

The src attribute of this element specifies the URL of an image to be requested via the HTTP GET method. That is, in order for the browser to produce the display shown in Figure 2.13, it must perform two GET requests: first, the GET to request the HTML document HtmlElements.html; then, after the browser has recognized the img element, the GET to request the graphic displayed in the lower right corner of the browser window. In this example, the image is being loaded from a server with fully qualified domain name www.w3.org. We'll learn in Section 2.5 a somewhat simpler way to load images when an HTML document and its associated images come from the same server.

The alt attribute on the img element specifies text that will be displayed by a browser that is unable to display images or that can be used to provide information about the image to visually impaired users. This text should therefore be descriptive of the image. Both the src and alt attributes are required. (Providing descriptive alt attributes is just one of many ways in which you can help make your web pages more accessible to people with disabilities; see [W3C-WAI] for a full set of accessibility guidelines.)

The optional height and width attributes can be used to tell the browser to scale an image to a size other than the one in which it was recorded. This can be useful for displaying a thumbnail version of an image, for example. Even if you do not want to rescale an image, it is good practice to include these attributes in each img start tag with values that represent the original (unscaled) size of the image. Specifying values for the height and width attributes in all img elements makes it possible for the browser to reserve space for page images before downloading them. Otherwise, the browser may reserve a default amount of space for each image in the page, initially display the document with a placeholder inserted in place of each image, and then adjust the layout of the document as it determines the actual size of each image during image downloading. If you've ever seen a document change layout in this way while you were trying to read it or click on one of its links, you may know how annoying this can be to a user.

The value specified for a width or height attribute is by default interpreted as a length in pixels. The term *pixel* is short for "picture element" and represents one "dot" on a display. A typical display is composed of a grid of such dots, and an image is formed on the monitor by causing each dot to be displayed in a particular color. The resolution of a display is specified in terms of pixels. For example, a display resolution of 1280 by 1024 corresponds to a grid of 1280 pixels across by 1024 pixels from top to bottom.

An alternative to specifying a length in pixels is to specify it as a percentage of the height or width of the client area of the browser. For example, markup such as

```
<img ... height="4" width="100%" ... />
```

could be used to create a custom horizontal rule that stretches an image out so that it spans the entire width of the browser's client area. That is, a height or width attribute value ending in a percent sign (%) is interpreted as a percentage rather than as a length in pixels.

By the way: if you don't know the pixel dimensions of an image that you want to include in an HTML document, you can load the image into Mozilla, right-click on it, and select Properties from the pop-up context menu. The dimension of the image in pixels will be displayed, along with other information.

Each image will by default be placed at the location of its img element in the document without any preceding or trailing line breaks. In other words, the browser by default includes each image in the document as if it were a single character. This default behavior can be overridden by the style attribute. For example, the img element in Figure 2.12 causes the associated image to be displayed side by side with text, as illustrated in Figure 2.13.

2.4.6 Links: The a Element

Finally, we come to the core "hypertext" part of HTML: the a, or *anchor*, element (the reason for this name will be discussed in a moment). This element is the primary means of creating a clickable link (a *hyperlink*) within a document. The anchor in our example appeared in the following context:

```
See
<a href="http://www.w3.org/TR/html4/index/elements.html">the
   W3C HTML 4.01 Element Index</a>
for a complete list of elements.
```

Most browsers display the textual content of an anchor element underlined and in a distinctive color, and the browser's cursor will normally change in some way when placed over this content to indicate that it is a hyperlink (although the default appearance of a hyperlink can be changed using style sheets). The href attribute of an anchor element specifies the URL of a document to be requested via the HTTP GET method if the link corresponding to the anchor is clicked by the user. When the browser receives a document in the HTTP response to this request, it will by default display this new document in place of the one containing the hyperlink. This default behavior can be overridden by certain attribute settings, as we'll learn later. In order to avoid possible browser incompatibilities, it is best to have no leading or trailing white space in the content of an anchor element, as shown.

Although the content of an anchor is typically text, anchor elements can also contain certain other elements. Images are probably the most frequent alternative to text within anchors. As an example of including an image in an anchor, consider the following HTML taken from the W3C site (these lines of markup can be included in any XHTML 1.0 document that passes the W3C's validator tests):

```
<a href="http://validator.w3.org/check/referer"><img
   src="http://www.w3.org/Icons/valid-xhtml10"
   alt="Valid XHTML 1.0!" height="31" width="88" /></a>
```

This markup causes a graphics-capable browser to display an image that, when clicked, will cause the browser to generate an HTTP request for the URL specified as the value of the href attribute of the anchor.

You may be wondering why an a element is called an anchor. According to Chapter 12 of the HTML 4.01 recommendation, [W3C-HTML-4.01]: " A link has two ends—called anchors—and a direction. The link starts at the "source" anchor and points to the "destination" anchor, which may be any Web resource . . . ".

What we have seen so far is the use of a as a source anchor. In XHTML, a destination anchor is specified by including an id attribute in the start tag of an a element. So, for example, an element such as

```
<a id="section1"></a>
```

could be included in a document, perhaps immediately before an h1 element with content Section 1. The syntax for legal strings that can be assigned to id attributes is given in Section 2.10.2. Also, note that HTML 4.01 browsers expect the name of a destination anchor to be specified using the name attribute of the a element rather than id. So it is wise to include specifications for both attributes, using the same value for both:

```
<a id="section1" name="section1"></a>
```

Furthermore, an attribute value that is intended to be used to identify a destination anchor should begin with a letter and consist entirely of letters, digits, and the four characters _:.- (underscore, colon, period, and hyphen).

To specify an anchor as the destination of a hyperlink, a string consisting of the anchor identifier along with a preceding crosshatch (#) is appended to a URL specifying the document containing the anchor (recall that such a string is called the *fragment* of the URL). So, for example, if a page with this destination anchor was at the URL http://www.example.org/PageWithAnchor.html, then the anchor could be referenced by a source anchor such as

```
<a href="http://www.example.org/PageWithAnchor.html#section1">...
```

If the hyperlink corresponding to this source anchor is clicked, the browser will load the referenced document and automatically scroll the page so that the location of the anchor specified by the fragment identifier is at the top of the page (or so that the page is scrolled to the bottom if the anchor is near the end of the page). Of course, if no anchor is specified in a URL, the browser scrolls the page so that the top of the page is at the top of the window. In essence, in this situation the browser acts as if there is a destination anchor at the very top of the document. We'll cover a shorter syntax for URLs containing fragments in Section 2.5.

2.4.7 Comments

A comment in HTML, like comments in other computer languages, is something that is intended to be read by programmers but to be ignored by the software processing the document. The comment in our example is

```
<!-- Notice that img must nest within a "block" element,
    such as p -->
```

As shown, a comment begins with the string of characters `<!--`, which must contain no white space. A comment ends with the string `-->`, again with no white space.

For obscure reasons related to XML's derivation from SGML, a pair of consecutive hyphens is not allowed following the initial `<--` of a comment except as part of the `-->` that closes the comment. So don't do anything like this:

```
<!-- This is NOT
  -- a good comment.
  -->
```

or even this:

```
<!-- Can't end with more than two hyphens! --->
```

2.4.8 Nesting Elements

Figure 2.12 shows several examples of *element nesting*, that is, including one element as part of the content of another element. For example, the markup

```
<tt><strong>hr</strong></tt>
```

nests a `strong` element within a `tt` element. This means that the text that is the content of the `strong` element will be displayed in a monospace font (every character has the same width) as well as a bold typeface (or some other "strong" fashion). Furthermore, in our example, both of these elements are part of the content of a `p` element. There is no HTML-imposed limit on the number of child elements that can be contained within a parent element or on the maximum depth of nesting of elements within a document. However, XHTML does require that every inner element must be ended before its enclosing outer element ends. So, for example,

```
<tt><strong>hr</tt></strong>
```

is not valid XHTML, even though most browsers will properly display the content.

It is also important to know which elements can and cannot nest within other elements. To a large extent, element nesting is related to which of two categories an element falls into, block or inline. Conceptually, a *block* element is an element such as `p` for which preceding and trailing line breaks are automatically generated by the browser. An *inline* element is one such as `span` that causes no automatic line break. In terms of nesting, generally speaking, block elements may have children that are either block or inline elements, but the children of inline elements must themselves be inline elements. So, nesting a `strong` element within a `tt` element is valid because both `tt` and `strong` are inline elements, but

```
<tt><p>hr</p></tt>
```

is invalid because we cannot nest the block element `p` within the inline element `tt`.

In Figure 2.12 I have put the start and end tags of block elements on lines by themselves, while for the most part I have written the tags for inline elements, well, "in line." If you compare this figure with Figure 2.13, the automatic line breaking effect of block elements should be apparent. As an aside, since the br element also generates a line break, you might conclude that it is a block element. However, generation of a line break is implicit for block elements, while for br it is the explicit purpose of the element. Therefore, br is considered an inline element.

As noted in the comment in Figure 2.12, the img element cannot appear directly as a child of the body element of a document. This is because—with few exceptions—the children of the body element must belong to the block category.

The detailed rules concerning how elements nest vary somewhat between HTML versions, and can be expected to continue to change somewhat in the future. After you have learned how to read XML grammars later in this chapter, you will be able to read the source for yourself to know exactly what the nesting relationships are in any version of XHTML. So I will not attempt to provide all of those details here. However, we will look in later sections at several types of elements—lists, tables, framesets, and forms—that each have fairly well-defined nested element content. Before moving to those elements, though, we will cover some details about URLs that are important for every HTML developer to understand.

2.5 Relative URLs

As we have seen, URLs are used as the values of some attributes in HTML documents. In this section, we'll look more closely at the forms of URLs that may be used as values within HTML documents and at how URLs are interpreted by web servers such as Tomcat.

First, recall that by default the webapps/ROOT subdirectory within your JWSDP 1.3 installation directory is the document base for the root URL path / of your Tomcat web server. In other words, given that you have installed a default JWSDP 1.3 on your machine and have started Tomcat, browsing on your machine to the URL http://localhost:8080/MultiFile.html will cause your server to look for a file named MultiFile.html in the webapps/ROOT directory.

Now let's assume that you have placed a file named MultiFile.html in your Tomcat ROOT directory that is identical to the document in Figure 2.12 except that the src attribute specification of the img element is changed to

```
src="valid-xhtml10.png"
```

(MultiFile.html is available for download from the textbook Web site listed in the Preface.) Furthermore, assume that you have placed a file (also available at the textbook site) named valid-xhtml10.png in the ROOT directory, and that this file contains the graphic shown in the lower right corner of Figure 2.13. Then if you browse to http://localhost:8080/MultiFile.html, you should see content identical to that shown in Figure 2.13.

As you might guess, the reason that this works is that the browser interprets a src attribute value that looks like a file name—such as valid-xhtml10.png—as shorthand for a URL. In this case, since the URL of the document containing the `src` attribute was `http://localhost:8080/MultiFile.html`, the browser will interpret the string `valid-xhtml10.png` as shorthand for the URL `http://localhost:8080/valid-xhtml10.png`. This URL in turn represents the file named `valid-xhtml10.png` in the Tomcat `ROOT` subdirectory, so this file will be returned by the server when this URL is requested.

In general, a string that is consistent with the URL path syntax given earlier (Sec. 1.6.2) is known as a *relative URL*; as we are about to learn, certain other strings are also valid relative URLs. A complete URL—one beginning with a scheme—is known as an *absolute URL*. Every relative URL is shorthand for some absolute URL. Unless otherwise noted, a relative URL can be used within an HTML document anywhere that an absolute URL can be used.

To convert a relative URL to an absolute URL, a *base URL* is used. When a browser requests an HTML document, by default the base URL used for converting any relative URLs contained within the document to absolute URLs is the document's URL, with any query string and fragment removed. Thus, for a document at `http://localhost:8080/MultiFile.html`, the default base URL is also `http://localhost:8080/MultiFile.html`. (The default base URL can be overridden by using the HTML `base` element; see the exercises.)

A relative URL that looks like a file name, such as `valid-xhtml10.png`, is converted to an absolute URL by replacing any characters following the final slash (/) in the base URL with the relative URL. This is why in the example just described the relative URL corresponded to `http://localhost:8080/valid-xhtml10.png`. Another valid relative URL is the empty string. In this case, the corresponding absolute URL is the entire base URL (any characters following the final slash are retained).

If a relative URL contains a query string and/or fragment, then the rules just given will be applied to the portion of the relative URL preceding the query and fragment strings, and then these strings will be appended to the generated absolute URL. For example, if a document at `http://www.example.org/PageWithAnchor.html` contained the markup

```
<a href="#section1">...
```

then the corresponding absolute URL would be `http://www.example.org/PageWithAnchor.html#section1` (because the relative URL with the fragment excluded is the empty string, which corresponds to the full base URL).

More sophisticated relative URLs can be formed using the syntax (similar to that used in file systems such as Linux) illustrated in Table 2.4. As shown, the string `../` in a relative URL means that a segment should be removed from the path component of the base URL before appending the remainder of the relative URL to the base. Repeating this string means that multiple segments should be removed. Beginning a relative URL with a slash (/) character means to replace the entire path component of the base URL with the given relative URL. Complete URL details, including unusual relative URLs such as `/../a.html`, are contained in [STD-66].

Such relative URLs are particularly useful if you store files in different directories on your web server. For instance, suppose that you would like to keep your HTML documents

TABLE 2.4 Absolute URLs Corresponding to Relative URLs When the
Base URL is `http://www.example.org/a/b/c.html`

Relative URL	Absolute URL
`d/e.html`	`http://www.example.org/a/b/d/e.html`
`../f.html`	`http://www.example.org/a/f.html`
`../../g.html`	`http://www.example.org/g.html`
`../h/i.html`	`http://www.example.org/a/h/i.html`
`/j.html`	`http://www.example.org/j.html`
`/k/l.html`	`http://www.example.org/k/l.html`

separate from image files, so you create directories named `doc` and `img` within the `ROOT` directory of your Tomcat server. You then put a copy of `MultiFile.html` in the `doc` directory and a copy of `valid-xhtml10.png` in the `img` directory. You could then modify this copy of `MultiFile.html` as follows:

```
src="http://localhost:8080/img/valid-xhtml10.png"
```

Then browsing to `http://localhost:8080/doc/MultiFile.html` would once again produce Figure 2.13. However, so would

```
src="../img/valid-xhtml10.png"
```

In addition to being shorter to type, the relative URL version of this attribute has the advantage that if you were to later move the `doc` and `img` directories to another location on your server—or even to a different web server entirely—you would not need to modify the `src` value. Thus, relative URLs should be used whenever possible to facilitate portability of HTML documents.

The next several sections consider specific HTML elements used for structuring data within a document.

2.6 Lists

Figure 2.14 illustrates the three types of lists supported by HTML:

- *Unordered:* A bullet list
- *Ordered:* A numbered list
- *Definition:* A list of terms and definitions for each

This figure was produced by the following HTML:

```
<ul>
  <li>Bulleted list item</li>
  <li>Bulleted list item 2</li>
</ul>
```

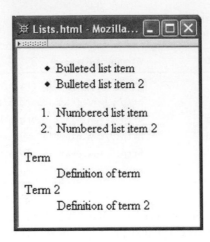

FIGURE 2.14 Browser rendering the three HTML list types.

```
<ol>
  <li>Numbered list item</li>
  <li>Numbered list item 2</li>
</ol>
<dl>
  <dt>Term</dt>
  <dd>Definition of term</dd>
  <dt>Term 2</dt>
  <dd>Definition of term 2</dd>
</dl>
```

As shown, the HTML syntax for all three types of lists is similar. First, the type of list is indicated by using either a ul (unordered list), ol (ordered list), or dl (definition list) start tag (each of the tag names ends in the letter "el," not the number "one"). All three elements are block elements, so a list by default begins on a new line when displayed in the browser. Each item in an unordered or ordered list is made the content of an li (list item) element. For a definition list, each term is made the content of a dt (definition term) element, and each term description is made the content of a dd element that immediately follows the dt element being described. For all three types of list, the list is terminated by following the last item in the list with the appropriate end tag.

Lists can be nested to produce an outline layout. For example, the markup

```
<ul>
  <li>Bulleted list item
    <ul>
      <li>Nested list item</li>
      <li>Nested list item 2</li>
    </ul>
  </li>
  <li>Bulleted list item 2</li>
</ul>
```

FIGURE 2.15 Browser rendering nested unordered lists.

can be used to produce the output shown in Figure. 2.15. The format of the bullets in this display (or the type of numbers used, if this was an ordered list) can be defined using style sheets as discussed in the next chapter.

2.7 Tables

HTML provides a fairly sophisticated model for presenting data in tabular form. Columns and rows will automatically size to contain their data, although there are also various ways to specify column widths; individual table cells can span multiple rows and/or columns; header and/or footer rows can be supplied; and so on. There are also various options for changing the visual appearance of a table, such as the widths of its internal cell-separating lines (*rules*) and external borders. Most of the visual features will be discussed in the next chapter on style sheets. In this chapter, some of the basic features of structuring and formatting HTML tables will be presented.

Simple tables are simple to represent in HTML. For example, a table of student grades could be written as follows and produces the table shown in Figure 2.16:

```
<table border="5">
  <tr>
    <td>Kim</td><td>100</td><td>89</td>
  </tr>
  <tr>
    <td>Sandy</td><td>78</td><td>92</td>
  </tr>
  <tr>
    <td>Taylor</td><td>83</td><td>73</td>
  </tr>
</table>
```

As shown in this example, the `table` element is used to define an HTML table. We will come back to the `border` attribute used in this tag in a moment. A `tr` (table row) element is used to contain each row. Within a row, a `td` (table data) element marks each element of the row. Notice that we don't need to specify the number of rows and columns in the table explicitly. Instead, these values are determined automatically: in a simple table, the number of rows is determined by the number of `tr` elements in the table, and the number of columns is determined by the maximum number of `td` elements contained within any row.

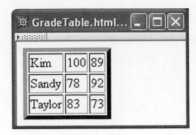

FIGURE 2.16 A simple table of grades.

In this example, since there are three tr elements, each containing three td elements, the table is 3 by 3. Finally, notice that the width of table columns is also automatically adjusted to contain the maximum width item in any column, although this can be overridden via the style attribute.

In this example, the border attribute in the table start tag tells the browser to display the table using a 5-pixel-wide border and 1-pixel-wide rules. In general, if any positive integer *n* is used for the value of border, then an *n*-pixel-wide border and 1-pixel-wide rules will be displayed. A value of 0 for this attribute turns off both the border and the rules. Additional table attributes are available that can be used to control the style of a table, but it is probably better to use style sheets for more advanced style settings, as discussed in the next chapter.

The table in this example is not very informative by itself. For example, there is no table caption, and there are no headers to define what the columns represent. This is easily corrected as shown in the next example and the accompanying Figure 2.17:

```
<table border="5">
  <caption>
    COSC 400 Student Grades
  </caption>
  <tr>
    <td> </td><td> </td><th colspan="2">Grades</th>
  </tr>
  <tr>
    <td> </td><th>Student</th><th>Exam 1</th><th>Exam 2</th>
  </tr>
  <tr>
    <th rowspan="2">Undergraduates</th><td>Kim</td><td>100</td><td>89</td>
  </tr>
  <tr>
    <td>Sandy</td><td>78</td><td>92</td>
  </tr>
  <tr>
    <th>Graduates</th><td>Taylor</td><td>83</td><td>73</td>
  </tr>
</table>
```

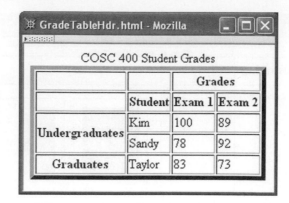

FIGURE 2.17 Table with headings and caption.

Two new elements are used in this example. The caption element, as the name implies, is used to define a caption for the table. If a caption element is used with a table, the caption start tag must must appear immediately after the start tag of the table element. The second new element, th (table header), is much like the td element, except that a typical browser will format the content of a th element in boldface and center it horizontally within the column.

Also notice in this example the use of empty table elements to skip a column. For example, the second row of the table begins with <td> </td> to indicate that the first column of the second row should be left blank. The   reference is included to ensure that the cell rules are displayed; my version of Internet Explorer 6, for one, will not display the cell rules if the content of a td element is empty or solely white space.

Finally, the example illustrates two new attributes that can be used with td and th elements: colspan and rowspan. Here colspan is used to tell the browser that a table element should cover more than one column, as is the case for the Grades heading in the example. rowspan is used for an element that covers more than one row, as illustrated by the Undergraduates heading in the example. Notice that on the row for student Sandy, no empty element is used: the row simply begins with an element containing Sandy. This is because the Undergraduates cell already occupies the first column due to the use of rowspan.

For performance and other reasons, if a large image is to be displayed on a web page, it will often be sliced into several smaller images that are downloaded separately and displayed next to one another to recreate the large image. Tables are frequently used to position the smaller images adjacent to one another so that they appear to be a single larger image. In order to achieve this effect, some table defaults must be overridden. Specifically, the table element has two attributes that control spacing within the table: cellspacing and cellpadding. Figure 2.18 illustrates how changes to the values of these attributes affect the spacing between table cells. The cellspacing attribute determines the amount of space between two adjacent cells, or between a side of the cell and the border of the table, while cellpadding determines the amount of space between the content of a cell (an image in this example) and the edge of the cell. In the top row of the example, the rule around each cell is visible, as is the border of the overall table containing the cells. In the second row, with

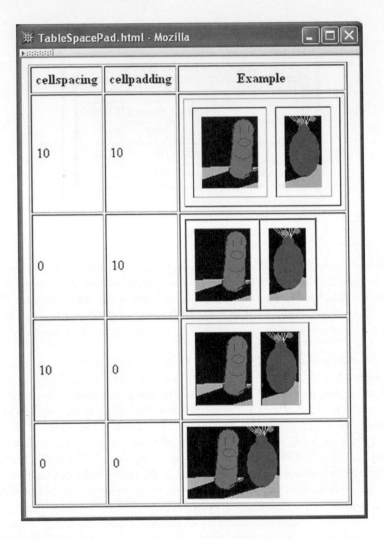

FIGURE 2.18 Effects of `cellpadding` and `cellspacing` attributes. Each element in the Example column is a table containing one row of two image elements. The top three Example tables have `border` set to 1 so that the table border and rules will be visible; the last Example table has `border` set to 0 so that there is no line between the two images. The image is courtesy of Ben Jackson.

`cellspacing` turned off, the cell rules are immediately adjacent to the table border and to one another. The third row shows that when `cellpadding` is turned off, the cell rules are immediately adjacent to the content of the cells. Finally, the last row uses the following table start tag:

```
<table border="0" cellspacing="0" cellpadding="0">
```

and, as shown, the two smaller images appear as if they are a single image.

In fact, this example illustrates another feature of HTML tables: tables can be recursively nested within tables. The markup that generated Figure 2.18 begins as follows:

```
<table border="1" cellpadding="5">
  <tr>
    <th>cellspacing</th><th>cellpadding</th><th>Example</th>
  </tr>
  <tr>
    <td>10</td><td>10</td>
    <td id="nested">
      <table border="1" cellspacing="10" cellpadding="10">
        <tr>
          <td>
            <img src="CFP1.png" style="display:block"
              alt="Cucumber and Flower Pot" height="86" width="67" />
          </td>
          <td>
            <img src="CFP2.png" style="display:block"
              alt="Cucumber and Flower Pot" height="86" width="45" />
          </td>
        </tr>
      </table>
    </td>
  </tr>
  ...
```

Notice that the content of the `td` element with `id` value `nested` (the third element of the second row of the outer table) is another table. This inner table could also contain tables, and so on to any desired depth of recursion.

Finally, you should also observe that each `img` element in this example assigns a value of `display:block` to its `style` attribute. This is required because images are considered inline HTML elements, and such elements by default are displayed with a little bit of space underneath them (allocated for the *descenders* of certain characters, such as p and q, that display below the baseline of text). The `style` attribute specification given overrides this default behavior by indicating that the image should be treated as a block element for display purposes.

Tables, then, are one way of laying data out on a display. We turn next to an alternative HTML layout mechanism that has some advantages—and disadvantages—compared with the more traditional table concept.

2.8   Frames

HTML frames are essentially a means of having several browser windows open within a single larger window. Figure 2.6 is an example of a browser window containing three frames (two on the left and one larger one on the right). Such a window is created by using one or more `frameset` elements after the `heading` element, rather than using a `body` element as all of our previous pages have used. The document type declaration is also different for framed pages than it is for standard web pages. For example, the window in Figure 2.6 could be created by HTML similar to the following:

```
<!DOCTYPE html
   PUBLIC "-//W3C//DTD XHTML 1.0 Frameset//EN"
   "http://www.w3.org/TR/xhtml1/DTD/xhtml1-frameset.dtd">
<html xmlns="http://www.w3.org/1999/xhtml">
  <head>
    <title>Java 2 Platform SE v1.4.2</title>
  </head>
  <frameset cols="20%,80%">
    <frameset rows="1*,2*">
      <frame src="overview-frame.html"
        id="upperLeftFrame" name="upperLeftFrame"></frame>
      <frame src="allclasses-frame.html"
        id="lowerLeftFrame" name="lowerLeftFrame"></frame>
    </frameset>
    <frame src="overview-summary.html"
        id="rightFrame" name="rightFrame"></frame>
  </frameset>
</html>
```

The first `frameset` statement says to create two rectangular subspaces, or views, within the browser window. The first (and therefore leftmost) of these subspaces covers 20% of the width of the browser window, and the second covers the remaining 80% of the window. Both subspaces cover the browser window from top to bottom, because only the `cols` (columns) attribute is specified. This top-level frameset element contains two child elements: another frameset and a frame (the one named `rightFrame`; as with fragment identifiers in anchors, `id` is the attribute used for naming frames in XHTML, and `name` in HTML 4.01). The child frameset specifies that its subspace (the left 20% of the browser window) is further divided into two views. Since these two views are specified using the `rows` attribute, they are stacked one on top of the other and both occupy the full width of the child frameset's subspace. The notation `1*,2*` indicates that the vertical space should be allocated so that the second (and therefore lower) view is twice as tall as the first view. If the value of the `rows` attribute had instead been `3*,2*`, the top view would have occupied 3/5 of the height of the subspace, and the lower view 2/5.

Framesets, then, can be viewed as something like tables: they can be used to lay out information within the browser. Also like tables, framesets can be defined recursively, with one frameset defined within another. A key difference between framesets and tables, however, concerns the contents: ultimately, at the leaves of a tree of frameset elements, frame elements are required. Each frame is essentially a browser window, which occupies a subspace of the screen as defined by the frameset(s) containing the frame. In the example considered, the frame named `upperLeftFrame` occupies the upper left corner (20% wide by 1/3 high) of the browser window, the frame `lowerLeftFrame` the lower left corner (20% wide by 2/3 high), and the frame `rightFrame` the right side (80% wide by 100% high).

The `src` attribute of a `frame` tells the browser the URL of a document to be loaded into the frame initially. If an HTML document is loaded into the frame and the user clicks a hyperlink within that frame, then the document named in the `href` attribute of the hyperlink's a element will be loaded into the frame. Other frames in the browser window will not be affected.

However, it is also possible for activity in one frame to cause a change in another frame, and this is in fact one of the main reasons for using frames. For example, the HTML contained in the frame named upperLeftFrame might contain an anchor such as the following:

```
<a href="java/applet/package-frame.html" target="lowerLeftFrame">
```

Because this anchor specifies lowerLeftFrame as the value of its target attribute, if the user clicks the link corresponding to this anchor, then the URL specified by the href attribute of the anchor will be loaded not into upperLeftFrame—the frame that contains the link—but instead into lowerLeftFrame.

One use of frames, then, is to provide a relatively easy means of writing HTML documents that provide navigation tools. That is, one page (a navigation page) can be written that contains a number of links to other documents in some collection of documents. This navigation page can be loaded into its own frame, and a second frame can be specified as a target for each of the anchor elements contained in the navigation page. A nonframe alternative is to include the navigation links directly in every page of the collection. This not only increases the difficulty of writing these pages, but also does not provide a separate scrollbar for the navigation links, which is an automatic and useful feature of a frame-based approach.

While frames can therefore be useful, there are also reasons to avoid using frames. The major reason is that frames can cause confusion for end users. For example, if the user is at a page that consists of multiple frames and clicks the browser's Print button, what is printed may not be what the user expected. The confusion can be especially acute for someone who is visually impaired and is attempting to "view" a frames-based document by using assistive software to translate the document into a verbal description. Another reason to avoid frames is that they assume that the document is going to be displayed on a monitor large enough to comfortably accommodate them. This is probably not a good assumption if the document is displayed on a cell phone.

For these and other reasons, many web developers avoid using frames. A key exception is that frames are still used for certain specialized technical applications—such as documents produced using the Javadoc™ documentation system—in which the end users may be expected to have the expertise needed to deal with the vagaries of frames and to be viewing documents on standard monitors.

2.9   Forms

An HTML *form* is used to allow a user to input data on a web page. Figure 2.20 is the form produced by the HTML form element of Figure 2.19.

We'll begin by considering the attributes used in this example's form element. The value of the required action attribute specifies a URL to which the information collected on the form should be sent when the user *submits* the form (more on form submission toward the end of this section). In this example, the form information will be placed in an HTTP request and sent to the URL www.example.org (which is a host name used for

```
<form action="http://www.example.org" method="get">
  <div>
    <label>
      Enter your name: <input type="text" name="username" size="40" />
    </label>
    <br />
    <label>
      Give your life's story in 100 words or less:
      <br />
      <textarea name="lifestory" rows="5" cols="60"></textarea>
    </label>
    <br />
    Check all that apply to you:
    <label>
      <input type="checkbox" name="boxgroup1" value="tall" />tall
    </label>
    <label>
      <input type="checkbox" name="boxgroup1" value="funny" />funny
    </label>
    <label>
      <input type="checkbox" name="boxgroup1" value="smart" />smart
    </label>
    <br /><br />
    <input type="submit" name="doit" value="Publish My Life's Story" />
  </div>
</form>
```

FIGURE 2.19 An example HTML form element.

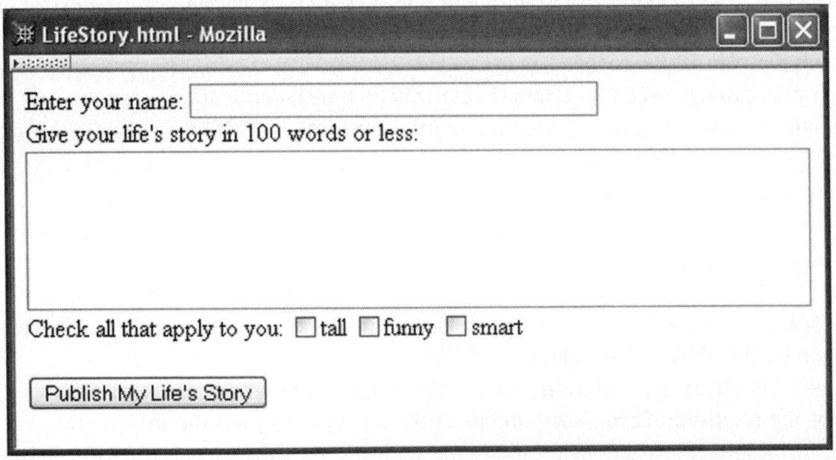

FIGURE 2.20 Example of an HTML form.

example purposes only, so submitting this form won't do anything interesting). The method attribute is used to specify the HTTP method that will be used to make the request. There are only two choices for this attribute value: get (the default value) and post. In XHTML, these values must be lowercase; however, the HTTP convention is to write these method names in uppercase, and I will follow this convention when referring to these methods in the text. We'll defer a discussion of when to use each method to Chapter 6. Suffice it to say that the GET method has been used here for example purposes and would normally not be the appropriate choice for a form such as this.

Next, notice that the first element contained within the form—and in fact the only immediate descendant of the form in the element tree—is a div element. div is almost identical to the span element encountered earlier: both elements are used to wrap other information in a document so that the wrapped information can be treated as a unit. The difference is that div is considered a block-type element, while span is an inline element. The div element is inserted here because the XHTML grammar requires that any child of a form element be a block, and most of the other elements we want to insert in the form are inline rather than block elements. Wrapping all of this other content of the form within a div is a simple way of satisfying the form element's constraint on its children. There are also other alternatives, such as using a table or a p element to wrap the form content. I have used a div here because it is a little simpler to use than a table for laying out this form, and it does not insert any vertical space at the beginning of the form, as a p element would.

The next element in this example is a label. This element is used to associate text with another element of the form. Only one form element may be contained in the content of a label element.

The input and textarea elements contained within the first two labels are examples of HTML *controls*. Each control provides a particular type of input element on a web page. The first control on this page is a *text field*, which is generated using an input element having a type attribute with value text. This control simply displays a box, one character tall by a number of characters wide that is specified using the size attribute (40 characters in this case). The text field acts like a small text editor, allowing the user to enter characters, modify previously entered information, cut and paste data in the field, etc. Default text can be included in a text field when the form is displayed by including a value attribute in the text field's input start tag; the value of this attribute is displayed as the default text. Finally, text fields, like every form control, should have a name attribute, for reasons discussed in later chapters.

The second control in this form is a *textarea*. This is similar to a text field, but allows the user to enter multiple lines of data. One other key difference is that input is an empty element (has no end tag), while textarea is not empty. Any character data placed between the start and end tags of a textarea is displayed as default text in the textarea box when the page is loaded. Another difference is that the size of a textarea is specified using the two attributes rows and cols, which specify the number of lines and the number of characters per line, respectively; the size attribute of text fields is not an attribute of textarea. Finally, like text fields, any information in the textarea can be edited by the user.

The next controls on this form are three checkboxes. A *checkbox* is a simple control: clicking on it toggles whether or not the checkbox appears to be *checked* (in Mozilla 1.4, a checked box is darker than an unchecked box). As shown here, the input element specifying a checkbox normally has a `value` attribute assigned to it. This value is the information that will be returned to the web server if the user checks the corresponding checkbox and *submits* the form as described toward the end of this section.

The checkboxes in this example can be checked or not in any possible combination. If instead we wanted to allow exactly one of several options to be selected, we would use a set of *radio button* controls. An example using radio buttons is

```
Your annual income is (select one):<br />
<label>
  <input type="radio" name="radgroup1" value="0-10" />
    Less than $10,000
</label><br />
<label>
  <input type="radio" name="radgroup1" value="10-50"
        checked="checked" />
    Between $10,000 and $50,000
</label><br />
<label>
  <input type="radio" name="radgroup1" value="&gt;50" />
    Over $50,000
</label>
```

which is displayed in Figure 2.21. The key HTML difference is that we would use a `type` value of `radio` rather than `checkbox`. One or more radio button controls that all have the same value for their `name` attribute form a radio button *set*. The browser will always display exactly one of the radio buttons in a set as the selected button (the middle button is selected in Fig. 2.21). An HTML form indicates which button in a set should be checked initially by including a `checked` attribute on the appropriate control, as shown. If this is not done, the browser will arbitrarily choose a radio button to check initially. The `checked` attribute can also be used with a checkbox control to initialize it to a checked state rather than to its default unchecked state. `checked` is an example of a *boolean attribute*, which is an attribute that has a value that is false by default and that is made true by assigning the attribute a value that is the attribute's name (e.g., `checked="checked"`). One other small point to notice is that I have used an entity reference rather than a greater-than symbol in the value of the third radio button. The browser will replace this reference with the character code for greater-than before using this value for any purpose.

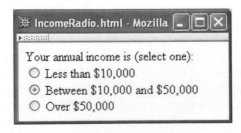

FIGURE 2.21 Form using radio buttons.

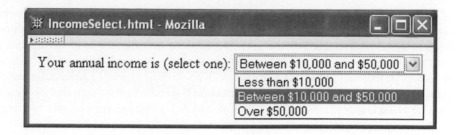

FIGURE 2.22 Form using `select` element. The user has just clicked the dropdown arrow to the right of the box representing the menu control. The "Between $10,000 and $50,000" value is initially shown in the menu box and is initially highlighted in the dropdown list.

Often, rather than using radio buttons to select a single option, a *menu* control is used. A menu is defined using yet another element, `select`. For example, we can rewrite the income controls using a menu rather than radio buttons as follows:

```
Your annual income is (select one):
<select name="income">
  <option value="0-10">Less than $10,000</option>
  <option value="10-50" selected="selected">
    Between $10,000 and $50,000
  </option>
  <option value="&gt;50">Over $50,000</option>
</select>
```

This markup produces the form shown in Figure 2.22. As shown in this example, the `option` element is used within a `select` to define a menu item. Notice two key differences between `option` and `input` with type `radio`. First, text is associated with a radio button only indirectly through the use of a label element, while the content of an `option` element directly specifies the text to be displayed in the menu. This can be an important difference, because it means that the look of a menu is not affected by resizing the browser window, whereas the look of text next to radio buttons can be significantly affected (Fig. 2.23).

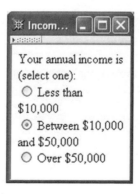

FIGURE 2.23 Resized window containing `IncomeRadio.html`.

A second difference is that the boolean `selected` attribute is used rather than `checked` to specify which option should be selected by default. As with radio buttons, it is good practice to write markup that sets the `selected` attribute on exactly one of the options of a menu to ensure that all users see the same initial menu value regardless of the browser used. However, there are situations where there is no obvious choice of an initial value for a menu. A common technique used in this situation is to add a menu item that essentially means "no value has been selected from this menu yet." In the present example, we might apply this technique as follows:

```
Your annual income is (select one):
<select name="income">
  <option value="select1" selected="selected">
    Select one of the following:
  </option>
  <option value="0-10">Less than $10,000</option>
  <option value="10-50">Between $10,000 and $50,000</option>
  <option value="&gt;50">Over $50,000</option>
</select>
```

This produces the form shown in Figure 2.24.

The final control in Figure 2.20 is a *submit button*, which is defined using an `input` tag with `submit` as the value of the `type` attribute. When a submit button is clicked, the *values* of the form—such as text entered into text fields and textareas and the data associated with `value` attributes of checked radio buttons and checkboxes and selected menu items—are normally sent to the web server that generated the page. Alternatively, it is possible to process the values of a form using program code downloaded as part of the web page itself. Much more will be said about processing form data in later chapters. For now, you'll notice that if you fill in the `LifeStory.html` form and submit it, the browser attempts to load the home page from `www.example.org` and the data entered on the form (possibly somewhat encoded) is included in the URL visited, as shown in the Location bar of the browser (Fig. 2.25).

Along with text input controls (text fields and textareas), checkboxes, radio buttons, menus, and submit buttons, there are several other controls defined in HTML. A

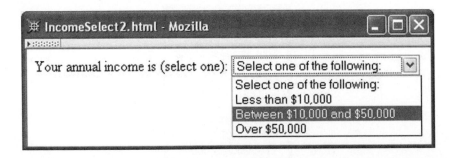

FIGURE 2.24 `Select` element with "select one" choice. The user is in the process of selecting the third item in the list.

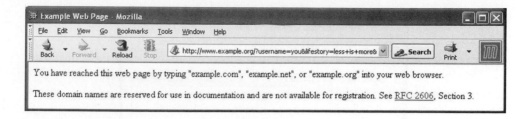

FIGURE 2.25 Page displayed when submit button is clicked after filling in the form. Note that several control names and values are displayed as part of the URL in the Location bar. The browser content is subject to copyright and used by permission of IANA.

complete list of nondeprecated form elements is contained in Table 2.5, and Figure 2.26 illustrates the visual appearance of the controls not already covered (button elements all have the same visual appearance regardless of the value of the type attribute, so only one button is shown). Detailed information about form controls is contained in the HTML 4.01 specification [W3C-HTML-4.01].

TABLE 2.5 HTML 4.01/XHTML 1.0 Nondeprecated Form Controls

Element	Type Attribute	Control
input	text	Text input
input	password	Password input
input	checkbox	Checkbox
input	radio	Radio button
input	submit	Submit button
input	image	Graphical submit button
input	reset	Reset button (form clear)
input	button	Push button (for use with scripts)
input	hidden	Nondisplayed control (stores server-supplied information)
input	file	File select
button	submit	Submit button with content (not an empty element)
button	reset	Cancel button with content (not an empty element)
button	button	Button with content but no predefined action
select	N/A	Menu
option	N/A	Menu item
optgroup	N/A	Heading in a hierarchical menu
textarea	N/A	Multiline text input
label	N/A	Associate label with control(s)
fieldset	N/A	Groups controls
legend	N/A	Add caption to a fieldset

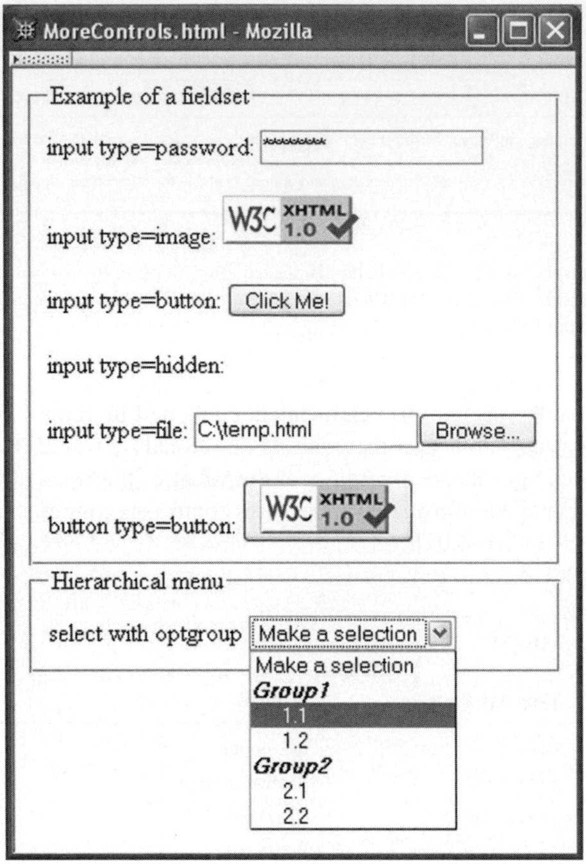

FIGURE 2.26 Additional HTML form controls.

2.10 Defining XHTML's Abstract Syntax: XML

Now that we understand basic XHTML concrete syntax and are familiar with the semantics of a number of XHTML elements, we're ready to see how the abstract syntax of a version of XHTML is defined using XML. By the end of this section, you should be able to read and understand the formal definition for any of the three flavors of XHTML 1.0.

The abstract syntax for each flavor of XHTML 1.0 is defined by a set of text files known collectively as an XML *document type definition* (DTD). To introduce you to the basic elements of a DTD, let's begin with a simple example drawn from an XHTML DTD:

```
<!ELEMENT html (head, body)>
<!ATTLIST html
  lang        NMTOKEN    #IMPLIED
  xml:lang    NMTOKEN    #IMPLIED
  dir         (ltr|rtl) #IMPLIED
```

```
    id          ID         #IMPLIED
    xmlns       CDATA      #FIXED 'http://www.w3.org/1999/xhtml'>
<!ENTITY gt     "&#62;">
```

The first of these lines is an example of an *element type declaration*. Element type declarations are used to specify the set of all valid elements in the language defined by the DTD. This example shows the actual element type declaration for the XHTML 1.0 html element. The information following the element type name is known as the *content specification* for the element; it provides information about the valid content of the element type being declared. This particular declaration says that, in XHTML 1.0 Strict, the html element must have two children, a head element followed by a body element. We'll describe content specifications in detail in Section 2.10.1.

The second line begins a tag that represents an XML *attribute list declaration*. As you might guess, this provides information about the valid attributes for an element, in this case for the html element. The attribute list declaration shown is equivalent to the actual XHTML 1.0 Strict declaration for html and says that this element type has five attributes: lang, xml:lang, dir, id, and xmlns. It also provides information such as the valid set of values for each attribute and default value information. More will be said about this in Section 2.10.2.

The final line is an example of an XML *entity declaration*. Such a tag is essentially a macro definition, associating the name gt (an *entity*) with the string >. We have already learned how to "call" such macros using entity references such as >. Now we can see more clearly how they are processed: the application reading a document containing an entity reference simply replaces the reference with the string represented by the entity, and then recursively processes this string. In this case, the string is a character reference, and the recursive processing will replace this reference with an appropriate encoding of the Unicode Standard value for the greater-than character. As we will learn in Section 2.10.3, the XHTML DTDs make extensive use of entity references within the DTDs themselves.

Each of the XHTML 1.0 DTDs is composed entirely of the three types of tag illustrated, along with entity references and comments (which have the same syntax as XHTML comments). So, at a high level, you now know about all of the pieces of these DTDs. In the next several subsections, we'll look at details of each of these three types of tags. We'll also see how DTDs are related to document type declarations.

2.10.1   Element Type Declarations

Let's begin by considering in more detail the html declaration from the XHTML 1.0 Strict DTD:

```
<!ELEMENT html (head, body)>
```

The string immediately following ELEMENT is the name of the *element type* being declared, in this case html. The XHTML DTD contains exactly one element type declaration for each element in the language. As already noted, the string following the element type name is the content specification for the element type (also referred to in some XML reference material

TABLE 2.6 Basic XML Content Specifications

Specification Type	Syntax	Content Allowed
Empty	EMPTY	None
Arbitrary	ANY	Any content (no restrictions)
Sequence	(elt1, elt2, ...)	Sequence of elements that must appear in order specified
Choice	(elt1 | elt2 | ...)	Exactly one of the specified elements must appear
Character data	(#PCDATA)	Arbitrary character data, but no elements
Mixed	(#PCDATA | elt1 | elt2 |...)*	Any mixture of character data and the specified elements in any order

as the *content model*). Several basic XML content specifications are shown in Table 2.6. These basic specifications are sufficient for defining the content model for many XHTML elements. For instance, the element type declaration for the br element is

```
<!ELEMENT br EMPTY>
```

In addition to the basic specifications shown, more sophisticated specifications may be formed by appending one of the iterator characters of Table 2.7 to the basic sequence and choice content specification types. So, for example, the XHTML DTD element type declaration

```
<!ELEMENT select (optgroup|option)+>
```

is a choice specification type modified with the + iteration character, and says that a select element may contain any number of optgroup and option elements in any order, as long as one or the other of these two elements appears at least once. Furthermore, sequence and choice specifications (optionally with iterator characters) can be nested, and an element name within a sequence or choice may have an iterator character suffixed to it. For example, the XHTML 1.0 Strict element type declaration for table is

```
<!ELEMENT table
    (caption?, (col*|colgroup*), thead?, tfoot?, (tbody+|tr+))>
```

TABLE 2.7 XML Content Specification Iterator Characters

Character	Meaning
?	Sequence/choice is optional (appears zero or one times).
*	Sequence/choice may be repeated an arbitrary number of times, including none.
+	Sequence/choice may appear one or more times.

This says that a `table` may optionally begin with a caption, followed optionally by either a sequence of `col` or `colgroup` elements, followed optionally by a `thead` and then optionally by a `tfoot` and finally a sequence of one or more `tbody` or `tr` elements. If you are familiar with BNF notation, you should see some clear similarities between the XML syntax for content specifications and BNF notation.

The keyword `#PCDATA` ("parsed character data") used in defining the character data and mixed content types represents any string of characters excluding less-than and ampersand, which are excluded because they represent the start characters for markup.

2.10.2   Attribute List Declarations

An *attribute list declaration* is included in the DTD for each element that has attributes. As noted earlier, an attribute list declaration begins with the keyword `ATTLIST` followed by an element type name and specifies the names for all attributes of the named element, the type of data that can be used as the value of each attribute, and default value information. For example, consider the example from the beginning of this section.

```
<!ATTLIST html
  lang        NMTOKEN    #IMPLIED
  xml:lang    NMTOKEN    #IMPLIED
  dir         (ltr|rtl)  #IMPLIED
  id          ID         #IMPLIED
  xmlns       CDATA      #FIXED 'http://www.w3.org/1999/xhtml'>
```

Each line after the first is a sequence of three elements: the attribute name, the attribute type, and the default declaration.

The *attribute type* specifies the type of data that may be specified as the attribute value. Table 2.8 gives the attribute types used in the definition of XHTML 1.0 Strict. The attribute type for the first two attributes of the `html` element is `NMTOKEN` (name token), which is an XML keyword for a string of characters representing a name ("word"). The ASCII characters that can be used in a `NMTOKEN` are letters, digits, and the four characters period (.), hyphen (-), underscore(_), and colon (:). A variety of non-ASCII characters that are included in the Unicode Standard can also be used; see [W3C-XML-1.0] for details.

TABLE 2.8 Key Attribute Types Used in XHTML 1.0 Strict DTD

Attribute Type	Syntax	Usage
Name token	NMTOKEN	Name (word)
Enumerated	(string1 | string2 | ...)	List of all possible attribute values
Identifier	ID	Type for `id` attribute
Identifier reference	IDREF	Reference to an `id` attribute value
Identifier reference list	IDREFS	List of references to `id` attribute values
Character data	CDATA	Arbitrary character data (except < and &)

The string (ltr|rtl) is an example of an *enumerated* attribute type. Specifically, the attribute list declaration just given specifies that the dir attribute can be assigned one of two values: either the string ltr or the string rtl. As shown, the allowable values for an enumerated type are separated by OR (|) symbols. Note that boolean attributes—such as checked attribute of the input element—are also enumerated types, but they have only a single allowable value. So, for example, the checked attribute is declared as follows:

```
checked    (checked)     #IMPLIED
```

The ID attribute type is illustrated by the id attribute of the html attribute list declaration. An id attribute, as the name implies, supplies an identifying name for its element. Every XHTML 1.0 element has an id attribute, and we have already seen some uses for it on the a and frame elements. We will see many more uses in later chapters. Syntactically, ID values are almost identical to NMTOKEN values, except that an ID value is required to begin with a letter, underscore, or colon. Furthermore, XML imposes the constraint that no two attributes in a document are allowed to be assigned the same ID value, while no similar constraint applies to NMTOKENs. In XHTML 1.0, this means that every id attribute must be assigned a value that is distinct from the value of every other id attribute in the document. So the following markup fragment cannot appear in a valid XHTML 1.0 document:

```
<html id="anId" xmlns="http://www.w3.org/1999/xhtml">
  <head id="anId">
  ...
```

An attribute type of IDREF (an id reference) indicates that the value of the associated attribute must be identical to the value of the id of some element of the document. Attributes of this type are used for linking one element with another element. For example, a label element can be linked with a form control (such as a text field) in two ways: by including the form control as a child of the label element, as illustrated in Section 2.9, or by explicitly linking to the form control using the for attribute of a label element, which is declared in the XHTML 1.0 Strict DTD as follows:

```
<!ATTLIST label
  ...
  for        IDREF         #IMPLIED
  ...
>
```

The explicit form of label-to-control linkage is demonstrated by the following markup:

```
<table>
  <tr>
    <td><label for="username">Your Name</label></td>
    <td><input id="username" type="text" name="username" /></td>
  </tr>
  ...
</table>
```

TABLE 2.9 XML Attribute Default-value Declarations

Default Type	Syntax
No default value provided by DTD, attribute optional	`#IMPLIED`
Default provided by DTD, may not be changed	`#FIXED` followed by any valid value (quoted)
Default provided by DTD, may be overridden by user	Any valid value (quoted)
No default value provided by DTD, attribute required	`#REQUIRED`

In a valid XHTML document, the value of each `for` attribute—since it is of type `IDREF`—must exactly match the value of some `id` attribute within the document. The `IDREFS` attribute type is similar, except that it allows for a white-space-separated list of `id` values rather than the single `id` value allowed by `IDREF`.

The last attribute in the `html` element's attribute list declaration, `xmlns`, has a data type of `CDATA`. In general, the XML keyword CDATA represents any string of characters that excludes the two characters less-than (<) and ampersand (&), much like the `#PCDATA` keyword used in element content specifications. In the context of an attribute value, a string of type `CDATA` must also not contain the quoting character (either " or ') used to enclose the attribute value, as described earlier in Section 2.3.5. As noted in that section, the quote character can be included in an attribute value by using an entity or character reference, such as " or ".

The *default declaration* for an attribute specifies what value should be used if no value is specified for the attribute in an element of the document or if a value is assigned but does not conform to the attribute's type (for example, if a number is specified as the value for an `id` attribute in an XHTML document). The default declaration for an attribute can take one of the forms shown in Table 2.9. A value of `#IMPLIED` means that the corresponding attribute need not be assigned a value in the start tag for the element and that the DTD does not define a default value for the attribute. Instead, it is left up to the application reading the XML document to determine an appropriate default value. For XHTML, this means that the browser assigns a default value of its choice for any attribute marked with the `#IMPLIED` default.

The DTD itself can also supply a default value for an attribute. The following attribute list declaration illustrates this form of default declaration:

```
<!ATTLIST form
  ...
  method     (get|post)     "get"
  ...
>
```

In some cases, the default value of an attribute is not allowed to be overridden by the document. The is indicated by preceding the default value by the XML keyword `#FIXED`, as illustrated by the `xmlns` attribute of the `html` element in the earlier attribute list declaration. So, for example, the following tag is not allowed in a valid XHTML 1.0 document:

```
<html xmlns="http://www.w3.org">
```

An attribute with a default declaration of either #IMPLIED or an explicit default value is not required to be assigned a value in the start tag of the element (at least, not by the DTD; the XHTML 1.0 recommendation requires the presence of the xmlns attribute even though the DTD itself does not). The last possible default declaration, #REQUIRED, indicates that a value must be specified for the corresponding attribute whenever the element containing that attribute appears in a valid document. For example, the attribute list declaration for the XHTML img element contains lines equivalent to the following:

```
src  CDATA  #REQUIRED
alt  CDATA  #REQUIRED
```

This implies that every img start tag in an XHTML document must contain assignments to these two attributes.

2.10.3 Entity Declarations

We have already learned that an XML DTD can contain entity declarations, each of which begins with the keyword ENTITY followed by an entity name and its replacement text, such as

```
<!ENTITY gt      "&#62;">
```

This statement defines the value of the entity reference > to be the string >, which in turn is an XML character reference to the greater-than character (which corresponds to the code point 62 in the Unicode Standard).

An entity such as gt is known as a *general entity* and can only be referenced from within documents defined by the DTD. XML also provides for a different type of entity that can be referenced from within DTDs and not from documents. Such entities are called *parameter entities*. A parameter entity declaration is indicated in the DTD by following the ENTITY keyword with a percent sign (%), as in these two declarations taken from the XHTML 1.0 Strict DTD:

```
<!ENTITY % LanguageCode "NMTOKEN">
<!ENTITY % URI "CDATA">
```

Such an entity is referenced by prefixing the entity name with a percent sign rather than with the ampersand used for beginning a general entity reference. So, for example, given that the LanguageCode parameter entity has been defined as we did, the entity declaration (which is also contained in the XHTML 1.0 Strict DTD)

```
<!ENTITY % i18n
  "lang        %LanguageCode; #IMPLIED
   xml:lang    %LanguageCode; #IMPLIED
   dir         (ltr|rtl)      #IMPLIED"
  >
```

is equivalent to the declaration

```
<!ENTITY % i18n
 "lang        NMTOKEN        #IMPLIED
  xml:lang    NMTOKEN        #IMPLIED
  dir         (ltr|rtl)      #IMPLIED"
 >
```

As another example of the use of parameter entities, the actual XHTML 1.0 Strict attribute list declaration for the html element is

```
<!ATTLIST html
  %i18n;
  id          ID             #IMPLIED
  xmlns       %URI;          #FIXED 'http://www.w3.org/1999/xhtml'
  >
```

You should now be able to see that that is equivalent to the version of this declaration given earlier.

2.10.4   DTD Files

At this point, you should understand XML well enough to be able to understand the DTDs for any of the three XHTML 1.0 flavors. But where are these DTDs located, and how does a browser know which DTD to use for a given XHTML document?

Recall that for the Strict flavor of XHTML 1.0, the document type declaration we have been using is

```
<!DOCTYPE html
        PUBLIC "-//W3C//DTD XHTML 1.0 Strict//EN"
        "http://www.w3.org/TR/xhtml1/DTD/xhtml1-strict.dtd">
```

As you might guess, the URL at the end of this tag is the location of a copy of the DTD for the document instance that follows the DOCTYPE tag. Technically, this portion of the DOCTYPE tag is known as the *system identifier* for the DTD. The string immediately following the PUBLIC keyword, on the other hand, is called the *formal public identifier* for the DTD. It is a name assigned to the DTD by the DTD's author according to SGML standards (which are not important to us here) and is essentially a URN for the DTD. While every XHTML 1.0 Strict document you write is required to begin with a DOCTYPE tag having the formal public identifier just given, the system identifier can be any URL of your choosing, as long as a copy of the DTD is available at the specified URL.

Actually, the file at the URL shown contains only a part of the overall XHTML 1.0 Strict DTD. Other portions of the DTD are contained in separate files that are imported into the DTD through a mechanism somewhat like the #include facility in C++. For example, the xhtml1-strict.dtd file contains the following lines of markup:

```
<!ENTITY % HTMLlat1 PUBLIC
   "-//W3C//ENTITIES Latin 1 for XHTML//EN"
   "xhtml-lat1.ent">
%HTMLlat1;
```

The first three lines are a special type of parameter entity declaration. This declaration is different from the ones we have seen previously in that its value is not a string but instead consists of a formal public identifier followed by a system identifier, much as would be found in a DOCTYPE tag. The system identifier in this case is a relative rather than absolute URL, and is considered to be relative to the URL of the document containing the entity declaration. So, if the system identifier in the DOCTYPE is as shown earlier, then the absolute URL corresponding to the relative HTMLlat1 system identifier would be http://www.w3.org/TR/xhtml1/DTD/xhtml-lat1.ent. If you visit this file, you will see a long list of entity declarations such as

```
<!ENTITY nbsp   " "> <!-- no-break space = non-breaking space,
                            U+00A0 ISOnum -->
```

A parameter entity such as HTMLlat1 that is associated with a file is known as an *external entity*, and the file it includes—which must contain only entity declarations, not declarations for elements or attribute lists—is known as an *entity set*.

Notice that the declaration of the HTMLlat1 entity is followed by a reference to the entity (%HTMLlat1;). This reference is needed because the entity declaration itself simply associates a name (HTMLlat1 in this case) with a file. The entity reference then causes the file to be imported into the DTD.

Finally, although you can find the XHTML 1.0 Strict DTD at the URL given and from there locate the entity sets that it includes, for human consumption I recommend viewing the marked-up DTD versions found at [W3C-XHTML-DTDS].

We now turn to the last topic in this chapter: how are HTML documents created in practice?

2.11 Creating HTML Documents

HTML documents can be created in a number of ways. One way is to open a simple text editor, such as Notepad in Microsoft Windows, and simply type in the markup and content of the document. However, this approach is seldom used in practice. A slightly more automated approach is to use an editor such as Emacs that can be customized to provide certain HTML/XML-specific features, such as tag highlighting, "smart" tabbing, automated generation of closing tags, and much more.

Higher-level tools that generate HTML from user input while for the most part hiding the underlying HTML syntax are also available. For example, most current word processors, such as Microsoft Word, allow you to save a document in HTML format (in Word, this may be accomplished by selecting the Web Page file type in the Save As window). So you can create a document using familiar word-processing features and have the word processor automatically convert the text formatting and other markup-type operations you applied to the document into an equivalent HTML document. This approach has the disadvantage that you do not have direct access to (or even much control over) the generated HTML.

Alternatively, several applications are available that provide word-processing-type functionality but also closely integrate access to an HTML representation of the document. For instance, the full Mozilla 1.4 package includes a Composer feature under the Window

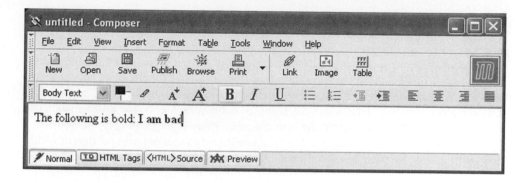

FIGURE 2.27 Example Composer window after user has entered text and boldfaced some of it.

menu. From a user perspective, Composer appears to be like many other word processors: it has WYSIWYG features for selecting text size and weight, creating bulleted and numbered items, performing text justification, inserting graphics, and so on (Fig. 2.27). But unlike typical word processors, Composer incorporates many HTML-specific features, such as the ability to insert named anchor elements and to directly edit the HTML generated by Composer. Other applications that provide similar or greater functionality include the Microsoft FrontPage® and Macromedia® Dreamweaver® software tools for Web site creation and management.

Given that there are tools for generating HTML from WYSIWYG input, you may wonder why we have covered HTML at all. Why not just use these tools whenever we want an HTML document? There are several answers to this question. One is that knowing HTML is somewhat like knowing assembly language: even if you never use it directly, it can be helpful in your use of other tools. Similarly, sometimes handwritten assembly code is better (by some measure) than compiler-generated code, and the same is sometimes true of handwritten vs. tool-generated HTML. Finally, and probably most importantly, many HTML documents are generated "on the fly" in response to HTTP requests rather than being generated in advance and stored as a file. That is, many HTML documents are produced by programs running on web servers. In later chapters we will learn how to write such programs, and our understanding of HTML will be invaluable to us then.

2.12   Case Study

We'll now apply what we've learned to developing some of the HTML documents for the blogging application described in Section 1.8. The files discussed here are located in the CaseStudy subdirectory of the chapter2 directory of the example files available from the textbook Web site (see the Preface for the address). What we'll be developing could be viewed as an early prototype version of the application: we won't have all of the features a commercial blogging system would provide, instructions will be incomplete, the user interface will be clumsy in places, and so on. That said, the application we develop will be operational and should illustrate a variety of topics.

Let's start with the document displayed when the blogger wants to log in and add an entry to the blog (Fig. 2.28). Notice that the left edges of the text boxes and button are aligned. As shown in Figure 2.29, this effect was produced by using a two-column table as the content of the form element, with the text labels in the left column of the table and the form controls in the right column. We'll learn another technique for aligning elements in the next chapter. One technique that you should avoid is using spaces to align elements (such as following the Password: label with several   entity references). The problem with this approach is that, as we'll learn in the next chapter, different browsers may use somewhat different fonts to render the document, which could lead to spaces having different widths among browsers. So what appears aligned in one browser may look jagged in another.

If you view the log-in page in a browser and click the Log in button, you will receive an error message. This is because we haven't yet written the server-side software that will process the information entered into the log-in form. So, although the value Login of the action attribute represents a valid relative URL, the server has not yet been told how to respond to requests to the corresponding absolute URL. We'll cover server-side software development beginning in Chapter 6.

If the server-side software was operational and the blogger logged in successfully, the application next displays an add-entry page (Fig. 2.30). As you might expect, the markup for this document is very similar to that shown in Figure 2.29, so I won't show the markup here (it is in the file addentry.html in the case study example downloads). There is, however, one small problem with using the earlier table-in-form technique on this page: by default, browsers center each of the elements in a row of a table vertically. And because the Body: label is in the same row as a multi-line text area, while I would like this label to appear immediately beneath the Title: label, it instead appears much farther down. We'll learn in the next paragraph how to fix this problem using a style property. The only other noteworthy aspect of this document is that it uses markup such as <b> to produce the tags displayed in the instructions at the top of the page. Using the markup <b> instead would of course have produced bold text rather than displaying the tag. (Yes, I designed the application to recognize the b and i elements rather than strong and em; for an end-user application, the b and i elements are easily remembered and less likely to be mistyped.)

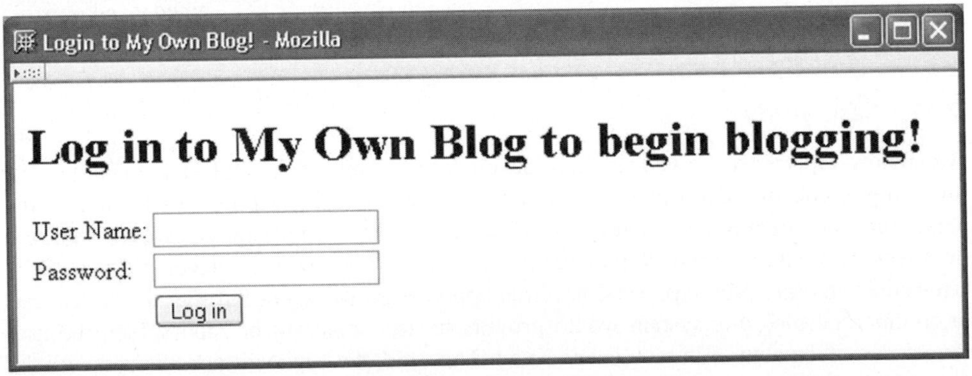

FIGURE 2.28 Log-in screen for blogging application.

```
<!DOCTYPE html
        PUBLIC "-//W3C//DTD XHTML 1.0 Strict//EN"
        "http://www.w3.org/TR/xhtml1/DTD/xhtml1-strict.dtd">
<!-- login.html -->
<html xmlns="http://www.w3.org/1999/xhtml">
  <head>
    <title>Login to My Own Blog!</title>
  </head>
  <body>
    <h1>
      Log in to My Own Blog to begin blogging!
    </h1>
    <form action="Login" method="post">
      <table border="0">
        <tbody>
          <tr>
            <td>User Name:</td>
            <td><input type="text" name="username" /></td>
          </tr>
          <tr>
            <td>Password:</td>
            <td><input type="password" name="pwd" /></td>
          </tr>
          <tr>
            <td> </td>
            <td><input type="submit" name="submit"
                       value="Log in" /></td>
          </tr>
        </tbody>
      </table>
    </form>
  </body>
</html>
```

FIGURE 2.29 HTML document generating the log-in screen for the blogging application.

Finally, let's consider the page that visitors to the blog site will see, the *view-blog* page (Fig. 2.31). Because this is intended to be the page seen by default, I've named it index.html. The screen shot shown here is somewhat different than the one in Figure 1.12 in that the latter includes style information, which is covered in the next chapter. The overall structure of the body of the HTML markup for this page is shown in Figure 2.32. As shown, the page consists of three basic parts: a banner image at the top, followed by a one-row table split into two elements: a left element containing the blog entries, and a right element containing links (in a fuller implementation, this element might also contain profile information, off-site links, and much more). The style attribute is used to ensure that the contents of each of these elements is displayed beginning at the top of the table row, rather than centered. This avoids the problem we saw in the add-entry page with the Body: label.

The image is wrapped in a div element in order to conform with the XHTML 1.0 DTD. If you look closely at Figure 2.31, you'll see that this image is not centered over the text of the document (it is more noticeable if the window is widened); we'll learn how to center elements in the next chapter.

FIGURE 2.30 Page for adding blog entries.

Now let's consider the content of the left side of the table. Each blog entry consists of text representing the date and time when the entry was added, an `h1` element containing the title of the entry, and text representing the body of the entry. A horizontal rule (`hr`) is used to separate entries. The first entry is

```
AUGUST 9, 2005, 5:04 PM EDT
<h1>I'm hungry</h1>
<p>
   Strange.  I seem to get hungry about the same time
   every day.  Maybe it's something in the water.
</p>
<hr />
```

The links on the right side of the table are formatted as a nested list, as shown in Figure 2.33. One thing to notice is that the entity reference & is used within the values of the last three `href` attributes. I actually want an ampersand (&) within these strings, but since the ampersand is an XML special character I must represent it via a reference. Also notice the use of the   (nonbreaking space) reference within the text of the hyperlinks. This ensures that each month and year is displayed on a single line. Without this, the browser might split a month and year into separate lines, particularly if the browser window is narrowed.

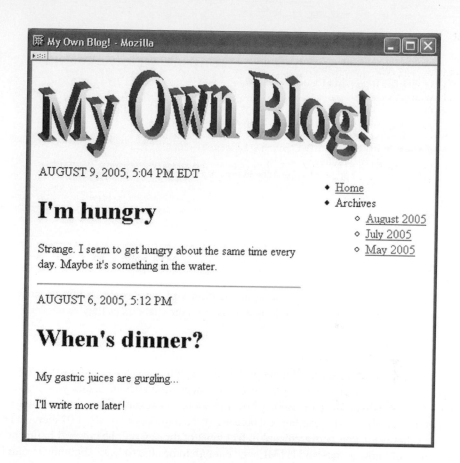

FIGURE 2.31 Screen displaying blog entries and navigation links.

```
<div>
  <!-- Banner image -->
  <img src="banner.gif" width="438" height="120"
       alt='"My Own Blog!" Banner' />
</div>
<table border="0">
  <tr>
    <!-- Blog entries -->
    <td style="vertical-align:top">
      ...
    </td>
    <!-- Side information -->
    <td style="vertical-align:top">
      ...
    </td>
  </tr>
</table>
```

FIGURE 2.32 Structure of the body of the HTML document generating the view-blog screen.

```
<ul>
  <li><a href="index.html">Home</a></li>
  <li>Archives
    <ul>
      <li><a href="index.html?month=8&amp;year=2005"
          >August 2005</a></li>
      <li><a href="index.html?month=7&amp;year=2005"
          >July 2005</a></li>
      <li><a href="index.html?month=5&amp;year=2005"
          >May 2005</a></li>
    </ul>
  </li>
</ul>
```

FIGURE 2.33 Side-information markup for the view-blog screen.

The final version of the blogging application will have some additional pages for displaying error information. We'll look at those in later chapters as they're needed.

2.13 References

At this point, you know quite a bit about the basic syntax of HTML documents. You also know about the basic functionality of several elements and attributes, and you know how to use an XHTML DTD to determine how elements can relate to one another and what types of data can be used in attributes. There are still a number of HTML 4.01 elements and attributes that we haven't covered, and in fact most of those won't be covered in this book. But you should now understand HTML well enough to be able to learn about the remaining elements from the HTML language references given here.

The authoritative reference for the XHTML 1.0 language is actually contained in two online documents: [W3C-XHTML-1.0] and [W3C-HTML-4.01]. The latter provides the semantic details of all of the various HTML 4.01/XHTML 1.0 elements (click the Elements link at the top of the page for a complete table of elements with links to details of each). This reference also provides some examples of element usage. However, these are HTML 4.01 examples, and many are not syntactically correct XHTML 1.0, so you should not cut and paste these examples into your own XHTML documents. The former reference carefully explains the syntax of XHTML 1.0 and how this differs from HTML 4.01. A set of annotated DTDs for the XHTML 1.0 language flavors is available at [W3C-XHTML-DTDS]. The specification for relative URLs is contained in [STD-66]. W3C-recommended guidelines for designing web pages for access by users with disabilities are provided at [W3C-WAI].

In order to write real-world HTML applications, you should also be familiar with the idiosyncrasies of various browsers, which may not perfectly implement the XHTML 1.0 recommendation. Covering browser idiosyncrasies in detail is beyond the scope of this book. However, generally speaking, virtually all modern browsers support all of the elements of the HTML 4.01/XHTML 1.0 recommendations (one exception is that Internet Explorer 6 does not support the abbr element). So, as far as basic HTML markup is concerned, if you follow the W3C recommendations and the syntax described in this chapter, your markup should be compatible with essentially all browsers. However, beyond basic markup there are some significant differences between browsers; for instance, many differences between Mozilla and IE6 will become evident in Chapter 5. Therefore, you should refer to developer documentation for complete details on each browser. For Internet Explorer, `http://msdn.microsoft.com/workshop/author/dhtml/reference/dhtml_reference_entry.asp` is a good documentation starting point; for Mozilla, `http://www.mozilla.org/docs/web-developer/` has links to documentation.

As discussed earlier, XHTML 1.0 is defined using XML 1.0. This means that the basic syntax of XHTML 1.0 and also the syntax of XML DTDs are defined as part of the XML specification. The authoritative XML 1.0 reference is [W3C-XML-1.0]. This reference makes extensive use of a form of extended BNF notation that is described in the final section of the document ("6 Notation"), which I recommend at least skimming before reading other parts of the document. We'll be covering XML in more detail in Chapter 7, so you shouldn't be concerned about understanding everything in the XML reference at this point.

Exercises

2.1. How many tags are contained in Figure 2.1? How many XHTML elements are contained in the figure? Not counting leading and trailing white space, how many characters of content are contained in the document shown in the figure?

2.2. Draw a complete element tree for the XHTML document shown in Figure 2.12. Assume that the head element of the document contains only a `title` element.

2.3. Many web pages are written for private use within a single company. How might developing HTML pages to be used within a company be easier than developing pages to be viewed as part of the World Wide Web?

2.4. Write XHTML markup that will display three paragraphs (each "paragraph" can contain just a few words of text). Write the markup so that there is more vertical space between the second and third paragraphs than there is between the first and second.

2.5. I recommended that two spaces between sentences be produced by using an ` ` reference followed by a space (Section 2.3.4). Why is this approach to producing two spaces between sentences better than either using a space followed by ` ` or using two ` ` references? (Hint: Think about how the sentences will appear as the browser window is resized.) Your answer should not only describe how the sentences might appear, but also explain why.

2.6. Write XHTML markup that assigns the value `"An example is written as <x, b>."` (including the quotes) to the `value` attribute of an `input` control of type `text`. (You may want to test your answer by including your markup in an XHTML document containing a form.)

2.7. Write a short XHTML document that demonstrates the six different heading elements and that also includes normal paragraph text. Compare the fonts used for the various headings with the default font used for paragraph text in Mozilla 1.4.

2.8. What is wrong with the following markup?

```
<pre>
  // Java code example
  if (a < b && c != d) {
    System.out.println("Time for donuts!");
  }
</pre>
```

2.9. If two displays have the same physical size but one has higher resolution than the other, then the same image displayed on both displays with the same width and height in pixels will appear how: smaller on the higher resolution display, larger on the higher resolution display, or the same size on both displays? Explain.

2.10. Using only XHTML as covered in this chapter, explain how you could provide a web page that contains an image that can be distorted by page visitors. Specifically, by manipulating their browsers, users should be able to stretch the image horizontally. The image may appear distorted when it is initially displayed.

2.11. Assume that the base URL for a web page is

```
http://www.example.com/hw1/detail/page7.html
```

Also assume that this page contains the relative URL

```
../images/icon5.gif
```

Give the absolute URL corresponding to this relative URL.

2.12. You are writing an HTML document that will reside in the `App1` subdirectory of the Tomcat `webapps/ROOT` directory. The `App1` directory contains a directory named `legal`. Write a relative URL that could be used within a document contained in `App1` to refer to a document named `copyright.html` in the `legal` directory. Write a second relative URL that could be used within `copyright.html` to refer to an image file named `logo.jpg` in the `App1` directory.

2.13. What is wrong with the following markup?

```
<strong>
  <dl>
    <dt>SGML</dt>
    <dd>Standard Generalized Markup Language</dd>
    <dt>XML</dt>
    <dd>Extensible Markup Language</dd>
  </dl>
</strong>
```

2.14. Rewrite the following example taken from the HTML 4.01 specification so that it complies with the requirements of the XHTML 1.0 standard as discussed in this chapter. The table produced by your version should look exactly the same as the table produced by the original version in a browser compliant with HTML 4.01.

```
<TABLE border="1"
          summary="This table gives some statistics about fruit
                    flies: average height and weight, and percentage
                    with red eyes (for both males and females).">
```

```
<CAPTION><EM>A test table with merged cells</EM></CAPTION>
<TR><TH rowspan="2"><TH colspan="2">Average
    <TH rowspan="2">Red<BR>eyes
<TR><TH>height<TH>weight
<TR><TH>Males<TD>1.9<TD>0.003<TD>40%
<TR><TH>Females<TD>1.7<TD>0.002<TD>43%
</TABLE>
```

2.15. The W3C recommends the use of the `object` HTML element for embedding multimedia—including Java applets—in a web page. However, while both IE6 and Mozilla 1.4 implement the `object` element, the attributes used with this element are generally different in the two browsers. For the most part, IE6 uses the value of the `classid` attribute (which is similar to a URN) to locate the software that will process the multimedia file. In Mozilla 1.4, on the other hand, the `type` attribute is typically used to specify a MIME type for the multimedia file, and browser preferences associate specific player software with the MIME type. Give one potential advantage of each of these approaches over the other.

2.16. The head element is declared as follows in the XHTML 1.0 DTD:

```
<!ENTITY % head.misc "(script|style|meta|link|object)*">
<!ELEMENT head (%head.misc;,
     ((title, %head.misc;, (base, %head.misc;)?) |
      (base, %head.misc;, (title, %head.misc;))))>
```

  (a) Describe in English what the `head.misc` entity represents.
  (b) Describe in English what the content specification of the `head` element represents. For this part of the problem, just translate the content specification directly into English. Also, you can use "head.misc" in your description; that is, you do not need to directly mention `script`, `style`, etc., in your description.
  (c) Now rewrite your description from the previous part of this problem more succinctly. That is, analyze the content specification and attempt to understand what it means, not just what it says literally. Once you understand the content specification, you should be able to describe it in English reasonably simply.

Research and Exploration

2.17. Review the HTML 2.0 specification (`http://www.w3.org/MarkUp/html-spec/`). What key HTML element discussed in this chapter is missing from this specification? List two `img` attributes covered in this chapter that are missing in this early specification.

2.18. A list of the elements included in XHTML Basic can be found in Sec. 3 of the XHTML Basic recommendation (`http://www.w3.org/TR/xhtml-basic/`). Give two XHTML 1.0 elements discussed in this chapter that are not part of XHTML Basic.

2.19. Create (or download) a copy of the HTML document of Figure 2.1. Then change the document type declaration to indicate that this is an HTML 4.01 document rather than XHTML 1.0, so that it will now be viewed as an SGML document rather than XML. Next, remove as many element tags as possible from the document while producing a document with the following properties:
  • The resulting document looks exactly the same as the original when viewed with Mozilla 1.4.

- The document is valid according to the W3C validator [W3C-VAL]. (The validator may warn you that it cannot find a character encoding. The default UTF-8 encoding that it assumes should be fine.)

2.20. Using references to entities supplied by XHTML 1.0, write XHTML markup that will cause a browser to display the following as shown, with italicized text, special characters, and spacing as shown. (This should display properly in a typical installation of Mozilla 1.4, but some of the characters may not display in Internet Explorer browsers.)

(a)

$$\int 2y \, dy$$

(b)

$$A \leq B \Rightarrow B \cap C = \emptyset$$

2.21. Some XHTML 1.0 elements must always have children in an element tree for any valid document. Other elements must always be leaves in an element tree, and still others can be either leaves or nonleaves. Give the content specification from XHTML 1.0 Strict DTD [W3C-XHTML-DTDS] for each of the following XHTML elements, and explain how the specification for each determines which of these three categories applies to the element:

(a) a

(b) tr

(c) br

2.22. Use the XHTML 1.0 Strict DTD [W3C-XHTML-DTDS] to identify at least three XHTML 1.0 Strict elements other than img and form that have required attributes. Specify the required attribute(s) for each. You can list elements not discussed in the text.

2.23. According to the XHTML 1.0 Strict DTD [W3C-XHTML-DTDS], which of the form controls in Table 2.5 can appear as children of a form element?

2.24. In Section 2.4.8, we informally discussed the concepts of inline and block elements. Now we will see exactly what these terms mean as far as the XHTML DTD is concerned.

(a) The XHTML 1.0 Strict DTD [W3C-XHTML-DTDS] defines a parameter entity called Block (note the capital B; there is also a different entity called block). Locate the entity definition of Block in the DTD, and rewrite it as an entity definition that contains no references. That is, expand out all entity references contained in the definition of Block, in the definitions of those entities, and so on, until no entity references remain. Don't be concerned that you do not recognize some of the elements included in these entity definitions; just write them down whether or not you recognize them (but feel free to look them up in the element list in [W3C-HTML-4.01] if you're curious).

(b) Find at least one element for which a reference to Block completely specifies the element's content.

(c) Repeat (a) and (b) for the Inline parameter entity (again, for the entity with name beginning with capital I).

2.25. The HTML elements recognized by Microsoft's Internet Explorer browser are documented at [MS-DHTML]. Find and briefly describe three elements recognized by IE that are not contained in the HTML 4.01 Transitional standard.

2.26. Read the W3C documentation at [W3C-HTML-4.01] on the base element in HTML, and then answer the following question: A collection of web pages has URLs of the form `http://www.example.com/page`*num*`.html`, where *num* is a different number for each page. You want to edit one of the pages, store it in a directory on your machine, and test the modified page. All of the other pages should remain on the web server, not be copied to your machine. The modified page contains several relative URLs of the form `page`*num*`.html`. What one statement would you add to the modified page so that these relative URLs refer to the appropriate pages on the web server?

2.27. The HTML `tabindex` attribute is used to establish a *tab order* among certain elements, primarily form controls such as `input`. That is, the `tabindex` attribute can be used to define the order in which certain elements will be visited as a user presses the Tab key on the keyboard.

   (a) To which elements does the `tabindex` apply in XHTML 1.0 Strict? Note: This is not exactly the same set of elements as those listed in [W3C-HTML-4.01]. Instead, you should examine [W3C-XHTML-DTDS].

   (b) Provide `tabindex` attribute specifications that will define the tab order for the following markup to be `input` elements named `username` and `password`, in that order; then the submit button; and finally the anchor element:

```
<form action="">
  <fieldset>
    <legend>
      Enter data here
    </legend>
    <label>User name:
      <input type="text" name="username" />
    </label>
    <a href="http://www.example.org/help">I forgot my username/
        password</a>
    <br />
    <label>Password:
      <input type="password" name="password" />
    </label>
    <br />
    <input type="submit" name="login" value="Log me in" />
  </fieldset>
</form>
```

2.28. The HTML `meta` element.

   (a) Research the HTML `meta` element, and briefly describe two uses for it (other than the one mentioned in the next part of this question). Give URLs for Web pages that use the element in each way.

   (b) Exercise 1.34 in Chapter 1 described the concept of a software *robot*. Read the second part of Section 4.1 of Appendix B of the HTML 4.01 Recommendation [W3C-HTML-4.01], and explain how you would use the `meta` element in an XHTML document in order to request that robots not crawl the document. Note that the examples in [W3C-HTML-4.01] are not valid XHTML. (See `http://www.robotstxt.org/wc/exclusion.html#meta` for more information on this form of robot exclusion.)

2.29. What is the purpose of the HTML `title` attribute (not element)? Describe a scenario in which this attribute might be particularly helpful to a Web site user.

Projects

2.30. HTML reference pages. Implement a subset of the following requirements as specified by your instructor.

(a) Create a set of HTML reference pages for the subset of HTML elements and attributes selected by your instructor. There should first be a page that contains a (short) list of two hyperlinks: one hyperlink to a page with a table of elements, and the other to a page with a table of attributes. The table of elements should contain two columns: the first listing the elements, and the second listing the attributes that are associated with each element. The attributes should be listed one per table row, and each element name should span the rows containing its attributes. Each element and attribute name in the table should be a hyperlink to a detail page describing that element or attribute. Each detail page should use a `dl` style list to define the element or attribute (your description can be short—a sentence or two—but it should be accurate). The table of attributes should be similar, except that the attribute names are in the first column and each attribute name will span a set of rows containing element names associated with the attribute. All pages should have meaningful titles, and tables should include meaningful captions.

(b) Modify the collection of pages in (a) to use frames. Specifically, the user should initially see a page containing three frames: upper left, lower left, and right (much like a Javadoc frames page, such as the one in Fig. 2.6). The upper left frame should contain the two-element list of two hyperlinks to the element and attribute pages. The lower left frame should initially contain the element table, but whenever the user clicks a link in the upper left frame, the lower left frame should display the appropriate table, either element or attribute. When a link is clicked in the lower left frame, the associated page should be displayed in the rightmost frame (initially, this frame should display the detail page for the first element in your element table).

(c) Write all of your pages to the XHTML 1.0 Strict or Frameset standard, as appropriate. Validate your pages at the W3C validator [W3C-VAL], and add a hyperlink with URL `http://validator.w3.org/check/referer` to all Strict pages to make it easy to verify that these pages validate. Note that this link will be able to perform the validation only if the page is viewed by visiting a Web server, and not if the page is available only on your machine or local network.

2.31. Order information form. Implement a subset of the following requirements as specified by your instructor.

(a) Create an HTML document (web page) that gathers information as part of an online product ordering system. This page will request shipping and billing name and address, credit card information, and contact information (e-mail address and phone number). It should provide a menu from which the type of credit card (from a list of approximately four options) can be selected; the default selection should be "Select a Credit Card." There should also be fields for entering the card number and expiration date. Furthermore, there should be a checkbox, initially checked, that is labeled "Please keep me informed about future product offerings." Finally, provide submit and clear buttons. All form controls should have appropriate `name` attributes. Use the GET method for form submission, and specify the empty string for the action.

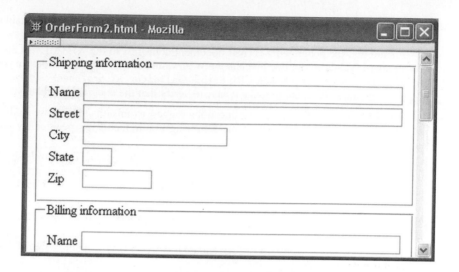

FIGURE 2.34 Example order form layout.

(b) Improve the layout of the form in (a), as illustrated in Figure 2.34. Use fieldset elements to enclose related controls in four groups: shipping, billing, credit card, and contact information (including the checkbox). The submit and clear buttons can be placed outside a fieldset. Within each fieldset, use tables to align the text boxes so that the left edges of the text boxes are all the same distance from the edge of the fieldset, even if the labels of the boxes are of different lengths.

(c) Ensure that your page conforms to the XHTML 1.0 Strict standard. Validate your pages at the W3C validator [W3C-VAL], and add a hyperlink with URL `http://validator.w3.org/check/referer` to all pages to make it easy to verify that your pages validate.

2.32. Entity table generator. Implement a subset of the following requirements as specified by your instructor.

(a) Write a Java program that reads an XHTML entity set and generates an XHTML document that can be used to test a browser's ability to display the entities declared in the entity set. Specifically, the user should enter the name of a file containing an entity set, such as one of the three entity sets imported into the XHTML 1.0 Strict DTD. The program should read the names of all entities declared in the entity set. You may assume for simplicity that each entity declaration begins in the first column of a line and has a single space between the `<!ENTITY` string and the entity name (this assumption is valid for the W3C XHTML 1.0 entity sets). The program should also input the name of a file to which an XHTML document will be written. The generated XHTML document should contain a two-column HTML table with each entity name read from the entity set in the first column and a reference to the entity in the second column.

(b) Rather than reading an entity set from a file, the program should input a URL and obtain the entity set from the given URL. You will probably want to use the `openConnection()` method of the `java.net.URL` class to obtain a `URLConnection` and use the `getInputStream()` method on this `URLConnection` object to obtain an `InputStream` representing the entity set.

(c) Ensure that the generated XHTML document conforms to the XHTML 1.0 Strict standard. Validate your document at the W3C validator [W3C-VAL], and have your program add a hyperlink with URL `http://validator.w3.org/check/referer` to the generated document to make it easy to verify that the document validates.

2.33. Case study extensions. The following questions suggest extensions to the case study of Section 2.12. Implement a subset of the following requirements as specified by your instructor.

(a) Add a profile section to the right element of the view-blog page. The profile should include an image and a list of profile entries, such as name, age, place of birth, place of residence, and occupation. Each entry in the list should consist of a bold label followed by a colon and then the appropriate information.

(b) Design and implement an HTML document that displays a single blog entry followed by comments entered by blog readers. Modify the document of Figure 2.32 so that it contains a hyperlink (with text "Comments") referencing the comments document.

(c) Add a form to the end of the document of part (b). The form should contain appropriate HTML controls allowing a user to enter a title for a comment and separately enter the body of the comment. The controls used to enter this information should be nicely aligned and labeled. Both submit and reset buttons should be provided.

(d) Add a set of five radio buttons to the form of the previous question. The buttons should allow a user to rate a blog entry, giving it from zero to four stars. A checkbox (initially unchecked) should precede the radio button set and be labeled "Rate this blog entry."

(e) Modify the radio buttons of the previous question so that they are "labeled" with appropriate graphics (four empty stars, one filled and three empty stars, etc.) rather than having text labels.

(f) Ensure that your pages conform to the XHTML 1.0 Strict standard. Validate your pages at the W3C validator [W3C-VAL], and add a hyperlink with URL `http://validator.w3.org/check/referer` to the all pages to make it easy to verify that your pages validate.

CHAPTER 3

Style Sheets
CSS

As we have learned, HTML markup can be used to indicate both the *semantics* of a document (e.g., which parts are elements of lists) and its *presentation* (e.g., which words should be italicized). However, as noted in the previous chapter, it is advisable to use markup predominantly for indicating the semantics of a document and to use a separate mechanism to determine exactly how information contained in the document should be presented. *Style sheets* provide such a mechanism. This chapter presents basic information about *Cascading Style Sheets* (CSS), a style sheet technology designed to work with HTML and XML documents.

CSS provides a great deal of control over the presentation of a document, but to exercise this control intelligently requires an understanding of a number of features. And, while you as a software developer may not be particularly interested in getting your web page to look "just so," many web software developers are members of teams that include professional web page designers, some of whom may have precise presentation requirements. Thus, while I have tried to focus on what I consider key features of CSS, I've also included a number of finer points that I believe may be more useful to you in the future than you might expect on first reading.

While CSS is used extensively to style HTML documents, it is not the only style-related web technology. In particular, we will study the Extensible Stylesheet Language (XSL)—which is used for transforming and possibly styling general XML documents—in Chapter 7.

3.1 Introduction to Cascading Style Sheets

Before getting into details, let's take a quick look at an XHTML document that uses simple style sheets to define its presentation. Specifically, let's consider once again the "Hello World!" document of Figure 2.1, but with the addition of two `link` elements in the `head` of the document (`CSSHelloWorld.html`, shown in Fig. 3.1). Notice that the body of this document is identical to that of Figure 2.1. However, viewing this document in Mozilla 1.4 produces the result shown in Figure 3.2, which is quite different from the way Mozilla displayed the original "Hello World!" document (Fig. 2.2).

The difference between the two browser renderings, of course, has to do with the `link` element, which imports a *style sheet* located at the URL specified as the value of its `href` attribute. In this example, the style sheet is written in the CSS language, as indicated by the MIME type value of the `type` attribute. The `style1.css` file contains the lines

```
<!DOCTYPE html
        PUBLIC "-//W3C//DTD XHTML 1.0 Strict//EN"
        "http://www.w3.org/TR/xhtml1/DTD/xhtml1-strict.dtd">
<html xmlns="http://www.w3.org/1999/xhtml">
  <head>
    <title>
      CSSHelloWorld.html
    </title>
    <link rel="stylesheet" type="text/css" href="style1.css"
        title="Style 1" />
    <link rel="alternate stylesheet" type="text/css" href="style2.css"
        title="Style 2" />
  </head>
  <body>
    <p>
      Hello World!
    </p>
  </body>
</html>
```

FIGURE 3.1 HTML source for "Hello World!" using style sheets.

```
body   { background-color:lime }
p      { font-size:x-large; background-color:yellow }
```

The first line simply says that, for rendering purposes, the `body` element of the document should be treated as if it contained the attribute `style="background-color:lime"`. The second line is similar, except that it specifies a style that should be applied to every `p` element of the document. The second line also specifies values for two different style *properties*, `font-size` and `background-color`. We'll learn details about these and many other style properties later in this chapter, but for now their meaning should be clear from their names and the effects shown in Figure 3.2.

The file `style2.css` contains the single line

```
p      { font-size:smaller; letter-spacing:1em }
```

This says that `p` elements should be set in a smaller than normal font size and that there should be space between adjacent letters. However, this style is not applied to the document

FIGURE 3.2 Browser rendering of `CSSHelloWorld.html`.

FIGURE 3.3 Selecting the style sheet to be used by Mozilla.

rendered in Figure 3.2, because this style sheet is specified as an *alternate style sheet* by the
rel (relationship) attribute of the link element that imports this sheet. A style sheet such
as the one in style1.css, which is referenced by a link element having a rel with value
stylesheet as well as a title specification, is known as a *preferred style sheet*. An alternate
sheet can be selected by the user, as illustrated in Figure 3.3. Notice that the values of the
title attributes of the link tags are displayed in the Use Style menu along with the default
Basic Page Style; preferred and alternate style sheet link elements must always contain
title attribute specifications. After the alternate style sheet is selected, the page renders in
the second style, as shown in Figure 3.4. (Alternate style sheets are not used often at the
time of this writing, because the user interface for IE6 does not support user selection of
alternate style sheets.)

Now that we have some understanding of what a style sheet is, we will discuss some
of the major features of CSS.

3.2   Cascading Style Sheet Features

The key property of style sheet technology is that it can be used to separate the presentation of information from the information content and semantic tagging. The content and

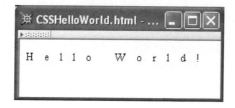

FIGURE 3.4 Browser rendering of CSSHelloWorld.html using style sheet from style2.css.

TABLE 3.1 Possible Values for media Attribute Defined by HTML 4.01 Standard

Value	Media Type
all	All types (default)
aural	Speech synthesizer
braille	Tactile device generating braille characters
handheld	Handheld device, such as a cell phone or PDA
print	Printer
projection	Projector, such as one used to display a large monitor image on a screen
screen	Computer monitor
tty	Fixed-width character output device
tv	Television (monitor with low resolution and little or no scrolling)

semantics of the "Hello World!" page did not change in the previous example: it consisted of a single paragraph containing some text. Put another way, the body elements of the HelloWorld.html and CSSHelloWorld.html files will have exactly the same abstract syntax tree. But by changing the style sheet used by the browser to display this tree, we can achieve different presentations of the same information.

There are significant advantages to having such a separation between the information contained in a document and its presentation. First, it allows the information in the document to be presented without change in a variety of ways. We have already seen an example of this feature with user-selectable alternative style sheets. But CSS can do even more than this. For example, the link element defines a media attribute that can be used to define the types of media for which a style sheet is designed, such as for display on a monitor or output to a printer (see Table 3.1 for a complete list of media types defined by the HTML 4.01 standard). So, for example, if we had used the link elements

```
<link rel="stylesheet" type="text/css" href="style1.css"
      media="screen, tv, projection" />
<link rel="stylesheet" type="text/css" href="style2.css"
      media="handheld, print" />
```

then the style sheet of style1.css would be used for display on monitors, televisions, and projectors, the style sheet of style2.css for output to handheld devices and printers, and the browser's default style sheet for all other forms of output. (The example file CSSHelloWorldPrint.html demonstrates this feature: try loading it into your browser and then printing it.) You'll notice that the title attribute does not appear in the link elements in this example. This is because these style sheets cannot be selected by the user, but instead will apply regardless of user actions. Such style sheets are called *persistent* and can be recognized by their lack of a title attribute specification in the link element referencing the style sheet.

From a developer's perspective, another useful feature of using style sheets is that it is relatively easy to give all of the elements on a page a consistent appearance. That is, if we want all of the h1 headers on a page to have a certain size, we can accomplish this easily using a style sheet. Furthermore, if at a later time we wish to change the size of the headers, we need only make the change in that one style sheet. More generally, if we use a single style sheet for all of the pages at a site, then all of the site pages will have a consistent style, and one that can be changed with little work.

In addition to these properties, which apply to any style sheet language—including older print-oriented style sheet languages—the cascading quality of CSS makes it particularly appealing for use with web documents. As we will learn, both the document author and the person viewing the document can specify aspects of the document style as it is displayed by the browser (or other user agent displaying the document). For example, a user may instruct their browser to display all HTML documents using only a white background, regardless of the setting of the background-color property in style rules supplied by the page author. This can be an important feature to, for example, a user who because of an eyesight limitation needs high contrast between text and its background.

It should also be noted that, though I am going to cover CSS in the context of providing style for HTML documents, it can also be used with non-HTML XML documents (Section 7.10 contains an example).

So, there are many reasons to learn about style sheet technology in general, and CSS in particular. We'll start by covering some of the core CSS syntactic elements. After that, we'll study the cascading aspects of CSS in more detail. Finally, we'll consider details of a number of specific style properties and apply CSS to the blogging case study.

3.3   CSS Core Syntax

As with HTML, there are several W3C-recommended versions of CSS. At the time of this writing, there are technically two W3C recommendations for CSS: CSS level 1 [W3C-CSS-1.0] and CSS level 2 [W3C-CSS-2.0] (often referred to as CSS1 and CSS2). Work is also underway on CSS level 3, and several specialized versions of CSS for limited devices, such as cell phones, low-cost printers, and televisions, are in various stages of standardization.

Although CSS2 has been a W3C recommendation since 1998, at this time no widely used browser implements the entire recommendation. Recognizing this fact, the W3C has been developing CSS 2.1, which is largely a scaled-back version of CSS2 that attempts to capture those features of CSS2 that are—as of the time of the recommendation's official publication—implemented by multiple browsers. Using the February 2004 candidate version of CSS 2.1 [W3C-CSS-2.1] as a guide, in this chapter I will specifically focus on key aspects of CSS2 that are implemented in both IE6—the latest generally-available version of Internet Explorer at the time of the writing—and Mozilla 1.4. For the most part, the basic CSS syntax is the same for both levels 1 and 2, so much of what is presented should also be compatible with older browsers. Furthermore, just as browsers generally ignore HTML elements that they do not recognize, they also generally ignore CSS style properties that they do not recognize. So, if you use CSS as described in this chapter, almost all browsers should be able to display your document (although some older ones may not style it properly). It will of course be advisable for you to monitor the progress of the CSS 2.1 and CSS 3 recommendations so that you can use newer style sheet features as they become widely available; see the References section (Section 3.12) for more on this.

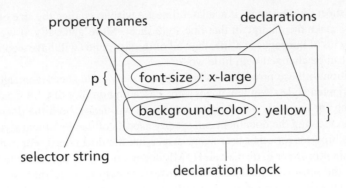

FIGURE 3.5 Parts of a single ruleset-type style rule.

One other word of warning is that versions of the Internet Explorer browser before IE6 supported style sheets but deviated from the CSS recommendation in several ways. Even in IE6, these deviations will be present unless you use a document type declaration such as the one for XHTML 1.0 Strict used in our examples. At the time of this writing, IE5 is still used on a substantial number of machines, although its usage is dwindling rapidly. So, if you develop real-world CSS style sheets in the near term, you may need to deviate somewhat from the material presented in this chapter. However, the concepts taught here are similar to those found in IE5, and as time goes on the details presented here should apply to the bulk of browsers in use. Again, see Section 3.12 for more information.

A CSS style sheet consists of one or more style rules (sometimes called *statements*). Each line in the `style1.css` file in Section 3.1 is an example of a rule. This form of rule is called a *ruleset* and consists of two parts: a *selector string* followed by a *declaration block*, which is enclosed in curly braces ({ and }) (see Fig. 3.5). The declaration block contains a list (possibly empty) of *declarations* separated by semicolons (;) (the final declaration can also be followed by a semicolon, and many style sheet authors follow this convention). The selector string indicates the elements to which the rule should apply, and each declaration within the declaration block specifies a value for one style property of those elements. While the example shows one rule per line, it is syntactically legal to split a rule over several lines or (though not recommended) write multiple rules on a single line. No special character is needed to mark the end of a rule (no semicolon as in Java), due to the use of the braces to distinguish the parts of the rule.

We'll have much more to say about the properties that may be set within declarations in a later section. For the moment, the properties that we use, such as `color` (text color) and `font-style`, should be fairly self-explanatory. Before considering other properties, we will focus on selector strings.

3.3.1 Selector Strings

In the following paragraphs, we will be referring to an example style sheet and HTML document shown in Figure 3.6 and Figure 3.7, respectively. Notice that comments are written using the Java-style multiline syntax; HTML-style comments are not recognized in

```
/* Headers have dark background */

h1,h2,h3,h4,h5,h6 { background-color:purple }

/* All elements bold */

* { font-weight:bold }

/* Elements with certain id's have light background */

#p1, #p3 { background-color:aqua }

/* Elements in certain classes are italic, large font,
   or both */

#p4, .takeNote { font-style:italic }
span.special { font-size:x-large }

/* Hyperlink ('a' element) styles */

a:link { color:black }
a:visited { color:yellow }
a:hover { color:green }
a:active { color:red }

/* Descendant selectors */

ul span { font-variant:small-caps }
ul ol li { letter-spacing:1em }
```

FIGURE 3.6 Style sheet file sel-demo.css used to demonstrate various types of CSS selectors.

CSS, nor are Java end-of-line (//) comments. A browser rendering of this HTML document using the given style sheet is shown in Figure 3.8.

Probably the simplest form of selector string, which we have already seen, consists of the name of a single element type, such as body or p. A rule can also apply to multiple element types by using a selector string consisting of the comma-separated names of the element types. For example, the rule

```
h1,h2,h3,h4,h5,h6 { background-color:purple }
```

says that any of the six heading element types should be rendered with a purple background. Therefore, in our example document, the markup

```
<h1>Selector Tests</h1>
```

has a purple background when displayed in the browser.

In the preceding style rule, each of the *selectors* (comma-separated components of the selector string) was simply the name of an element type. This form of selector is called a *type selector*. Several other forms of selector are also defined in CSS. One is the *universal*

```
<!DOCTYPE html
        PUBLIC "-//W3C//DTD XHTML 1.0 Strict//EN"
        "http://www.w3.org/TR/xhtml1/DTD/xhtml1-strict.dtd">
<html xmlns="http://www.w3.org/1999/xhtml">
  <head>
    <title>
      Selectors.html
    </title>
    <link rel="stylesheet" type="text/css" href="sel-demo.css" />
  </head>
  <body>
    <h1>Selector Tests</h1>
    <p id="P1" class="takeNote">
      Paragraph with id="P1" and class="takeNote".
    </p>
    <p id="p2" class="special">
      Second paragraph.  <span class="takeNote special cool">This span
      belongs to classes takeNote, special, and cool.</span>

      <ul>
        <li>Span's within this list are in <span>small-cap</span>
            style.</li>
        <ol>
          <li>This item spaces letters.</li>
        </ol>
      </ul>
    </p>
    <p id="p3">
      Third paragraph (id="p3") contains a
      <a href="http://www.example.net">hyperlink</a>.
      <ol>
        <li>This item contains a span but does not display it in
          <span>small caps</span>, nor does it space letters.</li>
      </ol>
    </p>
  </body>
</html>
```

FIGURE 3.7 HTML document used to demonstrate various types of CSS selectors.

selector, which is denoted by an asterisk (*). The universal selector represents every possible element type. So, for example, the rule

```
* { font-weight:bold }
```

specifies a value of bold for the font-weight property of every element in the document.

Another form of selector is the *ID selector*. Recall that every element in an XHTML document has an associated id attribute, and that if a value is assigned to the id attribute for an element then no other element's id can be assigned the same value. If a selector is preceded by a number sign (#), then it represents an id value rather than an element type name. So, for example, if a document contains the markup

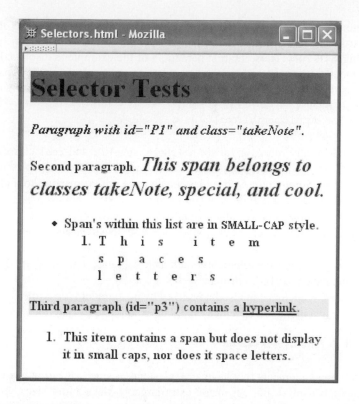

FIGURE 3.8 Browser rendering of `Selectors.html` after applying style sheet `sel-demo.css`.

```
<p id="p3">
  ...
</p>
```

then the following rule will cause this paragraph (and another element with `id` value `p1`, if such an element exists) to be displayed with an aqua background:

```
#p1, #p3 { background-color:aqua }
```

Note that `id` values are case-sensitive, so this rule will not apply to an element that has an `id` value of `P1`. This is why the first paragraph in Figure 3.8 does not have a background color.

Another HTML attribute that is frequently used with style sheets is `class`. This attribute is used to associate style properties with an element as follows. First, the style sheet must contain one or more rulesets having *class selectors*, which are selectors that are preceded by a period (.), such as `.takeNote` in the rule

```
#p4, .takeNote { font-style:italic }
```

Then any element that specifies `takeNote` (without the leading period) as the value of its `class` attribute will be given the properties specified in the declaration block of the corresponding style rule. Thus, the first paragraph of the example is displayed in an italic font. An element can be assigned to multiple style classes by using a space-separated list of class names as the value of the `class` attribute. For example, a `span` element with start tag

```
<span class="takeNote special cool">
```

will be affected by any rules for for the `takeNote`, `special`, and `cool` classes. Thus, the second sentence of the second paragraph of the example is italicized, since it belongs to the `takeNote` class, among others. If a class name does not correspond to a class selector in any of the style rules for a document (for example, `.cool` is not used as a class selector in `sel-demo.css`), then that class value is ignored.

Note that, like `id` values, `class` values are case sensitive and cannot begin with a decimal digit. However, unlike `id`, multiple elements can have the same value for their `class` attributes. All but a few elements, such as `html`, `head`, and elements that appear as content of `head`, have the `class` attribute.

ID and class selectors can also be prefixed by an element type name, which restricts the selector to elements of the specified type. For example, the style rule

```
span.special { font-size:x-large }
```

applies only to `span` elements that have a `class` value of `special`. So, in our example, the second paragraph itself is not set in the extra large (`x-large`) font size, but the second sentence of that paragraph is displayed using the extra large font, because the sentence is contained in a span with `class` value `special`. Also, an asterisk can be used in place of an element name in such a prefix, and (as with the universal selector) represents the set of all element names. In other words, the selectors `*.takeNote` and `.takeNote` are equivalent.

In addition to ID and class selectors, several predefined *pseudo-classes* are associated with a (anchor) elements that have an `href` attribute (source anchors). Table 3.2 lists these pseudo-class selectors. Figure 3.8 shows a link that has not been visited recently, and is therefore displayed in black. Positioning the cursor over that link without clicking the mouse button will cause the link to change to green, and clicking and holding the mouse button will change the color to red. If the link is visited, then the next time `Selectors.html` is

TABLE 3.2 Pseudo-Classes Associated with a Element Type

Selector	Associated a Elements
a:visited	Any element with `href` corresponding to a URL that has been visited recently by the user
a:link	Any element that does not belong to the `a:visited` pseudo-class
a:active	An element that is in the process of being selected; for example, the mouse has been clicked on the element but not released
a:hover	An element over which the mouse cursor is located but that does not belong to the `a:active` pseudo-class

loaded into the browser the link will be yellow. A fine point is that the current CSS 2.1 draft recommendation [W3C-CSS-2.1] allows a browser to ignore a pseudo-class style rule that would change the positioning of any elements within the browser. Color changes are therefore good choices as declarations for a rule that uses a pseudo-class selector, while even a seemingly innocuous declaration involving boldfacing should be used with caution (since boldfacing can increase the width of text and therefore move other elements).

Finally, a selector may be specialized so that it holds only within the content of certain element types. For example, the rule

```
ul span { font-variant:small-caps }
```

says that the text within a span element that is in turn part of the content of an unordered, or bulleted, list (ul element) should be displayed using a small-cap font form. Such a selector is known as a *descendant selector*. Notice that only the span within the bulleted list item in Figure 3.8 is displayed in the small-cap format.

Class selectors can also be included in the ancestor list; for example, the selector

```
.special span
```

would apply to any span element within the content of any element belonging to the class special. More generally, a white-space-separated list of element and/or class names may be used as a selector, representing a chain of elements each of which must be a descendant of the element to its left in order for the selector to apply. For example, the rule

```
ul ol li { letter-spacing:1em }
```

applies only to an li element within an ol (ordered, or numbered, list) element that is within a ul element. Thus, the numbered item in the second paragraph displays in the letterspaced format, because this paragraph's numbered list is contained within a bulleted list; but the numbered list in the third paragraph does not use this format, because it is not contained within a bulleted list.

3.3.2 At-Rules

So far, we have covered the ruleset form of style rules. The other form of rule is called an *at-rule*. The only at-rule that is widely supported and used at the time of this writing is the rule beginning with @import. This rule is used to input one style sheet file into another one. For example, a style sheet such as

```
@import url("general-rules.css");
h1, h2 { background-color: aqua }
```

will first read in rules from the file general-rules.css before continuing with the other rule in this style sheet. The url() function is used to mark its string argument as a URL. Single quotes can be used for this argument rather than double quotes; in fact, the quotes are not required at all. The URL can be absolute or relative. If it is a relative URL, like the one shown in this example, then it will be taken as relative to the URL of the file containing the import at-rule, rather than relative to the HTML document. The @import rule must end with a semicolon, as shown. Also, all @import rules must appear at the beginning of a style sheet, before any ruleset statements.

3.4   Style Sheets and HTML

So far, the style sheets we have used have been stored in files and included in an HTML document through the use of a link element. Such style sheets are known as *external* style sheets. Another option is to embed a style sheet directly in an HTML document as the content of the HTML style element, which can appear any number of times in the head content of a document. For example, an XHTML document might contain the following markup:

```
<head>
  <title>InternalStyleSheet.html</title>
  <style type="text/css">
    h1, h2 { background-color:aqua }
  </style>
</head>
```

As you would expect, this will have the same effect as if the given style rule had been contained in an external style sheet and included in the HTML document via a link element. A style sheet that is included in the content of a style element is known as an *embedded* style sheet.

I have two notes of caution about using embedded style sheets. First, if any XML special character, such as less-than (<) or ampersand (&), appears in the style rules, then the character must be replaced by the appropriate entity or character reference. On the other hand, such references should *not* be used in an external style sheet, because an external style sheet is not an XML document and therefore is not processed like one. Second, the HTML 4.01 specification suggests enclosing the content of a style element within an SGML comment, for example,

```
<style type="text/css">
  <!--
  h1, h2 { background-color:aqua }
  -->
</style>
```

This was suggested because some older browsers did not recognize the style element. Such a browser would ignore the style start and end tags but would still attempt to process the content of the element, as discussed in Chapter 2. Therefore, a style element could produce strange behavior in such browsers. To circumvent this problem, CSS was defined so that the SGML comment start and end delimiters <!-- and --> are ignored by style sheet processors (the delimiters themselves are ignored, but the content within the delimiters is not ignored). So an older browser would ignore both the style tags and the content in a style element written as shown, while a style-cognizant HTML 4.01 browser would process the `style` element as if the comment delimiters were not present.

However, using SGML comment delimiters in embedded style sheets is not recommended in XHTML, as XHTML parsers are allowed to strip out comments and their content regardless of what elements may contain the comments. So, in an XHTML-compliant browser an embedded style sheet enclosed within comment delimiters may be ignored. Given that almost all browsers in use today recognize the `style` element, and given this potential difficulty in XHTML browsers, I suggest that you not use SGML comment delimiters within `style` elements.

The `media` attribute described earlier can be used with the `style` element as well as with `link` elements, and therefore applies to both external and embedded style sheets. However, the `rel` attribute applies only to the `link` element, not to `style`. So an embedded style sheet is treated much the same as a persistent external style sheet: it cannot be selected or deselected by the browser user, but instead always applies to the document.

As we learned in the previous chapter, most HTML elements have a `style` attribute that can be used to define style properties for the element. Technically speaking, the value of a `style` attribute is not a style sheet, since it is not a set of style rules but is instead essentially a single list of style declarations that applies to a single document element. In fact, the use of style sheets is recommended over the use of `style` attributes, for a number of reasons. One reason is ease of coding: if you want all of the paragraphs in your document to have the same style applied, it is much easier to accomplish this by writing a single style rule than by adding a `style` attribute specification to every p element. Similarly, it is generally much easier to modify the style of a document that uses style sheets to define style than it is to modify one that uses `style` attributes. A `style` attribute value also cannot vary automatically with media type. This last observation is a special case of the more general recommendation that since markup is designed to carry structural and semantic information, it is generally best to keep all style information out of the body of an HTML document. All that said, there are times when the `style` attribute is convenient (e.g., to make an image cover an entire table cell, as in Section 2.7). So, while you shouldn't necessarily avoid its use altogether, try to use the `style` attribute wisely.

3.5   Style Rule Cascading and Inheritance

Before describing in detail many of the key CSS style properties, it will be helpful to understand two concepts: cascading of style sheet rules and element inheritance of style properties.

3.5.1   Rule Cascading

The style sheet of Figure 3.6 contains the rule

```
* { font-weight:bold }
```

which applies to every element of the HTML document. It also contains the rule

```
#p1, #p3 { background-color:aqua }
```

As we have seen, both of these rules applied to an element with `id` attribute value p3. That is, if multiple rules apply to an element, and those rules provide declarations for different properties, then all of the declarations are applied to the element. But what would happen if the rule

```
#p3 { font-weight:normal }
```

also appeared in a style sheet for the document? Which rule would apply to the `font-weight` property of the p3 element?

This is one example of a more general question: For every property of every element on a page, the browser must decide on a value to use for that property. How does it determine this value if multiple style declarations apply to that property of that element? Furthermore, what should the browser do if no declaration at all directly applies to that element property? We'll deal with the first question in this subsection, and the second question in the next.

In order to choose between multiple declarations that all apply to a single property of a single element, the browser (or other user agent) applies *rule cascading*, a multistage sorting process that selects a single declaration that will supply the property value. The very first step of this process involves deciding which external and embedded style sheets apply to the document. For example, if alternate external style sheets are available, only one will apply, and rules in the other alternate style sheets will be ignored. Similarly, if a media type is specified for an embedded or external style sheet and that type is not supported by the user agent rendering the page, then that style sheet's rules will be ignored.

Once the appropriate external and embedded style sheets have been identified, the next stage of the sorting process involves associating an origin and weight with every declaration that applies to a given property of a given element. The *origin* of a style sheet declaration has to do with who wrote the declaration: the person who wrote the HTML document, the person who is viewing the document, or the person who wrote the browser software that is displaying the document. Specifically, the origin of a declaration is one of the following:

- *Author:* If the declaration is part of an external or embedded style sheet or is part of the value specified for the `style` attribute of the given element, then it originated with the author of the document that is being styled.
- *User agent:* A browser or other user agent may define default style property values for HTML elements. In the Mozilla 1.4 **View|Use Style** menu, this is the style sheet represented by the "Basic Page Style" option. Appendix A of the CSS 2.0 recommendation [W3C-CSS-2.0] contains an example user agent style sheet.
- *User:* Most modern browsers allow users to provide a style sheet or to otherwise indicate style preferences that are treated as style rules.

In Mozilla 1.4, the user style rules can be defined in two ways. First, under the **Edit|Preferences|Appearance** category, the Fonts and Colors panels allow a user to select various style options, which will be treated as user style rules. Second, the user can explicitly create a style sheet file that the browser will input when it is started. However, this is not an easy-to-use feature in Mozilla 1.4: you must create a file with a certain filename (`userContent.css`) and place it in a certain directory (the `chrome` subdirectory of the

directory specified by the Cache Folder field of **Edit| Preferences | Advanced | Cache**).
Similar features are provided in IE6 under the **General** tab of the **Tools | Internet
Options** window. The Colors and Fonts buttons allow the user to set style options, and
a style sheet file can be read into IE by clicking the Accessibility button, checking the
checkbox in the User Style Sheet panel, and selecting the file.

In addition to an origin, every author and user style declaration has one of two *weight*
values: normal and important. A declaration has important weight if it ends with an exclamation mark (!) followed by the string `important` (or similar strings: case is not important,
and there may be white space before or after the exclamation mark). So the rule

```
p { text-indent:3em; font-size:larger !important }
```

gives important weight to the declaration of the `font-size` property. A declaration without the `!important` string—such as the declaration of the `text-indent` property in that
example—would have normal weight. All user-agent declarations can also be considered
to have normal weight.

Once the origin and weight of all declarations applying to an element property have
been established, they are prioritized (from high to low) as follows:

1. Important declaration with user origin
2. Important declaration with author origin
3. Normal declaration with author origin
4. Normal declaration with user origin
5. Any declaration with user agent origin

That is, we can think of each declaration as falling into one of five priority bins. We then look
through the bins, starting with the first, until we find a nonempty bin. If that bin has a single
declaration, the declaration is applied to the element property and we are done. Otherwise,
there are multiple declarations in the first nonempty bin, and we continue to the next sorting
stage in order to select a single declaration from among the candidates within this bin.

Before getting to this next stage, you may be wondering why important user declarations have higher priority than author declarations while normal-weight user declarations
have lower priority. The reason is accessibility. If a visually impaired web user must have
high contrast between text and background along with large bold fonts in order to read text
on a monitor, that user can be accommodated by writing declarations with important weight,
regardless of the page author's design decisions. On the other hand, a user who is merely
stating style preferences will generally not want their default preferences to override those
of a web site author who made specific style choices for his or her web site. One significant
change between CSS1 and CSS2 was the adoption of the sort order just listed, which is also
supported by the major modern browsers.

Now we return to the case in which the top nonempty bin of the weight-origin sort
contains multiple style declarations for a single element property. The next step is to sort
these declarations according to their *specificity*. First, if a declaration is part of the value
of a `style` attribute of the element, then it is given the highest possible specificity value

(technically, in CSS2 this specificity value can be overridden, but that feature does not seem to be widely implemented by current browsers). If a declaration is part of a ruleset, then its specificity is determined by the selector(s) for the ruleset. We begin by treating a ruleset with a comma-separated selector string as if it were multiple rulesets each with a single selector; that is, a ruleset such as

```
h1, #head5, .big { font-size:x-large }
```

is treated as the equivalent three rulesets

```
h1 { font-size:x-large }
#head5 { font-size:x-large }
.big { font-size:x-large }
```

Next, we conceptually place each ruleset in one or more bins, each bin labeled with a class of selectors. The bins we use for this purpose, from highest to lowest specificity, are:

1. ID selectors
2. Class and pseudo-class selectors
3. Descendant and type selectors (the more element type names, the more specific)
4. Universal selectors

A ruleset with a selector such as `li.special` would go in two bins, since this is both a class and a type selector. Now we select a ruleset from the first nonempty bin. If, say, two rulesets appears in this bin, we search lower bins for the first recurrence of either ruleset. If one of the rulesets recurs before the other, then it is chosen. So, for example, `li.special` would be chosen over `*.special`.

Even after this sorting process, two or more declarations may still have equally high weight-origin ranking and specificity. The final step in the style cascade is then applied, and is guaranteed to produce a single declaration for a given property of a given element. First, if there is a declaration in the `style` attribute for the element, then it is used. Otherwise, conceptually, all of the style sheet rules are listed in the order in which they would be processed in a top-to-bottom reading of the document, with external and imported style sheets inserted at the point of the `link` element or `@import` rule that causes the style sheet to be inserted. The declaration corresponding to the rule that appears farthest down in this list is chosen. As an example, if the file `imp1.css` contains the statements

```
@import url("imp2.css");
p { color:green }
```

and the file `imp2.css` contains the statement

```
p { color:blue }
```

and a document head contains the markup

```
<title>StyleRuleOrder.html</title>
<style type="text/css">
  p { color:red }
</style>
<link rel="stylesheet" type="text/css" href="imp1.css" />
<style type="text/css">
  p { color:yellow }
</style>
```

then the style rulesets are effectively in the order

```
p { color:red }
p { color:blue }
p { color:green }
p { color:yellow }
```

and p elements will be displayed with yellow text. Notice that since the import at-rules must always come at the beginning of a style sheet, any imported rules can always be overridden by rules in the body of the style sheet causing the import. This is sensible, since rules imported from a file are presumably meant to be of a reusable, general-purpose nature and therefore should be subject to revision for a specific task.

Finally, certain (often deprecated) HTML attributes other than style can be used to affect the presentation of an HTML document. For example, the height attribute of the img element type can affect presentation. But img also has a height style property that can be set to achieve the same effect. If both are defined for an img element, which should take precedence: the attribute or the style property? The general answer is that any CSS style declaration takes precedence over style-type declarations made via HTML attribute specifications. More specifically, the browser or user agent treats non-CSS attribute styling as if an equivalent CSS style rule had been inserted at the very beginning of the author (normal weight) style sheet with a specificity lower than that for the universal selector. So any important-weight user style rule as well as any style rule written by the document author will take precedence over style rules derived from attributes such as height, which in turn will take precedence over normal-weight user and user-agent style rules.

The style cascade is summarized in Figure 3.9. We're now ready to tackle the other question posed earlier: if a property of an element has no associated style declarations, how is the value of the property determined? The answer is that the value is inherited from ancestors of the element, as discussed next.

3.5.2 Style Inheritance

While cascading is based on the structure of style sheets, inheritance is based on the tree structure of the document itself. That is, conceptually an element *inherits* a value for one of its properties by checking to see if its parent element in the document has a value for that property, and if so, inheriting the parent's value. The parent may in turn inherit its property value from its parent, and so on. Put another way, when attempting to inherit a property value, an element (say with id value needValue) will search upward through its tree of ancestor elements, beginning with its parent and ending either at the root html element or

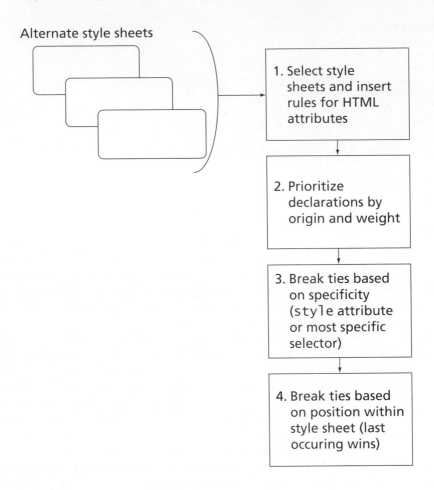

FIGURE 3.9 Steps in the CSS cascade.

at the first element that has a value for the property. If the search ends at an element with a value for the property, that value will be used by needValue as its property value. If no ancestor element has a value for the property, then as a last resort the property will be given a value specified for each property by the CSS specification [W3C-CSS-2.0] and known as the property's *initial value*. This terminology makes sense if you think of each element property as having its initial value assigned when the document is first read and then having this value changed if either the cascade or the inheritance mechanism supplies a value.

Figure 3.10 shows the source of an HTML document that illustrates inheritance. Notice that the style sheet for this document contains font-weight declarations for both the body and span element types. So for span elements, the font-weight is specified by an author rule, and no value will be inherited for this property. For other elements within the body, though, there is no author rule, and assuming that there is also no user or user-agent rule, the font-weight property value will be inherited from the body element. Therefore,

```
<!DOCTYPE html
        PUBLIC "-//W3C//DTD XHTML 1.0 Strict//EN"
        "http://www.w3.org/TR/xhtml1/DTD/xhtml1-strict.dtd">
<html xmlns="http://www.w3.org/1999/xhtml">
  <head>
    <title>
      Inherit.html
    </title>
    <style type="text/css">
      body { font-weight:bold }
      li { font-style:italic }
      p { font-size:larger }
      span { font-weight:normal }
    </style>
  </head>
  <body>
    <ul>
      <li>
        List item outside and <span>inside</span> a span.
        <p>
          Embedded paragraph outside and <span>inside</span> a span.
        </p>
      </li>
    </ul>
  </body>
</html>
```

FIGURE 3.10   HTML document demonstrating inheritance.

as shown in Figure 3.11, the word "inside" (which is the content of two span elements) appears with a normal font weight, while all other text is boldfaced. However, since there are no other property declarations for the two span elements, these elements do inherit other property values from their ancestors. The first span inherits italicization from its parent li element, while the second inherits a larger font size from its p element parent and italicization from its li element grandparent. The p element similarly inherits italicization from its li parent.

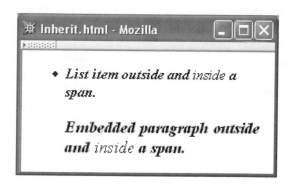

FIGURE 3.11   Rendering of document demonstrating inheritance.

A few final points should be mentioned about inheritance. First, while many CSS properties are inheritable, a number of other properties are not. In general, your intuition about whether or not a property will be inherited should be correct. For example, the `height` property of an element is not inherited from its parent, which is sensible, since often the parent has many children on many lines and therefore has a greater height than any one child. As I cover specific CSS properties in later sections of this chapter, you should assume that each property is inherited unless I explicitly say otherwise. Of course, you can consult the CSS specifications [W3C-CSS-2.0] if in doubt or for information about inheritance of properties not covered in this chapter.

A second point about inheritance has to do with exactly which of several possible property values is inherited. The value contained in a style declaration for a property is known as the *specified value* for the property. This value can be either relative or absolute. An *absolute value* is a value that can be understood without the need for any context, such as the value 2cm (two centimeters). A *relative value*, on the other hand, cannot be understood without knowing some context. For example, the property declaration `font-size:larger` uses the relative value `larger` to set the size of the font of an element. Exactly what this value is relative to is discussed in Section 3.6.3. For now, it's sufficient to know that the browser must perform a calculation—which depends on the particular relative value—to obtain a *computed value* for the property. In the case of the font-size value `larger`, this calculation might involve multiplying the base font size by a factor such as 1.2 to obtain the computed font size. If the specified value is absolute, then the computed value is identical to the specified value. Finally, the computed value may not be suitable for immediate use by the browser. For example, a specified font size—relative or absolute—may not be available for the font currently in use, so the browser may need to substitute the closest available font size. The value actually used by the browser for a property is known, appropriately enough, as the *actual value*.

In terms of inheritance, the computed value is normally inherited for a property, not the specified or actual value. The one exception to this among the properties discussed in this chapter is `line-height`; its inheritance properties will be described in detail in Section 3.6.4.

A final note about inheritance is that the CSS2 recommendation allows every style property to be given the value `inherit`, whether or not the property is inherited normally. When this value is specified for a property, the computed value of the property is supposed to be obtained from its parent. However, you should be aware that this inheritance feature is not supported by IE6, and therefore should be used with care if at all. I am mentioning it mainly because it appears often in the CSS2 recommendation. Since this value can be used for every CSS2 property, I will not mention it explicitly when listing possible values for properties in the following sections.

We are now ready to begin learning about many of the available CSS2 properties. We'll begin with a number of text properties.

3.6   Text Properties

In this section, we will cover many of the CSS properties related to the display of text. Specifically, we will learn about how to select a font and how to modify text properties such as color. We'll also cover in some detail how browsers determine the spacing between lines of text and how document authors can influence this spacing. Later sections will cover some other aspects of text, such as alignment, once we have covered necessary background material.

One note before beginning: CSS defines a `direction` property that can be thought of as defining the default direction in which text is written. It takes two possible keyword values: `ltr` indicates a left-to-right language, and `rtl` indicates right-to-left. This property affects the default behavior of many other CSS properties as well as some of their initial values. For example, the initial value for the `text-align` property, used to specify how a paragraph of text should be aligned, is `left` if `direction`'s value is `ltr` and is `right` otherwise. For simplicity, I will assume left-to-right languages throughout this chapter; if there is an asymmetry between left and right for a property (such as the initial value of `text-align`, which gives preference to `left`), simply switch the roles of left and right if you use a right-to-left language.

3.6.1   Font Families

Figure 3.12 is a browser rendering of an HTML document that displays characters using four different font families (we'll learn later how to write a document such as the one that generated this figure). A *font family* is a collection of related fonts, and a *font* is a mapping from a character (Unicode Standard code point) to a visual representation of the character (a *glyph*). Each glyph is drawn relative to a rectangular *character cell* (also known as the character's *content area*), which is shown shaded for each character in the figure. The fonts within a font family differ from one another in attributes such as boldness or degree of slantedness, but they all share a common design. The font families used in this example are, in order of use, Jenkins v2.0, Times New Roman®, Jokewood, and Helvetica™; they illustrate well how different font family designs can be from one another. (The Jenkins and Jokewood fonts may not be available on your machine, so this example may not appear the same in your browser as it does in Fig. 3.12.)

The font family to be used for displaying text within an HTML element is specified using the `font-family` style property. For example, the start tag

```
<p style="font-family:'Jenkins v2.0'">
```

FIGURE 3.12 Rendering of document illustrating four different font families.

indicates that the text within the paragraph started by this tag should use the Jenkins v2.0 font (unless a child element specifies a different font). Some font family names must be quoted and/or special characters contained in the names must be escaped; for simplicity, I recommend that you always quote font family names. Either single or double quotes can be used, which is especially convenient when the declaration appears within a `style` attribute as shown.

Most end-user computers contain files describing a variety of font families. However, there is no guarantee that a font family that you would like to display in an HTML document you are authoring will be available on all of the client machines viewing your document. Although IE6 has a mechanism for downloading fonts from the Web for use within an HTML document, this facility is not included in the current version of CSS 2.1 [W3C-CSS-2.1]. Instead, a recommended mechanism for specifying a font family in CSS is to use a comma-separated list of font families as the value of the `font-family` property, such as

```
font-family:"Edwardian Script ITC","French Script MT",cursive
```

The browser will attempt to use the first family specified (`Edwardian Script ITC` in this example), but if that family is not available on the browser's system, then the browser will proceed through the list until it finds a family that is available. The last element in the list (`cursive` in this example) should be the name of a *generic* font family. The generic font families defined by CSS are listed in Table 3.3. Unlike normal font family names, the names of generic families are CSS keywords and therefore must not be quoted within a `font-family` declaration.

The browser will attempt to associate a reasonable font family available on the user's system with each generic name. In Mozilla 1.4, the user can specify the actual font family associated with each generic family through a preference setting as illustrated in Figure 3.13.

TABLE 3.3 CSS Generic Font Families

Font Family	Description
serif	A *serif* is a short, decorative line at the end of a stroke of a letter. There are three serifs at the top of the W in Figure 3.12, for example. Most glyphs in a serif font family will have serifs, and such a family is typically *proportionately* spaced (different glyphs occupy different widths).
sans-serif	Usually proportionately spaced, but glyphs lack serifs, so they don't look as fancy as serif fonts.
cursive	Looks more like cursive handwriting than like printing.
fantasy	Glyphs are still recognizable as characters, but are nontraditional.
monospace	All glyphs have the same width. Since monospace fonts are often used in editors when programming, these font families are frequently used to display program code or other computer data.

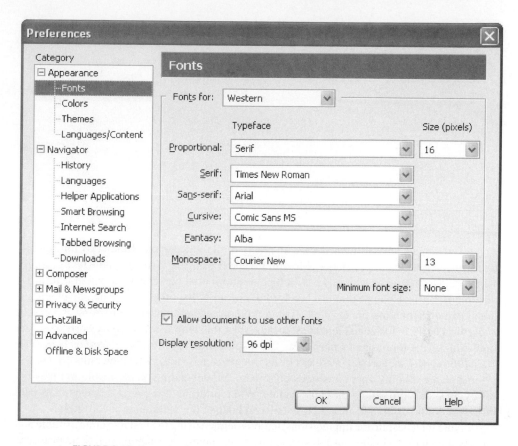

FIGURE 3.13 Example of associations of actual with generic font families in Mozilla.

3.6.2 Length Specifications in CSS

Font size is one of the key features used to distinguish between individual fonts within a font family. In CSS, the size of a font is specified using the `font-size` property. One type of value that can be assigned to `font-size` is a *CSS length*. In fact, CSS lengths can be assigned to many CSS properties, not just `font-size`. Therefore, we will cover length specification separately in this section before moving on to how to specify font properties such as size in CSS.

In CSS, a length value is represented either by the number 0 or by a number followed by one of the unit identifiers given in Table 3.4. Some example declarations involving length values are:

```
font-size:0.25in
font-size:12pt
font-size:15px
```

TABLE 3.4 CSS Length Unit Identifiers

Identifier	Meaning
in	Inch
cm	Centimeter
mm	Millimeter
pt	Point: 1/72 inch
pc	Pica: 12 points
px	Pixel: typically 1/96 inch (see text)
em	Em: reference font size (see text)
ex	Ex: roughly the height of the lowercase "x" character in the reference font (see text)

The first six units in Table 3.4 are, in practice, all related to one another by multiplicative scale factors. In particular, both Mozilla 1.4 and IE6 appear to maintain the relationships 1 in. = 2.54 cm = 25.4 mm = 72 pt = 6 pc = 96 px both on screen and when printing a document. Both also appear to use pixels to define all of the other units when displaying a document on a monitor. For example, if your monitor resolution is set to 1024 by 768 pixels and you specify a horizontal length as 1024px, then this length will roughly correspond to the width of the monitor's display area. The display area will also be treated as if it were $1024/96 \approx 10.7$ in. across, regardless of its true physical width. Thus, the units in, cm, mm, pt, and pc are all only approximations on screen, and depending on the resolution may be off by 50% or more (all by the same factor). When printing, however, it appears that both browsers define px as 1/96 in. (or close to it) and define the other units accordingly.

Note that, despite the imprecisions, lengths defined using the first five units in Table 3.4 are absolute lengths in the sense defined earlier: they do not depend on other style property values. Such units are referred to as *absolute units*. The other three units are *relative units*. Technically, CSS defines px as a relative unit, since its physical value should depend on the medium displaying the document. However, as indicated, in practice it seems to be treated by typical browsers as an absolute unit. We'll see why em and ex are relative units in a moment.

Before defining the em and ex units formally, it will be helpful to understand several details about fonts. First, all character cells within a given font have the same height. However, generally speaking, this height is not exactly the same as the computed or even the actual value of the CSS font-size property. For example, in Figure 3.12, a single font-size value—72 pt—applies to all of the characters, yet obviously the character cells vary somewhat in height. Thus a combination of the font family and the font-size property determines the actual height of character cells. The font-size computed value is known as the *em height;* for most font families, the cell height is 10–20% greater than the em height.

Another feature that the font defines is the baseline height. The *baseline height* is the distance from the bottom of a character cell to an imaginary line known as the *baseline*, which is the line that characters appear to rest on. As shown in Figure 3.12, when a single line of text contains characters from different fonts, the characters are by default aligned

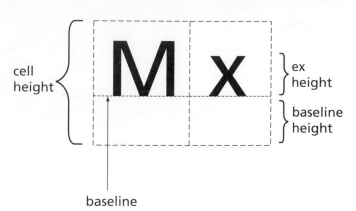

FIGURE 3.14 Some features and quantities defined by a font.

vertically by aligning their baselines. Thus, although we can see from the figure that the characters cells do not align vertically, the character glyphs themselves appear to all be written on a single horizontal line.

Yet another quantity defined by each font is the *ex height*. This quantity should be thought of as the font designer's definition of the height (above the baseline) of lowercase letters such as "x." Figure 3.14 illustrates this quantity and several other font features.

Now we can define the em and ex units. First, as noted in Table 3.4, these units are defined relative to a reference font (and are therefore relative units). With one exception explained in the paragraph after next, the reference font is just the font of the element to which the relative unit applies. So, for example, in the markup

```
<p style="width:20em">
```

the reference font is the font that applies (via a style rule or inheritance) to the p element.

Once the reference font is known, 1 em is simply the em height of the font, that is, the computed value of the font-size property of the reference font. So, continuing our example, if the computed value of the p element's font-size property is 0.25 in., then the computed value for its width property will be 5 in. Similarly, 1 ex is the ex height of the reference font.

The one exception when determining the reference font for these reference units is when one of them is used in a font-size declaration. In this case, the reference font is the font of the parent of the element to which the declaration applies. So in the markup

```
<div id="d1" style="font-size:12pt">
  <div id="d2" style="font-size:2em">
```

the reference font for the div with id attribute value d2 will be d1's font. Since the computed font-size for d1 will be 12 pt (because absolute units are used), the computed font-size for d2 will be 24 pt.

Now we are ready to more fully describe font-size and several other font properties.

3.6.3 Font Properties

The CSS font-size property, we now know, is used to specify the approximate height of character cells in the desired font within a font family. This property has an initial (default) value of medium, which is associated with a physical font size by the browser (these may vary with font family; Mozilla 1.4 defaults to 14 pt for proportional font families and 12 pt for monospace). A variety of other values can be specified for this property.

First, of course, a length value can be specified for font-size, using any of the length units described in the previous section. A second way that a font-size property may be specified is as a percentage of the computed font-size of the parent element. Since 1em represents the computed value of the parent's font-size, the following specifications are essentially equivalent:

```
font-size:0.85em
font-size:85%
```

Third, the font-size specification may be given using what is termed an *absolute size* keyword. One of these keywords is medium, the initial value for font-size. The remaining keywords are xx-small, x-small, small, large, x-large, and xx-large. The browser or other user agent creates a table of actual lengths corresponding to each of these size keywords. The CSS2 recommendation [W3C-CSS-2.0] is that each of these be approximately 20% larger than its next-smaller size.

Finally, the *relative size* keywords smaller and larger may be specified. Again, like the relative units em and ex, each of these keywords specifies the font size for the current element relative to the font size of its parent. These relative size keywords conceptually say "move one position in the font-size table." So, if the parent element has a font size of large, then a relative size specification of larger for its child is equivalent to an absolute size specification of x-large. If the parent font size is outside the range of the browser's font-size table, then an appropriate numerical font change (for example, 20%) is applied instead.

CSS also provides several other font style properties; three of the most commonly used are shown in Table 3.5. Several other font-related properties, including color, are covered later in this section.

TABLE 3.5 Additional Font Style Properties

Property	Possible Values
font-style	normal (initial value), italic (more cursive than normal), or oblique (more slanted than normal)
font-weight	bold or normal (initial value) are standard values, although other values can be used with font families having multiple gradations of boldness (see CSS2 [W3C-CSS-2.0] for details)
font-variant	small-caps, which displays lowercase characters using uppercase glyphs (small uppercase glyphs if possible), or normal (initial value)

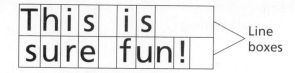

FIGURE 3.15 A box representing a p element that consists of two line boxes, each partially filled with character cells.

3.6.4 Line Boxes

We now want to consider how a browser determines where text should be rendered within an HTML element. We will assume in this section that the text is the content of an HTML p element, but the details are essentially the same for most other HTML block elements, such as div.

    The simplest case is the one in which the content of the p element consists solely of text. In this case, we can think of the p element as being rendered as a rectangular box composed entirely of a stack of imaginary boxes called line boxes. Each *line box* contains one line of text. The height of a line box is precisely the height of a character cell in the p element's font. Character cells representing the text are placed side by side in the topmost line box until it contains as many words (strings of contiguous non-white-space characters) as possible; a single space (with width defined by the font) separates each word. When the first line box can hold no more words, this process continues with the second line box, and so on until all of text of the p element has been added to line boxes. There will be just enough line boxes to contain the text, so the height of the box representing the p element will be the number of line boxes multiplied by the height of a character cell. Figure 3.15 illustrates the rendering of the text "This is sure fun!" using a monospace font within a p-element box that is only wide enough to hold 10 characters. Notice that the box consists entirely of two line boxes, and that neither of the line boxes in this case is completely filled by character cells.

    The browser's default setting of the height of line boxes can be overridden by specifying a value for the p element's line-height property. The initial value of this property is normal, which as we have seen sets the height of line boxes equal to the height of a character cell (a typical value might be 1.15 em, or 15% greater than the computed value of font-size). Other legal values for this property are a CSS length (using any of the units defined earlier), a percentage (treated as a percentage of the computed value of the p element's font-size), or a number without units. In the final case, the number is treated as if its units are em, except in terms of inheritance (we deal with this in a moment). Thus, the following declarations are all equivalent in terms of their effect on the p element itself:

```
line-height:1.5em
line-height:150%
line-height:1.5
```

    If the height of a line box is greater than the character cell height, then the character cells are vertically centered within the line box. The distance between the top of a character

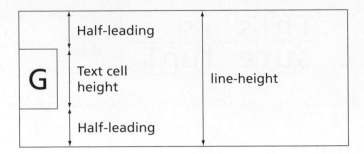

FIGURE 3.16 Default placement of text cell within a line box when the value of line-height exceeds the height of a text cell. An equal amount of space (half-leading) is inserted above and below the text cell.

cell and the top of a line box (which is the same as the distance between the bottom of a cell and the bottom of the line box) is sometimes called the *half-leading* (pieces of lead were often used to separate lines of type in early manual typesetting systems, hence the term). Thus, increasing the line-height value above its normal value not only increases the distance between lines, but actually moves the text of the first line down by the half-leading distance as well as increasing the distance between the last line of text and whatever follows the p element's box by the same distance (Fig. 3.16). We will learn how to override this default centering of text within tall line boxes later in this chapter.

A fine point about inheritance of this property: If normal or a number without units is specified as the value of line-height, then this specified value is inherited rather than the computed value. For any other specified value, such as 1.5em, the computed value is inherited. An exercise explores this further.

Now that we have learned about the line-height property, I can describe a convenient property called font. This property is an example of a CSS *shortcut property*, which is a property that allows values to be specified for several nonshorthand properties with a single declaration. As an example of the use of the font shortcut, the declaration block

```
{ font: italic bold 12pt "Helvetica",sans-serif }
```

is equivalent to the the declaration block

```
{ font-style: italic;
  font-variant: normal;
  font-weight: bold;
  font-size: 12pt;
  line-height: normal;
  font-family: "Helvetica",sans-serif }
```

Notice that the font shortcut always affects all six of the properties shown, resetting those for which a value is not specified explicitly in the font declaration to their initial (default) values. The font size and font family (in this order) must be included in the specified value for font. If values for any of style, variant, and weight appear, they must appear

TABLE 3.6 Primary CSS Text Properties

Property	Values
text-decoration	none (initial value), underline, overline, line-through, or space-separated list of values other than none.
letter-spacing	normal (initial value) or a length representing additional space to be included between adjacent letters in words. Negative value indicates space to be removed.
word-spacing	normal (initial value) or a length representing additional space to be included between adjacent words. Negative value indicates space to be removed.
text-transform	none (initial value), capitalize (capitalizes first letter of each word), uppercase (converts all text to uppercase), lowercase (converts all text to lowercase).
text-indent	Length (initial value 0) or percentage of box width, possibly negative. Specify for block elements and table cells to indent text within first line box.
text-align	left (initial value for left-to-right contexts), right, center, or justified. Specify for block elements and table cells.
white-space	normal (initial value), pre. Use to indicate whether or not white space should be retained.

before the font size and may appear in any order among themselves. To specify a value for line-height, immediately follow the font size value by a slash (/) and the line-height value. For example,

```
{ font: bold oblique small-caps 12pt/2 "Times New Roman",serif }
```

is a valid font declaration that explicitly sets all six font properties.

3.6.5 Text Formatting and Color

Beyond font selection, several other CSS properties can affect the appearance of text. These are listed in Table 3.6. All of these properties except text-decoration are inherited. And, while not inherited, text-decoration automatically applies to all text within the element, while skipping nontext, such as images. The decoration uses the element's color value. Some of these properties may interfere with one another. For example, since text justification (lining up text with a straight edge on both left and right sides) generally involves inserting space between letters and/or words, specifying justify for text-align and also specifying values for letter-spacing and word-spacing may not produce the results you expect. As usual, see the CSS2 recommendation [W3C-CSS-2.0] for details on such special cases.

Finally, as we learned in early examples in this chapter, the color property is used to specify the color for text within an element. There are many possible values for the color property, which we now cover. It should be noted that these values can also be specified for several other CSS properties, as discussed later.

CSS2 color properties can be assigned several types of values. The most flexible type is a numerical representation of the color. In particular, three numerical values are used

TABLE 3.7 Alternative Formats for Specifying Numeric Color Values

Format	Example	Meaning
Functional, integer arguments	rgb(255,170,0)	Use arguments as RGB values.
Functional, percentage arguments	rgb(100%,66.7%,0%)	Multiply arguments by 255 and round to obtain RGB values (at most one decimal place allowed in arguments).
Hexadecimal	#ffaa00	The first pair of hexadecimal digits represents the red intensity; the second and third represent green and blue, respectively.
Abbreviated hexadecimal	#fa0	Duplicate the first hexadecimal digit to obtain red intensity; duplicate the second and third to obtain green and blue, respectively.

to specify a color, representing intensities of red, green, and blue to be mixed together in order to simulate the desired color (the typical human eye can be "tricked" into perceiving light from multiple sources at various intensities and wavelengths as if it were from a single source with a single intensity and wavelength). The specific color model used involves specifying an integer between 0 and 255, inclusive, for each of the intensities of red, green, and blue, in that order (early Web pages used a limited range of intensities due to hardware limitations of many computers in use at the time, but most machines today can reliably display any of these intensities). Such an integer is known as an *RGB value*. Many readily available software tools, including Microsoft Paint, provide visual maps from colors to RGB values. Four different formats can be used to specify these three values, as shown in Table 3.7. All of the examples in this table specify the same color value. (A word of caution: it's easy to forget the leading # for the third and fourth formats.)

Many of our earlier style sheet examples used a second, more convenient way to specify common colors: many color values have a standard name associated with them. A list of the 16 colors named in CSS2 and their associated RGB values is given in Table 3.8. The current CSS 2.1 specification also adds orange (#ffa500) to the list. Furthermore, Mozilla 1.4 supports all and IE6 supports almost all (there are some exceptions containing gray or grey) of the 147 color names recognized as part of the W3C's Scalable Vector Graphics recommendation [W3C-SVG-1.1]. This provides 130 color names in addition to those of CSS 2.1, from aliceblue through yellowgreen (see http://www.w3.org/TR/SVG11/types.html#ColorKeywords for a complete list).

Finally, color values can be specified by referencing colors set for other purposes on the user's system. For example, the keyword Menu represents the color used for menu backgrounds, and MenuText the color used for text within menus. This can be useful, for example, if you plan to provide menus within your page and want them to use colors familiar to your users, regardless of user selected menu color preferences. A full list of these so-called system color names is provided in Section 18.2 of the CSS2 specification [W3C-CSS-2.0]. However, be advised that the draft for CSS3 current at the time of this writing deprecates such system color names.

TABLE 3.8 CSS2 Color Names and
RGB Values

Color Name	RGB Value
black	#000000
gray	#808080
silver	#c0c0c0
white	#ffffff
red	#ff0000
lime	#00ff00
blue	#0000ff
yellow	#ffff00
aqua	#00ffff
fuchsia	#ff00ff
maroon	#800000
green	#008000
navy	#000080
olive	#808000
teal	#008080
purple	#800080

We have referred throughout this section to the notion of a box corresponding to a
p element. In the next section, we begin to make this concept more precise.

3.7   CSS Box Model

In this section we define a number of CSS properties that relate to the boxes that a browser
renders corresponding to the elements in an HTML document. In subsequent sections we
will learn how browsers position these boxes relative to the browser client area and relative
to one another.

3.7.1   Basic Concepts and Properties

In CSS, each element of an HTML or XML document, if it is rendered visually, occupies
a rectangular area—a *box*—on the screen or other visual output medium. What's more,
every box consists conceptually of a nested collection of rectangular subareas, as shown
in Figure 3.17. Specifically, there is an innermost rectangle known as the *content area*
that encloses the actual content of the element (line boxes or boxes for other elements, or
both). *Padding* separates the content area from the box's *border*. There is then a *margin*
surrounding the border. The content and margin edges are not displayed in a browser, but
are drawn in Figure 3.17 for definitional purposes. Note the similarity between the CSS box
model and the concept of a cell in HTML tables. However, as we will see, style properties
in CSS provide finer-grained control over boxes than HTML provides for table cells.

Some other terminology related to the box model will also be helpful. The content
and margin edges of an element's box are sometimes referred to as the *inner* and *outer*
edges of the box, respectively. Also, as shown in Figure 3.18, the outer (margin) edges of a

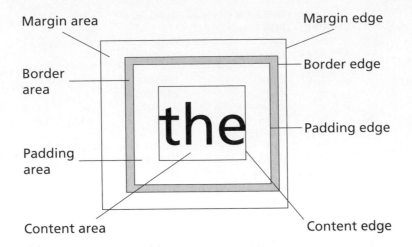

FIGURE 3.17 Definition of areas and edges in the CSS box model.

box define the *box width* and *box height*, while the inner (content) edges define the *content width* and *content height* of the box.

Figure 3.18 also gives the CSS property names corresponding to the 12 distances between adjacent edges in the box model. Notice that the border properties have the suffix -width. This suffix is used to distinguish border properties related to distances from other border properties that affect the color and style of borders (and have the suffixes -color and -style, respectively). Note that the same suffix is used for both horizontal and vertical distances, which can be confusing, since in the rest of the box model "width" normally refers to a horizontal distance.

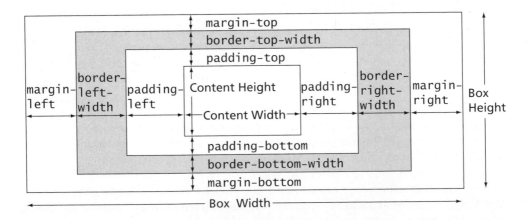

FIGURE 3.18 Definition of various lengths in the CSS box model.

```
<!DOCTYPE html
        PUBLIC "-//W3C//DTD XHTML 1.0 Strict//EN"
        "http://www.w3.org/TR/xhtml1/DTD/xhtml1-strict.dtd">
<html xmlns="http://www.w3.org/1999/xhtml">
  <head>
    <title>
      SpanBoxStyle.html
    </title>
    <link rel="stylesheet" type="text/css" href="span-box-style.css" />
  </head>
  <body>
    <p>
      The <span>first span</span> and <span>second span</span>.
    </p>
  </body>
</html>
```

FIGURE 3.19 HTML document demonstrating basic box model style properties.

As a simple example of what can be done with what we have already learned (and a few other things that we will learn shortly about border-style property values), consider the following style sheet:

```
/* span-box-style.css */
/* solid is a border style (as opposed to dashed, say). */
span { margin-left: 1cm;
       border-left-width: 10px;
       border-left-color: silver;
       border-left-style: solid;
       padding-left: 0.5cm;
       border-right-width: 5px;
       border-right-color: silver;
       border-right-style: solid }
```

and assume that this style sheet is contained in a file named span-box-style.css, as indicated by the comment. Then the HTML document shown in Figure 3.19 will be rendered by a CSS2-compliant browser as illustrated in Figure 3.20. Note that for span elements, any margin, border, or padding distance that is not specified by an author or user style sheet is given the value 0.

FIGURE 3.20 Rendering of document demonstrating basic style properties.

3.7.2 Box Model Shorthand Properties

CSS2 defines a number of shorthand properties related to the box model. For example, the declaration

```
padding: 30px;
```

is shorthand for four declarations:

```
padding-top: 30px;
padding-right: 30px;
padding-bottom: 30px;
padding-left: 30px;
```

Table 3.9 lists a number of such shorthand properties as well as the properties already covered and gives for each property its allowable values. None of the properties in this table is inherited.

The `auto` value that can be used when setting margin widths has a meaning that depends on its context, so we will defer discussing it to the appropriate later sections. I'll try to answer other questions you may have about Table 3.9 here.

First, notice that five of the properties in Table 3.9 (`padding`, `border-width`, `border-color`, `border-style`, and `margin`) take from one to four space-separated values. Each of these properties is a shorthand for specifying values for the four

TABLE 3.9 Basic CSS Style Properties Associated with the Box Model

Property	Values
`padding-{top,right,bottom,left}`	CSS length (Section 3.6.2).
`padding`	One to four length values (see text).
`border-{top,right,bottom,left}-width`	`thin`, `medium` (initial value), `thick`, or a length.
`border-width`	One to four `border-*-width` values.
`border-{top,right,bottom,left}-color`	Color value. Initial value is value of element's `color` property.
`border-color`	`transparent` or one to four `border-*-color` values.
`border-{top,right,bottom,left}-style`	`none` (initial value), `hidden`, `dotted`, `dashed`, `solid`, `double`, `groove`, `ridge`, `inset`, `outset`.
`border-style`	One to four `border-*-style` values.
`border-{top,right,bottom,left}`	One to three values (in any order) for `border-*-width`, `border-*-color`, and `border-*-style`. Initial values are used for any unspecified values.
`border`	One to three values; equivalent to specifying given values for each of `border-top`, `border-right`, `border-bottom`, and `border-left`.
`margin-{top,right,bottom,left}`	`auto` (see text) or length.
`margin`	One to four `margin-*` values.

TABLE 3.10 Meaning of Values for Certain Shorthand Properties that Take One to Four Values

Number of Values	Meaning
One	Assign this value to all four associated properties (top, right, bottom, and left).
Two	Assign first value to associated top and bottom properties, second value to associated right and left properties.
Three	Assign first value to associated top property, second value to right and left, and third value to bottom.
Four	Assign first value to associated top property, second to right, third to bottom, and fourth to left.

associated properties that include top, right, bottom, or left in their names. For example, border-style is a shorthand for specifying values for border-top-style, border-right-style, border-bottom-style, and border-left-style. Table 3.10 shows the meaning of the values for these properties. We have just seen an example of such a short-hand declaration, when a single padding declaration was equivalent to four declarations. As another example, the style declaration

```
margin: 15px 45px 30px
```

is equivalent to

```
margin-top: 15px
margin-right: 45px
margin-left: 45px
margin-bottom: 30px
```

You may also have a question about the border styles listed in Table 3.9. There is no precise definition for most of these border styles, so their visual appearance may vary somewhat when displayed in different browsers. For example, Figure 3.21 shows two paragraphs p1 and p2 displayed in two different browsers using the following style sheet:

```
/* border-styles.css */
#p1 {
        background-color: yellow;
        border: 6px maroon;
        border-style: solid dashed dotted double
}

#p2 {
        border: 16px teal;
        border-style: groove ridge inset outset
}
```

Obviously, you may want to experiment with these border-style values in browsers you are targeting before using these values. Also note that both of the border style values

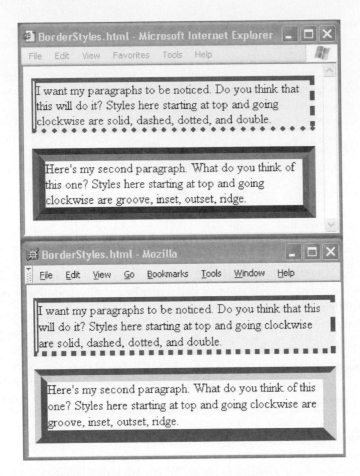

FIGURE 3.21 Illustration of some border styles in different browsers.

hidden and none effectively eliminate a border from a box element, but hidden behaves slightly different within HTML table elements in certain circumstances (refer to the CSS2 specification [W3C-CSS-2.0] for details).

Finally, you probably have noticed that shorthand properties make it possible to declare multiple values for a single property within a single declaration block. For example, the value of border-top-style can be specified by a direct declaration of this property as well as by declarations for the border-top and border shorthand properties. If multiple declarations within a single declaration block apply to a property, the last declaration takes precedence over any earlier declarations. So, for example, in the declaration block

```
{ border: 15px solid;
  border-left: 30px inset red;
  color: blue }
```

the border on the top, right, and bottom will be 15-px-wide solid blue, while the left border will be a 30-px-wide red inset style. This is because the first declaration sets all four borders to 15 px wide and solid, with the border color set to its initial value, which for border colors is the value specified for the element's color property (blue in this case). The second declaration effectively overrides these values for the `border-left` property.

3.7.3   Background Colors and Images

The `background-color` property specifies the color underlying the content, padding, and border areas of an element's box. The background color in the border area will normally be covered by the border itself, but will be visible if the border color is specified as `transparent` or partly visible if the border style is `dashed`, `dotted`, or `double` (see Fig. 3.21). Notice that the margin area is not affected by the background color. The margin area is always transparent, which allows the background color of the parent element to be seen in the margin area. Strictly speaking, the `background-color` property's value is not inherited; however, the initial value of `background-color` is `transparent`, and the background color of an element will be visible through transparent areas of child elements. In other words, for CSS box model purposes, we should think of the browser as rendering parent elements first and then rendering the nontransparent portions of the child elements over top of the parents.

A related property that is used in many Web pages is `background-image`. The acceptable values for this property are `none`, the initial value, or a URL specified using the same `url()` functional notation used with the `@import` style rule. By default, the image found at the specified URL will be *tiled* over the padding and content areas of the element to which this property is applied (such as the `body` element of an HTML document). *Tiling* simply means that if an image is too small to cover the element, either from left to right or from top to bottom or both, then the image is repeated as needed.

Like `background-color`, `background-image` is not inherited. Conceptually, the element to which the background image will be applied is first drawn, including its background color if any. Then the background image is drawn over top of the element, with the element showing through any transparent areas of the image. Finally, any child elements are drawn over top of the background image. The positioning of a background image and whether it is tiled or not can be specified using various CSS properties; see the CSS2 specification [W3C-CSS-2.0] for complete details.

This concludes our discussion of the basic CSS box model. We next turn to considering how this model relates to some specific HTML elements.

3.8   Normal Flow Box Layout

In a browser's standard rendering model (which is called *normal flow processing*), every HTML element rendered by the browser has a corresponding rectangular box that contains the rendered content of the element. The primary question we address in this section is where these boxes will be placed within the client area of the browser.

3.8.1 Basic Box Layout

First, recall that the `html` element is the root element of an HTML document. The browser generates a box corresponding to this element, which is called the *initial containing block*. The CSS2 recommendation does not specify the lengths (margin, padding, etc.) or dimensions (width and height) of this box, but instead leaves it to each browser to choose values for these parameters. In both IE6 and Mozilla 1.4, by default the border, margin, and padding lengths are all zero, so the inner (content) and outer edges of the box coincide. As for dimensions of the initial containing block box, if the browser's horizontal and vertical scrollbars are not active, then the box coincides with the browser's client area, and therefore has the same dimensions. On the other hand, if either scrollbar is active, then the the outer edges of the initial containing block are located at the edges of the underlying area over which the browser can be scrolled. Conceptually, it is as if the document is drawn on an imaginary *canvas*. The browser client area acts as a *viewport* through which all or part of the canvas is viewed. The initial containing block's height is the total height of this canvas, or the height of the browser's client area if that is greater than the canvas height. The width of the initial containing block is defined similarly. Figure 3.22 illustrates the relationship

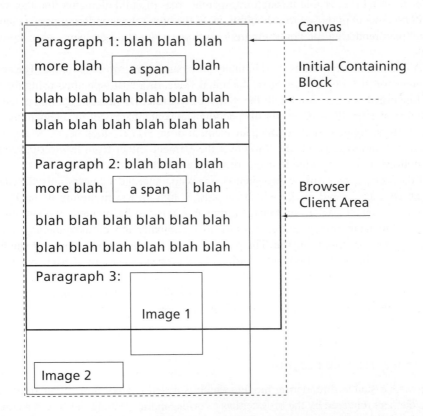

FIGURE 3.22 Initial containing block box when canvas is taller than client area but client area is wider than canvas.

between the canvas, client area, and initial containing block box when the canvas is taller than the client area but not as wide. Note that if the browser window is resized, the initial containing block's box will be resized automatically as needed.

All other CSS boxes within the client area are laid out (either directly or indirectly) relative to the initial containing block box. For an HTML document, the first such box to be added to the client area is the one corresponding to the body element. Because the body element is contained within the html element, the box corresponding to the body element is placed within the initial containing block box (which corresponds to the html element). This is the default behavior for all boxes: if one HTML element is part of the content of a second HTML element, then the box corresponding to the first element will be contained within the content area of the box for the second element. This default behavior is known as *normal flow* processing of boxes. Thus, if normal flow processing is used for an entire HTML document, all of the boxes corresponding to elements within the body element of the document will be contained within the box generated for the body, which in turn will be contained within the initial containing block box. In essence, in normal flow processing, the block corresponding to the body element is the canvas on which boxes for all other elements will be drawn.

By default, the body box will be placed so that its left, top, and right outer edges coincide with the left, top, and right inner (content) edges of the initial containing block. If the width of the browser window is changed, then the width of the body box may change as well, since the width of the initial containing block can change automatically when the browser width changes. The height of the body box, on the other hand, is determined by its content. You might think of the box as starting with the height of its content area set to 0. Then, as the browser generates boxes corresponding to elements contained within the body, it increases this height so that it is just sufficient to contain all the generated boxes. The height when this process is done determines the final height of the content area of the body element's box (the overall height of the box also depends on the values of style properties such as margin-top).

Similar rules apply to the default placement of boxes within the body box. That is, the first child element's box will be placed so that its left, top, and right outer edges coincide with the corresponding content edges of the body box. The height of this box will then be determined by generating boxes for all of the elements contained within the first element and laying these boxes out within this first child box (by recursively applying the layout rules being described). The second child element's box will be placed so that its top outer edge coincides with the bottom outer edge of the first child box (this isn't quite correct; see Section 3.8.3 for more details). The left and right edges of this second child box will also coincide with the left and right content edges of the body. The second child is then filled with all of its descendants' boxes. This process continues with the remaining children of the body.

Figure 3.23 is an HTML document that illustrates the layout concepts discussed thus far (I have used an embedded style sheet in this document and several others in this chapter for ease of reading, but in practice I would probably have used an external style sheet). Figure 3.24 shows how Mozilla 1.4 renders this document (the IE6 rendering is similar, although my copy of IE6 incorrectly draws the initial containing block's border so that it always coincides with the client area, regardless of how the browser window is sized).

```
<!DOCTYPE html
        PUBLIC "-//W3C//DTD XHTML 1.0 Strict//EN"
        "http://www.w3.org/TR/xhtml1/DTD/xhtml1-strict.dtd">
<html xmlns="http://www.w3.org/1999/xhtml">
  <head>
    <title>
      BlockBoxes.html
    </title>
    <style type="text/css">
      html, body { border:solid red thin }
      html { border-width:thick }
      body { padding:15px }
      div { margin:0px; padding:15px; border:solid black 2px }
      .shade { background-color:aqua }
      .topMargin { margin-top:10px }
    </style>
  </head>
  <body>
    <div id="d1">
      <div id="d2">
        <div id="d3" class="shade"></div>
      </div>
      <div id="d4" class="shade topMargin"></div>
    </div>
  </body>
</html>
```

FIGURE 3.23 HTML document containing nested div elements.

Figure 3.24 shows the borders of a number of boxes. The outermost border (thick red border at the edges of the browser's client area) is for the initial containing block box generated by the html element. The thin red border immediately inside the html element's box belongs to the body element's box. You'll notice that the body border does not touch the html border. This is because the Mozilla 1.4 user agent style sheet specifies a nonzero margin value (apparently about 8 px in Mozilla 1.4 and 10 px in IE6) for the body box, and the embedded author style sheet does not override this value. Inside the body block box there is a box with a medium-width black border generated by the div with ID d1. Inside this box are two child boxes, one for each of the div children of d1 (d2 and d4). Finally, the first of these child elements (d2) itself has a child div with id d3, which generates its own box. The boxes for the div elements d3 and d4, which have no content, are given a background color in Figure 3.24.

3.8.2 The display Property

The layout rules described so far only apply to HTML elements that CSS recognizes as *block elements*. These are elements for which the CSS display property has the value block. Of the elements covered in Chapter 2, standard user agent style sheets will define the following HTML elements as block elements: body, dd, div, dl, dt, fieldset, form, frame, frameset, hr, html, h1, h2, h3, h4, h5, h6, ol, p, pre, and ul. You may recall from the last chapter that

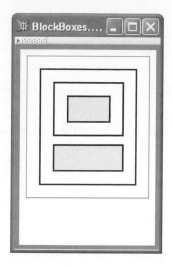

FIGURE 3.24 Nested boxes.

we informally introduced the concept of block elements as those elements for which the browser essentially generates a new line before and after the element. Now we see that what actually happens is that the browser stacks the boxes for these elements one on top of the next.

CSS defines a number of other possible values for the display property. Many of these values are associated with specific HTML elements. For example, there is a list-item value that is intended to be used as the display value for li elements, a table value for HTML table elements, and a table-row value for tr elements. In fact, nearly every element associated with the HTML table model has its own value for the display property (td and th share the table-cell value). We will not discuss these values further; see [W3C-CSS-2.0] for details.

In addition to these and other somewhat specialized values for display, there is another value that is shared by a number of HTML elements: inline. Again, recall from the previous chapter that inline HTML elements are those that do not interrupt the flow of a document by starting a new line as block elements do. Examples of inline elements were span and strong. In a typical browser, all of the HTML elements discussed in the last chapter except the block elements listed at the begining of this subsection, the li element, and table-related elements will be treated as having the value inline, which is the initial value for the display property.

As you might expect, the rules for laying out the boxes for elements with a display value of inline (which I'll refer to as *inline boxes*) are different from those for laying out boxes for elements with a display value of block (*block boxes*). In fact, how content is laid out within inline and block boxes also differs. We'll cover some more details concerning block boxes in the next few sections and then look more closely at inline boxes.

Before leaving this section, let me mention that an author style sheet can override the default value of an element's display property just as any other default property value can be overridden. For example, suppose that an HTML document has a large number of consecutive p elements but that for some reason we would like—with a minimal amount of change to the document—to have all of these separate paragraphs in the document displayed as one (long) paragraph. We can accomplish this by adding to the document the style rule

```
p { display:inline }
```

Obviously, this style rule significantly changes the expected semantics of the p element, so a rule such as this should be used with some caution.

3.8.3 Margin Collapse

Earlier I said that, roughly speaking, consecutive block boxes are positioned one on top of the next. I'll now explain why this isn't exactly the case.

When two consecutive block boxes are rendered (the first on top of the second), a special rule called *margin collapse* is used to determine the vertical separation between the boxes. As the name implies, two margins—the bottom margin of the first (upper) box and the top margin of the second (lower) box—are collapsed into a single margin.

Specifically, let m_1 represent the value of margin-bottom for the top box, and let m_2 represent the value of margin-top for the lower box. Without margin collapse, the distance between the borders of these boxes would be $m_1 + m_2$. With border collapse, the distance will instead be $\max(m_1, m_2)$ (see Fig. 3.25).

3.8.4 Block Box Width and Height

Each block element has a width property (not inherited) that defines the width of the content area of the element's block box. The initial value of this property is auto, which produces the width-defining behavior described earlier: the box will automatically be stretched horizontally so that its left and right outer edges align with the left and right content edges of its parent box. As an example, if the browser window shown in Figure 3.24 is widened, the block boxes displayed in the content area will also become wider (Fig. 3.26).

More precisely, if the value of width is auto, and if a value other than auto is specified for both margin-left and margin-right (the initial value for these properties is 0), then for display purposes width will be given the value

```
width = parent's displayed content width -
      (margin-left + border-left-width + padding-left +
       padding-right + border-right-width + margin-right)
```

This value is not in any way associated with the width property itself, as a specified or computed value is. Instead, it is used by the browser strictly for display purposes. Such a value is sometimes referred to as a property's *used value*.

In addition to auto, a length value can be specified as the value of the width property of a block element. The length value can use any of the units described in Section 3.6.2. Furthermore, the specified length value can be a *percentage*, which is a number (integer or decimal) immediately followed by a percent sign (%). In the case of the width property,

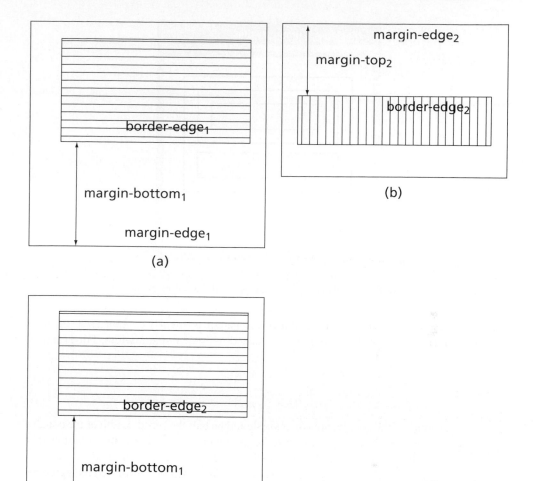

FIGURE 3.25 (a) A block box (only margin and border edges are shown). (b) A second block box with `margin-top` smaller than `margin-bottom` of first box. (c) First and then second boxes rendered, illustrating margin collapse.

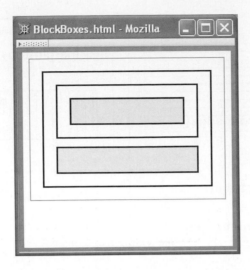

FIGURE 3.26 `BlockBoxes.html` displayed in a wider window.

this represents a percentage of the width of the parent element's content area, or more precisely, a percentage of the used value associated with the content width. For example, the declaration

```
width:50%
```

says that the width of the content area of a box should be half the (used) width of the content area of its parent box. Percentages can also be used with many other CSS properties that take a length value, although the length to which the percentage is applied varies from property to property. See the CSS2 recommendation [W3C-CSS-2.0] for details regarding properties not explicitly mentioned in this chapter.

You might expect (I did initially) that the percentage `width` declaration would cause an associated element to be centered within the parent box. However, this is not the case by default. Instead, the element will appear left-justified within its parent box. In essence, when only the `width` is specified for an element, the browser computes a used value for the `margin-right` property of the element's box so that the overall width of the box (sum of the element width plus left and right margins, borders, and paddings) is equal to the width of its parent's content area. The `margin-left`, however, is unchanged. To center an element, in addition to specifying a value for the element's `width` property, the value `auto` should be specified for both the `margin-left` and `margin-right` properties of the element. The browser will then use a single value for both margins, with the used value being computed so that the borders (but not necessarily the content) of the box will be centered within the content area of the parent box.

So, for example, assume that we create an HTML document `BlockBoxesWidth.html` from the earlier `BlockBoxes.html` example (Fig. 3.23) by adding the following two rules to the embedded style sheet:

```
#d3 { width:50% }
#d4 { width:50%; margin-left:auto; margin-right:auto }
```

Note that these rules will override the declarations having element selector div, due to the higher specificity of ID selectors. The new BlockBoxesWidth.html document will be rendered as shown in Figure 3.27. Notice that although both of the shaded boxes have specified widths of 50%, their actual widths are different because the percentage is applied to parent boxes that have different content widths. Also, keep in mind that the value of the width property defines the width of the content area of a box. Thus, the shaded boxes are both wider than half the width of their parents' content areas, because each box includes a total of 30 px of horizontal padding (15 px for each side) in addition to the content area.

In general, the value auto can be specified for any combination of width, margin-left, and margin-right. For example, if for a given box margin-left is auto, width is a specified length, and margin-right is 0, then the box will be right-justified within its containing block. See the CSS2 recommendation [W3C-CSS-2.0] for details on how CSS interprets other possible combinations for values of these three properties.

Block boxes also have a height property (not inherited) with an initial value of auto. As with the width property, the default block box height calculation described earlier can be overridden by specifying a value (length with units or percentage) for the block element's height property. If a percentage is specified, it is interpreted as a percentage of the value (if any) specified for the parent block's height property. If no value was specified for the parent's height, then the percentage specification is essentially ignored and treated as a specification of auto.

We're now ready to consider how inline boxes are rendered within a block box.

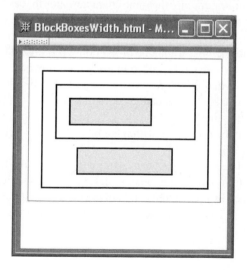

FIGURE 3.27 Rendering when widths of shaded boxes are specified as percentages. Lower box is centered because left and right margins are auto.

3.8.5 Simple Inline Boxes

Until now, we have thought of block boxes as either containing text (or more precisely, a stack of line boxes containing character cells) or containing other block boxes. But a block element can also contain inline elements, such as span and strong, and the browser will generate inline boxes corresponding to these elements. These inline boxes will be added to line boxes within the containing block box, much like text characters. In fact, we have already seen an example of this in Figure 3.20. In this section, we will look more closely at how browsers lay out *simple inline boxes*, that is, boxes for inline elements that contain only text or that are of type img. We'll briefly consider more complex inline elements in the next section.

We will first consider simple inline boxes consisting of text, generated by elements such as

```
<span style="font-size:36pt">BIG</span>
```

The height of the content area of such a box will be determined exactly as the height of a line box is determined: the height of a character cell (in the inline element's font) will be used unless the inline element's line-height property has a value other than normal, in which case this value will determine the content area height. Character glyphs are then added to the content area of the inline box as if they were being added to a line box, with half-leading added if needed to center the character cells vertically. Note that this process defines a baseline for the inline box: it is at the baseline height (as defined by the inline element's font) above the bottom edge of the content area of the inline box. We therefore now have a box that has a well-defined height (the height of the content area), width (the overall width of the box, including left and right padding, border, and margin lengths), and baseline height. These are essentially the same characteristics that a character cell has, so the browser can add this inline box to a line box as if it were a character cell, vertically aligning the baseline of the inline box with the baseline of the line box. If the inline box is too long to fit within the current line box, it may be broken on word boundaries into a sequence of shorter inline boxes that will each be added to a separate line box. If the top or bottom of an inline box extends beyond the corresponding edge of the line box, the line box height will automatically be expanded as needed to contain the inline box. If the line box height is extended upward, then the line box will be moved down within the containing block box by the same amount so that the line boxes within the block box will still effectively be stacked one on top of the other (Fig. 3.28).

You probably noticed that there is an asymmetry in how the height and width of the "character" representation of an inline box are determined. Specifically, the height of this "character" is determined by the content height of the inline box, but the width is determined by the overall box width. To illustrate, suppose we change the d3 element of the document of Figure 3.23 as follows:

```
<div id="d3" class="shade">
  Here are
  <span style="border:dotted silver 10px">some</span>
  lines of text.
</div>
```

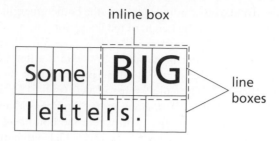

FIGURE 3.28 Two line boxes, the top box containing an inline box with a larger font size than the text elsewhere in the line boxes. Notice that the baselines are aligned in the top line box and that the line boxes stack despite having different heights.

Then the document will be rendered as in Figure 3.29. Notice that the word "some" is moved to the right to make room for the border, but the line height is unchanged, and in fact the border overlaps somewhat the text in the second line box.

The other type of simple inline element is an img. An img element is similarly treated, for rendering purposes, as a character to be added to a line box. However, the height and width of the "character" are the values specified for the height and width properties of the element (or, if these properties are not specified, the values of the height and width attributes, or, if these values are also not provided, then values contained within the image file itself). The baseline height of an image is always considered to be 0. Therefore, the bottom of the image will coincide with the baseline of the line box. As with inline boxes, if the top of an img box extends past the top of the line box, then the height of the line box

FIGURE 3.29 A span element with a border is added to the text.

will be increased to fit. Unlike other inline elements, the border, margin, and padding of an img element are considered part of the height of the image for purposes of determining the height of a line box containing the image.

The default vertical placement of an inline box within a line box can be overridden by specifying a value for the vertical-align property (not inherited) of the element generating the inline box. The initial value of vertical-align is baseline, which produces the default behavior described. Some other possible values are text-bottom, which aligns the bottom of the inline box with where the bottom of any character cell written into the line box would be located; text-top, which is similar except it aligns the top of the inline box with the top of the location for character cells; and middle, which aligns the vertical midpoint of the inline box with the *character* middle of the line box, a location that is one-half the ex height above the baseline of the line box. The CSS2 recommendation specifies several additional keyword values for vertical-align, but my copy of IE6 does not seem to handle them properly, so I will not cover them here.

In addition to these keywords, the value specified for vertical-align can be a length or a percentage (of the value of the height of an img element or the line-height of any other inline element). For both percentage and length specifications, a positive value indicates that the inline box should be raised by the specified distance relative to the default baseline position, and a negative value indicates that it should be lowered.

3.8.6 Nested Inline Boxes

How are text and boxes laid out within an inline element? We will consider the standard case for HTML, in which an inline element contains only text and other inline elements (see the CSS specification [W3C-CSS-2.0] for details on how a block box is handled within an inline box).

Actually, the layout of inline boxes and text within an inline box is essentially identical to the layout of inline boxes and text within a line box. In particular, the content area of the containing inline box is treated as a line box that initially has a height and baseline location defined by the font and line-height properties of the corresponding inline element. Characters and boxes are then added to this content area just as they would be to a line box, including having the vertical alignment of boxes determined by the vertical-align property. One difference is that the height of the content area is not adjusted to contain inline boxes whose top or bottom edges extend beyond the respective edges of the content area. However, when these boxes are eventually transferred from the content area to a line box, that line box's height will be adjusted. For example, changing the d3 element of the document of Figure 3.23 to

```
<div id="d3" class="shade">
  Here are some lines of text.
  This
  <strong style="line-height:3">bold</strong>
  word has a line-height of 3.
</div>
```

FIGURE 3.30 Effect of setting line-height on an inline element (the word "bold").

causes the browser to increase the height of the line box containing the word "bold," as shown in Figure 3.30. However, the heights of other line boxes are not affected.

3.9 Beyond the Normal Flow

What we have described so far is the default way in which a browser will format an HTML document. In this section, we'll learn that there are several CSS alternatives to the normal flow processing we have seen so far that can be used to control the position of boxes within a browser window. Three alternatives to normal flow positioning supported by both Mozilla 1.4 and IE6 are: relative positioning, in which the position is altered relative to its normal flow position; float positioning, in which an inline element moves to one side or the other of its line box; and absolute positioning, in which the element is removed entirely from the normal flow and placed elsewhere in the browser window.

We'll look at each of these three positioning schemes in detail in Sections 3.9.2–3.9.4. First, though, we'll briefly learn about the CSS properties used to indicate whether or not a box should use an alternative positioning scheme.

3.9.1 Properties for Positioning

The type of positioning for an element is defined by specifying two style properties. The position property takes the value static (the initial value) to indicate normal flow, relative and absolute to represent the respective flow positionings, or fixed, which is a special type of absolute positioning discussed in the exercises. The float property can be set for elements with either static or relative specified for position. Possible values for

FIGURE 3.31 HTML document using relative positioning to nudge text to the left.

float are none (the initial value), left, or right. The latter two values indicate that the element's box should move to the far left or far right side of the current line box, respectively. Neither position nor float is an inherited property.

Any element with a position value other than static is said to be *positioned*. If the position value of a positioned element is absolute or fixed, then it is said to be *absolutely positioned*; otherwise it is *relatively positioned*. Four (noninherited) properties apply specifically to positioned elements: left, right, top, and bottom. Each of these properties takes a value that is either a length, a percentage, or the keyword auto (the initial value). The meaning of these properties is explained for each positioning scheme in the following Sections 3.9.2–3.9.4.

3.9.2 Relative Positioning

Relative positioning is useful when you want to nudge a box a bit from the position where the browser would normally render it, and you want to do so without disturbing the placement of any other boxes. That is, all other boxes are positioned as if the nudged box had never moved.

For example, suppose that you were asked to produce the rendered HTML document shown in Figure 3.31. Notice that the first letter of each of the words "Red," "Yellow," and "Green" has a background that is partly shaded and partly not. This is not an effect that we would expect to produce in the normal flow processing model. But with relative positioning, it's easy: we use a style rule

```
.right { position:relative; right:0.25em }
```

and wrap each word to be moved in a span that specifies right for the value of its class attribute. As a side benefit, we get a little more separation between each word and the shaded box to its right than we would have had in normal flow processing, since the locations of these boxes is not affected by the relative shifting of the words.

Notice that for relatively positioned boxes, a positive value for the right property moves the box to the left by the specified amount. You can think of this as adding space to the right margin of the box. Recall that the initial value of left is auto; in this example, the corresponding computed value for the left property will be −0.25 em. Alternatively, if the style rule had been

```
.right { position:relative; left:-0.25em }
```

then the browser would have displayed the same rendering and `left` and `right` would have had the same computed values as they did with the original style rule. If, for some reason, both `left` and `right` have specified values other than `auto`, then the value of `left` will be used for the positioning, and the computed value of `right` will be set to the negative of the value of `left` (assuming `direction` is `ltr`). Similar rules apply to `top` and `bottom`, with `top` "winning" if both properties have non-auto values.

3.9.3   Float Positioning

Float positioning is often used when embedding images within a paragraph. For example, recall that the HTML markup

```
<p>
  <img
      src="http://www.w3.org/Icons/valid-xhtml10"
      alt="Valid XHTML 1.0!" height="31" width="88"
      style="float:right" />
  See
  <a href="http://www.w3.org/TR/html4/index/elements.html">the
    W3C HTML 4.01 Element Index</a>
  for a complete list of elements.
</p>
```

is part of the document displayed in Figure 2.13. The `float:right` declaration causes the image to be treated specially in several ways. First, the image is not added to a line box. Instead, the widths of one or more line boxes are shortened in order to make room for the image along the right content edge of the box containing the line boxes and image (the block box generated by the p element, in this case). The first shortened line box is the one that would have held the image if it had not been floated. Subsequent line boxes may also be shortened if necessary to make room for the image. Line boxes below the floated box extend to the full width of the containing block, producing a visual effect of text wrapping around the floated block (Fig. 3.32).

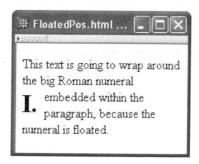

FIGURE 3.32 Wrapping of text around a floated box.

The markup used to generate this figure includes the following:

```
<style type="text/css">
  .bigNum { float:left; font-size:xx-large; font-weight:bold }
</style>
...
<p>
  This text is going to wrap
  around the
  <span class="bigNum">I. </span>
  big Roman numeral
  embedded within the paragraph, because the numeral is floated.
</p>
```

Notice that, unlike a relatively positioned box, the words "the" and "big" are not separated by the width of the floated span that separates these words in the source document. In other words, portions of this document that are part of the normal flow are formatted as if the floated element were not present at all (except for its effect on the width of line boxes). We say that float boxes are *removed from the normal flow* to indicate that making them float has an impact on how normal flow elements are rendered.

One small detail about floated boxes is that a floated inline box becomes a block box for display purposes; that is, an inline box's display property will have a computed value of block if the box is floated. This means, for example, that values can be specified for the height and width of a floated inline element.

For more details on float positioning, such as what happens when multiple floated boxes touch one another or when floated inline boxes extend below their containing block, see the CSS2 specification [W3C-CSS-2.0].

3.9.4   Absolute Positioning

Absolute positioning offers total control over the placement of boxes on the canvas. This power should be used with care: while you can create interesting visual effects this way, any information conveyed by these effects will generally not be available to users who are accessing the document in other ways (text-based browsing, speech synthesis, etc.). That said, there are certain times when it is useful to be able to place a box exactly where you want it.

For example, suppose that you would like to be able to easily add marginal notes to the left of paragraphs in an HTML document, as shown in Figure 3.33. Specifically, you'd like to be able to embed each note within the paragraph to which it applies, as in

```
<p>
  This second paragraph has a note.
  <span class="marginNote">This note is pretty long, so
  it could cause trouble...</span>
</p>
```

Then you would like the browser to automatically place the note next to the paragraph, starting vertically at the top of the paragraph.

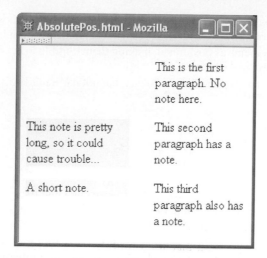

FIGURE 3.33 Absolute positioning used to create marginal notes.

This can be done easily using absolute positioning. When a box is absolutely positioned, as indicated by specifying `absolute` for the `position` property, the `left`, `top`, `right`, and `bottom` properties can be used to place the box relative to a containing block. The *containing block* for purposes of absolute positioning is defined as follows. First, we locate the nearest positioned ancestor of the absolutely positioned element (recall that a positioned element has `position` value other than `static`). If this ancestor is a block element (which we will assume; see the CSS2 recommendation for other possibilities), then the containing block is formed by the padding edge of the element's box, *not* the content edge as you might expect (the next example will show why this is a good choice of edge). If there is no positioned ancestor, then the initial containing block is used as the containing block.

Similar to relative positioning, specifying a value such as `10em` for the `left` property of an absolutely positioned box tells the browser to position the left outer edge of that box 10 ems to the right of the left (padding) edge of the containing block. Positive values for the other three positioning properties have similar effects, while negative values for these properties have the opposite effects (e.g., a negative value of `left` moves the box to the left rather than to the right). Like floats, if the box of an inline element is positioned absolutely, the box becomes a block box, and therefore can have its width set explicitly.

In our marginal note application, we would like each note to be positioned starting vertically at the top of the paragraph containing the note and horizontally to the left of the paragraph. This means that we want the paragraphs containing notes to be positioned, so that they can act as containing blocks for absolutely positioned elements. Also, we want to leave room next to paragraphs for the notes. So we will use the style rule

```
p { position:relative; margin-left:10em }
```

In relative positioning, if no value is specified for `left` or the other positioning properties, then the element is not moved. So the `position:relative` declaration has no visible effect. Instead, it marks p elements as positioned, making them eligible to act as containing blocks for absolutely positioned elements.

The rule for the `marginNote` class is longer, but not particularly difficult to understand. The rule is

```
.marginNote { position:absolute;
              top:0; left:-10em; width:8em;
              background-color:yellow }
```

This says to put any box belonging to the `marginNote` class and that is contained within a p element where we have said we would like it placed: beginning to the left of the top line of the paragraph. Notice that, for the given style rules, the outer left edge of a `marginNote` box will coincide with the outer left edge of the p element containing the `marginNote` element, regardless of the padding value of the p element (and assuming that the p element has no border). You can now see an advantage to positioning the box relative to the padding edge of the containing element rather than the content edge: we did not have to add in the padding distance in order to place our note in the margin.

As with float positioning, elements that are absolutely positioned are removed from the normal flow. This can be seen from the fact that there is no additional space between the second and third paragraphs in the figure. In contrast with float boxes, however, the normal flow will not flow around absolute boxes. In fact, absolute boxes will not flow around one another, either. For example, if we widen the browser window so that the second paragraph fits on a single line, the two marginal note boxes collide and the second obscures some of the text of the first (Fig. 3.34). This is another reason to use absolute positioning with care.

3.9.5 Positioning-Related Properties

A few additional CSS properties deserve mention in relation to positioning. The first of these is related to the overlay phenomenon that we have just discussed with absolute positioning.

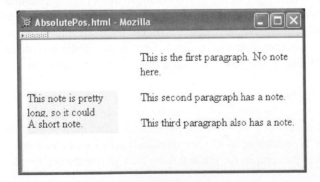

FIGURE 3.34 Absolutely positioned boxes can obscure one another.

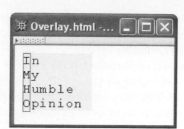

FIGURE 3.35 An overlay of one box on top of another.

There may be times when you want several boxes to overlie one another, at least partially, but you want to be certain that they overlie in a certain order. For example, you may want one box to be drawn first, then a second box to be drawn as an overlay over top of the first box, possibly obscuring some or all of the first box. Figure 3.35 illustrates this: a box containing text is drawn first, and then an empty box (basically just a border) is drawn over top of the text box.

The z-index property can be used to define a drawing order for positioned boxes. In its simplest form, the root element of each positioned box is assigned an integer z-index value (this assumes that normal flow is followed for all of the descendants of a positioned box). If this is done, then drawing will proceed as follows. First, the box with the most negative z-index value (if any) will be drawn. Other boxes with negative z-index values will then be drawn on top of this box, proceeding in ascending order, until the box with the negative value closest to 0 has been drawn. At this point, all of the elements that are not positioned are drawn. Finally, all elements with positive z-index values are drawn, again in ascending order. The full definition of z-index, including how ties are broken between elements with the same z-index value (or no value at all) is contained in Section 9.9.1 of the CSS2 specification. But for most purposes, the simple use of z-index described should be sufficient to guarantee the drawing order you want.

To produce the effect shown in Figure 3.35, I used the following style rules:

```
#text { position:absolute; top:10px; left:10px;
        font-family:"Courier",monospace; letter-spacing:0.1ex;
        background-color:yellow;
        z-index:1 }
#overlay { position:absolute; top:10px; left:10px;
           width:1.1ex; height:4.5em;
           border:solid red 1px;
           z-index:2 }
```

The first rule is applied to a div containing the text, and the second to an empty div. The key item to notice is that the z-index value of the second div is greater than that of the first, so the second div is drawn on top of the first.

We discussed the display property earlier, but it has a keyword value that we did not cover. Specifying none for the value of display tells the browser to, for display purposes, treat the element and all of its descendants as if they did not exist. In other words, the element is effectively removed from the normal flow and is also not displayed elsewhere. This is sometimes used with scripting to allow portions of a document to be easily added to or removed from the browser window.

The final property, `visibility`, is related. If the value of this property is `hidden`, then the element and its children—except those that specify `visible` for this property—will not be rendered. However, much as with relative positioning, the space occupied by the element will remain rendered. In other words, whether an element is visible or not does not affect the rendering of other nondescendant elements. Like `display`, this property is generally used in scripting contexts.

3.10 Some Other Useful Style Properties

While we have covered a significant portion of the CSS2 specification, we have also omitted a number of details and quite a few properties. A few of the remaining items are covered in this section.

3.10.1 Lists

The `list-style-type` property can be used to vary the default styles used for bulleted and numbered list items. In HTML, this property normally only applies to the `li` element type. However, it is inherited, so can be set on a parent `ol` or `ul` element in order to affect the style of all of that element's children. For bulleted lists, the values `disc`, `circle`, and `square` may be specified. For numbered lists, some of the normal values are `decimal` (1, 2, ...), `lower-roman` (i, ii, ...), `upper-roman` (I, II, ...), `lower-alpha` (a, b, ...), and `upper-alpha` (A, B, ...). A value of `none` can also be specified to indicate that no *marker* (leading bullet or number) should be generated for an `li` element.

A related `li` element type property is `list-style-image`, which has an initial value of `none`. If a URI is specified for this property (using the `url("...")` syntax described in Section 3.3), and if an image can be loaded from this URI, then this image will be used in place of the normal marker as specified by `list-style-type`. Once again, this property is inherited and is often set on parent elements rather than directly on `li` elements.

The `list-style-position` property can be used to change the location of the marker relative to the content of an `li`. A browser normally generates two boxes for an `li`: a special box to hold the marker, and a block box to hold the element content. If `list-style-position` has its initial value of `outside`, the marker box is outside the content block box. However, if the value is specified as `inside`, then the box generated for the marker will be the first inline box placed within the content block box. The visual effect in this case will be that the first line of the list item content is indented to make room for the marker.

Finally, the shortcut property `list-style` can be used to specify values for any or all of the mentioned properties, in any order.

3.10.2 Tables

For the most part, the box model properties discussed in this chapter, such as `border-style` and `padding`, can be used with elements related to tables (`table`, `td`, etc.), although their effect on table elements may vary slightly from their effect with other boxes. Furthermore, the values top, bottom, middle, and baseline may be specified for the vertical-align property of td and th elements. A top value causes the top of the content of the cell to coincide with the top of the row containing the cell, bottom makes the bottom of the content coincide with the row bottom, and middle centers the content within the row. If multiple cells specify baseline, then the baselines of their first lines of text will be aligned with one another. If baseline is specified for a cell containing a single img element, then the bottom of the image is treated as the baseline of the cell for alignment purposes. The baseline cells are displayed as high as possible within the row while keeping the content of all cells within the row.

CSS2 also specifies two different models for how borders should be handled: a *separate* model in which each cell has its own border, and a *collapse* model in which adjacent cell borders may be collapsed into a single border. The user agent style sheets for both Mozilla 1.4 and IE6 apparently specify the separate model as the default. You can override the default by assigning a value of collapse or separate to the border-collapse style property of a table element. Full details of CSS support for tables are well covered in Chapter 17 of the CSS2 specification, which should not be hard to understand if you have mastered the material in this chapter. So I will not cover tables further here.

3.10.3   Cursor Styles

CSS specifies a number of different cursor styles that can be used. The initial value for the cursor property is auto, which allows the browser to choose a cursor style as it deems appropriate. Mozilla 1.4, for example, will display a text cursor when the mouse is over text, a pointing finger when over a hyperlink, an arrow and hourglass when a link is clicked and a new document is loading, and an arrow in most other contexts. Other keywords that can be used to specify a value for the cursor property include default (often an arrow), text (used over text that may be selected), pointer (often used over hyperlinks), and progress (often used when a link is clicked). Some other keywords produce cursors that would normally be seen outside the browser client area, such as move (used to indicate window movement), various resizing arrows (e-resize, ne-resize, sw-resize, and other compass points), wait (program-busy, often an hourglass), and help (often an arrow with a question mark).

Like some other properties, cursor is normally used by scripts running within the browser, a topic covered in Chapter 5.

3.11   Case Study

We'll now create a style sheet suitable for our blogging application and also modify our previous view-blog document, formatting it using style properties rather than tables. For colors, fonts, and to a lesser extent spacing, our style sheet will be similar to the Oldstyle style sheet available as part of W3C's Core Styles project (http://www.w3.org/StyleSheets/Core/), giving us an opportunity to see some real-world styling (and something that looks much better than anything I would have produced). Ultimately, the style sheet and markup changes presented in this section will transform the view-blog page from that shown in Figure 2.31 to that shown in Figure 1.12.

```
/* The W3C Core Styles, Copyright © 1998 W3C (mit, inria, Keio). All
Rights Reserved. W3C liability, trademark, document use and software
licensing rules apply. See
http://www.w3.org/Consortium/Legal/ipr-notice.html

This is a modified version of the Oldstyle style sheet available
at http://www.w3.org/StyleSheets/Core/
A list of modifications made to the original Oldstyle style sheet is
at http://www.mathcs.duq.edu/~jackson/webtech/OldstyleMods.txt */
        /* Elements */
body    {
        background-color: #fffff5;
        font-family:    "Verdana", "Myriad Web", "Syntax", sans-serif;
        font-size-adjust: .58;
        margin:         1.5em 5%;
        }
p       {
        margin-top:     .75em;
        margin-bottom:  .75em;
        }
h1      {
        font-family:    "Georgia", "Minion Web", "Palatino",
                        "Book Antiqua", "Utopia", "Times New Roman",
                        serif;
        font-size-adjust: .4;
        font-size:      2.0em;
        font-weight:    600;
        color:          #C00;
        }
hr      {
        height:         1px;
        background-color: #999;
        border-style:   none;
        }
```

FIGURE 3.36 Style rules for nonanchor elements.

The style sheet rules we create will all be stored in a file named style.css. Each of the HTML documents for the application will be modified to include this style sheet file using markup such as

```
<link rel="stylesheet" href="style.css" type="text/css" />
```

in the head element of the document. Note that the relative URL used in the href attribute assumes that the HTML files and style.css file all reside within the same directory.

Figure 3.36 shows the first portion of the style.css file. The four rules shown each have a selector string that is a type selector. The first rule states that the background color of the body will be slightly off-white (recall that white is #ffffff). The default font family (unless overridden by another element) will be Verdana or, if Verdana is not available to the browser, one of three other font families listed (the final option is the generic sans-serif

```
        /* Hyperlinks */
a       {
        font-weight:    bold;
        text-decoration: none;
        }
a:link  {
        color:          #33F;
        background:     #fffff5;
        }
a:visited {
        color:          #93C;
        background:     #fffff5;
        }
a:active {
        color:          black;
        background:     #ccf;
        }
a:hover {
        color:          #fffff5;
        background:     #33F;
        }
```

FIGURE 3.37 Style rules for anchor elements.

family). The `font-size-adjust` property, which is not supported by IE6, has an effect if the first font family is not available. Given an appropriate specified value, the size of the selected font family is scaled so that its ex height is roughly the same as that of the first font family. This should make the letters appear to be about the same size regardless of the font actually used. Finally, notice that the left and right margins of the body are set at 5% of the width of the browser window, providing side margins that change as the window width changes.

The `p` and `h1` rules are reasonably straightforward, although the `h1` rule does use a numeric value for its `font-weight` property. This value corresponds to two steps bolder than `normal` and one step lighter than `bold`. The `hr` rule turns off the border, which the user agent style sheets for both IE6 and Mozilla 1.4 apparently turn on, and instead displays only a 1-pixel-high gray line. Note the use of both three-digit and six-digit color values.

Figure 3.37 shows the style rules related to hyperlinks (anchor elements). The first rule makes links bold and removes the underlining that would normally be associated with links. The remaining pseudo-class rules change the text and background colors of a hyperlink depending on its status, as described earlier.

So far, we have been slightly adapting the W3C Oldstyle Core style for our purposes. We next want to create a number of style rules specifically for the view-blog document. Recall that this document has three overall segments: an image above two segments, the blog entries on the left, and some navigation hyperlinks on the right. It is natural to lay out these segments by creating `div` elements and positioning them using CSS. Figure 3.38 shows the structure of the body of the new document (still called `index.html`).

The corresponding style rules are given in Figure 3.39. The first two rules center the top image and the body (main portion) of the document, which contains the blog entries and navigation links. It also fixes a width for the body portion of the document. This value

```
<div class="imgcentered">
  <!-- Banner image -->
  <img src="banner.gif" width="438" height="120"
       alt='"My Own Blog!" Banner' />
</div>
<div class="bodycentered">
  <div class="leftbody">
    <!-- Blog entries -->
    <div class="entry">
      ...
    </div>
    <hr />
    <div class="entry">
      ...
    </div>
  </div>
  <div class="rightbody">
    <!-- Side information -->
    ...
  </div>
</div>
```

FIGURE 3.38 Structure of the HTML document for the view-blog page using CSS rather than a table for layout.

```
        /* Classes for view-blog page */
.imgcentered {
        width:            438px;
        margin-left:      auto;
        margin-right:     auto;
        }
.bodycentered {
        width:            660px;
        margin-left:      auto;
        margin-right:     auto;
        }
.leftbody {
        width:            410px;
        float:            left;
        }
.rightbody {
        width:            230px;
        float:            right;
        }
.entry  {
        margin-top:       .75em;
        margin-bottom:    .75em;
        }
```

FIGURE 3.39 Style rules for div elements used for positioning.

```
<div class="datetime">AUGUST 9, 2005, 5:04 PM EDT</div>
<div class="entrytitle">I'm hungry</div>
<div class="entrybody">
  <p>
    Strange.  I seem to get hungry at about the same time
    every day.  Maybe it's something in the water.
  </p>
</div>
<hr />
```

FIGURE 3.40 Markup for a blog entry.

is narrow enough to be viewed without horizontal scrolling on almost any modern monitor, yet wide enough to display a reasonable number of words per line in the blog entries. The div's for the entries and navigation links are then floated to the left and right, respectively, within this body div. Notice that the sum of the widths of these div's is 20 px less than the width of the containing div, providing some visual separation between the blog entries and the navigation links. The final rule defines vertical spacing between blog entries, or more specifically, between blog entries and the horizontal rule separating them.

We can also use CSS to style the components of a blog entry. For example, the markup for the first entry of our example is shown in Figure 3.40, and Figure 3.41 gives style rules corresponding to this markup. Given the earlier discussion, these rules should not need any explanation.

Finally, let's use CSS to add a "displayed quote" feature, as illustrated in Figure 3.42. The basic idea is that if markup such as

```
.datetime {
        color:          #999;
        font-size:      x-small;
        }
.entrytitle {
        /* based on h2 of Oldstyle */
        font-family:    "Georgia", "Minion Web", "Palatino",
                        "Book Antiqua", "Utopia", "Times New Roman",
                        serif;
        font-size-adjust: .4;
        font-size:      1.75em;
        font-weight:    500;
        color:          #C00;
        margin-top:     .25em;
        }
.entrybody {
        font-size:      small;
        }
```

FIGURE 3.41 Style rules used for formatting components of a blog entry.

FIGURE 3.42 Example of a displayed quote (in a preview window, which suppresses the navigation links).

```
<span class='dquote'>It's more important than that.</span>
```

is included within text, then the content of the span will be displayed within the entry and also floated to the left of the enclosing text, enlarged, and enclosed within a three-sided, dotted border. This displayed-quote feature is not foolproof: if the span is included near the bottom of the text, then it might overlap with the next entry, since a floated element is taken out of the normal flow. But, if used carefully, it provides an interesting effect.

Figure 3.43 gives a suitable rule for producing the displayed-quote effect. One thing to notice is that the three-sided border was created using two declarations, and that the order of these declarations is important (the second rule overrides a portion of the first due to the cascade rules).

```
        /* For displaying a quote */
.dquote {
        float:          left;
        font-size:      larger;
        padding:        1px;
        margin-right:   5px;
        width:          10em;
        border-style:   dotted;
        border-left-style: none;
        border-color:   #999;
        }
```

FIGURE 3.43 Style rules for span element used to display a quote.

3.12   References

The primary reference for the material covered in this chapter is the CSS2 recommendation [W3C-CSS-2.0], and I have also consulted a version of the CSS 2.1 candidate recommendation [W3C-CSS-2.1] for guidance on which aspects of CSS2 seem most likely to find widespread support by browsers. The W3C home page for CSS, `http://www.w3.org/Style/CSS/`, contains links to all CSS recommendations as well as to CSS-related development software, books, tutorials, discussion groups, and other resources, including a CSS validator. Preliminary versions of CSS3 are also available at this site.

As mentioned earlier in Section 3.3, versions of Internet Explorer prior to IE6 did not fully support even CSS1, and IE6 also does not follow the CSS recommendation unless you use an appropriate document type declaration in your HTML document. See `http://msdn.microsoft.com/library/en-us/dnie60/html/cssenhancements.asp` for information on CSS in pre-IE6 versions of Internet Explorer as well as for details on how to turn on CSS-compliance in IE6. `http://www.mozilla.org/catalog/web-developer/css/` is Mozilla's documentation for CSS developers, which contains few details on Mozilla's support for CSS2 at the time of this writing (but see the next paragraph for other ways to learn about Mozilla's CSS support).

Going forward, as new browsers continue to emerge and older browsers become more rare, you will want to periodically acquaint yourself with emerging browser CSS capabilities. A preliminary set of CSS2 tests (and other helpful CSS information compiled by Eric Meyer, who has written extensively about CSS) is currently available at `http://www.meyerweb.com/eric/css/`. Presumably, a final CSS2 suite will eventually be available at the W3C site (a CSS1 suite is already available there). You can run such tests on various browsers yourself or rely on the results of tests performed by others. For example, as I wrote this chapter, I referred to the results of tests run by Christopher Hester (`http://www.designdetector.com/articles/CSS2TestSuiteFailures.php`) for information about CSS2 support (and lack thereof) in Mozilla and IE6. While this resource may or may not be up to date when you read this, a bit of Web searching for "CSS test suites" should provide the information you need.

Exercises

3.1. Practice writing simple style rules. In the following exercises, make use of the following declarations (one per line):
```
background-color: silver ;
font-size: larger ;
```
These will be referred to as "the background declaration" and "the text declaration," respectively.

(a) Write CSS style rules that apply the background declaration to `div` elements and the text declaration to `strong` elements.

(b) Write a single style rule that applies both the background and text declarations to both `p` and `em` elements.

(c) Write a single style rule that applies the background declaration to HTML elements having a value of `Nevada` for their `id` attributes as well as to elements belonging to the `shiny` class.

(d)   Write a style rule that applies the text declaration to `span` elements that belong to the `bigger` class.

(e)   Write a style rule that applies the text declaration to `span` elements that are descendants of other `span` elements.

(f)   Write a style rule that applies the background declaration when the cursor hovers over a hyperlink.

3.2.   Create three external style sheets, using a different subset of the style rules you wrote for the previous exercise in each style sheet. Then write a complete XHTML 1.0 Strict document that uses all of your style rules.

(a)   Your document should treat your style sheets as being of three different types:
- A non-persistent and preferred style sheet
- An alternate style sheet
- A style sheet used only if the XHTML document is printed

(b)   Use the `@import` rule to have the first of your style sheets import the second, which imports the third. Your XHTML document should treat the first style sheet as a persistent style sheet.

3.3.   Write an embedded style sheet (including the appropriate HTML tags) that sets the value of the `font-family` property to `Gill Sans Bold SmallCaps & OSF` for all elements of the document.

3.4.   Assume that the author, user, and user agent style sheets for an HTML document are as follows:

- Author:
```
div  { color:blue }
p    { color:green;
       font-size:smaller !important }
.hmm { color:fuchsia }
```
- User:
```
p    { color:white;
       background-color:black;
       font-size:larger !important }
body { color:yellow }
```
- User agent:
```
body { color:black }
```

Assume that these are the only style rules for the document (i.e., no `style` attributes appear).

(a)   What specified value will the browser use for the `color` property of p elements? For the `background-color` property of p elements? For the `font-size` property? Do any of your answers change if the p element belongs to the hmm class? Justify your answers.

(b)   What specified value will the browser use for the `color` property of `div` elements? Does your answer change if the `div` element belongs to the hmm class? Does the value depend on which element type contains the `div`? Justify your answers.

(c)   What `color` value will be given to a `ol` element that is a child of the body element, assuming that neither the `ol` element nor the body element belongs to the hmm class? Does your answer change if the body element (not the `ol` element) belongs to the hmm class? Justify your answers.

(d)   Assume now that the user agent rule is changed to
```
*    { color:black }
```
and answer the previous question.

3.5. (a) Write a style rule to create a class named quote. This rule should set the top and bottom margins to 0 and the left and right margins to 4em. The rule should contain a single (shortcut) declaration.

(b) Explain why em might be a better length unit to use for the task of indenting quoted text than px or one of the absolute length units.

3.6. Based on the textbook description of a typical browser's implementation of the CSS px (pixel) length measure, quantify how a 1px length changes if a monitor's resolution is changed from 1024 by 768 to 1280 by 1024.

3.7. Picture "framing."

(a) Write a style rule that will place a nice "frame" around img elements. The "frame" should be brown. The inside edges of the "frame" should touch the outside edges of the image. There should be 10-px distance between adjacent images (either horizontally or vertically). See the left image in Figure 3.44.

(b) Modify your style rule to "mat" your images. In particular, there should now be a 3-px gap between the outside edges of your images and the inside edges of the "frames." This gap should be a tan color. See the right image in Figure 3.44.

3.8. Figure 3.22 shows a client area wider than the canvas. Explain how such a situation could occur in an HTML document.

3.9. The em and ex units are both related to the height of characters; there is no unit related to character width. Give a rationale for this difference.

3.10. Create an HTML document and CSS style sheet that together produce the stairstep effect shown in Figure 3.45. The right sides of the steps should line up in the middle of the document, regardless of the width of the browser window. Also, each step should have the same height as all other steps, regardless of the number of lines of text contained in the step (see the lowest step in the figure, for example).

3.11. Assume that an HTML document uses the following style sheet:
```
body { margin:5px; border:0; padding:2px }
div { margin: 3px; border:1px solid blue; padding:4px }
```

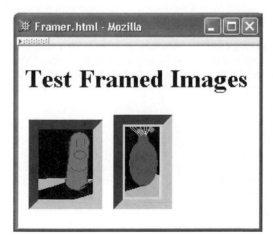

FIGURE 3.44 Two "framed" images. The right image is "matted." (Graphics courtesy of Ben Jackson.)

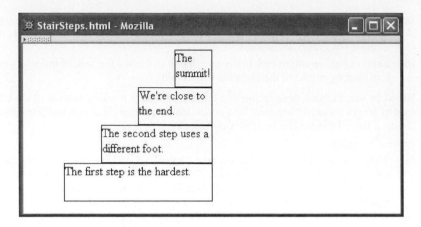

FIGURE 3.45 Stairsteps containing text.

Relative to the upper left corner of the initial containing block, for each of the three div elements in the following HTML body give the coordinates of the upper left corner of the content area of the block box generated by that div. Show/explain your work.

```
<body>
  <div id="div1">
    <div id="div2">
    </div>
  </div>
  <div id="div3"></div>
</body>
```

3.12. Assume that the normal value for the line-height property of a given font corresponds to the value 1.2em. Also assume that the height of the baseline above the bottom of a character cell in this font is 0.2em. If a value of 2em is specified for line-height, what is the corresponding half-leading value? What is the height of the baseline above the bottom of a line box containing only text in the given font and given that the line-height value is 2em?

3.13. Assume that the line-height value for a block box is 2em.

(a) Assume that one of the line boxes within this block box contains an image with height equal to 1.5em and a default value for vertical-align. If you knew the height of character cells as well as the height of the baseline within a character cell for the block box's font, how could you use this information to determine whether or not the height of the line box containing the image would need to be increased to make room for the image?

(b) If one of the line boxes contains an inline element having a specified font size twice the font size for the containing block box, will the baseline height of this line box necessarily be greater than it is in line boxes that contain only text in the default font? Explain.

3.14. (a) Identify at least three problems with the following style declaration:

```
font: 2em/12pt italic "Times New Roman" serif
```

(b) Rewrite the declaration so that it is syntactically correct.

(c) Assume that the corrected style declaration applies to an element E contained within an element to which the following declaration applies:

```
font-weight:bold
```

What will be the value of E's `font-weight` property?

3.15. The following HTML document produces an image followed by a label that is roughly vertically centered with respect to the image:

```
<!DOCTYPE html
        PUBLIC "-//W3C//DTD XHTML 1.0 Strict//EN"
        "http://www.w3.org/TR/xhtml1/DTD/xhtml1-strict.dtd">
<html xmlns="http://www.w3.org/1999/xhtml">
  <head>
    <title>
      CenteredText.html
    </title>
    <style type="text/css">
      .labeledImage { font-size:100px }
      .image { vertical-align:middle; height:100px }
      .label { vertical-align:middle;
                        font-size:medium; font-weight:bold }
    </style>
  </head>
  <body>
    <div class="labeledImage">
      <img src="../images/CFP1.png" alt="cucumber"
        class="image" />
      <span class="label">A cucumber.</span>
    </div>
  </body>
</html>
```

(a) How would the rendered document differ if the `vertical-align` declaration were removed from the `label` rule? Why?

(b) How would the rendered document differ if the `vertical-align` declaration were removed from the `image` rule? Why?

(c) There is a large space between the image and the label when the document is rendered. Why is such a large space present, and how can a smaller space be displayed instead?

3.16. Consider the following markup:

```
<p style="font-size:12pt; line-height:1.15em">
  This paragraph has
  <span style="font-size:30pt">line-height:1.15em</span>
  which is "normal".
</p>
```

FIGURE 3.46 Rendering of markup with different font sizes.

The Mozilla browser rendering of this markup in a narrow window is shown in Figure 3.46. Why does text in the second line overlap the others? What small change to the markup would fix this problem?

3.17. Both the `vertical-align` property and relative positioning can be used to move an inline box vertically. Give a style rule for each approach that could be used to move an inline box up a distance of 1 cm. In addition to moving the box up, what other display change(s) might occur if the `vertical-align` approach is used?

3.18. Some Web pages create a navigation bar (navbar) on the left side of the page and the main content in a wider column on the right side of the page. Write style rules that could be used to wrap the content around the navbar. That is, at the top of the canvas the navbar and content should each be displayed side by side. However, lower on the canvas, when the bottom of the navbar is reached, the content area should extend across the entire width of the browser client area.

3.19. Assume that you want to lay out a number of playing card images so that they overlap one another, as shown at the top and bottom of Figure 3.47. Would it be easier to use absolute or relative positioning to accomplish this? Explain.

3.20. Write a style sheet that will cause the `li` elements within any `ol` element to be numbered in an outline style: the top-level `li` elements should use uppercase Roman numerals, the next level uppercase letters, the next level lowercase Roman numerals, then lowercase letters, and finally decimal numerals at the fifth level.

Research and Exploration

3.21. Create a document that displays two boxes. The first box should have a thin border and a width of 6 in. The second box should have an equivalent width in pixels, using the relation 1 in. = 96 px. Now answer the following questions using the browser(s) assigned by your instructor:

(a) Do the two boxes appear to be the same length when displayed by your browser?

(b) Measure the first box with a ruler. How many inches (or centimeters) across is it? If the width of the second box differs from the first, measure it as well.

(c) Print your document. Now what are the actual widths of the boxes?

3.22. Locate a Web site (or visit a site specified by your instructor) that displays the colors of the so-called "browser-safe color palette," a collection of colors that can reliably be

FIGURE 3.47 Overlapping images of playing cards (face card and card back images courtesy of Ben Jackson)

displayed even using video cards that are capable of showing only 256 different colors simultaneously.

(a) How many colors are contained in this palette?

(b) Of the colors red, orange, yellow, green, blue, purple, and brown, identify the color(s) that seem to have the most different shades in the browser-safe palette and the color(s) that have the fewest.

(c) Visit some popular Web sites (as directed by your instructor) and analyze their use of CSS color values by viewing document and style sheet sources. Which sites use the browser-safe palette and which do not?

3.23. Identify all of the color keywords containing "gray" or "grey" at http://www.w3.org/TR/SVG11/types.html#ColorKeywords. Create an HTML document and CSS style sheet that can be used to test a browser's support for these keywords. Use your document to test and report on the support for these color keywords provided by IE6 (or other browser(s) as assigned by your instructor).

Refer to the CSS2 recommendation [W3C-CSS-2.0]—or a later W3C recommendation as specified by your instructor—in order to answer the following questions.

3.24. Give a style sheet rule for the body element of a document that will cause a background image to be repeated across the vertical center of the browser client area. The image should remain in the center of the window even if the window is scrolled (see Fig. 3.48, in which "Draft . . ." is an image).

3.25. Describe what the fixed value for the position style property does when viewing a document in a browser. Give an example of how this feature might be useful. Test to see which browsers (as assigned by your instructor) support this value for position (IE6 does not).

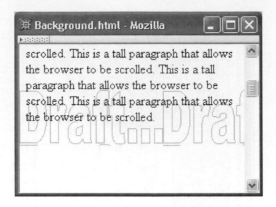

FIGURE 3.48 A background image containing "Draft . . ." is repeated across the center of the browser client area.

Projects

3.26. Create an external style sheet to be used with the HTML reference pages you wrote for Exercise 2.30 in order to accomplish the following (with minimal changes to your HTML source):

   (a) Use a `seashell` background color for all pages (`seashell` is one of the SVG color keywords).

   (b) Change the style of the bullets used in the short list of two hyperlinks (you choose the style).

   (c) Define alternative colors for all four of the anchor pseudo-classes.

   (d) Make table captions boldface, and table headers (`th` elements) normal weight but italicized.

   (e) Use a 14-pt sans serif font for all `td` elements.

   (f) Force text in cells that span multiple rows to be displayed at the top of the cell, rather than the default middle of the cell.

   (g) On the definition pages, cause each term and its definition to be displayed in a box that has a 3-px solid yellow border. The box should occupy 75% of the width of the client area (or frame, if you completed the framed version of the earlier assignment) and should be centered.

   (h) The W3C suggests the following markup be included in a Web page that is valid XHTML 1.0:

```
<p>
 <a href="http://validator.w3.org/check?uri=referer"><img
    src="http://www.w3.org/Icons/valid-xhtml10"
    alt="Valid XHTML 1.0!" height="31" width="88" /></a>
</p>
```

Use this markup on all of your valid XHTML 1.0 pages. Also include a `class` specification (of your choosing) in the `img` element. Then, without further change to this markup, write a style rule that will make these images appear on the right side of the browser client area and display the images at roughly half the height and width shown.

3.27. **(a)** Create an HTML document that renders similarly to Figure 3.47. Card images can be found in the `images/PlayingCards` directory of the example files download available at the Web site given in the Preface.

(b) Write a Java program that creates an HTML document such as the one just described. Your program should accept as input the number of cards to be held in each hand (the upper and lower parts of the figure represent hands held by players of a card game). The program should randomly select the images to display for all face-up cards (the right card in the second row and all of the cards in the lower hand). You will probably want to use the `java.util.Random` package for randomly selecting card images, but be careful not to display the same card image twice.

3.28. The following questions suggest extensions to the case study of Section 3.11. Implement a subset of the following requirements as specified by your instructor.

(a) Use CSS to style the comments document described in Exercise 2.33. First, link the comments document to the `style.css` file described in Section 3.11 (and available for download from the textbook Web site given in the Preface). Then add classes to `style.css` appropriate for styling various elements of the comments document, including each comment as a whole and the individual components of a comment: author name, comment heading, and comment body. Your class rules should center the comment heading over the comment body and right-justify the author name following the body. Finally, rewrite the document to use your new class definitions.

(b) Add a companion to the `dquote` class, named `drquote`, that is like `dquote` except that it floats text to the right instead of the left. Also, text within the floated box should be right-justified rather than left-justified, and the box border should be open on the right and closed on the left. Create an example document that demonstrates the use of your class.

(c) Use the validator at `http://jigsaw.w3.org/css-validator/` to ensure that the style sheet rules added in (a) and (b) are valid CSS. Turn in a copy of the Web page, showing your validation results.

CHAPTER 4

Client-Side Programming
The JavaScript™ Language

This chapter will introduce you to the JavaScript™ programming language, which is supported by nearly all traditional web browsers in use today. Our focus in this chapter will be on the study of JavaScript as a programming language, largely independently of how it might relate to a web browser. In the next chapter we will cover in more detail how JavaScript programs can interact with documents contained in a web browser by, for example, changing the style or even the content of a document. Therefore, this chapter will not include a section on the case study blogging application, which we defer to the next chapter.

While you may know that JavaScript is often used for relatively simple tasks within browsers, you should not be misled into thinking that it is therefore a language of limited power. To the contrary, as we will learn, it is in several respects a particularly powerful language, and in fact incorporates some programming language concepts that may be new to you. So, in addition to being useful for web programming, studying JavaScript may broaden your understanding of programming languages in general.

4.1 History and Versions of JavaScript

JavaScript was initially developed by Brendan Eich as part of the Netscape 2.0 release. The language was called LiveScript for a while in its early stages. But on December 4, 1995, before the final release of Netscape 2.0, the language was publicly announced as JavaScript. This name change was apparently intended to link the scripting language with the rising popularity of Sun's Java programming language, but has caused a fair amount of confusion over the years. Although there are strong similarities between the core syntaxes of JavaScript and Java (and C++, for that matter), and although JavaScript was designed to interact with Java applets, there are also tremendous differences between JavaScript and Java.

JavaScript became especially popular after the 1.1 release as part of Netscape's 3.0 browser. This version of JavaScript allowed web page developers to produce the familiar rollover effect: as the mouse moves over images, the images change (we'll learn how to produce this effect in Chapter 5). Other JavaScript versions followed as part of later Netscape browser releases. Meanwhile, Microsoft introduced the JScript® programming language (the JavaScript name was owned by Sun) in July of 1996, and this language similarly went through a series of revisions as new versions of Internet Explorer were released.

To confuse matters somewhat more, there is yet another flavor of JavaScript, known as ECMAScript. Soon after announcing JavaScript, Sun and Netscape approached an organization then known as the European Computer Manufacturers Association (ECMA) to produce a standard for JavaScript. The third edition of the ECMA-262 standard [ECMA-262] was released in 1999 and has been a significant help in bringing JavaScript and JScript closer together. JavaScript 1.5, the version implemented in Mozilla 1.4, conforms with ECMAScript Edition 3 (barring bugs), and JScript versions 5.5 (the version implemented in IE5.5) and beyond also appear to be compliant. Other browsers, such as Opera and Safari, also support the ECMAScript standard.

I will therefore focus on ECMAScript Edition 3 in this chapter, and refer to this simply as "JavaScript." All of the examples presented run in both Mozilla 1.4 and IE6, except as noted.

4.2   Introduction to JavaScript

I'd like to begin with a "Hello World!" JavaScript program. There's just one problem: JavaScript itself has no statement for performing output. Instead, the JavaScript language specification leaves it up to browsers to supply output (and input) methods. Happily, certain methods are supported by almost all modern browsers, even though technically they are not part of any standard. So we'll use one of these methods, `alert()`, to write a JavaScript "Hello World!" program (the `window` object is discussed in Section 4.3.1):

```
window.alert("Hello World!");
```

We can execute this program by referencing a file containing it from a `script` element within an HTML document. For example, if the JavaScript code given is placed within a file named `JSHelloWorld.js` in the same directory as the HTML document of Figure 4.1, then loading this document into a browser will cause the code to be executed. If this document is loaded into Mozilla 1.4, then the pop-up window shown in Figure 4.2 will appear. The browser window will be unresponsive until this *alert box* is dismissed, either by clicking the OK button or by closing the window (in Windows, as shown here, by clicking the × icon in the upper right corner of the alert box window). The client area of the browser window itself will be completely empty after the alert box is dismissed.

```
<!DOCTYPE html
        PUBLIC "-//W3C//DTD XHTML 1.0 Strict//EN"
        "http://www.w3.org/TR/xhtml1/DTD/xhtml1-strict.dtd">
<html xmlns="http://www.w3.org/1999/xhtml">
  <head>
    <title>
      JSHelloWorld.html
    </title>
    <script type="text/javascript" src="JSHelloWorld.js">
    </script>
  </head>
  <body>
  </body>
</html>
```

FIGURE 4.1 HTML document that loads and executes the JavaScript program in file `JSHelloWorld.js`.

FIGURE 4.2 Alert box generated by a JavaScript statement.

As with output, there is no input statement in JavaScript itself. Again, though, most browsers implement a `prompt()` method that can be called as illustrated by the following code:

```
var inString = window.prompt("Enter JavaScript code to be tested:",
                             "");
```

This pops up a window that displays the value of its first string argument and also provides a text box in which a user can enter information and that initially contains the string given by the second argument (Figure 4.3). The value returned by the `prompt()` method is the string entered by the user, assuming that the user clicks OK after entering the string (fuller details of `prompt()` are provided in Chapter 5).

Now that you've been introduced to JavaScript, let's briefly consider some of the ways in which developing JavaScript programs can differ from more traditional (Java/C++) program development before delving into details of the language.

4.3 JavaScript in Perspective

This section provides an overview of how JavaScript relates to various categories of programming languages and how this impacts development of JavaScript programs. We'll also look briefly at a few JavaScript software development tools so that you can experiment with your own code as you read the rest of the chapter.

FIGURE 4.3 Prompt pop-up window with user input entered.

4.3.1 Scripting Languages

As you probably noticed, we did not need to compile the "Hello World!" JavaScript program before executing it. Programming languages that do not need to be compiled before execution are known as *interpreted* languages. Software that reads and executes a program written in an interpreted language is known as an *interpreter*. Most modern browsers contain a JavaScript interpreter.

Programs written in interpreted languages are generally easier to maintain than programs written in compiled languages such as Java. For example, there's no need to remember to recompile interpreted programs after modifying them, and there are fewer files to manage, since there are no compiled versions of source files. Programs written in an interpreted language are also often simpler than equivalent programs written in a traditional compiled language. The one-line "Hello World!" program is one example of this. As another example, consider that while Java has a wide variety of numeric data types (int, float, double, etc.), JavaScript has a single Number data type. So some of the Java complexities of choosing an appropriate numeric data type and casting between types are not present in JavaScript.

There are, of course, some advantages to compiled languages. First, interpreted programs generally take longer to execute than similar programs written in compiled languages. One reason for this is that something like compilation has to occur during execution of an interpreted language, whereas it occurs before execution in a compiled language. Similarly, the simplicity of an interpreted language such as JavaScript comes at the cost of less efficient code. For example, the reason that Java provides many different numeric data types is so that the compiler can choose an implementation for an arithmetic operation that is optimized for the problem at hand. JavaScript, on the other hand, uses a generic—and therefore generally less than optimal—implementation for every arithmetic operation.

Many interpreted languages are, like JavaScript, also scripting languages. A *scripting language* is a specialized programming language designed to be used to automate tasks within a particular software environment. For example, if you have used Linux, you may have heard of *shell scripts*. These are generally small programs that issue Linux shell commands (the sorts of commands you type in within a shell prompt window) in order to cause the operating system to perform certain functions. For instance, shell scripting is a convenient way to change the file extension on all of the files within a directory. This could be done by hand, but scripting can be used to automate what might otherwise be a tedious process.

JavaScript is also intended to run within a certain software environment, or more precisely, within many software environments. The original LiveScript language was intended to be used as part of Netscape's LiveWire™ web server software as well as within Netscape browsers. JScript can similarly be run within Microsoft's IIS web server as well as within Internet Explorer browsers. In addition, many Microsoft operating systems also provide a Script Host application that essentially allows the Windows equivalent of Linux shell scripting to be performed using JScript. Certain other software applications also contain JavaScript interpreters, such as the Dreamweaver web-development tool.

To accommodate this diversity of script environments, each JavaScript implementation effectively consists of two software components. The primary component is a *scripting engine*, which includes a JavaScript interpreter as well as core ECMAScript functionality that must be present regardless of the script environment. The JavaScript scripting engine is the focus of this chapter. The second component of a complete JavaScript implementation is a *hosting environment*, which provides environment-specific capabilities to JavaScript programs running within the environment. The alert() and prompt() methods are part of the hosting environment of Mozilla and IE6. These and many other hosting environment features found in most modern browsers will be covered in Chapter 5.

All of the hosting environment capabilities as well as many scripting engine capabilities are provided through objects. Objects that are required by the ECMAScript definition and therefore provided by the scripting engine are known as *native* objects, and those provided by the hosting environment are known as *host* objects. In the JavaScript "Hello World!" example, window is the name of a native object (even though some of its methods are provided by the hosting environment). A *built-in* object is a native object that is automatically constructed during scripting engine initialization rather than being constructed as a result of a call to a constructor during program execution. The window object is an example of a built-in object, since it can be used immediately without constructing it explicitly.

4.3.2   Writing and Testing JavaScript Programs

JavaScript code can be written using various tools. Many JavaScript programs are small; for these, a simple text editor such as Windows Notepad is probably sufficient. If you use the GNU® Emacs editor (which runs on multiple platforms), it will colorize your JavaScript code if you include the following statements in the .emacs initialization file:

```
;; Turn on C++/other highlighting
(global-font-lock-mode)

;; Turn on a javascript mode for .js files
(require 'generic-x)
(add-to-list 'generic-extras-enable-list 'javascript-generic-mode)
```

For larger projects, commercial tools tailored to JavaScript development are available. For example, Microsoft's Visual InterDev® Web development system includes various JavaScript productivity features such as automatically providing lists of object properties and methods.

Once you've entered your JavaScript code, the next step is to execute your program, since JavaScript is not compiled and therefore does not require a compilation step before execution. While the lack of compilation streamlines the development process, it also means that there are no compiler error messages to alert you to potential problems before you execute a JavaScript program. Instead, any error messages are produced when you execute the program. What's more, to keep the language simple and flexible, JavaScript forgoes many safety features—commonly found in compiled languages—that help programmers to avoid hard-to-debug errors. For instance, it is not necessary to declare variables in JavaScript, which might seem like a programmer-friendly feature at first. But as an illustration of the problems this can cause, note that if you misspell the variable name on the left-hand side of a JavaScript assignment statement, then the scripting engine will silently create a new variable with the misspelled name. Obviously, you'll want to keep these sorts of problems in mind when you are debugging your JavaScript code.

As illustrated in Figure 4.1, executing a browser-based JavaScript program requires opening an HTML document in your browser. You can write your own documents to run each of your programs, or you can edit an existing document such as the one in Figure 4.1 so that it loads the file containing your program rather than JSHelloWorld.js. A simpler alternative using software available from the textbook Web site is described in the next section.

If you run your program and it does not behave as expected, the first step is to check for any browser-generated error messages. The details of this step of course depend on the browser you're using for your tests. If you have installed a full version of Mozilla as described in Appendix A, then error messages appear in its JavaScript console. You can open this console by selecting **Tools|WebDevelopment|JavaScript Console** from the browser menu. This console will display any syntax errors or run-time exceptions encountered (the code implementing Mozilla's features sometimes throws exceptions to this window, so I suggest opening the console and clicking its Clear button before running your JavaScript code). A nice feature of the Mozilla JavaScript console is that its error messages normally contain a hyperlink that, if clicked, will open a window displaying your JavaScript code and highlighting the offending line. This window is not an editor, though, so you'll still need to go back to your development software in order to make changes to your code.

IE6's response to JavaScript errors depends on the browser options you have selected as well as on whether or not certain other software is available on your system. A JavaScript problem is often indicated by the presence of a small yellow exclamation-mark icon in the lower left corner of the browser window (on the status bar). Clicking this icon will pop up a dialog box describing the error. However, instead of relying on this icon, I suggest selecting **Tools|Internet Options . . .** from the IE6 menu and click on the Advanced tab in the pop-up window that appears. Then check the "Display a notification about every script error" checkbox. The browser should then automatically pop up the error dialog box whenever a JavaScript syntax or run-time problem is encountered. Note that if you have debugging software installed and debugging enabled (also controlled via **Internet Options . . .**), instead of seeing this error window you will be asked whether or not you want to begin a debugging session (see Section 4.13 about JavaScript debuggers).

The Details section of the IE6 error window tells the type of error and its location (file name, line within the file, and character within the line). If multiple errors are encountered, the pop-up window will contain information about one of the errors and a Next button that will allow you to step through other error messages.

If your browser does not produce any error messages but your program does not behave as expected, you'll need to locate the source of the problem. The same sorts of bug location techniques that apply to other languages apply to JavaScript. Some common techniques are to desk check (simulate by hand) your program, add output statements so that you can see the results of intermediate computations, or run an interactive debugger. You'll need to understand certain JavaScript concepts in order to use an interactive debugger effectively, so this approach is covered in Section 4.13.

After locating the source of errors and changing your code, you can retest your program by reloading the HTML document containing the code into your browser. If your browser is currently accessing this document, this is as simple as clicking the Reload (Mozilla) or Refresh (IE6) button in the browser toolbar.

4.4 Basic Syntax

Much of JavaScript's basic syntax is identical to that of Java or C++. To illustrate these similarities, consider the JavaScript program of Figure 4.4, which plays the high-low guessing game with the user. That is, the program randomly picks a whole number between 1 and 1000, and the user attempts to guess the number. After each guess, the user is either told that the guess was correct or is told whether the guessed number is too high or too low. This continues until the user guesses the computer's number.

Let's begin by considering some ways in which JavaScript syntax is similar to Java and C++. First, comments in JavaScript are the same as those in Java: // begins a comment that ends at the end of the line containing the comment, and /* and */ may be used to contain multiline comments (not shown in this example). Also, JavaScript's use of braces to enclose statement blocks and its syntax for assignment statements and control constructs such as if and while should be familiar. Another similarity is that semicolons (;) can be used at the end of JavaScript statements as they are in Java and C++. Technically, most JavaScript statements do not require this, but for compatibility with compiled languages and to avoid possible hard-to-locate errors, I suggest always using semicolons just as you would in Java.

JavaScript uses the familiar dot notation to represent properties and methods of objects. So we can infer, for instance, that random() is a method of the Math object (which like window is a built-in object). This method returns a randomly chosen random

```javascript
// HighLow.js

var thinkingOf;  // Number the computer has chosen (1 through 1000)
var guess;       // User's latest guess

// Initialize the computer's number
thinkingOf = Math.ceil(Math.random()*1000);

// Play until user guesses the number
guess = window.prompt("I'm thinking of a number between 1 and 1000." +
                      "  What is it?", "");
while (guess != thinkingOf)
{

  // Evaluate the user's guess
  if (guess < thinkingOf) {
    guess = window.prompt("Your guess of " + guess +
                          " was too low.  Guess again.", "");
  }
  else {
    guess = window.prompt("Your guess of " + guess +
                          " was too high.  Guess again.", "");
  }
}

// Game over; congratulate the user
window.alert(guess + " is correct!");
```

FIGURE 4.4 JavaScript high-low program.

decimal number from 0 up to but not including 1, and `Math.ceil()` returns the smallest integer greater than or equal to its argument. The net effect of applying these methods in the program is that a random integer between 1 and 1000 is assigned to `thinkingOf`.

Some other similarities between Java and JavaScript that will be covered in more detail later in this chapter include the following. First, variable names in JavaScript are case sensitive, and the rules for choosing variable names are similar to those used in C++ and Java (although JavaScript of course has a somewhat different collection of reserved words that cannot be used as variable names). The syntax for argument passing in method calls and for array access (not shown in the example program in Figure 4.4) is also similar to Java's.

In addition, most of the strings used to represent various logical, string, and numeric operators, such as `!=`, `+`, and `*`, are identical to those used in Java and C++. (Recall that *operators* in a programming language appear within expressions, where an *expression* is a portion of a program that can be *evaluated* in order to obtain a value. For example, the expression `1+2` contains the operator `+` and, when evaluated, returns the value `3`. The `+` operator has two *operands*, `1` and `2`.)

While JavaScript thus has many similarities with Java and C++, there are also some significant differences. First, there is no `main()` function or method. Instead, the JavaScript scripting engine simply begins evaluating the first line of code it reads. Second, the variable declarations (statements beginning with the keyword `var`) do not specify a data type for the variables declared. Typed variables are another safety feature that is missing in JavaScript: if you assign a string value to a variable that you were intending to treat as a numeric variable, JavaScript will silently assign the string value to the variable. On the other hand, this can be viewed as adding to JavaScript's flexibility: if you want to (I don't recommend this), you can deliberately store a Number value in a variable at one time in a program's execution and at a later time store a String value in the same variable. In computer science terminology, JavaScript is a *dynamically typed* language whereas Java and C++ are *statically typed*.

This brings us to a third significant difference: JavaScript performs many conversions between data types automatically. In this program, the `prompt()` method returns a string value, so the values assigned to `guess` are all strings. But the value of `thinkingOf` is a number. In Java, an attempt to apply a relational operator such as `<` or `!=` to compare String and int operands would result in a compile error. But JavaScript automatically converts the string argument to a number so that the comparison can be performed. We'll learn more about JavaScript's type conversion rules later. For now, note that this automatic conversion feature, while convenient, comes at the expense of run-time computation required to detect the need for conversion and to choose an appropriate conversion to apply.

The JavaScript program of Figure 4.4—as well as every other example in this chapter that begins with a comment consisting of a file name—is part of the `chapter 4` directory of the download package available from the textbook supplements Web site (the URL is given in the Preface). The download package also includes an HTML document named `TestJs.html` that you can use to load and execute this chapter's examples. Simply open the `TestJs.html` file in your browser; in Mozilla, you can do this by selecting **File|Open File . . .** from the menu and navigating to the `TestJs.html` file in the file selector window that appears. When the file loads, the browser's client area will be blank, but a pop-up prompt box (as in Figure 4.3) will appear. Enter the name of the example file (such as `HighLow.js`) in this prompt box, and click OK. Your browser will then load the example file and execute the JavaScript code that it contains.

Now that you have some familiarity with the basic syntax of JavaScript, the next several sections will explore how JavaScript handles specific programming issues, including variables and data types, statements and operators, objects, arrays, and functions (methods).

4.5   Variables and Data Types

As previously mentioned, variables do not have data types in JavaScript. However, every variable has a value, and every value belongs to one of six JavaScript data types. Every numeric value is of type Number, string values are of type String, the literals `true` and `false` represent the two Boolean values, the literal `null` represents the one value of type Null, and every object is of type Object. The remaining type, Undefined, is the type of the value represented by any variable that has been declared but has not yet been assigned a value. Attempts to use such variables in Java will be flagged as errors by the Java compiler, but it is up to the programmer to avoid this situation in JavaScript. The five JavaScript data types other than Object are sometimes referred to as *primitive data types*.

In JavaScript, `typeof` is an operator that provides information about the data type of a value stored in a variable, as shown in Table 4.1. For example, the JavaScript code

```
// TypeOf.js
var i;
var j;
j = "Not a number";
alert("i is " + (typeof i) + "\n" +
      "j is " + (typeof j));
```

produces the output of Figure 4.5. A common use of the `typeof` operator is to test that a variable has been defined before attempting to use it. Notice, though, that `typeof` returns the string `undefined` for several different reasons, not only when a variable contains the value of type Undefined.

As mentioned previously, JavaScript can perform automatic conversions between data types. Tables 4.2, 4.3, and 4.4 show rules used to convert to Boolean, String, and Number types, respectively. NaN ("not a number") and Infinity, mentioned in these tables,

TABLE 4.1 Values Returned by `typeof` for Various Operands

Operand Value	String typeof Returns
null	object
Boolean	boolean
Number	number
String	string
Native Object representing function	function
Native Object not representing function	object
Declared variable with no value	undefined
Undeclared variable	undefined
Nonexistent property of an Object	undefined

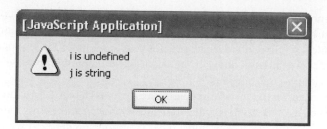

FIGURE 4.5 Result of executing `TypeOf.js`.

TABLE 4.2 Data Type Conversions to Boolean

Original Value	Value as Boolean
Undefined	`false`
`null`	`false`
0	`false`
NaN	`false`
`""` (empty string)	`false`
Any other value	`true`

TABLE 4.3 Data Type Conversions to String

Original Value	Value as String
Undefined	`undefined`
`null`	`null`
`true`, `false`	`true`, `false`
NaN	NaN
Infinity, −Infinity	`Infinity, -Infinity`
Other Number up to ≈20 digits	Integer or decimal representation
Number over ≈20 digits	Scientific notation
Object	Call to `toString()` method on the object

TABLE 4.4 Data Type Conversions to Number

Original Value	Value as Number
Undefined	NaN
`null`, `false`, `""` (empty string)	0
`true`	1
String representing number	Represented number
Other String	NaN
Object	Call to `valueOf()` method on the object

are special Number values that can occur if, for example, you divide by 0 (0/0 produces NaN while any positive number divided by 0 produces Infinity). toString() (Table 4.3) and and valueOf() (Table 4.4) are methods that are defined (either implicitly or explicitly) for every JavaScript object. We'll have more to say about these methods for some of JavaScript's built-in objects later in this chapter.

We learned earlier that, when comparing a String and a Number value with a comparison operator such as <, JavaScript will automatically convert the String value to a Number before performing the comparison. Some other common situations in which the scripting engine performs automatic type conversion are:

- The condition portion of statements such as if and while is automatically converted to Boolean.
- The value of the accessor portion of an array access (for example, the 3 in an expression such as records[3]) is automatically converted to String.

Additional type-conversion scenarios are covered in Section 4.7.

The strings used to name variables are called *identifiers*. Any string that begins with a letter or underscore (_), consists only of these characters and digits, and is not one of the reserved words listed in Figure 4.6 is a valid identifier in JavaScript. (The JavaScript specification also allows certain other characters in identifiers; see Section 7.6 of the ECMAScript specification [ECMA-262] for full details.) As mentioned previously, identifiers are case sensitive.

Finally, if a JavaScript program assigns a value to a variable without first declaring the variable (with a var statement), then the scripting engine will automatically create the variable. So, for example, the following is a legal JavaScript program that will create a variable, assign it a value, and then display the value in an alert box:

```
testing = "Does this work?";
window.alert(testing);
```

However, I strongly recommend using var to declare your variables. First, using var consistently to create variables makes it easier to determine all of the variables used in your program, which should facilitate future program maintenance. Moreover, you can avoid

abstract	boolean	break	byte	case	catch
char	class	const	continue	debugger	default
delete	do	double	else	enum	export
extends	false	final	finally	float	for
function	goto	if	implements	import	in
instanceof	int	interface	long	native	new
null	package	private	protected	public	return
short	static	super	switch	synchronized	
this	throw	throws	transient	true	try
typeof	var	void	volatile	while	with

FIGURE 4.6 JavaScript reserved words.

certain subtle errors if you use var rather than assignments to create all variables (but I'll leave the details to the exercises).

4.6 Statements

JavaScript has three types of statements. First, there is the *expression statement*, that is, a statement that consists entirely of an expression. Typical expression statements include assignment and increment statements, such as

```
i = 5;
j++;
```

The second type is the *block statement*, which is simply a set of statements enclosed in braces { and }. Finally, there are statements that begin with keywords such as var and if, which are (of course) called *keyword statements*.

We have already met the var statement, which is JavaScript's one statement for declaring a variable. Syntactically, the var keyword is followed by a variable declaration list, which is a comma-separated list of identifiers. Each identifier in a variable declaration list may optionally be followed by an equals sign (=) and then an arbitrary expression that acts as an initializer. So the JavaScript code

```
var i, msg="hi", o=null;
```

declares three variables named i, msg, and o, assigning them values of types Undefined, String, and Null, respectively.

Table 4.5 lists the JavaScript keyword statements that have direct analogs in Java and C++. I assume that you're already familiar with these statements as they're used in Java, so I won't cover them in detail here. Instead, Figure 4.7 illustrates the use of several of

TABLE 4.5 Some JavaScript Keyword Statements

Statement Name	Syntax
If-then	if *(expr) stmt*
If-then-else	if *(expr) stmt* else *stmt*
Do	do *stmt* while *(expr)*
While	while *(expr) stmt*
For	for *(part1 ; part2 ; part3) stmt*
Continue	continue
Break	break
Return-void	return
Return-value	return *expr*
Switch	switch *(expr)* { *cases* }
Try	try *try-block catch-part*
Throw	throw *expr*

these statements. This program will successively display three alert boxes. The first two boxes will contain the message A JavaScript exception can be anything, and the third will contain i = 3. Comments in the code point out small differences between some of the JavaScript keyword statements and their Java analogs.

4.7   Operators

In this section, we'll cover many of JavaScript's operators. Since most of these operators are similar to operators, in Java and C++, our focus will not be on the basic functionality of the operators, but instead on some specific ways in which JavaScript operators differ from those in Java.

Before covering the operators themselves, let's review some terminology related to operators. A *binary operator* is one such as * that has two operands. Other operators, such as ! (the logical NOT operator) and typeof, have a single operand and are called *unary operators*. A unary operator may be either *prefix*, meaning that it precedes its operand, or *postfix*, meaning that it follows.

JavaScript also has one *ternary operator* that takes three operands: the *conditional operator*, which separates its first and second operands with a question mark (?) and its second and third operands with a colon (:). Although this operator also appears in Java and C++, you may not have used it before, so I'll describe it briefly here. The conditional operator provides a convenient means to code if-then-else logic within a single statement: the first operand (preceding the question mark) is treated as a Boolean value, and the overall

```
// KeywordStmts.js

// Can use 'var' to define a loop variable inside a 'for'
for (var i=1; i<=3; i++) {

  switch (i) {

    // 'case' value can be any expression and data type,
    // not just constant int as in Java.  Automatic
    // type conversion is performed if needed.
    case 1.0 + 2:
      window.alert("i = " + i);
      break;
    default:
      try {
        throw("A JavaScript exception can be anything");
        window.alert("This is not executed.");
      }
      // Do not supply exception data type in 'catch'
      catch (e) {
        window.alert("Caught: " + e);
      }
      break;
  }
}
```

FIGURE 4.7 JavaScript program illustrating several keyword statements.

expression evaluates to either the value of the second operand, if the Boolean value is `true`, or the value of the third operand otherwise. For example,

```
window.alert( "Error " + (debugLevel>2 ? details : "") );
```

adds a string representing the value of the `details` variable to an output message if the relational expression `debugLevel>2` evaluates to `true`. Otherwise, the empty string is appended to the message.

4.7.1 Precedence

Table 4.6 lists the JavaScript operators covered in this chapter, in order of their operator precedence. Recall that, in an unparenthesized expression, an operator of higher *precedence* is performed before one of lower precedence. Table 4.6 lists operators from highest to lowest precedence. As in most languages, parentheses can be used to override these default precedences, with innermost parenthesized subexpressions evaluated before those farther out.

The assignment, conditional, and prefix unary operators are *right associative*, which means that if there is a tie among multiple operators at the same precedence level, the rightmost operator is applied first. For example, an expression such as

```
a *= b += c
```

is equivalent to

```
a *= (b += c)
```

TABLE 4.6 Precedence (High to Low) for Selected JavaScript Operators

Operator Category	Operators
Object creation	new
Postfix unary	++, --
Prefix unary	delete, typeof, ++, -- , +, -, ˜, !
Multiplicative	*, /, %
Additive	+, -
Shift	<<, >>, >>>
Relational	<, >, <=, >=
(In)equality	==, !=, ===, !==
Bitwise AND	&
Bitwise XOR	^
Bitwise OR	|
Logical AND	&&
Logical OR	||
Conditional and assignment	?:, =, *=, /=, %=, +=, -=, <<=, >>=, >>>=, &=, ^=, |=

The postfix unary operators cannot be applied repeatedly. For example,

```
i++ ++
```

is not a syntactically correct expression. Therefore, associativity does not apply to these operators. The remaining operators—those that are not in the conditional, assignment, or unary categories—are *left associative*, so ties among these operators are broken in favor of the leftmost operator.

Almost all of the operator symbols in Table 4.6 should already be familiar to you, either from your knowledge of Java or C++ or from material earlier in this chapter (two operators that are not found in Java or C++, === and !==, are covered in some detail later). However, many of these symbols have a somewhat different meaning in JavaScript than they do in Java or C++. We'll give an overview of the primary differences in the remainder of this section.

4.7.2 Type Conversion

One of the key differences between JavaScript and Java/C++ operators has to do with automatic type conversion. Let's begin with the additive and multiplicative operators +, -, *, /, and %. Each of these operators will convert its operands to Number (according to the rules of Table 4.4) if they are not already of this type. Thus, for example, the following is legal JavaScript code and outputs 3:

```
window.alert("5" - 2);
```

One exception to this conversion rule involves the + operator: much as in Java, if either or both of the operands of the + operator are of type String, then the non-String operand (if any) will automatically be converted to String and the two String operand values will be concatenated. (Use of the + operator in this way was illustrated in the calls to the alert() method within the high-low game program of Figure 4.4.)

Similarly, we learned earlier that if a String and a Number value are compared with a relational operator such as <, then the String will be converted to a Number before the comparison is performed. More generally, for each of the four relational operators listed in Table 4.6, unless both of its operands are of type String, the operands are converted to Number as needed before the comparison is performed. (Although a bit off the topic of conversions, note that relational expressions involving the special Infinity Number value generally behave as you would expect. For example, everything except Infinity is less than Infinity. The special NaN value, on the other hand, is treated as if it is not less than, equal to, or greater than any other value, including itself.)

If both operands to one of the relational operators or one of the operators == and != are of type String, then a lexicographic string comparison is performed. Recall that a *lexicographic comparison* of two strings s1 and s2 is performed as follows. String s1 is lexicographically less than string s2 if, at the first character position where the strings differ, the character value for s1 is numerically less than the corresponding character value for s2. If the strings do not differ in any character position, then s1 is lexicographically less than s2 if the length of s1 is less than the length of s2. If neither of these conditions holds, then the strings are lexicographically equal.

As you're probably aware, lexicographic comparisons of String objects in Java cannot be performed with relational or equality operators, but instead are normally performed with calls to methods such as equals() and compareTo(). For example, if str1 and str2 are two Java String objects, then to compare these strings lexicographically we would normally use code such as

```
if (str1.equals(str2)) { ... }
```

On the other hand, if str3 and str4 are JavaScript variables containing String values, JavaScript's automatic type conversion feature allows us to instead write

```
if (str3 == str4) { ... }
```

The type conversion rules for the == and != operators generally follow the pattern we have seen earlier: if the operands are not both of type String, then both are typically converted to Number for comparison purposes. However, there are several exceptions. First, the value of the Undefined type (the type of a declared variable that has not been assigned a value) is considered equal to null, the one value of the Null type. Also, if one of the operands is an Object value and this object is an instance of the Date built-in object (described in Section 4.12.3), then the Object is converted to String instead of Number. Finally, if one of the operands is an Object value representing a host object rather than a native object, then the type conversion of the object is implementation dependent.

To allow for (in)equality comparisons without type conversion, JavaScript provides the two *strict* operators. The strict equality (===) operator evaluates to true only if both operands are of the same type (without conversion) and have exactly the same value. The strict inequality (!==) operator is of course just the logical NOT of strict equality. For values of type Object, the values are "the same" only if both operands are references to exactly the same object. If you're not quite sure what an object reference is, this concept is covered in detail in Section 4.10.4. For now, it's enough to know that this is how Java defines its == operator when applied to two Java objects (and in fact the JavaScript == operator also behaves this way when applied to two Object values).

Certain other operators perform natural automatic conversions. For example, each of the unary + and - operators converts its operand to Number (this is in fact all that the unary + operation does). Likewise, the logical AND, logical OR, and logical negation (!) operators will all convert their operands to Boolean as needed. (Technically, the logical AND and OR operators behave somewhat differently than this. But if you only use them in the normal way—within the condition expression of statements such as an if or while statement—then they will effectively behave as just described.)

4.7.3 Bit Operators

A JavaScript programmer cannot access the internal bit representation of a Number value. However, JavaScript does supply the same bit-level operators found in Java: bitwise (ones complement) NOT(˜); the bitwise AND, XOR, and OR operators; and the shift operators (Table 4.6). The JavaScript operators first convert their operands to 32-bit twos-complement integers by converting them to Number (Table 4.4) if needed, then truncating decimal values to integers, and finally retaining only the low-order 32 bits for integers that exceed 32 bits. The operators are then applied as if they were operating within a machine with 32-bit registers, which implies, for example, that the result of a left shift operator << will be truncated to 32 bits if necessary. After the operator processing is completed, the 32-bit result is converted back to a Number value. For purposes of this final conversion, the 32-bit result is treated as an unsigned 32-bit integer by the unsigned right shift (>>>) operator and as a 32-bit twos-complement integer by the other operators.

As an example of using bit operators in JavaScript, consider the program

```
// ComplementOne.js
window.alert(~1);
```

This program will output −2, because ~1 evaluates to a string of 31 1 bits followed by a 0 bit, which represents −2 when treated as a signed twos-complement 32-bit integer for purposes of conversion to Number. On the other hand,

```
// ComplementOne.js (part 2)
window.alert((~1) >>> 0);
```

outputs 4294967294 ($2^{32} - 2$), which is the value of the same 32-bit string treated as an unsigned integer for purposes of conversion to Number.

4.8 Literals

The most basic elements of any programming language are its *literals*, that is, the strings of characters that directly represent values in the language. We've already noted that null is a JavaScript literal representing the (one) value of the Null data type, and that true and false are the literals representing the two Boolean values. This section provides some syntactic details about JavaScript number and string literals.

The JavaScript number literals are much like those in Java. For example, numbers can be written as integers (whole numbers) or decimals, and in either of these forms scientific notation can be used to indicate a power of 10. For example, -12.4e12 represents the value $−12.4 \times 10^{12}$. Java hexadecimal notation, e.g., 0xfa0, is also a valid form of number literal. Every JavaScript number literal represents a value belonging to the JavaScript Number data type. Since JavaScript has only one type of number, a Java literal that represents a number of a specified type (such as 27.3f, which represents a floating point value) is not a valid number literal in JavaScript. All Number values are represented using a 64-bit floating point format that provides approximately 16 decimal digits of precision for both integer and decimal values and can represent numbers with magnitudes as large as approximately 10^{308} and as small as approximately 10^{-323}. Literals beyond these limits will be represented as accurately as possible. For example, if a literal represents a value that is too large for the Number data type to represent accurately, then the literal will evaluate to the special Number value Infinity.

A string literal is a quoted string of characters all on a single line, and, as in HTML, the quoting characters may be either a pair of single quotes or a pair of double quotes. Note that this differs from Java, where a character contained in single quotes belongs to the char data type. It is much more efficient to store single characters using char than it is to use the Java String class. JavaScript, on the other hand, has only one data type for strings—named String—just as it has only one data type for numbers. This is another example of how JavaScript's design favors simplicity over efficiency.

Like Java, escape codes can be embedded in string literals to represent various characters. For example, \n represents the line feed (newline) character, and \" (\') can be used to represent a double (single) quote within a string literal that is enclosed in double (single) quotes. Of course, because the backslash character is special, it must be escaped within string literals; the escape code \\ can be used for this purpose. Finally, any 16-bit Unicode character value may be represented by immediately following the \u escape code with four hexadecimal digits. For instance, \u005c represents the backslash character.

4.9 Functions

The structure of the high-low program of Figure 4.4 is not typical of many JavaScript programs designed to be run within browsers. Instead, such programs often are structured as a set of functions. A *function* in JavaScript is much like a method in Java: it consists of a function name, an argument list, and code that is executed when the function is called. However, unlike Java methods, a function does not need to be associated with an object.

To illustrate, consider Figure 4.8, which is the initial portion of a revision of the high-low program from Figure 4.4 (the remainder of the revised HighLowWithFunction.js program is identical to the corresponding portion of the original HighLow.js). The code beginning with the keyword function and ending with the next closing brace is a *function declaration*. Every JavaScript function declaration follows the same syntax: the keyword function followed by an identifier followed by a parenthesized list of zero of more comma-separated identifiers followed by a curly-brace bracketed sequence of statements. The first identifier is the *function name*, the list of identifiers is the function's *formal parameter list*,

```
// HighLowWithFunction.js

var thinkingOf;   // Number the computer has chosen (1 through 1000)
var guess;        // User's latest guess

// This function returns a random number between 1 and
// the argument value 'high'.
function oneTo(high) {
  return Math.ceil(Math.random()*high);
}

// Initialize the computer's number
thinkingOf = oneTo(1000);

...
```

FIGURE 4.8 Initial portion of JavaScript high-low game program that defines and uses a function named oneTo() for computing a random number between 1 and a specified value.

and the statements represent the *function body*. In this example, the function name is oneTo, there is a single formal parameter named high, and the function body consists of a single return-value statement.

Unlike Java and C++, JavaScript does not require (or even allow) the data types of formal parameters or the data type of the return value of a function to be declared. (This shouldn't surprise us, since the data types of variables are also not declared in JavaScript.)

The code

```
oneTo(1000)
```

is a type of JavaScript expression known as a *function call*. Syntactically, the typical function call consists of an identifier followed by a parenthesized list of zero or more comma-separated *arguments*. In the example, the argument is 1000.

When a scripting engine evaluates a function call, the effect is similar to that of a method call in Java. First, the engine evaluates each of the arguments, producing a value for each. In our example, 1000 is a Number literal and therefore evaluates to a Number value. If the function call had instead been written as oneTo(999+1), the result of the function call would be the same, since the argument value would still be 1000. Next, after evaluating the arguments, the resulting values are associated with the appropriate formal parameters. In our example, the value 1000 will be associated with the formal parameter high. Next, the body of the function is executed. Finally, the value of the function call expression is determined as follows. If a return-value statement is executed, then the value of the expression in the return-value statement becomes the value of the function call expression. On the other hand, if a return-void statement is executed or if the final statement in the body has been executed and is not a return statement, then the Undefined value becomes the value of the function call expression. In our example, a return-value statement will be executed, and the value of the expression in this statement is of type Number. So a Number value will be assigned to thinkingOf.

As in Java, code within a JavaScript function body can assign values to the function's formal parameters, and such assignments will not change the values of any variables in the function call's argument list, even if the variable and the parameter use the same identifier. For example, the following JavaScript program will produce two alert boxes, the first with the message hi and the second with the message bye:

```
// ArgChange.js

var message = "bye";

function change(message) {
  message = "hi";
  window.alert(message);
  return;
}

change(message);
window.alert(message);
```

As we'll learn later, JavaScript's handling of object and array arguments is also similar to Java's.

In Java, a compile error is generated if a method call's arguments do not match the number and data types of the formal parameters of the method. In JavaScript, the arguments and parameters do not have data types, so there is no need to match their types. What's more, a function call does not need to have the same number of arguments as there are formal parameters in the function declaration. If too few arguments are supplied, the formal parameters without arguments will be given the Undefined value. If too many arguments are supplied, the excess arguments are ignored.

If a var statement appears within a function body, then the variable declared is called a *local variable*, while variables that are declared outside of any function are called *global variables*. The relationship between global and local variables is very similar to the relationship between the instance variables of a Java object—those variables declared outside of any method of the class—and the variables declared within its methods. Global variables can be accessed from any part of a program, while local variables can only be accessed from the function that declares them. Also, global variables exist from the beginning of execution of a program until the program terminates, while a local variable exists only from the time the function declaring the variable is called until the function returns (see Section 4.10.5 for an exception to this rule). If a function is called multiple times, new copies of its local variables are created every time the function is called.

The following program demonstrates JavaScript's behavior if a local and a global variable share the same identifier:

```
// LocalScope.js
var j=6;    // global variable declaration and initialization
function test()
{
  var j;    // local variable declaration
  j=7;      // Which variable(s) does this change?
  return;
}
test();
window.alert(j);
```

When the program is run, it displays an alert box containing 6, even though the test() function is called and assigns the value 7 to a variable named j. This assignment does not affect the value of the global variable by the same name because of JavaScript's *scope rules*, which dictate that if a variable reference is ambiguous (could refer to either a local or a global variable) then the scripting engine should associate the reference with the local variable. In such a situation, the global variable is said to be *shadowed* by the local variable with the same name.

To override JavaScript's default scope rules and access a shadowed global variable, you can prefix the name of the variable with window. Thus, if we changed the assignment statement within test() to

```
window.j = 7;
```

then the global rather than the local variable would be affected, and the output of the program would be 7 rather than 6. This works because global variables (as well as declared functions) are stored as properties of the `window` object. You'll want to keep this in mind if you run a debugger on a JavaScript program.

JavaScript supports recursive function calls. If a function calls itself recursively, each recursive execution will have its own local variables and formal parameter values. Thus, a recursive execution of a function does not have direct access to the parameters or local variables of other in-progress executions of the function. So, if you're familiar with the concept of a static local variable in C++ (a variable whose value is shared between calls to a recursive function or between successive nonrecursive calls to the same function), you should be aware that JavaScript has no direct support for this concept.

What if one function calls another function: does it matter which function is declared first in the program? No, it does not matter. This is because the scripting engine operates on a program in two *passes*, or phases. During the first pass, the scripting engine processes all `var` statements and function declarations. This creates global variables and function objects but doesn't actually execute any statements. In the second pass, the engine executes statements. So you can declare functions and variables in any order, because they will all be known to the scripting engine before it begins executing any statements that refer to the functions or variables.

Finally, JavaScript supplies some built-in functions that can be called just as you would call functions you have declared. In particular, the built-in functions `Boolean()`, `String()`, and `Number()` can be called to convert a value from any data type to a Boolean, String, or Number, respectively. Each function takes a single argument of any data type and returns a value of the specified type by applying the appropriate rules from Table 4.2, 4.3, or 4.4.

4.10   Objects

At this point, we've covered JavaScript's basic syntax, and we know a good deal about working with values belonging to the primitive (non-Object) data types. We'll now turn to JavaScript objects. The differences between JavaScript and Java are especially pronounced when it comes to objects, so if you've been skimming this chapter you may want to read this section more carefully.

4.10.1   Object Properties

An *object* in JavaScript is a set of *properties*, each of which consists of a unique *name* along with a *value* belonging to one of JavaScript's six data types. Properties in JavaScript are comparable to Java instance variables (i.e., nonstatic variables declared outside any method).

Like JavaScript variables, object properties themselves do not have data types; only the values assigned to properties have data types. For example, the following sequence of statements that successively assign Boolean, String, and Number values to a single property `prop` of an object `o` (assumed to be declared earlier) is syntactically valid in JavaScript, but would cause a compile error in Java or C++ regardless of how `o` was declared:

```
o.prop = true;
o.prop = "true";
o.prop = 1;
```

An even bigger difference with Java and C++ is that JavaScript programs do not define classes. There are some classlike features. For example, object constructors can be defined (as described later in this section) to create objects and automatically define properties for the objects created. Also, JavaScript uses a so-called *prototype* mechanism to provide a form of inheritance (this is an advanced topic that will not be covered in this chapter). However, unlike Java and C++, in which the class of an object defines its variables and methods, properties and methods can be added to or removed from a JavaScript object after it has been created.

For example, the following is valid in JavaScript:

```
var o1 = new Object();
o1.testing = "This is a test";
delete o1.testing;
```

We'll go into detail on these statements later in this subsection; for now, here's a brief description. The first line creates a variable named o1 and initializes it with a value of type Object by calling on the built-in constructor Object() using a JavaScript new expression. The second line then adds a property named testing to the o1 object and assigns a String value to this property. And the third line then deletes this property from o1.

Dynamic property creation is yet another example of JavaScript's flexibility, but also of its lack of certain safety features: if you misspell a property name in an assignment statement, you won't get an error message, but instead you'll create a new property. This is something to watch for when you're debugging JavaScript code.

Now we'll cover object creation and dynamic creation and removal of properties in somewhat more detail. First, as shown in the example, expressions beginning with the keyword new are used to create objects. Syntactically, a new expression begins with the new keyword followed by an identifier corresponding to an object constructor followed by a parenthesized list of zero of more arguments. We'll learn how to create user-defined constructors later in this chapter.

A new expression causes a new empty object to be created and then calls the specified constructor, supplying it with this new object plus the specified argument values. The constructor can then perform initialization on the object, which might involve creating and initializing properties, adding methods to the object, and adding the object to an inheritance hierarchy from which it can inherit additional properties and methods. In the case of the Object() constructor, no properties or methods are added directly to the new object by the constructor, but the object is modified so that it inherits several generic methods including default toString() and valueOf() methods used when converting the object to String and Number values, respectively. The values produced by these default methods are not particularly useful, but they at least prevent a run-time error in case an attempt is made to apply data type conversion to the object.

We next turn to property creation. As we saw, when a JavaScript statement attempts to assign a value to an object property, and the property does not exist in the object, then a property with the given name is created in the object and assigned the specified value. This happens even if the object has inherited a property with the same name, since an inherited property or method actually resides in a different object.

Finally, as shown, the keyword `delete` can be used to remove a property from an object. Syntactically, a `delete` expression begins with the `delete` unary operator followed by a reference to an object property, such as `o.testing`. You should not attempt to delete a nonexistent property (technically, this should be legal, but some browsers will throw an exception).

JavaScript provides a handy shortcut called an *object initializer* for creating an empty object (as if by a call to `new Object()`), creating properties on this object, and assigning values to these properties. For example, the statement

```
var o2 = { p1:5+9, p2:null, testing:"This is a test" };
```

creates an object with three properties p1, p2, and `testing` and assigns these properties the values 14, `null`, and `This is a test`, respectively. A reference to this object is then assigned to the variable o2.

4.10.2 Enumerating Properties

If properties can be dynamically created and destroyed, how can your program know which properties an object has at any given time? JavaScript provides a special for-in statement that can be used to iterate through all of the property names of an object. The following JavaScript code illustrates the use of this statement:

```
var hash = new Object();
hash.kim = "85";
hash.sam = "92";
hash.lynn = "78";
for (var aName in hash) {
  window.alert(aName + " is a property of hash.");
}
```

Executing this program will produce three alert boxes, each with one of the names kim, sam, or lynn. However, the order in which they appear is implementation dependent.

The syntax of a for-in statement is as shown: It begins with the reserved word for followed by a parenthesized portion followed by a statement (often a brace-enclosed block statement). The parenthesized portion begins with a variable identifier, optionally preceded by var if the variable was not previously declared. Then comes the reserved word in followed by an expression that evaluates to an object.

4.10.3 Array Notation

The code in the preceding example prints the property names. What if we want to print the values of these properties? The notation `hash.aName` represents the property named aName, which is not what we want. What we want is a notation that means "Evaluate the expression aName and convert it to a String if necessary. Then retrieve the property that has this string value as its name from the hash object."

As you might guess, JavaScript provides just such a notation: hash[aName] has exactly this meaning. So, for example, if we change the window.alert() call in the code to

```
window.alert(aName + " scored " + hash[aName]);
```

then the alert boxes output by the program will contain both the name and the value for each of the three properties in hash.

In short, JavaScript provides two different notations for accessing object properties. The first notation is the familiar dot notation, for example hash.kim. The second notation uses an array reference syntax in which the index is viewed as a String value, for example hash["kim"]. As we have seen, the array notation has the advantage that any expression, not just a string literal, can be used to represent the property name. So the array notation is more general, and in fact scripting engines view dot notation such as hash.kim as shorthand for the equivalent array notation hash["kim"].

Therefore, an object in JavaScript can also be viewed as a sort of array in which the elements are indexed by strings. Such an array is sometimes called an *associative array*. This is a powerful form of data structure, similar to Java's java.util.Hashtable class but built directly into the JavaScript language rather than provided by an API. In addition to the associative array feature of all JavaScript objects, JavaScript objects constructed using the Array() constructor (covered in Section 4.11) also have additional array-specific properties and methods.

4.10.4 Object References

Recall that if you execute the Java code

```
StringBuffer s1 = new StringBuffer("Hello");
StringBuffer s2 = s1;
```

then a single StringBuffer is created and both s1 and s2 will be references to it. This is because what is stored in a Java variable that represents an object is a reference (pointer) to the object and not the object itself. Thus, the second statement in the code copies the reference from s1 to s2 rather than making a copy of the entire object. Therefore, if the code is followed by

```
s2.append(" World!");
System.out.println(s1);
```

then even though it might appear that s2 is modified and s1 is not, the output will be Hello World!.

In the same way, JavaScript values of type Object are also references to objects, not actual objects themselves. So the following JavaScript code will also output Hello World!:

```
// ObjRef.js
var o1 = new Object();
o1.data = "Hello";
var o2 = o1;
o2.data += " World!";
window.alert(o1.data);
```

Similarly, when an Object value is used as an argument to a function or method, the object reference is passed and not a copy of the object itself. To illustrate this, consider the JavaScript program of Figure 4.9. The program creates two objects o1 and o2 and passes them as arguments to the function objArgs(). Thus, immediately after the function is called, param1 is a copy of the object reference contained in o1, and param2 a copy of o2 (part (a) of Figure 4.10). The first statement of the function changes the data property of the object referenced by param1 and o1 (Figure 4.10(b)). The function then changes param2 to be a copy of the object reference contained in param1. Note that this has no impact on the variable o2 or on the object referenced by this variable (Figure 4.10(c)). The output of the program will therefore be the two alert boxes shown in Figure 4.11.

```
// ObjArg.js

function objArgs(param1, param2) {
  // Change the data in param1 and its argument
  param1.data = "changed";
  // Change the object referenced by param2, but not its argument
  param2 = param1;

  window.alert("param1 is " + param1.data + "\n" +
               "param2 is " + param2.data);
  return;
}

// Create two different objects with identical data
var o1 = new Object();
o1.data = "original";
var o2 = new Object();
o2.data = "original";

// Call the function on these objects and display the results
objArgs(o1, o2);
window.alert("o1 is " + o1.data + "\n" +
             "o2 is " + o2.data);
```

FIGURE 4.9 JavaScript program illustrating the use of objects as arguments.

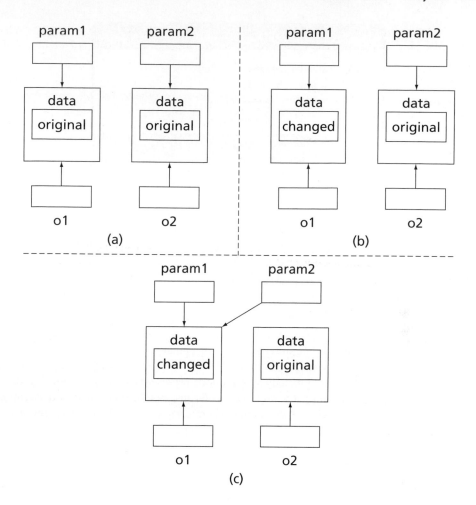

FIGURE 4.10 State of variables and parameters of the ObjArg.js program (a) immediately before the first statement of the function objArgs() is executed; (b) immediately after this statement is executed; and (c) immediately after the second statement of the function is executed.

4.10.5   Methods

If you read the description of the typeof operator (Table 4.1) carefully, you noticed that a value of type Object can represent a function. In fact, internally, JavaScript represents every function as an Object value. That is, when JavaScript processes a function declaration such as the one for objArgs(), it creates a specialized object that represents the function. A variable that has the same name as the function is also created, and a reference to the function object is assigned to this variable. Thus, when the program of Figure 4.9 is executed, it automatically creates a variable named objArgs that is a reference to an Object value representing the function objArgs().

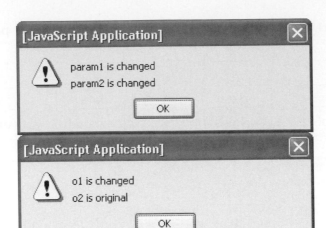

FIGURE 4.11 The two output alert windows produced by running `ObjArg.js`.

A *method* in JavaScript is simply a function that has been assigned as the value of a property of an object. For example, consider the JavaScript code of Figure 4.12, which creates a node object that could be suitable for use in a binary search tree data structure (see Section 4.10.7 for more on binary search trees). The code begins by declaring a function named `leaf()` that returns `true` exactly when a node represents a leaf (i.e., when both its `left` and `right` properties have the value `null`). As just noted, this function declaration also creates a variable named `leaf` that contains a reference to the object representing the function. The program subsequently contains the statement

```
node.isLeaf = leaf;
```

This creates a property named `isLeaf` and assigns to it a reference to the `leaf` function object. In other words, this creates a method on the `node` object. Although the method name can be the same as the function name, this is not necessary. The `isLeaf()` method is called later in the program with expressions such as

```
node1.isLeaf()
```

If you run the program, you'll see that the first node is not a leaf and the second one is a leaf.

As illustrated in the body of `leaf()`, the JavaScript keyword `this` is used to allow a method to access other properties of the object to which the method is assigned. That is, if `this` is used in an expression in the body of a function that is a method on some object, then when the method is called, `this` will evaluate to a reference to the object. So, when the `isLeaf()` method is called on `node1` causing `leaf()` to be called, the expression `this` within `leaf()` evaluates to a reference to `node1`.

```
// NodeWithMethod.js

// leaf() returns true iff this node is a leaf node.
// It is designed to be called as a method, not directly
// as a function.
function leaf() {
  return this.left == null && this.right == null;
}

// makeBTNode(value) creates a binary tree node and
// initializes its value to the given argument.
// It also adds an isLeaf() method to the node.
function makeBTNode(value) {
  var node = new Object();
  node.left = node.right = null;
  node.value = value;
  node.isLeaf = leaf;
  return node;
}

// Create and initialize two node objects, making the second
// a child of the first.
var node1 = makeBTNode(3);
var node2 = makeBTNode(7);
node1.right = node2;

// Output the value of isLeaf() on each node
window.alert("node1 is a leaf: " + node1.isLeaf());
window.alert("node2 is a leaf: " + node2.isLeaf());
```

FIGURE 4.12 Program that creates a node object containing a `clear()` method.

Notice that the function `leaf()` is declared as a function but is intended to be used only as a method, not a function. To make this intention clear (which could be helpful to someone else maintaining this program, for example), it would be better if we could avoid declaring the function at all and instead simply create a method directly. In fact, we can do this by removing the declaration of `leaf()` and replacing the assignment to `node.isLeaf` as follows:

```
// NodeWithMethod2.js
// Remove leaf() declaration found in NodeWithMethod.js
...
  node.isLeaf =
    function leaf() {
      return this.left == null && this.right == null;
    };
```

When a `function` keyword appears where an expression is expected, such as on the right-hand side of an assignment statement, it marks the beginning of a *function expression*. Such an expression evaluates to an Object value representing a function, just as a function declaration does. However, a key difference is that the scripting engine does not create a variable for the object created by a function expression. Therefore, if we create the isLeaf() method using a function expression, then it is no longer possible to to call leaf() directly.

I should explain one syntactic aspect of this code: Notice that there is a semicolon following the final closing brace of the leaf() function expression. This semicolon marks the end of the statement that assigns a value to the isLeaf property. While JavaScript does not always require this (since the syntax rules often allow semicolons to be omitted), it's good practice to include it.

One final note: If a function declares a local variable and also evaluates a function expression, and if the function expression contains a reference to the local variable, then the local variable will continue to exist after the function declaring the variable returns.

4.10.6 Constructors

The function makeBTNode() in the previous example acts as a kind of constructor for objects representing nodes in a binary search tree. While this code is fairly simple, it can be made even simpler by using JavaScript's constructor mechanism.

Figure 4.13 illustrates the use of a JavaScript constructor. It will help you to read this code if you understand that every function can be called not only as a function and as

```
// BTNode.js

// BTNode(value) is a constructor for a binary tree node.
// It initializes its value to the given argument.
// It also adds an isLeaf() method to the node.
function BTNode(value) {
  // Notice that we no longer need to create an Object
  // and that we use "this" to reference the object
  // initialized.
  this.left = this.right = null;
  this.value = value;
  this.isLeaf =
    function leaf() {
      return this.left == null && this.right == null;
    };
  // Notice that we no longer return a value.
}
// Create and initialize two node objects, making the second
// a child of the first.
// Notice the use of "new" to call a function as a constructor.
var node1 = new BTNode(3);
var node2 = new BTNode(7);
node1.right = node2;

// Output the value of isLeaf() on each node
window.alert("node1 is a leaf: " + node1.isLeaf());
window.alert("node2 is a leaf: " + node2.isLeaf());
```

FIGURE 4.13 Program that defines and uses an object constructor.

a method, but also as a constructor. That is, every JavaScript function you declare is also automatically a constructor. Therefore, the BTNode() function declared at the beginning of Figure 4.13 can be used as a constructor, even though its declaration is no different than any other function declaration.

You tell the scripting engine that you want to call a function as a constructor by prefixing the call with the new keyword. Thus, in the statements initializing node1 and node2, we are calling BTNode() as a constructor rather than as a standard function. When a function is called as a constructor, the scripting engine automatically creates an empty object and associates the this keyword with this object within the body of the function. This is why we do not need to explicitly create an object in the BTNode() function as we did in the earlier makeBTNode() function. This is also why we use the keyword this in the assignment statements in the body of BTNode().

Finally, although the BTNode() function does not return a value, each new expression used to call this function as a constructor will return as its value the object that was automatically created by the scripting engine and initialized by the code in the body of BTNode(). So, as before, the output of this program will show that the first node is not a leaf and the second is.

Thus, although JavaScript does not have a class concept exactly like that found in Java and C++, we see that the constructor mechanism can be used to provide somewhat similar functionality. In fact, when we construct an object in JavaScript using new, the constructed object is known as an *instance* of the function (object) used as the constructor. In the preceding example, we could call node1 and node2 instances of BTNode. The JavaScript instanceof operator can be used to test whether one object is an instance of another object. For example, adding the code

```
// Test that node1 is an instance of BTNode
window.alert("node1 is instance of BTNode: " +
          (node1 instanceof BTNode));
```

to the end of the BTNode.js file produces the output node1 is instance of BTNode: true.

4.10.7   Example: Binary Tree

We'll end this section on JavaScript objects by writing code for creating and using a simple binary search tree. Recall that in a binary tree, every node has a left and a right child, although either or both children may be empty (null). In a binary search tree, each node N has the property that all values (if any) stored in nodes in the left subtree of N are smaller than N's value, and all values stored in its right subtree are larger than N's value. Therefore, we can search to see whether or not a value is stored in such a tree by first comparing the search value with the root node's value. If the values match, we're done. Otherwise, if the search value is smaller than the root value, we continue our search in the left subtree, because we know that the search value must be there if it is in the tree at all. Similarly, we need only search the right subtree if the search value is larger than the root value.

Figures 4.14 and 4.15 show JavaScript code for a constructor function SearchTree() that creates a binary search tree object having methods insert() and search(). The

```
// SearchTree.js (part 1)

// Constructor for BTNode objects
function BTNode(value) {
...
}

// Constructor for SearchTree objects
function SearchTree() {

  /**** Variables ****/
  this.root = null;

  /**** Methods ****/

  // locate(value) returns a reference to the node
  // containing the value if the given value is in the search tree,
  // returns null if the search tree is empty,
  // and otherwise returns a reference to the node that
  // should be this value's parent.
  // This method is only intended to be used by other
  // methods, not called directly.
  this.locate =
    function locate(value) {
      var curr = this.root;  // Node currently being visited
      var parent = null;     // Parent of current node
      // Search for value, remembering parent nodes
      while (curr != null && curr.value != value) {
        parent = curr;
        if (value < parent.value) {
          curr = parent.left;
        }
        else {
          curr = parent.right;
        }
      }

      // If curr is null, we did not locate the value.
      // Return parent (which is null if tree is empty) instead.
      if (curr == null) {
        curr = parent;
      }
      return curr;
    };
```

FIGURE 4.14 Initial portion of program for creating a binary search tree.

insert() method first searches for the value to be inserted and, if the value is not found, creates a BTNode (using the constructor of Figure 4.13). It then inserts this node into an appropriate location so that the tree retains the binary search property described in the preceding paragraph. Both methods rely on another method named locate() that performs the actual search for a value in the tree and returns a value that either indicates that the search

```
// SearchTree.js (part 2)

    // insert(value) adds the given value to the search
    // tree if it is not already present.
    this.insert =
      function insert(value) {

        // Search for location of value or its parent
        var location = this.locate(value);

        // If value is not present (location is non-null
        // and location.value is not same as given value),
        // then create a node containing the value
        // and insert it at the appropriate location.
        var node = new BTNode(value);
        if (location == null) { // Empty tree
          this.root = node;
        }
        else if (location.value != value) { // location is parent
          if (value < location.value) {
            location.left = node;
          }
          else {
            location.right = node;
          }
        }
      };

    // search(value) returns true iff the given value is
    // present in the tree
    this.search =
      function search(value) {

        // Search for location of value or its parent
        var location = this.locate(value);

        // Found value iff location is not null and value
        // of location is the given value
        return location != null && location.value == value;
      };
}
```

FIGURE 4.15 Remainder of constructor for binary search tree program.

succeeded or provides information that can be used to insert the value into the appropriate location within the tree. Figure 4.16 then shows code that constructs a tree, inserts values into the tree, and searches the tree. When run, this code will indicate that the value 12 is contained in the tree but that 6 is not.

This program illustrates several points. First, notice that a method can declare local variables (such as curr in locate()) just like any other function, and that these variables are referenced within a method just as they would be within a normal function.

```
// SearchTree.js (part 3)

// Create a search tree and insert values
var tree = new SearchTree();
tree.insert(7);
tree.insert(3);
tree.insert(12);
tree.insert(12); // Try inserting a second time

// Search the tree
window.alert("Search for 12 produces " + tree.search(12));
window.alert("Search for 6 produces " + tree.search(6));
```

FIGURE 4.16 Code for using binary search tree constructor and calling methods on constructed tree object.

Second, note that if one method (such as `insert()`) wants to call another method (such as `locate()`) of the same object, the call must be prefixed with `this`. Otherwise, the scripting engine would interpret a call without the leading `this`—such as `locate(value)`—as a call to a regular function and not to a method. Third, notice that although `locate()` is intended to be called only by other methods within a `SearchTree` object, there is no `private` declaration in JavaScript to enforce such an intention. Since most JavaScript programs are small, this simplification compared with Java and C++ is a reasonable trade-off.

Although the test program in Figure 4.16 uses integer values for nodes, notice that `SearchTree` and `BTNode` objects can accommodate values of any type. In fact, values of different types can be stored in a single `SearchTree`, because JavaScript's comparison operators (`!=`, `<`, etc.) can be used to compare arbitrary data types, as explained in Section 4.7. However, note that because the code uses the nonstrict equality operators `!=` and `==`, values belonging to two different data types might map to a single node. For example, if the statement

```
window.alert('Search for "3" produces ' + tree.search("3"));
```

is added to the end of the `SearchTree.js` program, this search will evaluate to `true`, even though no node in the tree contains the String value 3. We could avoid this effect by using the strict equality operators `!==` and `===` in place of the nonstrict operators in the comparisons involving the `value` property of `BTNode`'s.

4.11 Arrays

We learned earlier that all object properties can be accessed using an arraylike notation, and that objects can therefore be viewed as associative arrays. In addition, JavaScript supplies a native function object named `Array` that can be used to construct objects that have special array characteristics and that inherit a number of array-oriented methods. In this section, we'll learn more about creating and using `Array` instances, which we'll refer to simply as *arrays*.

4.11.1   Creating an Array

One way to create an array is to use the `Array` constructor directly in a call with no arguments:

```
var ary1 = new Array();
```

Alternatively, an array can be constructed and initialized with values by supplying two or more arguments to the `Array` constructor:

```
var ary2 = new Array(4, true, "OK");
```

After this statement is executed, `ary2[0]` will have the Number value 4, `ary2[1]` the Boolean value `true`, and `ary2[2]` the String value `OK`. Keep in mind that array notation is just a way of specifying the name of a property in JavaScript. So an expression such as `ary2[0]` evaluates to the value of the property with the name 0 (a String consisting of a single numeric character) belonging to the object referenced by the variable `ary2`. On the other hand, attempting to execute the expression `ary2.0` would generate a syntax error in JavaScript. This is because an identifier must be used for the property name in dot notation, and the syntax rules for identifiers require that they must not begin with a numeric character. There is, however, no such restriction on the actual names that can be used for properties: any string can be used.

I will refer to properties of an array object that have names that are string representations of natural numbers as the *elements* of the array. So `ary2` in the second example has three elements immediately after the `Array` constructor is executed. An array object can also have other nonelement properties. In fact, every array object is automatically given a special property named `length`. When an array is constructed with a no-argument constructor (as in the case of `ary1` in the first example), the value of `length` will be 0. When constructed with two or more arguments, `length` is set to the number of arguments. Thus, after the statement creating the variable `ary2`, `ary2.length` will have the value 3. We'll have more to say about this property in the next section.

Another way to create and initialize an array that produces identical results to those of the previous example is

```
var ary3 = [4, true, "OK"];
```

An expression such as the one on the right side of the assignment in this example is called an *array initializer*. This is essentially a shorthand that implicitly calls the `Array` constructor for us.

The elements of a JavaScript array can be any JavaScript values, including other instances of `Array`. This feature can be used to create multidimensional arrays. For example, one way to create a two-dimensional array is

```
// array2d.js
var ttt = [ [ "X", "O", "O" ],
            [ "O", "X", "O" ],
            [ "O", "X", "X" ] ];
```

In this example, the outer one-dimensional array (named `ttt`) contains three elements, each itself a one-dimensional array. The notation `ttt[1]` will evaluate to a reference to the second of these internal arrays (the 0 x 0 array). Since this is an array object itself, the notation `ttt[1][2]` will evaluate to the value of the third element of this array, 0. Higher-dimensional arrays can be created and accessed similarly.

4.11.2 Dynamically Changing Array Length

Just as we can dynamically add properties to any JavaScript object, we can add properties to an array. In particular, in Section 4.11.1, we could follow the code creating `ary2` (which had three elements) with the statement

```
ary2[3] = -12.6;
```

This will create a new property named (as a String) 3 with the value -12.6. In addition, the `length` property of `ary2` will be changed to 4. Thus, unlike arrays in Java, the effective size of JavaScript arrays can change dynamically. In this way, JavaScript arrays are more like instances of the `java.util.Vector` class than they are like Java arrays.

Elements can also be removed from a JavaScript array by decreasing the value of the `length` property. For example, if we next executed the statement

```
ary2.length = 2;
```

then the properties 2 and 3 would automatically be removed from `ary2`.

While we're on the topic of the `length` property, let me mention a special case that might cause you trouble if you're not aware of it. If the `Array` constructor is called with a single Number argument, then this argument value is assigned to the `length` property but no array elements are actually created. As an example, the expression

```
new Array(200)
```

creates an array having `length` 200 but does not actually create or initialize the properties with names 0 through 199. Similarly, if you increase the `length` value of an array object, this does not automatically add any elements (properties with numeric names) to the array. Thus, your code should not assume that `length` always represents the actual number of elements in an array.

4.11.3 Array Methods

Every array object automatically inherits a number of useful methods. Many of these methods are described briefly in Table 4.7, and some additional details are given in this subsection. Full algorithmic details of every method are provided in Section 15.4.4 of the ECMAScript specification [ECMA-262].

The argument to the `sort()` method should be an object representing a function. This function in turn should take two arguments representing array elements and return a Number value. A negative return value indicates that the element corresponding to the first argument should come before the element corresponding to the second in the sorted array,

TABLE 4.7 Methods Inherited by Array Objects. Unless Otherwise Specified, Methods Return a Reference to the Array on Which They are Called.

Method	Description
toString()	Return a String value representing this array as a comma-separated list.
sort(Object)	Modify this array by sorting it, treating the Object argument as a function that specifies sort order (see text).
splice(Number, 0, any type)	Modify this array by adding the third argument as an element at the index given by the first argument, shifting elements up one index to make room for the new element.
splice(Number, Number)	Modify this array by removing a number of elements specified by the second argument (a positive integer), starting with the index specified by the first element, and shifting elements down to take the place of those elements removed. Returns an array of the elements removed.
push(any type)	Modify this array by appending an element having the given argument value. Returns length value for modified array.
pop()	Modify this array by removing its last element (the element at index length−1). Returns the value of the element removed.
shift()	Modify this array by removing its first element (the element at index 0) and shifting all remaining elements down one index. Returns the value of the element removed.

a positive value indicates that the second should come before the first, and 0 indicates that the elements can be in either order (for sorting purposes, they are equivalent). For example, in the program of Figure 4.17, the return value will be positive if the first argument is greater than the second and negative if the first is less than the second. This will result in an array of Number values being sorted into ascending order, as shown. Also notice that the argument to sort() can be a function expression rather than the name of a function declared elsewhere.

```
// ArrayMethods.js
var numArray = [1,3,8,4,9,7,6,2,5];

// Sort in ascending order
numArray.sort(
  function compare (first, second) {
    return first - second;
  }
);
// numArray.toString(): 1,2,3,4,5,6,7,8,9

numArray.splice(2, 0, 2.5);
// numArray.toString(): 1,2,2.5,3,4,5,6,7,8,9

// output of following: 5,6,7
window.alert(numArray.splice(5,3).toString());
// numArray.toString(): 1,2,2.5,3,4,8,9
window.alert(numArray.toString());
```

FIGURE 4.17 Program illustrating use of several of the methods inherited by array objects.

Figure 4.17 also illustrates two versions of the `splice()` method, which is used both for inserting an element into an array (and automatically making room for the new element by shifting other elements) and for removing one or more elements from an array (and automatically shifting other elements to take the place of those removed). Notice that the version of `splice()` that removes elements also returns an array containing the elements removed.

The `push()`, `pop()`, and `shift()` methods make it easy to implement basic stack and queue data structures using arrays (if you're not familiar with these data structures, you may want to either read about them in any textbook on data structures or skip the remainder of this section). In the case of a stack, the `length` property acts as the stack pointer, with an empty stack indicated by a 0 value. The following code illustrates usage of these methods to implement a stack:

```
// stack.js
var stack = new Array();

stack.push('H');
stack.push('i');
stack.push('!');

var c3 = stack.pop(); // pops '!'
var c2 = stack.pop(); // pops 'i'
var c1 = stack.pop(); // pops 'H'
window.alert(c1 + c2 + c3);  // displays "Hi!"
```

You can similarly implement a basic queue structure using `push()` to add elements to the end of the queue and `shift()` to remove elements from the front of the queue. In this case, `length` will point to the back of the queue, and the front of the queue will be at index 0. Other array methods can be used for additional functionality. For example, `splice()` could be used to insert an element at a location other than the end of the queue, which might be useful as part of an implementation of priority queues.

4.12   Built-in Objects

In this section, we will briefly overview several of JavaScript's built-in objects. Chapter 15 of the ECMAScript reference [ECMA-262] describes all built-in objects and should be consulted for details.

4.12.1   The Global Object (`window`)

In every JavaScript host environment, some object is designated as the *global object*. In common browsers, this object is named `window`. It is called the global object because, as mentioned earlier, all global variables declared by your program are actually stored as properties of this object. What's more, other built-in objects, such as `Object`, `Array`, and other objects described later, are also stored as properties of the global object. For example, the `Object` object is stored in `window.Object`.

Furthermore, all host objects are stored (directly or indirectly) as properties of the global object. I've emphasized this fact in the JavaScript code in this chapter by prefixing `window.` before the calls to the `alert()` and `prompt()` host methods. Usually, though, this isn't necessary, because if your code calls a function or refers to a variable and JavaScript can't locate the function or variable among your function declarations and local variables (and formal parameters, if the code is in a function body), then it will look for a property by the given name in the `window` object.

In addition to properties representing built-in and host objects, the global object contains several other useful properties. For instance, the global object property `Infinity` contains the Number value representing Infinity, which is sometimes useful (as an initial value in code for finding the minimum value in an array, for example). See the ECMAScript specification [ECMA-262] for additional global object properties.

4.12.2 String, Number, and Boolean

We're previously learned that JavaScript has built-in functions `String()`, `Number()`, and `Boolean()` that can be used to convert values to each of these data types. If any of these functions is called as a constructor, it will not only convert its argument value to the appropriate type if necessary, but will also wrap the converted value in an object that is an instance of the constructor object. For example,

```
// WrappedNumber.js
var wrappedNumber = new Number(5.625);
```

creates an object that is an instance of `Number`. This object will inherit certain methods associated with the `Number` object. One of these methods will be a version of `valueOf()` that returns the wrapped value (a value of type Number in the case of an instance of `Number`). So, for example, executing

```
// WrappedNumber.js (part 2)
window.alert(typeof wrappedNumber.valueOf());
```

will indicate that `wrappedNumber.valueOf()` is of type Number.

In addition to `valueOf()`, `Number` instances inherit several methods that can be used to format a numeric value for output purposes. For example,

```
// WrappedNumber.js (part 3)
window.alert(wrappedNumber.toFixed(2));
```

will output `5.63`, which is the value of the original number rounded to two decimal places. The `toExponential(Number)` method is similar:

```
// WrappedNumber.js (part 4)
window.alert(wrappedNumber.toExponential(2));
```

TABLE 4.8 Some of the Methods Inherited by `String` Instances

Method	Description
charAt(Number)	Return string consisting of single character at position (0-based) Number within this string.
concat(String)	Return concatenation of this string to String argument.
indexOf(String, Number)	Return location of leftmost occurrence of String within this string at or after character Number, or −1 if no occurrence exists.
replace(String, String)	Return string obtained by replacing first occurrence of first String in this string with second String.
slice(Number, Number)	Return substring of this string starting at location given by first Number and ending one character before location given by second Number.
toLowerCase()	Return this string with each character having a Unicode Standard lowercase equivalent replaced by that character.
toUpperCase()	Return this string with each character having a Unicode Standard uppercase equivalent replaced by that character.

will output 5.63e+0. Finally,

```
// WrappedNumber.js (part 5)
window.alert(wrappedNumber.toString(2));
```

outputs 101.101, which is 5.625 represented in binary (base 2). This method can be used to output a number in any standard number base, including base 8 (octal) and base 16 (hexadecimal).

The `Number` object itself also provides properties `Number.MIN_VALUE` and `Number.MAX_VALUE`, which contain values that are the smallest and largest (in absolute value) numbers that can be represented in JavaScript.

Every `String` instance has a property named `length`, which is a Number value representing the number of characters in the internal string value. In addition, instances of `String` inherit a number of methods, including those shown in Table 4.8. Note that none of these methods change the value of the `String` instance on which they are called. Instead, they return a value that uses the instance's underlying String value as an input.

Finally, JavaScript's automatic type conversion allows you to apply `String` and `Number` inherited methods directly to primitive values of type String and Number, respectively. For example, the following is syntactically legal JavaScript that will output `Str`:

```
// slicestring.js
var primitiveString = "a String value";
window.alert(primitiveString.slice(2,5));
```

When the scripting engine encounters this code, it automatically wraps the String value contained in `primitiveString` within a `String` object instance, since the String value is being used where an Object value is expected (preceding a dot). Thus, the code given is a shorthand for

```
// slicestring.js (part 2)
window.alert((new String(primitiveString)).slice(2,5));
```

In fact, you can even use a string literal as the "object" on which a String method is called:

```
// slicestring.js (part 3)
window.alert("a String value".slice(2,5));
```

4.12.3 Date

The expression

```
new Date()
```

returns an instance of the built-in Date object representing the current date and time on the host machine (which, when JavaScript is run within a browser, is the machine running the browser). Date instances can be used for a variety of purposes. One common use is to generate a string representing the current date and time in the user's time zone; this string can then be displayed in the browser (using techniques discussed in Chapter 5) to make a web page appear fresh. The inherited toLocaleString() method, when called on a Date instance, returns a date/time string formatted according to the conventions used in the user's location (as determined by browser settings). Alternatively, toLocaleDateString() and toLocaleTimeString() can be used to obtain only the date or time, respectively. Other methods allow you to extract the year, month, day within the month or week, hour, and so on. See Section 15.9.5 of the ECMAScript reference [ECMA-262] for a complete list of inherited methods.

Another use of Date instances is to determine how much time has elapsed between two events. For example, consider the following JavaScript code:

```
// ElapsedTime.js

var startTime = new Date();

// Perform some processing
...

var endTime = new Date();
window.alert("Processing required " +
             (endTime - startTime)/1000 +
             " seconds.");
```

Recall that when JavaScript attempts to perform arithmetic involving Object values (such as Date instances), it first casts the objects to Number values by calling valueOf() on each object. The valueOf() method inherited by a Date instance returns an integer representing the number of milliseconds that have elapsed between the date and time represented by the instance and a certain fixed date and time (midnight universal (UTC) time on January 1, 1970). So taking the difference of two Date instances gives the number of milliseconds that have elapsed from the date and time represented by the first instance to the date and time of the second. Dividing this difference by 1000 gives the elapsed time in seconds.

Similarly, if `date1` and `date2` are `Date` instances, then the following code will execute the block statement controlled by the if statement only if the date and time represented by `date1` is prior to that represented by `date2`:

```
if (date1 < date2) { ... }
```

You should understand why this code works in view of the preceding discussion. It's worth noting that to compare dates in Java requires a method call. Thus, this code once again illustrates how intuitive JavaScript code can be due to its use of automatic type conversion.

4.12.4 Math

The `Math` object is like the global object in that you do not construct instances from it, but instead you call methods directly on it. For instance, to perform a square root operation, you can use an expression such as

```
Math.sqrt(15.3)
```

All of the methods of this object are listed in Table 4.9. In addition to these methods, `Math` has several properties with values of type Number, including `E` and `PI`, which represent

TABLE 4.9 Methods of the Math Built-in Object

Method	Return Value
`abs(Number)`	Absolute value of Number
`acos(Number)`	Arc cosine of Number (treated as radians)
`asin(Number)`	Arcsine of Number
`atan(Number)`	Arctangent of Number (range `-Math.PI/2` to `Math.PI/2`)
`atan2(Number, Number)`	Arctangent of first Number divided by second (range `-Math.PI` to `Math.PI`)
`ceil(Number)`	Smallest integer no greater than Number
`cos(Number)`	Cosine of Number (in radians)
`exp(Number)`	`Math.E` raised to power Number
`floor(Number)`	Largest integer no less than Number
`log(Number)`	Natural logarithm of Number
`max(Number, Number, ...)`	Maximum of given values
`min(Number, Number, ...)`	Minimum of given values
`pow(Number, Number)`	First Number raised to power of second Number
`random()`	Pseudo-random floating point number in range 0 to 1
`round(Number)`	Nearest integer value to Number
`sin(Number)`	Sine of Number
`sqrt(Number)`	Square root of Number
`tan(Number)`	Tangent of Number

the base of the natural logarithm and the ratio of the circumference to the diameter of a circle, respectively.

4.12.5 RegExp

JavaScript provides regular expression capabilities through instances of the built-in `RegExp` object. A *regular expression* is a certain way of representing a set of strings. Regular expressions are frequently used to test that a string entered in an HTML form has a certain format, or, in the terminology of regular expressions, belongs to the set of strings that have the correct format.

As a simple example, the set of strings that consist of exactly three digits—which might represent, for example, the set of valid area codes in a phone number—can be represented by the JavaScript regular expression

```
\d\d\d
```

In a JavaScript regular expression, the string `\d` stands for the set of digit characters 0 through 9. Concatenating this string with itself three times as shown represents the set of all possible strings of three consecutive digits.

We could use this regular expression as follows to test whether or not a String value contained in a variable named `areaCode` consists of exactly three digits:

```
var acTest = new RegExp("^\\d\\d\\d$");
if (!acTest.test(areaCode)) {
  window.alert(areaCode + " is not a valid area code.");
}
```

(We'll soon see why this regular expression doesn't look exactly like the preceding one.) The `test()` method of a `RegExp` instance returns `true` if its String argument is a member of the set of strings represented by the instance's regular expression, and returns `false` otherwise. In this example, we want to output a message if `areaCode` is not in the set of valid area codes, so we complement the value returned by `test()` in the condition of the `if` statement.

There are several differences between the string argument supplied to the `RegExp()` constructor and the regular expression given earlier. First, there are more backslash characters (\\) in the string. This is because, within a String literal, the backslash character is normally used to begin an escape code used to represent some Unicode character (Section 4.8). But within a regular expression the backslash is used to represent, not a Unicode character, but a special subexpression within the larger regular expression. Therefore, when a backslash appears in a String literal as part of a regular expression, the backslash must be escaped by preceding it with another backslash.

The other difference is that the string argument passed to `RegExp()` begins with a caret (^) and ends with a dollar sign ($). These are necessary because of the way JavaScript interprets the argument to `RegExp()`. Specifically, although the regular expression `\d\d\d` represents strings *consisting of* three consecutive digits, when it is passed to `RegExp()` it is treated as though it represents all strings *containing* three consecutive digits. The caret and dollar sign characters can be used to override this `RegExp()` interpretation.

In particular, in a JavaScript regular expression, the caret and dollar sign characters represent the beginning and end of a string, respectively. Thus, the argument represents any string in which the beginning of the string is immediately followed by three consecutive digits, the last of which is immediately followed by the end of the string. These characters can be used for other purposes as well. For example, if we removed the dollar sign from the argument to RegExp we obtain

```
var acTest = new RegExp("^\\d\\d\\d");
```

which represents the set of all strings that begin with three digits.

JavaScript provides an alternate syntax for creating a RegExp instance that avoids the need to duplicate backslashes. For example, the preceding declaration of acTest can be rewritten as

```
var acTest = /^\d\d\d/;
```

The expression on the right-hand side of the assignment is known as a *regular expression literal*. The scripting engine conceptually converts such an expression to a call to the RegExp() constructor, automatically escaping any backslash characters contained in the regular expression literal. Notice that it is still necessary to use the caret and/or dollar sign characters if you desire to override the RegExp() treatment of regular expressions. JavaScript regular expressions are normally written using this literal syntax.

Now that you know something about what regular expressions are and how they can be used in a JavaScript program, the remainder of this section will discuss several regular expression features that are frequently used in browser-based JavaScript programs. Refer to the ECMAScript reference [ECMA-262], particularly Section 15.10, for complete details.

The simplest form of regular expression is a character that is not one of the regular expression special characters, which are

```
^ $ \ . * + ? ( ) [ ] { } |
```

For example, underscore (_) is not one of the special characters, so _ is the regular expression that represents the set of all strings that contain the underscore character. A special character is escaped by preceding it with a backslash. As an example, \$$ represents the set of strings that end with a dollar sign.

Another simple regular expression is the period (dot) ., which represents any character except for a line terminator. In other words, dot is the wildcard character in regular expressions. *Escape code* regular expressions, such as \d, similarly represent multiple characters. Table 4.10 lists all of the JavaScript escape codes representing multiple characters.

Simple regular expressions can be composed into more complex regular expressions using one of three types of operators. We've already seen an example of the first of these operators, *concatenation*. In general, the concatenation of two regular expressions represents the set of strings that consist of any string represented by the first regular expression concatenated with any string represented by the second expression. Thus,

```
^\d\. \w$
```

TABLE 4.10 JavaScript Multicharacter Escape Codes

Escape Code	Characters Represented
\d	Digit: 0 through 9
\D	Any character except those matched by \d
\s	Space: any JavaScript white space or line terminator (space, tab, line feed, etc.)
\S	Any character except those matched by \s
\w	"Word" character: any letter (a through z and A through Z), digit (0 through 9), or underscore (_)
\W	Any character except those matched by \w

represents the set of strings beginning with a single digit followed immediately by a period, a space, and terminating a "word" character (letter, digit, or underscore). Notice that white space is significant within a regular expression. For instance, the set of strings represented by the last regular expression does not include either of the strings

3.A   or   7. J

—the first because it has no space, and the second because it has two spaces.

When we want to concatenate a regular expression with itself multiple times, we can use the *quantifier* shorthand notation. For example, the set of all strings of exactly three digits is represented by the regular expression

\d{3}

This notation, viewed as a postfix unary operator, has higher precedence than both concatenation and union (discussed next). Therefore,

-\d{3}

represents strings that begin with a - followed by three digits.

The second regular expression operator is *union*, which is represented by the pipe symbol |. For example,

\d|\s

represents the set consisting of all digit and white space characters. The concatenation operator takes precedence over union, so the set of strings represented by the regular expression

\+|-\d|\s

consists of + (escaped because it is a special character), the two-character strings beginning with - followed by a digit, and the white space characters. The default precedence can be overridden using parentheses. Thus,

```
(\+|-)\d|\s
```

represents the set of two-character strings beginning with either a + or – followed by a digit plus the white space characters.

It would be tedious (and error prone) to use the union notation directly to represent a set such as the set of all lowercase letters. JavaScript provides a *character class* notation that can be used for such purposes. For instance, the set of lowercase letters can be represented by

```
[a-z]
```

Similarly, the escape code \w is equivalent to the regular expression

```
[a-zA-Z0-9]|_
```

Notice that, while - is not normally a special character in regular expressions, it is special within a character class and must be escaped by a preceding backslash in order to represent the - character itself.

A variation of the quantifier notation can be used to represent unions of concatenations. For example,

```
\d{3,6}
```

is shorthand for any string of from three through six digits, that is,

```
\d\d\d|\d\d\d\d|\d\d\d\d\d|\d\d\d\d\d\d
```

By definition, zero concatenations of any string with itself results in the empty string. Thus, the regular expression

```
(\+|-){0,1}\d
```

represents the set of strings that begin with either the empty string or a plus or minus sign, followed by a digit. In other words, the leading sign character is optional. JavaScript uses the symbol ? for this purpose. That is to say, the quantifier {0,1} occurs so often that it has its own shorthand symbol, ?. Therefore, the expression displayed would normally be written as

```
(\+|-)?\d
```

So far, the regular expressions we've seen have all represented finite sets of strings. The final operator, the *Kleene star*, allows us to represent infinitely large sets. For example, the regular expression

```
\d*
```

represents the set of strings of any number of digits, including the string of no digits at all (the empty string). In general, the Kleene star following a regular expression represents the set created by concatenating strings from the original set with one another an arbitrary number of times. This postfix unary operator has the highest precedence of all regular expression operators.

For example, assume that a certain application requires the use of passwords and that each password must contain at least one digit and at least one letter and may only contain digits, letters, and underscores. The following is a JavaScript regular expression that represents the set of valid passwords for this application:

```
\w*(\d\w*[a-zA-Z]|[a-zA-Z]\w*\d)\w*
```

4.13   JavaScript Debuggers

At this point, you should know quite a bit about writing JavaScript programs. We'll now briefly learn about debugging JavaScript programs using interactive debugging software. I'll also mention some of the ways in which JavaScript debugging differs from, say, Java debugging.

The first question is whether or not you already have a debugger and, if not, where to obtain one. If you are debugging your JavaScript code using IE6, your system may or may not already have a debugger present. To find out, select **Tools|Internet Options ...** from the IE6 menu and click on the Advanced tab in the popup window that appears. Make sure that the checkbox for "Disable Script Debugging (Internet Explorer)" is unchecked, and click the OK button in the pop-up. Now load a JavaScript program into IE6 that has an error in it (the file error.js, available at the textbook Web site, can be used). If a pop-up window appears asking if you would like to debug, then you have a debugger installed. Otherwise, Microsoft provides a free Script Debugger that is currently available at http://msdn.microsoft.com/downloads/list/webdev.asp.

On the other hand, if you are debugging using Mozilla and you downloaded Mozilla according to the instructions in Appendix A, then you automatically have an interactive JavaScript debugger named Venkman. Since Venkman can be run on all major operating systems, I'll use it as a specific example in this section. Other interactive debuggers, such as Microsoft's Script Debugger, generally have similar features, although of course details will differ. You should see the manufacturer's documentation for your debugger for complete details. For Venkman, the documentation can be accessed through the Venkman **Help** menu.

To debug a JavaScript program with the Venkman debugger, begin by starting Mozilla and then opening the debugger window (Figure 4.18) by selecting **Tools|Web Development|JavaScript Debugger** from the Mozilla menu. Next, in the browser window, open the HTML document that loads the JavaScript program to be debugged. The Loaded Scripts panel in the upper left portion of the debugger window will display the name of your JavaScript file. Right-clicking the file name and selecting Find File from the pop-up context menu then loads the file into the source code panel in the upper right portion of the debugger window.

Figure 4.18 shows the Venkman debugger window after I loaded the TestJs.html document into Mozilla and then entered LocalScope.js when prompted. TestJs.html

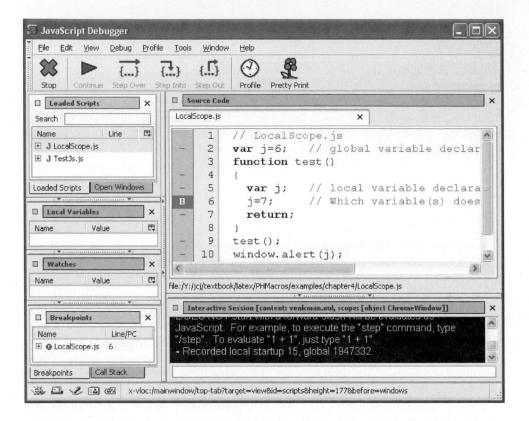

FIGURE 4.18   The Venkman JavaScript debugger with a breakpoint set in a loaded JavaScript file.

loaded TestJs.js, which in turn loaded LocalScope.js. Thus, the Loaded Scripts panel shows two JavaScript files. I then selected LocalScope.js for debugging as just described. Next, I set a *breakpoint* on line 6 of this file by clicking to the left of the line number, which caused a B to appear where I clicked. The breakpoint is also listed in the Breakpoints panel at the bottom left of the debugger window.

Now if I return to my browser window, reload it, and again enter LocalScope.js when prompted, the scripting engine will *break* (pause) just before executing line 6 of LocalScope.js. I can then use the Step buttons to step through the code one line at a time. The Step Over button causes the scripting engine to execute until reaching the next line of code within the current file, so this would take me to line 7 of LocalScope.js. The Step Into button behaves similarly unless the current line is a call to a user-defined function or method, in which case the scripting engine enters that function or method and then breaks. Step Out, on the other hand, executes a function or method until it has returned to the calling statement, at which point a break occurs. Clicking Step Out after the break at line 6 of LocalScope.js will cause the scripting engine to execute until reaching the end of line 9, the statement that called the test() function containing line 6. These Step buttons enable you to carefully examine the flow of control through the program. Alternatively, clicking on Continue will cause the scripting engine to execute until either another breakpoint or the end of the program is reached.

In addition to control flow, we are often interested in examining the values of variables as a program executes. The Local Variables panel in Venkman provides this information, but in a way that is somewhat confusing due to JavaScript's internal representation of variables. To begin with, I suggest clicking on the small box in the upper left corner of the Local Variables panel; this will float the panel out into a separate window that can be independently resized (Figure 4.19).

As shown in Figure 4.19, the Local Variables panel has just two top-level variables: scope and this. This particular figure shows the local variables at the time of the break at line 6 of LocalScope.js. When local variables are examined in the midst of executing a function or method, scope represents an object that contains the local variables and formal parameters of the function as properties. So the j under scope represents the local variable declared at line 5 of LocalScope.js. The variable's value is shown as void (Venkman's representation of the Undefined value) because line 6 has not yet been executed, so the local j has not yet been assigned a value. If we view Local Variables at a point in the execution that is outside all functions and methods, then scope will represent the window (global) object. Similarly, except when executing a method, this represents the window object. In a method, as mentioned earlier, this represents the object on which the method is called.

What about global variables? As indicated earlier, global variables are stored as properties of the window object. Therefore, if either scope or this represents the window object, then all global variables will appear as properties and can be examined by clicking the + to the left of the object name. So, in this example, we would find the global j (with value 6) as a property under the this object. However, be warned that window is given a great many other properties automatically, so your program's global variables will not be immediately apparent. If neither scope nor this represents the window object (which is the case if a method is being executed), then the window property under the this object will represent the global object and can be examined for the values of global variables.

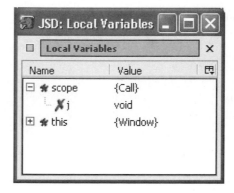

FIGURE 4.19 The Venkman Local Variables panel floated into a separate window.

4.14 References

The primary reference for this chapter, of course, is the ECMAScript 3.0 Language Specification [ECMA-262]. A good starting point for information about Mozilla's implementation of JavaScript is `http://www.mozilla.org/docs/web-developer/#scripting`, while `http://msdn.microsoft.com/library/en-us/script56/html/js56jsoriJScript.asp` provides links to both tutorial and reference information on Microsoft's JScript language.

Be advised that many JavaScript references on the Web are not just about the JavaScript language itself, but also about how JavaScript interacts with web browsers. Such material will probably make more sense once you have read the next chapter.

Exercises

4.1. While the value of the Null data type is represented by the JavaScript keyword `null`, the Undefined type has no associated keyword in the JavaScript language. Assume that the variable `testVar` has been declared in a JavaScript program. Write JavaScript code that could be inserted into this program that will output the string `undefined` if `testVar` has the Undefined type's value and output `defined` otherwise.

4.2. What is output if the following JavaScript program is executed by a typical web browser? Explain.

```
var i=5;
function duh()
{
    var i;
    window.i=6;
}
duh();
window.alert(i);
```

4.3. To what does the following JavaScript expression evaluate? Explain in detail how JavaScript arrives at this result.

```
Number("007") == "007"
```

4.4. What is output if the following JavaScript program is executed by a typical web browser? Explain.

```
var o1 = new Object();
o1.j = 9;
var o2 = o1;
function test(o1)
{
  o1.j=10;
  return;
}
test(o1);
window.alert(o2.j);
```

4.5. Write JavaScript code that will create an Object with a property named `color` having a String value of red.

4.6. JavaScript code used by a Web document must be in a file that can be read by anyone who can access the document. In an attempt to keep others from using their code, some JavaScript authors *obfuscate* their code—that is, attempt to reduce the intelligibility of their code—in various ways. What does the following obfuscated code do, and why?

```
var weird = "al" + "father".slice(4, 6) + "t";
window[weird]("Weird, but it works.");
```

4.7. Insert parentheses in the following expression in order to make the operator precedence relationships clear.

```
a = b ? z /= y ? x : w ? v : u : d += e
```

4.8. Some applications, such as random number generators and certain cryptographic algorithms, are explicitly designed to use arithmetic *overflow* as part of their computation. An overflow can occur in Java, for example, when two large int's are multiplied together and the result is stored in an int. If the result of the multiplication exceeds 32 bits, only the lower 32 bits are stored (recall that a Java int stores 32 bits, with the most significant being the sign bit). The higher-order bits, including the original sign bit, are lost, and the new most-significant bit becomes the new sign bit. Explain how such an overflow can be simulated in JavaScript using one of the JavaScript bit operators.

4.9. Consider the following JavaScript program:

```
function addTo(value) {
  myVar += value;
  return;
}
// Create an object with property myVar
// and method addTo
var o = new Object();
o.myVar = 0;
o.addTo = addTo;
// Call the addTo method
o.addTo(12);
```

This program will throw an exception. Which statement causes the exception? Why? How should this code be corrected?

4.10. What is the output of the following JavaScript program? Explain why this output is produced.

```
function rusty(a) {
  this.x = a;
  return;
}
var o1 = new Object();
var o2 = new Object();
o1.rusty = rusty;
o2.rusty = o1.rusty;
o1.rusty(1);
o2.rusty(2);
window.alert(o1.x + "," + o2.x);
```

FIGURE 4.20   Output produced by drawGrid() when passed ttt array as an argument.

4.11. Write a JavaScript function drawGrid() that takes a two-dimensional array as its sole argument. Your function should produce an alert box that displays the array with grid lines separating the elements. For example, Figure 4.20 shows the output when the function is called with the array ttt of Section 4.11.1. While this array is rectangular, your function should work for ragged arrays as well (a two-dimensional array is *ragged* if the one-dimensional arrays that compose it are not all of the same length).

4.12. Write a function median() that accepts a one-dimensional array containing an odd number of integers as its single argument and returns the median value stored in the array (this is the value of the middle element of a sorted version of the array). The argument array should not be modified.

4.13. Using a RegExp instance, write a JavaScript function isValid() that accepts a String argument and returns true if the argument matches one of the following phone-number formats and returns false otherwise:

```
(123)456-7890
(123) 456-7890
123/456-7890
123-456-7890
123 456 7890
1234567890
```

Research and Exploration

4.14. If a JavaScript program attempts to access the value of a variable that does not exist, the scripting engine will throw an exception. For what inputs will the following program throw an exception, and why?

```
var answer = window.prompt("Enter a number", "");
if (answer < 0) {
  isNeg = true;
}
window.alert("Number is negative: " + isNeg);
```

Will the program still throw an exception if the statement

```
var isNeg;
```

is appended following the call to alert()? Why or why not? Answer the same questions if instead of appending this statement the body of the if statement is changed to

```
var isNeg = true;
```

4.15. When a function is called, it automatically has access to an object named arguments that represents the arguments passed to the function. Read about this object in Section 10.1.8 of the ECMAScript reference [ECMA-262], and then write a JavaScript function summer that accepts any number of arguments of type Number and returns the sum of all the numbers. For example,

```
summer(5, 3, -6, 1)
```

should return the value 3. Calling the function with no arguments—summer()—should return 0.

4.16. Use the toString() method inherited by Number instances to convert a number to hexadecimal. Experiment with your code in the browser(s) assigned by your instructor and report on the format of the string produced, noting details such as the case of letters and how the base of the number is represented, if at all. Also experiment with some other common number bases (such as 2 and 8) as well as at least one uncommon base (such as 24), and report on the results.

4.17. Every user-defined JavaScript function is an instance of the built-in object Function and inherits certain properties as a result. One of the inherited properties is a method (function object) named call(). Read Section 15.3.4.4 of [ECMA-262] and then explain what the following code does:

```
function simple () {
  this.count = 10;
}
var anObj = new Object();
simple.call(anObj);
```

(Note: In [ECMA-262] terminology, every Object that represents a function has a [[Call]] property, which can be thought of as containing the code for the function. Also, ToObject() represents an internal JavaScript function that converts its argument to an Object as explained in Section 4.12.2.)

4.18. A JavaScript program can direct the scripting engine to execute on a string that is created at run time by calling the built-in eval() function. For example,

```
var expr = window.prompt("Enter an arithmetic expression", "");
window.alert(eval(expr));
```

will prompt the user to enter an arithmetic expression (such as 3 + 5 * 2) and will then output the value of this expression (13 in this example). Perform experiments building on this example in order to answer the following questions:

(a) Can an expression passed to eval() access variables declared elsewhere in the program?

(b)　Can the string passed to eval() represent one or more statements rather than simply an expression?

(c)　If a variable is created by the code in the argument to eval(), where (in what object) is that variable created? Does your answer change if eval() is called from within the body of a function?

4.19. Consider the following JavaScript program:

```
// makeAdd.js
function makeAdd(op1) {
   return function adder (op2) { return op1 + op2; };
}
var add4 = makeAdd(4);
window.alert(add4(6));
```

makeAdd() evaluates a function expression for a function named adder(), which creates a function object. This function object, in turn, remembers the value of op1 as it exists at the time makeAdd() is called. So, when makeAdd() is called with the argument 4, the adder() function created remembers the value of op1 as 4. The object representing this function is returned by makeAdd() and assigned to the variable add4. When add4() is then called as a function with the argument 6, the adder() function contained in the add4 object is actually called, and its op2 parameter is given the value 6. This function then adds the remembered value of op1 to the argument value associated with op2, returning the value 10. In general, an object that combines a function with values remembered from the scope in effect at the time the function was created is called a *closure*. Thus, JavaScript function expressions actually create closures, not merely functions. Beginning with the given program, experiment with closures in JavaScript, addressing the following questions:

(a)　What happens if you call add4() with a value other than 6?

(b)　Add code that calls makeAdd() a second time with a different argument value and assigns the result to a second variable. Does your new closure behave as you would expect? Does the original closure (add4()) still behave as it did before, or is it affected by the creation or execution of a second closure? Explain your observations.

(c)　Add a global variable op3 to the program, and change the body of the function expression to

```
return op1 + op2 + op3;
```

Does changing the value of op3 after the call makeAdd(4) change the value returned by a subsequent call to add4()? Explain.

Projects

4.20. Write portions of a *discrete event simulation* in JavaScript. Discrete event simulations are often used to analyze customer service operations, such as an airline ticket counter. An *event* in such a simulation represents something of note that happens, such as a customer arriving at the counter or a customer transaction being completed. The heart of the simulation is an *event queue*, which is a time-ordered list of upcoming events. In addition to the time at which the event will occur, each element of the event queue has a field indicating the type of event (such as "transaction complete"). The program iterates through the event queue, each time removing and processing the event at the front of the queue. This may cause other events to be added to the queue (they will not necessarily be added to the end, but instead are added so that the event times remain ordered; so this is actually a priority queue). This iteration continues until the queue is exhausted, at which time information gathered during program execution (such as the average time customers spent waiting in line for an agent) is output.

(a) Write a constructor for a class Event; the instances of this class will be used to represent simulation events. Each instance should have properties time (assume that this is a Number) and type (of arbitrary type). Your constructor should have two arguments corresponding to these properties, so that the properties can be initialized easily when an instance is constructed.

(b) Write a constructor and methods for a class EventQueue representing an event queue. There should be a method empty() that returns true if and only if the queue is empty; a method add() that takes an Event object as its argument and adds it to the queue; and a method removeNextEvent() that removes the Event with the smallest time value (breaking ties arbitrarily) from the event queue and returns this object.

(c) Use the classes of (a) and (b) to write a simple airline ticket counter simulation. Input the number of ticket agents working at the counter. The event queue should be initialized by adding a number of customer-arrival events at various times, each time being an integer representing the number of minutes since the ticket counter opened. The program should then begin processing the event queue by removing the first event. If no agent is free when a customer-arrival event occurs, an element containing the current time should be pushed onto a data structure representing the waiting line at the ticket counter (so each element of the line structure represents a customer by the time at which the customer entered the line). If an agent is free when a customer-arrival event occurs, then the number of busy agents is incremented and a transaction-complete event is scheduled to occur three minutes later. When a transaction-complete event occurs, if any customers are in the waiting-line structure, then the first customer is removed from the line and the length of time that customer waited in line is added to an accumulator variable; the number of busy agents is unchanged. Otherwise, if no customers are waiting, an agent becomes free. The simulation ends when no events remain in the event queue. At this time, average customer wait time (accumulated wait time divided by number of customers) is output.

4.21. Write a JavaScript program that will allow a user to test the speed at which alert boxes are generated by a particular browser running on a particular system. Specifically, the program will display an alert box, then display a second alert box after OK is clicked in the first alert box, display a third alert box when the second is acknowledged, and so on. The program will stop displaying these alert boxes once 10 seconds has elapsed from the time the first box was displayed (so dividing by 10 will give the number of boxes displayed per second). Then, for 2 seconds, the program should repeatedly display alert boxes that report on the number of clicks per second recorded during the first 10 seconds (the reason for doing this for 2 seconds is so that you can see the results even if you accidentally click OK on one or more of the result alert boxes). For timing, use only the built-in Date object and its methods; that is, don't use any other timing-related host objects that might be available in your browser. Report on the results of testing with various browsers and systems.

4.22. Write a JavaScript program that generates 10 random math problems. Each math problem should consist of three operands (random integers between −10 and 10, inclusive) and two operators (randomly drawn from +, -, *, and %). For example, a problem might be -4 + 7 % 3. Display each problem in a prompt box, and allow the user to enter an integer representing the value of the problem (following standard JavaScript operator precedence rules). After all 10 problems have been answered, output the number of correct answers. (Hint: Use eval() (Exercise 4.18) to compute the correct answers.)

4.23. Consider a two-player game played with pegs of six different colors. One player (the *encrypter*) selects four pegs of different colors and places them in a certain order (leftmost through rightmost). This is the *encrypted message,* and is not shown to the second player (the *decrypter*). The decrypter then selects four pegs and places them in an order from left to right; this is the decrypter's guess about what the encrypted message is. Next, the encrypter *leaks* information about the encrypted message by placing small black or white pegs next to the guessed pegs; these pegs define a *score* for the guess. A black scoring peg indicates that one of the guessed pegs is exactly right: right color and in the right position. A white scoring peg indicates that a guessed peg is the right color but in the wrong position. So two black scoring pegs and one white would mean that three of the guessed pegs are of the right color and that two of these are in the correct position within the guessed peg ordering. Once a guess has been scored, the decrypter guesses a second time, and the encrypter scores this guess. (See Figure 5.35 for a graphical representation of such a game after two guesses have been scored.) This continues until the decrypter fully guesses the secret code (score of four black pegs).

Write a JavaScript program that plays a text version of this game. The program should simulate the encrypter, and the human player will be the decrypter. Specifically, the program will randomly select a secret code consisting of four numbers between 1 and 6. The numbers should all be different. The program will then input and score each guess made by the decrypter (human player). In particular, the user will input four numbers in a prompt box, and the computer will score this guess against the secret. The computer will then output to an alert box the user's guess and score (so many black and so many white pegs). If the score is 4 black, the game ends and the computer displays the total number of guesses made. Otherwise, the computer asks for another guess consisting of four numbers. Notice that the human is expected to write down his or her guesses and scores, because the computer will only output the most recent guess and score by the user each time. Your program does not need to verify that the user enters numbers between 1 and 6, since entering something else can only hurt the user's chances of winning. You may also assume that all of the user's four inputs for a guess are different numbers.

4.24. Write two versions of a base2() function that takes a String argument and returns a Boolean value indicating whether or not the argument begins with a 1 followed by any number of 0 or 1 characters and ending with the string _2. For example, it should return true if called with 10010_2 but false with 0_2. One version should use regular expressions, and the other should not.

4.25. Consider a word game in which a 4-by-4 grid of letters is displayed. Your task is to find as many words as possible in the grid. A word occurs in the grid if, starting at a position in the grid that contains the first letter of the word, the second letter is in a grid position next to (including diagonally) the first, the third letter is in a position next to the second, and so on. No grid position can be used twice in making a word. So, if the grid of letters is

```
e|w|t|h
-------
r|d|v|x
-------
q|p|a|w
-------
z|y|b|m
```

then it contains words such as "paw" and "red" but does not contain "ewe" because the upper-left corner of the grid would have to be used twice to make this word.

(a) Write a program that allows a user to play a solitaire, three-letter version of the game described. Your program should incorporate a dictionary of all (or at least most) three-letter words; a JavaScript file shortwords.js containing over 400 such English words is included as part of the download available from the textbook supplements Web site (see the Preface for the URL). The program should begin by selecting 16 letters at random. Display these letters as a 4-by-4 grid in an alert box (this probably won't look perfect because of the fonts used in alert boxes). When the user clicks OK in this box, a prompt box should be displayed in which the user is asked to enter a word. If the word entered is in the dictionary and in the grid and hasn't been entered before, the program should increment a counter. Next, the alert box with the grid should again be displayed, followed by the prompt box and a check of the word entered. This should continue until the user enters the word quit. The program should then display a final alert box showing the grid and the number of distinct words found by the user.

(b) Modify your program so that it displays a message at the beginning of each alert box after the first. The message should tell the user that the previously entered word was a duplicate, was not on the board or in the dictionary, or was accepted.

(c) Modify your program so that it will be more likely to choose some letters (such as vowels) than it is other letters.

(d) Modify your program so that when it terminates it displays a list of all of the words not found, along with the other information.

(e) Modify your program so that it automatically terminates once 3 minutes have elapsed from the time the first alert box was displayed. That is, clicking OK in either the alert or prompt box after 3 minutes have elapsed should cause the program to terminate and the final alert box to be displayed. The word entered in a final prompt box (one submitted after 3 minutes have elapsed) should not be counted.

4.26. Crazy Eights is a simple game played with a standard deck of 52 playing cards. The rules for a two-player version are as follows: The deck is shuffled, seven cards are dealt to each player, one card is placed face up to begin a discard pile, and the remaining cards are placed face down and form a draw pile. The first player can play one card from his or her hand face up on the discard pile if that card matches the suit or the number of the card currently on the discard pile. Alternatively, if the player holds an 8 (any suit), this card can be played, and the player also names the suit that this card represents. For example, if the top discard card is a 4 of spades, I can play an 8 of hearts and specify that the suit is now clubs. The next card played to the discard pile by either player must either be an 8 or a club. If the first player does not play, then he or she must take one card from the top of the draw pile. The second player then plays similarly. Play alternates until one of the players is out of cards; this player wins.

(a) Write a JavaScript program (and an HTML document that loads the program and any other necessary files) that allows a human to play Crazy Eights against a computer. Specifically, the program should simulate the initial shuffle and dealing of cards by creating appropriate data structures. It should next display a prompt box telling the user what cards he or she holds and what card is on top of the discard pile (prompt boxes in IE6 display only two lines, so you should use short card names such as 6c and kh). The user should then enter in the prompt box either a p indicating that a card should be picked from the draw pile, or a string (such as 6c) representing a card to be played. If the card is not legal (either not in the hand or not of the correct suit/number), prompt the user again. After simulating the user's play, play the computer's hand, always playing a card if possible. Alternate allowing the user to play and playing the computer's hand until one of the players wins, at which time the program should announce the winner.

For this version of the program, if an 8 is played, assume that the suit of the card played is the suit named by the player. For example, if the computer plays the 8 of diamonds, the suit will be diamonds.

Shuffling can be performed as follows: if there are n cards, choose a random number r_1 between 0 and $n - 1$. Swap the card at index r_1 with the card at index $n - 1$. Then choose a random number r_2 between 0 and $n - 2$, and swap the card at r_2 with the one at $n - 2$. Continue this process $n - 1$ times. The JavaScript code

```
Math.floor(Math.random()*(n+1))
```

evaluates to a random number between 0 and n.

(b) If the game continues for a long time, the draw pile may become empty. Modify your program so that if this happens, a new draw pile is created by shuffling the cards underneath the top card of the discard pile. Following this operation, the discard pile will consist of just the single card that was originally on top of the pile.

(c) Modify the program so that the user can name the suit after playing an 8. That is, if the user plays an 8, prompt the user a second time for the suit it is to represent. Be careful: you should not actually change the suit of the 8 played, since the discard pile may be shuffled later to form a new draw pile. Instead, the player (and your program) is supposed to remember what suit was named.

(d) Write and use in your program a JavaScript class named `Cards` that can be used to represent the shuffled deck, the players' hands, and the discard pile. This class should have at a minimum methods for adding individual cards to and removing cards from an instance, "looking at" cards (for example, obtaining a reference to the third card in a hand), and shuffling the cards in an instance.

(e) Add a sort method to the `Cards` instance. This will be used to sort an instance representing a player's hand, so that the cards appear in a logical order. For example, the primary sort might be by suit, with a secondary sort placing cards in ascending order of their number (2 through 10 followed by jack, queen, king, and ace).

(f) Write and use in your program a JavaScript class named `Card` that can be used to represent individual cards. The constructor for this class should take two arguments representing the suit and number of a card. Write at least two methods for the class: one that returns a string representing the card suitable for output to the user (such as 6c), and the other that returns a Number representing the *sort order* of the card. This is a value that can be used to sort the cards appropriately. For example, the 2 of clubs might be given a sort order of 0, the 3 of clubs 1, the ace of clubs 12, the 2 of diamonds 13, and so on.

CHAPTER 5

Host Objects
Browsers and the DOM

In the previous chapter we studied the JavaScript programming language. Although the programs we developed were run by a web browser, they had relatively little interaction with either the browser itself or the document displayed by the browser. In this chapter we will focus our attention on the Document Object Model (DOM), an API (application programming interface) that defines how JavaScript programs can access and manipulate the HTML document currently displayed by a browser. (In Chapter 7, we'll learn that the DOM can also be used by other programming languages, such as Java, to input and process XML documents.) In addition, we'll learn how JavaScript programs can be informed of user interactions, such as mouse movements or clicks.

JavaScript programs access the DOM through a host object named `document`. Commonly used browsers also provide a number of other host objects. Unlike `document`, these objects are not covered by any formal standard. However, a de facto standard exists in that quite a few host objects are common to both IE6—by far the most popular browser at the time this was written—and Mozilla 1.4—a browser designed to conform closely with DOM standards. So, in addition to covering the `document` object, this chapter will also briefly cover a number of other common host objects. These objects provide services such as allowing a JavaScript program to navigate the browser to another URL or to resize the browser window.

5.1 Introduction to the Document Object Model

The JavaScript language itself, as we have learned, contains no facilities for interacting with a browser or with the document contained in the browser. Instead, such facilities are provided by the browser in the form of host objects that are stored as properties of the JavaScript global object, which is named `window` in IE6 and Mozilla 1.4 (and, as far as I know, in every other desktop browser). We learned in the previous chapter about two host objects that are commonly provided by browsers: `alert` and `prompt`. As noted in the opening paragraphs of this chapter, we will be focusing on another host object, which is normally stored in the `document` property of the JavaScript global object. The definition of the properties of this object, many of which are themselves objects with their own properties, is known as the *Document Object Model* (DOM).

As an introductory example, let's see how the familiar *rollover* effect (an image changes when you place the mouse over it, and changes back when the mouse moves away from the image) can be produced using the DOM. Figure 5.1 shows an HTML document with an `img` element that includes two attributes, `onmouseover` and `onmouseout`, whose values are JavaScript function calls. These are examples of *intrinsic event attributes*, which

```
<!DOCTYPE html
        PUBLIC "-//W3C//DTD XHTML 1.0 Strict//EN"
        "http://www.w3.org/TR/xhtml1/DTD/xhtml1-strict.dtd">
<html>
  <head>
    <title>Rollover.html</title>
    <script type="text/javascript" src="rollover.js">
    </script>
    <meta http-equiv="Content-Script-Type" content="text/javascript" />
  </head>
  <body>
    <p>
      <img id="img1" src="CFP2.png" alt="flower pot"
        height="86" width="44"
        onmouseover="show('img1', 'CFP22.png');"
        onmouseout="show('img1', 'CFP2.png');" />
    </p>
  </body>
</html>
```

FIGURE 5.1 HTML document with calls to JavaScript function.

we will learn more about later. For now, it's enough to note that the onmouseover attribute specifies JavaScript code that will be executed when the mouse cursor is placed over the img element, and the onmouseout attribute specifies code to be executed when the cursor subsequently moves away from the img. The code in both cases is a call to a function named show(). (The browser knows that this is JavaScript code because of the meta element earlier in the document, which is also discussed later.)

Intrinsic event attributes and the meta element are part of the HTML specification, so we haven't yet seen anything directly related to the DOM. But we will when we look at the JavaScript show() function (Figure 5.2). First, the function calls the getElementById() method of the document object, passing it the value of the first argument passed to it (which is the String img1 in both calls to show()). This method takes a String and returns a JavaScript Object that represents the document element having the specified String as its id attribute value. This object, in turn, has a method setAttribute() that allows JavaScript code to assign values to the attributes of an img element, such as the src attribute (Figure 5.3). So the show() function uses this method to assign the value of its second argument (a String representing a URL) to the src attribute of the img element. After this change is made, the browser causes a different image to be displayed for this img element.

```
// rollover.js

function show(eltId, URL) {
  var elt = window.document.getElementById(eltId);
  elt.setAttribute("src", URL);
  return;
}
```

FIGURE 5.2 JavaScript function accessing the DOM.

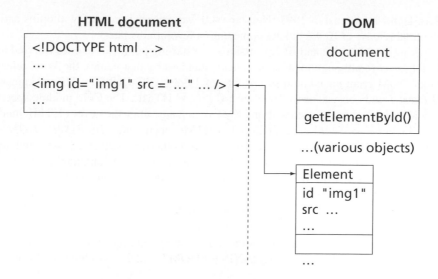

FIGURE 5.3 Each element in an HTML document has a corresponding Object (an instance of Element) that can be accessed using getElementById(). HTML attributes of an element can be specified using the setAttribute() method.

Putting this all together, we can see that the net effect is that the browser initially displays the image at relative URL CFP2.png. When the mouse moves over this image, the show() function is called with a second argument of CFP22.png, so the image is replaced with the one located at URL CFP22.png. When the mouse moves away, show() is again called, and the original image is restored.

Now that we've been introduced to the DOM, let's briefly look at some of its history.

5.2 DOM History and Levels

A relatively simple document object model was incorporated in the Netscape 2.0 browser so that JavaScript could interface with this browser. The model included a write() method, which could be used to dynamically add content to a document. It also provided access to form controls and anchor elements, so aspects of these controls and elements could be changed dynamically by a JavaScript program. However, many elements of the document displayed by the browser, including the document's images, could not be modified through this early model. The Netscape 3.0 browser's document object added the ability to modify images, enabling the rollover effect that we have just seen, which proved to be a popular feature. Internet Explorer 3.0 contained a similar document object model.

The 4.0 versions of the Netscape Navigator and Internet Explorer browsers opened up essentially the entire document along with style information to access from scripts, but the two browsers implemented their document object models in substantially different ways. In fact, these differences in document object models were in many ways more difficult for developers to handle than the differences in HTML between the browsers. The W3C responded quickly to these emerging differences, beginning formal work on developing a standard DOM in August of 1997 (Netscape 4.0 was released only a few months earlier, and the final release of IE 4.0 did not come until a few months later).

Taking the Netscape and IE 3.0 versions as a starting point (sometimes referred to as the *DOM Level 0*, although there is no official standard by that name), the W3C released its initial DOM recommendation in October of 1998 [W3C-DOM-1]. This is known as *DOM Level 1* and consists of two modules: Core and HTML. The Core module specifies functionality designed to be used with any XML document, while the Level 1 HTML module specifies higher-level DOM access tailored to HTML documents. The *Level 2 DOM* also contains Core and HTML modules along with several others, particularly Events and Style, that extend Level 1 functionality. Level 2 HTML is in some ways incompatible with Level 1 HTML and is viewed by the W3C as obsoleting it. Portions of a Level 3 DOM have become W3C recommendations, but browser support for this level is still evolving at the time of this writing, and for the most part the changes from Level 2 do not impact typical HTML document handling as much as they do more general XML document processing. Given this history and the support available in modern browsers and other software (such as the Sun™ Java API for XML Processing, JAXP) for DOM Level 2, I will focus in this chapter on this level.

One of the primary contributions of the W3C effort has been to generalize the DOM beyond its use solely as a means for a scripting language to access HTML documents within a browser. Instead, the DOM as defined by the W3C applies to arbitrary XML documents as well as to HTML, and the DOM is designed to be used by standalone applications written in languages such as Java in addition to being used by scripts running within browsers. This generality comes at the price of some additional complexity. In order to reduce this complexity somewhat, in this chapter I will only cover JavaScript access to the DOM of an HTML document contained within a browser. Java access to XML documents via the DOM will be explored in Chapter 7. Also, while there are actually six different W3C recommendations that collectively define DOM Level 2, I will only cover portions of four of them: DOM 2 Core [W3C-DOM-2-CORE], Events [W3C-DOM-2-EVENTS], Style [W3C-DOM-2-STYLE], and HTML [W3C-DOM-2-HTML]. Full details on DOM 2 can be found in the DOM section of the W3C web site `http://www.w3.org`.

The next several sections will proceed as follows. First, we'll look in more detail at the HTML intrinsic event attribute facility, which as we've seen is often used in conjunction with JavaScript functions accessing the DOM. Next, we'll see how DOM calls can be used to modify the style of elements in a document. These features are sufficient to do much of the DOM processing typically found in a JavaScript program. Then we'll look at several more advanced topics that facilitate capabilities such as dropdown menus; some of these features will also be useful when we learn about DOM processing of XML documents. We'll also explore some of the ways in which browsers deviate from the DOM recommendations, learn how to detect these deviations, and consider ways of dealing with them. Finally, I'll briefly cover some other host objects that are commonly found in modern browsers.

5.3 Intrinsic Event Handling

For the most part, browser-based JavaScript programs are *event-driven*. That is, JavaScript functions are normally not called directly from the top level of a JavaScript program. Instead, functions are called in response to various user actions, such as clicking a button or moving the mouse over a certain element. The rollover program in Section 5.1 is an example of the event-driven program structure.

In this section, we'll learn more about HTML intrinsic event attributes such as onmouseover. In later sections, we'll learn that the DOM also provides an alternative, more general mechanism for associating browser events with JavaScript functions.

First, a little terminology. An *event* in a browser is an occurrence of potential interest. Example events are the mouse moving over an element, a mouse button being clicked, or a key being pressed. Each type of event has an abbreviated name associated with it; e.g., "mouseover" is the name of the event that occurs when the mouse moves over an element. An intrinsic event attribute, as we have seen, is used to provide scripting code that is called when a particular event associated with the element containing the attribute occurs. Finally, the name of each event attribute is on followed by the name of the associated event.

The complete list of intrinsic event attributes defined by the HTML 4.01 recommendation is given in Table 5.1. Unless otherwise noted, these attributes apply to the body element and to virtually all elements that are represented visually in an XHTML 1.0 Strict document (the br element is the one exception).

TABLE 5.1 HTML Intrinsic Event Attributes

Attribute	When Called
onload	The body of the document has just been fully read and parsed by the browser (this attribute pertains only to body and frameset).
onunload	The browser is ready to load a new document in place of the current document (this attribute only pertains to body and frameset).
onclick	A mouse button has been clicked and released over the element.
ondblclick	The mouse has been double-clicked over the element.
onmousedown	The mouse has been clicked over the element.
onmouseup	The mouse has been released over the element.
onmouseover	The mouse has just moved over the element.
onmousemove	The mouse has moved from one location to another over the element.
onmouseout	The mouse has just moved away from the element.
onfocus	The element has just received the keyboard focus (this attribute pertains only to certain elements, including a, label, input, select, textarea, and button).
onblur	The element has just lost the keyboard focus (attribute pertains only to the same elements as onfocus).
onkeypress	This element has the focus, and a key has been pressed and released.
onkeydown	This element has the focus, and a key has been pressed.
onkeyup	This element has the focus, and a key has been released.
onsubmit	This element is ready to be submitted (applies only to form elements).
onreset	This element is ready to be reset (applies only to form elements).
onselect	Text in this element has been selected (highlighted) in preparation for editing (applies only to input and textarea elements).
onchange	The value of this element has changed (applies only to input, textarea, and select elements).

As noted earlier and illustrated in Figure 5.1, any time you use an intrinsic event attribute you should also include a meta element in the the head of the document. In general, a meta element is used to specify information that would normally be found in the HTTP header field of the response message containing the HTML document: http-equiv is used to specify the name of the HTTP header field, and content its value. The particular HTTP header field defined by the meta element in Figure 5.1 is Content-Script-Type, which is used to specify the default language for scripts within the document (recall that JavaScript, while the most popular, is not the only scripting language that can be used within web documents). So the net effect is that the meta element

```
<meta http-equiv="Content-Script-Type" content="text/javascript" />
```

tells the browser that intrinsic event attributes are written in JavaScript. (Most browsers will default to JavaScript if the Content-Script-Type header field is not defined for a document; furthermore, if an intrinsic attribute value begins with the string javascript:, most browsers will interpret this to mean that the remainder of the value is JavaScript code. But neither of these conventions is a formal standard.)

Figure 5.4 shows an example HTML document that calls window.alert in response to a variety of events. You might find it helpful to load this document into your browser and experiment with it, trying keypresses, tabs, and button clicks on various elements, navigating away from and back to the page, and minimizing and restoring the window. If you try these experiments in different browsers, you may notice that the definitions of events can vary somewhat between browsers. For example, Mozilla 1.4 treats pressing the Tab key as a keypress, while IE6 does not, and Mozilla 1.4 detects a select event when the user tabs to an empty text field, while IE6 does not. In short, when writing JavaScript event handling code, you should keep in mind that browsers treat special cases in different ways, and in general attempt to write your code so that it is not dependent on special-case behaviors.

5.4 Modifying Element Style

DOM access is often used to change the style of an HTML document element in response to a user-initiated event. For example, consider a simple navigation bar (navbar) consisting of a table of links placed to the left of other content (Figure 5.5). Using JavaScript and the DOM, it is simple to change the appearance of items in the navbar as the mouse moves over them. In particular, HTML markup such as

```
<td onmouseover="highlight(this);"
   onmouseout="lowlight(this);"><a
     href="http://www.example.org"
     >Products</a>
</td>
```

will cause a JavaScript function named highlight to be called when the cursor enters the region of the screen occupied by a td element, and will cause lowlight to be called when the cursor exits this region. These functions are then supposed to change the background color (to silver and gray, respectively) of the td element that generated the function calls.

```
<!DOCTYPE html
        PUBLIC "-//W3C//DTD XHTML 1.0 Strict//EN"
        "http://www.w3.org/TR/xhtml1/DTD/xhtml1-strict.dtd">
<html xmlns="http://www.w3.org/1999/xhtml">
  <head>
    <title>
      IntrinsicEvents.html
    </title>
    <meta http-equiv="Content-Script-Type" content="text/javascript" />
  </head>
  <body onload="window.alert('Body loaded.');"
        onunload="window.alert('Unloading...');">
    <form action="http://www.example.org"
          onsubmit="window.alert('Submitting...');"
          onreset="window.alert('Resetting...');">
      <p>
        <input type="text" name="someText"
               onkeypress="window.alert('Text field got character.');"
               onselect="window.alert('Text selected.');" />
        <br />
        <input type="button" name="aButton" value="Click Me"
               onclick="window.alert('Button clicked.');" />
        <input type="submit" name="aSubmit" value="Submit"
               onfocus="window.alert('Submit button got focus.');" />
        <input type="reset" name="aReset" value="Reset" />
      </p>
    </form>
  </body>
</html>
```

FIGURE 5.4 HTML document using several intrinsic event attributes.

FIGURE 5.5 Navbar to the left of page content. The cursor (not shown) is hovering over the second item in the navbar, causing the item to be highlighted.

(The markup is somewhat hard to read because I wanted to eliminate some extraneous spaces that would otherwise have been displayed if I had written easier-to-read markup.)

Each of these functions passed the argument `this`. Recall that, within a method, `this` is a reference to the object on which the method is called. Within an intrinsic event attribute value, `this` is a reference to a JavaScript object representing the element to which the attribute applies, in this case a td element (recall the correspondence between HTML elements and DOM objects illustrated by Figure 5.3). The host object corresponding to the td element has a number of properties, including a `style` property that is itself an object. The `style` object, defined in the DOM2 Style recommendation [W3C-DOM-2-STYLE], has properties corresponding to all of the CSS2 style properties of the td element (notice the two different uses of "properties" here, first in an object-oriented sense, then in a style sheet sense). One of these `style` object properties is named `backgroundColor`; setting this object property changes the specified value of the `background-color` CSS property of the corresponding td element. Therefore, the `highlight` function can be defined as follows:

```
// NavBar.js
function highlight(element) {
  element.style.backgroundColor = "silver";
  return;
}
```

Each CSS style property has a corresponding `style` object property, and the names are identical as long as the CSS property name has no hyphens (-). However, since the hyphen is not a legal character within a JavaScript identifier, any CSS property name containing a hyphen has a corresponding `style` object property name that is derived from the CSS name, as we have just seen demonstrated by `background-color`: hyphens are removed, and letters that originally followed hyphens are capitalized. Alternatively, in DOM2 (but not in IE6; see Section 5.7) the `style` object provides a `setProperty()` method that can be used to modify style properties using their CSS property names:

```
// NavBar.js (part 2)
function lowlight(element) {
  element.style.setProperty("background-color", "gray", "");
  return;
}
```

The third argument to `setProperty()` is the weight to be associated with the property specification, and should be either the String value `important` or the empty string (as shown).

Sometimes, it is useful to retrieve as well as to set property values. For example, if an element explicitly specifies the value `gray` for its `background-color` style property, then the following JavaScript function can be called by both the `onmouseover` and `onmouseout` methods:

```
// NavBar.js (part 3)
function changeLight(element) {
  if (element.style.backgroundColor == "gray") {
    element.style.backgroundColor = "silver";
  } else {
```

```
        element.style.backgroundColor = "gray";
    }
    return;
}
```

When a style property value is retrieved, the specified value for the property is returned. If no property is specified for the style property, the empty string will be returned as its value, even if the property has some other actual value (obtained through inheritance or as an initial value, for example). Because of this, we included a `style` attribute on the `td` element, so that the first time `changeLight()` is called on the element, the `element.style.backgroundColor` property will have a nonempty value.

In DOM2, the `style` object also supplies a `getPropertyValue()` method (again, not supported in IE6) that complements the `setProperty()` method just described. Thus, in Mozilla 1.4 and other browsers supporting this aspect of DOM2, a valid alternative to the if statement in the `changelighte` function is

```
if (element.style.getPropertyValue("background-color") == "gray") {
```

DOM Level 2 also specifies a number of methods and objects that can be used to operate on style sheets, rather than on the style associated with an individual element. See the DOM Level 2 Style specification [W3C-DOM-2-STYLE] for details.

5.5   The Document Tree

Recall that the elements of a syntactically correct HTML or XML document form a tree structure. For example, in a Strict XHTML 1.0 document, the `html` element is the root of the document tree and has child elements `head` and `body` (the root may also have additional child elements representing any white space included within its content). The Document Object Model makes this tree of elements accessible to JavaScript programs. This section focuses on DOM2 support for document tree access and modification within a browser that has loaded an HTML document.

5.5.1   Node Object

The document tree accessible to JavaScript programs running within a DOM2-compliant browser consists of a variety of node types. Some nodes of the tree are JavaScript objects corresponding to HTML elements such as `html` or `body`. Other nodes may contain text representing the content of an element or the white space between elements. Yet other nodes may represent the text of HTML comments. There is even a node representing the document type declaration. Each of these types of nodes is represented by instances of a particular host object. For example, document elements are represented by instances of a host object named `Element`, while text and interelement white space are represented by instances of the `Text` host object. In order to simplify the definition of these various host objects, the DOM defines a generic `Node` host object that contains properties that are also part of any object that might be found in the document tree, including `Element`, `Text`, and several other host objects. Some of the key properties of the `Node` object are given in Table 5.2, Table 5.3, and Table 5.4. (IE6 does not provide the `Node` object, so

TABLE 5.2 Nonmethod Properties of Node

Property	Description
nodeType	Number representing the type of node (Element, Comment, etc.). See Table 5.3.
nodeName	String providing a name for this Node (form of name depends on the nodeType; see text).
parentNode	Reference to object that is this node's parent.
childNodes	Acts like a read-only array containing this node's child nodes. Has length 0 if this node has no children.
previousSibling	Previous sibling of this node, or null if no previous sibling exists.
nextSibling	Next sibling of this node, or null if no next sibling exists.
attributes	Acts like a read-only array containing Attr instances representing this node's attributes.

TABLE 5.3 Some Possible Values for the nodeType Property of Node Instances (the Symbolic Constants are not Provided by IE6)

Value	Symbolic Constant	Host Object Type
1	Node.ELEMENT_NODE	Element
2	Node.ATTRIBUTE_NODE	Attr
3	Node.TEXT_NODE	Text
8	Node.COMMENT_NODE	Comment
9	Node.DOCUMENT_NODE	Document
10	Node.DOCUMENT_TYPE_NODE	DocumentType

TABLE 5.4 Method Properties of Node

Method	Functionality
hasAttributes()	Returns Boolean indicating whether or not this node has attributes.
hasChildNodes()	Returns Boolean indicating whether or not this node has children.
appendChild(Node)	Adds the argument Node to the end of the list of children of this node.
insertBefore(Node, Node)	Adds the first argument Node to the list of children of this node immediately before the second argument Node (or at end of child list if second argument is null).
removeChild(Node)	Removes the argument Node from this node's list of children.
replaceChild(Node, Node)	In the list of children of this node, replace the second argument Node with the first.

the symbolic constants listed in Table 5.3 are not available to JavaScript programs running within this browser.)

The Element instance representing the html element of a document is stored in the documentElement property of the document object. Starting at this node, it is easy to use Node methods to walk through the document tree in order to obtain information about the tree. For example, the JavaScript code in Figure 5.6 can be used to produce an outline representation

```javascript
// TreeOutline.js

// treeOutline returns a string representing an
// outline of the Element nodes in the document tree.
function treeOutline() {
  return subtreeOutline(document.documentElement, 0);
}

// subtreeOutline returns a string representing
// an outline corresponding to the tree
// structure of a Node tree rooted at "root".
// "level" indicates indentation level of root.
function subtreeOutline(root, level) {
  var retString = "";  // String to be returned

  // Work around browsers that don't support Node
  var elementType = window.Node ? Node.ELEMENT_NODE : 1;

  // If this root is an Element node, then print its name
  // and recursively process any children it has.
  if (root.nodeType == elementType) {
    retString += printName(level, root.nodeName);
    var children = root.childNodes;
    for (var i=0; i<children.length; i++) {
      retString += subtreeOutline(children[i], level+1);
    }
  }
  return retString;
}

// printName creates a string consisting of
// the given string "thisName", indented
// as indicated by "level".
function printName(level, thisName) {
  var retString = "";
  for (var i=0; i<level; i++) {
    retString += "..";
  }
  retString += thisName + "\n";
  return retString;
}
```

FIGURE 5.6 JavaScript function treeOutline for producing outline representing the tree of elements within a document.

of the Element nodes contained in a document tree. This code can be included in an HTML document as shown in Figure 5.7, which calls the outlining function if a button is clicked and displays the results in an alert box (Figure 5.8).

As shown, the nodeName property for an Element instance is the name of the element's type. However, although the element type names are lowercase in the document of Figure 5.7, they are output in uppercase in Figure 5.8. The reason for this difference is that my server specified a MIME type of text/html for the HTML document of Figure 5.7, so the browser treated this document as an HTML document even though it contains an XHTML DTD. The values of the nodeName property for Element instances are always uppercased for HTML documents. However, in an XML document the value of nodeName for an Element instance is identical in case to the corresponding type name. So, if the server had specified an XML MIME type (such as application/xhtml+xml) for this same document, then the element names output in Figure 5.8 would all have been lowercase. Therefore, when testing nodeName values, you may want to use a JavaScript String method such as toUpperCase() or toLowerCase() to convert the nodeName to a known case before testing it.

The code of Figure 5.6 also illustrates a coding convention that I will generally follow in this chapter: write code as if all browsers adhere to the DOM standard, and then deal with

```
<!DOCTYPE html
        PUBLIC "-//W3C//DTD XHTML 1.0 Strict//EN"
        "http://www.w3.org/TR/xhtml1/DTD/xhtml1-strict.dtd">
<html xmlns="http://www.w3.org/1999/xhtml">
  <head>
    <title>
      TreeOutline.html
    </title>
    <!-- Import treeOutline() function -->
    <script type="text/javascript" src="TreeOutline.js">
    </script>
  </head>
  <body>
    <p>
      Text within a "p" element.
    </p>
    <ol>
      <li>First element of ordered list.</li>
      <li>Second element.</li>
    </ol>
    <!-- Call function producing an outline of this document's
         element tree -->
    <form action="">
      <p><input type="button" name="button" value="Click to see outline"
                   onclick="window.alert(treeOutline());" /></p>
    </form>
  </body>
</html>
```

FIGURE 5.7 HTML document that uses treeOutline function to display an element tree for the document.

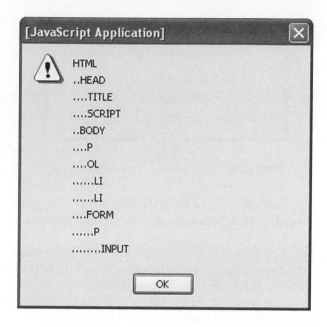

FIGURE 5.8 Alert box produced by `TreeOutline.html`.

known exceptions. In this code, I wanted to use the named constant `Node.ELEMENT_NODE` to test the `nodeType` of each `Node` in the document tree. However, IE6 does not define a `Node` property of the `window` object, so this named constant (and several others) are not available in IE6. To handle this deviation from the standard, I created a local variable `elementType` and assigned it either the named constant's value if the browser defines the `Node` property or the numeric value (from Table 5.3) equivalent to this constant otherwise. (Recall from Chapter 4 that when evaluating the statement

```
var elementType = window.Node ? Node.ELEMENT_NODE : 1;
```

JavaScript will automatically cast the expression `window.Node` to Boolean, producing the value `false` if `Node` is not a property of `window` and `true` if the value of `Node` is of type Object.)

5.5.2   Example: List Reordering

As an example of how some of the tree-modifying methods of Table 5.4 can be used, assume that we would like to display a list in the browser that can be reordered by the user. Specifically, if the user clicks on a list item, then it will be swapped with the item below it in the list (nothing happens if the last item in the list is clicked). For example, if the user clicks on the first item in the list of Figure 5.9, then the browser content should become that shown in Figure 5.10. (Not your standard web page, is it?)

We can accomplish this by writing a single JavaScript function `switchItems()` and calling this function from the `onclick` attribute of each `li` element in the list (Figure 5.11).

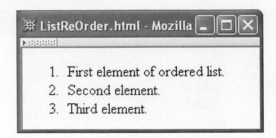

FIGURE 5.9 Initial rendering of `ListReOrder.html`.

The JavaScript code implementing the `switchItems()` function is given in Figure 5.12. There are just two steps. First, we search through the linked list of nodes that are siblings of the `Node` corresponding to the list item that was clicked. We perform this search by using the `nextSibling` property until we find the `Node` for the list item following the one clicked. Second, we remove the `Node` for the list item following the one clicked from the document tree and reinsert this `Node` before the `Node` for the clicked item. If no list item follows the clicked item (as indicated by a `null` value for `nextSibling` at some point in the sibling chain), then we leave the document tree unchanged. If this function does change the tree, the browser will automatically update what it displays accordingly.

5.5.3 The document Node

As hinted at in Table 5.3, technically the `document` object itself is considered to be a Dom tree node (with `nodeType` 9, DOCUMENT_NODE) and therefore also has all of the properties and methods listed in Table 5.2 and Table 5.4. In fact, while the `html` element is the root of an HTML document, in the DOM the `document` object is treated as the root of the `Node` tree: it is the parent of the `html` Element instance, while its own `parentNode` value is `null`. Thus, `document` provides a parent for nodes representing markup outside the `html` element, such as comments or the document type declaration (which has a `nodeType` value of `Node.DOCUMENT_TYPE_NODE`).

In addition to the properties it has by virtue of being a node, the `document` object has a number of additional properties. We have already mentioned one of

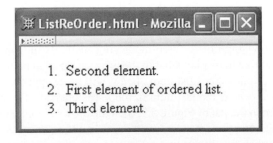

FIGURE 5.10 Rendering of `ListReOrder.html` after user clicks the first list item.

```
<ol>
  <li onclick="switchItems(this);">First element of ordered list.</li>
  <li onclick="switchItems(this);">Second element.</li>
  <li onclick="switchItems(this);">Third element.</li>
</ol>
```

FIGURE 5.11 HTML markup from `ListReOrder.html` of a list containing clickable items.

these: documentElement. Many other especially useful document properties are summarized in Table 5.5.

5.5.4 Element Nodes

Nodes of type ELEMENT_NODE (1) are instances of the Element host object, and like document have certain properties in addition to those belonging to Node. The one nonmethod property unique to Element is tagName, which is in essence just another name for the nodeName property. Some key methods of Element are listed in Table 5.6.

```
// ListReOrder.js

// Switch item in an ordered list with
// the item following it, if there is one.
function switchItems(itemNode) {

  // Work around browsers that don't support Node
  var elementType = window.Node ? Node.ELEMENT_NODE : 1;

  // Locate the item following itemNode, skipping
  // over any non-Element nodes (white space, comments,
  // etc.).  The XHTML DTD only allows li elements
  // as content of an ol, so any Element following
  // itemNode should be an li.  But we'll test the nodeName
  // property just to be safe.
  var nextItem = itemNode.nextSibling;
  while (nextItem &&
         !(nextItem.nodeType == elementType &&
           nextItem.nodeName.toLowerCase() == "li")) {
    nextItem = nextItem.nextSibling;
  }

  // If there is a next item, remove it and re-insert
  // it before itemNode
  if (nextItem) {
    itemNode.parentNode.removeChild(nextItem);
    itemNode.parentNode.insertBefore(nextItem, itemNode);
  }
  return;
}
```

FIGURE 5.12 JavaScript code implementing the `switchItems` function.

TABLE 5.5 Some Properties of the document Object

Property	Value
doctype	An Object representing the document type declaration, if present, or null if not. Key properties are publicId and systemId, which are String values corresponding to the declaration's public and system identifier, respectively.
title	String representing the content of the title element (can be modified).
body	Object representing the body element of the document.
cookie	String representing the cookies associated with the current document; see Chapter 6 for more on cookies.
URL	String representing absolute URI for the document (read-only).
domain	String representing domain portion of URL, or null if a domain name is not available (read-only).
referrer	If this document was loaded because a hyperlink was clicked, this String is the URI of the page containing the hyperlink. Otherwise, it is the empty string.
createElement(String)	Given argument representing an element type name (such as div), returns an Element instance corresponding to the specified element type.
createTextNode(String)	Returns a Text instance containing the given String as its data value.
getElementById(String)	Given argument corresponding to the value of the id attribute of an element, returns that Element instance, or returns null if no document element has the specified id attribute value.
getElementsByTagName(String)	Given a String value representing an element type name, returns a "collection" (essentially an array) of Element instances corresponding to each element in the document having the given element type name.

5.5.5   Text Nodes

Instances of the Text DOM object are used to represent character data, that is, anything in the HTML document that is not markup. The nodeType for these elements is Node.TEXT_NODE (3). The primary property of Text instances is data, which is the text represented by the Text node. Assigning a value to this property changes the corresponding text content displayed by the browser.

There is no guarantee that the character data content of an element will be placed in a single Text node; instead, the Element node may have several Text nodes that are siblings of one another. The normalize() method of Node can be used to modify subtrees so that this does not occur; see Exercise 5.14.

5.5.6   Example: Collapsible Elements

To illustrate the potential utility of the document, Element, and Text properties and methods listed in the preceding subsections, let's write a function that can be used to make elements of a web page collapsible. To see what I mean by "collapsible," consider

TABLE 5.6 Some Methods of Element Instances

Method	Purpose
getAttribute(String)	Returns value of attribute having name given by the String argument, or the empty string if no value (even a default) is available for the given attribute name.
setAttribute(String, String)	Creates an attribute with a name specified by the first argument String and assigns to it the value of the second argument String. If an attribute with this name already exists, it is overwritten with the new value specified, or an exception is thrown if the attribute is read-only.
removeAttribute(String)	Removes the specified attribute, or throws an exception if the attribute cannot be deleted.
hasAttribute(String)	Returns Boolean value indicating whether or not the Element has an attribute with the specified name.
getElementsByTagName(String)	Like the method with the same name on document, but only returns those Element instances that are descendants of this Element.

Figure 5.13, which shows a web page before a collapse button is clicked, and Figure 5.14, which shows the page after the button is clicked. In essence, clicking the button makes the selected element (an unordered list in this case) disappear, and the browser collapses the remainder of the document into the space formerly occupied by the collapsed element.

I want to accomplish this in a way that does not impact the HTML. In particular, an element to be collapsed shouldn't look any different than any other element, except that I will require that it have an id attribute. So the markup for the unordered list in Figures 5.13 and 5.14 is just

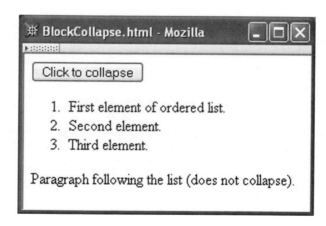

FIGURE 5.13 Initial rendering of BlockCollapse.html.

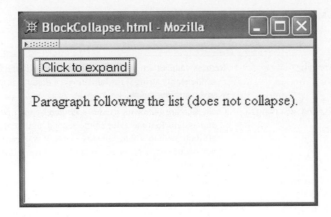

FIGURE 5.14 Rendering of BlockCollapse.html after button is clicked once (or any odd number of times).

```
<ol id="collapse1">
  <li>First element of ordered list.</li>
  <li>Second element.</li>
  <li>Third element.</li>
</ol>
```

What's more, I want the collapse button to be generated automatically by JavaScript code when the document is loaded. Specifically, the body start tag will be

```
<body onload="makeCollapsible('collapse1');">
```

and a JavaScript function makeCollapsible() will be defined so that the call to this function modifies the document tree to add a button element before the list, as if the following markup were contained in the document:

```
<div>
  <button type="button"
          onclick="toggleVisibility(this,'collapse1')">
    Click to collapse
  </button>
</div>
<ol id="collapse1">
...
```

(The button element is placed within a div element due to the content model requirements of the XHTML DTD.) By creating the button in this way rather than entering the button markup directly into the document, we can easily generate similar collapse buttons in other documents.

As shown, the button element generated by makeCollapsible() will, when clicked, call on another function that we'll need to write, toggleVisibility(). This function will toggle the CSS display property of the collapsible element between the values block and none, which will have the effect of alternately displaying the element as a CSS block box or not displaying it at all (and not even reserving any space for it). This function will also change the text on the button (see Figure 5.14).

The code for the `makeCollapsible()` and `toggleVisibility()` functions is given in Figure 5.15. While I think that the code should be fairly self-explanatory for the most part, let me mention one small point. Notice that immediately after creating a node I insert it into the document tree, before doing anything else with the node. Although the DOM Level 2 standard does not explicitly require this order of operation, my experience has been that some browsers may behave badly if you do not follow this convention.

```
// BlockCollapse.js

// Add a button before the specified element (assumed
// to be block style) that will make the element
// disappear when clicked once and re-appear when
// clicked a second time.
// The button is placed within a div to ensure that
// the markup we generate is valid XHTML.

function makeCollapsible(elementId) {
  var element = window.document.getElementById(elementId);
  if (element) {
    var div = window.document.createElement("div");
    element.parentNode.insertBefore(div, element);
    var button = window.document.createElement("button");
    div.appendChild(button);
    button.setAttribute("type", "button");
    var buttonText = window.document.createTextNode("Click to collapse");
    button.appendChild(buttonText);
    button.setAttribute("onclick",
                        "toggleVisibility(this,'" + elementId + "');");
  }
  return;
}

// Function called when the button is clicked.

function toggleVisibility(button, elementId) {
  var element = window.document.getElementById(elementId);
  if (element) {
    if (element.style.display == "none") {
      element.style.display = "block";
      button.childNodes[0].data = "Click to collapse";
    } else {
      element.style.display = "none";
      button.childNodes[0].data = "Click to expand";
    }
  }
  return;
}
```

FIGURE 5.15 JavaScript code for `makeCollapsible()` and `toggleVisibility()` functions.

5.5.7   HTML Convenience Properties

The DOM's HTML module defines a number of deprecated convenience properties that can be used to set and retrieve element attribute values without calling setAttribute() and getAttribute(). I mention these primarily because they are widely used in JavaScript DOM code, so you are likely to see them in practice.

For example, if the value of a variable element is an Element instance, then the following two statements have the same effect:

```
element.setAttribute("id", "element3");
element.id = "element3";
```

In general, I recommend using setAttribute() and getAttribute() rather than these convenience properties. First, this has the advantage that it is clear to anyone reading your code that you are accessing HTML attributes rather than merely properties of a JavaScript object. Also, there are some special cases you have to remember when using the convenience properties. For example, you cannot write element.class, because class is a reserved word in JavaScript. Instead, you must write element.className. On the other hand, there are no special cases if you use the recommended methods.

We will, however, learn later that the HTML convenience property syntax is necessary for certain tasks related to forms. We'll also see that certain tasks in IE6 require this syntax. So, while I recommend avoiding this syntax when you can, it may not always be possible.

5.6   DOM Event Handling

We have already learned how to add calls to JavaScript event handling code via HTML attributes such as onmouseover. This can be viewed as a special case of a more powerful event model provided by browsers that conform to the DOM Level 2 Event module specifications [W3C-DOM-2-EVENTS]. This more powerful model is covered in this section.

You should note that this section is specifically about DOM event handling. While all of the code in this section can be executed in Mozilla 1.4, much of it will not work properly in IE6. Conceptually, though, event handling in IE6 is similar to that in the DOM; the differences are primarily syntactic. Section 5.7 contains syntactic details of IE6 event model.

5.6.1   The Event Object and Event Listeners

In the DOM event model, when an event occurs, an instance of a host object named Event is created. This instance contains information about the event, including the type of event (click, mouseover, etc.) and a reference to the document node corresponding to the markup element that generated the event; this node is called the *event target*. The Event instance properties type and target, respectively, provide this information.

Once an Event instance is created, it is sent to certain event listeners. In the JavaScript version of the DOM, an *event listener* is simply a function that takes a single argument that is an instance of Event. A call to the addEventListener() method on a node object associates an event listener with a type of event occurring on that node. For example, suppose a document contains an element with an id of msgButton and the following JavaScript code is executed:

```
// EventHello.js

var button = window.document.getElementById("msgButton");
button.addEventListener("click", sayHello, false);

function sayHello(event) {
  window.alert(
    "Hello World!\n\n" +
    "Event type: " + event.type + "\n" +
    "Event target element type: " + event.target.nodeName);
  return;
}
```

Then whenever the mouse is clicked on the msgButton element, the alert box of Figure 5.16 will be displayed.

The third (Boolean) argument to addEventListener() is discussed later in connection with event capture; for now, we will always set this to false. The second argument is of course the identifier of an event listener. The first argument is a case-insensitive String specifying the type of event listened for. Many of the DOM2 event types are the same as those used for HTML intrinsic event attributes (and are obtained by removing the prefix on from the attribute names in Table 5.1). However, three of the intrinsic event types do not have DOM2 counterparts at all: keypress, keydown, and keyup. Furthermore, there is also no DOM2 double-click event (that is, no event corresponding to the ondblclick attribute), although we will learn in a moment how double clicks can be detected using the DOM2 event model.

5.6.2 Mouse Events

Event instances associated with the six DOM2 mouse events—click, mousedown, mouseup, mousemove, mouseover, mouseout—have several properties in addition to type and target. These properties are described in Table 5.7. Notice that the detail property can be used to detect a double-click event: a double click is represented by an Event instance with a type of click and a detail value of 2. Note, however, that a total of six Event instances will be generated, in the following order: mousedown, mouseup, click, mousedown, mouseup, click.

FIGURE 5.16 Alert box produced by sayHello() function.

TABLE 5.7 Properties Added to Event Instances Representing DOM2 Mouse Events

Property	Value
clientX, clientY	These properties specify the x and y offsets (in pixels) of the mouse from the upper left corner of the browser client area. Apply to all events.
screenX, screenY	These properties specify the x and y offsets (in pixels) of the mouse from the upper left corner of the display. Apply to all events.
altKey, ctrlKey, metaKey, shiftKey	These properties each have a Boolean value indicating whether or not the corresponding keyboard key was depressed at the time this Event instance was generated. Apply to all events.
button	Which mouse button was depressed: 0=leftmost, 1=second from left, etc. (reversed for left-handed mouse). Applies to click, mousedown, and mouseup events.
detail	Number of times the mouse button has been depressed over the same screen location. Applies to click, mousedown, and mouseup events.
relatedTarget	If event is mouseover, then target is node being entered, and relatedTarget is node being exited. If event is mouseout, then target is node being exited, and relatedTarget is node being entered.

As one simple example of the potential functionality added by having event information available, suppose that we would like to add a *trail* to the mouse cursor. This is fairly simple (at least, as long as the user does not scroll the browser window): we simply add a mousemove event listener to the document, and, each time this listener is called, we position a small div in the browser window at the location of the mouse cursor. If we do this, say, 10 times, then a trail will appear to follow the mouse as it moves (Figure 5.17). On the eleventh call to the listener, we will move the first div to the current location of the mouse, on the twelfth call move the second div, and so on, so that div elements are always placed at the 10 most recent mouse locations.

Figure 5.18 shows the style sheet I used for this document, and the JavaScript code is shown in Figure 5.19 and Figure 5.20. The HTML document merely includes these files and then calls the init() function of Figure 5.19 when the document has been completely loaded, using the markup

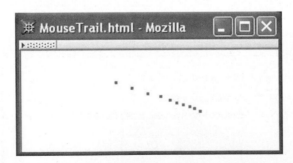

FIGURE 5.17 Trail of blips marking the last 10 locations (as recorded by mousemove events) of the mouse cursor.

```
/* MouseTrail.css */
.mouseTrailClass {
    background-color:green;
    height:3px; width:3px;
    position:absolute;
    left:0; top:0;
    display:none }
```

FIGURE 5.18 Style sheet defining initial style properties for mouse trail blip div elements.

```
<body onload="init();">
```

The init() function, in turn, creates 10 div elements (initially not displayed), assigns a unique id to each along with a CSS class, and adds each to the end of the HTML document's body. It also registers the function updateDivs() (Figure 5.20) as a listener for mousemove events anywhere within the document. The id prefix and CSS class name are chosen so that the id and class values for these 10 div elements are unlikely to conflict with values of other elements of the document. Choosing such names makes it likely that this style sheet and JavaScript code could be used without change in other documents, if desired.

```
// MouseTrail.js (part 1)

// Number of "blips" (divs) used to form the mouse trail
var NUM_BLIPS = 10;
// Each div's id will be this string followed by an integer
var DIV_ID_PREFIX = "mouseTrailDiv";
// CSS class for the "blips"
var CSS_CLASS = "mouseTrailClass";

// Create "blip" divs and add mousemove listener.
function init() {

  // Create div elements that will be "blips" trailing the mouse.
  // Style for these is provided by a separate style sheet.
  for (var i=0; i<NUM_BLIPS; i++) {
    var aDiv = window.document.createElement("div");
    window.document.body.appendChild(aDiv);
    aDiv.setAttribute("id", DIV_ID_PREFIX + i);
    aDiv.setAttribute("class", CSS_CLASS);
  }

  // Listen for every mouse move.
  window.document.addEventListener("mousemove", updateDivs, false);
  return;
}
```

FIGURE 5.19 Definitions of global constants and the init() function of JavaScript code for producing a mouse trail.

```
// MouseTrail.js (part 2)

// Blip 0 will be the first to have its position changed
// when the mouse begins to move.
var nextToChange = 0;
// Has the mouse moved at all yet?
var moved = false;

// mousemove event listener.
function updateDivs(event) {

  var aDiv; // object corresponding to a blip div element

  // If first mouse movement, initialize all blips to be at
  // the mouse cursor location and make them visible.
  if (!moved) {
    moved = true;
    for (var i=0; i<NUM_BLIPS; i++) {
      aDiv =
        window.document.getElementById(DIV_ID_PREFIX + i);
      aDiv.style.left = event.clientX + "px";
      aDiv.style.top = event.clientY + "px";
      aDiv.style.display = "block";
    }

  // On subsequent calls, change the location of one
  // blip and update a counter indicating which blip
  // should change location after the next mouse move.
  } else {
    aDiv =
        window.document.getElementById(DIV_ID_PREFIX + nextToChange);
    aDiv.style.left = event.clientX + "px";
    aDiv.style.top = event.clientY + "px";
    nextToChange = (nextToChange+1) % NUM_BLIPS;
  }
  return;
}
```

FIGURE 5.20 Definitions of some global variables and the updateDivs() function of JavaScript code for producing a mouse trail.

Notice the statements such as

```
aDiv.style.left = event.clientX + "px";
```

Recall that CSS length values, such as the values assigned to left, are string values that must include units (unless the value is 0). Also recall that the + operator is interpreted as string concatenation if either or both of its operands are Strings. So this statement converts the numeric value of event.clientX to a string and appends the appropriate unit designation, px.

Also notice that the use of the mod operator % makes it easy to cycle through the div elements as the event listener is called. As updateDivs() is successively called in response to mouse movements, the global variable nextToChange, which is initialized to 0, will take on the values 1, 2, 3, 4, 5, 6, 7, 8, 9, 0, 1, 2, etc. So each `div` element will be modified on every tenth call.

The code given is not "industrial strength." A key problem is that the `Event` instance returns the mouse location relative to the upper left corner of the client area of the browser window, not relative to the upper left corner of the document. But the absolute placement of `div` elements in this code is relative to the initial containing block, which is effectively the upper left corner of the document. So, if the user scrolls the window, the mouse trail produced by this code will be offset from the location of the cursor by the distance scrolled. A smaller problem is that the trail continues to be displayed even when the mouse stops moving; we might expect it to collapse (all `div` elements drawn at the mouse cursor location) when the mouse stops moving for, say, half a second. Both of these problems could be addressed using features of appropriate host objects described in Section 5.8.

5.6.3   Window-Level Events

Beyond the events corresponding to HTML intrinsic events, DOM2 also defines a number of additional events in modules HTMLEvents, UIEvents, and MutationEvents. Of these, I will mention just three HTMLEvents here (Table 5.8). These events are typically defined on the `window` object, using code such as

```
window.addEventListener("error", showMsg, false);
```

5.6.4   Event Propagation

In addition to defining `Event` instances, the DOM2 event model also provides control over *event propagation*. When a mouse event occurs, its target node is the most deeply nested (within the document tree) of those nodes that are visible on the screen and that cover the location of the mouse. For example, if the mouse moves over an anchor (hyperlink) that is within a paragraph element that is in turn within a `td` that is nested within a hierarchy of table elements that is, finally, part of the body element of a document, then the target of the mouseover event is the anchor node.

Although an event has a single target node, it may cause many event listeners to be called. First, this can occur because several listeners for this event may have been added to the target node. For example, if the target anchor node is associated with the variable `aNode`, then code such as

TABLE 5.8 Some DOM HTMLEvents Module Events That Do Not have Corresponding HTML Intrinsic Event Attributes

Event	Cause
error	An error (problem loading an image, script error, etc.) has occurred.
resize	View (window or frame) of document is resized.
scroll	View (window or frame) of document is scrolled.

```
aNode.addEventListener("mouseover", listener1, false);
aNode.addEventListener("mouseover", listener2, false);
```

would associate two different listeners with each mouseover event targeted at aNode.

In addition, event listeners associated with any of the ancestors of aNode in the document tree may be called. Specifically, when an event occurs, a DOM2-compliant browser conceptually creates an ordered list of event listeners and calls the listeners according to this order. There are three types of event listeners in this list, which appear in the following order: capturing listeners, target listeners, and bubbling listeners. A *capturing event listener* is a listener associated with an ancestor (in the document tree) of the target node and that was created with a call to addEventListener() that had its third argument set to true. A *target listener* is one of the listeners specifically added to the target node with its third argument false. And a *bubbling listener* is a listener associated with an ancestor of the target node and that was created with a call to addEventListener() that had its third argument set to false.

So, for example, given the markup

```
<p id="p1">
  <a id="a1" href="somewhere">Over the rainbow</a>
</p>
```

then with respect to click events on the a1 element, the following JavaScript code would register listener1() as a capturing event listener, listener2() as a target listener, and listener3() as a bubbling listener:

```
var target = document.getElementById("a1");
var ancestor = document.getElementById("p1");
ancestor.addEventListener("click", listener1, true);
ancestor.addEventListener("click", listener3, false);
target.addEventListener("click", listener2, false);
```

Thus, if the user clicks the a1 element and if all of the listeners are called (as we will see, they might not be), then the listener1() function will be called first, then listener2(), and finally listener3(). Notice that the order in which calls are made to addEventListener() does not determine the order in which the listeners are called.

If there are multiple ancestors with capturing listeners, then these listeners are ordered starting with those nearest the root of the document tree and proceeding down the tree toward the target node. The bubbling listeners are ordered in reverse, beginning with listeners associated with nodes nearest the target and proceeding up the tree toward the root. For a few types of events, including load, unload, focus, and blur, the listener list includes only capturing and target listeners; bubbling listeners are not added to the list for these event types.

Once this ordered list of listeners has been created, the browser calls the listeners in the list, one after the other. Two DOM2 properties of Event that were not mentioned previously provide information to a listener function regarding event propagation. First, the eventPhase property has a Number value, which represents the *event processing phase* of the browser: 1 indicates that the listener is being called as a capturing event listener (i.e., the browser is in the capture phase); 2 a call as a target listener; and 3 a call as a bubbling listener. The second property, currentTarget, contains a reference to the node on which the listener was registered.

The browser may not call all of the listeners in the ordered list if any of the listeners calls the stopPropagation() method (which takes no arguments) on its Event instance argument. In particular, once stopPropagation() is called, any other listeners that would be called during the current phase of processing and that are registered as listeners on the current node (currentTarget) will be executed, but after they have been executed further listener processing for this event will be terminated. However, a call to stopPropagation() in an event listener for one event (e.g., click) only stops processing for that event, not for other events.

Capturing event listeners are particularly suitable for tasks—such as the earlier cursor trail example—that are associated with the highest levels of the document tree. We normally want such tasks to be performed on every possible event. By capturing the event before it reaches listeners at lower levels of the tree, we guarantee that the capturing listener can process the event even if a listener later in the ordered listener list calls stopPropagation().

5.6.5   Example: Dropdown Menus

Having ancestors handle events targeted at their descendants can be extremely useful. For example, JavaScript is often used to implement dropdown menus on web pages. A rudimentary menu system initially displays a menu bar and makes different dropdown menus visible as the mouse moves over each menu bar item (Figure 5.21). The dropdown menus themselves are similar to the navigation bars that we saw earlier: the background color changes as the mouse moves into and out of the various menu boxes. A dropdown menu should remain visible until the mouse moves outside both the menu and its associated menu bar item, at which point it should disappear.

We can create such a menu in HTML by using a one-row table to hold the menu bar items and using an absolutely positioned div element to contain the dropdown menu associated with each of these items. Figure 5.22 shows portions of the markup for such a

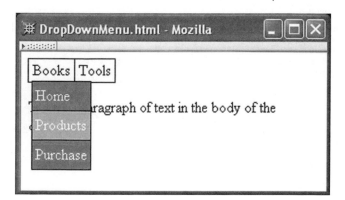

FIGURE 5.21 Example of rudimentary dropdown menu, with two-element menu bar and a dropdown menu visible under the first menu bar item. The second item in the dropdown menu is highlighted.

```
<body onload="addEventHandlers();">
  <table cellpadding="0" cellspacing="0" class="menubar">
    <tbody>
      <tr>
        <td>
          <div id="MenuBar1"
            >Books<div id="DropDown1">
            <table cellpadding="3" cellspacing="0" class="navbar">
              <tbody>
                <tr>
                  <td id="DropDown1_1"><a
                      href="http://www.example.com"
                      >Home</a>
                  </td>
                </tr>
                <tr>
                  <td id="DropDown1_2"><a
                      href="http://www.example.org"
                      >Products</a>
                  </td>
                </tr>
                ...
              </tbody>
            </table>
            </div>
          </div>
        </td>
        <td>
          <div id="MenuBar2"
            >Tools<div id="DropDown2">
            <table cellpadding="3" cellspacing="0" class="navbar">
              <tbody>
                <tr>
                  <td id="DropDown2_1"><a
                      href="http://www.example.com"
                      >Sockets</a>
                  </td>
                </tr>
                ...
              </tbody>
            </table>
            </div>
          </div>
        </td>
      </tr>
    </tbody>
  </table>
</body>
```

FIGURE 5.22 Portions of HTML markup for an example dropdown menu.

menu. Notice that I actually used two nested div elements within each menu bar item td. The outer div (e.g., MenuBar1) will act as the containing block for the inner div (e.g., DropDown1). That is, we will make the outer div a positioned element (by applying a position:relative style declaration to it) so that the inner div containing the dropdown menu can be positioned relative to this outer div.

The style rules for these outer and inner div elements are:

```
.menubar div { position:relative;
               line-height:1.5em;
               padding:0 0.5ex;
               margin:0 }
.menubar div div { position:absolute;
                   top:1.5em; left:0;
                   z-index:1;
                   display:none }
```

Notice that the top value of the inner div (e.g., DropDown1) is the same as the line-height value of the outer div, which contains the text of the menu bar item (e.g., "Books"). The dropdown menu will therefore appear immediately under the text of the menu bar. This means that it will overlap the border of the menu bar, as you can see if you look closely at Figure 5.21. It is important that there be no space between the bottom of the menu bar and the top of the dropdown menu: recall that we want the dropdown menu to disappear when the mouse leaves both the menu bar item and its dropdown menu, and if there is any space between the two, then the dropdown menu could disappear as the user attempts to move from the menu bar item to the menu. So this slight overlap is preferable to a small gap, which might be present due to the difference between specified and actual values of style properties if we tried to position the dropdown menu more exactly.

Now we develop the JavaScript event listeners (all of the following code is contained in a file DropDown.js). Four functions will be used: one to cause a dropdown menu to become visible, one to make it invisible again, and two to change the background colors of menu boxes as the cursor moves into and out of them. We'll begin with the first two of these functions, which will be named showDropDown() and hideDropDown(), respectively. We will add event listeners referencing these functions to the outer div for each menu bar item by including initialization code such as the following in the addEventHandlers() function called immediately after the HTML document has been loaded by the browser:

```
var menuBar1 = window.document.getElementById("MenuBar1");
menuBar1.addEventListener("mouseover", showDropDown, false);
menuBar1.addEventListener("mouseout", hideDropDown, false);
```

For convenience, we'll also store a reference to the inner div (the one containing the menu) as a property of the outer div's DOM object, so that we don't have to search through the children of the outer div for this inner div object:

```
menuBar1.dropDown = window.document.getElementById("DropDown1");
```

The listener functions themselves, along with a utility function called by one of these functions, are shown in Figure 5.23. The core of each listener is straightforward: specify a value for the display style property of the div containing the dropdown menu in order to make this menu either visible or invisible. As just noted, a reference to this div was stored by initialization code in the dropDown property of the outer div object, which is the object that is the currentTarget for the event, since the event listener is registered on the outer div. So, actually, changing the visibility of the menu is easy.

```
// mouseover listener for a menu bar item
function showDropDown(event) {

  // If mouse is over a menu bar item, then display
  // the drop-down menu associated with this menu bar item
  if (event.target == event.currentTarget) {
    var dropDown = event.currentTarget.dropDown;
    dropDown.style.display = "block";
  }
  return;
}

// mouseout listener for a menu bar item
function hideDropDown(event) {

  // If this menu bar item is not an ancestor of the node to which
  // the mouse is moving, hide the drop-down menu associated with
  // this menu bar item
  if (!ancestorOf(event.currentTarget, event.relatedTarget)) {
    var dropDown = event.currentTarget.dropDown;
    dropDown.style.display = "none";
  }
  return;
}

// Is ancestorElt an ancestor of descendElt?
// This treats a node as an ancestor of itself.
function ancestorOf(ancestorElt, descendElt) {
  var found;

  // Base cases: descendElt is null or same as ancestorElt
  if (!descendElt) {
    found = false;
  } else if (descendElt == ancestorElt) {
    found = true;

  // Recursive case: check descendElt's parent
  } else {
    found = ancestorOf(ancestorElt, descendElt.parentNode);
  }
  return found;
}
```

FIGURE 5.23 Event listeners called for mouseover and mouseout events related to menu bar items.

However, each function also contains an if statement, which is where event propagation becomes involved. First, note that the only time the menu needs to be made visible is when the mouse moves over the menu bar item for this menu (the outer `div` element). Any mouseover event in a descendant of the outer `div` can be ignored, and for efficiency purposes probably should be ignored. The if statement in `showDropDown()` guarantees that mouseover events generated by descendant elements are ignored. Without this statement, all mouseovers in descendants would bubble to this event listener and cause the outer `div`'s `display` property to be changed needlessly.

The if statement in `hideDropDown()` makes use of a utility function `ancestorOf()` that returns `true` if and only if its first argument is an ancestor of the second argument in the document tree. So the net effect of this if statement is that `hideDropDown()` only hides the dropdown menu if the mouse is moving to an element (as indicated by `relatedTarget`) that is not a descendant of the outer `div` element (which is the `currentTarget`, since it is the element on which the event listener is registered). Since the HTML content of this outer `div` consists of both the menu bar item and the dropdown menu (and nothing else), and since we want to hide the dropdown menu when the mouse moves outside both of these entities, this short test captures exactly the effect we want. You might want to try to code a dropdown menu without using event bubbling in order to appreciate just how much this feature can simplify event handling code.

We still need two functions for changing the background color of menu items as the mouse moves into and out of them. Recall that we used functions `highlight()` and `lowlight()` for this purpose in the earlier navbar example, and we could use the same functions now by registering them as event listeners on the `td` elements of the menu, as in

```
var dropDown1_1 = window.document.getElementById("DropDown1_1");
dropDown1_1.addEventListener("mouseover", highlight, false);
dropDown1_1.addEventListener("mouseout", lowlight, false);
```

However, now that we know more about event propagation, we can modify these functions slightly to make our menu system more efficient. For example, we now know that if the mouse moves over the anchor element contained within a menu box's `td` element, this will generate a mouseout event for the `td` element and a mouseover for the `a` element. In this situation, our old code should have made the `td` background gray in response to the mouseout, then made the `td` background silver again in response to the mouseover bubbled up from the `a` element. The browser display probably was not modified by this (because there was no net change, and the browser probably did not attempt to update its display while the script was executing), but this still does not constitute "clean" code. We can avoid this problem by again using the `ancestorOf()` utility (see `lowlight()` in Figure 5.24). Specifically, a menu `td` element's background will be made gray only if the mouse moves to an element that is not a descendant of this `td` element. With this change, moving the mouse to an `a` element within a `td` will not cause any change to the style of the `td`.

Similarly, the new version of `highlight()` only changes the background color of a `td` element if it hasn't already been changed. This means that bubbling events from descendants will not cause redundant style changes. Also notice that the `highlight()` function stops propagation of the mouseover event. If it did not, the event would bubble to the

```
// mouseover listener for a drop-down menu item
function highlight(event) {

  // If this menu item is not already highlighted, make it so
  if (event.currentTarget.style.backgroundColor != "silver") {
    event.currentTarget.style.backgroundColor = "silver";
  }

  // Drop-down is already showing, so no need for ancestor
  // menu bar item to see this event
  event.stopPropagation();
  return;
}

// mouseout listener for a drop-down menu item
function lowlight(event) {

  // If this menu item is not an ancestor of the node to which
  // the mouse is moving, then unhighlight this item
  if (!ancestorOf(event.currentTarget, event.relatedTarget)) {
    event.currentTarget.style.backgroundColor = "gray";
  }
  return;
}
```

FIGURE 5.24 Event listeners called for mouseover and mouseout events related to dropdown menu items.

showDropDown() listener. But if highlight() is being called, then the dropdown menu must be visible, which means that showDropDown() does not need to be called.

5.6.6 Event Canceling and Form Validation

My earlier description of the browser's ordered list of event listeners was slightly incomplete. For certain events on certain HTML elements, the browser provides a default event listener that is called after all other listeners for all other events on the element have been called. An example default listener is the one that processes a click event on a hyperlink, causing the browser to load a document from a specified URI in place of the current document. Another default listener is the one called after a submit button is clicked on a form. This listener creates a query string representing the form data and submits it in an HTTP request to the URL specified for the form's action attribute.

Default event listeners are not placed in an ordered event list and therefore are not affected by calls to stopPropagation(). However, many event types, including click and submit, are *cancelable*, which means that the browser can be told not to perform any default action associated with the event. Calling the preventDefault() method (which takes no arguments and returns no value) on an Event instance cancels the browser's default event listener.

Canceling the browser's default action is often used in conjunction with form validation. For example, consider an HTML document FormValidation.html containing a text box named requiredField within which the user is supposed to enter data before clicking the submit button on a form named validatedForm. Then we could validate the user's data entry as follows. First, we would associate a listener with the submit event on the form:

```
// FormValidation.js
// ...
  var form = window.document.getElementById("validatedForm");
  form.addEventListener("submit", validateForm, false);
```

The code for the function called by the listener might then be something like

```
function validateForm(event) {
  var textfield = window.document.getElementById("requiredField");
  var fieldValue = textfield.value; // getAttribute doesn't work here!

  // If text box contains only white space, do not submit form.
  // This test uses a regular expression; it will be true if
  // the text box is empty or contains only white space.
  if (/^\s*$/.test(fieldValue)) {
    window.alert("Data must be entered in the field\n" +
                 "before submitting the form");
    event.preventDefault();
  }
  return;
}
```

Notice that to obtain the current content of the text box control as displayed in the browser, I used the expression textfield.value rather than textfield.getAttribute("value"). The reason is that the value property of an Element corresponding to an HTML text field provides access to the data displayed for that field in the browser, while the value HTML attribute of the text field acts as an initial value. So a call to getAttribute() in a DOM2-compliant browser should return the initial value rather than the value actually entered by the user (although IE6 and at least some versions of Firefox return the displayed value). The value displayed on the form can also be modified by a JavaScript statement such as

```
textfield.value = "CHANGE THIS";
```

Again, this will not change the attribute value, but only what is displayed in the text field.

5.6.7 Generating Events

Ideally, when data entered in a text box is invalid, we would like to not only tell the user that there is an error, but also select the contents of the box (both to bring attention to the information and so that the contents will be replaced automatically when new information is entered). In effect, we'd like the browser to change its display as if the user had selected the contents of the text box using the mouse. Notice that this would also cause a select event to occur.

TABLE 5.9 DOM2 Methods for Generating Common Events

Method	Applicable Elements
blur	anchor, input, select, textarea
click	input (type button, checkbox, radio, reset, or submit)
focus	anchor, input, select, textarea
select	input (type text, file, or password), textarea

DOM2 defines four methods that can be used to simulate such effects (Table 5.9). Each method, which takes no arguments and has no return value, generates an event of the type indicated by the name of the method; the object on which the method is called becomes the target value for the Event. In addition, any visual changes that would normally be associated with the event, such as selecting the text within a text box, are displayed by the browser. (A caution: I've had some trouble with these methods in Mozilla 1.4, particularly if called from within intrinsic event functions rather than from within event listeners registered via addEventListener().)

For example, returning to the example in Section 5.6.6, we might add the code

```
textfield.select();
```

following the call to window.alert(). When this statement is executed, it will generate a select event as if the user had selected text within the text box. Furthermore, the browser display will be modified as if this had happened, so that any text in the box will be highlighted and the text box will have the focus.

As another example, the click() method can be used to submit a form in response to a user input other than clicking the submit button. Let's say that a form includes a menu (select element) of country names. If the user selects one of these, we may want to immediately submit the form to the server so that it can return a second form that looks much like the first but also adds a menu of city names appropriate for the selected country. We could do this by associating with the country menu a listener for the change event (the event corresponding to the onchange intrinsic event attribute). This listener, when called, would in turn call the click() method on the submit button of the form containing the menu.

The four methods described, while sufficient for many standard purposes, are actually special cases of a more general DOM mechanism that can be used to generate arbitrary events; see Section 1.5 of [W3C-DOM-2-EVENTS] for details.

5.7 Accommodating Noncompliant Browsers

Mozilla 1.4 and a number of other browsers support all of the DOM2 features described in this chapter. However, IE6—the most widely used browser at the time this was written — deviates from DOM2 in a number of ways, although often the deviations are more syntactic than substantive. Of course, other browsers both now and in the future may also deviate from DOM2. This section provides some suggestions for dealing with browser noncompliance in general and for supporting IE6 in particular, since IE6 will likely be in use on many machines for several years to come.

5.7.1 Detecting Host Objects

In an earlier example, I used the code

```
var elementType = window.Node ? Node.ELEMENT_NODE : 1;
```

and said that the expression `window.Node` was in essence a test for the existence of the DOM2 `Node` object. This is a specific example of a general rule: before accessing DOM API features—particularly those that are known not to be supported by one or more browsers in widespread use—your JavaScript code should determine that the feature is provided by the browser in which the code is running. Failure to follow this rule may result in your code throwing unexpected exceptions in some browsers, causing the function containing the code to terminate prematurely.

Testing for existence of DOM features can be accomplished in a variety of ways. The first, as just illustrated, is to directly test for each feature before using it. Before moving on to other techniques, I'll mention some fine points concerning such tests. Consider the following attempt at testing for the existence of the `setProperty()` method of a `style` object:

```
if (element.style.setProperty) {
```

This code could throw an exception for a number of reasons, for instance, if `element` is not defined, or if `style` has the value `null`. Possibilities such as these can be eliminated by writing the test more carefully:

```
if (element && element.style && element.style.setProperty) {
```

I'll leave it as an exercise to work out why the condition in this case never throws an exception as long as `element` has been declared. For now, the general form of such tests should be clear from this example, and I encourage you to use tests of this form whenever you have any doubt about the existence or value of one or more of the components of a property accessor.

Another way to test for the existence of a feature is to use a feature of the DOM itself. A DOM2-compliant browser is supposed to provide an `implementation` host object that has, among other properties, a `hasFeature()` method. If you pass this method two String arguments representing the name of a DOM2 module (such as `Core` or `Events`) and a DOM version (such as `2.0`), it returns `true` if the browser fully implements this module and `false` otherwise. There are some issues involved with using this method, however. First, you may want to use some other technique to ensure that the `implementation` object exists and has a `hasFeature()` method. A more critical issue is that it is not uncommon for browsers to implement a subset of the recommendations for a DOM module. In this case, the `hasFeature()` method returns `false`, providing no indication that some portions of the module are implemented. I therefore don't recommend using this method.

Finally, a common approach to testing for DOM features is to attempt to recognize which browser is running your JavaScript code. The idea is that if you know which browser is running your code, and you know which DOM features are supported by which browsers, then this one test can be used in place of a number of individual tests elsewhere. Code implementing this form of feature testing might look something like

```
var ie =
  // Code recognizing Internet Explorer browsers...
  ;
// Other code ...
if (!ie) {
  element.style.setProperty("background-color", "gray", "");
} else {
  element.style.backgroundColor = "gray";
}
```

While this approach is widely used, I recommend avoiding it. Even if your code successfully recognizes all browsers on the market today (and there's a good chance that it will not), and even if you know precisely the features supported by every browser, there will be new browsers tomorrow or the next day that your code might not properly recognize or for which its feature information might be incorrect. Thus, code of this type will not age well. What's more, there is no absolutely reliable way to detect which browser is executing your code. For example, the appName property of the host object navigator, mentioned in Section 5.8, is one popular way to detect the type of browser. But some browsers allow the user to set the value of this property, so it cannot be relied upon. And again, as new browsers come on the market, the value of this property will change, perhaps in unexpected ways.

Now that we've considered some general techniques for detecting whether or not a browser provides a certain host object, let's focus specifically on some of the DOM objects that are missing in IE6 along with some ways to simulate these features.

5.7.2   IE6 Details

We have seen earlier one small way in which IE6 does not fully implement DOM2: it does not supply a Node object, and therefore certain named constants (such as Node.ELEMENT_NODE) are not available in IE6. Earlier code shows how to work around this problem simply by using a conditional expression. IE6 also does not supply the setProperty() or getPropertyValue() methods of the style object, but this can for the most part (except for assigning a weight to a property) be circumvented by using style attributes such as backgroundColor as described in Section 5.4. Similarly, in my version of IE6, a call to setAttribute() or getAttribute() with the string class as the first argument does not behave as it should (the className convenience property can be used instead). Another issue is that IE6 appears to force the height of an empty div or span to at least the character height, even if the element's height property is set to a lower value. This is normally not a problem, but can show up in specialized documents such as the earlier MouseTrail application.

Of the DOM features covered in this chapter, the remaining area in which IE6 deviates from the DOM is in the area of event listeners. Here the differences are significant. I will only cover some basics of the IE6 event model here; for details, see the Microsoft Development Network Web site (at the time of this writing, `http://msdn.microsoft.com/workshop/author/om/event_model.asp` is a good starting point).

First, IE6 does not support the general notion of multiple JavaScript event listeners associated with a single event type on a single element. This means that the `addEventListener()` method is not available. So the intrinsic event model is the only one available to programs running in IE6.

Furthermore, recall that in an earlier DOM example we used the following code to specify a value for an HTML intrinsic event attribute:

```
button.setAttribute("onclick",
                    "toggleVisibility(this,'" + elementId + "');");
```

This particular code specifies a value for the `onclick` attribute of an `Element` object named `button`. The value specified is a string representing a call to a JavaScript function named `toggleVisibility()`. This function call includes two arguments: the keyword `this` and a string representing an element's `id` value.

To set a value for an `onclick` attribute in IE6 from within a JavaScript program, code such as the following must instead be used:

```
button.onclick = toggleVisibility;
```

There are two key differences between this code and the `setAttribute()` method call. First, the value assigned by `setAttribute` is always of type String, but the identifier `toggleVisibility` assigned to the `onclick` property will evaluate to an Object representing a function. In short, the IE6 code is assigning an Object to the `onclick` attribute, rather than a String representing a call to a function. This brings up the second difference, which is that it is not possible to pass arguments to the `onclick` function using the IE6 approach. Instead, when a click event occurs, the IE6 browser calls the specified function with no arguments. It does, however, define an object named `event` within the global (`window`) object, which provides many of the same properties that would be provided by an `Event` object passed to a DOM event listener. More on this later in this subsection.

We can detect the IE6 approach to event processing by testing the `onclick` property of an object, which is initially `null` in IE6 but should not have this value in a DOM-compliant browser (because in the DOM it is String-valued, and `null` is not a String value in JavaScript). In particular, code such as the following should work both in IE6 and in DOM-compliant browsers:

```
if (button.onclick === null) { // e.g., in IE
  button.onclick = toggleVisibility;
} else {
  button.setAttribute("onclick",
                      "toggleVisibility(this,'" + elementId + "');");
}
```

There is still the issue that the toggleVisibility() function is called with differing numbers of arguments. This can also be handled without too much difficulty. First, notice that in IE6 the function toggleVisibility() is actually a method of the button object. What's more, IE6 effectively calls this function as a method, which means that in IE6 the value of the keyword this within toggleVisibility() will be a reference to button. But that is exactly the value of this used as an argument to toggleVisibility in the DOM approach. So we do not need to pass this argument in IE6. Furthermore, we can store any other argument values (the value of elementId in our example) as properties of the button object rather than passing them as arguments. For instance, we can modify the code by adding the line

```
button.elementId = elementId;
```

to the "then" part of the if statement. This stores the value that would have been the second argument to toggleVisibility() in a property of the button object. Once this is done, the beginning of the toggleVisibility() function can be rewritten as follows:

```
// BlockCollapseIE.js (part 2)
function toggleVisibility(inButton, elementId) {

  // Local variables whose values will be defined
  // based on the event model supported.
  var button, element;

  // If DOM browser, inButton is an object and
  // elementId is a non-empty, non-Number String,
  // so this condition is true.
  if (inButton && elementId) {
    button = inButton;
    element = window.document.getElementById(elementId);
  }
  // Otherwise, if window.event exists assume this
  // is IE6
  else if (window.event) {
    button = this;
    if (button) {
      element = window.document.getElementById(button.elementId);
    }
  }
  if (element) { // remainder as in BlockCollapse.js
```

The technique just illustrated should work for intrinsic event attributes in general. But what if we have written a more general DOM event listener that expects to be passed an Event instance? For example, recall the updateDivs() event listener used in the earlier MouseTrail example. This function used many properties of its Event instance object. IE6 provides similar properties, but most have different names and some have different semantics. Writing code to take account of all of these differences seems problematic.

However, it's not necessarily difficult to generalize DOM code so that it runs correctly in IE6 as well. For example, `updateDivs()` can be modified as follows:

```
function updateDivs(event) {

  // Convert IE event object to DOM Event instance if necessary
  if (needEventConversion(arguments)) {
    event = eventConvert(window.event, this);
  }

  var aDiv; // object corresponding to a blip div element
  ...
```

(Exercise 4.15 covers the `arguments` object.) The `needEventConversion()` function attempts to test whether or not the browser calling it is compliant with the DOM event model. The function shown in Figure 5.25, for example, tests that the event listener has received exactly one argument and that it is an instance of `Event`, which would seem to be a fairly reliable test.

If conversion is needed, the `eventConvert()` function extracts information from the IE6 `window.event` object and uses it to construct an `Event` object with the same information (or close to it). Figure 5.26 contains an implementation of such a function. While I don't claim that it's perfect, it can be used to generalize all of the examples in this chapter so that they work in both Mozilla 1.4 and IE6. In any event, you can learn about some of the similarities and differences between the IE6 and DOM event-related objects by examining the body of the `eventConvert()` function.

Finally, recall that in the DOM we create a capturing event listener by setting the third argument to `addEventListener()` to `true`. IE6 also supports a form of event capturing, which is enabled by calling the IE-specific `setCapture()` method on an object that has a listener for any of the mouse events (click, mouseover, etc.). However, the semantics of event capture are substantially different in IE6 than they are in DOM2; see documentation on `setCapture()` and related methods at [MS-DHTML] for details. Because of the differences in capture semantics, I did not attempt to simulate the `eventPhase` property in `event Convert()`.

```
// EventConvert.js

// Attempt to determine whether or not event conversion is needed.

function needEventConversion(args) {
  return !((args.length == 1) &&
           window.Event &&
           (args[0] instanceof window.Event));
}
```

FIGURE 5.25 Function `needEventConversion()` for testing whether or not a function was called in a manner consistent with the DOM2 event model.

```
// EventConvert.js (part 2)
// Convert from IE6 event object to DOM event object.
function eventConvert(ieEvent, currentTarget) {

  var event = new Object();
  try {

    // Do a (poor) simulation of IE dblclick
    // using DOM2 click event and detail property.
    // Let other event types pass through unchanged.
    event.detail = 1;
    if (ieEvent.type == "dblclick") {
      event.type = "click";
      event.detail = 2;
    } else {
      event.type = ieEvent.type;
    }
    event.target = ieEvent.srcElement;
    event.currentTarget = currentTarget;

    // Define DOM functions that call comparable IE functions.
    // cancelBubble only cancels bubbling, not execution of capturing
    // or target listeners, so only approximates stopPropagation.
    event.stopPropagation = function () {ieEvent.cancelBubble = true;};
    event.preventDefault = function () {ieEvent.returnValue = false;};
    event.screenX = ieEvent.screenX;
    event.screenY = ieEvent.screenY;
    event.clientX = ieEvent.clientX;
    event.clientY = ieEvent.clientY;
    event.altKey = ieEvent.altKey;
    event.ctrlKey = ieEvent.ctrlKey;
    // No meta key defined in IE event object
    event.shiftKey = ieEvent.shiftKey;
    switch (ieEvent.button) {
      case 1: event.button = 0; break;
      case 4: event.button = 1; break;
      case 2: event.button = 2; break;
    }
    switch (ieEvent.type) {
      case "mouseover": event.relatedTarget = ieEvent.fromElement; break;
      case "mouseout": event.relatedTarget = ieEvent.toElement; break;
    }
  } catch (e) {
    // Return whatever we have and hope for the best...
  }
  return event;
}
```

FIGURE 5.26 Function `eventConvert()` for creating an object that simulates portions of a DOM2 Event instance from an IE6 `window.event` object.

5.8   Additional Properties of `window`

We have now covered the DOM API in quite a bit of detail. In addition to the host objects defined by the DOM, most browsers supply many other useful host objects as properties of the `window` object. Examples of such host objects are `alert()` and `prompt()`. In this section, I will provide an overview of these and several other frequently used host objects that are available in both Mozilla 1.4 and IE6 (and presumably many other browsers). Since none of these objects are currently covered by any formal standard, you should consult the documentation of all browsers that you wish your software to run on for details of these properties as well as to learn about other properties not covered here. Currently, good starting points for learning more about host objects supplied by the `window` object are [MS-DHTML-WINDOW] for IE6 and [MOZ-DOM-WINDOW] for Mozilla.

Table 5.10 and Table 5.11 list a number of method host objects provided by both IE6 and Mozilla 1.4. The first three methods of Table 5.10 (including two that we've already used) are user interface methods that cause various dialog windows to be displayed. The next two methods allow a JavaScript program to open new browser windows and also to close windows. Other methods in this table allow a window to be modified in various ways, such as by moving or resizing it. The four methods in Table 5.11 provide facilities for scheduling function calls.

To illustrate the use of several of these methods, consider the following somewhat contrived example. JavaScript code running in one window will create a second browser window (a pop-up). Every second, the pop-up window will move and grow by a small amount. As this happens, text in the original window will show a countdown, starting at 10 and proceeding toward 0. If the user clicks a button in the original window, the countdown will be reset to 10. When the countdown finally reaches 0, the pop-up will be closed.

Figure 5.27 illustrates the two browser windows sometime after the first window has been loaded. The HTML source of the document loaded into the original window is given in Figure 5.28. Notice that a function named `init()` is called after the document is loaded, that the body of the document has a `span` (with `id` value `countdown`) containing the text string `10`, and that a function named `resetCountdown()` is called if the button contained within the body of the document is clicked.

Figure 5.29 contains the definitions of the JavaScript functions `init()` and `reset` `Countdown()` called by the `HostObjects.html` HTML document, along with one more function definition named `messWithPopUp()`. As shown, the main task for `init()` is to create a pop-up window by calling `window.open()`. The value returned by this call is a JavaScript Object reference that represents the global object for this new window. This object will differ from the global object of the original window because each window effectively runs its own JavaScript scripting engine. The Object reference returned by `open()` allows JavaScript code in the original window to access properties in the pop-up window, including host objects of the pop-up. For example, the `popup.focus();` statement in `resetCountdown()` calls the `focus()` method of the pop-up window's global object (we explain what this does in the next paragraph). The `init()` function also creates an interval timer that calls the `messWithPopUp()` function once per second until the timer is cleared. Finally, for the convenience of the other two functions, `init()` creates an object reference to the `countdown` `span` element.

TABLE 5.10 Some Common window Methods

Method	Functionality
alert(String)	Display alert window displaying the given String value.
confirm(String)	Pop up a window that displays the given String value and contains two buttons labeled OK and Cancel. Return boolean indicating which button was pressed (true implies that OK was pressed).
prompt(String, String)	Pop up a window that displays the first String value and contains a text field and two buttons labeled OK and Cancel. Second String argument is initial value that will be displayed in the text field. Return String representing final value of text field if OK is pressed, or null/undefined (browser-dependent) if Cancel button is pressed.
open(String, String)	Open a new browser window, and load the URI specified by the first String argument into this window. The second String specifies a name for this window suitable for use as the value of a target attribute in an HTML anchor or form element. Optional String third argument is comma-separated list of "features," such as the window width and height; see example in text. Returns an object that is a reference to the global object for the new window.
close()	Close the browser window executing this method.
focus()	Give the browser window executing this method the focus.
blur()	Cause the browser window executing this method to lose the focus. The window that gains the focus is determined by the operating system.
moveTo(Number, Number)	Move the upper left corner of the browser window executing this method to the (x, y) screen location (in pixels) specified by the argument values, which should be integers. The upper left corner of the screen is at $(0, 0)$.
moveBy(Number, Number)	Move the upper left corner of the browser window executing this method right and down by the number of pixels specified by the first and second, respectively, argument values. These values should be integers.
resizeTo(Number, Number)	Resize the browser window executing this method so that it has width and height in pixels as specified by the first and second, respectively, argument values. These values should be integers.
resizeBy(Number, Number)	Resize the browser window executing this method so that its width and height are changed by the number of pixels specified by the first and second, respectively, argument values. These values should be integers.
print()	Print the document contained in the window executing this method as if the browser's Print button had been clicked.

The resetCountdown() function is conceptually simple: it sets the text string contained within the countdown span to 10. It also gives the pop-up window the focus, which for most browsers and operating systems ensures that the pop-up window is displayed on top of all other windows on the user's display. If this were not done, then when the user clicked on the button in the original window, this window might gain the focus and obscure the pop-up window.

Finally, the messWithPopUp() function, called each second, decrements the number contained within the countdown span. If the resulting value is 0, then the interval timer is cleared and the pop-up window is closed. Otherwise, the function "messes with" the pop-up

TABLE 5.11 Common window Methods Related to Time

Method	Functionality
setTimeout(String, Number)	Execute (once) the JavaScript code represented by the first argument value after the number of milliseconds specified by the second (integer) argument value has elapsed, unless the timeout is cleared (see next method). Return Number representing an ID for the timeout that can be used to clear it.
clearTimeout(Number)	Clear the timeout having the ID specified by the Number argument.
setInterval(String, Number)	Repeatedly execute the JavaScript code represented by the first argument value every time the number of milliseconds specified by the second (integer) argument value has elapsed, unless the interval timer is cleared (see next method). Return Number representing an ID for the interval timer that can be used to clear it.
clearInterval(Number)	Clear the interval timer having the ID specified by the Number argument.

window, moving and resizing it slightly. The net effect is that the pop-up will move southeast on the display and grow slightly larger every second. Once again, the pop-up window is given the focus in this case to ensure that it is visible.

Let me add a few words of caution before moving on. As you may be aware, pop-up windows are often (but not always) used to display advertisements or other information that

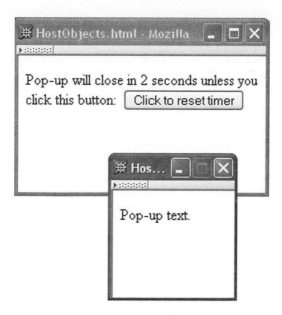

FIGURE 5.27 Pop-up window displayed in front of initial browser window containing HostObjects.html document.

```
<!DOCTYPE html
        PUBLIC "-//W3C//DTD XHTML 1.0 Strict//EN"
        "http://www.w3.org/TR/xhtml1/DTD/xhtml1-strict.dtd">
<html xmlns="http://www.w3.org/1999/xhtml">
  <head>
    <title>
      HostObjects.html
    </title>
    <meta http-equiv="Content-Script-Type" content="text/javascript" />
    <script type="text/javascript" src="HostObjects.js">
    </script>
  </head>
  <body onload="init();">
    <p>
      <label>Pop-up will close in <span id="countdown">10</span>
        seconds unless you click this button: 
        <button type="button"
                onclick="resetCountdown();">Click to reset timer</button>
      </label>
    </p>
  </body>
</html>
```

FIGURE 5.28 HTML document used to illustrate the use of several common host object methods.

many users would rather not see. Some browsers, such as Mozilla, provide features that allow users to block pop-up windows except those originating from specified Web sites. Furthermore, even when used for innocuous purposes, pop-up windows can be confusing to many users. Having multiple windows can also add noticeably to the complexity of JavaScript code. In general, then, it is best to avoid pop-ups unless their use significantly simplifies a user interface design. Finally, for security and privacy reasons your code normally cannot access the Dom of a pop-up window that is loaded from a different domain than your code.

Table 5.12 lists some nonmethod properties of the `window` object that are provided by both IE6 and Mozilla 1.4. You might wonder why a `closed` property is needed. It is because other windows might contain references to the closed window. In the preceding example, for instance, the code references the pop-up window through the `popup` variable. If the user closes the pop-up window, then a statement such as `popup.moveBy(10,10);` will cause an exception to be thrown, because the window referenced by `popup` no longer exists. So our code could be improved by having the `messWithPopUp()` function begin with a statement such as

```
if (!popup.closed) {
```

in order to avoid closure-related exceptions.

The `navigator` host object has several String properties that provide human-readable information about the browser, including `appName`, `appVersion`, and `userAgent`. As mentioned earlier, it is not uncommon for JavaScript programs to examine these properties in order to try to customize themselves for the browser on which they are running, although

```
// HostObjects.js

/* Functions to create a small pop-up window and move/resize
   it every second until 10 seconds have elapsed without the
   user clicking a button. */

var popup;          // Reference to pop-up window's global object
var intervalID;     // ID of one-second interval timer
var countdownElt;   // span containing number of seconds until
                    //    pop-up closes

// init is called when document has loaded.
// It creates a pop-up window and a one-second interval timer.
function init() {
  popup = window.open("HostObjectsPopUp.html", "popup",
                      "width=100,height=100");
  intervalID = window.setInterval("messWithPopUp();", 1000);
  countdownElt = window.document.getElementById("countdown");
  return;
}


// resetCountdown is called when user clicks button.
// It changes a "countdown" value that is displayed in the HTML document.
function resetCountdown() {
  countdownElt.childNodes[0].data = "10";
  popup.focus();   // Make sure the pop-up is still visible.
  return;
}


// messWithPopUp is called every second by the interval timer.
// It decrements the "countdown" value, closes the pop-up window
// if the countdown has reached 0, and otherwise moves and resizes
// the pop-up.
function messWithPopUp() {
  var secondsLeft = countdownElt.childNodes[0].data - 1;
  countdownElt.childNodes[0].data = String(secondsLeft);
  if (secondsLeft == 0) {
    window.clearInterval(intervalID);
    popup.close();
  } else {
    popup.moveBy(10,10);
    popup.resizeBy(2,2);
    popup.focus();
  }
  return;
}
```

FIGURE 5.29 JavaScript functions that call on several common host object methods.

TABLE 5.12 Some Common Non method Properties Added to the `window` Object by Browsers

Property	Value
`closed`	Boolean indicating whether this window is open or closed.
`location`	String representing URL currently loaded into this window. Setting this property to a String value causes the browser to load the URL represented by this String.
`name`	The name value assigned to this window by the second argument to the `open` method.
`opener`	Object reference to window that opened this window. Need not be present in every `window` object.
`parent`	If this document is loaded in a `frame`, this is an object reference to the global object for the `frameset` containing the `frame`. In a window opened with `window.open`, this is a reference to the window itself. In an initial browser window, this property may not be present.
`top`	Similar to parent, but is a reference to the top of the hierarchy rather than to the immediate ancestor.
`navigator`	Object providing information about the browser (see text).
`screen`	Object providing information about the display on which the browser window is viewed (see text).

I don't recommend this approach in general. So I won't say more about these properties here.

Another common host object is `screen`. This object provides several Number-valued properties including `height` and `width`, which represent the size of the user's entire display (in pixels), as well as `availHeight` and `availWidth`, which give the dimensions (in pixels) of the area of the display that is not covered by window manager components (such as the Taskbar in Windows). The `colorDepth` property of `screen` returns the number of bits used per pixel on the display. These values can all be helpful in choosing how to present information to this user (how large to make the browser window, what colors to use, and so on).

5.9 Case Study

We're now ready to use JavaScript to incorporate some additional features into our blogging application.

Let's begin with scripting for the add-entry page (Figure 5.30). Notice that there are three buttons at the bottom of this page. The middle of these, Add Entry, is the submit button (`input` element of type `submit`) for the form. Recall that when a submit button is clicked, the browser creates a query string from the data contained in the form and sends this string in an HTTP request to the server. The last button, Clear, is a reset button (`input` of type `reset`); the browser will clear the form's text box and textarea when this button is clicked. The first button, Preview, is an `input` of type `button`, which has no default browser behavior. The behavior we want for this button is similar to that of a submit button: we want a query string representing the form to be sent to the server. However, there will be two differences. First, we want the query string to indicate to the server that this is a preview request, which will affect both the processing of the request and the format of the

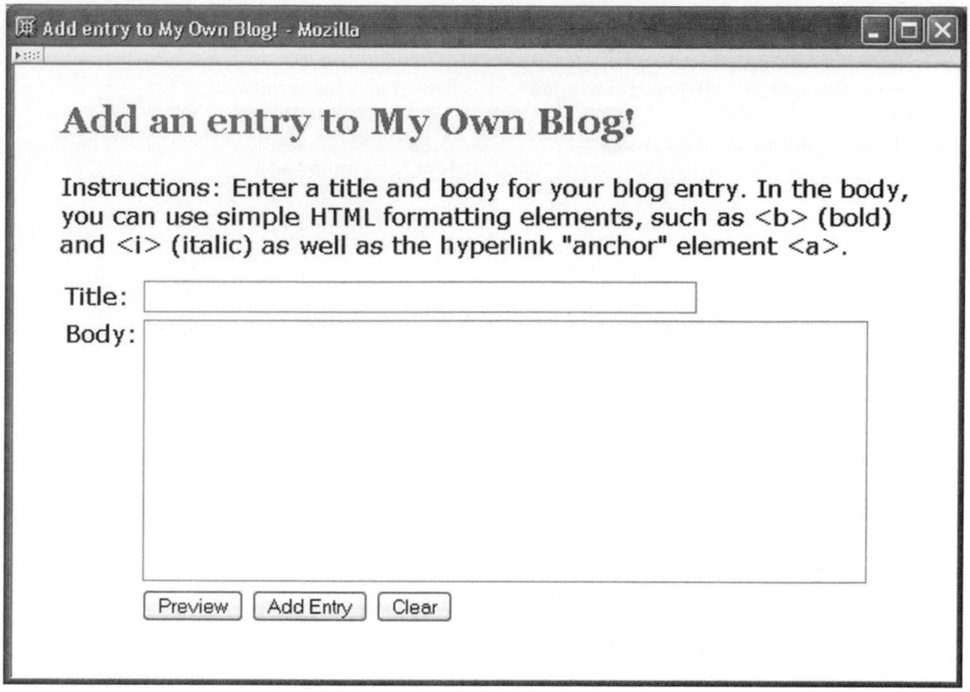

FIGURE 5.30 Add-entry page with CSS styles applied.

response page (see Figure 3.42 for an example of a preview page). Second, we want the HTML document that is returned by the server to be displayed in a different window, so that the add-entry page will not be disturbed.

The Preview button behavior will be implemented by a JavaScript function named showPreview(), which will be called by defining an onclick HTML intrinsic event attribute on the input element:

```
<input type="button" name="preview" id="preview"
       value="Preview" onclick="showPreview();" />
```

An implementation of showPreview() is given in Figure 5.31. The basic idea is to modify the original form somewhat and then to simulate a click of the submit button. The browser will then send the contents of the modified form to the server and display the response. The modified form will both inform the server that this is a preview request and instruct the browser to display the response in a separate window.

The function begins with a call to window.open(), which does nothing if a window named MOBPreviewWindow is already open or otherwise opens a new window with this name. Most browsers, including IE6 and Mozilla, follow the convention that if the first argument to window.open() is about:blank then an empty browser window will be opened (normally, this argument is a URL to be loaded into the new window).

```
/* Show a preview of the blog entry in a separate window. */
function showPreview() {

    var windowName = "MOBPreviewWindow"; // Name for new window

    // Open a separate window
    var previewWindow = window.open("about:blank", windowName);

    // Target the response to the form at the new window
    var addForm = document.getElementById("addForm");
    addForm.setAttribute("target", windowName);

    // Indicate to the server that this is a preview
    var doPreview = document.getElementById("doPreview");
    doPreview.value = "true";

    // Submit the form
    document.getElementById("addentry").click();

    // Reset form to original values
    doPreview.value = "false";
    addForm.setAttribute("target", "");

    // Give the new window the focus
    previewWindow.focus();
    return;
}
```

FIGURE 5.31 JavaScript function for sending a preview request to the server and displaying the returned HTML document in another window.

The next two lines of showPreview() retrieve the JavaScript object representing the form element (which has id value addForm) and set the value of the target attribute of this element to the name of the newly opened window. Recall that if target is declared for a form, then when the browser submits the form to the server, it will display the response document in the named window rather than in the window containing the form.

Next, the browser sets the value of a hidden element (input of type hidden) in order to inform the server that it is receiving a request for a preview, not a request to add an entry to the blog. The markup for this element is

```
<input type="hidden" name="doPreview" id="doPreview"
        value="false" />
```

Such an element is not visible in the browser window, but its value is sent to the server when the form containing this element is submitted.

Next, the function sends a click event to the Add Entry (submit) button, which has id value addentry. This causes the form's control values to be encoded in a query string and sent to the server. The function ends by reversing the changes it made to the form so that when the Add Entry button is later clicked by the user, the browser will send a nonpreview request to the server and display the results in the window containing the add-entry page. The call to focus() causes the new window to be placed on top of all other open windows, ensuring that it will be visible to the user.

We would also like to improve on the default functionality of the Clear (reset) button. By default, clicking on this button immediately clears the text from the form. It would be better to confirm that the user wants to do this before actually clearing the text. We can do this by adding a click event listener to this button. The listener function displays a confirmation window and prevents the browser from performing the clear action if the user does not confirm the clear.

Figure 5.32 performs this task. The init() function, which will be called in the onload intrinsic event attribute of the body element, adds the event handling function confirmClear() to the Clear button (which has id value clear). The confirmClear() function displays a confirm box and, if the user does not want to clear the form, instructs the browser not to perform its default processing, which in the case of the reset button is clearing the form. Much of the code deals with detecting and appropriately handling browsers that do not follow the DOM event model.

We will create a file named addentry.js containing the three functions just discussed and add to the head element of the addentry.html document the markup

```
/* Add event handlers to buttons. */
function init() {

  var clear = document.getElementById("clear");
  if (clear.onclick !== null) {
    clear.addEventListener("click", confirmClear, false);
  }
  else {  // non-DOM browser; assume IE6
    clear.onclick = confirmClear;
  }
  return;
}

/* Confirm that user wants to clear form. */
function confirmClear(event) {
  var OK = window.confirm("Clear the form?");
  if (!OK) {
    if ((arguments.length == 1) && window.Event &&
        (arguments[0] instanceof window.Event)) {
      event.preventDefault();
    }
    else { // non-DOM browser; assume IE6
      window.event.returnValue = false;
    }
  }
  return;
}
```

FIGURE 5.32 JavaScript functions for confirming that the add-entry form should be cleared.

```
<script type="text/javascript" src="addentry.js"></script>
<meta http-equiv="Content-Script-Type"
      content="text/javascript" />
```

You might be wondering about error handling. The confirmClear() function assumes that if a browser does not conform with the DOM event model, then it is IE6 and therefore that window.event is an object. However, this assumption may well be wrong, in which case executing the statement

```
window.event.returnValue = false;
```

will throw an exception. Since there is little that the code could do if it caught the exception, and since exceptions normally are not displayed by browsers to end users, this is probably acceptable behavior. Alternatively, the body of each function could be wrapped in a try-catch to prevent any exceptions from being thrown to the browser.

This try-catch approach is illustrated by our final function, which is also named init() and is stored in the file viewblog.js (Figure 5.33). As you might guess, this function

```
// viewblog.js

/* Make local times show as tool tips when mouse is over
   the date/time of an entry in the view-blog page. */
function init() {

  try {
    // For each div that has class attribute value
    // datetime
    var allDivs = document.getElementsByTagName("div");
    for (var i=0; i<allDivs.length; i++) {
      if (allDivs[i].className == "datetime") {

        // Normalize this div's text and get the content
        // of its first child element (assumed to be a Text node).
        // Use this text to construct a Date object representing
        // the given date and time, then use the toLocaleString()
        // method to get a string representing the time local
        // to the browser.  Assign this string to the title
        // attribute of the div, which produces the tool tip
        // effect.
        allDivs[i].normalize();
        allDivs[i].setAttribute("title",
          new Date(allDivs[i].childNodes[0].data).toLocaleString());
      }
    }
  }
  catch (e) {
  }
  return;
}
```

FIGURE 5.33 JavaScript function for adding local time as a tool tip to the view-blog page.

will be called when the document that displays the blog entries (index.html) is loaded. Because the viewblog.js and addentry.js files are used by separate HTML documents, using a single name for two different functions does not cause a conflict.

This function makes use of a *tool tip* feature supported by most browsers. If the title attribute of an element of an HTML document is assigned a value, the document is displayed in a browser, and the cursor is stopped over this element, then the browser will momentarily pop up a small window containing the title text. For example, Figure 5.34 shows the view-blog page with a tool tip (covering part of the title of the first entry). The JavaScript code of Figure 5.33 associates such a tool tip with the div's belonging to the style class datetime, which (referring back to Figure 3.40) are the div's containing the date and time at the beginning of each blog entry. The goal is to have the tool tip show the time of the entry converted to the user's local time and preferred formatting of dates. In Figure 5.34, the user is in the Eastern U.S. time zone while the time displayed on the page is Pacific U.S. time, which is three hours earlier. Thus, the tool tip shows a time that is three hours later than the time on the page.

The only feature of the code itself that has not already been covered is the Date() constructor used. When called with a string argument, the constructor creates an instance of Date that represents the given time. The rest of the code should be relatively easy to understand, based on earlier material and the comments.

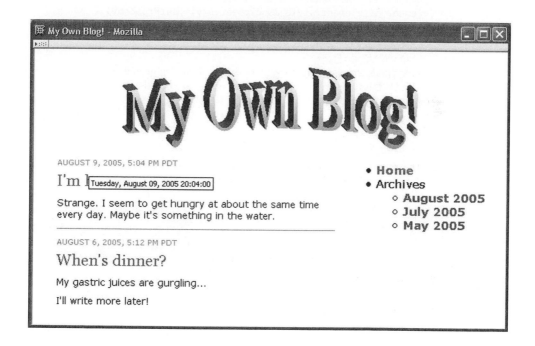

FIGURE 5.34 View-blog page with tool tip displaying the local equivalent of a time displayed on the page.

5.10 References

As mentioned early in this chapter, the W3C has issued six separate recommendations for DOM Level 2, four of which ([W3C-DOM-2-CORE], [W3C-DOM-2-EVENTS], [W3C-DOM-2-HTML], and [W3C-DOM-2-STYLE]) have been covered to some extent in this chapter. The remaining two specifications are available in the DOM section of http://www.w3.org. Each of these documents uses a two-tiered approach to specifying its portion of the DOM API. First, the bulk of each document describes its portion of the API using the OMG Interface Definition Language (IDL)^{TM} notation, a language created by the Object Management Group for the purpose of describing software interfaces in a language-independent way. You should be able to read definitions written in this language without much difficulty, but for full details see the documentation available from http://www.omg.org. Second, each DOM2 recommendation contains an appendix that gives the JavaScript syntax (but no semantic information) for each feature of the API. In addition, each document also contains another appendix describing the Java syntax of the API, which will be useful to us in later chapters.

Presently, a good starting point for understanding DOM support in Mozilla can be found at [MOZ-DOM] and for IE6 at [MS-DHTML]. Other host objects supplied by the window objects of these browsers are covered at [MS-DHTML-WINDOW] for IE6 and [MOZ-DOM-WINDOW] for Mozilla.

Exercises

5.1. Carefully explain why the condition of the if statement
```
if (element && element.style && element.style.setProperty) {
```
will not cause an exception to be thrown, assuming that element has been declared in a var statement. Hint: As in Java, the second operand of && is only evaluated if the value of the first operand is true.

5.2. Give JavaScript code for assigning the value 5 to the z-index value of an Element instance named anElt. Do this two ways: using setProperty() and using the appropriate property defined on the style object.

5.3. Describe a situation in which the value of the third (weight) argument to the setProperty() method of the style object would make a difference in what is displayed by a browser.

5.4. Rewrite the changeLight() function of Section 5.4 so that the backgroundColor style property of the specified element will be set to silver if either the current value is gray or if no value has been specified for the property.

5.5. Assume that you are adding JavaScript code to an HTML document that contains a form with a submit button. You did not modify any of the HTML or add an event listener for the click event on this button, and yet the button stopped working after you added your code to the document. Give at least two possible explanations.

5.6. Consider the following HTML markup:
```html
<body id="body1">
  <div id="div1">
    <button type="button" id="button1">
      Click Me
    </button>
  </div>
</body>
```

and assume that the following JavaScript code has been executed:

```
function h1(event) {
}
function h2(event) {
  event.stopPropagation();
}

var body1 = document.getElementById("body1");
var div1 = document.getElementById("div1");
var button1 = document.getElementById("button1");
body1.addEventListener("click", h1, true);
body1.addEventListener("click", h2, false);
div1.addEventListener("click", h1, true);
div1.addEventListener("click", h2, false);
button1.addEventListener("click", h2, true);
button1.addEventListener("click", h1, false);
```

Give the sequence in which the event listeners will be called by a DOM2-compliant browser when the button is clicked, specifying the values of `currentTarget` and `eventPhase` in the `Event` instance argument in each call. Then determine the results in one or more browsers as directed by your instructor.

5.7. Assume that an HTML document contains a text field (`input` element of type `text`) having an `id` attribute value of `msg`. Write DOM2-compliant JavaScript code that displays the string 1 < 2 within this text field. Pay particular attention to the question of whether you should use a reference for the less-than (<) symbol or not.

5.8. Contrast the IE6 and DOM approaches to modifying an intrinsic event attribute, giving at least one advantage of each approach over the other.

Research and Exploration

5.9. Follow the suggestion at the end of Section 5.3, and experiment with intrinsic event handling in at least two different browsers as assigned by your instructor. Perform at least five different experiments (including the two mentioned at the end of Section 5.3), and report your results. Design at least one experiment that requires a modification to the code of Figure 5.4, and modify the code appropriately.

5.10. The `meta` element discussed in Section 5.3 is used for a variety of purposes. Research this element, and describe at least two other tasks for which it is commonly used. Only one task should be related to search engines.

5.11. Study the DOM2 Style recommendation [W3C-DOM-2-STYLE] and the JavaScript language binding (Appendix C of [W3C-DOM-2-STYLE]), and answer the following questions:
1. What is the JavaScript name of the property of the `document` object that represents the collection of style sheets associated with a document?
2. Given an object `ssheet` representing a style sheet, what property of `ssheet` represents the collection of style rules for the style sheet? (Note: In IE6, this property is named `rules` instead.)
3. Name at least one other property of a style sheet object such as `ssheet`.
4. Given a style rule object `srule`, which property of `srule` represents the selector string for the rule?

     5. Given `srule` as in the preceding question, how would you modify the associated style rule so that it specifies the value `none` for the `display` property?

5.12. When the Tomcat web server installed as part of JWSDP 1.3 returns a file to a client browser, Tomcat decides what MIME type to provide in the HTTP response, based on the extension of the file's name. For example, by default a file name ending in `.html` is given a MIME type of text/html. The default mappings used by Tomcat are contained in the file `conf/web.xml` within the JWSDP installation directory. Using the mapping from `html` to text/html as an example, add a default mapping from the extension `xhtml` to the MIME type application/xhtml+xml. Copy the files of Figure 5.6 and Figure 5.7 to the `webapps/ROOT` directory of your JWSDP installation, and copy `TreeOutline.html` to the file `TreeOutline.xhtml`. Finally, restart your Tomcat server, and browse Mozilla 1.4 to `http://localhost:8080/TreeOutline.xhtml` (assuming that you are running a default Tomcat installation on the same machine as your browser). How does the alert box displayed when you click the button differ from that of Figure 5.8? Experiment with displaying both `TreeOutline.html` and `TreeOutline.xhtml` in several different browsers as assigned by your instructor, and report the results.

5.13. The function `makeCollapsible()` in Figure 5.15 inserts nodes into the document tree with calls to `insertBefore()` or `appendChild()` immediately after creating them with calls to `createElement()` or `createText()`. In the browser(s) assigned by your instructor, experiment with variations of this code in which you set attribute values on newly created nodes before adding them to the document tree. Report on the behavior of the browser, noting not only what the browser displays but also any exceptions thrown.

5.14. I mention at the end of Section 5.5.6 that an `Element` node may have several children that are sibling `Text` nodes. For one or more browsers assigned by your instructor, write JavaScript code that outputs (in an alert box) the `nodeType` of the child nodes of the `p` `Element` and the content of any of its `Text` children after the browser reads the following markup:

```
<p>
  This &amp; That.
</p>
```

Refer to the DOM2 Core recommendation [W3C-DOM-2-CORE] to learn about the `normalize()` method of `Node` instances. Apply this method to the `p` `Element` corresponding to the markup given, and describe the effect on the collection of child nodes in each of the assigned browsers.

5.15. Write code to perform experiments in the browser(s) assigned by your instructor with the methods listed in Table 5.9 to answer the following questions: If your code causes a blur event on an element, does another element automatically gain focus? Does a call to `click()` on an element also give the element focus? What about a call to `select()`? If your code gives the focus to a text field, where is the cursor located within the field? Does this vary depending on the location of the cursor when the text field last had the focus?

5.16. Many browsers, including Mozilla 1.4 and some versions of IE6, include tools for blocking pop-up windows. Experiment with the pop-up-blocking browser(s) assigned by your instructor, and attempt to develop a JavaScript function `popupOK()` that will reliably detect whether or not the browser allows pop-ups. Demonstrate your function by writing an

HTML document that when loaded calls JavaScript code that in turn calls your function, navigating the browser to the URL of an HTML document containing an error message if the browser does not allow pop-ups. (Note: Even with pop-up blocking enabled, a web browser by default may not block documents served from your machine or even other machines within your Internet domain. See your browser documentation for details and information on possibly overriding such settings.)

Projects

5.17. Event debugging: Alert boxes are often used for debugging JavaScript code, but they may not work well for debugging event listeners, because the mouse or keyboard activity needed to close an alert pop-up window generates unwanted events. An alternative is to use the DOM to add debugging output to the document itself.

    (a) Write a JavaScript object DebugArea with two methods init() and println(). When init() is called, it adds a textarea to the end of the document. Calling println() with a single argument causes its argument to be cast to a String and appended to the textarea followed by a newline character (\n).

    (b) Modify init() to accept two optional arguments. If specified, the first argument specifies the number of lines of text, and the second the number of characters per line in the generated textarea.

    (c) Incorporate your DebugArea object into the dropdown menu example of Section 5.6.5 so that every time one of the event listeners is called, the name of the event listener, the nodeName of the target, and the id attribute of the target (if available) are appended to the debug textarea.

5.18. Date and time. Section 15.9.5 of [ECMA-262] describes methods of Date instances that you will need to complete this project.

    (a) Write a JavaScript digital clock function. The function should be called with the id of an HTML element within which the time is to be displayed. If the first child of this element is a Text node, then the content of that node should be replaced with the current time; otherwise, a new Text node should be created containing the current time and inserted as the first child node of the HTML element. The time should be written in the form HH:MM:SS (hours followed by minutes followed by seconds). The minutes and seconds should have a leading zero if either is a one-digit number. That is, display 4:07:22 rather than 4: 7:22.

    (b) Write a similar function that displays the current date in the form September 9, 2004 (full month name followed by day of the month followed by a comma followed by the year).

    (c) Modify your time function so that it automatically updates the displayed time once a second.

    (d) Modify your date function so that it automatically updates the displayed date at midnight of the current day and then every 24 hours after that.

    (e) Write an HTML document and supporting JavaScript code to test your function(s).

5.19. Validating and reformatting user data.

    (a) Write a JavaScript function formatPhoneNum() that is designed to be called when a text box loses focus. If the text box contains a phone number in any of the formats specified for Exercise 4.13 when the box loses focus, then formatPhoneNum() should replace the number with a number in the hyphen-separated format 123-456-7890. If the box does not contain a phone number in one of the specified formats, then the event listener should display an alert box asking the user to reenter the phone number. Also write an HTML document containing a text box that can be used to test your function.

(b) Modify your JavaScript code so that it can be called as an event listener in either IE6 or Mozilla 1.4. Write a second function that registers `formatPhoneNum()` as an event listener on a text box with an `id` value of `phonenum`. Modify your HTML document so that it calls the second function after the document is loaded, and remove any other intrinsic event attributes from the document.

(c) Modify your JavaScript code so that after alerting the user about a bad number the contents of the text box will be selected. (Note: In Mozilla 1.4, this only works for me if I am using a DOM2 event listener rather than an intrinsic event listener and if the selection occurs after the alert box is displayed.)

5.20. Add a graphical user interface to the program of Exercise 4.23.

(a) Write an HTML document and JavaScript code that allows the user to play the game of Exercise 4.23 using only a mouse. A possible interface is suggested by Figure 5.35, which shows a game after the user (decrypter) has made two guesses. The user clicks on a color in the palette area and then on one of the holes in the Board area. The program then colors the background of that hole with the selected

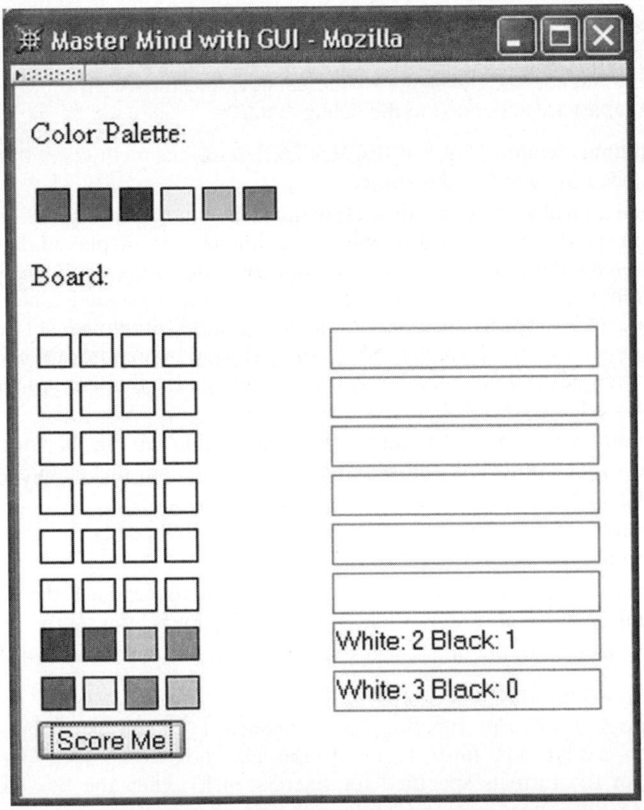

FIGURE 5.35 Graphical user interface for program of Exercise 5.20 after two guesses have been made.

palette color. The color of a hole can be changed by clicking on a different color in the palette and then clicking the hole. When the user is satisfied with the colors on the row representing the current guess (guesses proceed from bottom to top on the board), the Score Me button is clicked. The program then computes the score for that guess and displays it in the text box to the right of the guess.

(b) Modify your program so that if the user's eighth guess is not correct, an alert box is displayed saying that the game is over. Reset the game when the alert box is acknowledged, just as if the user had reloaded the HTML document.

(c) Modify your program so that it alerts the user about invalid guesses, such as a guess that uses the same color more than once or a guess that hasn't selected a color for every hole. When a guess is invalid, the same board row should be processed again the next time the scoring button is pressed.

(d) Modify your program so that the guess scores are displayed graphically (using black and white "pegs") rather than textually.

5.21. Add a graphical user interface to the Crazy Eight program of Exercise 4.26.

(a) Display graphical card images for both the user's hand and the computer's hand (showing card fronts for the user and card backs for the computer's hand, so that the user can see how many cards the computer has left). Similarly, the deck from which cards are drawn should be represented by a card back, and the top card of the discard pile should be showing. Figure 3.47 is an example, with the computer's hand at the top, the deck and discard pile in the middle, and the user's hand at the bottom. You may want to use a solution to Exercise 3.27(a) as a starting point. While you do not have to follow the format of Figure 3.47 precisely, your cards must overlap one another (they are offset 15 pixels in Figure 3.47, but you can vary that some if you like). You can still use prompt boxes to input the user's play as well as the user's choice of suit when an eight is played. After the user chooses a legal play, the computer should choose a play and then the displayed cards should be appropriately updated and the user prompted for the next play.

(b) Create event listeners so that clicking on the deck will cause a card from the deck to be added to the user's hand, and clicking on a card in the player's hand will either cause that card to be played to the discard pile if it is a legal play, or display an alert box if the play is illegal. Once the user has selected a legal play, the computer should automatically play and the display should be updated appropriately, showing the results of both the user's and computer's plays. When the user plays an eight, the choice of suit can be made via an alert box.

(c) Modify your program so that the user's cards are always displayed in sorted order (refer to Exercise 4.26(e) for an example sort order).

(d) Modify your program so that the choice of suit when the user plays an eight is made graphically. For example, when the user chooses to play an eight, the program might display a div containing the suit symbols for clubs, diamonds, etc. (you may want to use the XHTML-defined character entities ♣, ♦, ♥ and ♠). The user could then click on a suit symbol to select a suit and close the div.

(e) Modify your program so that the display is updated twice after a user selects a play. First, the display is updated to show the user's play. Then, after a two-second delay, the display is updated to show the computer's play. Any clicks by the user during the pause between displaying the user's and computer's plays should be ignored.

(f) Modify your program so that when a card in the user's hand is clicked, the card will appear to move from the hand to the discard pile. That is, your program should display the card at several locations between its starting position and the discard pile, with a short delay between the displays at successive locations (the shorter the delay between successive locations, the smoother the card movement will appear). Any clicks by the user while a card is moving should be ignored.

5.22. The following questions suggest extensions to the case study of Section 5.9. Implement a subset of the following requirements as specified by your instructor.

    (a) Extend the example view-blog document so that it includes a list of several comments following the first entry. However, the comments should be contained in a div that is not visible when the view-blog document is first loaded into the browser. Instead, a hyperlink with the text "Comments . . ." should appear immediately below the blog entry. When this hyperlink is clicked, the comments should become visible, and the text of the hyperlink should change to "Hide comments." Clicking this hyperlink should return the browser to the initial condition in which comments are not visible.

    (b) Modify the preceding document so that the "Comments . . ." hyperlinks are not contained in the document itself. Instead, these hyperlinks should be automatically generated by JavaScript code executed immediately after the view-blog document is loaded (that is, code that is part of or called by the init() function of viewblog.js).

    (c) Add a hyperlink containing the text "Add a comment" immediately below each entry on the view-blog page. Clicking this link should cause a comment-entry form (as described in Exercise 2.33) to be loaded into the browser. The links should be created by JavaScript code executed when the view-blog page is loaded. Furthermore, an id attribute should be added to each blog entry div (the div's having class entry). The URL in the href attribute of each generated hyperlink should contain a query string with a entryId parameter having as its value the value of the id attribute for the corresponding blog entry.

    (d) Add JavaScript code to viewblog.js that will automatically create a table of contents for the view-blog page. Each entry in the table of contents should be a hyperlink with text that is the title and date and time of a blog entry. Clicking a link should scroll the browser window to the selected blog entry. The table of contents should be added to the div containing the navigation links (the div with class attribute rightbody).

CHAPTER 6

Server-Side Programming
Java Servlets

In this chapter we continue our study of programming web-based systems. However, we now move from client-side programming involving web browsers to server-side programming. Specifically, in this chapter we study Java servlet programming. Servlets can be thought of as providing a way to extend the capabilities of a web server so that the server is tailored to provide certain services to web users. As we will learn in Chapter 8, in addition to being useful by themselves for developing web applications, servlets are also the basis for a higher-level web development technology, JavaServer Pages (JSP).

6.1 Servlet Architecture Overview

As we have learned in previous chapters, HTML documents that contain JavaScript (or that embed other technologies, such as Java applets) can change the content and structure of the browser's representation of the document in response to various events, pop-up dialog windows, and so on. The combination of HTML plus JavaScript and the DOM is sometimes referred to as *Dynamic HTML (DHTML)*, and an HTML document that contains scripting is called a *dynamic* document. On the other hand, a simple HTML document without scripting is known as a *static* document.

In an analogous way, the responses by a web server to an HTTP request can be classified as static or dynamic. In a static response, when the browser has requested an HTML document—or perhaps a style sheet or image referenced by the document—the server satisfies the request by returning a file stored in the file system on the server. The web server is not responsible for actually generating the content of the response, but simply for finding and sending content that was generated by some other process. In a dynamic response, on the other hand, the content of the response is directly generated by software on the server. For example, when you visit a search engine Web site, the document sent to your browser in response to a search request is typically generated on the fly in response to your request, not retrieved from the file system of the server.

Java servlet technology is one of many technologies available for generating responses dynamically when an HTTP request is received (related technologies are considered at the end of this chapter and in Chapter 8). In essence, a *servlet* is just a Java class that a web server instantiates when the server is started. A particular method is called on this instance when the server receives certain HTTP requests. Code in the servlet method can obtain information about the request and produce information to be included in an HTTP response by calling methods on parameter objects passed to the method. When the servlet returns control to the server, the server creates an HTTP response from the information dynamically generated by the servlet. Figure 6.1 illustrates the interaction between server and servlet.

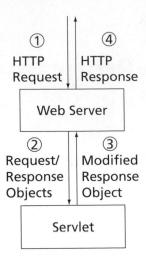

FIGURE 6.1 High-level web-server–servlet interaction.

In somewhat more detail, a web server handling a servlet request generally operates as follows:

1. When an HTTP request message is received by a servlet-capable server, it first determines—based on the URL of the request—that the request should be handled by a servlet. For example, a server might be configured to treat any request to any URL for which the path component begins with `servlet` as a request that should be handled by a servlet.

2. The server next determines from the URL which servlet should handle the request and calls a method on that servlet. Two parameters are passed to the method: an object implementing the `HttpServletRequest` interface, and an object implementing the `HttpServletResponse` interface. Both of these interfaces are defined as part of the Java Servlet API, which is implemented by the server. The first object provides methods that can be used by the servlet to access the information contained in the HTTP request message received by the server. The second object can be used to record information that the servlet wishes to include in the HTTP response message that the server will send to the client in reply to the request.

3. The servlet method executes, typically calling methods on the `HttpServletRequest` and `HttpServletResponse` objects passed to it. The information stored in the latter object by the servlet method typically includes an entire HTML document along with some HTTP header information, such as the document Content-Type. When the servlet method has finished its processing, it returns control to the server.

4. The server formats the information stored in the `HttpServletResponse` object by the servlet into an HTTP response message, which it then sends to the client that initiated the HTTP request.

Now that we have a basic idea of how servers and servlets interact, let's take a look at an example of a simple but complete servlet. Throughout this chapter, we will be studying examples that comply with Version 2.4 of the Java Servlet API Specification [SUN-SERVLETS-2.4], which is the version supported by the server software you will have if you follow the server installation instructions in Appendix A. The examples in this chapter should also work with later versions of the API.

6.2 A "Hello World!" Servlet

Figure 6.2 shows a simple Java Servlet named ServletHello that responds with the HTML "Hello World!" document of Figure 2.1 in response to an HTTP GET request. As noted earlier, a servlet is simply a Java class. In particular, the servlets we will study are all subclasses of HttpServlet, a class provided by the javax.servlet.http package, which in turn depends on the javax.servlet and java.io packages. So every servlet you write will need to import these three packages.

In order to respond to GET requests, the servlet class must override the doGet() method of HttpServlet, as shown in this example. This method has two parameters as discussed earlier, and may also throw the two exceptions shown. A production servlet (one that has been deployed for use in an operational system) should normally catch and handle all exceptions internally rather than throwing any to the server. For simplicity, however, the example servlets in this chapter will throw exceptions to the server rather than catching them. If you installed JWSDP 1.3 as outlined in Appendix A, then you will be using the Tomcat web server, which will write a trace for the exception in the jwsdp_log.*.txt log file; see Section 1.7.5 for the location of Tomcat's log files. In addition, when the Tomcat server catches an exception, it may return an HTML page to the client that displays a partial exception trace (an exercise explores the exact conditions under which the trace is displayed). Note also that if your servlet prints a stack trace itself with a call to printStackTrace(), or if it writes debugging output to System.out or System.err, this output will be appended to the file launcher.server.log in the Tomcat log directory.

The body of a doGet() method generally performs the following actions in the order shown:

1. Set the HTTP Content-Type header of the response. The MIME type portion of this header will typically be text/html, and it is also good practice to include the type of character encoding used, as shown (the default character encoding is ISO-8859-1).

2. Obtain a PrintWriter object from the HttpServletResponse parameter object by calling this object's getWriter() method. The getWriter() method must not be called before the Content-Type is set by a call to setContentType().

3. Output a valid HTML document to the PrintWriter object.

4. Close the PrintWriter object.

It is the third item, generating an HTML document, that typically changes from servlet to servlet, while the other items normally change little if at all.

You may find it helpful to compare the structure of a basic servlet with a "Hello World!" Java program. First, a servlet does not have a main method, because the Tomcat server

```
import java.io.*;
import javax.servlet.*;
import javax.servlet.http.*;

/**
 * Hello World! servlet
 */
public class ServletHello extends HttpServlet
{
    /**
     * Respond to any HTTP GET request with an
     * HTML Hello World! page.
     */
    public void doGet (HttpServletRequest request,
                       HttpServletResponse response)
      throws ServletException, IOException
        {
           // Set the HTTP content type in response header
           response.setContentType("text/html; charset=\"UTF-8\"");

           // Obtain a PrintWriter object for creating the body
           // of the response
           PrintWriter servletOut = response.getWriter();
           // Create the body of the response
           servletOut.println(
"<!DOCTYPE html \n" +
"    PUBLIC \"-//W3C//DTD XHTML 1.0 Strict//EN\" \n" +
"    \"http://www.w3.org/TR/xhtml1/DTD/xhtml1-strict.dtd\"> \n" +
"<html xmlns='http://www.w3.org/1999/xhtml'> \n" +
"  <head> \n" +
"    <title> \n" +
"      ServletHello.java \n" +
"    </title> \n" +
"  </head> \n" +
"  <body> \n" +
"    <p> \n" +
"      Hello World! \n" +
"    </p> \n" +
"  </body> \n" +
"</html> ");
           servletOut.close();
        }
}
```

FIGURE 6.2 "Hello World!" Java servlet.

provides the main. Instead, doGet() (or related methods, such as doPost(), discussed in Section 6.5.3) acts as a sort of main for the servlet. A conceptually larger difference is that, while a Java application can interact with a user via a GUI or System.in/System.out method calls, a servlet cannot interact directly with a user. Instead, as we will learn in more detail in Section 6.5, all input to the servlet is stored in the HttpServletRequest object before doGet() is called, and all output is written (directly or indirectly) via the HttpServletResponse object. A final difference to notice for now is that the primary output from a servlet is typically HTML, while of course this is not the case for most Java applications.

The general steps to follow in order to run a servlet are:

1. Compile the servlet using an appropriate compiler version (see Appendix A).

2. Copy the resulting .class file to the appropriate directory for your Java-servlet-capable web server. If you have installed JWSDP 1.3 as outlined in Appendix A, then you can copy the class file to the subdirectory shared/classes of the JWSDP 1.3 installation directory. (This is not an optimal way to install a servlet, but it is simple and will serve our purposes in this chapter. Better mechanisms for deploying servlets and related software are covered in Chapter 8.)

3. Start (or restart) your server. (This will not be necessary when we move to more sophisticated methods for deploying servlets.)

4. Navigate to the URL corresponding to your servlet. With the default JWSDP 1.3 version of Tomcat, assuming that your browser is on the same machine as your JWSDP installation, an appropriate URL for the ServletHello example would be

```
http://localhost:8080/servlet/ServletHello
```

Note that the class name, not the file name (ServletHello.class), appears in the URL.

6.3   Servlets Generating Dynamic Content

The "Hello World!" servlet of the previous section is not very interesting, since it doesn't do anything more than can be done by a static HTML file. Figure 6.3 shows how ServletHello can be changed so that in addition to printing "Hello World!" it also outputs the number of times the servlet has been visited since the server hosting the servlet was last started. Figure 6.4 shows an example page produced by this servlet. Clearly, this page is no longer static, but produces slightly different output each time it is accessed.

Conceptually, each time the doGet() method of the HelloCounter servlet is executed by the web server, a counter variable visits will be incremented and its value output as part of the HTML document produced by the servlet. Notice that we are assuming here that when the web server starts it creates a single instance of the HelloCounter class and executes the doGet() method on this instance to handle each request for the HelloCounter servlet. This is the default behavior of any server complying with the Java Servlet 2.4 Specification. Many commercial web applications are replicated over multiple servers and therefore do not conform with the single-instance assumption. It is also possible for a single server to create multiple concurrent instances of a single servlet; this could be particularly useful on a multiprocessor system. However, we will content ourselves with studying the single-instance case, which should provide a solid foundation if you later need to learn about multi-instance servlets.

```
[...] // removed import's, same as ServletHello
public class HelloCounter extends HttpServlet
{
    // Number of times the servlet has been executed since
    // the program (web server) started
    private int visits=0;

[...] // removed doGet() declaration and initialization

            // Obtain a PrintWriter object for creating the body
            // of the response
            PrintWriter servletOut = response.getWriter();

            // Compute the number of visits to the URL for this servlet
            visits++;

[...] // removed output of initial portion of HTML document

"      <p> \n" +
"         Hello World! \n" +
"      </p> \n" +
"      <p> \n" +
"         This page has been viewed \n" +
            visits +
"         times since the most recent server restart. \n" +
"      </p> \n" +

[...] // removed remainder of doGet()
```

FIGURE 6.3 Excerpts from modified "Hello World!" servlet adding a visit counter.

It turns out that even for the case of a server running a single instance of this simple servlet, the servlet might not always produce the output that you would expect. Specifically, if multiple users access this servlet at nearly the same time, the multiple executions of the servlet's doGet() method may interleave in a way that causes different users to see the same visit count. We'll come back to this issue in Section 6.11, where we will also present some

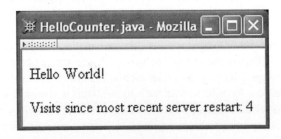

FIGURE 6.4 Example page produced by HelloCounter.

Java techniques for dealing with this and similar problems. But before that, we'll cover some of the key features of the Java servlet API.

6.4   Servlet Life Cycle

The HelloCounter servlet of Figure 6.3 initialized the visits variable by including an initializer (=0) in the variable declaration. The Java servlet API also provides facilities to support more sophisticated initialization tasks, such as opening files or establishing database connections when a servlet is first visited.

Specifically, when a server loads and instantiates a servlet class (which may be either when the server is started or the first time the servlet is requested, depending on how the server is configured), it also performs servlet initialization tasks. This includes calling an init() method on the servlet. By default, this method does nothing. Overriding this method allows you to perform any desired initialization on the servlet. The init() method must return successfully before any other servlet processing (calls to doGet(), for example) will be performed. If your initialization processing encounters an error—such as a file not found—then it should throw an UnavailableException (a subclass of ServletException). So, for example, if we had wanted to initialize the value of visits from a text file and prevent further servlet processing if the file was not found or was improperly formatted, we could have created a modified version of HelloCounter called HelloCounterWithInit that includes the init() method shown in Figure 6.5.

There are two other servlet life-cycle methods, service() and destroy(). service() is the method actually called when an HTTP request is received; this method, in turn, calls doGet() (or, as we will learn in Section 6.5.3, possibly some other method, such as doPost()). Normally, you should not override service(). The destroy() method will be called when the server is in the process of taking a servlet out of service, usually when the server itself is shutting down. Overriding the default, do-nothing destroy()

```
public void init()
    throws ServletException
{
    try {
        BufferedReader br =
            new BufferedReader(new FileReader("aFile"));
        visits = (new Integer(br.readLine())).intValue();
    }
    catch (FileNotFoundException fnfe) {
        throw new UnavailableException("File not found: " +
                                    fnfe.toString());
    }
    catch (Exception e) {
        throw new UnavailableException("Data problem: " +
                                    e.toString());
    }
}
```

FIGURE 6.5 Method init() that could be used to initialize the HelloCounter variable visits from a file.

method allows a servlet to terminate cleanly, for example by closing database connections or any open files. Of course, if the server itself does not shut down cleanly (due to a server software crash, power failure, etc.), the destroy() method will not be called. So, for example, if you want to guarantee that certain data is written to a file after processing an HTTP request, you must write the data to the file immediately in the appropriate method called by service() rather than waiting to output the data from destroy().

Other servlet classes, known as *listeners*, can be created and registered with the server so that they will be called when certain events occur, including life-cycle events. One common use for listeners is to initialize a web application consisting of multiple servlets rather than a single servlet. The details are beyond the scope of our discussion in this chapter.

6.5   Parameter Data

Almost all servlets access data contained in the HTTP request sent to the server from the browser. As indicated earlier, a servlet can access this data by calling methods on the HttpServletRequest parameter supplied to the servlet's doGet() method. In this section we'll focus on methods for accessing the most frequently used portion of the HTTP request, the so-called *parameter data* of the request. Later sections will cover methods for accessing some of the other information contained within a request.

6.5.1   Parameter Data and Query Strings

In some sense, navigating to a URL that is associated with a servlet can be viewed as similar to calling a method in Java. That is, when we navigate to the URL, the server calls the doGet() method of the servlet for us and essentially returns to us a (long HTML) string representing the "return value" of the method. However, an actual call to a Java method can include parameter values, such as the string value aString in the following method call:

```
System.out.println("aString");
```

While we can't pass parameters when visiting a URL in exactly the same way, we can get much the same effect. In particular, consider a URL such as the following:

```
http://www.example.com/servlet/PrintThis?arg=aString
```

Recall from Chapter 1 that, within a URL, a question mark (?) marks the end of the path portion of the URL and the beginning of the query portion of the URL, and that the query portion of the URL consists of a *query string*. In this case, the query string contains one *parameter*, named arg, which is assigned the string value aString. Note that all query string parameter values are treated as strings, and that they should not be quoted. More generally, multiple parameters can be included in the query string of a URL by separating adjacent parameter name-value pairs with ampersands (&). For example, the following URL's query string contains two parameters:

```
http://www.example.com/servlet/PrintThis?arg=aString&color=red
```

Order of parameters is not important, so the following URL contains exactly the same parameter data as the preceding URL, although at a surface level the two query strings appear to be different:

```
http://www.example.com/servlet/PrintThis?color=red&arg=aString
```

A parameter name or value can be composed of any sequence of 8-bit characters, including control characters and other nonprinting characters. However, if a name or value contains any nonalphanumeric characters, then the name or value will undergo a transformation known as *URL encoding* before being included in the query string. URL encoding of a string can be described by the following pseudocode algorithm:

```
initialize the result to the empty string
for each 8-bit character in the original string
   if the character is an alphanumeric
     concatenate the character to the result
   else if the character is a space
     concatenate a plus sign (+) to the result
   else
     concatenate a percent sign (%) followed by
       the two-digit hexadecimal value of the character
       to the result
   endif
endfor
return result
```

For instance, if we wanted to send the string `'a String'` (including the space and quotes) as the parameter value instead of `aString` in the first example, the URL would be

```
http://www.example.com/servlet/PrintThis?arg=%27a+String%27
```

It should be clear that the URL encoding transformation can be reversed, giving back the original unencoded string. The reverse transformation is called *URL decoding*.

The empty-string value can be assigned to a parameter by either following the equals sign (=) after the parameter name with an ampersand, if there is another parameter name-value pair in the query string, or by ending the query string with the equals sign. So to send an empty-string value for the `arg` parameter along with the value `red` for the `color` parameter we could use either

```
http://www.example.com/servlet/PrintThis?arg=&color=red
```

or

```
http://www.example.com/servlet/PrintThis?color=red&arg=
```

As we will see, there is a difference between including a parameter with an empty string value and not including the parameter at all.

6.5.2   Servlets and Parameter Data

Query strings can be included in any URL, even one that corresponds to a static web page. For a static page, the query string will be ignored by the web server. On the other hand, if a query string is included in the URL used to access a servlet, the servlet can obtain the query string as well as the parameter data contained in the query string by using the `HttpServletRequest` methods shown in Table 6.1 (technically, several of these methods are inherited by `HttpServletRequest` from its parent class `ServletRequest`). The last of these methods, `getParameterValues()`, should be used if there is a possibility that the parameter name passed as an argument to `getParameterValues()` might appear multiple times in the query string. If such a parameter exists in a query string and `getParameter()` is called on this parameter rather than `getParameterValues()`, then only one of the values associated with this parameter in the query string will be returned. (We'll see examples of how recurring parameters arise in the next subsection.)

As a simple example of accessing parameter data from a servlet, Figure 6.6 shows the body of the `doGet()` method of a servlet `PrintThis` that creates a web page displaying two paragraphs, the first containing the query string of the URL used to access the servlet, and the second containing either the URL-decoded value of the `arg` parameter, if this parameter is present in the query string, or the default text "Hello World!" Furthermore, if the `color` parameter is present, the value of this parameter is used as the color of the text in the second paragraph. Figure 6.7 is an example of a web page produced by accessing this servlet with the query string displayed in the first paragraph of the figure. Notice that parameter values, such as the value of `arg`, are automatically URL-decoded by the `getParameter()` method, while decoding is not performed by `getQueryString()`.

Recall that the ampersand (&) and less-than (<) symbols are not allowed to appear in the character data or attribute values of an XHTML document, and that in certain circumstances the greater-than (>) symbol also must not appear. But we expect that the query string will often contain one or more ampersands, and we cannot guarantee that the `color` and `arg` parameters will not also contain one or more special characters. So before writing the query string or the values of these parameters to the HTML document

TABLE 6.1 Some `HttpServletRequest` Methods for Accessing Parameter Data

Method	Purpose
`String getQueryString()`	Returns the entire query string in its original (URL encoded) form.
`Enumeration getParameterNames()`	Returns `Enumeration` of `String` values representing all parameter names (URL-decoded) in the query string.
`String getParameter (String name)`	Returns string representing value (URL-decoded) of parameter named name, or `null` if parameter is not present in the query string.
`String[] getParameterValues (String name)`	Returns array of strings representing all values (URL-decoded) of parameter named name, or `null` if parameter is not present in the query string.

```
              // Set the HTTP content type in response header.
              response.setContentType("text/html; charset=\"UTF-8\"");

              // Obtain a PrintWriter object for creating the body
              // of the response
              PrintWriter servletOut = response.getWriter();

              // Create the first part of the body of the response
              servletOut.println(
"<!DOCTYPE html \n" +
"     PUBLIC \"-//W3C//DTD XHTML 1.0 Strict//EN\" \n" +
"     \"http://www.w3.org/TR/xhtml1/DTD/xhtml1-strict.dtd\"> \n" +
"<html xmlns='http://www.w3.org/1999/xhtml'> \n" +
"   <head> \n" +
"     <title> \n" +
"       PrintThis.java \n" +
"     </title> \n" +
"   </head> \n" +
"   <body> \n" +
"     <p>Query string: " +
        WebTechUtil.escapeXML(request.getQueryString()) + "</p>" );

              // Decide whether or not to set color
              String color = request.getParameter("color");
              if (color == null) {
                  servletOut.println(
"      <p> " );
              } else {
                  servletOut.println(
"      <p style='color:" +
                      WebTechUtil.escapeQuotes(WebTechUtil.escapeXML(color)) +
"'> " );
              }

              // Decide which string to output
              String arg = request.getParameter("arg");
              if (arg == null) {
                  arg = "Hello World!";
              }

              // Create remainder of response body
              servletOut.println(
"      " + WebTechUtil.escapeXML(arg) + "\n" +
"      </p> \n" +
"   </body> \n" +
"</html> ");
              servletOut.close();
```

FIGURE 6.6 Body of doGet() method for Java servlet accessing and displaying parameter data.

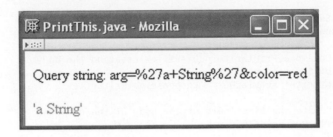

FIGURE 6.7 Example output of `PrintThis.java`.

output by the servlet, all ampersand, less-than, and greater-than symbols in these strings are replaced by appropriate entity references. The servlet performs this replacement by calling a static method `escapeXML(String)` that belongs to a class `WebTechUtil`. The `escapeXML()` method returns a `String` that is exactly the same as the input string except that the three special characters are replaced as described. Similarly, quote characters should be replaced by references in a string that will appear as part of the value of an attribute in an XHTML document. The `escapeQuotes()` method of `WebTechUtil` performs this task and is applied to the `color` parameter string before this string is output as part of a `style` atribute value.

The `WebTechUtil` class is available for download along with the textbook example files from the Web site referenced in the Preface. So in order to run this example, you will need to download and compile the `WebTechUtil` class as well as `PrintThis` and copy both class files to the appropriate directory of your server's file system.

For any application designed to be accessed on the public Web, it is vitally important that your servlets escape all of the data entered by users before incorporating that data in the documents generated by your servlets. As an example of the type of problem that can occur if user data is not escaped, consider the following scenario. You have written a Web application that receives user comments via an HTML form and displays the comments—without escaping—on a public Web page. A malicious user, Mal, enters a "comment" on your form that contains an HTML `script` element. When another user, Mark, visits the page displaying comments, the content of the `script` element will be executed by Mark's browser. The script could then take various malicious actions: modifying (via the DOM) content and links on the comments page displayed in Mark's browser, redirecting Mark's browser to another page entirely, even transmitting Mark's cookie information (which might include session information) to a server operated by Mal! This is known as a *cross-site scripting attack* (sometimes called a CSS attack, but note that it has nothing to do with style sheets).

By escaping all XML special characters in user-entered comments, the attack just described can be avoided, since all elements within these comments (including the `script` element) will then be viewed as text by the browser rather than as HTML elements. Other precautions that should be taken when writing server applications include always setting the content type of a generated HTML document (so that there is agreement between client and server about which character codes represent the special characters) and always escaping quote characters within generated attribute values. See `http://www.cert.org/advisories/CA-2000-02.html` for a detailed description of the cross-site scripting problem and recommended solutions.

6.5.3   Forms and Parameter Data

While query strings can be appended to a URL as shown above in Section 6.5.1, they are typically created automatically by browsers when the submit button on an HTML form is clicked. Recall the `LifeStory.html` form of Figure 2.19, which has a text field named `username` (that is, the value of its `name` attribute is `username`), a textarea named `lifestory`, three checkboxes all named `boxgroup1`, and a submit button named `doit`. Assume that this form has been filled in as shown in Figure 6.8. Then the browser will create the following query string (all one line with no white space, but this example is split into two lines for readability):

```
username=you&lifestory=less+is+more&boxgroup1=funny
&boxgroup1=smart&doit=Publish+My+Life%27s+Story
```

As shown, there is a parameter name-value pair for nearly every control on the form. Also notice that the parameter `boxgroup1` appears twice, because all of the checkboxes have this name. The one control that does not appear in the query string is the checkbox labeled "tall," which was not checked. In general, for each of the controls on the form that represents input from the user, as well as for every hidden control, the browser creates a pair consisting of the string assigned to the `name` attribute of the control along with the current value of the control. The value of a control depends on the particular control; see Table 6.2. In Mozilla 1.4, you can view the current values of all form controls (including those that will not be submitted to the server) by selecting **View** | **Page Info** from the menu, clicking

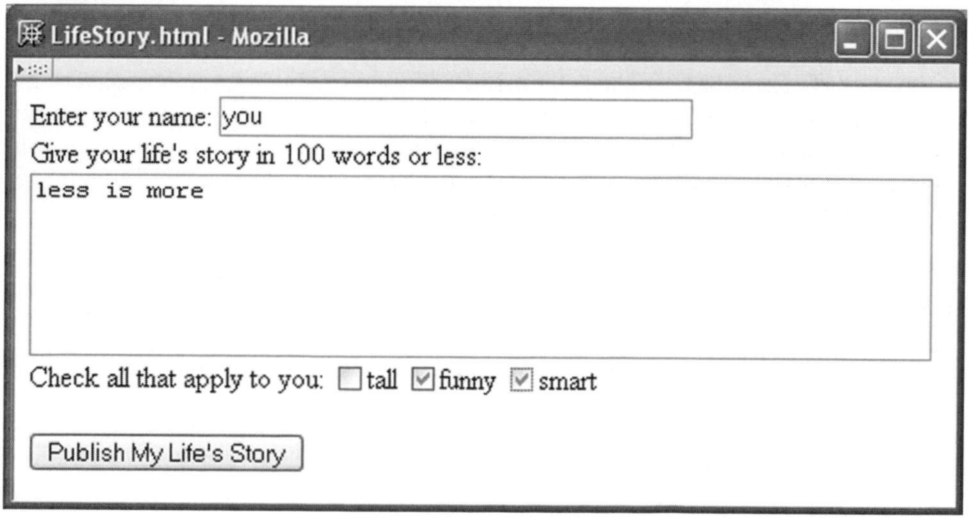

FIGURE 6.8 Filled-in form

the **Forms** tab, and making sure that Current Value is selected for view in the **Fields** box. The one control not covered in Table 6.2 is the input/file control, which is designed to transmit files in a MIME format that is not supported at a high level by the Java servlet API and is therefore not discussed here.

If the method attribute of a form element is assigned the value get, then the browser will append the query string it constructs to the form's action URL and perform an HTTP GET using the resulting URL. On the other hand, if the method is set to post, then the same query string will be constructed, but it will be passed to the server via the body of the HTTP request rather than as part of the URL.

A nice feature of the Java servlet API is that the same methods can be used to access parameter data regardless of whether it is passed to the server through a GET or a POST method. However, in order to handle POST requests, the servlet must override the HttpServlet doPost() method. The method signature for doPost() is exactly the same as for doGet(), and in fact, the methods are similar in almost every respect. Essentially the only difference is that one method is called by the server to handle GET requests and the other to handle POSTs. One other difference is that if your code calls the getMethod() method on the HttpServletRequest parameter, the return value will be either the string GET or POST, depending on which HTTP method was used in the request. (The standard is not entirely clear on whether or not these strings will always be uppercase, so I recommend using a case-insensitive string comparison if you test the return value of getMethod().)

While GET and POST processing are similar on the server side, generally speaking, the POST method should be chosen for HTTP requests generated by forms. First, a POST request can send a query string of essentially any length in the body of the request, while a GET request sends the query string as part of the URL, and the length of URLs accepted by many servers is limited to several thousand characters or less. So if a form contains a textarea or for some other reason might generate a particularly long query string, the POST request method should definitely be used. Also, almost all browsers will display a warning message if a user attempts to send a POST request more than once. For example, if you are using Mozilla 1.4 to view a page that is the response to a POST request and you attempt to Reload the page (which would cause the POST request to be resent to the server), the browser will display the pop-up window shown in Figure 6.9. This is a warning that if you continue with the Reload, the data in the POST request will be resent to the web server. Obviously, if this data would, say, cause your credit card to be charged a second time for

TABLE 6.2 Values for HTML Form Controls (Except input/file)

Control(s)	Value
input/text, input/password, textarea	Text present in control when form is submitted.
input/checkbox, input/radio, input/submit, input/image, button/submit	String assigned to corresponding value attribute. Control must be selected/clicked for parameter to be returned.
input/hidden	String assigned to corresponding value attribute.
select	String assigned to value attribute of selected option(s), or content of any selected option for which value is not defined.

FIGURE 6.9 Message displayed when user attempts to reload page requested via HTTP POST method.

a purchase, you would be glad to see this message and have the opportunity to cancel. However, reloading a page produced by a GET request will not produce this warning. So any form that produces a query string that should not be accidentally resent should also use the POST method.

On the other hand, GET is the recommended method when the form contains data that is only intended to be used to request information, not to cause information to be stored or updated on the server. A primary example of such a form is one that is intended to be sent to a search engine, such as the Google™ search engine, since the search terms entered on such a form are only intended to be used to request a search. An advantage of using GET in this case is that the query string of the URL requested by the search form will contain the search terms entered. For example, the URL generated by the Google search engine when I entered the search terms "form GET POST" contains these terms, as shown by the Location bar in Figure 6.10 (I've shortened the URL somewhat to make the search

FIGURE 6.10 Example of search page generated by a form using an HTTP GET method. The Location bar shows the URL (with some parameters removed for simplicity) generated by the form. (This Web page is reproduced by permission of Google Inc.)

terms readily visible). Anyone who visits the URL shown will cause the same search to be performed again, at least as long as the parameter named q in google.com URLs retains the same semantics. Similarly, if I were to bookmark this page, visiting this bookmark again at a later date would reexecute my search. On the other hand, if the Google search engine used the POST method for its search forms, then the URL of the search result page would not contain the search terms and could not be used in this way.

At this point, you should have a fairly complete understanding of parameter processing with servlets. We'll look next at the primary mechanism used by servlets to recognize multiple HTTP requests as all originating from the same user, an important task for many e-commerce and other web applications.

6.6   Sessions

In order to facilitate usability, many web sites are designed to obtain information from site visitors over a series of pages rather than in one large page. For example, a user may enter product ordering information on one page, a shipping address on another, and credit card information on a third. But if the web site is handling requests from hundreds of users, how does the server know which HTTP requests are coming from which users? I for one certainly don't want to do business at a site that might think that my credit card information should go together with someone else's order!

This problem is a bit trickier than you might think. It turns out that none of the information that is required to be part of an HTTP request can be used to reliably associate multiple requests with a single user. Instead, a separate convention for passing user-identifying information between browsers and servers has been developed. Specifically, each HTTP request is examined by the server to see if it contains a special identifier known as a *session ID* (we'll have more to say about exactly where the session ID is stored within the request in the next section). If a request does not contain a session ID, then the request is assumed to be from a new user and the web server generates a new unique session ID that is associated with this user. When the HTTP response message is created by the web server, the session ID will be included as part of the response. If the browser receiving this response supports the session convention (details on this also in the next section), it will store the session ID contained in the response and send it back to the server as part of subsequent HTTP requests. Notice that this convention, when successful, will allow a servlet to recognize all of the HTTP requests coming from a single user. Such a collection of HTTP requests, all associated with a single session ID, is known as a *session*. Figure 6.11 illustrates a server establishing and maintaining sessions with two clients.

6.6.1   Creating a Session

A server complying with the Java servlet API supports the session concept by associating an `HttpSession` object with each session maintained by the server. Each object stores the session ID for its session as well as other session-related information discussed in the following subsections. An `HttpSession` object is created by the server when a servlet calls the `getSession()` method on its `HttpServletRequest` parameter and the associated HTTP request does not contain a valid session ID; the `getSession()` method returns the

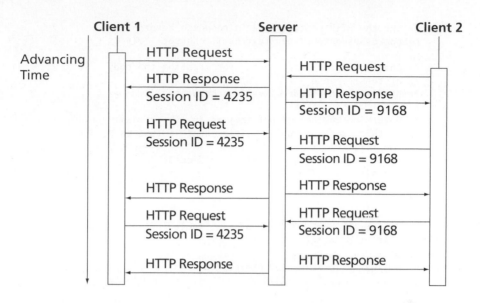

FIGURE 6.11 A server establishing and maintaining sessions with two clients.

newly created object in this case. On the other hand, if the HTTP request contains a valid session ID, then a call to getSession() returns the previously created HttpSession object containing this session ID. The servlet can determine whether the HttpSession object returned by getSession() has been newly created or not by calling the boolean method isNew() on the HttpSession object.

We will do much more with HttpSession objects in a moment, but let's pause to see one thing that we can already do with what we've learned. The VisitorCounter servlet shown in Figure 6.12 modifies the earlier HelloCounter servlet (Figure 6.3) so that the number of visitors to the page, rather than the number of visits, is displayed. The difference is that in the original servlet a single user could visit the page multiple times, and each page visit would increment the visit count. In the new version, this will not happen (at least not if the multiple visits all occur within a short time of one another; we'll say more about this in Section 6.6.3). This is because the visit counter is now only incremented on the first visit by a user to the page, which can be detected by checking to see whether or not a new session has begun. Specifically, if the session is not new, then the user has visited the page before, and the counter is not incremented.

6.6.2 Storing and Retrieving Attributes

We'll now see how the Java servlet session facility can be used to associate multiple web pages with a single user. Figure 6.13, Figure 6.14, and Figure 6.15 show three web pages produced by a simple servlet of this type. When a user initially visits this Greeting servlet, the user is asked to sign in (Figure 6.13). After entering a sign-in name, the user is thanked by name (Figure 6.14). Finally, if the user revisits the servlet, for example by clicking on

```
            // Set the HTTP content type in response header
            response.setContentType("text/html; charset=\"UTF-8\"");

            // Obtain a PrintWriter object for creating the body
            // of the response
            PrintWriter servletOut = response.getWriter();

            // Determine whether or not this is the first visit
            // by this user, and update visit count if this is
            // the first visit
            HttpSession session = request.getSession();
            if (session.isNew()) {
                visits++;
            }

            // Create the body of the response, including visit count
            servletOut.println(
"<!DOCTYPE html \n" +
"    PUBLIC \"-//W3C//DTD XHTML 1.0 Strict//EN\" \n" +
"    \"http://www.w3.org/TR/xhtml1/DTD/xhtml1-strict.dtd\"> \n" +
"<html> \n" +
"  <head> \n" +
"    <title> \n" +
"      VisitorCounter.java \n" +
"    </title> \n" +
"  </head> \n" +
"  <body> \n" +
"    <p> \n" +
"      Hello World! \n" +
"    </p> \n" +
"    <p> \n" +
"      This page has been viewed by \n" +
        visits +
"      visitors since the most recent server restart. \n" +
"    </p> \n" +
"  </body> \n" +
"</html> ");
            servletOut.close();
```

FIGURE 6.12 Body of doGet() method of VisitorCounter servlet that counts number of individual visitors.

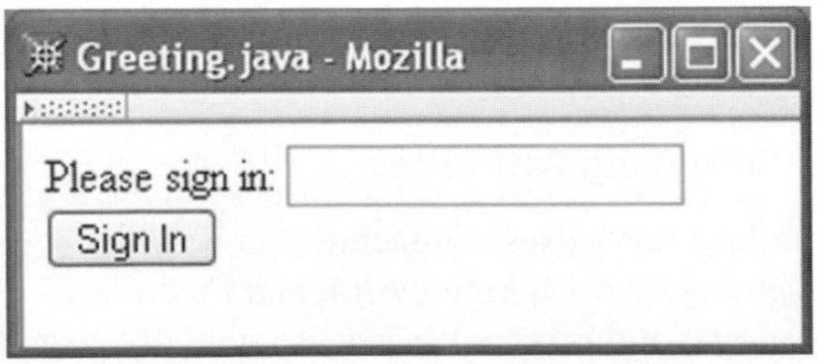

FIGURE 6.13 Sign-in page of the Greeting servlet.

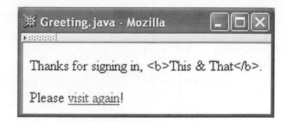

FIGURE 6.14 Thank-you page of the `Greeting` servlet. The user signed in as `<b>This & That</b>`; notice that the XML special characters are displayed rather than being treated as markup.

the "visit again" link in the thank-you page, then he or she is greeted by name (Figure 6.15) on a welcome-back page rather than seeing the sign-in form. Figure 6.16 illustrates the client-server interaction producing this sequence of pages.

This servlet is implemented by storing and retrieving an attribute value in the `HttpSession` object for the user. A *session attribute* is simply a name-value pair that is stored in the `HttpSession` object. (Recall that the term "attribute" is also used in HTML to describe name-value pairs within the start tag of an element. The way in which this term is being used, as HTML element or session attribute, should be clear from context.) Two methods of `HttpSession` are used to store and retrieve attributes: `setAttribute(String name, Object obj)` to create or overwrite an attribute having the given name with the given `Object` value; and `getAttribute(String name)`, which returns the value (of type `Object`) for the attribute with the given name, or `null` if there is no attribute with this name in the `HttpSession` object.

Figure 6.17 shows the `doGet()` method and Figure 6.18 the `doPost()` method of the `Greeting` servlet. Consider the `doGet()` method first. Notice that, as for `VisitorCounter`, the `doGet()` method of `Greeting` uses the `isNew()` method to determine whether or not this is the user's first visit to the servlet. If this appears to be a first visit, either because the session is new or because the `signIn` attribute used to store the user's sign-in name has not been defined in an existing session, then the servlet calls a `printSignInForm()` method (shown in Figure 6.19) in order to display a sign-in form (Figure 6.13). We will see how the `signIn` attribute is set in the `doPost()` method. For now, notice that the value returned by a call to `getAttribute()` is of type `Object`, so it must be explicitly cast to its actual

FIGURE 6.15 Welcome-back page of the `Greeting` servlet.

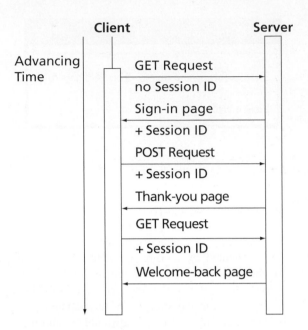

FIGURE 6.16 Client-server interaction resulting in display of three web documents in the order shown in Figures 6.13–6.15. Note that the two GET requests are distinguished by whether or not a session ID is present in the request.

data type (String in this case). In response to GET requests that are not the first—that is, that contain a valid session ID and for which the session object contains a signIn attribute—the servlet displays the value of the signIn attribute within a welcome-back page (Figure 6.15) by calling a printWelcomeBack() method, which is straightforward and therefore not shown.

Key aspects of the printSignInForm() method are shown in Figure 6.19. Three things should be noted. First, the HTTP method used by the form is POST. Second, the second parameter of printSignInForm() is used as the value of the form's action attribute. Since the call to this method in doGet() passes the value Greeting for this parameter, the action of the form is being set to this value. When the form is submitted, the browser will treat this action as a relative URL and will therefore send an HTTP POST request containing the form's query string back to our Greeting servlet. Finally, note that the name of the text field is signIn, the same name we have used for our session attribute. Although different names could be chosen, it is natural to name any session attribute that stores a parameter value after the parameter stored.

Because the sign-in form generated by printSignInForm() uses the POST method, the doPost() method of Greeting will be called when the form is submitted. As shown in Figure 6.18, this method attempts to retrieve the signIn parameter value (the value of the form's text field). If this parameter exists in the HTTP request's query string, the thank-you page (Figure 6.14) is displayed and the value of the parameter is stored in the signIn session attribute, where it can be accessed by subsequent GET requests. The Greeting argument value in the call to the printThanks() method (again simple and therefore not shown)

```
/**
 * Respond to any HTTP GET request with either a sign-in or a
 * welcome-back page, depending on whether or not this is the first
 * visit.
 */
public void doGet (HttpServletRequest request,
                   HttpServletResponse response)
    throws ServletException, IOException
{
    // Set the HTTP content type in response header
    response.setContentType("text/html; charset=\"UTF-8\"");

    // Obtain a PrintWriter object for creating the body
    // of the response
    PrintWriter servletOut = response.getWriter();

    // If first visit by user, display sign-in form.  Otherwise,
    // welcome the returning visitor back using name stored in the
    // session object on the first visit.
    HttpSession session = request.getSession();
    String signIn = (String)session.getAttribute("signIn");

    if (session.isNew() || (signIn == null)) {
        printSignInForm(servletOut, "Greeting");
    } else {
        printWelcomeBack(servletOut, signIn);
    }

    // Clean up and return
    servletOut.close();
}
```

FIGURE 6.17 doGet() method of Greeting servlet.

that generates the thank-you page is again a relative URL, this time for use as the value of the href attribute of the hyperlink displayed on this page. If the signIn parameter is not present in the request (Exercise 6.4 asks you to think about how this might happen), then an error of sorts has occurred. I have chosen to handle this situation by sending the user back to the sign-in form without any error message.

One other small point to notice is that, as shown in the figures, a user might want to sign in using characters that are not allowed as part of the character data of an XML document. Therefore, as was the case with the PrintThis servlet, we must replace each of the XML special characters in the value of signIn with an entity or character reference before writing signIn's value to the response. The printThanks() and printGreeting() methods use the escapeXML() method described in Section 6.5.2 to perform the character replacement.

6.6.3   Session Termination

I have said that the Greeting servlet will display its welcome-back page rather than its sign-in page once the user has submitted the sign-in page, and the implication was that

```
/**
 * Respond to any HTTP POST response with a thank you, and store
 * the sign-in name supplied in the session object.
 */
public void doPost (HttpServletRequest request,
                    HttpServletResponse response)
    throws ServletException, IOException
{
    // Set the HTTP content type in response header
    response.setContentType("text/html; charset=\"UTF-8\"");

    // Obtain a PrintWriter object for creating the body
    // of the response
    PrintWriter servletOut = response.getWriter();

    // If signIn parameter present in request, output "thank you"
    // message and store sign-in within session object.
    // Otherwise, an unexpected behavior has occurred; display
    // signIn form again.
    String signIn = request.getParameter("signIn");
    HttpSession session = request.getSession();
    if (signIn != null) {
        printThanks(servletOut, signIn, "Greeting");
        session.setAttribute("signIn", signIn);
    } else {
        printSignInForm(servletOut, "Greeting");
    }

    // Clean up and return
    servletOut.close();
}
```

FIGURE 6.18 doPost() method of Greeting servlet.

```
    private void printSignInForm(PrintWriter servletOut,
                                 String action)
    {
        ...
        servletOut.println(
"    <form method='post' action='" + action + "'><div> \n" +
"      <label> \n" +
"        Please sign in: <input type='text' name='signIn' /> \n" +

        ...
```

FIGURE 6.19 Portions of the printSignInForm() method used to generate the sign-in page (Figure 6.13).

this would be the case in perpetuity after the sign-in. But, in fact, a sign-in will only be good until the session *expires* or is *invalidated*. The HttpSession interface defines a setMaxInactiveInterval(int interval) method that takes an integer argument interval representing a number of seconds. If more than interval seconds elapse between any two HTTP requests to the servlet from the user represented by this HttpSession object, then the user's session will expire before the second of these two requests can be processed. More precisely, the web server effectively sets a timer of duration interval for the session after each HTTP request containing this session's ID is received. If the timer completes before the next request containing this session ID is received, then the server calls the invalidate() method on the session object, terminating it. Servlet code can also call the invalidate() method directly at any time in order to terminate a running session. This would typically be done when a user clicks a "log out" link on a web page that is part of a session, for example.

There are some other fine points about session termination that should be mentioned. First, if setMaxInactiveInterval() is called with a negative argument, then the session will not expire, although it could still be terminated by a call to invalidate(). Second, if setMaxInactiveInterval() is not called explicitly for a session object, then the server will determine the default expiration behavior of the object; a common default is for a server to expire sessions after 20 minutes or so. Finally, server restart will typically invalidate all sessions managed by the server, although some servers may support *persistent* sessions that survive server restarts. We will not cover this feature here.

Of course, sessions are maintained by communication between clients and servers, so a session can also potentially be terminated by the client. In fact, the next section deals with the primary mechanism used to implement the session concept—so-called *cookie* processing—and we will see that the client has significant control over this mechanism.

6.7 Cookies

A *cookie* is a name-value pair that a web server sends to a client machine as part of an HTTP response, specifically through the Set-Cookie header field. Browsers will typically store the cookie pairs found in the response in a file on the client machine. Then, before sending a request to a web server, the browser will check to see if it has stored any cookies received from this server. If so, the browser will include these cookies in the Cookie header field of its HTTP request.

The cookie mechanism is a natural means of implementing the session concept automatically as part of the processing performed by the getSession() method. Specifically, if a server uses cookies to maintain a session, then a call to getSession() will cause the server to look for a cookie named JSESSIONID in the Cookie header field of the request. If a JSESSIONID cookie is found, its value is used to search the server's list of valid session objects for an object with the same session ID. If found, a reference to this object is returned as the value of the getSession() call. Otherwise, if no JSESSIONID cookie is found or if the cookie value does not match the session ID of any valid session object, a new session object is created. A JSESSIONID cookie having the session ID of this new object as its value is then created, and this cookie is added to the Set-Cookie header field of the HTTP response (or more precisely, the cookie is stored on the server and will be sent in the Set-Cookie header field when the servlet sends its HTTP response). The new session object is then returned to the servlet.

Servlets can also explicitly create and use cookies. The Java servlet API provides a class called `Cookie` for this purpose. Each instance of this class corresponds to a single cookie. This class can be used to create internal representations of new cookies and to access the name-value data in existing `Cookie` objects (see the first three rows of Table 6.3). Two other methods are used to transfer the information between this internal representation and the representation of a cookie in an HTTP header: the `getCookies()` method on the `HttpServletRequest` parameter returns an array of `Cookie` objects corresponding to the cookies sent by a browser in the HTTP request; and the `addCookie(Cookie cookie)` method on the `HttpServletResponse` parameter tells the server to add the information in the given `cookie` to the Set-Cookie header field when the server later sends its HTTP response to the client.

Cookies, like sessions, can expire, but the expiration is performed by the client, not the server. A browser will not send an expired cookie in subsequent HTTP requests. By default, a cookie expires when the browser that accepted the cookie is closed, but the server can request that this behavior be overridden using the `setMaxAge()` method shown at the end of Table 6.3. There are also several other `Cookie` methods, not shown here, that determine which servlets on a server and which servers within a domain receive a cookie as well as whether or not a cookie should be sent only over secure (encrypted) connections. Details of all `Cookie` methods are provided in [SUN-SERVLETS-2.4].

As an example of how cookies can be used, consider the following variation on the visit counter theme. We would now like to maintain a separate counter for each different visitor to our servlet. Each counter should record the number of times that its associated user has visited the servlet. Furthermore, the counter should not be reset unless it has been a full year since the user has visited the servlet. The essential portions of the `doGet()` method of a `CookieCounter` servlet for accomplishing this task are shown in Figure 6.20, and an example of the output produced by this servlet appears in Figure 6.21.

There are a few items to notice about this servlet's code. First, I called `addCookie()` early in the `doGet()` method. This was not arbitrary: all calls to `addCookie()` should be made before writing any HTML output to the `HttpServletResponse` parameter. The Tomcat server, at least, ignores calls made to `addCookie()` after printing to the `PrintWriter` object has begun. Also, while it is not shown here, you can add multiple cookies to the response by calling `addCookie()` multiple times. However, the browser may limit the number of cookies

TABLE 6.3 Key `Cookie` Class Methods

Method	Purpose
`Cookie(String name, String value)`	Constructor to create a cookie with given name and value.
`String getName()`	Return name of this cookie.
`String getValue()`	Return value of this cookie.
`void setMaxAge(int seconds)`	Set delay until cookie expires. Positive value is delay in seconds, negative value means that the cookie expires when the browser closes, and 0 means delete the cookie.

```
    private static final int oneYear = 60*60*24*365;

    public void doGet (HttpServletRequest request,
                       HttpServletResponse response)
        throws ServletException, IOException
{
        // Get count from cookie if available, otherwise
        // use initial value.
        int count = 0;
        Cookie[] cookies = request.getCookies();
        if (cookies != null) {
            for (int i=0; (i<cookies.length) && (count==0); i++) {
                if (cookies[i].getName().equals("COUNT")) {
                    count = Integer.parseInt(cookies[i].getValue());
                }
            }
        }
        // Increment the count and add request to client to store it
        // for one year.
        count++;
        Cookie cookie = new Cookie("COUNT",
                                        new Integer(count).toString());
        cookie.setMaxAge(oneYear);
        response.addCookie(cookie);

        // Set the HTTP content type in response header
        response.setContentType("text/html; charset=\"UTF-8\"");
        . . .
"  <body> \n" +
"    <p>You have visited this page " + count + " time(s) \n" +
"        in the past year, or since clearing your cookies.</p> \n" +
"  </body> \n" +
        . . .
```

FIGURE 6.20 Portions of doGet() method of a servlet that counts the number of times a user visits a URL.

that it accepts from a single site. The cookie specification calls for the browser to accept at least 20 cookies, or possibly fewer if the cookies require a significant amount of storage. So, just as with edible cookies, don't overdo it.

Another thing to notice in the code is that I have used uppercase alphanumerics for the cookie name (COUNT). For maximum compatibility with various browsers, following this practice is advisable, although not strictly required. Also, because cookie values are strings,

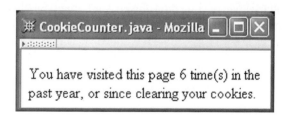

FIGURE 6.21 Output of CookieCounter.java after six visits to the servlet's URL.

I have had to use the `Integer` class to perform conversions between the integer value that I need in order to perform increment operations and the `String` value that is stored in the cookie. The code shown here illustrates a standard technique for performing these types of conversions by using the `parseInt()` and `toString()` methods of `Integer`.

This servlet is fairly robust. For instance, restarting the server will not affect the count, since the count is stored on the client, not the server. Restarting the client also will not affect the count, because the client stores the count in a cookie file. However, as hinted at in the text of Figure 6.21, users can remove their cookies. In Mozilla 1.4, for example, cookie removal can be performed by selecting **Tools | Cookie Manager | Manage Stored Cookies**. A user can also choose to *block* (refuse to accept) cookies from particular web sites, or to block cookies entirely. Some browsers also allow cookies to be blocked based on whether or not a site maintains a *privacy policy* and, if there is a policy, what the policy says (see [W3C-P3P] for information on creating a site privacy policy). The Mozilla 1.4 browser can be instructed to consider privacy policies under **Edit | Preferences, Category:Privacy&Security | Cookies**, by selecting "Enable cookies based on privacy settings." Mozilla also allows users to specify separate cookies policies for *first-party* cookies vs. *third-party* cookies. A first-party site is the web site that you intended to visit, the one whose URL is displayed in the Location bar of your browser. A third-party site is a site other than the one you intended to visit but that nonetheless supplies some of the content of the page you see, such as images (including banner ads).

In short, servers cannot rely on the availability of the cookie mechanism in order to implement the session abstraction, since many browsers can and do block cookies. However, there is an alternate method that can be used to maintain sessions, which we discuss next.

6.8   URL Rewriting

An alternative to passing a session ID between server and client through HTTP headers is to pass it via the HTML documents themselves. That is, an alternative is for the server to write the session ID within every HTML document it returns to the client in such a way that the URLs that the client subsequently requests will contain the session ID. The server accomplishes this by adding the session ID to every servlet URL appearing in any page sent to the client. This typically involves rewriting every URL referencing the servlet in the `href` attribute of any anchor and the `action` attribute of any form output by the servlet. Then, whenever the server receives an HTTP request, it must check the URL it receives for session ID information and, if found, use the session ID just as it would if it had been passed to the server via a cookie.

The `HttpServletResponse` interface supports this approach to maintaining session by defining an `encodeURL(String url)` method. Given a `url` argument, this method returns the same URL plus, if appropriate, a session ID (when it is "appropriate" to add a session ID is explained later in this section). The session ID is added via a little-used URL feature known as a *path parameter*. For example, if the `url` argument's value is, say, `URLEncodedGreeting` (a String representing a relative URL), and it is appropriate to add a session ID to this URL, then `encodeURL(url)` will return something like

```
URLEncodedGreeting;jsessionid=0157B9E85127D047E2BD464ECE116701
```

As shown, a path parameter is added to a URL by appending a semicolon to the URL followed by a name-value pair. While the path parameter looks much like a parameter in a query string, it is not, and will be invisible to query-string processing methods such as `getParameter()`.

The server checks for the presence of session information within the request URL when `getSession()` is called. In particular, when `getSession()` is called, it will first search for a JSESSIONID cookie in the header of the HTTP request. If found, then the server will record that cookie processing can be used to maintain this session and proceed with its session object processing as described in the previous section. If a JSESSIONID cookie is not found, the server will check for a `jsessionid` path parameter in the request URL. If this is found, the server records that this session must be maintained using URL rewriting. It then continues with its session processing, using the session ID contained in the path parameter just as it would if the ID had come from a cookie. Typically, the mechanism used by the server to maintain session is transparent to the servlet code, but if desired the boolean `HttpServletRequest` methods `isRequestedSessionIdFromCookie()` and `isRequestedSessionIdFromURL()` can be called by the servlet code to determine how the session ID was transmitted in the current HTTP request.

Now we can return to the issue of when it is appropriate for `encodeURL()` to add the session ID to a URL. If, at the time this method is called, the servlet has already called `getSession()` and the server has not recorded that cookies can be used to maintain this session, then the session ID will be added to the URL. Otherwise, if either of these conditions does not hold, then `encodeURL()` will return its argument URL unchanged.

It's easy, then, to create a modified version of the `Greeting` servlet that incorporates URL rewriting and that will therefore maintain session even for users that disallow cookies from this servlet. We'll call the modified servlet `URLEncodedGreeting`. The only significant modification is that all of the (relative) URL's output to the response are now passed through `encodeURL()` prior to output. So, for example, instead of

```
printSignInForm(servletOut, "Greeting");
```

we will now have

```
printSignInForm(servletOut,
                response.encodeURL("URLEncodedGreeting"));
```

and other method calls containing "Greeting" are similarly changed. These changes plus changing the class name are all that is needed in order to maintain session without cookies. You might want to test this yourself: tell your browser to block cookies from your servlet server (using the Cookie Manager in Mozilla), and then run both `Greeting` and `URLEncodedGreeting`. `Greeting` will now fail to recognize you when you return after signing in, but `URLEncodedGreeting` should welcome you warmly, just as `Greeting` did before you turned cookies off. The only significant difference that you will see between running `Greeting` with cookies enabled and `URLEncodedGreeting` with cookies disabled is that in the latter case the `jsessionid` path parameter is displayed in the browser's Location bar.

Note that if URL rewriting is to be used to maintain session, it's important that *every* URL referencing the servlet be rewritten. Otherwise, if cookies are disallowed and the user requests a servlet URL that has not been rewritten, then no session ID will be transmitted to the servlet in the request. And if there is no session ID in a request, then `getSession()` will create a new session, effectively losing all earlier session information.

In summary, with little effort on the part of a servlet developer—the addition of one method call for every servlet-referencing URL output by the servlet—session can be maintained with any client, whether or not the client allows cookies. That said, Exercise 6.7 explores a subtle security issue that should be considered when deciding whether or not to add URL rewriting to a servlet.

6.9 Other Servlet Capabilities

At this point, we've covered most of the major capabilities provided by servlets. This section briefly mentions several more servlet methods.

6.9.1 Additional HttpServletRequest Methods

Table 6.4 lists several methods on `HttpServletRequest` that return information that is part of the HTTP request received from the client. The method `printInfo()` shown in Figure 6.22 illustrates how these methods can be used to produce output such as that shown in Figure 6.23.

6.9.2 Additional `HttpServletResponse` Methods

Table 6.5 lists several methods that can be called on the `HttpServletResponse` parameter (`response` object) in order to control various aspects of the HTTP response generated.

TABLE 6.4 Additional `HttpServletRequest` Methods

Method	Purpose
`String getRemoteAddr()`	Return IP address of the client machine making this request.
`String getRemoteHost()`	Return fully qualified name of the client making this request, or its IP address if name is not available.
`String getProtocol()`	Return the type and version of communication protocol used by the client to make this request (e.g., "HTTP/1.1").
`boolean isSecure()`	Return boolean indicating whether or not this request was made over a secure communication channel.
`StringBuffer getRequestURL()`	Return a StringBuffer containing the URL used to access this servlet, excluding any query string appended to the URL as well as any `jsessionid` path parameter.
`Enumeration getHeaderNames()`	Return an Enumeration of String objects representing names of all header fields in the request.
`String getHeader(String fieldName)`	Given a valid header field name, return a String representing the value of the field, or `null` if header field is not present in request. The match of `fieldName` against header field names is case insensitive.

```java
/**
 * Add tables of HTTP protocol and header information to
 * servletOut object
 */
private void printInfo(HttpServletRequest request,
                       PrintWriter servletOut)
    throws IOException
{

    // Output protocol information
    servletOut.println(
"   <table border='0'> " +

"      <tr><th align='right'>Client IP address:</th><td>" +
         request.getRemoteAddr() + "</td></tr>" +
"      <tr><th align='right'>Client host name:</th><td>" +
         request.getRemoteHost() + "</td></tr>" +
"      <tr><th align='right'>HTTP protocol:</th><td>" +
         request.getProtocol() + "</td></tr>" +
"      <tr><th align='right'>Secure channel:</th><td>" +
         request.isSecure() + "</td></tr>" +
"      <tr><th align='right'>Request URL:</th><td>" +
         request.getRequestURL() + "</td></tr>" +
"   </table>" );
    // Output HTTP header fields
    String headerName;        // holds name portion of one header field
    String headerValue;       // holds value portion of one header field
    Enumeration headerNames = request.getHeaderNames();
    if (headerNames == null) {
        servletOut.println(
"   <p style='color:red'>Cannot access headers</p> " );
    } else {
        servletOut.println(
"   <table border='1'> " +
"   <caption>HTTP Header Fields</caption> " +
"     <tr><th>Name</th><th>Value</th></tr>" );
        while (headerNames.hasMoreElements()) {
            headerName = (String)headerNames.nextElement();
            headerValue = request.getHeader(headerName);
            servletOut.println(
"     <tr><td>" + headerName + "</td> " +
"        <td>" + headerValue + "</td></tr>");
        }
        servletOut.println(
"   </table>" );
    }
}
```

FIGURE 6.22 Method for displaying HTTP communication and header information.

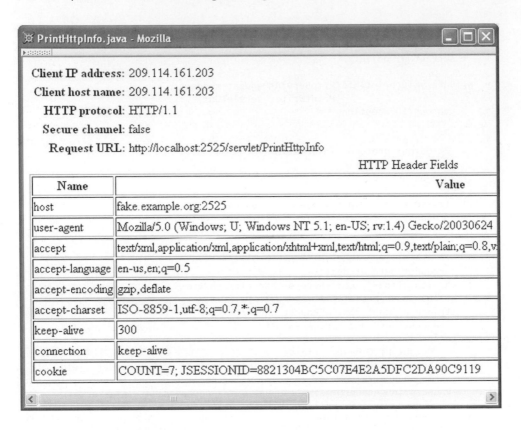

FIGURE 6.23 Example output produced using `printInfo()`.

In order to effectively use many of these methods, it is important to understand how the server generates an HTTP response. All output sent to the `PrintWriter` object of the `HttpServletResponse` is stored in a data structure known as the *response buffer*. When this buffer becomes full, the server *flushes* the buffer, that is, sends its content to the client and clears the buffer in preparation for storing additional information. However, before this buffer can be flushed the first time, the HTTP headers of the response must be sent to the client, since the HTTP protocol requires that the header precede the body of the response. Therefore, all calls to methods that set HTTP header fields or the status code must be made before the first buffer flush, since later calls cannot cause additional header fields to be sent to the client. Methods that must be called before the first buffer flush include `setHeader()`, `setDateHeader()`, `setContentLength()`, `setStatus()`, `sendError()`, and `sendRedirect()`. As noted in the table, `setBufferSize()` has the more stringent requirement that it must be called before any data is written to the buffer.

You might, then, be tempted to set the buffer size extremely large to ensure that the entire page generated by the servlet will fit in the buffer. This would have at least two advantages. First, the HTTP header fields and status code could be set at any time during generation of the page. Second, if the entire page fits within the buffer, then the server will automatically set the Content-Length header field before sending the HTTP response containing the page. This is useful because the TCP/IP connection over which the server and client communicate via HTTP can be kept open if content length information is contained in the response, and keeping the connection open means that subsequent requests can be made without taking the time to establish another connection. On the other hand, if the page content generated by your servlet will exceed the size of the buffer and you want the connection kept open, then your servlet should determine the total length of the content and set the Content-Length field explicitly by a call to setContentLength() before the first buffer flush.

Of course, there are disadvantages to using a large buffer as well. An obvious one is that a large buffer will require more memory than a small buffer. Another is that the client will not be able to begin processing the response until the servlet has completed generating the entire response, because the entire page will reside within the buffer on the server until flushed at the end of processing. On the other hand, if the page content is written to a small buffer that is flushed several times as content is generated, then the client can work on the data from these buffer flushes while the server continues generating additional data.

Notice that two of the methods listed in Table 6.5—sendError() and sendRedirect()—do more than just set parameters or headers: these methods actually cause

TABLE 6.5 Additional HttpServletResponse Methods

Method	Purpose
void setHeader(String name, String value)	Include a header field with the given name and value in the HTTP response.
void setDateHeader(String name, long value)	Include a date header field (such as Expires) with the given name in the HTTP response. The given value is converted from milliseconds since 00:00 01 January 1970 UTC to an equivalent time in HTTP date format.
void setContentLength(int len)	Set the Content-Length header field to the given value.
void setBufferSize(int size)	Set the desired size of the response buffer (see text). The server may override the specified size and use a larger value. This method must be called before any data is written into the response buffer.
int getBufferSize()	Return an integer representing the actual size of the response buffer.
void setStatus(int statusCode)	Set the status code in the HTTP response (status code is 200 (OK) by default). Any information contained in the response buffer is cleared. Use only for nonerror status codes.
void sendError(int statusCode, String msg)	Set the status code in the HTTP response to the given error statusCode (status code beginning with 4 or 5), and in the body of the response send a server-generated HTML error page containing the given msg.
void sendRedirect(String url)	Cause HTTP response with status code 307 (Temporary Redirect) to be sent to the client, causing the client to send a new HTTP request to the given url. Client will behave as if it had sent request to the specified url.
void encodeRedirectURL(String url)	Perform URL rewriting (for session management) on url that will be used for redirection.

a response to be sent to the client. Therefore, no prints can occur on the PrintWriter object of the response after either of these methods has been called.

Finally, dealing with dates in Java can be tricky, so you might find an example of using the setDateHeader() method helpful. Recall that web browsers typically use the Expires response HTTP header as advice about how long the returned document should be kept in the browser cache. Roughly speaking, if the user revisits the page before the cached copy has expired, then the browser will return the copy from the cache. Otherwise, if the cached copy has expired, the browser will send another HTTP request to the server.

Now suppose that we would like to write servlet code that sets the Expires header field of a response so that the page contained in the response expires 10 seconds after it is served. We could do this using code such as the following:

```
import java.util.Calendar;
    . . .
        // Tell client to use cache for 10 seconds following an access
        Calendar expires = Calendar.getInstance();
        expires.add(Calendar.SECOND, 10);
        response.setDateHeader("Expires", expires.getTime().getTime());
```

Two getTime() method calls are needed on the expires object because the first returns a Date object and the second, on this returned object, returns a long representing the time in milliseconds, which is the date form we need. See the Java API Calendar documentation for additional methods and properties supplied by this class.

6.9.3   Support for Other HTTP Methods

In addition to doGet() and doPost(), five other methods defined by HttpServlet corresponding to HTTP 1.1 request methods can be overridden. These methods all have the same signatures as doGet() and doPost(). They are doDelete(), doHead(), doOptions(), doPut(), and doTrace(). Both doOptions() and doTrace() have default implementations that typically should not be overridden. The doHead() method is also automatically defined if the doGet() method is overridden by the servlet code.

6.10   Data Storage

Nearly all web applications—that is, software systems that include dynamic generation of HTML documents—interact with some form of data storage, usually either a file system or a database management system. For example, if you order a textbook from a Web site, the software implementing the site must have access to the current inventory of books being offered at the site and will also typically save your order in a data store of some type. Proper choice of a data storage mechanism and efficient implementation of software interacting with this mechanism is often crucial to developing a responsive and reliable web application.

However, storing data from within a web application is to a large extent the same as storing data from within any other software application, and therefore is not itself a web technology. Thus, many data storage topics—efficient use of file systems, database management, and so on—are beyond the scope of this textbook.

We do, however, cover a few Java topics related to data storage, for those not already familiar with these topics. To facilitate writing small example web applications, Appendix B covers Java object serialization, which provides a convenient (although not necessarily efficient) mechanism for storing data from a Java object in a file system. If you are already familiar with databases, Appendix C provides some guidance on connecting to a database from within a Java program using the Java Database Connectivity (JDBC™) API. The Microsoft Access and MySQL® database management systems are used as examples.

There is one aspect of data storage from within web applications that deserves further attention here: web applications generally involve concurrent processing, while many non-web applications do not. This, in turn, can significantly affect the way in which a program interacts with its data store, particularly when the data store is a file system. Concurrent processing within Java servlets is discussed in the next section.

6.11   Servlets and Concurrency

This section does not present any new Java servlet features. Instead, it deals with a server feature—concurrency—that can cause hard-to-find servlet errors if it is not understood and managed carefully.

6.11.1   Concurrency in Web Servers

Concurrent processing is a topic that is typically encountered in the study of operating systems, which must manage multiple user and system programs simultaneously. But concurrency is also encountered within certain software applications, particularly web-based applications. For example, if you have noticed a web browser loading several images at the same time, or have observed that the web browser can respond to your mouse clicks while it is still downloading information from a web server, then you have seen concurrent processing in action on the client side. However, while such concurrency is present in the browser itself, a client-side software developer typically doesn't need to deal explicitly with issues related to concurrent processing in his or her code. This is because each JavaScript function runs to completion, without interruption by other JavaScript functions.

On the server side, the situation is different. While there is a single user on the client side, there can be hundreds or even thousands of users accessing a web site nearly simultaneously. In order to efficiently handle all of these users, concurrent processing is vital. For example, if the servlet code handling an HTTP request from one user begins a disk input or output operation, a concurrent web server running on a single-processor system might temporarily suspend further instruction processing by that servlet while it allows a second servlet, handling an HTTP request for another user, to begin executing its instructions. The second servlet might then run to completion before the server chooses to continue the first servlet's instruction processing (see Figure 6.24).

Without concurrent processing, the second user's HTTP request could not begin to be processed until the first user's request was completed, and the CPU might sit virtually idle while waiting for the input/output operation of the first servlet to complete. Generally speaking, this idle time will lead to longer overall processing times if servlets are run sequentially—each running to completion before the next can begin—rather than concurrently. Furthermore, if many users are attempting to access a web site simultaneously,

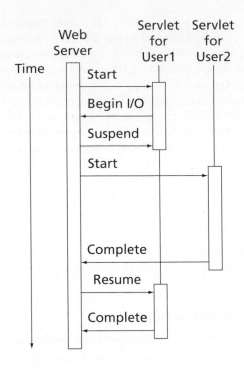

FIGURE 6.24 Schematic of server running servlets for two users concurrently.

the difference in processing times between sequential and concurrent processing can be substantial. Concurrent processing by web servers, therefore, is the norm.

6.11.2 Threads

In the example of concurrency in the preceding subsection, we said that processing of the first servlet was "suspended" at one point in time and then "resumed" at another time. In order to understand the problems that can arise as a result of this suspending and resuming, we need a more detailed understanding of these processes.

First, let me correct an oversimplification in the description of concurrent processing. It is actually not the web server that manages concurrent processing, but the Java Virtual Machine (Java VM) within which the server executes. The server's role is to create a thread for each HTTP request that it receives. A *thread* is the Java VM's abstract representation of the processing to be performed to accomplish a particular task, possibly concurrently with other tasks. In the case of a web server, the type of task we will be interested in is one that processes a single HTTP request in order to produce an HTTP response.

The Java VM maintains a data structure containing information about each of the threads that it is managing. So when we say that the server creates a thread for each HTTP request that it receives, we are, in essence, saying that it adds another element to the Java VM's thread data structure. We will call the information stored in this data structure concerning a thread the *state* of the thread. We can think of the state of a newly created request-processing thread as being the location of the first method that should be executed (the doGet() method of a particular servlet instance, for example) along with references to the HttpServletRequest and HttpServletResponse objects created by the server to be passed to this method.

The Java VM also records for each thread whether or not it is currently executing. In a single processor system (which we will assume for simplicity), at most one thread can be executing at any one time. As the thread executes, its state changes. After each statement is executed by the thread, the Java VM may choose to suspend the running thread. If the thread is suspended by the Java VM, then its state is saved in the Java VM's thread data structure. The state of another thread is then loaded into the Java VM, and execution proceeds for that thread until the thread is suspended or completes execution. Then the state for this thread is saved, if necessary, and another thread is resumed. These thread management activities continue as long as the Java VM is running.

What is crucial to understand about all of this is exactly what is and what is not part of a thread's state. That is, what information does the Java VM save and restore for a thread, and what information is not saved and is therefore subject to change between the time when a thread is suspended and when it is resumed? The state of a thread consists of the following information:

- Which statement is to be performed next: object, method, and line number. We will refer to the method containing this statement as the *current* method of the thread.
- The statement that will be executed when the current method returns, and the statement that will be executed when the method containing that statement returns, and so on for all methods that have not yet returned. We will call these the *active* methods of the thread.
- The values of parameters to the current method and all other active methods of the thread. The combination of this information with the preceding information is sometimes referred to as the *call stack* for the thread.
- The values of all of the servlet's *local variables*, that is, variables defined within the current method and all other active methods.

The following are examples of the types of information that are not part of a thread's state:

- *Instance variables*, that is, variables that are declared outside of any method in a class.
- *Class variables*, that is, variables that are declared outside any method and in addition have the keyword static in their declaration.
- Files, databases, other servers, and any other resources external to the Java VM.

A few servlets, such as ServletHello (Figure 6.2), make no use of instance or class variables or any other information outside of that which is part of a thread's state. The presence of concurrency will not alter the behavior of such servlets. However, most servlets— even simple ones—do use information beyond their thread's state, and this can lead to some unintended behaviors, as we will see next.

6.11.3   Threading Issues

To illustrate the type of problem that can occur when a servlet is run in a concurrent environment, let's return to the simple HelloCounter servlet of Section 6.3 (Figure 6.3). Recall that this servlet attempts to maintain a count of the number of times it has been accessed and to display an updated count each time. Now assume that a thread processing an HTTP request directed to this servlet executes the statement visits++; and is then suspended. Notice that visits is declared as an instance variable, not a local variable or a method parameter. Therefore, the value of visits is not part of the thread state, so this value is not saved when the Java VM suspends this first thread.

If a second thread executes the entire HelloCounter servlet from beginning to end while the first thread is suspended, the second thread will also increment visits and then output an HTML page that contains the value of this variable. Since visits is incremented twice before being output by the second thread, the value it outputs will be 2 greater than the value in the previous output page. For example, if the value of visits was 17 before the first thread began execution, then the second thread would output an HTML page saying that 19 page views had occurred. What's more, when the first thread resumed execution, the value of visits would again be undisturbed. So the first thread, which would continue at the call to the println() method, would also output a page saying that 19 page views had occurred! That is, someone who was able to see the entire sequence of pages output by this servlet would see the pages-viewed sequence 17, 19, 19 (see Figure 6.25).

Now even though we might not have expected this behavior, in this example at least it's probably not a problem. That is, it's okay if two visitors are both told that 19 page views have occurred, because this is in some sense correct: the servlet has in fact begun execution 19 times before either user is informed of the page-view count. However, if we were required to write a servlet that assigned a unique view identification number on each access (perhaps for customer service reasons), then we would obviously need more sophisticated code than that used for the HelloCounter servlet. We will see how to write such code in the next subsection.

6.11.4   Thread Synchronization

Now that we have some understanding of threading and some of the problems that can arise when multiple threads can run concurrently, the next question is how to address these problems. The short answer is to use Java's lock mechanism (described shortly) in order to force threads to access shared data in a way that guarantees the behaviors we want. In fact, the relatively simple and powerful mechanisms for handling threading issues in Java are one reason to prefer Java over some other languages for server-side web programming.

As an illustration of Java's power to address threading issues, we will see that a one-word addition to the HelloCounter servlet will cause it to output a distinct count in response to each page view. Specifically, we will add the synchronized keyword to the beginning of the doGet() method declaration:

```
synchronized public void doGet (HttpServletRequest request,
                    HttpServletResponse response)
```

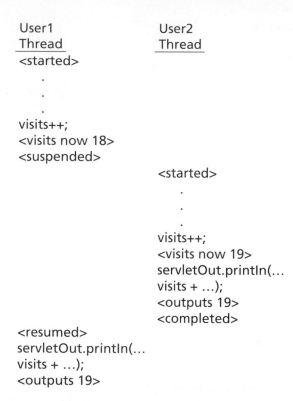

FIGURE 6.25 Two threads running in `HelloCounter` concurrently. The initial value of `visits` is assumed to be 17.

The Java run time automatically creates a *lock* for any object that contains a method with the `synchronized` keyword in its declaration. When a thread attempts to execute a synchronized method of such an object, the Java VM either decides (how it decides is described shortly) to suspend execution of the thread or allows the thread to begin executing the method immediately. If the thread is allowed to execute immediately, then it is said to *hold* the lock for the object until it completes executing the method, at which point the thread *releases* the lock. At most one thread is allowed to hold the lock for an object at any one time. So the Java VM will allow a thread to execute a synchronized method if no other thread holds the lock and will *block* the thread otherwise, causing the thread's execution to be suspended. After a thread releases the lock, the Java VM will check to see if any threads have been suspended to wait for this lock, and if so will choose one of these threads, give it the lock, and begin its execution on the method for which it was waiting.

Figure 6.26 illustrates the locking idea. In this figure, two HTTP requests are accessing the same servlet at nearly the same time. The thread for the first user's request calls a synchronized method `synchMethod()` defined elsewhere within the servlet object. Because no other thread is running at this time in this servlet, the first thread obtains the lock for the servlet object and begins executing in the synchronized method. However, before this

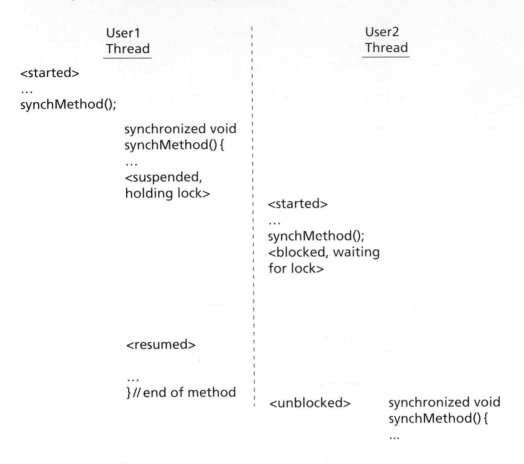

```
          User1                          User2
          Thread                         Thread
          _____                         _____

<started>

...

synchMethod();

          synchronized void
          synchMethod() {

          ...

          <suspended,
          holding lock>

                                <started>

                                ...

                                synchMethod();
                                <blocked, waiting
                                for lock>

          <resumed>

          ...
          } // end of method
                                <unblocked>      synchronized void
                                                 synchMethod() {

                                                 ...
```

FIGURE 6.26 Two servlets invoking a synchronized method.

thread returns from the method, its processing is suspended, perhaps waiting for an input operation to complete. The thread corresponding to the second user's HTTP request then attempts to execute synchMethod(). However, since the first thread still holds the lock, the second thread will be blocked. At some later time, the first thread resumes processing and eventually returns from synchMethod(), releasing the lock. At some subsequent time, the Java VM will see that the second thread is waiting for the lock, will give that thread the lock, and will allow it to execute in synchMethod().

In our HelloCounter example, by adding the synchronized keyword to the declaration of doGet(), we are guaranteeing that only one thread can execute this method at a time. In other words, we are forcing this method to be run sequentially rather than concurrently. With this change, any thread that increments the visit counter will also output the counter value produced by this increment operation before any other thread can increment the counter. This guarantees that each user sees a distinct page-view value.

The simple technique illustrated here can be used to solve concurrency problems in any single servlet that processes only HTTP GET requests. However, as explained in the next section, it will not help if two or more servlets attempt to share a resource such as a file. Furthermore, this technique defeats the whole purpose of concurrency: because we are synchronizing on the doGet() method, threads cannot run concurrently within this servlet at all! The next subsection will show how to address both of these issues.

6.11.5 Servlet Synchronization

Often, two or more servlets will need to access a shared resource. The shared resource may itself provide functionality that can be used to handle concurrency issues; this is generally the case if the resource is a database management system. For other shared resources, such as files, the servlet programmer must handle concurrency issues directly.

In the case of synchronizing multiple servlets, the simple use of the synchronized keyword on one or more methods within each servlet will not work. The problem is that the lock that a thread obtains when it executes in a synchronized method is the lock for the object that contains the method. Holding this lock does not prevent a second thread from executing a synchronized method in a different object. Since each servlet is a separate object (instantiated by the server and conforming to the HttpServlet interface), each servlet has its own synchronization lock. Therefore, one thread running in a synchronized method belonging to one servlet does not prevent a different thread from running in a synchronized method belonging to a different servlet.

As a concrete example of the problem of sharing resources between multiple servlets, consider a slightly more sophisticated version of the HelloCounter application. The new application will consist of two cooperating servlets. The first, called CounterWriter, displays a "Hello World!" page and—unknown to the page visitor—increments a visit counter each time the servlet is accessed. The second, called CounterReader, displays the number of visits made to CounterWriter since CounterReader was last accessed (Figure 6.27). (Actually, it displays the number of page views, but to simplify the discussion I will assume that every user visits this page only once and call this a visit count.) The idea is that the first servlet is designed to be accessed by visitors to a web site, while the second is designed to be used only by the web site administrator in order to gather site usage data. The visit count for this application will be stored in a file so that it can be shared between the two servlets. This also has the side benefit that the counter will no longer be reset when the web server is restarted, since it is stored in the file system rather than in main memory.

Pseudocode outlines of the processing to be performed by each of these servlets are presented in Figure 6.28 and Figure 6.29. While this processing certainly looks

FIGURE 6.27 Web page produced by CounterReader servlet.

```
Input count from file
Increment count
Overwrite file with updated count
Display "Hello World!" page
```

FIGURE 6.28 Pseudocode for CounterWriter functionality.

straightforward, once again, concurrency issues can cause the servlets to behave differently than we would expect.

As an example of a problem that could occur, assume that two HTTP requests are received nearly simultaneously by the server, the first to be handled by the CounterReader servlet and the second by CounterWriter. Furthermore, assume that the CounterReader servlet inputs the count from the file but is then immediately suspended. While this servlet is suspended, the CounterWriter servlet is executed in its entirety. Finally, the CounterReader servlet completes its execution, overwriting the file and displaying the count that it read from the file before it was suspended.

If you trace through this execution sequence with example data, you'll discover that something is wrong (Figure 6.30). For example, if we assume that the count in the file is initially 24, then at the end of the processing just described the CounterReader user will see a web page displaying 24 and the count in the file will have been reset to 0. But these are exactly the same results we would see if the second user had never visited the CounterWriter servlet. In other words, our application lost the visit by the second user. Even worse, it's not hard to see that if not one but several users visit the CounterWriter servlet while execution of the CounterReader servlet is suspended, *none* of these visits will be counted.

A little thought shows that we could fix this problem if we could just collapse the first two steps of CounterReader into a single step that could not be interrupted by a thread running in either servlet. Some more analysis shows that we also want the first three steps of CounterWriter to run without interruption. That is, as long as all of the steps in each servlet that deal with the shared file can be executed without interference from the other servlet, the application will not produce any strange behavior as a result of concurrency. Also notice that if synchronization is performed in this way, the Display processing by each servlet will not be synchronized, so concurrent processing can still occur.

We can achieve the desired noninterruption effect in Java by creating a class CounterFile that contains two synchronized methods, one (incr()) containing the three steps of CounterWriter and the other (readAndReset()) containing the two steps of CounterReader. These methods are shown in Figure 6.31, and supporting methods are shown in Figure 6.32. Because both methods are in the same class separate from the

```
Input count from file
Overwrite file with 0 to reset count
Display HTML page containing count read from file
```

FIGURE 6.29 Pseudocode for CounterReader functionality.

```
Servlet 1 (CounterReader)                 Servlet 2 (CounterWriter)
-------------------------                 -------------------------
Input count from file (24)
<suspended>
                                          Input count from file (24)
                                          Increment count (25)
                                          Overwrite file with count (25)
<resumed>                                 Display "Hello World!" page
Overwrite file with 0
Display count (24)
```

FIGURE 6.30 Example trace through unsynchronized execution of CounterReader and CounterWriter pseudocode, assuming count in file is initially 24.

servlets, we avoid the problem discussed earlier involving synchronized methods in separate classes.

Notice that we have declared the incr() and readAndReset() methods to be static. This keyword indicates that the methods do not belong to individual instances of the class, but instead belong to the CounterFile class itself. Since a class is also an object in Java, this means that the lock associated with these methods is a lock for the CounterFile class object. We'll explain why we've done this in a moment. For now, note that one of the results of this decision is that we have had to declare several other entities within the class to be static. This is because every class entity accessed by a static method—these entities include the filename variable and the writeCount() and readCount() methods—must also be declared static.

We're now ready to write the CounterWriter and CounterReader servlets. Combining the earlier pseudocode with the methods defined in CounterFile and our knowledge of servlets, we can see that each servlet should be simple: call a method in CounterFile and write appropriate HTML to the PrintWriter obtained from the HttpServletResponse parameter. Figure 6.33 and Figure 6.34 sketch the bodies of the doGet() methods for each of these servlets.

Note that the methods of Figure 6.31 are called differently than typical methods. Typically, we might expect to call one of these methods using code such as

```
CounterFile counterFile = new CounterFile();
counterFile.incr();
```

But since these are static methods that belong to the class itself, we use the (simpler) notation shown. Notice that if we had instead declared these methods without the static keyword and had created an instance of CounterFile in each servlet, then we would have again had a synchronization problem. The problem is that if each servlet created an instance of CounterFile, then there would be two locks, one for each instance, and we would be back to the very synchronization problem that we recognized at the beginning of this subsection.

In general, each shared resource that needs to have explicit concurrency management can be handled in a similar way, by creating its own class containing synchronous methods

```java
import java.io.*;
/**
 * This class uses synchronized class methods to synchronize thread
 * access to a file containing a counter.
 */
public class CounterFile
{
    private static final String filename = new String("count.dat");

    /** Increment the counter, creating a file if it does not exist */

    synchronized public static void incr()
        throws IOException
    {
        int count;                  // Value stored in file

        // Create File object associated with the count file
        File countFile = new File(filename);

        // Get count from file if it exists, and use default value 0 o.w.
        count = readCount(countFile);
        // Update the count and output it to the file
        count++;
        writeCount(countFile, count);
    }

    /** Return current value of the counter and reset to 0 */

    synchronized public static int readAndReset()
        throws IOException
    {
        int count;                  // Value stored in file

        // Create File object associated with the count file
        File countFile = new File(filename);

        // Get count from file if it exists, and use default value 0 o.w.
        count = readCount(countFile);

        // Output reset value to the file
        writeCount(countFile, 0);

        // Return the count read from the file
        return count;
    }
```

FIGURE 6.31 First portion of CounterFile class providing synchronized access to a shared file.

```
/** Create output stream for countFile and output count. */

private static void writeCount(File countFile, int count)
    throws IOException
{
    DataOutputStream outstream =
        new DataOutputStream(new FileOutputStream(countFile));
    outstream.writeInt(count);
    outstream.close();
}

/** Input count from file, returning 0 if file does not exist */

private static int readCount(File countFile)
    throws IOException
{
    int count = 0;            // Default value if file does not exist
    if (countFile.exists()) {
        DataInputStream instream =
            new DataInputStream(new FileInputStream(countFile));
        count = instream.readInt();
        instream.close();
    }
    return count;
}
}
```

FIGURE 6.32 Second part of `CounterFile` class providing synchronized access to a shared file.

```
// Obtain a PrintWriter object for creating the body
// of the response
PrintWriter servletOut = response.getWriter();

// Increment the number of visits to the URL for this servlet
CounterFile.incr();
```

FIGURE 6.33 Portion of `CounterWriter` servlet for incrementing visit count. HTML output is the same as that of `ServletHello`.

```
// Obtain a PrintWriter object for creating the body
// of the response
PrintWriter servletOut = response.getWriter();

// Compute the number of visits to the URL for this servlet
visits = CounterFile.readAndReset();
```

FIGURE 6.34 Portion of `CounterReader` servlet for displaying and resetting visit count. HTML output is the same as that of `HelloCounter`.

that "collapse" related sequences of accesses to the shared resource so that the sequence cannot be interrupted. However, beware: once an application has two or more locks, it is possible to reach a state in which there are two threads, each holding a lock for which the other is waiting. The threads are then said to be *deadlocked*, and typically neither will complete execution. Deadlock is often reasonably easy to avoid if you are aware of the possibility. A general discussion of deadlock avoidance is beyond the scope of this book; refer to a typical operating systems textbook for details.

6.11.6 Summary and Concluding Remarks

We have examined some of the key issues that can arise from concurrency in web servers and have presented Java-based solutions to these problems. However, as you have probably realized by now, correctly handling concurrency issues in complex applications can be difficult. The good news is that the primary shared resource in most web-based systems is a database, and database management systems typically provide facilities such as table locking and transaction management that can be used to manage concurrency. How to use these facilities is outside the scope of this text, but details are provided in standard database textbooks. The techniques outlined in this section should go a long way toward handling most other concurrency issues, which are often simpler than those arising in databases.

Java does provide several other synchronization features as well, including the application of the synchronized keyword to blocks of code rather than to methods, as well as the methods wait(), notify(), and notifyAll(). These synchronization features are usually not needed within servlets and are therefore not covered here. See the Java API documentation [SUN-J2SE-1.4.2] for information on these methods, and the Java language reference [SUN-JLS-2] for information on block-level code synchronization.

6.12 Case Study

We're ready now to develop server-side code for our blogging application, which will finally give us a functional system (although it could have some problems with XML special characters; we'll solve these problems in the next chapter).

Recall that the blogging application has two forms, one for logging in (Figure 2.28 is an unstyled version of this form) and one for previewing/adding an entry to the blog (Figure 2.30). We will write servlets Login and AddOrPreview to handle the form data from each of these forms. We will also write a third servlet, ViewBlog, that generates the HTML document representing the main (view-blog) page (Figure 1.12). This servlet will receive requests when the user clicks on any of the navigation links on the right side of the view-blog page. Also, after the AddOrPreview servlet adds an entry to the blog, it will redirect the request to ViewBlog (by calling sendRedirect()). The browser will then send a request to ViewBlog and display the response received from this servlet. Thus, if the user adds an entry (via a request to AddOrPreview) and then clicks the browser Refresh button, the refresh request will be sent to ViewBlog, not AddOrPreview. If we did not use the redirect but instead had AddOrPreview generate the view-blog page directly, clicking Refresh would resend the add-entry form data to AddOrPreview, which could produce an unwanted duplicate blog entry.

In addition to the three servlets, we will write some support classes. First, the Entry class represents a single blog entry. The constructor for this class is

```
Entry(String rawTitle, String rawText) {
    this.entryID = -1; // Valid ID assigned when stored
    this.rawTitle = rawTitle;
    this.cookedTitle = cookTitle(rawTitle);
    this.rawText = rawText;
    this.cookedText = cookText(rawText);
    this.createDateTime = Calendar.getInstance();
    }
```

As shown, this constructor takes a blog title and body, stores both *raw* and *cooked* versions of these strings, and also stores the date and time at which the Entry instance is created (the getInstance() method of the java.util.Calendar class returns an object representing the current date and time). In this chapter, cooking the strings involves escaping all XML special characters in them by calls to WebTechUtil.escapeXML(). The entryID instance variable is discussed in the next paragraph. The remainder of this class is simply variable declarations, implementations of the cookTitle() and cookText() methods, and methods for setting/getting various instance variables. In particular, getTitle(), getText(), and getCreateDateTime() return cookedTitle, cookedText, and createDateTime, respectively.

We will rely on a DataStore class in order to store the blog information in the file system. A full implementation of this class should provide several public static methods:

- void initialize(): must be called before any other methods are called. If called more than once, calls after the first have no effect.
- java.util.Vector getEntries(int month, int year): returns a vector of all Entry objects created during the specified month and year. The entries appear in the vector in reverse chronological order (most recent first).
- java.util.Vector getAllMonths(): returns a vector of Calendar objects, one for each month for which there is a blog entry. The objects appear in the vector in chronological order.
- void addEntry(Entry entry): adds entry to the blog data store. This method also sets the entryID variable of entry to a unique value.
- Entry getEntry(int entryID): return the Entry that has the given entryID, or null if there is no such object.
- void updateEntry(Entry entry): called to notify the data store that entry has been modified.

The getEntry() and updateEntry() methods are not used in our implementation of the blogging application, but would be useful if the application were extended with, say, the ability to edit an entry. One possible implementation of the first four methods of DataStore, based on object serialization, is discussed in Appendix B.

The final support class is DisplayBlog, which generates the actual HTML for the view-blog and preview pages. This class has a single public method display(). As shown

```
static void display(PrintWriter servletOut,
                    Vector entries, Vector months)
{
    displayProlog(servletOut);
    displayEntries(servletOut, entries);
    if (months != null) { // null means previewing an entry
        displaySideInformation(servletOut, months);
    }
    displayEpilog(servletOut);
    return;
}
```

FIGURE 6.35 Java function used to generate HTML for the view-blog page.

in Figure 6.35, this method takes the `PrintWriter` passed to it by a servlet class along with two vectors representing a collection of blog entries and months for which entries are available in the data store. It then calls several private methods. `displayProlog()` simply prints the initial portion of the view-blog HTML document to the `PrintWriter` object, from the `DOCTYPE` tag through the `div` immediately preceding the main body of the document. `displayEpilog()` prints several closing tags, including the final `</html>` tag. The interesting methods are `displayEntries()` and `displaySideInformation()`. We'll look at only the first of these here; the other one is similar.

First, you may want to review Figure 3.40, which shows the markup for an example blog entry. We want to write Java code that will print a sequence of such entries, one for each `Entry` object contained in the `entries` argument vector. Figure 6.36, which is the main loop of the `displayEntries()` method, performs this task. While the code is

```
        // Output each entry, following all but the last with
        // a separator.
        Iterator entryGetter = entries.iterator();
        while (entryGetter.hasNext()) {
            Entry entry = (Entry)entryGetter.next();
            servletOut.println(
"       <div class='entry'> \n" +
"         <div class='datetime'>" +
            dateFormat(entry.getCreateDateTime()) + "</div> \n" +
"         <div class='entrytitle'>" +
            entry.getTitle() + "</div> \n" +
"         <div class='entrybody'> \n" +
"         " + entry.getText() + "\n" +
"         </div> \n" +
"       </div>" );
            if (entryGetter.hasNext()) {
                servletOut.println(
"       <hr />" );
            }
        }
```

FIGURE 6.36 Main loop within the `displayEntries()` method.

ugly visually, it is reasonably simple functionally. The DisplayBlog's dateFormat() method (not shown) takes a Calendar argument and uses the java.text.SimpleDateFormat class to produce a formatted string representation of the date and time contained in the argument object.

Now that we have an overview of the support classes, we can develop the servlet classes themselves. We'll begin with the Login servlet that handles data from the log-in form (the HTML for this form is contained in Fig. 2.29). The doPost() method of this class (its only method) is shown in Figure 6.37. This servlet begins by attempting to retrieve the user name and password from the query string passed to it as part of the HTTP request. For a variety of reasons (including purposely misformed requests), these parameters may not be present, so we test for them to avoid throwing an exception. We then verify that the user name and password entered are those identifying the blogger (obviously, in a fuller implementation these values would not be hardcoded and a better password would be used). If successful, we create a session object with a loggedIn attribute. We'll test for the presence of this attribute in the AddOrPreview servlet in order to verify that the user is indeed logged in. Finally, if all tests succeed, then we redirect the user's browser to the add-entry page (Figure 2.30). If for any reason we cannot log the user in, the browser is redirected to the log-in page. (In a fuller implementation we would generate this page dynamically so that an error message could appear indicating that log-in had failed.)

You may have noticed that the relative URLs used in the sendRedirect() method calls begin with the string /MOBFiles. Recall from Section 1.7.4 that, by default, any files in the webapps/ROOT subdirectory of the JWSDP 1.3 installation directory are accessible via relative URLs beginning with /. We will create a MOBFiles subdirectory of ROOT and place all of the static files (HTML, image, CSS, and JavaScript) for our application within MOBFiles. Thus, the addentry.html and login.html documents will be accessible using the relative URLs shown. If our application had many static files, we might create

```
public void doPost(HttpServletRequest request,
                   HttpServletResponse response)
    throws ServletException, IOException
{
    String username = request.getParameter("username");
    String password = request.getParameter("pwd");
    if (username != null && password != null &&
        username.equals("nice") &&
        password.equals("try")) {
        HttpSession session = request.getSession();
        session.setAttribute("loggedIn", new Boolean(true));
        response.sendRedirect("/MOBFiles/addentry.html");
    }
    else {
        response.sendRedirect("/MOBFiles/login.html");
    }
}
```

FIGURE 6.37 doPost() method of the Login servlet.

subdirectories of MOBFiles to further organize our files (JavaScript in one directory, images in another, etc.).

We're now ready to work on the AddOrPreview class, which will handle requests generated by the add-entry page. This class will implement the init() method as well as doPost(). Recall that init() is called once when a servlet is instantiated by the web server (servlet container). Since our servlet is going to access the data store, and since the DataStore object must be initialized by a call to its initialize() method before any other operations can be performed on the data store, we will make this call in the init() method of the servlet.

The doPost() method of AddOrPreview causes one of three responses to be sent to the browser. First, if there is no loggedIn attribute in the HttpSession object, then an error page is displayed (Figure 6.38). The code (I'm deleting comments to keep this short) in doPost() that accomplishes this is

```
HttpSession session = request.getSession();
if (session.getAttribute("loggedIn") == null) {
    response.sendRedirect("/MOBFiles/loginRequired.html");
}
```

Second, recall from Section 5.9 that the doPreview parameter of the add-entry form is used to indicate whether the Preview or Add Entry button was clicked. If the doPreview parameter is present and has the value false, we will assume that we should add an entry to the blog and display the updated blog (by redirecting to the ViewBlog servlet, for reasons given earlier). Building on the classes defined earlier, this is straightforward:

```
else if (request.getParameter("doPreview") != null &&
         request.getParameter("doPreview").equals("false")) {
    Entry entry = new Entry(request.getParameter("title"),
                            request.getParameter("entry"));
    DataStore.addEntry(entry);
    response.sendRedirect("ViewBlog");
}
```

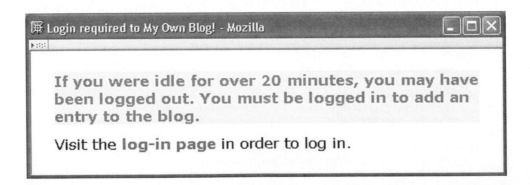

FIGURE 6.38 Page displayed if a POST request is sent to the AddOrPreview servlet and the user is not currently logged in.

Finally, if the user is logged in but the request does not indicate that an entry should be added to the blog, a preview page will be returned to the browser. A preview page (Figure 3.42) can be generated by passing to the `DisplayBlog.display()` method a `PrintWriter`, a vector containing a single `Entry` object representing the data contained in the request, and a `null` value for the vector of months (indicating that the side navigation information should not be displayed). The code for this is

```
else {
    response.setContentType("text/html; charset=\"UTF-8\"");
    PrintWriter servletOut = response.getWriter();
    Entry entry = new Entry(request.getParameter("title"),
                            request.getParameter("entry"));
    Vector oneEntry = new Vector();
    oneEntry.add(entry);
    DisplayBlog.display(servletOut, oneEntry, null);
    servletOut.close();
}
```

The remaining servlet is `ViewBlog`. Since this servlet receives requests that are generated by clicking a hyperlink or by a redirect from `AddOrPreview`, it will implement `doGet()` rather than `doPost()`. Also, because `ViewBlog` accesses the data store and might be instantiated before `AddOrPreview`, `ViewBlog` will implement an `init()` method identical to the one described earlier for `AddOrPreview`.

The `doGet()` method begins with the usual servlet initialization (calls `setContentType()` and defines `servletOut`). It then tests for the presence of month and year parameters, which are included in the query strings for archive hyperlinks (see Fig. 2.33). If present, we convert the values from `String` to `int` using the `Integer.parseInt()` method. If the parameters are not present, then the `Calendar` class is used to retrieve the current month and year. Once the appropriate `int` values are stored in variables `month` and `year`, the remaining code simply calls on methods in the support classes described earlier:

```
// Retrieve the appropriate entries from the data store.
Vector entries = DataStore.getEntries(month, year);

// Retrieve months for which blog entries are available
Vector months = DataStore.getAllMonths();

// Display the blog entries for the selected month/year.
DisplayBlog.display(servletOut, entries, months);

// Clean up
servletOut.close();
```

To run our application, HTML files such as `login.html`, `addentry.html`, and `loginRequired.html`, as well as the other static files developed earlier for our application (`style.css`, `addentry.js`, etc.), will be placed in the `ROOT/MOBFiles` directory described earlier. The six Java classes described in this section will be compiled and the class files placed in the shared/classes directory under the JWSDP 1.3 installation directory, along with the class file for WebTechUtil (which is used by Entry). After restarting the Tomcat server, you can navigate to http://localhost:8080/MOBFiles/login.html and log in as user nice with password try. Then you're ready to start adding entries to your own blog. Anyone with access to your machine (users on other machines on your local network, for example) can view your blog entries by browsing to the /servlet/ViewBlog path at the 8080 port of your machine.

6.13 Related Technologies

Java servlets are only one of many ways of providing dynamic server content. The earliest standardized technology used for this purpose was the Common Gateway Interface (CGI). A web server supporting CGI recognizes certain URLs as requests for CGI-generated dynamic content in much the same way that servlet requests are recognized. For instance, a URL with a path beginning with /cgi-bin/ is interpreted by many servers as a request for CGI-generated content. Once the server recognizes a CGI request, it assigns values representing most of the data in the request to a number of operating system environment variables. For example, it assigns to the QUERY_STRING environment variable the value of the query string portion of the request URL, and assigns to REQUEST_METHOD the HTTP request method used. HTTP header fields are assigned to environment variables beginning with HTTP_ followed by the header field name, uppercased and with underscores (_) replacing hyphens (-). For example, the User-Agent field value would be assigned to the HTTP_USER_AGENT environment variable.

Once all of the environment variables have been defined, the server executes the program named in the request URL. For example, if the URL path is /cgi-bin/test.pl, then the server would execute a program named test.pl located in a certain directory as defined by the server configuration files. If the HTTP request uses the POST method, the body of the request (still URL-encoded) is piped to the standard input stream of the executed program. The program communicates back to the server by writing to the program's standard output stream. The first few lines of the output are one or more directives to the server. Typically, there is a single directive indicating the content type of the remainder of the output. Other possible directives allow the program to specify the HTTP status code for the response and a redirection URL. The program output that follows the directives will be used by the server as the body of its HTTP response. This portion of the program output is typically an HTML document.

A major advantage of CGI programming is its flexibility: any language can be used to write a CGI program. In practice, CGI programs have often been written in the Perl scripting language. Perl is popular for a number of reasons. First, since it is a scripting language, there is no need to compile a Perl program, so there is no need to maintain separate source and binary versions of the program. In addition, Perl provides a number of language shortcuts that appeal to many programmers. For example, the operand of many operations is implicit, which saves typing and reduces the chance of typographical errors. Also, a Perl module (similar to a Java package or a C++ library) called CGI.pm simplifies many CGI-related tasks, such as generating form elements and accessing parameter and other data contained in the environment variables and input stream passed to a Perl CGI script. Furthermore, it is easy to interface with other software or system utilities from within a Perl script.

While a number of web-based systems are still based on CGI, it appears that most software professionals have turned to other technologies. One of the problems with the CGI approach is efficiency. With basic CGI programming, every time a CGI program is executed, a new operating system process must be created to run the program, which can be expensive computationally. Also, since CGI programs run in separate processes, synchronization of concurrent CGI programs is generally slower and more difficult to code than is synchronization in Java. Furthermore, some of the servlet objects, such HttpSession and Cookie, have no comparable concept in the CGI protocol. In CGI programming, such concepts need to be either programmed from scratch or provided by a third-party package, which may limit code portability.

Beyond these generic problems with CGI programming, there are some specific problems related to the use of Perl. The fact that Perl is interpreted rather than compiled means that in addition to the process creation overhead, a Perl script itself will generally execute more slowly than a comparable program in a compiled language. Data types do not play a major role in Perl, which may make Perl programs more susceptible to certain run-time errors than programs written in a compiled language with stronger type checking, such as Java. In addition, Perl is not as widely known as Java, which can lead to difficulties with maintaining and enhancing Perl code. Along these same lines, Perl is not inherently object oriented, which can be a distinct disadvantage with respect to the development and reuse of Perl-based software.

While most if not all of these CGI deficiencies can be overcome by careful programming or by using advanced server functionality, there is still another difficulty that both CGI programming and servlets share: entanglement of logic and HTML generation. You have probably noticed that the example servlet programs in this chapter are somewhat ugly: in my attempt to maintain HTML structure in the output statements, the overall Java code has become hard to read. Worse than this, most large development teams have both designers and programmers (they go by a variety of names, but I'll use these generic designations here). The designers know a lot about HTML and style sheets and how to create attractive and usable web pages, but they generally know little about writing code. And programmers, while we tend to believe that we know how to create functional web pages, are generally much too technically savvy to be able to put ourselves behind the monitors of the general public. That is, we are (generally speaking) lousy designers. But with both CGI and servlet programming, web page (design) and logic (programming) are intricately intertwined, making it difficult for designers and programmers to cleanly divide labor and work together efficiently.

In Chapter 8, we'll look at another technology—JavaServer Pages™, or JSP™—that builds on Java Servlets technology and supports a stronger separation of design from logic. While JSP might be viewed as an alternative to Java servlets, it is probably more accurate to view it as an extension that provides higher levels of abstraction and that can be used in concert with servlets in larger web applications. Chapter 8 also contains a brief discussion of several technologies related to JSP that are used for server-side programming, including ASP.NET and PHP.

6.14   References

The authoritative reference for Java servlets is [SUN-SERVLETS-2.4]. In addition to explaining all of the major servlet features, this document includes API descriptions of the `javax.servlet` and `javax.servlet.http` packages (the APIs for these packages are also available in Javadoc form by opening in a browser the file `docs/api/index.html` under your JWSDP 1.3 installation directory). Most of the classes and interfaces discussed in this chapter—including `HttpServlet`, `HttpServletRequest`, `HttpServletResponse`, `HttpSession`, and `Cookie`—are defined in the `javax.servlet.http` package. `javax.servlet` defines `ServletException` and several inherited methods, such as `setHeader()`. HTTP cookie header fields are defined in [RFC-2109]; by default, the Netscape version of cookies described in this document is used to implement the `Cookie` class. Developers of sites that use cookies in any way should provide a privacy policy at their site that complies with the Platform for Privacy Preferences Project (P3P®) privacy recommendation. Although the P3P recommendation is not covered in this text, it is freely available at [W3C-P3P]; see Section 3.1 of the version 1.0 specification for two complete examples of privacy policies. The authoritative reference on Java language support for threads is the Java Language Specification [SUN-JLS-2], primarily Chapter 17. Information about CGI, including a link to the CGI/1.1 standard that is implemented by many servers, can be found at the W3C Web site [W3C-CGI].

Exercises

6.1. What is the URL encoding of the string `B&O Railroad down 3.2%`?

6.2. One of the methods on `HttpServletRequest` is `getRequestURL()`. Based on your knowledge of the Internet and web servers, give at least two reasons why this method might be needed. That is, explain why a servlet writer cannot always know in advance what URL will be used to access the servlet, even if the servlet class file is known to be physically stored on a particular server and in a particular location within the file system of that server.

6.3. The `Greeting` servlet's `doPost()` method (Figure 6.18) always calls `getSession()`. However, the `session` object returned by `getSession()` is only used if the `signIn` parameter is present in the query string. Are there any circumstances under which the response generated by the servlet would change if the statement defining the `session` object was moved as shown below? Explain.

```
if (signIn != null) {
    HttpSession session = request.getSession();
    printThanks(servletOut, signIn, "Greeting");
    session.setAttribute("signIn", signIn);
```

6.4. The `Greeting` servlet's `doPost()` method (Figure 6.18) included code to deal with the possibility that a POST request to the servlet would not contain the `signIn` parameter. Describe at least two different scenarios that might lead to such POST requests being sent to the servlet.

6.5. Give at least one good reason why the Java servlet URL rewriting mechanism should add session ID as a path parameter rather than as a query string parameter.

6.6. A new visitor sends a request to the URL of a servlet that uses URL rewriting. Do you think that the servlet response will contain the session ID in the HTTP header, in URLs written to the body of the response, in neither, or in both? Justify your answer. How could you test your hypothesis?

6.7. As the `Greeting` servlet (Figure 6.17 and Figure 6.18) demonstrated, session can be used as a means of determining whether or not a user has signed in and, if signed in, including user-specific data on subsequent pages. Explain how Kim, a user of such a servlet, could accidentally allow one or more friends to access this servlet as if they were also signed in as Kim, even though the friends don't know Kim's sign-in name and don't have access to Kim's machine. (Hint: What is the major difference from a user viewpoint between sessions maintained by cookies and by URL rewriting?)

6.8. Figure 6.31 contains a synchronized method named `readAndReset()` that inputs a value from a file and then writes to the file. Explain how thread-related errors could occur if this method were rewritten as two separate synchronized methods, one performing the input and the other performing the write. (This illustrates the fact that individually synchronizing every access to a shared resource does not necessarily prevent every possible synchronization error.)

6.9. Assume that the `incr()` method of Figure 6.31 was not synchronized. Describe two different scenarios that could produce unwanted behaviors by the `CounterReader/CounterWriter` application as a result of concurrency.

Research and Exploration

6.10. In the JWSDP 1.3 version of Tomcat, if a servlet throws an exception to the Tomcat server (rather than catching exceptions in the servlet itself), then the server may or may not return an HTML document containing an error message to the browser.

    (a) Try writing one or more servlets that purposely throw exceptions, and perform experiments with your servlet(s) in order to determine the conditions that must be met in order for an error message to be displayed in the client browser when an exception is thrown.

    (b) View the server logs to determine which log file contains server-generated exception tracebacks.

    (c) Write a servlet that generates a complete HTML document that is displayed in the client browser (so that from the user's perspective processing is successful) while also throwing an exception that is recorded in the server log (so that from the server's perspective processing is not successful).

6.11. Cookies and security.

    (a) Assume that someone eavesdropping on a network has obtained another user's session ID from an HTTP request sent by that user. How could this information be used to spoof the servlet that generated the session ID into allowing the eavesdropper to access the servlet as if the eavesdropper were sending a request that was part of the same session?

    (b) Consider a servlet that is accessed using the secure HTTPS protocol. Imagine that the servlet sets a cookie named SECRETDATA on each client that accepts cookies. Also assume that the document returned by the servlet contains HTTP (not HTTPS) references to images on the same server that hosts the servlet. Explain why, if no precautions are taken, an eavesdropper could obtain that value of SECRETDATA. Look up the `setSecure()` method of the `Cookie` class, and show how it could be used to avoid this problem with SECRETDATA.

(c) Combining your answers to the previous two parts of this question, if a JSESSIONID cookie is used to store the session ID for a servlet accessed using the HTTPS protocol, what can you assume about this cookie in any "good" implementation of the Java Servlet API?

(d) How could you test your server to determine whether or not it implements the JSESSIONID cookie as it should? Perform the test and report your findings.

(e) How can storing log-in information in cookies be a security risk, even if the cookies storing this information are always sent using secure communications and assuming that the server itself is secured against external attacks? Illustrate the problem by writing a servlet that sets a cookie (that is "secure" because `setSecure()` has been called on it) and showing how to obtain the cookie's value without the need for eavesdropping or knowing anything about the server's code.

6.12. One of the criteria used by `encodeURL()` to decide whether or not to include a session ID on a URL is whether the server has evidence that the client supports cookies. Give another criterion—related to the URL to be rewritten—that should be considered from a security viewpoint before adding session ID to a URL. Test your server to see whether or not it uses this criterion, and report your results.

Projects

6.13. Automatic log-in.

(a) Implement a servlet that presents a new user with a form containing fields for entering a user name and password (the latter should use an appropriate type of `input` element). The form should also contain a checkbox, initially unchecked, labeled "Check to log in automatically in the future." If the user checks the box and successfully logs in (that is, the user name and password are both "CSisCoolStuff"), then the user name and password should be stored in two cookies (you may assume that cookies are enabled on the client). After successfully logging in, the user should see a page that says "Logged In Successfully." An unsuccessful attempt to log in should return the user to a page with an error message followed by the original log-in form, with the checkbox checked if it was checked on the previous form and unchecked otherwise. On subsequent visits, the servlet should attempt to log the user in using cookie information, if available. If this fails, the user should see the original log-in form, without any error message. If it succeeds, the user should see a "Welcome Back" page. Set the cookies to expire after six months.

(b) Extend the program in (a) so that if it tries to store the user name and password in cookies but fails, it will display a message on the "Logged In Successfully" page informing the user that cookies must be enabled in order to automatically log in.

6.14. High-low game.

(a) Write a servlet that plays the too-high–too-low number guessing game. If the servlet receives an HTTP GET request, it should pick a number between 1 and 1000 randomly (using `java.util.Random`) and display a form on which the user can enter a guess (Figure 6.39). It should also start a session containing, as an attribute, the number that this user must guess (it may assume for now that cookies are enabled). The session may contain other attributes as well, if desired. If the servlet receives an HTTP POST request with a valid session ID, it should test the guess contained in the POST against the number stored in the session. If the guess is correct, a page should be output congratulating the user. Otherwise, the user should be told whether

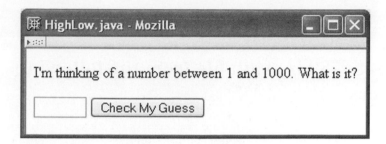

FIGURE 6.39 Initial page produced by servlet playing the high-low game.

the guess was too high or too low and be presented with a form on which the next guess can be entered.

(b) Modify your servlet so that if it receives a POST request that does not correspond to a valid session ID, it displays an appropriate message on the form used to input guesses (Figure 6.40).

(c) Modify the high-low servlet so that it will function properly even if the client does not allow cookies.

6.15. Book exchange.

(a) Write one or more servlets that will facilitate buying and selling used textbooks. Users should be able to post books for sale and search for books to buy by ISBN. Specifically, book sellers should enter their identifying information—name, e-mail address, phone number—one time per session, and then enter one or more books to be offered for sale. Information about each book should be entered on a separate page and include ISBN, condition of the book, and price. Sellers should be able to submit arbitrarily many book description pages. Book buyers should be able to enter an ISBN and see a table listing all copies of the book available for sale (Figure 6.41). If no copies of the specified book are available, a message to this effect should be displayed.

You may want to use something like the following data structure to store the information entered by users. The overall structure is a Hashtable that uses ISBNs as the keys. For each ISBN key present in the Hashtable, I store an ArrayList

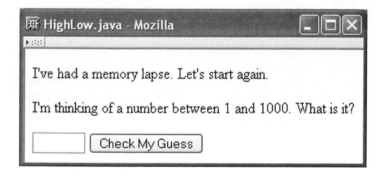

FIGURE 6.40 Page displayed if POST request to high-low servlet does not contain a valid session ID.

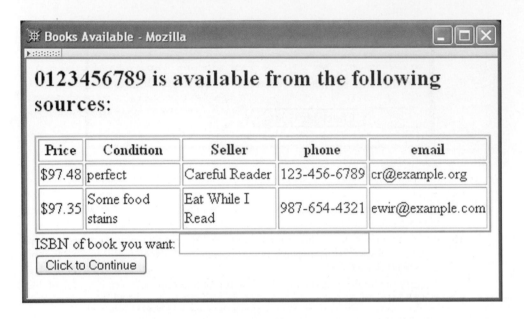

FIGURE 6.41 Example list of books produced by book-selling servlet.

containing one entry for each copy of the book that is available for sale. I used a five-element String array to hold the data for each book (price, condition of the book, and three seller-information elements), but you might prefer a different approach, such as defining a Book object.

(b) Modify your servlet so that the book information entered persists even if the server is restarted. This means that you will need to store this information in one or more files as it is entered. See Appendix B for guidance on storing Java objects as files.

(c) Use Java thread synchronization appropriately to guarantee that your servlet will behave as expected regardless of any concurrency issues that might arise.

6.16. Write a Crazy Eights game Web site (this project can also be adapted to other games). The site should allow users to play Crazy Eights against the computer, using the JavaScript software you developed in Exercise 5.21. The wins and losses for each user should be recorded for the duration of the user's session and displayed after each game is completed.

(a) A basic application should consist of a single Java servlet that generates two different HTML documents: a play-game page if a GET request is received without any parameters in the URL; and a statistics page if a GET request is received that contains a `result` parameter (used to indicate whether the user has won or lost a game against the computer). The play-game page should load the JavaScript file developed in Exercise 5.21, modified so that when the game is over the script causes the browser to navigate to the statistics page by loading an appropriate URL into the `location` property of the `window` object (see Table 5.12). (Recall from Section 1.7.4 that if you place your JavaScript file, say `crazy8.js`, in the webapps/ROOT subdirectory of the JWSDP 1.3 installation directory, it can be accessed by a relative URL such as `/crazy8.js`.) The first time that the statistics page is invoked for a session, the servlet should initialize the session object with the appropriate score (either one win for the user and none for the computer or vice versa, depending on the value of the result parameter). Subsequent invocations of the page should cause the servlet to update the session object's score data appropriately. In either case, after initializing or updating the session object, the servlet should display the user's wins and losses. The page displayed should also contain a hyperlink that the user can click to play again. You may assume that the user has cookies enabled.

(b) Modify your servlet to add two pages: a log-in page and a sign-up page. The sign-up page displays a form with text boxes for user name and password (use the appropriate form control) and a submit button. A user name and password entered on this page are stored by the application (using appropriate synchronization) in either a file or a database, as directed by your instructor, and statistics will now be stored along with the user name and password rather than being stored in session. After submitting the sign-up page, the statistics page will be displayed next (and will show no wins and no losses immediately after sign-up). The statistics page should now show the user name (appropriately escaped) as well as the wins and losses. The log-in page will be displayed if a GET with no parameters is received. This page will show a log-in form (user name, password, and submit button) and also will contain a hyperlink to the sign-up page. If the user name and password entered on the log-in form match a user name and password previously entered on the sign-up page, the user will be taken to the statistics page. (Note: If the application data is stored in a file, use a simple file name, such as mydata.ser, rather than one that includes machine-specific directory path information, such as /home/me/hw/mydata.ser, so that your servlet can be tested on other machines without modification.)

(c) Add error-handling code to your servlet. Specifically, if the user name and password entered on the log-in page do not match any of the stored user-name–password combinations, then redisplay the log-in page with an error message. Similarly, if the user name entered on the sign-up page has already been taken, or if the user name or password is not present in the HTTP request, redisplay the sign-up page with an error message.

6.17. The following questions suggest extensions to the case study of Section 6.12.

(a) Modify the blogging application so that the log-in page is dynamically generated by a DisplayLogin servlet rather than being a static page. If another servlet detects an error and redirects the user to the log-in page as a result, the log-in page should display an appropriate error message.

(b) Modify the blogging application so that readers can anonymously contribute comments about a blog entry. See Exercise 2.33 for a description of how the user interface might be designed. The DataStore API and Entry class described in Section 6.12 should be extended to handle comments.

(c) Modify the comment capability so that users must log in before commenting on a blog entry. The log-in page should also allow users to register by providing a user name and password. Registration information should be stored permanently (not merely as session information). Modify the comment display format to show the user name as well as the comment itself.

(d) Extend the blogging application so that the blogger can remove all comments made by a specified user.

CHAPTER 7

Representing Web Data
XML

In Chapter 2, we were introduced to the Extensible Markup Language, XML. In that chapter we learned how to read XML Document Type Definition (DTD) files and looked specifically at the DTD for XHTML. More generally, XML DTDs can be used to define markup languages for a wide range of applications, from financial information to textbooks like this one. At its core, XML can be thought of as a general means of representing any sort of structured data. While there are other technologies that have a similar purpose, XML is the most widely used for transmitting structured data over the Web.

In this chapter we will consider several different technologies related to XML. We'll begin with some details about XML itself, including the concept of an XML namespace, which allows different XML "vocabularies" to be mixed within a single XML document. Next, we'll learn how JavaScript client programs can communicate directly with servers via XML documents. We'll then consider several standard approaches that Java programs can use to input, manipulate, and output XML documents. We'll focus especially on the Extensible Stylesheet Language, XSL, which was mentioned in Chapter 3. Finally, we'll briefly learn how to associate style sheet information with XML documents loaded into web browsers. The chapter ends with a continuation of the case study.

XML is used extensively in many web servers. In fact, this chapter lays the foundation for most of the material in the remaining two chapters of this book. So our focus in this chapter will be primarily on the XML technologies themselves, and the remaining chapters will provide some concrete applications of these and other XML technologies. In fact, we will defer covering one of the core XML technologies, XML Schema, to Chapter 9 so that we can cover it in the context of one of its key applications, web services.

7.1 XML Documents and Vocabularies

The following is a simple example XML document:

```
<text>
  Hello World!
</text>
```

This should look familiar: overall, this document looks like an HTML element (of type `text`) containing the text "Hello World!"

In fact, most of the syntactic rules we learned in Chapter 2 for XHTML apply to all XML documents. The basic XML syntax rules are as follows (these are covered only briefly here, since they all should be familiar from our earlier study of XHTML):

- An XML document consists of markup and character data.
- There are two types of markup: tags and references.
- Tags begin with a less-than (<) character and end with a greater-than (>) character.
- References in an XML document begin with an ampersand (&) and are of two types: character references (such as) and entity references (such as <).
- All XML documents may make references to the entities lt, gt, amp, apos, and quot, which map to the characters less than (<), greater than (>), ampersand (&), single quote ('), and double quote ("), respectively. Other entities may also be defined, depending on the XML DTD used and/or application processing the document.
- If not used to begin markup, the characters < and & must be escaped (an exception is that escaping is not necessary within comments and CDATA sections; see the remarks following this list).
- Element tags are of three types: start tags, end tags (which begin with </), and empty-element tags (which end with />).
- Character data may only appear within a nonempty element.
- Start and end tags must be paired and must be properly nested with other pairs of start and end tags.
- Attribute specifications may appear within start tags or empty-element tags. Every attribute specification consists of an attribute name followed by an equals sign (=) followed by a quoted attribute value. An attribute value may not contain the character <; if the character & appears, it must be the first character in a character or entity reference. A pair of either single quotes or double quotes may be used to quote an attribute value. Attribute specifications are white-space-separated from one another.
- Element and attribute names are case sensitive.
- The XML white space characters are the same as in XHTML (Table 2.1): space, carriage return, line feed, and tab.
- XML comments begin with <!--, end with -->, and may not contain the string -- elsewhere within the content of the comment.

One XML feature that has not been mentioned previously is the *CDATA section*. The content of a CDATA section is interpreted as character data, even if it contains characters such as < and & that would normally be interpreted as markup. A CDATA section begins with the string <![CDATA[and ends with the string]]>. For example, the following is valid XML markup containing a CDATA section:

```
<message>
  The markup
<![CDATA[
  <message>This & that</message>
]]>
  is not valid XML because the &amp; must be escaped.
</message>
```

The CDATA section could be replaced with the equivalent markup

```
&lt;message&gt;This &amp; that&lt;/message&gt;
```

Any document that follows the syntactic rules in the preceding list and that has a single root element is an example of a *well-formed XML document*. So the "Hello World!" example document at the beginning of this section is a well-formed XML document, while a syntactically correct document with two root elements, such as

```
<root1>
</root1>
<root2>
</root2>
```

is not considered well formed.

A Java program that processes an XML document typically has two parts. One part normally calls on an API for an *XML parser* (called an *XML processor* in [W3C-XML-1.0]) to convert between the XML document and some internal data format, such as a tree structure. This part of the program is often just a few lines of code. This is one of the reasons for the popularity of XML: it is usually easy to import XML data into and export XML data from a program.

The other part of an XML processing program is the actual application software that processes data represented by the XML document. This part of the program needs to know about the *semantics* of the XML document: what element types and attribute names is it expected to contain, and what do these element types and attribute names mean? For example, Figure 7.1 is an XML document that represents a so-called *RSS feed*, a document designed to provide summary information about a Web site (the acronym RSS has been used by different developers to stand for different things; one such phrase, "rich site summary," is probably as good a description as any of how RSS feeds tend to be used). An application program processing this file needs to be aware that RSS feed documents have element types such as rss, title, link, and so on, and needs to understand what each of these elements represents (we'll briefly define these later). An *XML vocabulary* is created by specifying a complete description of the elements and attributes for a specific type of XML document. (An XML vocabulary is also sometimes referred to as an *XML application*, but I will use the term "application" to refer to software that processes an XML document.) While XHTML is one of the first and also probably the best-known of the many XML vocabularies that have been defined, there are many other XML vocabularies that are also in widespread use. One of these vocabularies, SOAP, is covered in Chapter 9. We'll also see several examples of special-purpose XML vocabularies in the remaining chapters of this book.

An XML vocabulary can be specified in a variety of ways. Simple XML vocabularies intended to be used by a small group of developers may be specified informally using natural language. Vocabularies intended to be made publicly available are normally specified more formally. For example, the specification for such an vocabulary might include an XML DTD (DTDs were described in detail in Section 2.10) in order to provide an unambiguous definition of the valid contents of element types, the attributes for each element type and their data types, entity definitions, and so on.

If a DTD is available for an XML vocabulary, then an XML document written according to the vocabulary can include a *document type declaration* in order to associate the document with the appropriate DTD, just as XHTML documents included a document

```
<rss version="0.91">
  <channel>

    <title>www.example.com</title>
    <link>http://www.example.com/</link>
    <description>
      www.example.com is not a site that changes often...
    </description>
    <language>en-us</language>

    <item>
      <title>Announcing a Sibling Site!</title>
      <link>http://www.example.org/</link>
      <description>
        Were you aware that example.com is not the
        only site in the example family?
      </description>
    </item>
    <item>
      <title>We're Up!</title>
      <link>http://www.example.net/</link>
      <description>
        Our new RSS feed is up.  Visit us today!
      </description>
    </item>
  </channel>
</rss>
```

FIGURE 7.1 Example RSS feed XML document.

type declaration. So, for example, we might have begun the RSS document example of Figure 7.1 as follows:

```
<!DOCTYPE rss
    SYSTEM "http://my.netscape.com/publish/formats/rss-0.91.dtd">
<rss version="0.91">
```

You may notice that this document type declaration differs somewhat from those we used with XHTML documents. The form of declaration used in XHTML documents was dictated by the XHTML recommendation, not by XML itself. In fact, generally speaking, document type declarations are optional in XML documents unless the vocabulary specification requires them. Furthermore, although XHTML requires a certain form of document type declaration including the keyword PUBLIC, XML in general allows the alternative syntax just shown using the keyword SYSTEM. The string following this keyword is a URI known as the *system identifier* for the document's DTD (the URI given in this example is, at the time of this writing, the URL of a copy of the DTD for RSS version 0.91). If a relative URI is specified, then it will be taken as relative to the location of the XML document containing the document type declaration. Generally speaking, the PUBLIC form of DOCTYPE is used for widely used DTDs (such as XHTML), while the SYSTEM form is sufficient for DTDs that are intended for use within, say, a single corporation. For more information on document type declarations containing the PUBLIC keyword, see [RFC-3151], which contains references to standards describing the syntax of strings such as "-//W3C//DTD XHTML 1.0 Strict//EN" (known as a *formal public identifier*) and explains how to register an organization so that its public identifiers are guaranteed unique.

An XML parser may conform with the XML 1.0 recommendation [W3C-XML-1.0] at one of two levels. A *nonvalidating parser* is required to verify that an input XML document is well formed. Even if a document type declaration is present in the XML document, a nonvalidating parser is not required to read a DTD that is external to the document (but see the following paragraphs for more on DTDs and nonvalidating parsers). A *validating parser* requires that any document it parses contain a document type declaration. The validating parser will read the DTD, verify that the document conforms with DTD, and also verify that the document meets *validity constraints* defined by the XML 1.0 recommendation. An example validity constraint is that each assignment to an attribute with data type ID must be distinct from the values assigned to all other such attributes (in XHTML, this means that all id attributes must have unique values, since ID is the data type for id attributes in XHTML).

In addition to error checking, an advantage of validating parsers is that every correct implementation of a validating parser should produce essentially the same results when parsing a given XML document. This means that if you write an XML processing application using one validating parser implementation and later decide to use a different parser, you should be able to substitute the new parser into your application without making any changes to the application code you have written (more on how this substitution can be performed in Java in Section 7.5). On the other hand, since nonvalidating processors may read all, some, or none of a DTD (if present), one implementation might read the entity declarations and default attribute values contained in a DTD while another implementation might not. This means that different implementations of nonvalidating parsers may produce different results when parsing the same XML document.

Nonvalidating parsers have the advantage that they will generally run faster than validating parsers because they perform less validation. Thus, you might want to use a validating parser during development of an application and a nonvalidating parser in the production version. If it is important that certain aspects of the DTD be processed by the parser whether or not it is validating, this can be accomplished by including some or all of the DTD in the XML document itself. The syntax for including DTD declarations in an XML document is illustrated by the following markup:

```
<!DOCTYPE rss
    SYSTEM "http://my.netscape.com/publish/formats/rss-0.91.dtd"
 [
<!ENTITY vsn "0.91">
<!ENTITY unused "This entity is not used.">
 ]
>
<rss version="&vsn;">
```

DTD declarations enclosed within square brackets at the end of the document type declaration are collectively called the *internal subset* of the DTD. The internal subset is read by every parser, validating or not; see the XML 1.0 recommendation [W3C-XML-1.0] for more details on the internal subset.

If either a validating or a nonvalidating parser detects an error while parsing a document, the parser generally signals the error to the application program that called the parser API. Handling of the error depends on the application. For example, as we learned in Chapter 2, browsers simply ignore undefined element types and attribute names appearing in XHTML documents. On the other hand, software for, say, a financial XML application might abort further processing if such an error was encountered.

The XML parser implementation used by JWSDP 1.3 can be run in either validating or nonvalidating mode. In either mode, it signals errors by throwing exceptions to the application program. We'll learn about XML parsing with JWSDP 1.3 in some detail later in this chapter. But first, we'll cover a few details of XML documents themselves.

7.2 XML Versions and the XML Declaration

XML was developed under the auspices of the World Wide Web Consortium as a language for representing documents to be communicated over the World Wide Web. The group that developed XML was formed in 1996 and published a first working draft of XML in the same year. XML 1.0 was officially adopted as a W3C recommendation in early 1998. Despite the relatively short development cycle during a time of rapid change for the Web in general, XML 1.0 has been widely adopted without the need for substantial modification. Although the W3C released an XML 1.1 recommendation in 2004, the W3C at the same time encouraged those who do not need 1.1's (relatively few) new features to continue to use XML 1.0. I will therefore cover XML 1.0 [W3C-XML-1.0] in this chapter.

The XML recommendations suggest (but do not require) that every XML document begin with a special tag known as an *XML declaration*. This is used to specify the version of XML used to write the document and optionally some additional meta-information about the document, such as the character set/encoding used. If a minimal XML 1.0 declaration was added to the earlier "Hello World!" example, the result would be

```
<?xml version="1.0"?>
<text>
  Hello World!
</text>
```

Note that because of its potential impact on the character set of an XML document, if an XML declaration is contained in an XML document, then it must begin at the very first character of the document: not even white space or comments are allowed to precede it. The default character encoding for an XML document is UTF-16 if the document begins with the two-byte character 0xfeff (which is used only for determining the encoding, and is otherwise ignored) or UTF-8 if the document begins with any other character. All software for reading XML documents is required to support these encodings (and may also support other encodings). An encoding other than one of these default encodings may be specified by including an *encoding declaration* within the XML declaration. For example, to specify that an XML document is encoded using the ISO-8859-1 character set, the following XML declaration could be used:

```
<?xml version="1.0" encoding="ISO-8859-1"?>
```

Unlike attributes in element tags, the `version` and `encoding` declarations must appear in the order shown.

7.3   XML Namespaces

Recall that RSS is one example of an XML vocabulary. Brief descriptions of several of the key element type names specified for RSS version 0.91 are given in Table 7.1. Programs known as *RSS aggregators* read RSS feeds and display their contents in a human-readable form. For example, a Java-based aggregator known as the Juicy News Network (JNN is available at `https://jnn.dev.java.net/`) is shown in Figure 7.2. In the figure, JNN has read a number of RSS feeds and listed the `title` of the `channel` element from each document in its left pane. The user clicked on the highlighted title, causing JNN to display the `title` values for the `item` elements within that RSS feed in its upper right pane. Finally, when the user selected one of these items, JNN generated the lower right pane, which displays the `item` title (now hyperlinked to the `link` URL of the `item`) followed by the `description` of the `item`.

Something to notice here is that the `description` displayed in Figure 7.2 contains a hyperlink. In fact, the RSS markup for this `description` element begins as follows:

```
<description>I've been spending the weekend at the
<a href=http://airrace.org>Reno Air Races</a>.
```

But the a element type is not listed in Table 7.1. In fact, a is not part of the RSS 0.91 vocabulary, which is the version of RSS used by this feed. Of course, XHTML—another XML vocabulary—does define an a element. Thus, JNN is apparently designed to recognize

TABLE 7.1 Several of the RSS 0.91 Element Types

Element Type Name	Description
rss	Root element. Specifies (via attribute) version of RSS used.
channel	Contains the content of the document (similar to body in an HTML document).
item	Represents one item of interest at the Web site serving the RSS document.
title	Brief (at most 100 characters) description of the channel or item containing the title element.
description	A somewhat longer (at most 500 characters) description of the channel or item containing the description element.
link	A URL linking a channel or item to a Web document.

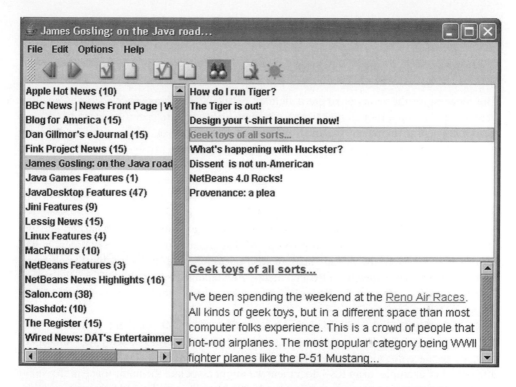

FIGURE 7.2 Example RSS aggregator. (The content of this screen shot is copyright © 2006 Sun Microsystems, Inc. All rights reserved. Reproduced by permission of Sun Microsystem Inc.)

at least some XHTML elements embedded within an RSS 0.91 document. The semantics of such elements are defined by XHTML, not by the RSS 0.91 vocabulary.

Actually, it is not uncommon for XML elements defined by one vocabulary (such as XHTML) to be embedded within an XML document written using another vocabulary (such as RSS). But notice that this can lead to name conflicts. For example, both XHTML and RSS define `link` element types, each with its own content models, attributes, and semantics. While an RSS aggregator might assume that any `link` element it sees belongs to the RSS vocabulary, how can such name conflicts be solved more generally?

The W3C's XML Namespace recommendation [W3C-XML-NAMESPACE-1.1] provides a mechanism for identifying each element and attribute name within a document with a specific XML vocabulary. An *XML namespace* is a collection of element and attribute names associated with a particular XML vocabulary (such as XHTML) through an absolute URI known as the *namespace name*. An example namespace name is `http://www.w3.org/1999/xhtml`, which is specified as the namespace name for XHTML 1.0 by its recommendation [W3C-XHTML-1.0]. We have seen this namespace name frequently in earlier examples. In fact, XHTML 1.0 requires that every XHTML document be associated with this namespace name by including an xmlns attribute specification in the root element of the document:

```
<html xmlns="http://www.w3.org/1999/xhtml">
```

The meaning of the xmlns attribute is defined by the XML Namespace recommendation. When specified on a root element as shown, the xmlns attribute specifies a *default namespace* for the entire document. So, in an XHTML document, the xmlns specification indicates that all element type names within the document—including html—belong by default to the XML namespace having namespace name http://www.w3.org/1999/xhtml. Specifying a default namespace has no effect on attributes, which belong to no namespace unless explicitly associated with a namespace via mechanisms described in the rest of this section.

Many XML documents—such as the RSS 0.91 examples shown earlier—do not specify a default namespace. Of course, if an RSS aggregator is reading a document, it will normally assume that the document is an RSS document and therefore that the elements are (unless otherwise specified) RSS elements. But, technically speaking, if no namespace is specified for an element via the xmlns mechanism, then that element does not "belong" to any XML namespace.

Now, what about embedded elements, such as XHTML elements within an RSS document? First, the document must associate a *namespace prefix* with the namespace containing the embedded element types. This is done using a special form of the xmlns attribute. For example, in an RSS document we might associate the namespace prefix xhtml with the namespace name http://www.w3.org/1999/xhtml as follows:

```
<rss version="0.91" xmlns:xhtml="http://www.w3.org/1999/xhtml">
```

An xmlns attribute specification of this form is called a *namespace declaration*.

Once a namespace has been associated with a namespace prefix through a namespace declaration, we can mark any element (or attribute) name as belonging to the namespace by preceding the name with the prefix. For example, in an RSS document containing the given namespace declaration, we can mark an a element as belonging to the XHTML namespace as follows (notice that both the start and end tags contain the namespace prefix):

```
<item>
  <title>Announcing a Sibling Site!</title>
  <link>http://www.example.org/</link>
  <description>Were you aware that
     <xhtml:a href="example.com">example.com</xhtml:a>
     is not the only site in the example family?</description>
</item>
```

The XML namespace concept was defined some time after XML itself was initially defined and, as we have noted, is covered in a separate W3C recommendation. Therefore, some software may fully comply with the XML recommendation and yet not be *namespace-aware*. In software that is namespace-aware, all element and attribute names (except for xmlns attributes) are referred to as *qualified names*, whether or not they are prefixed. Associated with each qualified name is an *expanded name*, which is a pair consisting of a namespace name and a *local name*. The local name is just the qualified name with any namespace prefix removed; for example, in the qualified name xhtml:a, a is the local name. In typical Java XML software, if a qualified name is not in any namespace, then the namespace-name component of its expanded name is represented by null.

Although the RSS example just given showed a namespace declaration in the root element of the document, namespace declarations can appear in any element. If an element name is prefixed and also declares the prefix used, then the element belongs to the namespace named in its namespace declaration. On the other hand, if the element is prefixed but does not itself declare the prefix, then the element belongs to the namespace named in the nearest ancestor element declaring this prefix. So, for example, in the XML markup

```
<ns1:elt1 xmlns:ns1="http://www.example.com/ns">
  <ns1:elt2 xmlns:ns1="http://www.example.org/namespace">
    <ns1:elt3 />
  </ns1:elt2>
</ns1:elt1>
```

elt1 belongs to the namespace named http://www.example.com/ns, while elt2 and elt3 belong to the namespace named http://www.example.org/namespace.

It should be noted that if you design an XML vocabulary and wish to conform with the XML namespace recommendation, the element and attribute names you define must not use colons (for obvious syntactic reasons). Similarly, an XML document conforming with XML namespace may not contain colons in prefix names or in the values specified for attributes of the XML data type ID (this corresponds to values for id attributes in XHTML).

7.4   JavaScript and XML: Ajax

In Chapter 5 we learned how to use the JavaScript implementation of the DOM API to access an XHTML document loaded into a browser. More generally, the JavaScript DOM can be used to access any type of XML document, not just one written according to the XHTML vocabulary. This capability is often used in conjunction with a JavaScript host-object constructor named XMLHttpRequest, which we've waited until this chapter to cover because of its relationship with XML.

An instance of XMLHttpRequest, as its name implies, allows a JavaScript program to send an HTTP request to a server and receive back a response containing an XML document. Normally, an instance of XMLHttpRequest is used for a single request and response. To illustrate the use of XMLHttpRequest, we will modify the HelloCounter example of Section 6.3. In that example, the servlet maintained a count of visits and returned this count to a client on request as part of an XHTML document. If, a few minutes after this document had been loaded, the user wanted to see an updated visit count, it was necessary to reload the document. Using the XMLHttpRequest object in conjunction with JavaScript DOM processing, we will now create a modified servlet that generates an XHTML document within which a visit counter appears to update itself automatically, without reloading the document.

The new VisitCountUpdate servlet will have both doGet() and doPost() methods. The doGet() method will be very similar to that of the HelloCounter servlet (Figure 6.3) with a few small changes. In particular, the XHTML document generated by a call to doGet() will import a JavaScript file named VisitCountUpdate.js that is assumed to be located in the Tomcat ROOT directory; the body start tag will cause an init() method to be called when the document has loaded; and the number of visits will be wrapped in a span element with id value visits. An example html element generated by the doGet() method is shown in Figure 7.3.

The doPost() method of VisitCountUpdate will be accessed by XMLHttpRequest instances to obtain the current visit count. As shown in Figure 7.4, this method generates an XML document having a single element named count that contains the current value of the servlet's visit counter variable visit (recall that this variable is incremented each time the doGet() method is called). Notice that the Content-Type of the document is set to application/xml; we'll discuss the reason for this choice later.

Now we are ready to consider the JavaScript code that will be executed by the XHTML document generated by the servlet. As shown in Figure 7.5, the init() method simply arranges for the function getVisits() to be called every 3 seconds. This latter function creates an instance of XMLHttpRequest and sends a POST request to VisitCountUpdate. It also specifies, by assigning a function value to the instance property onreadystatechange, that the function updateVisits() should be called when the response to this request is received. The function assigned to onreadystatechange is called with no arguments; notice the use of a function expression to in essence convert this no-argument call to a call containing the XMLHttpRequest instance as an argument.

```
<html xmlns='http://www.w3.org/1999/xhtml'>
  <head>
    <title>
      VisitCountUpdate.java
    </title>
    <script type='text/javascript' src='/VisitCountUpdate.js'>
    </script>
    <meta http-equiv='Content-Script-Type' content='text/javascript' />
  </head>
  <body onload='init();'>
    <p>
        Hello World!
    </p>
    <p>
        This page has been viewed
        <span id='visits'>12</span>
        times since the most recent server restart.
    </p>
  </body>
</html>
```

FIGURE 7.3 An XHTML document (shown without its document type declaration) generated by servlet VisitCountUpdate.

```
public void doPost  (HttpServletRequest request,
                        HttpServletResponse response)
  throws ServletException,  IOException
  {
     // Set the HTTP content type in response header
     response.setContentType("application/xml;  charset=\"UTF-8\"");

     // Obtain a PrintWriter object for creating the body
     // of the response
     PrintWriter servletOut = response.getWriter();

     // Output the count
     servletOut.println(
"<?xml version='1.0' encoding='UTF-8'?> \n" +
"<count>" + visits + "</count>");
        servletOut.close();
     }
```

FIGURE 7.4 doPost() method of servlet VisitCountUpdate.

Before looking at updateVisits(), several small points should be noted. First, IE6 does not supply XMLHttpRequest as a host object constructor, but instead makes available an ActiveX object that can be used to construct an XMLHttpRequest instance as illustrated in Figure 7.5. Second, I suggest using POST rather than GET to send requests via XMLHttpRequest, as some browsers (notably IE6) may return a cached response to a GET request rather than actually sending the request to the server. We'll have more to say about caching later in this section. The third argument to open() (true) indicates that we want the scripting engine to continue execution immediately after executing the send() method; that is, we want to handle the response from the server asynchronously. Using false as this argument value would cause the scripting engine to suspend following the send() call until the response was obtained, in essence suspending all other JavaScript processing. While this approach has the advantage that it is not necessary to specify a function to handle the readystatechange event, I don't recommend using it except perhaps for testing. Finally, the argument to send() (the empty string in this example) is passed as the query string in the body of the POST request. Note that you are responsible for URL encoding each name or value in the query string that might contain nonalphanumeric characters. This can be accomplished by calling the JavaScript encodeURIComponent() method of the global object:

```
// Assume that 'textfield' represents a text box object.
var aName = textfield.value;
connection.send("name=" + window.encodeURIComponent(aName));
```

The updateVisits() function is shown in Figure 7.6. This function is called each time the value of the readyState property of the XMLHttpRequest instance changes. The value 4 indicates that the entire response has been received, so our function returns immediately if readyState has any other value. Similarly, if the HTTP status code value is

```
// VisitCountUpdate.js

// Start a timer that every three seconds retrieves from the
// server the current number of visitors to our site.
function init() {
  window.setInterval("getVisits()", 3000);
  return;
}

// Use XMLHttpRequest to request the current number of
// visitors to our site.
function getVisits() {
  var connection; // Object used to send HTTP requests to server
                  // and receive HTTP responses from server

  // Create the connection object using the appropriate constructor.
  if (window.XMLHttpRequest) {
    connection = new XMLHttpRequest();
    }
    else if (window.ActiveXObject) {
      try {
        connection = new ActiveXObject("Microsoft.XMLHTTP");
      }
      catch (e) {
      }
    }
    if (connection) {

      // Associate this XMLHttpRequest object with a specific URL.
      connection.open("POST",
                      "/servlet/VisitCountUpdate",
                      true);

      // Send an HTTP request to the server after specifying the
      // function that should be called when the response is received.
      connection.onreadystatechange =
        function update () { updateVisits(connection); };
      connection.setRequestHeader("Content-Type",
                                  "application/x-www-form-urlencoded");
      connection.send("");
  }
  return;
}
```

FIGURE 7.5 Portion of JavaScript code for automatic visit count updating.

other than 200 (recall that this code indicates success), the function will ignore the response. The order of tests is significant: we want to ensure that the entire response has been received before testing the status value.

Once we have received a complete and successful response, we can use the JavaScript DOM API to extract information from the XML document contained in the response

```
// VisitCountUpdate.js (part 2)

// Update the associated HTML document when the HTTP response
// containing the visit count is received.
function updateVisits(connection) {
  if (connection.readyState == 4 && connection.status == 200) {
    var visits = document.getElementById("visits");
    var count = connection.responseXML.documentElement;
    visits.childNodes[0].data = count.childNodes[0].data;
  }
  return;
}
```

FIGURE 7.6 Remainder of JavaScript code for automatic visit count updating.

message. The `responseXML` property of the `XMLHttpRequest` instance represents a node of type `Document`, which is the type of the `window.document` object. Thus, the function has access to two `Document` nodes: `document`, the root of the tree representing the document displayed in the client area of the browser; and `connection.responseXML`, the root of the tree representing the XML response from the server. The code in the function uses DOM processing to replace the text within the `visits` element of the browser's tree with the character data in the response XML document's root element.

Each instance of `XMLHttpRequest` also has a `responseText` property that represents the body of the HTTP response as a JavaScript String. Thus, in our example, we could have returned the visit count as a simple string in the response rather than embedding this string within an XML document. However, even for a simple response as in this example, there are some advantages to sending the response as XML. For instance, we might in the future want to serve the visit count to a second client that would like to know the time of the last visit as well as the visit count. By adding this time as an attribute of the count element, a single XML document could be served to both clients, and our example client would not need any changes. Wrapping a string in an XML element also provides at least some level of documentation of the meaning of the string within the document itself, which can be helpful when debugging an application. And we can add XML comments to the document to provide further documentation without needing to change the client software at all.

On the other hand, there are some costs involved in using XML rather than a simple string for data transfer. The most obvious cost is that an XML document is larger than a simple string, so more characters must be transmitted if XML is used. In addition, the scripting engine must parse the received XML document, which requires some processing time. Along these lines, IE6 will only parse the XML document if `application/xml` is specified as the value of the Content-Type header field of the server's response, which is why we used this value in Figure 7.4.

There are a few issues to keep in mind when using `XMLHttpRequest`. One is that, for security reasons, the URL argument in the `open()` method must be in the same domain as that from which the XHTML document executing the call to the method is served. Generally speaking, this restriction will not cause you trouble as long as you always use a relative URL for this argument, as we did in Figure 7.5.

One other issue involves caching. By default, IE6 caches the response to each GET request that it generates. Furthermore, if a URL is visited first by a GET request and then by subsequent POST requests via XMLHttpRequest instances, IE6 might reply to the POST requests with the response cached as a result of the GET request. This will obviously cause problems for our implementation of the VisitCountUpdate servlet, which is initially visited via a GET and subsequently by POST requests seeking updated visit counts. To avoid this difficulty, the servlet's doGet() method includes the statement

```
response.setHeader("Cache-Control", "no-cache");
```

before adding any content to the servlet's response buffer. The resulting Cache-Control header field in the server's response instructs IE6 not to cache the GET response.

While other techniques exist for communicating data between web clients and servers, the successful use of XMLHttpRequest for sophisticated tasks such as the Google Maps™ mapping application has made this a particularly popular approach. In fact, the combined use of XML, HTML, CSS, JavaScript, the JavaScript DOM, and the asynchronous communication mode of the XMLHttpRequest host object to provide highly interactive user interfaces for web applications has been given its own name, *Asynchronous JavaScript and XML (Ajax).*

7.5 DOM-Based XML Processing

We'll now turn to considering how to write server-side Java software for processing XML documents. The Java examples here and elsewhere in this chapter assume that you have installed the JWSDP 1.3 software and set your CLASSPATH environment variable as explained in Appendix A. No other software is required to run the examples, although some examples (those accessing an XML document stored at a URL, for instance) must be executed on a computer connected to the Internet.

There are several standard approaches to processing XML documents in Java. In this section, we'll cover an approach based on the Document Object Model, which we covered in some detail in Chapter 5. Later in this chapter we will consider several other Java XML packages.

In DOM-based XML processing, an XML document is first input and parsed, creating a tree of nodes representing elements, text, comments, and so on. After the tree has been constructed, methods similar to those described in Chapter 5 can be called to modify the tree, extract data from it, and so on. The Java DOM API is defined by the org.w3c.dom package as part of the standard Java API [SUN-JAVA-API-1.4.2]. The Java DOM API specifies a number of interfaces that correspond to DOM objects and classes we studied in the context of JavaScript, such as Node, Document (which is the interface implemented by an object corresponding to the window.document object in JavaScript), Element, and Text (the last three are all subinterfaces of Node). One key difference in Java is that many of the JavaScript nonmethod properties of DOM objects are accessed using methods in Java. The method name is normally formed by capitalizing the first letter of the JavaScript property name and then prefixing the name with the string get. For example, the parentNode property of JavaScript Node instances is replaced with a getParentNode() method in Java. So, a JavaScript statement such as

```
var parent = aNode.parentNode;
```

would be written in Java as

```
Node parent = aNode.getParentNode();
```

We will learn some advantages of following this naming convention when we cover aspects of the JavaBeans specification in the next chapter.

Another difference is that any method such as getElementsByTagName() that returned an arraylike list of Node instances in JavaScript will in Java return an object implementing the NodeList interface. Such an object has just two methods: getLength(), which returns an int representing the number of Node objects in the NodeList; and item(), which takes an int argument and returns the Node object at the corresponding (0-based) position within the list of nodes contained in the NodeList. So, while in JavaScript we might write an expression such as

```
document.getElementsByTagName("link")[0]
```

to produce a reference to the first Node of element type link (assuming that at least one such Node exists in the document), in Java we could not use this arraylike syntax. Instead, we would write (assuming that document is an object implementing the Document interface) something like

```
document.getElementsByTagName("link").item(0)
```

Given this introduction to the Java DOM API, let's consider the Java program of Figure 7.7. This program performs the following task: input from a user-specified file an RSS document such as the one shown in Figure 7.1, and output the number of link elements contained in the input document. So, for example, if the example RSS document of Figure 7.1 was contained in a file named ExampleContentFeed.xml and the Java program was named DOMCountLink, then a run of the program might look like (user input is italicized)

```
$ java DOMCountLinks ExampleContentFeed.xml
Input document has 3 'link' elements.
```

The heart of this program consists of the three statements

```
Document document = parser.parse(new File(args[0]));
NodeList links = document.getElementsByTagName("link");
System.out.println("Input document has " +
                   links.getLength() +
                   " 'link' elements.");
```

```
// JAXP classes
import javax.xml.parsers.DocumentBuilderFactory;
import javax.xml.parsers.DocumentBuilder;

// DOM classes
import org.w3c.dom.Document;
import org.w3c.dom.NodeList;

// JDK classes
import java.io.File;

/** Count the number of link elements in an RSS 0.91 document */
class DOMCountLinks {

    /** Main program does it all */
    static public void main(String args[]) {
        try {
            // JAXP-style initialization of DocumentBuilder
            // (XML parser that builds DOM from document)
            DocumentBuilderFactory docBuilderFactory =
                DocumentBuilderFactory.newInstance();
            DocumentBuilder parser = docBuilderFactory.newDocumentBuilder();
            // Parse XML document from file given by first argument
            // into a DOM Document object
            Document document = parser.parse(new File(args[0]));

            // Process the Document object using the Java API version of
            // the W3C DOM
            NodeList links = document.getElementsByTagName("link");
            System.out.println("Input document has " +
                            links.getLength() +
                            " 'link' elements.");
        }
        catch (Exception e) {
            e.printStackTrace();
        }
        return;
    }
}
```

FIGURE 7.7 DOM-based program for displaying the number of links in an RSS 0.91 document.

The first of these statements opens the file specified by the first command-line argument and parses the XML document contained in this file, producing a Document object that is the Java counterpart to window.document in JavaScript. The second statement calls on the getElementsByTagName() method (described in Table 5.5) to retrieve a list of Node objects corresponding to elements of type link in the XML document. Finally, outputting the number of objects in this list completes the program's task.

The first portion of the program,

```
DocumentBuilderFactory docBuilderFactory =
    DocumentBuilderFactory.newInstance();
DocumentBuilder parser = docBuilderFactory.newDocumentBuilder();
```

illustrates a standard technique for obtaining a DOM-based parser in a Java program using the Sun Java API for XML Processing (JAXP) [SUN-JAXP-1.2]. As already mentioned, there are several Java APIs for processing XML documents. Typically, each API specifies how a program can interact with an XML parser, but the API may or may not specify how to create an instance of the parser in the first place. JAXP provides a unified approach to creating parser instances through a factory mechanism. A *factory* is just an object that is used to create other objects.

In JAXP, a two-stage approach is used to create a parser. For example, in the case of creating a DOM-based parser, in the first stage the factory itself is created by a call to the static `newInstance()` method of `DocumentBuilderFactory`. Notice that this method returns an instance of `DocumentBuilderFactory`. Once the factory instance has been created, it is used to create the actual DOM-based parser by a call to the factory's `newDocumentBuilder()` method. As we will see, a similar factory approach is used to create other parsers, although of course the class names and some method names will differ.

You may wonder why this factory mechanism is used rather than standard object creation using a constructor and the `new` keyword. The basic answer is that it allows a single compiled Java program to be run using different DOM-based parsers. For example, if the `javax.xml.parsers.DocumentBuilderFactory` system property is set to the name of a class (on the Java class path) that implements the `DocumentBuilderFactory` API, then the specified class will be used rather than the default class. The default class, if you are using JWSDP 1.3, is `org.apache.xerces.jaxp.DocumentBuilderFactoryImpl`. But if you wanted to run the `DOMCountLinks` program using the Free Software Foundation's implementation of the `DocumentBuilderFactory` API instead, you could do so (assuming you've downloaded the software and placed it on your class path) by running the program with the following command (all on one line):

```
java -Djavax.xml.parsers.DocumentBuilderFactory=gnu.xml.dom.JAXPFactory
  DOMCountLinks ExampleContentFeed.xml
```

On the other hand, if the factory facility (or something similar) were not used, then two different programs with different `import` statements would be needed to load the different DOM implementation packages. The feature allowing different implementations of an API to be used by a single program is known as *pluggability*.

By default, a `DocumentBuilderFactory` instance creates a parser that is non-validating and not namespace-aware. These defaults can be overridden by calling the methods `setValidating(true)` and `setNamespaceAware(true)`, respectively, on the `DocumentBuilderFactory` instance before creating the `DocumentBuilder` instance. So, for example, the code

```
DocumentBuilderFactory docBuilderFactory =
    DocumentBuilderFactory.newInstance();
docBuilderFactory.setNamespaceAware(true);
DocumentBuilder parser = docBuilderFactory.newDocumentBuilder();
```

creates a parser that is nonvalidating but namespace-aware.

In order to support namespace-aware processing, the W3C's DOM API includes several methods that extend those methods that we covered in Chapter 5. One of these methods is getElementsByTagNameNS(), which returns a NodeList for a given element type name much like getElementsByTagName(). However, getElementsByTagNameNS() takes two String arguments: a namespace name (URI) followed by a local name (recall that such a pair of strings is known as an expanded name). So, if we were using a namespace-aware parser, then the code

```
NodeList links =
  document.getElementsByTagNameNS(null, "link");
```

could be used to retrieve a NodeList containing all of the link elements in the document that belong to no namespace. For example, if this code were run on the document of Figure 7.1, which does not declare a default namespace, then this code would retrieve the same NodeList as the earlier code containing a call to getElementsByTagName(). On the other hand, if this code were run on a valid XHTML document containing link elements, then an empty NodeList would be returned. This is because a valid XHTML document declares the default namespace http://www.w3.org/1999/xhtml, so the link elements in a valid XHTML document belong to this namespace. To retrieve these elements using getElementsByTagNameNS() would require a call of the form

```
NodeList links =
  document.getElementsByTagNameNS(
    "http://www.w3.org/1999/xhtml", "link");
```

The DOM API also defines several other namespace-aware variants of methods discussed in Chapter 5. For instance, createElementNS() takes two String arguments representing an expanded name (namespace name followed by local name) and creates an Element object having the given element type name within the appropriate namespace. In general, any DOM method that takes an element or attribute name as an argument has a namespace-aware variant. See [W3C-DOM-2-CORE] and the org.w3c.dom package within the Java API Specification [SUN-JAVA-API-1.4.2] for full details on namespace-aware DOM methods.

Finally, it should be noted that although we have used the DocumentBuilder class only to parse existing documents, it also provides a method newDocument() that can be called in order to create an empty Document object. DOM API methods, such as createElement() or createElementNS(), can then be called to construct an internal representation of an XML document. We'll learn later some of the things we can do with such a created document.

One drawback of processing an XML document using the DOM approach is that the entire document tree must be created, even if only a fraction of the document is actually pertinent to the software processing the document. For instance, our link-counting example does not need access to a complete parse tree of the document in order to accomplish its task. In fact, loading the entire tree for such a simple task will almost certainly use much more memory than is necessary, and will probably use more CPU time as well (for allocating memory, creating data structures, etc.). We'll cover an alternative to DOM-based parsing next that is often much less computationally expensive. We'll also begin to see how XML processing can be incorporated into web applications.

7.6   Event-oriented Parsing: SAX

As already noted, the DOM approach to XML processing is to first read and parse an entire XML document into a tree representation and then process this tree. In effect, all communication between the parser and the application is by way of the document tree. An alternative to the DOM approach is to have the parser interact with an application as it reads an XML document. This is the approach taken by SAX (Simple API for XML). In the SAX view of XML processing, as an XML parser is reading an XML document, certain events occur. For example, reading an element start tag is an event, as is reading its end tag or reading text contained within an element. SAX allows an application to register event listeners with the XML parser, much as the DOM event model described in Section 5.6 allowed a JavaScript program to register event listeners with a browser. A SAX parser calls these listeners as events occur and passes them information about the events.

There is no formal standard defining SAX, and in fact no one owns the SAX API (it is in the public domain). However, SAX is, according to the official SAX Web site (http://www.saxproject.org/), "the first widely adopted API for XML in Java, and is a 'de facto' standard." The version described here is SAX 2.0.1, often referred to as SAX2 [SAX-2.0.1].

Figure 7.8 and Figure 7.9 contain a SAX2 recoding of the link-counting program from Figure 7.7. As with the earlier DOM-based program, the JAXP factory approach can be used to obtain the parser, and once again the API implementation used is pluggable (see [SUN-JAXP-1.2] for details). There is one more step in this factory code than in the DOM example: a factory is used to obtain a SAXParser (via a call to the newSAXParser() method), which in turn is used to obtain the actual XMLReader parser. This extra step is not absolutely necessary, since a SAXParser instance can be used directly as a parser (it provides a syntax similar to that of the DocumentBuilder DOM parser class). However, SAXParser is a wrapper class specified by JAXP over top of the XMLReader class specified by the SAX2 API [SAX-2.0.1]. So, for portability purposes, it is probably advisable to use XMLReader rather than SAXParser, and my examples will follow this approach.

Once the parser has been obtained, a two-step process is followed to input an XML document. First, the parser is passed—via a call to its setContentHandler() method—an instance of a Java class that defines the event-handling methods to be called by the parser; more on this class shortly. Second, the parse() method of the parser is called with an argument representing the URL of the XML document to be parsed. In this example, the URL for an RSS content feed from java.net (which happens to have a channel title of

```
// JAXP classes
import javax.xml.parsers.SAXParserFactory;
import javax.xml.parsers.SAXParser;

// SAX classes
import org.xml.sax.XMLReader;
import org.xml.sax.Attributes;
import org.xml.sax.SAXException;
import org.xml.sax.helpers.DefaultHandler;

/** Count the number of link elements in an XML document */
class SAXCountLinks {

  /** Source for RSS feed */
  static String FEED_URL = "http://today.java.net/rss/21.rss";

  /** Initialize XMLReader and set up event handlers */
  static public void main(String args[]) {
    try {
      // JAXP-style initialization of SAX parser
      SAXParserFactory saxFactory = SAXParserFactory.newInstance();
      XMLReader parser = saxFactory.newSAXParser().getXMLReader();

      // SAX-style processing of RSS document at FEED_URL
      parser.setContentHandler(new CountElementsHelper());
      parser.parse(FEED_URL);
    }
    catch (Exception e) {
      e.printStackTrace();
    }
    return;
  }
```

FIGURE 7.8 Initial portion of SAX-based program for displaying the number of links in an RSS 0.91 document.

"Java Web Services and XML Features") is passed to the parser. All further processing is performed by the parser and event handler class, so this is the end of the main program.

The SAX2 API class DefaultHandler provides a default set of essentially do-nothing event handlers for all of the core SAX2 events. As shown, a Java program using the SAX2 API typically creates a subclass of DefaultHandler that overrides some or all of the default event handler methods. This subclass—named CountElementsHelper in this example— encapsulates all of the event handling performed by the program.

Three of the key SAX2 event-handling methods are overridden in CountElementsHelper. The startDocument() and endDocument() methods are called at the beginning and end of document processing, respectively. The startElement() method is called each time the start of an element is encountered by the parser. The element start could be indicated by either a start tag or an empty-element tag (a tag such as <br />). As shown in the example, this method has four parameters. By default, the third parameter, qName, holds the qualified name of the element that is being started, and

```java
/** Helper class containing SAX event handler methods */
private static class CountElementsHelper extends DefaultHandler {

  /** Number of 'p' elements seen so far */
  int numElements;

  /** Constructor (allows for superclass initialization) */
  CountElementsHelper() {
    super();
  }

  /** Perform initialization for this instance */
  public void startDocument() throws SAXException {
    numElements = 0;
    return;
  }

  /** Process the start of an element */
  public void startElement(String namespaceURI, String localName,
                           String qName, Attributes atts)
      throws SAXException
  {
    if (qName.equals("link")) {
      numElements++;
    }
    return;
  }

  /** Done with document; output final count */
  public void endDocument() throws SAXException {
    System.out.println("Input document has " +
                       numElements +
                       " 'link' elements.");
    return;
  }
}
}
```

FIGURE 7.9 Helper class portion of SAX-based program for displaying the number of links in an RSS 0.91 document.

the empty string will be assigned to the first two parameters, namespaceURI and localName. However, if setNamespaceAware(true) is called on the SAXParserFactory instance before newSAXParser() is called, then for any element name that belongs to a namespace, namespaceURI and localName will represent the respective components of the expanded name for the element. Element names not belonging to any namespace will still be passed via the qName parameter.

The last parameter, atts, represents the attribute specifications contained in the element tag being processed. This object provides a getLength() method that returns the number of attribute specifications; methods getQName(), getURI(), and getLocalName() that, given an integer index, return the qualified name, namespace name

(URI), and local name, respectively, of the attribute at the given index within atts; and several versions of a getValue() method for obtaining the value of an attribute. As an example, if a start tag such as the following is processed by a SAX parser:

```
<a id="anc34" href="details">
```

then atts.getValue(1) and atts.getValue("href") will both return the string details. That is, an attribute's value can be obtained either by specifying the attribute's 0-based position within the attribute list or by specifying the attribute's qualified name. Several other methods are also provided by the Attributes class; see the SAX2 API [SAX-2.0.1] for details.

 If an event handling method throws a SAXException, then the parse() method will also throw this exception. A SAXException may be constructed from a string, from an Exception object, or from a string and an Exception (the parameters appear in that order). Throwing a SAXException provides a mechanism for an event handler to signal a syntactic error to the calling program. In fact, the parse() methods of both DocumentBuilder and XMLReader also throw a SAXException if the parser detects that the input XML document is not well formed. Warnings and validation errors are ignored by default in the JWSDP parsers; we'll learn shortly how to override this behavior.

 One small point that should be noted for purposes of portability is that while the default XMLReader produced by JAXP-compliant software (such as that supplied by JWSDP 1.3) is not namespace-aware, the SAX2 API specifies that XMLReader should be namespace-aware by default. You should also note that when a default SAX2-compliant parser encounters a qualified element name in a start tag, it is allowed to pass the empty string "" as the value of the qName parameter in the parser's call to startElement() (the event handler needs to consult the namespaceURI and localName for the name of the element in this case). The JAXP XMLReader, on the other hand, by default always supplies a non empty qName. A SAX2-compliant parser can be told to behave this way as well by making the following call immediately after creating the parser:

```
parser.setFeature("http://xml.org/sax/features/namespace-prefixes",
                  true);
```

To facilitate interoperability with non-JAXP XMLReader's, you may want to include this code in any JAXP SAX programs you write. Also note, as with DocumentBuilderFactory, the SAXParserFactory produces a nonvalidating parser by default. You can override this default (or make it explicit) by calling setValidating() with the appropriate boolean argument before creating the SAX XMLReader object.

 Another key DefaultHandler method is characters(), which is the primary method called when the parser encounters character (nonmarkup) data in a document. This method takes three arguments: an array of type char followed by two int's. The first int is the index of the first character in the array, and the second is the number of characters in the array. So a call such as characters(someChars, 6, 4) indicates that the characters() method should process character data contained in array elements someChars[6] through someChars[9]. While this might seem on the surface to be an inconvenient way to pass data to `characters()`, the Java `String` class has a constructor that takes three arguments in the same order and produces a `String` object containing the appropriate characters. The `StringBuffer` class provides a similar three-argument `append()` method; see Figure 7.10 for an example using this method.

Note that there is no guarantee that all of the character data within an element will be passed to `characters()` in a single call. Instead, the data may be passed in multiple calls with arbitrary numbers of characters in each call. In practice, this tends to occur if the character data includes entity references, such as `&lt;`. The parser passes the character(s) represented by an entity reference to `characters()`, not the characters representing the reference itself. For example, in markup such as

```
<p>A &lt; character must be escaped.</p>
```

a SAX parser might call `characters()` three times: first to process the two characters A, then to process the character <, and finally to process the remaining character data within the p element. But the `&lt;` string itself will not be passed to `characters()`.

While most character data is passed to an application by calls to `characters()`, there is an exception that should be noted. When a validating parser encounters white space characters within an element that does not allow character data in its content—that is, an element that does not include `#PCDATA` in its content model—the parser will call `ignorableWhitespace()` rather than `characters()`. `ignorableWhitespace()` takes the same three arguments as `characters()`, and as with `characters()`, there is no guarantee that all of the relevant character data will be passed in a single call to `ignorableWhitespace()`. Such white space is "ignorable" because it has no semantic purpose; it is allowed only for purposes of formatting the XML document. Nonvalidating parsers have the option of calling either `ignorableWhitespace()` or `characters()` when they encounter ignorable white space; the JWSDP parser always calls `characters()` when it has the option.

As you might expect, the `DefaultHandler` also defines a do-nothing `endElement()` method. `endElement()` is called whenever an end tag is encountered. Also, when an empty-element tag is encountered, `endElement()` is called immediately after the `startElement()` method is called for that tag. The `endElement()` parameters are the same as the first three parameters of `startElement()`, and they have the same semantics.

The class `PrintElementsHelper` of Figure 7.10 illustrates the use of the `endElement()` and `characters()` methods. If an instance of this class is passed to an `XMLReader`'s `setContentHandler()` method, then the character data of each `link` element of the XML document parsed by the `XMLReader` will be printed to `System.out`. For instance, if run on the XML document of Figure 7.1, the following output will be produced:

```
Link data: http://www.example.com/
Link data: http://www.example.org/
Link data: http://www.example.net/
```

```java
/** Helper class containing SAX event handler methods */
private static class PrintElementsHelper extends DefaultHandler {

  /** Whether or not we are in a link element */
  boolean inLink = false;

  /** Character data collected for the current link element */
  StringBuffer charData;

  /** Constructor (allows for superclass initialization) */
  PrintElementsHelper() {
    super();
  }
  /** Process the start of an element */
  public void startElement(String namespaceURI, String localName,
                           String qName, Attributes atts)
      throws SAXException
  {
    if (qName.equals("link")) {
      inLink = true;
      charData = new StringBuffer();
    }
    return;
  }


  /** Process character data */
  public void characters(char chars[], int firstChar, int nChars)
      throws SAXException
  {
    if (inLink) {
      charData.append(chars, firstChar, nChars);
    }
    return;
  }
  /** Process the end of an element.  If link, output
      collected character data. */
  public void endElement(String namespaceURI, String localName,
                         String qName)
      throws SAXException
  {
    if (qName.equals("link")) {
      System.out.println("Link data: " + charData.toString());
      inLink = false;
    }
    return;
  }
}
```

FIGURE 7.10 Instance of DefaultHandler that prints the character data contained with the link elements of an XML document. This class is part of SAXPrintLinks.java.

Notice that this class assumes that the `qName` argument to both `startElement()` and `endElement()` is nonempty, which can be guaranteed by ensuring that the `namespace-prefixes` SAX feature is enabled as described earlier in this section.

Earlier, we learned that a `SAXException` is thrown when the parser is given an XML document that is not well formed. If a validating parser reads an XML document and a validation error is detected (such as the wrong content for an element), then the parser will call the `error()` method of the event handling class (the subclass of `DefaultHandler` passed to `setContentHandler()`). This method has the signature

```
public void error(SAXParseException spe) throws SAXParseException {...}
```

where `SAXParseException` is a subclass of `SAXException` discussed in the following. The default `error()` method supplied by `DefaultHandler` does nothing. A simple way to cause the parser to throw an exception when a validation error occurs is to override the default method with one that throws its argument:

```
public void error(SAXParseException spe) throws SAXParseException {
  throw spe;
}
```

The parser will then throw this `SAXParseException` to the calling application.

If the application catches a `SAXParseException` (or casts a caught `Exception` or `SAXException` to `SAXParseException`), then it can obtain information on the approximate location within the XML document of the error by calling on the `getLineNumber()` and `getColumnNumber()` methods of `SAXParseException`. In addition, any `SAXException` object—including a `SAXParseException`—may wrap another `Exception`. If so, a call to `getException()` will return a nonnull value representing the wrapped `Exception`. If such a wrapped exception is present, it is generally more useful to call debugging aids such as `printStackTrace()` on this object rather than directly on the `SAXException` object. Thus, the following exception-handling code would be better in most applications than that shown in Figure 7.8:

```
catch (SAXParseException spe) {
  System.err.println("Parse error at line " +
                     spe.getLineNumber() +
                     ", character " +
                     spe.getColumnNumber());
  if (spe.getException() != null) {
    spe.getException().printStackTrace();
  }
  else {
    spe.printStackTrace();
  }
}
catch (SAXException se) {
  if (se.getException() != null) {
    se.getException().printStackTrace();
  }
```

```
  else {
    se.printStackTrace();
  }
}
catch (Exception e) {
  e.printStackTrace();
}
```

Finally, although the parse() method in the example of Figure 7.8 takes a URI as its argument, this is not unique to SAX parsing. In fact, the DOM-based DocumentBuilder class also has a parse() method that takes a string argument representing a URI. Since XML was designed from the outset to be used to transmit data over the Web, it should not be surprising that XML parsers would make it relatively easy to access XML documents via URIs. In addition, a second form of the XMLReader parse() method takes an instance of org.xml.sax.InputSource as its argument. An InputSource instance, in turn, can be constructed from a java.io.InputStream or a java.io.Reader. So SAX-style processing can readily be applied to a variety of sources of XML input. In fact, in the next section we'll learn (among other things) that SAX processing can even be applied to a document represented by a DOM tree.

7.7 Transforming XML Documents

A SAX parser can be viewed as a mechanism for transforming an XML text document into a stream of events corresponding to the markup and character data contained in the original document. Similarly, a DOM parser transforms an XML document into a DOM tree. In fact, JAXP provides standardized APIs for transforming from any of these three representations— XML document, SAX event stream, or DOM tree—to either of the others. Furthermore, JAXP allows a Java program to use the Extensible Stylesheet Language (XSL) to extract data from one XML document, process that data, and produce another XML document containing the processed data. XSL can be used, for example, to extract information from an XML document and embed it within an XHTML document so that the information can be viewed using a web browser.

In this section, we will learn how to perform JAXP transformations between XML representations (text, DOM, and SAX events) and will introduce the JAXP API for XSL. In later sections we will cover two key components of XSL itself: XPath and XSLT.

7.7.1 Transforming between XML Representations

In earlier sections, we learned how to convert a text-formatted XML document into a DOM object tree by using a JAXP factory method. We also learned that we can modify a DOM tree via Java DOM API methods such as createElement(), appendChild(), and so on. But we didn't learn how to "reverse" the parsing operation and produce a textual representation of an internal DOM tree. We'll begin our study of XML transformations by showing how to convert a DOM tree into an XML text document.

This task can be accomplished in JAXP as illustrated by the program of Figure 7.11. This program begins by reading a text XML document into a DOM Document object and then modifying this object (recall that in the Java DOM API the getParentNode()

```
// JAXP classes
import javax.xml.transform.TransformerFactory;
import javax.xml.transform.Transformer;
import javax.xml.transform.dom.DOMSource;
import javax.xml.transform.stream.StreamResult;
import javax.xml.parsers.DocumentBuilderFactory;
import javax.xml.parsers.DocumentBuilder;

// DOM classes
import org.w3c.dom.Document;
import org.w3c.dom.NodeList;

// JDK classes
import java.io.File;

/** Input an RSS document, remove the first "item" element, and
    output the resulting RSS document to System.out */
class DOMtoText {
    public static void main(String args[]) {

        try {
            // Input an RSS document into a DOM Document object
            DocumentBuilderFactory docBuilderFactory =
                DocumentBuilderFactory.newInstance();
            DocumentBuilder parser = docBuilderFactory.newDocumentBuilder();
            Document document = parser.parse(new File(args[0]));

            // Use the DOM API to remove the first item element
            // (this code assumes that there is at least one item...)
            NodeList items = document.getElementsByTagName("item");
            items.item(0).getParentNode().removeChild(items.item(0));

            // Use JAXP methods to output the modified Document object
            TransformerFactory tFactory = TransformerFactory.newInstance();
            Transformer transformer = tFactory.newTransformer();
            transformer.transform(new DOMSource(document),
                                  new StreamResult(System.out));
        }
        catch (Exception e) {
            e.printStackTrace();
        }
        return;
    }
}
```

FIGURE 7.11 Program converting a DOM Document object to an XML text representation.

method is used to obtain the parent of a Node, while in JavaScript we used the parentNode property of Node instances). The program then uses yet another JAXP factory class, this time called TransformerFactory, to create an instance of Transformer. The Transformer instance then performs the actual conversion from the DOM Document object to a text XML document by a call to the Transformer's transform() method.

The `transform()` method takes two arguments, the first implementing the interface `javax.xml.transform.Source` and the second implementing `javax.xml.transform.Result`. JAXP supplies several classes implementing the `Source` interface: `javax.xml.transform.dom.DOMSource`, `javax.xml.transform.sax.SAXSource`, and `javax.xml.transform.stream.StreamSource`, representing a DOM, SAX, or text representation of an XML document, respectively. A `DOMSource` is often constructed from a `Document` object, as shown in this example, and for the most part is simply a wrapper for the `Document`. More generally, any DOM `Node` object can be used as the argument to the `DOMSource` constructor, which allows the `Transformer` to operate on a subtree of the document rather than on the entire document tree. We'll discuss the `SAXSource` class before concluding this subsection. A `StreamSource` can be constructed from a `java.io.File`, `java.io.Reader`, or `java.io.InputStream` object associated with an XML text document, or from a `String` representing a URL at which an XML text document is located.

The `Result` interface is similarly implemented by JAXP classes `DOMResult`, `SAXResult`, and `StreamResult`, each located in the same package as its `Source` counterpart. The constructors for `DOMResult` and `StreamResult` also take the same types of arguments as their `Source` counterparts. The primary constructor for `SAXResult` takes a `ContentHandler` as its argument; this is one of the interfaces implemented by `DefaultHandler`. So, for example, if in some application `transformer` is a `Transformer` instance as in the program in Figure 7.11, if `document` is a `Document` object representing an RSS document, and if `CountElementsHelper` is the class shown in Figure 7.9, then the statement

```
transformer.transform(new DOMSource(document),
                new SAXResult(new CountElementsHelper()));
```

will output the number of link elements contained in the DOM tree represented by `document`.

For completeness, what follows is a brief description of the `SAXSource` class; its use is an advanced topic that I will not cover in detail. Typically, the `SAXSource` represents two objects: a SAX `InputSource` and an object representing a parser. The `InputSource` does not necessarily represent an XML document; instead, the parser object is written to parse the type of document represented by the `InputSource`. When a `Transformer` instance's `transform()` method is called with such a `SAXSource`, the `Transformer` calls a `parse()` method on the parser object, passing to this method the `InputSource` from the `SAXSource`. The parser, in turn, reads the `InputSource` and makes a series of calls to SAX event methods—`startElement()`, `characters()`, and so on—that are implemented by the `Transformer` object. In essence, the parser transforms the `InputSource` into a stream of SAX events, which the `Transformer` treats as a representation of an XML document (regardless of the actual format of the `InputSource`). The `Transformer` then transforms this SAX event stream into whatever XML representation is specified by the result argument to `transform()`.

Finally, while the JAXP API defines all of the `Source` and `Result` classes just covered, some XML parsers may not provide implementations for all of the classes. Your code can test for the availability of an implementation for a particular `Source` or `Result` by calling the boolean `getFeature()` method on the `TransformerFactory` object. Each `Source` and `Result` class supplies a FEATURE property that can be passed as an argument to getFeature() to determine whether or not that class is supported. For example, the program in Figure 7.11 might be modified to wrap the call to transform in Figure 7.11 within an if statement beginning with

```
if (tFactory.getFeature(DOMSource.FEATURE) &&
    tFactory.getFeature(StreamResult.FEATURE)) {
```

7.7.2   Introduction to XSL

The transformations discussed in the preceding subsection are useful for converting a document between various XML representations. In this subsection, we'll begin looking at a different type of transformation, one that extracts information from one XML text document and uses that information to create another XML text document.

The "programming language" used to direct this type of transformation is the Extensible Stylesheet Language (XSL). XSL is an XML vocabulary; that is, XSL documents are well-formed XML documents. So the transformation "program" is an XML document. An XSL document normally contains two types of information: *template data*, which is text that is copied to the output XML text document with little or no change; and XSL markup, which controls the transformation process.

An example XSL document is shown in Figure 7.12. The first thing to notice is that it uses two namespaces. http://www.w3.org/1999/XSL/Transform is the namespace name for the XSL namespace, and of course http://www.w3.org/1999/xhtml is the XHTML namespace name. So, in this document, XHTML is the default namespace, and elements prefixed with xsl belong to the XSL namespace. Elements belonging to the XSL namespace are part of the XSL "programming language" and direct the transformation, while elements in other namespaces form part of the template data of the XSL document.

```
<?xml version="1.0" encoding="UTF-8"?>

<xsl:transform version="1.0"
  xmlns:xsl="http://www.w3.org/1999/XSL/Transform"
  xmlns="http://www.w3.org/1999/xhtml">

  <xsl:template match="/">
    <html>
      <head>
        <title>
          HelloWorld.xsl (transformed)
        </title>
      </head>
      <body>
        <p><xsl:value-of select="child::message" /></p>
      </body>
    </html>
  </xsl:template>
</xsl:transform>
```

FIGURE 7.12 An example XSL document HelloWorld.xsl.

```
<?xml version="1.0" encoding="UTF-8"?>
<message>Hello World!</message>
```

FIGURE 7.13 Simple XML document `HelloWorld.xml` to be transformed.

We'll cover the semantics of many XSL elements—including those shown in Figure 7.12—in detail later in this chapter. For now, it is enough to know that if the `HelloWorld.xsl` document is input to software performing an XSL transformation along with an XML document such as the one shown in Figure 7.13, then the software will output the content of the `xsl:template` element (template data) but with the `xsl:value-of` element replaced by the content of the XML document's `message` element. There may also be other small differences in the output version of the template data, such as the elimination of ignorable white space. Figure 7.14 is the output produced by running an XSL transformation using `HelloWorld.xsl` and `HelloWorld.xml` as its input.

A JAXP `Transformer` instance can be used to perform XSL transformations, although a slightly different method is used to construct the `Transformer` than we saw earlier. For example, consider the Java program `XSLTransform` of Figure 7.15. This program is designed to be called with two command-line arguments. The first of these is the name of a file containing an XSL document, and the second the name of a file containing an XML document. As illustrated in Figure 7.15, the XSL document is passed as a `Source` argument (in this example as a `StreamSource`) in the call to `newTransformer()` that constructs the `Transformer` instance. The `transform()` method of this instance is then called as before, with the source argument representing the input XML document. The result argument of the `transform()` method (`System.out` in this example) will then receive the transformed document. So if this program is called as

```
java XSLTransform HelloWorld.xsl HelloWorld.xml
```

where `HelloWorld.xsl` and `HelloWorld.xml` are as defined in Figure 7.12 and Figure 7.13, respectively, then the HTML document of Figure 7.14 will be written to standard output.

7.7.3 XSL Component Overview

XSL actually is a collection of three separate W3C recommendations:

- XSL Transformations (XSLT), which defines the semantics of the various elements and attributes of the XSL namespace;

```
<?xml version="1.0" encoding="UTF-8"?>
<html xmlns="http://www.w3.org/1999/xhtml"><head><title>
        HelloWorld.xsl (transformed)
    </title></head><body><p>Hello World!</p></body></html>
```

FIGURE 7.14 XHTML document produced by transforming `HelloWorld.xml` XML document according to `HelloWorld.xsl` XSL document.

```
/** Apply the XSL transform contained in the file named by
    the first command-line argument to the XML document
    named by the second argument and write the resulting
    document to standard output. */
class XSLTransform {
    public static void main(String args[]) {

        try {
            TransformerFactory tFactory = TransformerFactory.newInstance();
            Transformer transformer =
                tFactory.newTransformer(
                    new StreamSource(new File(args[0])));
            transformer.transform(
              new StreamSource(new File(args[1])),
              new StreamResult(System.out));
        }
        catch (Exception e) {
            e.printStackTrace();
        }
        return;
    }
}
```

FIGURE 7.15 Java program XSLTransform for performing XSL transformations. import statements, not shown, are similar to those of earlier programs.

- XML Path Language (XPath), which defines the syntax and semantics of many of the attribute values used in XSL elements for accessing portions of the input XML document; and
- XSL Formatting Objects (XSL-FO), a separate XML vocabulary for defining style properties of an XML document.

The XSL document of Figure 7.12 illustrates elements of both XSLT and XPath. Specifically, the values of the match and select attributes are XPath expressions, while the transform, template, and value-of elements along with their attributes are defined by the XSLT recommendation.

In our example, the template data was primarily XHTML markup, and the result document was an XHTML file (although not one that perfectly conforms with XHTML 1.0 recommendations, as it lacks a document type declaration). We could instead have used XSL-FO markup as the template data, and the resulting document would have then been suitable for input to an *XSL formatter*. An XSL formatter is an application that takes an XSL-FO document as input and typically produces as output a document in a printer-oriented format, such as the Adobe® Portable Document Format (PDF).

A strength of XSL-FO is that it can be used to produce on demand individualized print documents, such as user's manuals specialized to a particular model or even serial number of a product. However, XSL-FO does not seem to be widely used for Web applications at this time; XSLT and XPath appear to be used much more frequently. So, although XSL has three component technologies, I will only cover XPath and XSLT. We'll begin by learning some basics of XPath, since XSLT depends on it.

7.8 Selecting XML Data: XPath

XPath is a syntax for specifying a collection of elements or other information contained within an XML document. I will describe version 1.0 of XPath [W3C-XPATH-1.0], which is the current version at the time of this writing.

Conceptually, XPath assumes that the XML document to which XPath expressions will be applied has been parsed into an internal tree representation. The XPath tree model is similar to the DOM tree. For example, the nodes in an XPath tree are of different types, such as element, text, and comment nodes. In addition, unlike the DOM model, the XPath tree model also uses nodes to represent attribute name value pairs.

The root of the XPath parse tree is known as the *document root*. Like an instance of Document in the DOM, this node of the XPath parse tree has a child node representing the root of the element hierarchy in the parsed document; this node is called the *document element*. In Figure 7.13, the root element is of type message. Thus, for this example XML document, an XPath element node of type message will be a child of the document root node in the XPath parse tree.

With this conceptual introduction, we're ready to begin learning about some specific XPath expressions.

7.8.1 Location Paths

As noted earlier, we have already seen some simple examples of XPath expressions in Figure 7.12. For example, in the markup

```
<xsl:template match="/">
```

the value of the match attribute (/) is an XPath expression. This particular XPath expression represents the XPath document root. An XPath expression such as this that represents one or more nodes within an XPath parse tree is known as a *location path*. As another example, in the markup

```
<xsl:value-of select="child::message" />
```

the value of the select attribute (child::message) is a location path. Unlike the / location path, we cannot say which nodes are represented by this second location path without knowing some additional information. In particular, this location path is defined relative to some XPath parse tree node known as the *context node* for the location path. We'll learn more later about how the context node is defined; for now, it is enough to know that it plays an important role in interpreting many XPath expressions.

In this second example, the location path consists of a single *location step*. More generally, a location path can consist of multiple location steps separated by slash (/) characters; we'll see examples of such location paths later. Each location step consists of at least two parts: an *axis name* followed by two colons (::) and a *node test*. In this example, `child` is the axis name and `message` is the node test.

The axis name in a location step can be thought of as specifying a "direction" in which the XPath-processing software should search relative to its current context node. The child axis, for example, says that we are going to look at the nodes that are immediate descendants of the context node. Some commonly used axis names are given in Table 7.2. With the exception of `attribute`, each of these axis names corresponds to a list of element, text, and/or comment nodes (and possibly some other, less common nodes that I won't cover here). The `attribute` axis corresponds to a list of nodes representing the attribute name-value pairs for the context node (assuming that that node is an element node).

The node test portion of a location step is generally one of two types. The node test in the location step `child::message` is a *name test*, which consists of specifying a qualified name that represents an element type name (or attribute name in the case of the `attribute` axis). Only those nodes having the specified name are selected for inclusion in the list representing the value of the XPath expression. In addition, an asterisk (*) may be used as the name test, which means that all element (or attribute, for the `attribute` axis) nodes on the axis are included in the node list. The other common node test is a *node-type test*: some standard node-type tests are `text()`, `comment()`, and `node()`, which select nodes representing character data, comments, or any type, respectively. So the XPath location step expression

```
descendant::text()
```

evaluates to a list of all of the text nodes that are descendants of the context node, while

```
descendant::node()
```

TABLE 7.2 Some XPath 1.0 Axis Names

Name	Relationship with Context Node
`self`	The context node itself
`child`	Any immediate descendant
`descendant`	Any proper descendant
`descendant-or-self`	Any descendant, including the context node itself
`parent`	Immediate ancestor
`ancestor`	Any proper ancestor, including the document root (unless the context node is the document root)
`ancestor-or-self`	Any ancestor, including the context node itself
`preceding-sibling`	Any sibling of the context node that precedes the context node in the document
`following-sibling`	Any sibling of the context node that follows the context node in the document
`attribute`	Any attribute defined for the context node

represents all element, text, and comment nodes that are descendants of the context node.

Optionally, a location step can contain one or more *predicates*. An XPath predicate can be thought of as a boolean function which is applied to every node in a node list. If the predicate returns `true` for a node, then that node is copied to a new list (the *filtered list* produced by the predicate). Nodes on which the predicate returns `false` are not copied to the filtered list.

Syntactically, predicates follow the axis name and node test in a location step, and each predicate is enclosed in square brackets (`[ ]`). Semantically, the node list produced by the axis-name–node test portion of the location step is filtered by the first predicate. This list is then further filtered by the second predicate, and so on until all predicates have been applied to the list. The filtered list produced by the final predicate is the value of the location step.

For example, the expression

```
child::chapter[attribute::display="visible"][position()=last()]
```

says that a list of all of the element nodes that are children of the context node and that have element type `chapter` should first be generated. Next, this list should be filtered so that it includes only those elements which contain an attribute named `display` having value `visible` (this and other predicates are described in more detail at the end of this subsection). Finally, this filtered list should be further filtered so that the only node that remains is the "last" node, that is, the node in the filtered list (of "visible" chapter nodes) whose start tag occurs farthest down in the document.

XPath provides a wide variety of possible predicates; Table 7.3 lists some of the common ones. Several comments are in order. First, notice that, as in JavaScript, string literals in XPath expressions—such as `Overview` and `visible` in Table 7.3—can be enclosed in either single or double quotes. Also, while the XPath `last()` function always returns the number of nodes in the list being filtered, the value of the `position()` function depends on the axis of the location step. If the axis name is `ancestor`, `ancestor-or-self`, or

TABLE 7.3 Some XPath Predicates

Predicate Type	Example	Example Predicate Is true If ...
Related node exists.	`child::title`	Node has child element of type `title`.
Related node exists with certain text content.	`child::title="Overview"`	Node has child element of type `title` that has string value (concatenation of all text content of descendants) of `Overview`.
Attribute exists.	`attribute::display`	Node has attribute named `display`.
Attribute exists with certain value.	`attribute::display='visible'`	Node has attribute named `display` that has value `visible`.
Node is at a certain position in the list of nodes being filtered.	`position()<=3`	Node is one of the first three in the node list (see text concerning node ordering).

preceding-sibling, then the nodes are ordered from latest node in the document toward the earliest. For all other axes discussed here, the nodes are ordered earliest to latest. In either case, the first element in the ordering has a position() value of 1. So the location step

```
ancestor::section[position()=last()]
```

would evaluate to the ancestor of the context node that has a section element type and that is the *earliest* occurring in the document, while the location step

```
ancestor::section[position()=1]
```

produces the nearest section ancestor of the context node.

Notice that =, not ==, is used for equality testing in XPath predicates. Also keep in mind that if you use a relational operator such as <= in an XPath expression that is in turn an attribute value within an XSL document, XML syntax rules require that you escape the < symbol by using a reference, such as <.

Predicates can also be combined using the Boolean operators and and or. An example is the predicate

```
position() != 1 or descendant::para
```

The filtered list returned by this predicate will consist either of all of the nodes in the original list or of all but the first node, if the first node does not have a para element as one of its descendants.

Before moving on to a description of how location steps can be combined to form location paths, several abbreviations should be mentioned. First, the axis specification in a location step is optional, and if omitted defaults to child::. So the location steps child::para and para are equivalent. Similarly, @ can be used in place of the axis specifier attribute:: . Thus [@display="visible"] can be used in place of [attribute::display="visible"]. In addition, parent::node() can be abbreviated as ..(two dots), and self::node() as . (a single dot); this syntax is similar to that used in relative URLs (Section 2.4.6). One final abbreviation, the notation //, will be explained in Section 7.8.3.

7.8.2   Location Paths with Multiple Steps

As noted earlier, a location path can consist of several location steps separated by / characters, as in

```
child::para/child::strong
```

or, using the more common abbreviated syntax, simply

```
para/strong
```

Such a location path is evaluated as follows. First, the leftmost location step is evaluated, producing a node list. In our example, this would be the list of all para elements that are children of the context node. Next, each node in the list produced is used as the context node for one evaluation of the second location step. So, in our example, the location step child::strong would be evaluated using each para node in turn as the context node. Then a list is produced that is the union of the results of these evaluations. Returning to our example, we would now have a list containing every node that is a strong element and that has its parent in the list produced by evaluating the first location step.

If a location path has a third location step, the first two steps are first evaluated, producing a list of nodes. Each node in this list is then used as the context node for one evaluation of the third location step, with the lists produced by these evaluations unioned to give the final value of evaluating the location path. Paths with more steps are evaluated in the obvious way.

Let's consider an example evaluation of the given location path with respect to the following simple XML document:

```
<body>
  <para id="p1">
    This is <strong id="s1">important</strong> to know.
    And I do mean <strong id="s2">important</strong>.
  </para>
  <para id="p2">
    This is not as important.
    <em><strong id="s3">Is this?</strong></em>
  </para>
  <strong id="s3">What about this?</strong>
  <para id="p3">
    <strong id="s4">Is anyone listening?</strong>
  </para>
</body>
```

If the context node is the body element and the XPath expression para/strong is evaluated, then the value of the expression will be a list consisting of the strong nodes with id values s1, s2, and s4. Contrasting this with predicates, note that the value of para[strong] with the same context node would be a list of the para nodes p1 and p3.

7.8.3   Absolute and Relative Location Paths

As hinted at earlier in this section, there are two types of location path. A path such as para/strong is a *relative location path*. The other type is an *absolute location path*. Syntactically, the difference between these two types of paths is that an absolute path begins with a slash (/) while a relative path does not. So an example of an absolute path is /para/strong. Semantically, the difference is similar to the difference between relative URLs that begin with a slash and those that do not. Specifically, a relative location path defines a set of nodes relative to the context node, while an absolute location path defines a set of nodes relative to the document root. Put another way, for purposes of evaluating an absolute location path, the context node is the document root. For example, in the XML document in the preceding subsection, in which the body element is the document element, /para/strong corresponds to an empty list of nodes, since the document root has no para children.

The abbreviation // mentioned earlier is short for the absolute location path /descendant-or-self::node()/. So, for example, //strong is an abbreviation for /descendant-or-self::node()/strong, and therefore is an absolute location path representing all of the strong nodes in the document. On the other hand, the expression .//strong expands to self::node()/descendant-or-self::node()/strong, which is a relative location path representing the subset of all strong nodes among the set of nodes rooted at the context node.

7.8.4   Combining Node Lists

The pipe symbol (|) can be used to represent a node set produced by taking the union of the node sets returned by multiple location paths. Thus, the XPath expression

```
child::strong|descendant::emph
```

represents a node set containing all of the strong children of the context node as well as all of its emph descendants.

7.8.5   Function Calls as XPath Expressions

Finally, although XPath expressions are often location paths that evaluate to node lists, other XPath expressions are also available. Function calls are one such expression. Though we learned in Section 7.8.1 that a function call can be used as part of an XPath predicate, they are also XPath expressions in their own right. I will mention just three of these functions that will be particularly useful to us later; a complete list of XPath functions is provided in Section 4 of the XPath recommendation [W3C-XPATH-1.0].

If the string() function is called on an XPath expression that evaluates to a node list, the function returns a string representing the concatenation of all text contained in the first node of the list, including that node's descendants. This text is concatenated in the order in which it appears in the document corresponding to the XPath tree. For example, if string(/) is evaluated and the document being processed is

```
<testing>
 1
 <more>2</more>
 3
</testing>
```

then a string equivalent to
 1
 2
 3
 will be returned (recall that
 is an XML character reference that evaluates to the line feed character). Notice that the XPath expression argument to the string() function should not be quoted.

The normalize-space() function takes a string as its argument and returns a *normalized* version of the string. As in a normalized attribute value (Section 2.3.5), in a normalized string, leading and trailing white space is removed, all remaining XML white space characters (tabs, newlines, and carriage returns) are converted to space characters, and consecutive space characters are collapsed to a single space. So if `normalize-space()` is called on the string returned by the preceding example, the result will be `"1 2 3"`.

If the `id()` function is called with a string of white-space-separated identifiers, a list of the nodes having `id` attributes with these identifiers as their values is returned. For example, `id("node4 para10")` returns the two nodes with `id` values `node4` and `para10`, if there are any such nodes.

7.9 Template-based Transformation: XSLT

At this point, you should have a reasonable understanding of many features of XPath. We're now ready to turn to XSLT.

7.9.1 "Hello World!" Revisited

Let's begin our study of XSLT by looking more closely at the example XSLT document of Figure 7.12. First, the root element of an XSLT document can be named either `transform`, as shown in this example, or `stylesheet`. There is no semantic difference between these elements, but I suggest using `transform` for XSLT documents that do not generate XSL-FO markup, and `stylesheet` for those that do. I will therefore use `transform` as the root element in all of my XSLT examples. The `version` attribute of the root element is required. For the version of XSLT described in [W3C-XSLT-1.0], which is the reference for the material in this section, `1.0` must be specified as the value of the `version` attribute.

By convention, the XSLT namespace `http://www.w3.org/1999/XSL/Transform` is normally associated with the namespace prefix `xsl`, as illustrated in Figure 7.12. Also, when XSLT is used for general-purpose transformation from one XML application to another, the default namespace for the XSLT document is normally set to that of the target application. In this example, since the goal is to generate an XHTML document, the XHTML namespace is specified as the default namespace for the XSLT document.

The content of the root element often consists of one or more `template` elements; there is just one such element in the example. Each template represents a *template rule*, which typically consists of two parts: an XPath expression specified as the value of the `template` element's `match` attribute and known as the template rule's *pattern*; and the content of the template rule, which is known as the *template* portion of the rule.

Software for performing an XSLT transformation, such as JAXP, is known as an *XSLT processor*. Recall that an XSLT processor is given two inputs—an XSLT document and a source XML document—and produces a single result XML document. Internally, an XSLT processor represents each of these documents as an XPath tree, called the *source tree*, the *style-sheet tree*, and the *result tree*, respectively. Since all three trees are XPath trees, nodes in any of these trees (or more generally, lists of nodes) can be referenced using XPath expressions.

One other thing to note about the trees built by an XPath processor is that, by default, any text node in either the source tree or style sheet tree that contains only white space is removed from the tree (one exception is white space contained in an `xsl:text` element of an XSLT document; this element is discussed later). For the most part, this means that white space inserted for readability between elements in an XSLT or XML source document will not be reflected in the final XML result document. White space that is part of the content of an element, on the other hand, is normally kept without change. We'll deal with white space issues more in Sections 7.9.3 and 7.9.4; for now, I just want you to be aware that, by default, XSLT processors remove all ignorable white space from the trees they construct, but that they do not collapse white space within elements that include #PCDATA content as browsers do when displaying HTML documents.

Once the source and style sheet trees have been loaded and the result tree has been initialized, XSLT processing software performs a traversal of the source tree—starting with the document root node—in search of nodes that are matched by some template rule. A template rule *matches* a node if, when the pattern of the rule is evaluated, the node list produced contains the node being matched. In our example, the XPath pattern / evaluates to the node list consisting of only the document root node, and therefore the template rule matches the document root. More details on the traversal algorithm and matching will be provided in the next subsection.

After locating a source tree node matched by a template rule, the XSLT processor next *instantiates* the template of the matching rule. Instantiation conceptually involves copying the non-XSLT elements and their content (including text, but by default not comments) to the result tree. XSLT elements are not copied to the result tree; instead, they are replaced with other content, which depends on the XSLT element type and on the source XML document.

In our example, the template contains a single XSLT element of type value-of. This type of XSLT element causes a text node to be added to the result tree. The content of this text node is formed by first evaluating the XPath expression that is the value of the select attribute (child::message in our example), producing a node list. The XPath context node used in this evaluation is the node that was matched by the template rule whose template is being instantiated (the document root node in our example). Given that the input for our XSLT example is the XML document of Figure 7.13, the XPath expression child::message evaluates to a node list containing a single document element node of type message. Next, after the node list has been produced, the XSLT processor in effect calls the XPath string() function on the node list. That is, all of the text in the first node ("first" here meaning the first in the order of document appearance) and in its descendants is concatenated (in order of document appearance) into a single string. This string becomes the content of the text node added to the result tree. So, in our example, a text node containing Hello World! is added to the result tree. Because the value-of element was a child of a p element in the style-sheet tree, the text node generated will be a child of the corresponding p element in the result tree, as shown in Figure 7.16.

One final detail of this transformation concerns namespace declarations: notice that there is a default XHTML namespace declaration in the html start tag in the XHTML result document (Figure 7.14), but not in the html start tag of the input XSLT document (Figure 7.12). The reason for this is that the XSLT processor records namespace information for each of the nodes contained in the result tree. Because the html element in the style sheet tree belongs to the XHTML namespace (by virtue of the default namespace declaration in the transform start tag of the input XSLT document), this information is recorded for the html

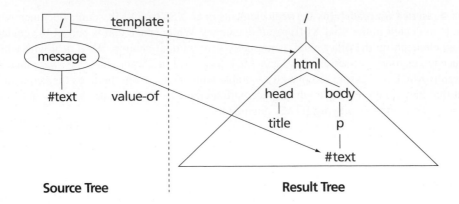

Source Tree **Result Tree**

FIGURE 7.16 Illustration of construction of result tree from template instantiation. Source tree node in box was matched by a template rule, producing result tree structure indicated by triangle. Text node of p element in result tree was produced by instantiating `value-of` XSLT element, which selected the circled source node and converted it to text. Text nodes are represented by `#text`.

element in the result tree. When this tree is output at the end of the XSLT processing, the XSLT processor includes this namespace information in the XHTML document produced by including a default namespace declaration on the root element (`html`). Namespace information is also associated with the other elements in the result tree, but this is of course covered by the declaration in the root element, so the only namespace declaration generated by the XSLT processor is in the root element.

A small but important syntactic restriction also deserves mention: patterns can use only a limited portion of the XPath language. One of the main limitations is that only the `child` and `attribute` axes can be used directly, although the `//` abbreviation (which—recall—is short for `/descendant-or-self::node()/`) is also allowed. Also, a pattern must evaluate to a node list, so most function-call expressions (such as a call to `string()`) are not allowed to be used as patterns. One exception is that a call to the `id()` function can be used as a pattern (it must be called with an argument that is a string literal, not a more general expression). The pipe symbol `|` is legal in patterns as well, and is often used in them. See Section 5.2 of the XSL Transformation recommendation [W3C-XSLT-1.0] for a complete specification of legal patterns. These restrictions do not apply to most other uses of XPath expressions in XSLT. For example, the value of the `select` attribute in a `value-of` element can be any XPath expression.

What we have covered so far can be generalized somewhat. For example, a template can contain multiple `value-of` elements drawing from different portions of the source tree. While what we have learned so far is useful for some applications, a major limitation is that the result document has a fixed element structure, since `value-of` elements can only add text node children to existing elements. We'll next learn about a key XSLT mechanism for generating result trees whose element structure depends on the source XML document as well as on the XSLT document. We will also cover the XSLT algorithm for matching template rules with nodes in more detail.

7.9.2 Recursive Template Processing

Assume now that we would like to convert an RSS document such as the one in Figure 7.1 into an XHTML document that displays a list of the titles of the items contained in the original RSS document. The body of the document will begin with a heading providing information taken from the `title` element of the `channel` (we will assume, as specified by RSS 0.91, that there is only one channel in the document). An XSL transformation for accomplishing this task is shown in Figure 7.17, and the result of applying it to the example RSS feed of Figure 7.1 is given in Figure 7.18. Figure 7.19 illustrates schematically how information flows from the source and style sheet trees to the result tree.

The basic algorithm followed by an XSLT processor in order to accomplish such a transformation is described by the pseudo-code of Figure 7.20. The transformation begins with a call to `applyTemplates` with the `resultNode` set to the document root of the result tree and the `currentNodeList` set to the document root of the source tree.

Tracing the execution of the algorithm on the source document of Figure 7.1 given the XSLT document of Figure 7.17 will give us some insight into its operation. The algorithm

```
<?xml version="1.0" encoding="UTF-8"?>

<xsl:transform version="1.0"
  xmlns:xsl="http://www.w3.org/1999/XSL/Transform"
  xmlns="http://www.w3.org/1999/xhtml">

  <xsl:template match="/rss">
    <html>
      <head>
        <title>
          RSStoXHTML
        </title>
      </head>
      <body>
        <h1>
          <xsl:value-of select="channel/title" />
          RSS feed links:
        </h1>
        <ul>
          <xsl:apply-templates select="channel/item" />
        </ul>
      </body>
    </html>
  </xsl:template>
  <xsl:template match="item">
    <li>
      <xsl:value-of select="title" />
    </li>
  </xsl:template>

</xsl:transform>
```

FIGURE 7.17 XSL transformation to convert portion of an RSS feed to XHTML.

```
<?xml version="1.0" encoding="UTF-8"?>
<html xmlns="http://www.w3.org/1999/xhtml"><head><title>
        RSStoXHTML
    </title></head><body><h1>www.example.com
     RSS feed links:
    </h1><ul><li>Announcing a Sibling Site!</li>
    <li>We're Up!</li></ul></body></html>
```

FIGURE 7.18 XHTML output produced by the preceding XSL transformation. There are only six lines in the output; the last line (starting with </h1>) has been broken into two lines for readability.

begins by attempting to match one of the two template rule patterns of Figure 7.17 to the source document root. Each match attempt, in turn, will set the context node to the document root and evaluate the pattern expression. The first pattern evaluates to the rss node, while the second evaluates to an empty list (no item is a child of the document root). Since neither of these lists contains the document root (the node we are attempting to match), both matches fail. Thus, the for each templateRule loop of applyTemplates() completes execution without finding a match.

However, since the source document root has child nodes, the XSLT processor will automatically recurse, attempting to find template rule pattern matches to each of the children of the document root. Each matched child, if any, will generate a child subtree of the document root in the result tree.

One of the children of the source document root is the rss node. When applyTemplates() attempts to match the /rss pattern with this node, it will succeed. This will lead to the template associated with the first template rule being instantiated. The value-of element within this template will be replaced as before with a value obtained by evaluating the expression channel/title with context node set to the rss node (since this was the node matched).

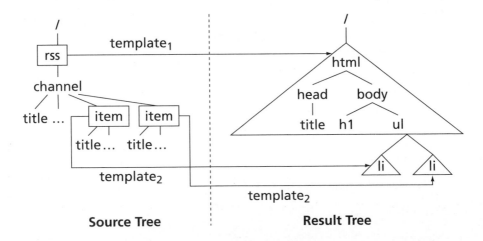

FIGURE 7.19 Illustration of recursive construction of result tree element structure from template instantiation. Source nodes in boxes were matched by template rules, producing result structure indicated by triangles.

```
// Return true if templateRule matches candidateNode
boolean match(pattern, candidateNode)
  for contextNode starting at candidateNode and changing to
      contextNode.parent until contextNode becomes null
    if evaluating pattern with context node set to
        contextNode produces node list that contains candidateNode
      return true
    endif
  endfor
  return false // failed to match node with rule


// update result tree by adding children to resultNode
// based on processing source tree nodes in currentNodeList
void applyTemplates(resultNode, currentNodeList)
  for each currentNode in currentNodeList
    matchFound = false
    for each templateRule in style-sheet tree while not matchFound
      if match(templateRule.pattern, currentNode)
        matchFound = true
        instantiate templateRule.template, including:
          for each occurrence of apply-templates element
            newResultNode = node in result tree corresponding
                to parent of apply-templates element
            nodeList = list produced by evaluating "select"
                XPath expression of apply-templates element,
                using currentNode as context node if
                XPath expression is relative
            applyTemplates(newResultNode, nodeList)
          endfor
      endif
    endfor
    if not matchFound and currentNode has child(ren)
      // automatically recurse:
      applyTemplates(resultNode, currentNode.children)
    endif
  endfor
```

FIGURE 7.20 Outline of XSLT processing algorithm.

When the `apply-templates` element is encountered in the template, this amounts to a recursive call to the `applyTemplates()` procedure. The result node to which children will be appended by instantiating this element will be the `ul` element in the result tree corresponding to the `ul` element that is the parent of `apply-templates` in the source tree. The nodes that `applyTemplates()` will attempt to match are those in the list produced by evaluating the XPath expression `channel/item`, again using the `rss` node as the context node for evaluating this relative expression. In our example RSS document of Figure 7.1, the list will consist of two `item` nodes.

When `applyTemplates()` attempts to match the first template to the first `item` node, it will fail. In addition, the first pass through the `for` loop of `match()` will fail for the second template rule pattern, which is `item`. Specifically, evaluating `child::item` with context node set to the first item node will produce an empty node list, since the item nodes have no item children. However, in the second pass through the for loop the context node will be channel, and evaluating item with this context node does produce a node list containing the first item node (in fact, it will contain both item nodes). Therefore, the second template rule pattern matches the first item node, and similar reasoning shows that it matches the second item as well. The second rule's template will therefore be instantiated twice, once with each of the item nodes acting as the context node for purposes of evaluating the value-of's select expression title. This completes the processing of the recursive call to applyTemplates() generated by the apply-templates element, which in turn completes the automatic recursive call to applyTemplates(), which in turn completes the overall XSLT processing.

In addition to template rules contained in the XSLT document input to the XSLT processor, the processor itself provides some *built-in template rules*. One of these rules is equivalent to the following:

```
<xsl:template match="text()">
  <xsl:value-of select="." />
</xsl:template>
```

Unless overridden by another template rule, if a currentNode in applyTemplates() is a text node, then the node will be matched and the instantiated template will effectively copy the text node from the source tree to the result tree. This behavior may not always be desirable, particularly if automatic recursive calls to applyTemplates() occur. You can turn off this default behavior by including a template rule such as the following in your XSLT document:

```
<xsl:template match="text()">
</xsl:template>
```

This rule pattern will match source text nodes but will not copy the nodes to the result tree.

One remaining detail concerns the way in which the XSLT processor chooses a template rule if multiple rules match a node. By default, the rule of thumb is that the more specific a pattern is, the more priority is given to its associated template rule. A pattern that is a location path consisting of two or more location steps, such as channel/item, is more specific than a pattern consisting of a single location step, such as item. Any nonwildcard name test is more specific than a prefixed wildcard test, such as pref:* for some namespace prefix pref, which in turn is considered more specific than an unprefixed wildcard * or a node-type test such as text(). In addition to these default rules, the priority of a template rule can be set explicitly by specifying a value (positive or negative decimal number) for the template element's priority attribute. The greatest default priority is 0.5, so any greater value will override all default rules (see Section 5.5 of the XSLT specification for the complete set of default priority values). You should also be aware that it is considered an error if among the template rules matching a node there are two or more with the highest priority value, so you should design your XSLT documents to avoid this possibility.

You should now have a fairly complete understanding of the overall XSLT processing framework. We'll next learn about some additional facilities that XSLT provides for adding information to a result tree and controlling the format of the final result document.

7.9.3   Generating Result Tree Content

We have already learned that result tree content is generated by instantiating templates, which in turn consist of character data, non-XSLT elements (which are sometimes called *literal result elements*), and XSLT elements. The two XSLT elements appearing in templates that we have covered so far are `value-of` and `apply-templates`.

XSLT provides several other elements that, like those, can be used to generate content in the result tree. For example, suppose that we would like to modify the XSLT document of Figure 7.17 so that the items in the generated list are hyperlinks. Specifically, the `link` value of each `item` element from the source tree should be specified as the value of the `href` attribute in each hyperlink (a element) generated in the result tree. Also, suppose that we would like to specify the `description` value of each `item` as the value of the `title` attribute of the generated a elements. As described in Section 5.9, both Mozilla and IE6 will pop up a small window (a *tool tip*) containing the `title` text if the mouse hovers over the hyperlink (Figure 7.21). To accomplish these tasks, we can use the XSLT `attribute` element to add attribute information to an element, as illustrated in Figure 7.22. Processing the RSS document of Figure 7.1 with the XSLT document of Figure 7.17 modified as shown in Figure 7.22 produces the XHTML document of Figure 7.23.

The content of an `attribute` element should be character data and/or XSLT markup that will generate one or more text nodes in the result tree. The character data and text nodes will be concatenated together to form the specified value for the attribute. Recall that `value-of` generates a text node, and, as you might expect, `value-of` is probably the most common content for an `attribute` element.

FIGURE 7.21 A tool tip window in IE6 produced by hovering the mouse over the first hyperlink.

```
<xsl:template match="item">
  <li>
    <a>
      <xsl:attribute name="href">
        <xsl:value-of select="link" />
      </xsl:attribute>
      <xsl:attribute name="title">
        <xsl:value-of select="description" />
      </xsl:attribute>
      <xsl:value-of select="title" />
    </a>
  </li>
</xsl:template>
```

FIGURE 7.22 Replacement for second template rule in Figure 7.17 that generates a element with two attributes specified.

You'll notice that the `title` elements generated in the result XHTML document contain `&#10;` strings and multiple adjacent space characters, since XSLT preserves this white space by default. The net result is that the tool-tip window produced in IE6 has extraneous space, as can be seen in Figure 7.21 (even worse, in Mozilla 1.4 the line feed characters produce small black boxes in the tool-tip window). This can be avoided by using the XPath `normalize-space()` function in the `value-of` generating the value for the `title` elements as follows:

```
<xsl:value-of select="normalize-space(string(description))" />
```

After this change, the second `title` attribute specification would be output as

```
title="Our new RSS feed is up. Visit us today!"
```

```
<?xml version="1.0" encoding="UTF-8"?>
<html xmlns="http://www.w3.org/1999/xhtml"><head><title>
        RSStoXHTML2
      </title></head><body><h1>www.example.com
        RSS feed links:
      </h1><ul>
<li><a href="http://www.example.org/"
title="&#10;    Were you aware that example.com is
not the &#10;    only site in the example family?
&#10;      ">Announcing a Sibling Site!</a></li>
<li><a href="http://www.example.net/"
title="&#10;    Our new RSS feed is up.  Visit us today!
&#10;      ">We're Up!</a></li></ul></body></html>
```

FIGURE 7.23 Output produced by running RSStoXHTML2.xsl of Figure 7.22 on RSS document of Figure 7.1. The last line has been split for readability.

XSLT provides a convenient shorthand notation known as an *attribute value template* that can be used to specify the values for attributes of non-XSLT elements. The a element of the preceding example could be rewritten using this shorthand notation as

```
<a href="{link}"
   title="{normalize-space(string(description))}">
  <xsl:value-of select="title" />
</a>
```

Syntactically, any pair of curly braces ({ and }) within an attribute value specification are viewed by an XSLT processor as an attribute value template. The template is replaced with a string obtained by evaluating the XPath expression contained in braces and then invoking the string() XPath function on the result if the result is not already a string. If the attribute value template is part of a larger string representing an attribute value, its value is concatenated with its neighbors. For example,

```
<a title="{link}:{description}" ...>
```

specifies an attribute value consisting of the string value of the link XPath expression followed by a colon and then the value of description.

Attribute value templates can also be used to specify some attributes of certain XSLT elements. Of the XSLT elements we have learned about so far, only the name attribute of the attribute element can take an attribute value template rather than a fixed string as its value. Another XSLT element that has a name attribute that can take an attribute value template as its value is element, which is used to generate an element of the type specified by name in the result tree. For example, if the XPath expression child::level evaluates (as a string) to 3, then the XSLT markup

```
<xsl:element name="h{child::level}">
  <xsl:value-of select="data" />
</xsl:element>
```

will generate an h3 element in the result tree (with content representing the first node of the node list returned by evaluating the XPath expression data).

So far, we have seen how to extract text from the source tree and add it to the result tree. But what if we would like to copy an entire subtree from the source to the result tree? This can be useful if, say, we want to use XSLT to reformat an input XHTML file, producing the reformatted XHTML file as output. For example, suppose that we would like to create an XHTML document which contains only the h1 elements from an input XHTML document (this created document could be considered a high-level outline of the original document). The new document should contain not only the text of the h1 elements, but also any markup they contain. For instance, given the XHTML input file of Figure 7.24, we would like an output such as that of Figure 7.25.

The XSLT copy-of element can be used to accomplish this task, as shown in Figure 7.26. Each node in the node list returned as the value of the XPath expression specified for the select attribute of copy-of is copied to the result tree. Copying an element node

```
<!DOCTYPE html
         PUBLIC "-//W3C//DTD XHTML 1.0 Strict//EN"
         "http://www.w3.org/TR/xhtml1/DTD/xhtml1-strict.dtd">
<html xmlns="http://www.w3.org/1999/xhtml">
  <head>
    <title>
      H1ExtractTest.html
    </title>
  </head>
  <body>
    <h1>First heading</h1>
    <h2>Lower heading</h2>
    <h1>Second
      <span style="font-size:larger">major</span>
      heading
    </h1>
    <h2>Another lower heading</h2>
    <h3>And even lower</h3>
    <h1>Last heading</h1>
  </body>
</html>
```

FIGURE 7.24 Example XHTML document containing multiple h1 elements, one with a child span element.

involves creating an element of the appropriate type in the result tree, creating copies of all of the attribute nodes of the element, and recursively copying the child nodes of the element. In the special case in which the document root is a node in the selected node list, the child elements of the document root are copied to the result tree, but the document root itself is not copied.

This example is the first one in which the input XML document (Figure 7.24) has made use of a namespace. This necessitated that we include some namespace information in the XSLT document of Figure 7.26. Specifically, in addition to declaring the XHTML namespace to be the default namespace, we also needed to declare a namespace prefix (I chose xhtml) for this namespace. All of the XPath expressions use this namespace prefix when referring to source tree elements. This is needed because the default namespace declared for the XSLT document applies only to the XSLT document's elements, not to XPath expressions in attribute values. An XPath expression such as /html therefore refers

```
<?xml version="1.0" encoding="UTF-8"?>
<html xmlns="http://www.w3.org/1999/xhtml"
xmlns:xhtml="http://www.w3.org/1999/xhtml"><head><title>
         H1Extract
       </title></head><body><h1>First heading</h1><h1>Second
     <span style="font-size:larger">major</span>
     heading
   </h1><h1>Last heading</h1></body></html>
```

FIGURE 7.25 Desired output (except for white space) obtained by applying an XSLT document to the XHTML document of Figure 7.24.

```
<?xml version="1.0" encoding="UTF-8"?>

<xsl:transform version="1.0"
  xmlns:xsl="http://www.w3.org/1999/XSL/Transform"
  xmlns:xhtml="http://www.w3.org/1999/xhtml"
  xmlns="http://www.w3.org/1999/xhtml">

  <xsl:template match="/xhtml:html">
    <html>
      <head>
        <title>
          H1Extract
        </title>
      </head>
      <body>
        <xsl:apply-templates select=".//xhtml:h1" />
      </body>
    </html>
  </xsl:template>

  <xsl:template match="xhtml:h1">
    <xsl:copy-of select="." />
  </xsl:template>

</xsl:transform>
```

FIGURE 7.26 XSLT document for extracting h1 elements and their descendants from an XHTML document.

to an element in the null namespace. Since the elements of the source tree are all in the XHTML namespace, this expression would evaluate to an empty node list rather than to the node list containing the document element. On the other hand, the XPath expression. appearing in the copy-of tag of the example needs no namespace prefix, because it refers directly to a node (specifically, the current node) rather than to an element by name.

As we have seen, white space in an XSLT document is often lost in the final XML result document. Not only is the result document generally ugly, but loss of white space can even lead to documents that are syntactically different from what is intended. For example, consider the XSLT template rule of Figure 7.27. If we were to process an XSLT document containing this template rule, the output file would include the following:

```
<ul><li/>...</ul>
```

which could cause problems for some older browsers, because li is not an empty HTML element but <li/> is an empty-element tag. What happened? In the source document, the li element contains only white space, so its content is removed when the template is read into the style sheet tree. On output, XML allows elements with no content to be written using the empty-element notation, and the JWSDP 1.3 XML software chooses to do so, as shown. How can we prevent such behavior, and more generally, preserve interelement white space?

```
<xsl:template match="/">
  <html>
    <head>
      <title>
        EmptyElement
      </title>
    </head>
    <body>
      <ul>
        <li> </li>
        ...
      </ul>
    </body>
  </html>
</xsl:template>
```

FIGURE 7.27 XSLT template rule illustrating white space effects.

The XSLT `text` element can be used for this purpose. The content of this element must be character data (character and entity references may appear within the element, but all entity references must expand to character data). Instantiating a `text` element adds a text node containing the element's character data to the result tree. A key feature of the `text` element is that if it contains only white space, this white space is retained in the style-sheet tree. Thus, if the content of the `ul` in the example of Figure 7.27 were

```
<ul>
  <li> </li>
  <li><xsl:text> </xsl:text></li>
</ul>
```

then the output would include

```
<ul><li/><li> </li></ul>
```

The `text` element (as well as `value-of`) can also be used to turn off escaping of XML special characters. By default, when the result tree is output as an XML document, the XML processor escapes any less-than (<) or ampersand (&) characters appearing within text nodes (and certain other characters, such as greater than (>), may also be escaped). However, this default behavior prevents writing an entity reference such as ` ` into the result XML document. Instead, if a normal text node in the result tree contains this string of characters, a string such as ` ` will be output to represent it. A browser will display this as ` ` rather than as a nonbreaking space.

To override this default behavior, the `text` and `value-of` elements provide a `disable-output-escaping` attribute. If the value `yes` is specified for this attribute, then the character data content of the `text` or `value-of` element will not be escaped when the result tree is converted to an XML document. So, to create an `li` element such that in the result XML document this element contains a reference to a nonbreaking space character, we could write

```
<li>
  <xsl:text
    disable-output-escaping="yes"> </xsl:text>
</li>
```

The XML output corresponding to this XSLT fragment is

```
<li> </li>
```

as desired. Note carefully how this works: on input into the style sheet tree, the XSLT processor converts the reference & to an ampersand character, so the text node stored in the style sheet tree contains the six-character string . If output escaping were not disabled, this would be output as . On the other hand, if in the input XSLT document we had tried to use

```
<li>
  <xsl:text
    disable-output-escaping="yes"> </xsl:text>
</li>
```

then an XSLT processing error would have occurred. This is because the nbsp entity is not defined for XSLT (it is defined as part of the XHTML DTD, which is why we can reference it within XHTML documents).

7.9.4   XML Result Document Formatting

The XML documents produced by XSLT thus far have been hard to read, largely because white space contained in the XSLT document has been lost. Also, we have not yet learned how to add an XML declaration and/or document type declaration to the XML result document. In this section we address these deficiencies.

Although white space can be preserved by inserting text elements in an XSLT document, doing so would make the XSLT document itself harder to read. Instead, if we would like to preserve most or all of the white space within an XSLT document, we can use the following approach. The XML recommendation requires all XML applications to recognize the attribute xml:space on all elements. Either preserve or default can be specified as the value of this attribute. If preserve is specified for an element (either XSLT or non-XSLT), then white space within that element and its descendants will be preserved (unless a descendant overrides this setting for itself and its descendants by specifying default for its xml:space attribute). So simply adding the attribute specification

```
xml:space="preserve"
```

to the transform (root) element of an XSLT document causes the XSLT processor to preserve all white space within the document, which can greatly improve the formatting of the XML result document. For example, with this simple change to the XSLT document of Figure 7.17 and Figure 7.22 (producing a file RSStoXHTML3.xsl), the ul element of the output produced becomes (I have wrapped the a elements for readability, but all other white space was produced by the XSLT processor):

```
    <ul>

<li>
  <a title="Were you aware that example.com is not
            the only site in the example family?"
     href="http://www.example.org/">
    Announcing a Sibling Site!
  </a>
</li>

<li>
  <a title="Our new RSS feed is up. Visit us today!"
     href="http://www.cxample.net/">
    We're Up!
  </a>
</li>

    </ul>
```

The indentation still does not appear to be perfect: the li elements are indented less than the ul element, whereas they should be indented more. We can see the reason for this if we look closely at the XSLT markup of Figure 7.22: the indentation produced is identical to the indentation of the templates in the XSLT document. So we could further improve the output indentation by simply modifying the indentation of these XSLT templates.

Finally, XSLT provides an output element, which can be used to control several aspects of the XML result document. If this element appears in an XSLT document, it is generally the first child of the root element transform. Here is an example output element appropriate for producing an XHTML 1.0 Strict document having no XML declaration (the RSStoXHTML3.xsl file includes this element):

```
<xsl:output
  method="xml"
  version="1.0"
  encoding="UTF-8"
  doctype-public="-//W3C//DTD XHTML 1.0 Strict//EN"
  doctype-system="http://www.w3.org/TR/xhtml1/DTD/xhtml1-strict.dtd"
  omit-xml-declaration="yes"
/>
```

The version attribute specifies the version of XML to be followed in generating the result XML document, and encoding the character encoding that should be used when generating the document. If an XML declaration was included in the output (the default, which is overridden in this example), these values would be included in it. The doctype-public and doctype-system attributes specify the public and system identifiers, respectively, to be used in the document type declaration. This example output element causes the XML result document to begin with (split onto multiple lines for readability):

```
<!DOCTYPE html
  PUBLIC "-//W3C//DTD XHTML 1.0 Strict//EN"
  "http://www.w3.org/TR/xhtml1/DTD/xhtml1-strict.dtd">
```

There are many more programming-type features in XSLT, such as conditional and loop processing capabilities, sorting, number generation, and so on. But the basic features we have covered are sufficient to perform many interesting transformations and should give you a good basis for further study.

7.10   Displaying XML Documents in Browsers

At this point, we've covered several core XML technologies—DOM, SAX, XPath, and XSLT—from a server-side perspective. Web browsers also offer various levels of support for XML processing. Because such browser support is not uniform and this capability does not seem to be in widespread use on the Web at this time, I will cover browser support for XML only briefly here.

First, there is a standard mechanism for associating style information (either CSS or XSLT) with XML documents via an XML processing instruction. A *processing instruction* is a special XML tag that has a syntax similar to that of an XML declaration: the tag begins with <? and ends with ?>. Semantically, a processing instruction is viewed by an XML application as an instruction to the application itself rather than as part of the markup and character data contained in the document. Each processing instruction begins with a name known as the *target* of the processing instruction and may contain other character data as well.

The processing instruction used to associate style information with an XML document has target xml-stylesheet. An example of a document that uses this processing instruction to associate an XML document with an XSLT document is given in Figure 7.28. The character data in this instruction has the appearance of attribute specifications, although the "attribute" values are parsed slightly different (most entity references are not allowed in these values, for example). The "attributes" in a processing instruction are therefore referred to as *pseudo-attributes*. For the most part, the pseudo-attributes that are allowed in an xml-stylesheet are the same as the attributes that may appear in an HTML link element that specifies stylesheet for its rel attribute, and each pseudo-attribute has the same meaning as its associated link attribute (see [W3C-XML-STYLE-1.0] for full details). Thus, in the example of Figure 7.28, the processing instruction indicates that a document of MIME type text/xsl should be loaded from the (relative) URL HelloWorld.xsl. Although text/xsl is not an IANA-registered MIME type (as I write this), it is recognized by both Mozilla 1.4 and IE6 as representing XSLT documents.

```
<?xml version="1.0" encoding="UTF-8"?>
<!-- HelloWorldStyled.xml -->
<?xml-stylesheet type="text/xsl" href="HelloWorld.xsl"?>
<message>Hello World!</message>
```

FIGURE 7.28 XML document containing an xml-stylesheet processing instruction that associates the XML document with an XSLT document.

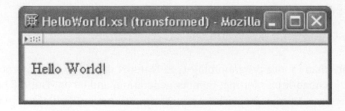

FIGURE 7.29 Browser rendering of XML document from Figure 7.28 after XSLT transformation has been applied.

If the XSLT document of Figure 7.12 is located at the URL `HelloWorld.xsl`, then if either Mozilla 1.4 or IE6 loads the XML document of Figure 7.28, the browser will apply the XSLT document to the XML document and then display the resulting XHTML document as if it had been loaded into the browser rather than the XML document. The final result in Mozilla is shown in Figure 7.29; by looking at the browser title bar, you can tell that the browser is not simply displaying the character data from the XML document. If you were to view the source of the document, however, you would see only the original XML document, not the generated XHTML.

Alternatively, a CSS style sheet can be applied to an XML document using the `xml-stylesheet` processing instruction. For example, if `HelloWorld.css` is a URL for the style sheet

```
/* HelloWorld.css */
message { display: block;
          margin: 8px;
          font-weight: bolder }
```

and the XML document

```
<?xml version="1.0" encoding="UTF-8"?>
<!-- HelloWorldStyledCSS.xml -->
<?xml-stylesheet type="text/css" href="HelloWorld.css"?>
<message>Hello World!</message>
```

is loaded into Mozilla 1.4, then the browser will style the XML document as shown in Figure 7.30.

FIGURE 7.30 Browser rendering of XML document styled using CSS.

7.11 Case Study

The blogging application developed thus far works well when blog entries consist of plain text. But what if the blogger would like to add a little markup to his or her entries, such as simple formatting or hyperlinks? While this would be nice, we want to limit the HTML elements that can be used so that the view-blog page isn't accidentally broken by blogger-entered markup. For example, the blogger shouldn't be allowed to declare id attributes on elements, because these might accidentally conflict with id attributes defined elsewhere in the page.

In this chapter, we'll develop a class TextCooker that will process the text of an entry, allowing some XHTML elements to remain in the text and escaping the XML special characters of other elements. For the allowed elements, most attributes will be removed. The class will also recognize a special non-HTML element displayquote. This element will be replaced by a span having the dquote style class that produces a floated comment (Figure 3.42). The text of the displayquote will also be repeated outside the span, so that the user only needs to enter the text once, but it will appear twice, once as part of the normal entry and once as a displayed quote.

To illustrate, if the blogger enters on the add-entry form (Figure 5.30) the text

```
<p>
An <a href="http://www.example.com" id="test">anchor</a>
is <displayquote>a simple test</displayquote>,
but it's better than nothing.  Now we can <b>bold</b>
and <i>italicize</i>, but not <u>underline</u>.
</p>
<p>
If this is a separate paragraph, then &lt;p&gt; tags are working.
</p>
```

and the user clicks the Preview button, then the preview window should contain the document shown in Figure 7.31.

We will require that the blogger enter valid XML markup (of course). This way, the page ultimately produced should be valid XML, and we will be able to use one of the XML technologies described in this chapter to process the blogger-entered markup. (In a more fully developed application, we would probably provide graphical tools to mark up the text rather than having the blogger do this manually. But that's beyond our scope.)

Now that we know approximately what we want to accomplish, let's turn to developing the code. The primary change to the application developed in the previous chapter is to the method used to cook the text of an entry. The previous version of this method, found in the Entry class, was

```
/**
 * Cook text: for now, escape all XML special characters.
 * TO DO: Process certain tags in the text.
 */
private String cookText(String rawText) {
    return WebTechUtil.escapeXML(rawText);
}
```

FIGURE 7.31 Preview of blog entry containing a variety of tags, some functional and others converted to plain text.

The new version of this code will be

```
private String cookText(String rawText)
    throws Exception
{
    return (new TextCooker()).cook(rawText);
}
```

The Entry constructor will also now throw Exception. Exceptions will be generated if the rawText is not valid XML. Throwing the exceptions allows appropriate error messages to be displayed to the user, as we'll see later.

For now, let's focus on the TextCooker class. The first question is, which of the XML technologies should we use to implement this class? Although XSLT or DOM processing could be used, SAX is particularly well suited to this task. XLST and the DOM would both create a tree representation of the input, which is extraneous for our application. A string-oriented approach would be much more appropriate than a tree-oriented one, and this is precisely what SAX provides.

The `TextCooker` class, therefore, begins with the following code:

```
/** Result ("cooked") document. */
StringBuffer cookedText = new StringBuffer();

/** Method for "cooking" raw text. */
public String cook(String rawText)
    throws Exception
{
    SAXParserFactory saxFactory = SAXParserFactory.newInstance();
    XMLReader parser = saxFactory.newSAXParser().getXMLReader();
    parser.setContentHandler(new CookHelper());
    String rootedText = "<root>" + rawText + "</root>";
    parser.parse(new InputSource(new StringReader(rootedText)));
    return cookedText.toString();
}
```

Recall that a well-formed XML document must have a single root element. This is why we wrap the `root` element around the raw text. We'll ignore these tags later in the processing. This code also illustrates a technique for applying the SAX parser to a `String`, rather than to a URL or a file as in the earlier examples. Besides this, the code is essentially identical to earlier SAX examples.

We turn next to the event handling class `CookHelper` (which I included in the `TextCooker.java` file). This class begins as follows:

```
private class CookHelper extends DefaultHandler {

    /** Whether or not we are in a displayquote element. */
    boolean inQuote = false;

    /** Character data collected for current displayquote
        element. */
    StringBuffer charData;

    CookHelper() {
        super();
    }
```

Note that `CookHelper` has access to two `StringBuffer`s: `charData`, which `CookHelper` declares, and `cookedText`, which `TextCooker` declares. `cookedText` holds the text that will ultimately be returned by the `cook()` method. `charData` is used to collect all the characters within a `displayquote` element so that the resulting string can be duplicated as described earlier, once within a `span` and once as plain text.

Figure 7.32 shows the `startElement()` method of `CookHelper`, which (recall) is called automatically by the parser as each start tag is encountered. If this is the start of a `b`, `i`, or `p` element, then the start tag is added to the output string but any attributes are discarded. An `a` start tag is output with only the `href` attribute, and any XML special characters in the value of this attribute are escaped. A `displayquote` start tag normally initializes `charData` to receive the characters within the `displayquote`. However, a nested `displayquote` will

```
public void startElement(String namespaceURI,
                         String localName, String qname,
                         Attributes atts)
    throws SAXException
{
    if (qname.equals("b") || qname.equals("i") ||
        qname.equals("p")) {
        cookedText.append("<" + qname + ">");
    }
    else if (qname.equals("a")) {
        cookedText.append(
            "<a href='" +
            WebTechUtil.escapeQuotes(
            WebTechUtil.escapeXML(atts.getValue("href"))) +
            "'>");
    }
    else if (qname.equals("displayquote") && !inQuote) {
        inQuote = true;
        charData = new StringBuffer();
    }
    else if (qname.equals("root")) {
        // discard
    }
    // Unrecognized element: escape < and >
    else {
        cookedText.append("&lt;" + qname);
        for (int i=0; i<atts.getLength(); i++) {
            cookedText.append(
                " " + atts.getQName(i) + "='" +
                WebTechUtil.escapeXML(atts.getValue(i)) +
                "'");
        }
        cookedText.append("&gt;");
    }
    return;
}
```

FIGURE 7.32 The startElement() method of the CookHelper class.

instead be treated as text. As noted earlier, the root element was added for parsing purposes and will not appear in the output string. Finally, any other start tag will be converted to text by escaping the less-than and greater-than characters of the tag. Escaped versions of all attributes within the tag will also be output. The net result is that when the cooked text for such a tag is displayed in a browser, it should appear exactly (except for white space) as the blogger entered it.

Figure 7.33 shows the characters() method of CookHelper, which is called for all character data encountered by the SAX parser. We want to escape all such data. This might seem unnecessary: won't the parser throw an exception if, say, a stray less-than character is contained in the character data? It will in this case, but it won't throw an exception if it encounters <. Instead, this will be converted to the less-than character and passed to characters(). Thus, we must apply escaping in order to convert this character back to a

```
public void characters(char chars[],
                        int firstChar, int nChars)
    throws SAXException
{
    String escapedChars =
        WebTechUtil.escapeXML(
            new String(chars, firstChar, nChars));
    if (inQuote) {
        charData.append(escapedChars);
    }
    else {
        cookedText.append(escapedChars);
    }
    return;
}
```

FIGURE 7.33 The characters() method of the CookHelper class.

reference so that it can be safely included in HTML documents. The characters passed to characters() are collected in one of CookHelper's two StringBuffer's depending on whether we are currently within a displayquote element or not.

The final method implemented by CookHelper is endElement() (Figure 7.34). This is for the most part similar to startElement() except for the handling of a displayquote end tag, which performs the processing described earlier (outputs the text content of displayquote both as content of a span and as character data).

```
public void endElement(String namespaceURI,
                        String localName, String qname)
    throws SAXException
{
    if (qname.equals("b") || qname.equals("i") ||
        qname.equals("p") || qname.equals("a")) {
        cookedText.append("</" + qname + ">");
    }
    else if (qname.equals("displayquote") && inQuote) {
        inQuote = false;
        cookedText.append("<span class='dquote'>" +
                        charData +
                        "</span>" +
                        charData);
    }
    else if (qname.equals("root")) {
        // discard
    }
    else {
        cookedText.append("&lt;/" + qname + "&gt;");
    }
    return;
}
```

FIGURE 7.34 The endElement() method of the CookHelper class.

The `TextCooker` class is not perfect; for example, it will produce odd results if, say, an `i` element is nested within a `displayquote`. It will also turn an empty-element tag, such as `<hr />`, into separate start and end tags (or text representing the tags). But it does illustrate the potential utility of SAX processing for such a task.

Finally, we must also modify the `AddOrPreview` servlet—which is the servlet that constructs `Entry` instances—so that it handles the exceptions now thrown by the `Entry` constructor. For example, the code for adding an entry to the blog is wrapped in a try-catch block as follows:

```
try {
    Entry entry =
        new Entry(request.getParameter("title"),
                  request.getParameter("entry"));
    DataStore.addEntry(entry);
    response.sendRedirect("ViewBlog");
}
catch (SAXParseException spe) {
    displaySAXException(response, spe);
}
catch (Exception e) {
    throw new ServletException(e);
}
```

That is, if a `SAXParseException` is thrown when we attempt to construct an `Entry`, then we will create an HTML response containing information from this exception. Figure 7.35 shows an example of such a response generated when the blogger enters text with a starting `p` tag without a matching end tag. The blogger can then correct the entry and attempt to add it again. As shown, the code throws any exception other than a `SAXParseException` (we don't expect any such exceptions) to the server to handle. The same try-catch block will be wrapped around the code that creates an `Entry` for preview purposes.

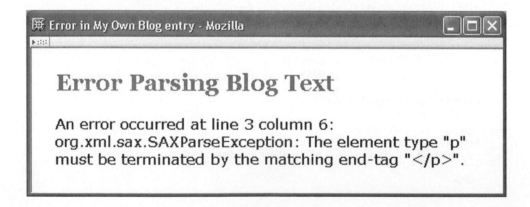

FIGURE 7.35 Rendering of HTML document describing a SAX parse exception.

The `displaySAXException()` method obtains a `PrintWriter` object and prints HTML to it. After some initial static text, it contains the code

```
    servletOut.println(
"      An error occurred at line " + spe.getLineNumber() +
" column " + spe.getColumnNumber() + ": ");
        if (spe.getException() != null) {
            servletOut.println(
                WebTechUtil.escapeXML(spe.getException().toString()));
        }
        else {
            servletOut.println(
                WebTechUtil.escapeXML(spe.toString()));
        }
```

We escape the string representation of the exception because it may contain XML special characters, as shown in Figure 7.35.

7.12 Related Technologies

Microsoft has provided significant software support for XML processing since early in XML's development. In the .NET Framework, most of this support is provided as part of the System.Xml "namespace" (a namespace in the .NET Framework is similar to a package in Java). Although there are syntactic differences between the Java and .NET approaches to XML processing, the concepts used are often similar. For example, the following .NET code fragment written in the Microsoft C# programming language loads an XML document from the relative URL `test.xml` into a DOM tree and creates a variable named `firstChild` that represents the first child element of the root element of the document; it should be reminiscent of JAXP code we have seen earlier:

```
XmlDocument doc = new XmlDocument();
doc.Load("test.xml");
XmlElement firstChild =
  (XmlElement) doc.DocumentElement.FirstChild;
```

The System.Xml namespace supports DOM processing (Level 1 and 2 Core), SAX-like processing via its `XmlReader` class, and XSLT transformations (including XPath expression evaluation) via the `XslTransform` class of the System.Xml.Xsl namespace. Currently, reference documentation for System.Xml can be found at `http://msdn.microsoft.com/library/en-us/cpref/html/frlrfSystemXml.asp`, and the overall starting point for Microsoft's XML developer documentation is `http://msdn.microsoft.com/xml/`.

Portions of the .NET Framework, including some classes in the System.Xml namespace API, have become international standards of the ECMA and ISO bodies (see `http://msdn.microsoft.com/net/ecma/` for details and links to reference materials). Based on these standards, Mono, an open source project (`http://www.mono-project.com`), has reimplemented significant portions of the .NET development platform for execution on Linux and Macintosh systems as well as Windows. At the time of this writing, DOM-oriented processing is not yet supported by Mono, but SAX-style parsing and XSLT support are implemented.

Support for DOM Level 2 processing, event-based (SAX-style) parsing, and XSLT is also available for PHP, a server-side scripting language discussed briefly in Section 8.9.3. In version 5 of PHP, this support is provided by the DOM, XML parser, and XSL extensions of PHP. The PHP Manual—available in a variety of languages at `http://www.php.net/docs.php`—provides information on installing and enabling these extensions.

As mentioned earlier, this chapter has covered only some of the more basic XML-related technologies. In particular, in Chapter 9 we will learn about XML Schema, which can be thought of as an extension to XML DTDs that adds significantly more data type information, among other features. This data type information makes it possible to import an XML document directly into programming language data structures, including typed variables, objects, and arrays; likewise, data structures can be directly exported to XML documents.

7.13   References

Complete syntactic rules for basic XML 1.0 documents and DTDs are given in [W3C-XML-1.0]. However, this reference does not contain anything about XML namespaces; instead, XML namespace concepts and syntax are described in [W3C-XML-NAMESPACE-1.1]. The JAXP API is described at [SUN-JAXP-1.2] as well as via the `javax.xml.*` packages in the Java 1.4.2 API [SUN-JAVA-API-1.4.2]. Details of the JWSDP 1.3 implementation of JAXP can be found in chapters 6 through 9 of the Java Web Services Tutorial [SUN-JWS-TUTORIAL-1.3]. References for the Document Object Model were given in Section 5.10; also see the `org.w3c.dom` package in the Java 1.4.2 API for documentation of the Java version of the DOM API. The Java API `org.xml.*` packages also supplement the SAX2 reference material [SAX-2.0.1]. XPath and XSLT are documented at [W3C-XPATH-1.0] and [W3C-XSLT-1.0], respectively. Using the `xml-stylesheet` processing instruction to associate style information with XML documents is described at [W3C-XML-STYLE-1.0].

Exercises

7.1. Suppose that you are writing software to process RSS feed documents that all contain the document type declaration

```
<!DOCTYPE rss
    SYSTEM "http://my.netscape.com/publish/formats/rss-0.91.dtd">
```

If this software is designed to execute on a machine that lacks a network connection, would you use a validating or a nonvalidating parser in your software? Explain.

7.2. Determine the expanded name for each of the elements in the following XML markup:

```
<e1 xmlns="http://www.example.net/ns/default">
  <ns1:e2 xmlns:ns1="http://www.example.org/ns">
    <e3 xmlns:ns1="http://www.example.com/ns/also">
      <ns1:e4 />
```

```
    <e5 />
  </e3>
 </ns1:e2>
</e1>
```

7.3. Rewrite the JavaScript function `makeCollapsible()` of Figure 5.15 as an equivalent Java method. Specifically, assume that you are writing a Java method `makeCollapsible()` for a class that contains an instance variable document of type `org.w3c.dom.Document`. Also assume that this variable has been initialized with a DOM document before your method is called. Your method should perform the same operations on document as are performed by the JavaScript function on `window.document`.

7.4. Write an `ignorableWhitespace()` method that will cause its SAX event-handling class to treat ignorable white space exactly as it treats any other character data.

7.5. Is the XPath expression / a location step or not? Explain.

7.6. Describe in English the node list represented by each of the following XPath expressions.

    (a) `child::*`
    (b) `child::text()`
    (c) `child::child`
    (d) `child`
    (e) `descendant::p[self::node()="Blah!"]`
    (f) `descendant::p[div][span]`
    (g) `descendant::p[div][span][position()=1]`
    (h) `ancestor::p/div`
    (i) `ancestor::p/div[position()=1]`
    (j) `/div[@id="div4"]`
    (k) `//div[@id="div4"]`
    (l) `.//div[@id="div4"]`
    (m) `//div[@id="div4" or p]`
    (n) `//div[@id="div4"]|p`

7.7. Write an XPath expression that produces a list of all of the attribute nodes for all of the children of the context node that have an attribute with name `id`.

7.8. What is the output if the XSLT transform

```
<xsl:transform version="1.0"
  xmlns:xsl="http://www.w3.org/1999/XSL/Transform"
  xmlns="http://www.example.org/UnrealNamespace">

  <xsl:template match="/">
    <ohYeah>
       <xsl:apply-templates select="next/item" />
       <xsl:apply-templates select="previous/item" />
    </ohYeah>
  </xsl:template>

  <xsl:template match="item">
    <xsl:copy-of select="." />
  </xsl:template>
</xsl:transform>
```

is run on the following XML source document?

```
<next>
  <previous>
    <item>A</item>
  </previous>
  <item>B</item>
  <item>C</item>
</next>
```

7.9. Explain how the behavior of the pre element would be different if the declaration for the xml:space attribute of the XHTML 1.0 pre element were changed to

```
<!ATTLIST pre
  ...
  xml:space (preserve|default) 'preserve'
  >
```

7.10. For each of the following tasks, which of the XML processing technologies as described in this chapter—DOM, SAX, or XSLT—would be most appropriate? Why?

  (a) Read an XHTML document. For each ul element, reorder the li elements it contains so that the first words of these elements appear in alphabetical order. Output the reordered document.

  (b) Test an XML document for validity. Output a message giving the line number of the error if the document is not valid.

  (c) Change all elements having local name ul in an XML document to elements having local name ol. Do not disturb any other aspects of the document, such as namespace prefixes of the element names or attribute specifications of the elements.

7.11. Consider the following XSLT document:

```
<xsl:transform version="1.0"
  xmlns:xsl="http://www.w3.org/1999/XSL/Transform"
  xmlns="http://www.w3.org/1999/xhtml">
  <xsl:template match="/">
    <html><head><title>RSSTitles</title></head>
      <body>
       <ul>
         <xsl:apply-templates select="rss" />
       </ul>
      </body>
    </html>
  </xsl:template>

  <xsl:template match="title">
    <li>
      <xsl:value-of select="." />
    </li>
  </xsl:template>

  <xsl:template match="text()">
  </xsl:template>
</xsl:transform>
```

(a) If this transformation is applied to the XML document of Figure 7.1, what will the result document be?

(b) How would the output differ if the last `template` element were not present?

7.12. Write XSLT markup that adds an element of type `site` having an attribute named `desc` to the result tree. The value of the attribute should be the string value of the first (in document order) `title` node of the source tree. Write your markup using:

(a) The XSLT `attribute` element.

(b) An attribute value template.

7.13. Write XSLT markup that adds an empty element to the result tree with an element type name obtained from the string value of the first (in document order) `eltName` node in the source tree.

Research and Exploration

7.14. Refer to [RFC-3151] to answer the following questions:

(a) Is a DTD formal public identifier more like a URL or a URN? Explain.

(b) What are the values of the class description, language, and owner fields in the XHTML 1.0 Strict formal public identifier?

7.15. In addition to the `version` and `encoding` declarations, the XML declaration can contain a `standalone` declaration. Syntactically, if this declaration appears within an XML declaration, it must follow the `version` and `encoding` declarations, if present. Study the description of the `standalone` declaration given in Section 2.9 of the XML 1.0 recommendation [W3C-XML-1.0], and then write a valid XHTML 1.0 Strict document that includes an XML declaration with the value `yes` for its `standalone` declaration. Pay particular attention to the validity constraint given in this section of the recommendation.

7.16. Refer to the DOM Level 2 Core recommendation [W3C-DOM-2-CORE], and make a list of the signatures of all of the namespace-aware Java DOM methods (those ending with `NS`) belonging to the `Element` class.

7.17. Parser features.

(a) Using the JAXP `getFeature()` method, test the default JWSDP 1.3 implementation of JAXP to determine whether or not it supports the `SAXSource` class.

(b) Design and conduct experiments with the default JWSDP 1.3 SAX parser in non-validating mode in an attempt to determine whether or not it reads entity declarations and default attribute values from an external DTD.

(c) Using the pluggability capability supported by the JAXP API, repeat your experiments with a different parser, such as the one available as part of the GNU JAXP project (see `http://www.gnu.org/software/classpathx/jaxp/`).

7.18. Assume that you are running XSLT on a source XHTML document that contains the following p element:

```
<p>Copyright &copy; 2005.</p>
```

where the `copy` entity is defined by XHTML to represent the copyright symbol (Unicode Standard character 0x00a9). If this element is copied from the source tree to the result tree, which is then output as an XML document, what do you think the output will be? Run an experiment to test your hypothesis. Explain the experimental results. Based on the material covered in this chapter, is there a way to produce an exact copy of this element in the result document using XSLT?

Projects

7.19. Write a Java servlet that modifies XHTML documents so that every ol element in the document is collapsible. Specifically, your servlet should accept a parameter `targetDoc` that is expected to be the URL of an XHTML document. The servlet inputs this document and adds a "Click to collapse" button before every ol element it contains, much like the JavaScript code in Section 5.5.6 (also see Exercise 7.3). The response from the servlet contains the modified XHTML document. Write your servlet using the DOM API. Test your servlet with an XHTML document on your server. Note that you should be careful with the use of relative URLs in the document, since the browser will use as the base URL the URL of your servlet and not the URL of the document itself.

7.20. Write a Java servlet that reads a source XHTML document and produces a result XHTML document containing a list of the a elements from the source document. Specifically, your servlet should accept a parameter `targetDoc` that is expected to be the URL of an XHTML document. The result document it produces should contain a ul element with one li for each a in the source document. Each a element in the result should copy the `href` attribute specification from the corresponding source element, but no other attributes should be copied. The text of the source a element, if any, should be used as the content of the result a element. If a source element has no text (for instance, if the content of the element is an img), then the string `no text` should be used as the content of the result a element.

7.21. Table-of-contents generator.

(a) Write a Java Servlet that uses XSL transformations in order to add a table of contents to the beginning of valid XHTML documents. Specifically, the start page for your servlet should provide the user with a simple form on which he or she can enter an absolute URL and click a submit button. Your servlet should use an XSL transformation (that you write) to convert the XHTML document at the specified URL into a copy of the document that has a table of contents representing all of the document's heading (h1 through h6) elements added to the beginning of its body element. Each line of the table of contents should display the text from one of the heading elements, but the lines should not be heading elements (that is, all lines should be the same font height and weight, regardless of the heading elements from which their text is taken). A horizontal rule should separate the table of contents from the original body content. (Hint: keep in mind that the elements of a valid XHTML document are in the XHTML namespace.)

(b) Modify your servlet so that it only places heading elements that have an id attribute specified in the table of contents and so that clicking on any line in the table of contents scrolls the browser to the selected heading element.

(c) Modify your servlet so that the amount of indentation of each line of the table of contents depends on the heading level of the corresponding element: h1 is indented least (possibly not at all), and h6 is indented most. Achieve this indentation effect by inserting   references at the beginning of a line.

(d) Modify your servlet so that any attributes—except id—specified on the heading element are applied to the corresponding line in the table of contents. (The reason for excluding the id attribute is that it is not valid to have two elements with the same id value in a single XHTML document.)

(e) Modify your servlet so that the document produced begins with an XHTML 1.0 Strict document type declaration and so that the text of the document is reasonably formatted. Ensure that the result is a valid XHTML 1.0 Strict document.

7.22. The following questions suggest extensions to the case study of Section 7.11.

(a) The given implementation of the blogging application does not properly handle tags within a `displayquote` element. Modify the implementation so that if a recognized tag (such as `<i>`) appears within a `displayquote` element, then the tag has the expected effect both in the body of the text and in the floated element. On the other hand, an unrecognized tag should be escaped so that the tag itself appears in both the text body and in the displayed element.

(b) Note that the parsed text in the given implementation includes the `root` start and end tags. The line and column numbers provided by a parse exception will be based on this parsed text rather than the original text. Therefore, these numbers might not always accurately locate the error within the original text. Modify the application to fix this problem.

(c) Extend the set of elements recognized by the cooking process as directed by your instructor. For example, you might recognize `img` elements and the attributes `src`, `alt`, `height`, and `width` on such elements.

CHAPTER 8

Separating Programming and Presentation
JSP™ Technology

Using Java servlets or CGI programming, a web server can run a program to produce a dynamic response to an HTTP request. The servlet/CGI class of dynamic server technologies, while powerful and flexible, tightly interleaves programming logic with HTML generation. One disadvantage of this approach that we have already seen is that a program that intermixes code and portions of HTML generated by that code may be hard to read, because we are trying to use indentation for two different purposes: to denote the structure of the program and to denote the structure of the HTML generated by the program. A more serious problem with tightly coupling programming logic and HTML generation is that it interferes with a natural division of labor in web site development. As mentioned in Chapter 6, a large web site is often developed by a team of individuals with different skills. Some team members (often called "designers" or "page authors") are primarily responsible for designing the look and feel of the site, while others ("developers" or "programmers") are primarily responsible for developing the programming logic. It is not hard to imagine the difficulties that can be encountered if designers and developers work simultaneously on developing a web site using Java servlets.

In this chapter, we will focus on the JavaServer Pages (JSP) technology, one instantiation of a class of related technologies that facilitate separate development of a web site's presentation and logic. The key conceptual contribution of these technologies is to embed program code related to presentation within a web document rather than to embed the document within code, as is the case with CGI and servlets. The result is a document that is much easier for designers to read and work with than a servlet would be. Program code related to data processing is encapsulated in a way that makes it relatively easy to access from a web document. When using JSP, this code is normally encapsulated in JavaBeans™ technology, which we therefore cover briefly. We'll also see that what we learned about servlets is useful in JSP-based systems, as servlets are often used for controlling the overall processing flow.

We will see several examples of the use of XML in this chapter. In particular, the version of JSP I cover here is an XML vocabulary. This has several advantages: the syntactic validity of XML-based JSP documents can be checked easily, XML tools such as XSLT can be used to process them, and existing syntax can be used for features such as associating identifiers with namespaces. However, let me add that JSP originally was not an XML vocabulary, and many JSP pages are still written using an older, non-XML syntax. I'll have more to say about this older JSP syntax, as well as about related technologies such as ASP and PHP, near the end of this chapter.

8.1   Introduction to JavaServer Pages

Let's begin by looking at a simple JSP document. Specifically, in Figure 8.1 I have rewritten the HelloCounter servlet of Figure 6.3 using the XML version of JSP. An example of an HTML document produced by running this JSP document via a JSP-capable web server such as Tomcat 5.0 is given in Figure 8.2.

The root element of this JSP document is html, just as it is for an HTML document. Thus, on the surface, this JSP document looks like a web page with some extra tags embedded within it. One advantage of this is that HTML development tools, such as Mozilla's Composer, can be used on JSP documents such as the one shown. That is, while Composer (as of Mozilla 1.4) does not "understand" JSP-specific tags, it will for the most part simply

```
<html
  xmlns="http://www.w3.org/1999/xhtml"
  xmlns:jsp="http://java.sun.com/JSP/Page"
  xmlns:c="http://java.sun.com/jsp/jstl/core">
  <jsp:directive.page contentType="text/html" />
  <jsp:output
    omit-xml-declaration="yes"
    doctype-root-element="html"
    doctype-public="-//W3C//DTD XHTML 1.0 Strict//EN"
    doctype-system="http://www.w3.org/TR/xhtml1/DTD/xhtml1-strict.dtd" />

  <head>
    <title>
      HelloCounter.jspx
    </title>
  </head>
  <body>

    <jsp:scriptlet>
      /* Initialize and update the "visits" variable. */
    </jsp:scriptlet>
    <c:if test="${empty visits}">
      <c:set var="visits" scope="application" value="0" />
    </c:if>
    <c:set var="visits" scope="application" value="${visits+1}" />
    <p>
      Hello World!
    </p>
    <p>
      This page has been viewed
        ${visits}
      times since the most recent
      application restart.
    </p>
  </body>
</html>
```

FIGURE 8.1 JSP visit counter document.

```
<!DOCTYPE html PUBLIC "-//W3C//DTD XHTML 1.0 Strict//EN"
 "http://www.w3.org/TR/xhtml1/DTD/xhtml1-strict.dtd">
<html xmlns="http://www.w3.org/1999/xhtml"><head><title>
      HelloCounter.jspx</title></head><body><p>
      Hello World!</p><p>
      This page has been viewed
        3
      times since the most recent
      application restart.</p></body></html>
```

FIGURE 8.2 Example HTML document generated by JSP document of Figure 8.1. The DOCTYPE element appears on a single line but has been wrapped onto a second line for readability.

ignore them and allow for the HTML elements of the page to be edited via its graphical user interface. Therefore, once the JSP structure of a document has been written and initial HTML elements have been properly placed within the document, it is often relatively easy for designers or other members of a development team to modify the document's look and feel using simple GUI-based tools. Let me also mention that, although in this chapter I will only illustrate the use of JSP to generate XHTML documents, it can more generally be used to generate documents conforming with any XML vocabulary.

As illustrated in Figure 8.1, a JSP document typically uses several different namespaces in addition to a default HTML namespace. The namespace name for JSP itself is `http://java.sun.com/JSP/Page`, while `http://java.sun.com/jsp/jstl/core` is the name of the core namespace of the JSP Standard Tag Library (JSTL). A JSP *tag library* is a mechanism for incorporating functionality in a JSP document beyond that defined by the JSP standard itself. The JSP Standard Tag Library is included as part of the JWSDP 1.3 version of the Tomcat 5.0 distribution and provides a number of useful functions, as we will learn.

The JSP `directive.page` and `output` elements can be used for setting certain properties of the HTML document that will be produced by a JSP document. In this case, the `directive.page` element directs the server to set the Content-Type header field of the HTTP response to the `text/html` MIME type (this overrides the default `text/xml`, which might confuse some browsers). The JSP `output` element is similar to the XSLT `output` element, controlling aspects of the XML declaration and document type declaration at the beginning of the document. In this example, the `output` element causes the XML declaration to be suppressed in the XHTML document produced and provides all of the content for the document type declaration: the name of the root element along with the public and system identifiers.

Immediately following these elements are several lines of XHTML *template data* (the `head` start tag through the `body` start tag). Template data is conceptually passed through without alteration to the result XHTML document. Again, this is much like template data in XSLT documents.

Following this template data the JSP `scriptlet` element is used to include a scriptlet in the document. A *scriptlet* is a fragment of Java code that is embedded within the JSP document; I'll have much more to say about the relationship between JSP documents and Java code in the next section. For now, it should be noted that the content of a `scriptlet` element is not treated as template data, so it is not passed through to the output XHTML document. Normal XML comments, on the other hand, are treated as template data and therefore do appear in the output document. Thus, as illustrated, one use for scriptlets is to embed comments in your JSP document that will not appear in the output XHTML document.

Following the scriptlet are several lines of XML markup that perform all of the computations needed by this application. As you might suspect, the `if` element of the JSTL's core namespace conditionally executes the `set` element it contains, and the `set` element performs an assignment to a variable. Specifically, whether or not the first `set` element is executed depends on the value of the `test` attribute of the `if` element. This particular `test` will evaluate to `true` if a variable named `visits` is "empty," which includes not existing at all. In this case, the `visits` variable will be created and assigned the value 0. Declaring the scope of the variable to be `application` is a means of saving the value of the variable for use by future visits to the JSP document. If `visits` already exists when the `if` element is encountered, then the `set` element it contains will be skipped and the value of `visits` will not be affected. After this conditional processing has been performed, the subsequent `set` element increments the `visits` variable.

Syntactic and semantic details needed to write such markup will be covered later in this chapter. For now, notice that these tags are all valid XML markup. In essence, the JSTL provides (among other things) a simple XML-based programming language.

The remainder of the document in Figure 8.1 is more template data with the exception of `${visits}`, which is a reference to the `visits` variable. This reference will be replaced with a string representing the value of the variable in the result XHTML document, as shown in Figure 8.2.

8.2   JSP and Servlets

The description of the JSP document of the previous section may have given you the impression that the web server interacts directly with the content of a JSP document, "executing" `if` and `set` elements and evaluating expressions such as `visits+1`. In fact, what actually happens is that every JSP document is translated into a Java servlet, which is then compiled. This translation and compilation normally occurs the first time the JSP document's URL is requested. Tomcat places translated JSP documents and their class files under the `work` subdirectory of the JWSDP 1.3 installation directory. For example, the servlet corresponding to the `HelloCounter.jspx` document in the `HelloCounter` web application in Section 8.1 will be placed at `work/Catalina/localhost/HelloCounter/org/apache/jsp/HelloCounter_jspx.java`. After translating and compiling a JSP document, the server then executes the resulting servlet class to produce the response to the request. Every subsequent visit to the document's URL causes the server to again invoke the compiled servlet. Depending on how the server is configured, if a revised JSP document is placed in the web application directory, then the next time the JSP document is visited, the translation and compilation process may be automatically performed again before executing the servlet to produce a response.

This two-step approach has advantages and disadvantages relative to direct interpretation of the JSP document itself. One disadvantage is in debugging: if a servlet translated from a JSP document throws an exception to the server, the exception will refer to the servlet code and not to the original JSP document (although comments within the code may point back to the JSP source). There can also be a noticeable delay the first time a JSP document is requested. The primary advantage is that, after the first access to a JSP document, subsequent accesses tend to be relatively fast because they are running a compiled program rather than causing interpretation of a text file.

Conceptually, translation of a JSP document into a Java servlet proceeds as follows. The translator creates a subclass of HttpServlet that also implements the javax.servlet.jsp.HttpJspPage interface. This interface includes a method _jspService() that is called by the server rather than doGet() or doPost() when an HTTP request for the JSP document is received. The _jspService() method begins by defining a number of *implicit objects* that are available to scriptlet code embedded within the document. The implicit objects related to classes covered in Chapter 6 are listed in Table 8.1; we'll learn about one more implicit object in the next section. The implicit object out can be used much like the PrintWriter returned by a call to getWriter() in a Java servlet, but it actually is a separate object that by default automatically passes its data through to the PrintWriter object when its buffer is full. Generally speaking, you can simply think of out as the PrintWriter object, as for the most part it behaves similarly.

Once these (and other) implicit objects have been defined, the _jspService() method contains Java code that implements the JSP document being translated. For example, template data from the JSP document is added to the HTTP response by calls on the object out. Specifically, when Jasper, the component of Tomcat 5.0 responsible for translating a JSP document into a Java servlet, is run on the JSP document of Figure 8.1, the servlet code generated includes the lines

```
out.write("<head>");
out.write("<title>");
out.write("\n      HelloCounter.jspx");
out.write("</title>");
out.write("</head>");
out.write("<body>");
```

corresponding to the initial template data in the document. Notice that *ignorable* white space (in the sense described in Section 7.6) may be removed from the template data.

TABLE 8.1 Some Java Implicit Objects Automatically Created when a JSP Document is Translated into a Servlet

Object Name	Instance of
request	javax.servlet.http.HttpServletRequest
response	javax.servlet.http.HttpServletResponse
session	javax.servlet.http.HttpSession
out	javax.servlet.jsp.JspWriter

The content of a scriptlet element is copied directly into the generated servlet. Thus, in the servlet translated from the JSP document of Figure 8.1, the comment

```
/* Initialize and update the "visits" variable. */
```

immediately follows the last of the `out.write()` calls just listed. If we replaced this scriptlet with

```
<jsp:scriptlet>
  out.write("<p>Hello " +
            request.getParameter("username") +
            "!</p>");
</jsp:scriptlet>
```

then the body of the HTML document generated by the translated servlet would begin with a paragraph saying "Hello" to the user specified by the `username` parameter in the request query string (or saying "Hello null!" if the query string did not contain a `username` parameter).

Many older JSP documents make extensive use of scriptlets rather than JSTL elements to perform computations. Scriptlets make the full power of the Java programming language available within the JSP document itself, which comes with both advantages and disadvantages. The advantage is obvious: you can do essentially anything using a JSP document that you can do with a servlet. But there is a major disadvantage, related to the rationale we gave for considering JSP in the first place: we are still mixing potentially sophisticated programming with presentation within a single document. Also, the scriptlet code itself is text, so XML tools cannot be used to manipulate it directly. JSTL, on the other hand, provides simple programming constructs in an XML-compatible format. Furthermore, as we will learn later, if more sophisticated processing than that provided by JSTL is required in a JSP document then separate Java classes can be accessed by JSP elements. Using this approach, the JSP document itself can remain largely if not entirely free of Java code while still having indirect access to arbitrarily sophisticated Java classes.

The translation of JSP and tag library elements into Java servlet code depends on the element being translated and the specific translator used. As an example, when Jasper translates our example JSP document, the `directive.page` element becomes

```
response.setContentType("text/html;charset=UTF-8");
```

(UTF-8 is the default character encoding for JSP documents), and the `output` element becomes (this is a single line wrapped for readability)

```
    out.write("<!DOCTYPE html PUBLIC
\"-//W3C//DTD XHTML 1.0 Strict//EN\"
\"http://www.w3.org/TR/xhtml1/DTD/xhtml1-strict.dtd\">\n");
```

as you might expect. A variable reference such as `${visits}` appearing outside a tag is translated to code that invokes `out.write()` with the value of the variable.

One thing to note is that the servlet code sequentially writes text representing an HTML document to the object out. This means that if the `_jspService()` method executes a `return` before reaching the end of its processing (the Jasper-generated code often contains multiple `return` statements), then the HTML document produced in response to an HTTP request directed to JSP document may be incomplete and therefore not a well-formed XHTML document.

This brief overview of the relationship between servlets and JSP documents should help to clarify some concepts covered later, and may be particularly valuable if you need to debug a JSP document. However, for the reasons given earlier, I suggest avoiding scriptlet code within your JSP documents. Therefore, the remainder of this chapter will focus on developing JSP documents without resorting to scriptlets.

8.3   Running JSP Applications

In this section we'll learn a method for executing JSP documents via a web server. Before providing detailed instructions, though, it will be helpful to understand some JSP-related concepts, beginning with the concept of a web application.

8.3.1   Web Applications

For the most part, the server-side programming examples in Chapter 6 consisted of a single servlet, and that servlet provided the complete functionality required to accomplish some task. For larger tasks, however, there will generally be a large collection of resources—servlets, JSP documents, utility and support Java classes, static HTML documents, style sheets, JavaScript files, images, and so on—that work together in order to provide what appears to an end user to be a single software application. Such a collection of resources is known as a *web application*. A single Web site may include a number of separate web applications. For example, a financial services site might have one web application that provides stock quotes, another for entering buy and sell orders, and yet another to assist customers with financial planning by providing functionality such as a retirement "calculator."

From the point of view of JSP and servlet developers, perhaps what is most significant about a web application is that data can easily be shared among the *components* of the web application, that is, among the servlet instances—either coded directly or generated from JSP documents—that belong to the application. In a servlet, the shared data structure is accessed by calling the servlet's `getServletContext()` method, which takes no arguments and returns a reference to an object implementing `ServletContext`. Within generated-from-JSP servlets, in addition to out and the other implicit objects listed in Table 8.1, the `application` implicit object is automatically associated with the `ServletContext` object. Assuming that all of the components of a web application are running within a single Java VM (which is the default, and which I will assume throughout this chapter), the `ServletContext` class is instantiated once when the server loads the web application, and this single instance is shared among all of the application's components. That is, a call to `getServletContext()` always returns a reference to this existing instance rather than creating a new instance.

Two basic types of data can be stored in the `ServletContext` object of a web application. First, as we will learn shortly, initialization data can be stored in a file associated with a web application. When the web application is initialized by the web server, this data is read from the file and stored in the ServletContext object, from which it can be retrieved by any of the web application's components using methods described later. Second, the ServletContext object has setAttribute() and getAttribute() methods that behave just like those on an HttpSession object, except that of course these methods store data within the ServletContext object rather than in an HttpSession object. Thus, data stored using setAttribute() on the ServletContext object can be retrieved by any other component of the same web application by calling getAttribute() on this object. As we will learn in more detail later, when in our earlier example we specified application as the value of the scope attribute in JSTL elements such as set, we were instructing JSP to use these methods on the ServletContext object in order to store and retrieve the visits variable.

It should also be noted that each HttpSession object is shared among all of the components of a web application. However, keep in mind that there is (conceptually, at least) one session object per user, so a given session object will only be shared between threads running in response to requests by a single user. On the other hand, the ServletContext object is shared among all threads running in all components of a web application. In other words, the scope of data stored in the ServletContext object is broader than the scope of data store in any single HttpSession object.

One other term that should be defined before going further is "container." The collection of server software that translates a web application's JSP documents, instantiates its servlet classes as objects, invokes methods such as doGet() or _jspService() on these objects, and provides the implementation of the Java servlet APIs is known as the *container* for the web application's components. You may recall from Chapter 1 that the container portion of Tomcat is called Catalina. Many Web sites run Catalina by itself (without the Coyote HTTP-handling portion of Tomcat) as a back-end processor that is called by a primary web server (such as Apache) to handle requests for URLs corresponding to servlets or JSP documents. In these environments, it is useful to distinguish between "web server" and "container," since they are two different software packages. Because I will be assuming in this chapter that Tomcat is being run as the primary web server and not as a back end, I will often blur the distinction between "web server" and "container."

8.3.2   Installing a Web Application

A web application can be installed in a container in a variety of ways. In Chapter 6 I explained how to install a servlet by adding it to the shared/classes directory of Tomcat 5.0. We were in essence adding these servlets to one large default web application. While sufficient for our purposes in that chapter, this approach cannot be used for JSP documents (and has a number of drawbacks even for servlet installation). In this section, I will illustrate a method for explicitly creating a web application by creating a HelloCounter application consisting of the single JSP document of Figure 8.1.

The first step in this method is to create a directory under the webapps subdirectory of the directory in which you installed JWSDP 1.3. As the name implies, webapps is the default Tomcat 5.0 root directory for web applications (the name of the directory Tomcat uses for this purpose can be changed by modifying the Application Base field of the Host object within the Tomcat 5.0 Administration Tool). The name of the subdirectory we create will also by default serve as the initial portion of the URL path used to access this application (recall that the path of a URL is the portion following the authority and preceding the query string). So, if we use the name `HelloCounter` for this directory and our Tomcat server is running at port 8080 of `www.example.org`, then URLs beginning with `http://www.example.org:8080/HelloCounter/` will be used to access documents associated with this web application.

Next, within this new subdirectory we will place our JSP document. By default, Tomcat will recognize any file with the extension `jspx` as a JSP document written in XML format. So we will copy our JSP document to the `webapps/HelloCounter` directory with the name `HelloCounter.jspx`.

We must now notify the server that a new web application is available. This step is known as *deploying* the application to the server. Deployment with the JWSDP 1.3 version of Tomcat 5.0 can be performed through a simple web interface. First, make sure that your server is running, and then visit its `/manager/html` path. For example, if the server is running on the same machine as your browser and is listening on the default port 8080, then you would browse to `http://localhost:8080/manager/html`. You will be prompted for a user name and password; enter the values you provided when you installed JWSDP 1.3. If you have forgotten the values, they can be found in the `conf/tomcat-users.xml` file within your JWSDP installation directory.

As shown in Figure 8.3, the JWSDP Web Application Manager application (yes, the Manager itself is a web application) lists each of the web applications currently deployed to the server (or, more precisely, to the appropriate virtual host of the server). It also provides

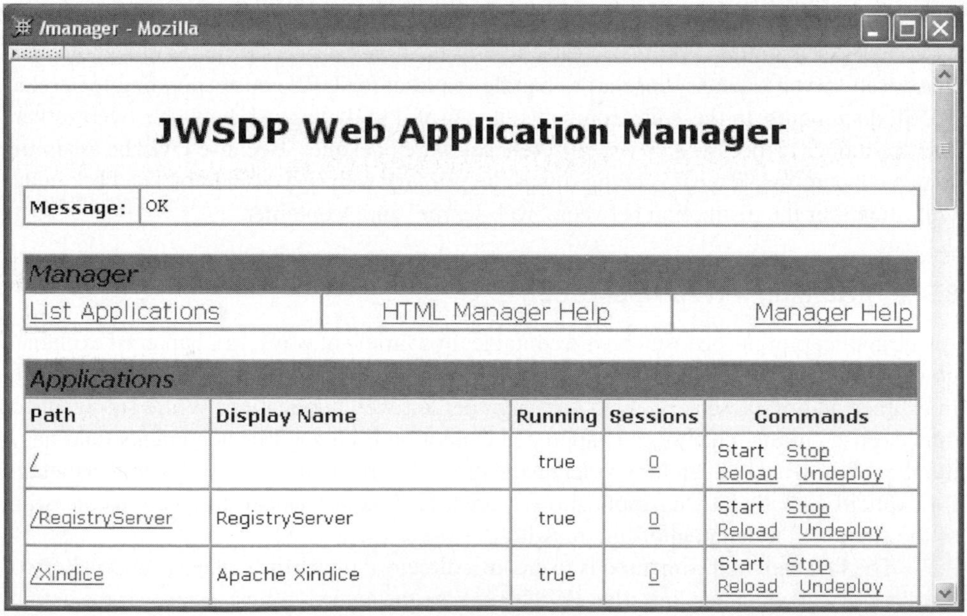

FIGURE 8.3 JWSDP 1.3 Web Application Manager application list. (The content of this screen shot is copyright © 2006 Sun Microsystems Inc. All rights reserved. Reproduced by permission of Sun Microsystems Inc.)

some status information and clickable command links for each deployed application. If an application is not running (the Stop link has been clicked), then the server acts as if the application does not exist, returning an HTTP 404 status code for any access to the path associated with the application. It may be useful to stop a web application if other services that the application depends on, such as a database, are temporarily unavailable. The Start link becomes active when an application is stopped; clicking this link restarts the application. Reloading an application causes it to shut down and immediately restart using the latest JSP and Java class files available. You will probably use this command frequently during development. Undeploying an application causes the application to be stopped, to become unavailable to the server, and—note this carefully—to have its webapps subdirectory and all files underneath its subdirectory deleted. There is no opportunity to cancel any of these commands, so once you click Undeploy for an application, it will be undeployed (and its directory deleted). Obviously, you'll want to be careful when clicking near an Undeploy link. In fact, you should only put copies of files under the webapps directory, never originals.

Below the application list are two forms that allow you to deploy an application (Figure 8.4). In our example, deployment is particularly easy: we enter the name of the directory we created in the "WAR or Directory URL" field and click the Deploy button immediately below this field. The browser will then refresh the application list, and our new web application should appear (Figure 8.5). We can now run our web application by

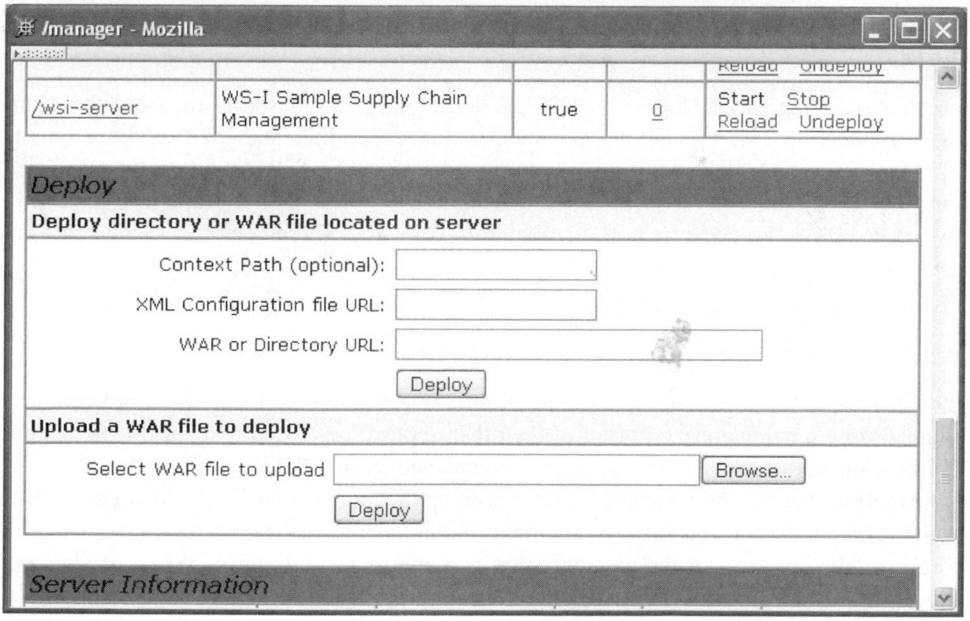

FIGURE 8.4 JWSDP 1.3 Web Application Manager deployment forms. (The content of this screen shot is copyright © 2006 Sun Microsystems Inc. All rights reserved. Reproduced by permission of Sun Microsystems Inc.)

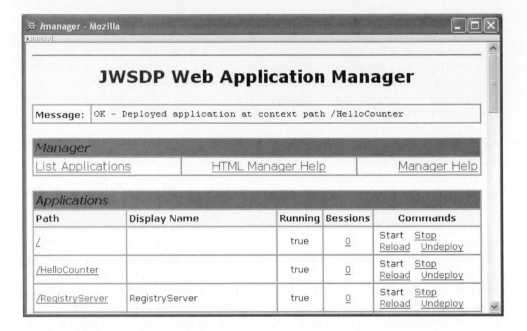

FIGURE 8.5 JWSDP 1.3 Web Application Manager after HelloCounter application has been deployed. (The content of this screen shot is copyright © 2006 Sun Microsystems Inc. All rights reserved. Reproduced by permission of Sun Microsystems Inc.)

either navigating to /HelloCounter/HelloCounter.jspx on our server or, from the Manager application list, by clicking on the /HelloCounter link and then clicking on the HelloCounter.jspx link. After a delay (during which the JSP document is translated and the resulting servlet is instantiated and initialized), you should see a web page saying that 1 visit has occurred. Reloading this page will increment the displayed visit count.

8.3.3   Defining Web Application Parameters

You may have noticed that the Display Name field for the HelloCounter application is blank, while a name appears for all of the other applications listed (except for the default application with path /). The value to be displayed in this field is one of the pieces of information that can be associated with a web application via an XML document called a *deployment descriptor*. The root element of this document has element type web-app; Table 8.2 lists several of the elements that can appear as children of this root element. Chapter 13 of [SUN-SERVLETS-2.4] and Chapter 3 of [SUN-JSP-2.0] provide complete details on deployment descriptors for servlets and JSP documents, respectively. My purpose here is simply to inform you that certain deployment features exist and to illustrate basic usage of some of those most commonly used.

TABLE 8.2 Some Elements of Web Application Deployment Descriptors

Element	Use (as Child of web-app)
display-name	Provides name to be displayed for application (for example, in Manager's Display Name field).
description	Provides text describing the web application for documentation purposes.
context-param	Provides parameter value that can be used by components for initialization.
servlet	Associates a name with either a servlet class or a JSP document and optionally sets other options and parameters for the servlet or JSP document.
servlet-mapping	Associates a URL (or a set of URLs) with one of the servlet names defined by a servlet element.
session-config	Specifies the default for the length of time that a session can be idle before being terminated.
mime-mapping	Associates file extensions with MIME types.
welcome-file-list	Specifies a list of files. If an HTTP request is mapped to a directory within this application, the server will search within the directory for one of these files and respond with the first file found. If no file is found, the directory contents are displayed by default.
error-page	Specifies a resource (static web page or application component) that will provide the HTTP response when either a specified HTTP error status code is generated or a specified Java exception is thrown to the container.
jsp-config	Associates certain information with the JSP documents of an application, such as the location of tag library files and settings for certain JSP options.
security-role	Defines a "role" (e.g., manager, customer) to be used for purposes of allowing or denying access to certain resources of a web application.
security-constraint	Specifies application resources that should be access-protected and indicates which user roles will be granted access to these resources.
login-config	Specifies how the container should request user-name and password information (which will subsequently be mapped to one or more roles) when a user attempts to access a protected resource.

An example deployment descriptor for the HelloCounter application is given in Figure 8.6. In order to associate this descriptor with the web application, the document should be given the name web.xml and placed in a directory named WEB-INF that is a subdirectory of the HelloCounter directory we created earlier. The WEB-INF directory is treated in a special way by the web server: any attempt to access this directory or its contents will receive an HTTP status code of 404 (resource not available) in the response. In addition to the deployment descriptor, other resources that should not be accessed directly by end users are normally placed within WEB-INF. For example, the normal location for servlet and other Java class files is in the classes subdirectory of WEB-INF. Such classes are automatically loaded as part of the web application.

A deployment descriptor compliant with the Java Servlet 2.4 specification must include the default namespace declaration shown in the web-app start tag and must also specify 2.4 as the value of the required version attribute. While not required, it is also

```
<web-app
  xmlns="http://java.sun.com/xml/ns/j2ee"
  xmlns:xsi="http://www.w3.org/2001/XMLSchema-instance"
  xsi:schemaLocation="http://java.sun.com/xml/ns/j2ee/web-app_2_4.xsd"
  version="2.4">

  <display-name>HelloCounter</display-name>
  <description>
    Creates a counter variable at the application level and increments
    and displays this variable on each visit.  Uses JSP Document (XML)
    syntax.
  </description>
  <!-- The following element creates an initialization parameter
       (unused by current web application). -->
  <context-param>
    <param-name>initialVisitsValue</param-name>
    <param-value>527</param-value>
  </context-param>
  <servlet>
    <servlet-name>visit_count</servlet-name>
    <jsp-file>/HelloCounter.jspx</jsp-file>
  </servlet>
  <servlet-mapping>
    <servlet-name>visit_count</servlet-name>
    <url-pattern>*.jsp</url-pattern>
  </servlet-mapping>
  <servlet-mapping>
    <servlet-name>visit_count</servlet-name>
    <url-pattern>/visitor/*</url-pattern>
  </servlet-mapping>
  <session-config>
    <session-timeout>1</session-timeout>
  </session-config>
</web-app>
```

FIGURE 8.6 Example deployment descriptor for the HelloCounter web application.

good practice to include a source location for the Servlet 2.4 deployment descriptor schema (see below), which can be accomplished by including in the start tag the two attribute specifications

```
xmlns:xsi="http://www.w3.org/2001/XMLSchema-instance"
xsi:schemaLocation="http://java.sun.com/xml/ns/j2ee/web-app_2_4.xsd"
```

A *schema* is much like an XML DTD: it is used to define the elements and attributes of an XML vocabulary. We will cover XML Schema, the vocabulary used to define schemas, in the next chapter.

The child elements of web-app may appear in any order, and most of them are allowed to appear any number of times (including no times at all). The three exceptions are the "-config" elements (session-config, jsp-config, and login-config), which each may appear at most once.

We'll now consider various child elements in the order of their appearance in the example deployment descriptor. First, each context-param element in a deployment descriptor defines a *context parameter* that can be used to initialize an application; we'll see how to access context parameters from within JSP documents later. Often, the bulk of a deployment descriptor consists of the next two child element types illustrated, servlet and servlet-mapping. A servlet element provides a short name for either the fully qualified name of a Java servlet class (specified as the content of a servlet-class element, not shown) or the path to a JSP document relative to the application's *document base directory* (the directory containing the WEB-INF subdirectory, which is the HelloCounter directory in our example). A servlet-mapping then specifies a *URL pattern* to be associated with a particular component.

A URL pattern is interpreted as follows. When the server receives a request for a URL, it first selects the web application that will handle this request. Specifically, it chooses the application that has the longest *context path* (the Path field in the Web Application Manager list) matching a prefix of the path portion of the URL. So, the context path /HelloCounter associated with our web application will match with the following URLs, assuming that these are entered on the machine running our Tomcat server and that our server is listening for requests on port 8080:

```
http://localhost:8080/HelloCounter/HelloCounter.jspx
http://localhost:8080/HelloCounter/visitor/welcome
http://localhost:8080/HelloCounter/visitor.jsp
http://localhost:8080/HelloCounter/images/nifty.png
```

Once the server has chosen a web application, the portion of the URL path following the context path (with any path parameters, such as jsessionid, removed) is used for matching by URL patterns. I'll refer to this as the *postcontext path*. For the URLs listed, the postcontext paths will be, respectively,

```
/HelloCounter.jspx
/visitor/welcome
/visitor.jsp
/images/nifty.png
```

URL patterns can be one of the four forms shown in Table 8.3. The server attempts to match (case-sensitively) a postcontext path with a server resource in the order shown, beginning with any exact URL patterns, then attempting a path-prefix match if all exact patterns fail. Path-prefix patterns must begin with / and end with *, and can contain no embedded * characters. The string /* is a valid path-prefix pattern and matches any postcontext path. If multiple path-prefix patterns match, then the longest matching pattern is selected, so /visitor/* would have preference over /*. If all exact and path-prefix patterns fail to match, then extension matching is attempted. If this also fails, and if the default pattern / has been specified as a url-pattern, then this pattern will match any postcontext path. Notice, however, that if the special path-prefix pattern /* is specified, then any extension

TABLE 8.3 Forms of URL Patterns

Name	Example	Postcontext Path Matched
Exact	`/HelloCounter.jspx`	The path `/HelloCounter.jspx`
Path-prefix	`/visitor/*`	The path `/visitor` or any path beginning with `/visitor/`
Extension	`*.jsp`	Any path ending in `.jsp`
Default	`/`	Any path

and default patterns will effectively be ignored. Finally, if no pattern at all matches the postcontext path, then the server falls back to its default nonservlet processing: it attempts to locate a resource (such as an image or HTML document) by treating the postcontext path as a path in the file system rooted at the document base directory. The post-context path `/images/nifty.png`, for example, would cause the server to look for an `images` subdirectory of the `HelloCounter` directory and, if found, to look for a `nifty.png` file within this subdirectory.

Returning to the four example postcontext paths given earlier and assuming that a deployment descriptor had exactly four `servlet-mapping` elements, each using one of the four example URL patterns given in Table 8.3 as the value of its `url-pattern` element, then the first postcontext path would be matched by the first pattern in Table 8.3, the second path would not be matched by the first pattern but would be matched by the second, and so on.

Let me add that the `HttpServletRequest` object provides several methods that enable a servlet to learn about the URL that invoked it. `getContextPath()` returns the context portion of the URL (beginning with a / but not ending with one), `getServletPath()` returns the portion of the URL matched by the URL pattern—excluding any portion of the path corresponding to the `/*` at the end of a path-prefix pattern—and `getPathInfo()` returns any portion of the URL path following the `getServletPath()` portion (if nonempty, this always begins with a /).

Finally, recall that sessions automatically time out after some length of time; `session-config` is used to set this time. Its value, which must be an integer, represents a time in minutes.

8.4   Basic JSP

Now that we've covered several preliminaries, we'll consider many of the facilities provided by JSP as they would be used in writing a JSP document. Our focus will be on writing documents without the use of embedded Java scriptlets. In later sections, we'll look behind the scenes to see how to write Java code so that it can be accessed from JSP documents via tags. Combining these techniques allows us to write JSP documents that are Java-free while still having indirect access to the full power of the Java language and APIs.

Overall, every valid JSP document consists of at most three types of information: JSP markup, JSP Expression Language (EL) expressions, and template data. The JSP markup is the XML markup that belongs to a namespace recognized by the JSP container. EL expressions, such as `${visits+1}`, are defined by JSP's Expression Language facility, which will be described in some detail in Section 8.4.1. All other non-white space in the document—usually HTML markup and character data—is template data. We'll begin this section by considering EL and return later to the various features provided by JSP markup.

8.4.1 JSP Expression Language (EL)

As we have seen in the `HelloCounter` example, variables can be created and manipulated within JSP elements. However, it was not always as easy to work with variables within JSP documents as this example might lead you to expect. In fact, most early JSP developers relied heavily on Java code within scriptlets to create and manipulate variables, and many JSP documents in use continue to adopt this approach. However, beginning with JSP version 2.0, JSP incorporates an Expression Language (EL) that can be utilized along with elements from the JSP Standard Tag Library to accomplish many simple presentation-oriented programming tasks without any need for embedding Java code.

An EL expression can be invoked in one of two contexts: within template data and within certain attribute values in JSP markup. In both cases, within a JSP document an EL expression must be preceded by `${` and followed by `}`. As discussed earlier, when used as part of template data, such as in

```
This page has been viewed
  ${visits}
times since the most recent
application restart.
```

the enclosed EL expression is evaluated (as described later in this subsection) and, if it is not already a `String` value, converted to a `String`. This `String` is then written to the implicit `out` object. When used in an attribute specification, as in

```
<c:set var="visits" scope="application" value="${visits+1}" />
```

the enclosed EL expression is evaluated and converted to a data type that depends on the context of the evaluation. In this example, the value resulting from evaluating this expression is ultimately stored as an object, which in this case would mean using a Java wrapper class such as `Integer` to hold the primitive value resulting from the evaluation. We'll have more to say about how EL values are stored.

The literals in EL are the booleans `true` and `false`, decimal integer and floating point—including scientific notation—numbers, strings enclosed in either single or double quotes, and the reserved word `null`. A variable identifier must follow the syntactic rules for Java identifiers: begin with a *Java letter* (character for which `Character.isJavaIdentifierStart()` returns `true`; the ASCII characters of that kind are letters, underscore, and dollar sign) and consist entirely of *Java letters* and *Java digits* (characters for which `Character.isJavaIdentifierPart()` returns `true`). In addition, a variable identifier must not be one of the EL reserved words. The complete list of 16 EL reserved words is

```
and     div     empty    eq     false    ge     gt    instanceof
le      lt      mod      ne     not      null   or    true
```

Most of the EL reserved words are synonyms for other symbols. For example, and, or, and not are synonyms for the familiar Boolean operators &&, ||, and !. The and is particularly convenient because, of course, & is a special character in XML and therefore must be escaped within a JSP document. Similarly, le and lt are synonyms for the relational operators <= and <, which would also require escaping. Other synonyms are eq for ==, ne for !=, ge for >=, gt for >, div for / (division), and mod for % (remainder after division). The operator empty is a prefix unary operator that evaluates to true if its operand's value is null or represents an empty object (the empty string, an array with no elements, etc.). Otherwise, it evaluates to false. The reserved word instanceof is not currently used in EL, but is reserved for possible future use.

The remaining operators in EL are addition, subtraction, and multiplication (+, -, and *), unary minus, the ternary conditional operator involving ? and :, parentheses to group operators for precedence purposes, and the array access operator [] discussed later in this subsection. Addition is always numeric in EL (the + symbol does not also represent string concatenation as it does in some languages). With this exception for +, the rules for automatic type conversion within EL expressions are for the most part similar to those in JavaScript; see Section 2.8 of [SUN-JSP-2.0] for complete details.

A variable reference such as visits within an EL expression is resolved in one of two ways. First, if the variable reference is identical to the name of one of the *EL implicit objects* listed in Table 8.4, then the reference evaluates to the indicated implicit object. For the most part, the EL implicit objects are derived from JSP implicit objects that we have

TABLE 8.4 EL Implicit Objects

EL Implicit Object Name	Represents
pageContext	Container for JSP implicit objects
pageScope	Values accessible via calls to page.getAttribute()
requestScope	Values accessible via calls to request.getAttribute()
sessionScope	Values accessible via calls to session.getAttribute()
applicationScope	Values accessible via calls to application.getAttribute()
param	Values accessible via request.getParameter()
paramValues	Values accessible via request.getParameterValues()
header	Values accessible via request.getHeader()
headerValues	Values accessible via request.getHeaders()
cookie	Map from cookie names to their associated Cookie values (data obtained via request.getCookies())
initParam	Values accessible via application.getInitParameter()

already discussed. One exception is the EL implicit object `pageScope`, which is based on the JSP implicit object `page`, which was not covered previously. The `page` object is simply a reference to the `HttpServlet` object itself. The other exception is `pageContext`, which is a reference to an instance of the class `javax.servlet.jsp.PageContext`. For JSP purposes, the primary use of this class is to provide direct access to the JSP implicit objects `request`, `out`, and so on. For instance, the EL expression `pageContext.request` represents a reference to the `request` JSP implicit object. We'll learn how to use such objects directly from a JSP document (without scriptlets) later when we discuss the JavaBeans technology.

With the exception of `pageContext`, each of the EL implicit objects is a `java.util.Map` derived from data in a JSP implicit object. The `Map` interface defines a `get()` method that takes an `Object` *key* and returns a corresponding `Object` representing the value associated with the key (you should be familiar with the key-value terminology if you've used the `java.util.Hashtable` class, which implements `Map`). As an example of how one of these `Map` objects is derived from a JSP implicit object, consider the `param` object. If the JSP implicit object `request` contains parameters named `p1` and `p2` with values `15` and `4`, respectively, then the EL implicit object `param` will be a `Map` with key `p1` associated with value `15` and key `p2` associated with value `4`.

The EL syntax for accessing `Map` objects is similar to the JavaScript array-object access syntax. For example, the EL expression `param['p1']` evaluates to the value associated with the `p1` key in the `param` object, and therefore to the same value as the Java code `request.getParameter("p1")`. Since the array accessor is a string literal, the above EL expression can be written equivalently (as in JavaScript) as `param.p1`. We'll learn later that the same array and object notations can be used to access the properties of JavaBeans objects. Similarly, if an EL variable `aVar` represents either a Java array or any object implementing the `java.util.List` interface, and if `index` is an EL variable that can be converted to an integer, then `aVar[index]` returns the value of the element numbered `index` in `aVar`.

The `initParam` object provides access to the name-value pair defined in a `context-param` element of the deployment descriptor. So, given the deployment descriptor of Figure 8.6, the EL expression `initParam.initialVisitsValue` would evaluate to 527. As shown in Table 8.4, within a servlet the values of `context-param` elements are accessible via calls to `getInitParameter()` on the `ServletContext` object.

Like the JSP implicit objects `session` and `application`, both `page` and `request` have `getAttribute()` and `setAttribute()` methods that can be used to associate data with these objects. These methods are invoked automatically by JSP-generated code as follows: If an EL variable reference does not match one of the EL implicit object names in Table 8.4, then the JSP implicit objects `page`, `request`, `session`, and `application` are searched—in that order—for an attribute having the given variable name. That is, a reference to the variable `visits` will generate a call to `getAttribute()` on the `page` object; if this returns `null`, then a call to `getAttribute()` on `request`, and so on until a nonnull value is returned by one of the method calls or calls have been made on all four objects. The first nonnull value returned is used as the value of the variable, and since `getAttribute()` returns a Java `Object`, this value will be an `Object`. If all four objects are searched and no attribute with the specified name is found, then the EL variable's value is `null`. (JavaScript uses a similar technique to implement inheritance: if a property is not found in an object, and that object inherits from another object, then the second object will be searched, and so on with any object from which the second object inherits until the property is found or the inheritance list is exhausted.)

You can see from this discussion that every variable reference in EL—implicit or otherwise—resolves either to a Java `Object` or to `null`. Similarly, when the JSP `set` element is used to assign a value to an EL variable, the value is stored using a call to `setAttribute()` and therefore must be stored as an `Object`. JSP automatically handles conversions between simple data types and their corresponding wrapper classes, such as `Integer`.

Finally, EL also allows function calling, although the language itself defines no functions. Instead, all functions are defined as part of the tag library mechanism described later. Syntactically, an EL function call is simply a function name followed by parentheses which optionally contain a comma-separated list of arguments, such as

```
fn:toLowerCase(param['username'])
```

Note that the function name is considered a qualified name and may be prefixed, as illustrated in this example. The namespace prefix allows JSP to determine which tag library defines the function.

8.4.2   JSP Markup

JSP markup can appear anywhere within a document where markup is syntactically allowed by XML. There are three categories of JSP element types: scripting, directive, and action. We will deal with each of these categories in turn.

The `scriptlet` element of Figure 8.1 is one type of *scripting element*, that is, an element that can be used to directly insert Java statements or expressions into the servlet translated from a JSP document. As indicated earlier, for the most part we would like to have a clear separation between Java code and the JSP layer of a web application, so I won't cover scripting elements further here.

The `directive.page` element of Figure 8.1 is an example of a JSP *directive element*, that is, an element used to provide direction to the JSP translator itself. There are only two types of directive available for use in a JSP document: *page* and *include*. The page directive (`directive.page` element) has a variety of attributes that may be set. We have already seen that the `contentType` attribute is used to set the value of the Content-Type header field of the HTTP response. Note that this attribute can also be used to override the default UTF-8 encoding of the result document by using markup such as

```
<jsp:directive.page contentType="text/html;charset=ISO-8859-1" />
```

Some of the other page directive attributes are listed in Table 8.5. Multiple page directive attributes can be included in a single page directive using the standard XML syntax of separating attribute specifications with white space. Alternately, multiple `directive.page` elements may be included in a single document, although for all of the attributes shown, any attribute appearing in multiple elements must have the same value in every element. Also, if the `contentType` attribute appears, then it should appear at the beginning of the

TABLE 8.5 Some JSP Page Directive Attributes

Attribute	Values
session	true (the default) indicates that session implicit object should be created; false means that no session or sessionScope object is available to this document.
buffer	none indicates that data written to out should be passed immediately to the response object's PrintWriter rather than being buffered; a positive integer followed immediately by "kb" indicates that out represents a JspWriter with a buffer of at least the number of kilobytes specified. Default is 8kb.
errorPage	Relative URL of application resource to be requested if an uncaught exception occurs in this JSP document. Default is any error page defined in the deployment descriptor, or container-specific otherwise.
isErrorPage	true indicates that this document is intended to be used to process exceptions generated in other JSP documents or servlets and should have an exception JSP implicit object defined representing the exception thrown by the other page; false (the default) indicates that no exception object is available.

document (since it translates into a call to response.setContentType(), which in turn should be called before any response data is generated). A number of other page directive attributes are available; the complete list can be found in Section 1.10.1 of [SUN-JSP-2.0].

The include directive (element directive.include) imports text from another file into the JSP document at the point at which the directive appears. This happens during the translation of the document into a servlet. For example, a JSP document with the directive

```
<jsp:directive.include file="../common/disclaimer.jspf" />
```

imports the content of the file disclaimer.jspf located in the directory common, which is a sibling of the directory containing this JSP document. If the imported file is written using XML syntax, then it must be well-formed XML. In particular, this means that start and end tags within the file must appear in pairs, and there must be a single root element. A file that is intended for inclusion in a JSP document (or in another file to be included in a JSP document) is known as a *JSP segment*. A top-level JSP document plus all of the segments it includes—either directly, or indirectly through include directives in segments—is known as a *translation unit*, because the translator effectively assembles all of the text from these files into a single JSP document, which is then translated.

Finally, the third category of JSP element is the *action element*, which is an element that is translated into Java servlet code that performs some action. These elements provide so-called *standard actions*, that is, actions that are required by the JSP specification to be provided by any JSP-compliant container. The JSP tag library mechanism allows additional action elements to be used within a JSP document, which provide *custom actions*. The JSP Standard Tag Library (JSTL) is a primary source of custom actions, although other tag libraries can also be used.

Several custom actions from the JSTL core functional area are covered in the next subsection. Some standard actions, particularly those related to JavaBeans instances, are covered later.

TABLE 8.6 JSTL Functional Areas

Functional Area	Namespace Name Suffix
Core	core
XML Processing	xml
Functions	functions
Database	sql
Internationalization	fmt

8.4.3   JSTL Core Actions

The JSTL is divided into several separate functional areas, each with its own name-space. The prefix of every JSTL namespace name is `http://java.sun.com/jsp/jstl/`. Table 8.6 lists all of the JSTL functional areas along with the suffixes of the respective namespace names. So, for example, the namespace name for the functions area is `http://java.sun.com/jsp/jstl/functions`.

Most of this section is devoted to covering several of the key JSTL actions belonging to the core functional area. However, the other functional areas also provide many useful capabilities. The XML processing area, for example, allows a range of XML-related functions to be performed by a JSP document, including XSLT processing. The functions area provides a variety of standard string processing functions—such as `indexOf()` and `toLowerCase()`—that can be included in EL expressions. The functions area also supplies a `length()` function that can be used to obtain the number of elements in a `Map` or other collection. The database area allows a JSP document to directly access a database rather than accessing it indirectly through JavaBeans objects (described later), while the internationalization area allows strings representing data such as currency or dates to be formatted appropriately for a given locale. Complete details on the noncore JSTL functional areas are contained in [SUN-JSTL-1.1].

In the remainder of this subsection we will describe the basic features of the JSTL core functional area actions listed in Table 8.7. Before getting into the details of the JSTL elements implementing these actions, a few naming conventions should be noted. When the

TABLE 8.7 Some JSTL Core Actions

Action	Purpose
set	Assign a value to a scoped variable, creating the variable if necessary
remove	Destroy a scoped variable
out	Write data to out implicit object, escaping XML special characters
url	Create a URL with query string
if	Conditional (if-then) processing
choose	Conditional (if-then-elseif) processing
forEach	Iterate over a collection of items

attribute var is specified in a JSTL element, it represents the name of a scoped variable that is being assigned a value by the element. A *scoped variable* is a nonimplicit EL variable, that is, an attribute of one of the page, request, session, or application objects. The object containing the attribute is called the *scope* of the variable; hence the name "scoped variable." Syntactically, the value of var must be a valid EL variable name; object references, such as obj.prop, are not allowed. The scope attribute in JSTL elements is by convention used to specify the scope of a scoped variable, and must be one of the four values page, request, session, or application if specified. If not specified, page is the default scope unless otherwise indicated. Also note that a given variable name should only appear in at most one of the scopes.

The var and scope attributes are also special in that their values must be string literals. With only a few exceptions noted later, the specification for virtually every other JSTL attribute can include one or more EL expressions, as illustrated by specification of the value attribute in the earlier example markup

```
<c:set var="visits" scope="application" value="${visits+1}" />
```

We're now ready to discuss the JSTL core actions listed in Table 8.7 in some detail. I'll go through them in their order of appearance in the table.

First, the set action can be used to assign a value to one of three different types of variables: a scoped variable, an element of a java.util.Map, or a property of a JavaBeans object. The example markup just given illustrates the standard syntax used for assignment to a scoped variable. If the variable does not already exist, it is first created. Otherwise, the specified value is assigned to the specified scoped variable.

The syntax for applying set to a Map is slightly different. Recall that conceptually a Map consists of a collection of key-value pairs. The target attribute of set is used to specify the Map to be modified, property is the key, and value is the value to be assigned to the given key. For instance, recalling that the EL implicit object applicationScope is a Map, this means that the following markup syntactically represents assigning the value obtained by evaluating the EL expression visits+1 to the visits key of applicationScope:

```
<c:set target="${applicationScope}"
       property="visits"
       value="${visits+1}" />
```

However, the JWSDP 1.3 version of Tomcat does not allow assignments to EL implicit variables such as applicationScope, so although this markup would compile properly, it would cause a run-time exception if executed.

As with assignments to scoped variables, if set assigns a value to a key that does not exist in a Map (that allows assignments), then the key will automatically be added with the specified value. Using set with JavaBeans objects will be covered in a later section.

The remove action has only two attributes: var and scope. It removes the specified scoped variable from its scope object. More precisely, it removes the attribute with the name given by var from the JSP implicit object named by scope (and from the corresponding EL implicit object). If scope is not specified, the EL scope chain is searched in the same order it is searched when a variable is referenced: starting with page, and ending with application. The attribute is removed from the first scope object containing it (if any). Notice that although the reference to the object representing the scoped variable is removed, the object itself will continue to exist if there are still other references to it within the web application.

The out action has a required value attribute that specifies a value to be written to the out JSP implicit object. By default, the XML special characters <, >, and & along with the quote characters " and ' are escaped (that is, represented by XML references such as <). As noted in Chapter 6, it is important to escape any character data in a generated HTML document that is obtained from the HTTP request to a servlet. Otherwise, at a minimum the HTML document may not display properly in browsers; what's worse, your web application may be open to security risks such as cross-site scripting attacks.

If the value to be written by an out action is null, then by default the empty string (that is, nothing) will be written. This default behavior can be overridden either by specifying a value for the default attribute or by including character data as the content of the out element. In either case, if value is null, then the specified default value will be output. Leading and trailing white space will be trimmed from any character data content of an out element.

The only required attribute of the url action is value, which should be given a value that is a URL, either absolute or relative. If the URL begins with a /, then it is treated as relative to the web application context path. If session is enabled, cookies are disabled, and the URL is relative, then URL rewriting will be performed. Furthermore, the element may contain param elements, which will be used to define parameters (name-value pairs) that will be added to the query string of the URL. The values of these parameters will automatically be URL encoded. So, for example, if the context path of your web application is /myApp and URL rewriting is not performed, then the JSP markup

```
<c:url value="/somewhere">
  <c:param name="username" value="Kim Sam" />
</c:url>
```

will write the string /myApp/somewhere?username=Kim+Sam to the implicit object out. Alternatively, if var is specified for the url action, then instead of writing the string to out, it will be assigned to the specified scoped variable.

Actually, value is not a required attribute for either set or param. If value is not specified, then these actions will perform JSP processing on their content, but use the resulting String value as if it had been specified for value rather than writing the string to the out implicit object. Leading and trailing white space is also removed from the string. For example, the following markup assigns an XML-escaped version of the String value of scoped variable messy to the variable clean:

```
<c:set var="clean">
  <c:out value="${messy}" />
</c:set>
```

Let me emphasize that the action out in this case does not write anything to the implicit object out, even though the action's name might lead you to expect that it always writes output.

The action if can be used in either or both of two ways. In the earlier example

```
<c:if test="${empty visits}">
  <c:set var="visits" scope="application" value="0" />
</c:if>
```

the action is being used as a means of controlling whether or not its body content will be processed. If the condition specified as the value of test evaluates to true (after automatic conversion to a boolean), then the content of the if is processed and any contained template data is written to the object out. Otherwise, the content of the element is not processed.

By the way: You'll notice that the test in the example returns false if visits exists in any scope object, not just in application. If we had wanted to test specifically for the presence of visits in application alone, we could have used the markup

```
<c:if test="${empty applicationScope.visits}">
```

In if's second form, the action is used to evaluate a condition and assign the resulting boolean value to a scoped variable. This version includes the attribute var and optionally scope. If the if element is empty, then its only purpose is to assign a value to the scoped variable. If it is not empty, then (as before) its content is processed if the condition evaluates to true. For example, the following markup creates (or sets, if the variable already exists) a scoped variable named testResult in the default page scope and, if the condition is true, sends the contained character data to the out object:

```
<c:if test="${visits gt 3}" var="testResult">
  You're becoming a regular!
</c:if>
```

The action if is limited in that it does not provide an else clause. An else clause can often be simulated by writing a second if with a test that is the negation of the original if's test. Alternatively, the more general action choose can be used. The content of a choose element must consist entirely of when elements optionally followed by a single otherwise element. Each when element must specify a test attribute and must be nonempty. An otherwise element, like choose itself, has no attributes, but unlike choose has no constraints on its content. The entire choose element functions as an if-then-elseif: the content of the first when having a test that evaluates to true is processed, and if none of these tests evaluates to true, then the content of the otherwise (if present) is processed.

The primary action for iteration in JSTL is forEach. This action can be used in two different ways. First, it can be used as a standard for loop, with a scoped variable taking on successive values from a specified starting value through a specified ending value. When used this way, the content of the forEach element is processed once for each value assigned to the variable. The syntax in this case is illustrated by the following example:

```
<c:forEach var="i" begin="2" end="8" step="2">
  ${i}
</c:forEach>
```

which will write the digits 2, 4, 6, and 8 (plus white space) to the out object. If the variable is not needed within the loop, the var attribute does not need to be specified. Likewise, if step is not specified, then it defaults to 1. Unlike many programming languages, the step value must be positive. If the end value is less than the begin value, then the content of the forEach element will not be processed at all.

The second form of forEach action is used to iterate over a data structure, much like the JavaScript for-in statement. Iteration can be performed over a wide variety of Java collection-style data structures, including arrays and any class that implements one of the java.util interfaces Map, Collection, Iterator, or Enumeration. (However, note that iteration should normally be performed only once per JSP document over any object implementing Iterator or Enumeration, since there is no JSP mechanism for resetting the object following iteration through it.)

As an example of the syntax of this form of the forEach element, consider the following markup, which iterates through the header EL implicit object and outputs a list containing one item for each header field in the HTTP request being processed (we'll see how to format the header field output presently):

```
<ul>
  <c:forEach var="aHeader" items="${header}">
    <li><c:out value="${aHeader}" /></li>
  </c:forEach>
</ul>
```

As with the other form of forEach, the var attribute is optional. Also, the begin and end and, optionally, step attributes may be specified in this form. If these attributes are specified, the content of the forEach will be processed at most the number of times it would have been processed if items was not specified. So, for example, if there are eight items in the header implicit object, the content of

```
<ul>
  <c:forEach var="aHeader" items="${header}" begin="1" end="4">
    <li><c:out value="${aHeader}" /></li>
  </c:forEach>
</ul>
```

will be processed only four times, so only four header fields will be output. Notice that whenever items is specified, the scoped variable var takes on values from items, whether or not begin and end are also specified.

The exact output produced by the forEach actions in these examples is implementation dependent. The reason is that forEach assigns java.util.Map.Entry objects to var when the value of items is a Map object (and recall that the header EL implicit object is a Map). So the actual output depends on how this object is cast to a String for output. However, Map.Entry objects have two EL-accessible properties, key and value, representing the key and value for one element of the Map. So we could produce a formatted list of header names and values using markup such as

```
<ul>
  <c:forEach var="aHeader" items="${header}">
    <li>
      <strong><c:out value="${aHeader.key}:" /></strong>
      <c:out value="${aHeader.value}" />
    </li>
  </c:forEach>
</ul>
```

Finally, unlike scoped variables in the other actions we've seen, the scoped variable of forEach is always placed in page scope; the scope attribute cannot be specified on forEach. Furthermore, the variable will be removed from the page object when processing of the forEach action is complete. This is known as a *nested scoped variable*.

8.5   JavaBeans Classes and JSP

As you can see from what we have covered so far, JSP markup and the EL language make it relatively easy to perform simple, presentation-oriented programming tasks within a JSP document. For example, as illustrated by the last example of the previous section, it is straightforward to display all of the key-value pairs of a Map object as a list. However, for more sophisticated computations we may still want to use Java directly. In these situations, we would like to have a simple mechanism to call Java methods from within a JSP document. JSP provides such a mechanism through its support for JavaBeans classes.

In this section, we'll begin by learning how to write a class so that it can be recognized as a JavaBeans class by JSP. We'll then see how JSP and JavaBeans objects interact.

8.5.1   JavaBeans Technology Basics

If a Java class is written so as to conform with certain aspects of the JavaBeans Specification [SUN-JAVABEANS-1.01], then certain methods of this class can be called from a JSP document. For example, consider the following class my.TestBean:

```
package my;
public class TestBean {
    private String greeting = "Hello World!";
    public String getWelcome() {
        return greeting;
    }
}
```

If this class is compiled and placed in the WEB-INF/classes/my directory of a web application named BeanTester, then accessing a JSP document associated with this web application that contains the following markup within its html element will cause a heading containing Hello World! to be displayed:

```
<jsp:useBean id="testBean" class="my.TestBean" />

<head>
  <title>
    BeanTester.jspx
  </title>
</head>
<body>
  <h1>
    <c:out value="${testBean.welcome}" />
  </h1>
</body>
```

A Java class conforms with the JavaBeans specification for JSP purposes if it:

- Is public and not abstract.
- Has one or more public methods that follow one of the simple property design patterns of the JavaBeans specification (to be described).

Furthermore, if the class is going to be instantiated via the useBean standard action, as shown in this example, then the class must have a public no-argument constructor (which may be the constructor that is supplied automatically by Java when no constructor is explicitly declared). The class should also be contained in a named package, such as my, rather than in the default package (you'll need to import the class if it is not in a named package).

The class TestBean just defined conforms with these requirements. In particular, the getWelcome() method follows one of the two JavaBeans simple property design patterns, as explained in the next paragraph, and the class has a no-argument constructor (supplied automatically by Java, since no constructor is declared explicitly). Therefore, the useBean standard action shown successfully instantiates an object belonging to the TestBean class and associates the object with an EL variable name (testBean in this example). We'll refer to an object that is an instance of a class conforming with the JavaBeans specification requirements stated above as a *bean*. We'll cover useBean in detail in the next subsection.

If a method of a JavaBeans class is written in a way that conforms with one of the two JavaBeans *simple property design patterns*, then the method can be accessed by EL expressions as if it were a property of an object rather than a method. In the example, the getWelcome() method conforms with the *getter* simple property design pattern, which requires that the method be public, return a value (that is, it cannot be void), take no arguments, and have a name starting with get followed by an uppercase letter. Because getWelcome() conforms with the getter design pattern, it has the effect of associating a *bean property* named welcome with each instance of TestBean (the rules for obtaining the property name from the method name are described in the next paragraph). In our example, the getWelcome() method will be called automatically when a JSP document attempts to retrieve the value of the `welcome` bean property of a `TestBean` object. Thus, since the markup

```
<c:out value="${testBean.welcome}" />
```

attempts to retrieve the value of `welcome`, `getWelcome()` is called automatically and the value returned by this method is used as the value of the `welcome` bean property. In addition, EL supports JavaScript-like array access syntax for reading bean properties, so the following markup will produce the same output:

```
<c:set var="propName" value="welcome" />
<c:out value="${testBean[propName]}" />
```

The bean property name corresponding to a getter method is obtained from the getter method's name by first removing the `get` prefix. If the remaining name begins with more than one uppercase letter, then the remaining name is used without further modification as the property name. So if a getter method is named `getAValue()` then the corresponding bean property is named `AValue`. On the other hand, if the remaining name begins with a single uppercase letter then this letter is converted to lowercase to obtain the bean property name. This is why, in our example, `welcome` is used as the name of the bean property in the JSP document, while the getter method is named `getWelcome()`.

The JavaBeans specification allows an alternate getter design pattern in the case of a boolean-valued bean property, substituting `is` for `get`. For instance,

```
public boolean isEven() {}
```

defines a boolean bean property named `even`. If both `isEven()` and `getEven()` methods are defined within a single JavaBeans class, the `isEven()` method takes precedence and will be invoked by a reference to the `even` bean property.

The other JavaBeans simple property design pattern is for a *setter* method, which is called automatically when a JSP document attempts to assign a value to the corresponding property of a JavaBeans object. The design pattern in this case requires that the method name must begin with `set` followed an uppercase letter and the method itself must be public, must not return a value (that is, it must be `void`), and must take a single argument. The bean property name is derived by removing the `set` prefix from the method name and following the same case conversion rules used for getter methods. If there is a corresponding getter for the same bean property, the setter's argument must be of the same data type as that returned by the getter method. So the method

```
public void setWelcome(String welcome) {
    greeting = welcome;
}
```

is a setter for the `welcome` bean property.

In JSP, bean properties are assigned values much as `Map` objects are assigned values: using a `set` core action with the `target` and `property` attributes specified. One difference is that in the case of assigning to a bean property, the value of `property` is coerced to a `String` representing the bean property name (in the case of `Map` objects, the `property` value is used as is in a call to the `containsKey()` method of the `Map` interface). Suppose the setter just defined is added to the `TestBean` class, and the following markup is added to the end of the body of the `BeanTester.jspx` document:

```
<h1>
  <c:set target="${testBean}" property="welcome" value="Howdy!" />
  <c:out value="${testBean.welcome}" />
</h1>
```

Then visiting this document would produce a second heading with `Howdy!` following the `Hello World!` heading. Note that if this markup were included in the JSP document and the `welcome` property had only a getter method, then an error would occur, since a bean property will effectively be read-only if it has a getter but no setter method associated with it. Similarly, a bean property is write-only if it has an associated setter but no getter.

8.5.2   Instantiating Bean Objects

As illustrated in the preceding subsection, the `useBean` standard JSP action can be used to instantiate a bean object within a JSP document. Most of this subsection describes some of the common uses of this action. First, though, let me mention that bean objects are often instantiated by servlets rather than JSP documents and stored by the servlets as scoped variables, and in such cases `useBean` is not needed. For example, the code

```
import my.TestBean;
...
HttpSession session = request.getSession();
TestBean testBean = new TestBean();
session.setAttribute("testBean", testBean);
```

creates a `TestBean` object and assigns it to the session attribute (scoped variable) `testBean`. If a JSP document is subsequently executed in the same session, then the EL expression `sessionScope.testBean` provides a direct reference to the object without the need for a `useBean` element. That said, there are times when `useBean` can be handy, so we'll cover it next.

First, if an appropriate JavaBeans instance exists when `useBean` is invoked, then it will generally do nothing. For instance, the markup

```
<jsp:useBean id="testBean" class="my.TestBean"
scope="session" />
```

will create the variable `testBean` (with session rather than the default page scope) only if it does not already exist. If the `testBean` variable already exists in the specified scope and refers to an instance of `my.TestBean` or to an object that could be assigned to a `my.TestBean` variable, then this action does nothing. If the variable exists but has a value

that is not an object that can be assigned to a `my.TestBean` variable, an error will occur. So
if our previous example is modified to

```
<jsp:useBean id="testBean" class="my.TestBean" scope="session" />

<head>
  <title>
    BeanTester.jspx
  </title>
</head>
<body>
  <h1>
    <c:out value="${testBean.welcome}" />
  </h1>
  <h1>
    <c:set target="${testBean}" property="welcome" value="Howdy!" />
    <c:out value="${testBean.welcome}" />
  </h1>
</body>
```

then the first time that this page is visited by a user, the response will contain two headings,
the first with content `Hello World!` and the second with content `Howdy!`. However, if the
user visits the page again while his or her session is still active, then the page will show two
`Howdy!` headings. This is because the `TestBean` instance created by the first visit is stored
in the `session` object associated with the user, and therefore a new instance will not be
created for subsequent requests occurring while the session remains valid. Once the session
expires, a new `HttpSession` object will be created on the next visit. Since the new session
object will not have a `testBean` attribute, a new instance of `my.TestBean` will be created and
the user will once again see a `Hello World!` heading.

Note carefully that the `useBean` action does *not* search the EL scope chain for the
scoped variable, but only looks in the specified scope object (or in the `page` implicit object
if no scope is specified). This is an example of a more general principle: typically, standard
actions (those defined by JSP itself and not JSTL) do not employ the EL variable reference
scope chain but instead refer to one specific scope object, which is `page` by default.

If a `useBean` element has a nonempty body, then this body is processed if and only
if the `useBean` action actually creates a bean rather than doing nothing. This provides a
convenient means for initializing a newly created JavaBeans object from within the JSP
document that created it. For instance, if we replace the first line of the preceding example
with the markup

```
<jsp:useBean id="testBean" class="my.TestBean" scope="session">
  <c:set target="${testBean}" property="welcome" value="Greetings!" />
</jsp:useBean>
```

then the first heading of the first visit in a session will display `Greetings!`. All other
headings displayed while the session is active will display `Howdy!`.

Finally, there are some syntactic constraints that you should be aware of. First,
string literals (not EL expressions) must be used to provide the value of all of the `useBean`

attributes we have discussed. Also, the id value specified in a useBean action must be unique with respect to all other useBean actions within the same translation unit (JSP document and imported JSP segments).

8.5.3   Using JavaBeans Objects

While on the surface it might appear that the JavaBeans interface can only be used for simple data access and storage in Java objects, it can in fact be used for much more than that. For example, suppose that we would like to use JSP to write a web application MortgageCalc that performs mortgage calculations. Specifically, the user will supply an initial loan amount, repayment period (number of months), and interest rate, and the web application will respond with the corresponding monthly payment amount. We could implement this using a JavaBeans class such as the following (the actual calculation of the payment amount is not shown):

```
package mortgage;
public class Mortgage
{
    private double amount = -1.0;
    private int nMonths = -1;
    private double intRate = -1.0;

    public void setAmount(double amount) {
        this.amount = amount;
    }
    public void setMonths(int nMonths) {
        this.nMonths = nMonths;
    }
    public void setRate(double intRate) {
        this.intRate = intRate;
    }
    public double getPayment() {
        return ... ;
    }
}
```

The key here is that we have used a getter method not merely as a mechanism for retrieving the value of a variable stored in a bean, but as a means to perform a computation.

This JavaBeans class might be used by JSP markup such as the following, which takes parameter values obtained from an HTML form (or directly from a query string in the URL) as input and outputs the payment amount computed by the JavaBeans object as part of an HTML document:

```
<jsp:useBean id="calc" class="mortgage.Mortgage" />
<p>The monthly payment for the values you entered would be
  <c:set target="${calc}" property="amount"
        value="${param.mortgageAmount}" />
```

```
<c:set target="${calc}" property="months"
       value="${param.period}" />
<c:set target="${calc}" property="rate"
       value="${param.rate}" />

  ${calc.payment}
</p>
```

Notice that EL automatically converts the `String` values obtained from the `param` implicit object to the data types appropriate for the properties of the `Mortgage` JavaBeans object (`double` and `int`).

JavaBeans objects are also often used to provide indirect access to persistent data stored either on a file system or in a database. For example, the properties of a JavaBeans object might be set using `set` JSP actions, and a getter method might be implemented that stores this property data when called. From the JSP perspective, accessing this getter method looks like retrieving a bean property value. In this case, the value returned might be a code indicating whether the store operation was successful or not.

8.5.4   Getters/Setters on Nonbean Objects

Now that you're familiar with JavaBeans coding conventions, you may notice that many Java Servlet API classes have methods that follow the getter-setter syntax. For instance, the `HttpServletRequest` class has a `getPathInfo()` method that takes no arguments and returns a `String`. Generally speaking, such methods can be accessed from JSP documents using the bean property syntax, whether or not the class defining the methods has a no-argument constructor. So, for example, if the EL expression

```
${pageContext.request.pathInfo}
```

appears outside other markup, then it is equivalent to the Java scriptlet

```
<jsp:scriptlet>
  out.write(request.getPathInfo()}:
</jsp:scriptlet>
```

8.6   Tag Libraries and Files

While the JavaBeans interface is quite flexible, it can be cumbersome to use, particularly if there are many properties to be set. For instance, in the mortgage application in Section 8.5.3 we used three separate `set` actions and then needed to get the value of a bean property in order to retrieve the computed value. In addition to being cumbersome to write, such markup is also hard to maintain and likely to lead to coding errors: it would be easy to forget to include one of the `set` actions, or to inadvertently have two `set` actions with the same property name (as a result of cut-and-paste markup).

For many reasons, then, it would be preferable to write markup such as the following in a JSP document:

```
<p>The monthly payment for the values you entered would be
  <myTag:mortgage amount="${param.mortgageAmount}"
                  period="${param.period}"
                  rate="${param.rate}" />
</p>
```

Now we have replaced the three separate actions plus an EL variable reference from the earlier markup with a single action. Furthermore, notice that this markup does not directly reference the `Mortgage` JavaBeans object, so there is no need to include a `useBean` action in this JSP document. What's more, as we will learn, the three attributes in the `mortgage` element can be marked as required: a translation-time error will be generated if one of the attributes is not present. So this approach can also help to avoid potential coding problems with missing values.

In fact, we can do all of this if the markup of Figure 8.7 is stored in the file `WEB-INF/tags/mortgage.tagx` and the namespace declaration

```
xmlns:myTag="urn:jsptagdir:/WEB-INF/tags"
```

is included in the JSP document containing the `mortgage` element. A file such as the one in Figure 8.7 is known as a JSP *tag file*. A tag file, in turn, is one of several JSP mechanisms for defining a custom action. A collection of definitions of custom actions is known as a JSP *tag library*. In this example, the `mortgage.tagx` file along with any other tag files in

```
<jsp:root version="2.0"
  xmlns:jsp="http://java.sun.com/JSP/Page"
  xmlns:c="http://java.sun.com/jsp/jstl/core">

<jsp:directive.attribute name="amount" required="true" />
<jsp:directive.attribute name="period" required="true" />
<jsp:directive.attribute name="rate" required="true" />

  <jsp:useBean id="calc" class="mortgage.Mortgage" scope="application" />

    <c:set target="${calc}" property="amount"
           value="${amount}" />
    <c:set target="${calc}" property="months"
           value="${period}" />
    <c:set target="${calc}" property="rate"
           value="${rate}" />

    ${calc.payment}

</jsp:root>
```

FIGURE 8.7 Tag file defining a custom action with three required attributes.

the /WEB-INF/tags directory would form a tag library for our application, which we'll call MortgageCalcUsingTag.

When a custom action is defined using a tag file, the custom action is conceptually a method that is "called" by including in a JSP document an element of the type defined by the tag file (mortgage in this example). I will call such an element in the JSP document a *referencing element*. The attribute values of the referencing element act as the arguments of the "method call" made by the element. As shown here, the JSP *attribute directive* is used within a tag file to define the attributes that may be specified on a referencing element. The attribute directive may only be used in tag files, not in JSP documents. The required attribute of this directive indicates whether or not the attribute given by name must be specified in the referencing element; the default value of required is false.

When an element referencing a custom action is encountered in a JSP document, a new object is created to hold tag file variables having page scope. Thus, the page-scoped variables in the JSP document are completely separated from the page-scoped variables of any tag file called by the document, and each tag file's page-scoped variables are also separated from every other tag file's variables. Each tag file's page scope object is initialized by creating a variable for each attribute specified in the referencing element and assigning to each variable its corresponding attribute value. If an attribute is not specified in the referencing element, then no page-scoped variable is created for it. Other than specified attributes, the tag file's page-scope object has no other variables initially. For most other implicit objects—and in particular for the request, session, and application objects that form the rest of the EL scope chain—the tag file and JSP document refer to the same objects. This means, for example, that the application-scope object referred to by the useBean action in the example tag file is the same object referred to from anywhere else within the web application.

Once the tag file's page-scope object has been initialized, the markup contained in the tag file is processed with the page implicit variable (and derived pageScope EL implicit variable) defined to refer to this new object rather than to the page object of the JSP document itself. Thus, the EL variable references in the value attributes of the set actions of Figure 8.7 will resolve to the corresponding attribute values passed to the tag file by the referencing element.

An XML-formatted tag file such as the one in Figure 8.7 must be well formed, which implies that the file must have a single root element. As a convenience, JSP supplies a root element that can be used as the root element of documents—such as our tag file—that are to be processed by a JSP translator but for which there is not a natural root element. The root element can be used in JSP documents as well, although it is optional if the document already has a single root element (such as html). If root is used in a document, its version attribute is required and indicates the version of JSP followed when writing the document.

While there are other ways to make a tag file accessible to a JSP document, placing the file in the WEB-INF/tags subdirectory is the simplest. Tag files placed in any other directory will by default be treated as documents rather than as tag files. The extension of an XML-formatted tag file must be tagx. The portion of the file name preceding the extension is used as the custom tag name within a referencing JSP document; since we used the tag name mortgage in our example, the file needed to be named mortgage.tagx. The namespace name used for the tag library must be a URN consisting of the string urn:jsptagdir: followed by a path—relative to the context base directory—to the subdirectory containing the tag file(s). It should be clear from this why we used the namespace name that we did in this example.

While what we have learned about custom tags is useful, much more sophisticated tags can be developed. For example, custom tags can perform iterative or conditional processing over their content (much like the forEach and choose tags of the JSTL core) and can create variables (much like set), among other capabilities. Refer to Chapters 7 and 8 of the JSP Specification [SUN-JSP-2.0] for complete details.

8.7 Support for the Model-View-Controller Paradigm

While for the most part this book is concerned with covering key concepts of web technologies rather than with software development issues, certain JSP features are best understood in the context of how they might typically be used when building a web application. In particular, many web applications are developed within a conceptual framework known as the model-view-controller (MVC) paradigm, and several JSP facilities are often used when developing within this framework. This section provides an overview of MVC and of related JSP features. It will also illustrate how the various JSP technologies we've discussed can work together.

8.7.1 MVC Basics

Most real-world web applications are of course much larger than the examples in this chapter and may contain a large number of components (servlets and JSP documents) as well as numerous support files (such as JavaBeans classes). While there are many possible ways of organizing the components and support files for such an application, one approach, called the *model-view-controller paradigm*, is widely used in one form or another in many web applications. In fact, the MVC paradigm was elucidated long before the Web existed, and can be applied in any system that has both data processing and data presentation requirements. But our focus will be on its use with web applications.

A web application following the MVC organizational paradigm will typically have a single *controller* that receives all incoming HTTP requests. Because the controller provides a single point of entry to the application, application-wide tasks such as initialization, logging, and controlling access to the application are often performed by the controller. The controller may also interact with *model* components of the application. These are software components that represent the persistent data of the application and server-side processing performed on this data. Finally, when the controller and model software have performed all necessary preprocessing of a request, the controller selects an appropriate *view* (presentation) component and forwards the HTTP request to that component. The view component will generally obtain data from the request and/or model components and then generate an HTTP response that presents a formatted view of this data.

In a web application written using JSP, the controller portion is often implemented as one or more Java servlets. The model components will typically consist of JavaBeans classes and/or a database (or other storage mechanism). Each view component is normally a JSP document. Each such JSP document might also access JavaBeans objects and tag libraries to obtain model data for inclusion in the response it generates. Furthermore, portions of the response might be generated by calling on other servlets or JSP documents within the web application.

Now that we have an overview of the MVC paradigm, we will consider some features of JSP and Java Servlets that support MVC-style web applications. We'll begin by considering servlet features that support controller functionality, and then turn to MVC-related JSP features.

8.7.2   Servlet Request Dispatching

In an MVC-structured web application, it is common for a single Java servlet to receive every incoming HTTP request intended for the application. This servlet may initiate some processing of the request data, typically via interactions with JavaBeans objects and/or a database. When this data processing is completed, the controller servlet will select an appropriate JSP view component and *forward* the HTTP request on to that component. The selected JSP document then produces an HTTP response based on information in the forwarded HTTP request as well as information obtained from other model data sources, such as JavaBeans objects.

A Java servlet forwards an HTTP request by calling the forward() method on a javax.servlet.RequestDispatcher object obtained from the application container. Servlet code such as the following can be used to obtain a RequestDispatcher:

```
RequestDispatcher dispatcher =
  getServletContext().getRequestDispatcher(contextRelativeURL);
```

where contextRelativeURL is a URL that must begin with a / and that is interpreted as a URL relative to the context path. For example, for the earlier HelloCounter example web application, /HelloCounter.jspx would be an appropriate argument to use in order to forward to the HelloCounter.jspx document.

Alternatively, for any servlet or JSP document that is given a name in a servlet element of the web application's deployment descriptor, a RequestDispatcher for this component can be obtained by passing the servlet name as an argument to the getNamedDispatcher() method of the application's ServletContext object. Suppose, for example, that the following markup is part of a web application's deployment descriptor:

```
<servlet>
  <servlet-name>visit_count</servlet-name>
  <jsp-file>/HelloCounter.jspx</jsp-file>
</servlet>
```

Then the following Java code could also be used to obtain a RequestDispatcher object for the HelloCounter.jspx component:

```
RequestDispatcher dispatcher =
  getServletContext().getNamedDispatcher("visit_count");
```

Whether calling getRequestDispatcher() or getNamedDispatcher(), if the JSP container cannot find the requested resource, then the method call returns null.

Once a RequestDispatcher has been obtained, the servlet can forward the HTTP request on to the associated application component by calling the RequestDispatcher object's forward() method with two arguments: the HttpServletRequest and HttpServletResponse objects passed to the servlet. The component to which the request is forwarded behaves as if it received the HTTP request directly rather than via the servlet. In fact, the HttpServletRequest object is automatically modified so that methods such as getRequestURL() will return values as if the forwarded-to component had been requested directly. Furthermore, if the servlet has written any data to the HttpServletResponse object's PrintWriter buffer, this data will be discarded so that the forwarded-to component starts with an empty buffer. (A fine point is that if the PrintWriter buffer was not only written to by the servlet but also flushed, then calling forward() generates an error.)

To illustrate, suppose that we would like to modify the earlier visit-counting web application so that a user with an active session will be asked to visit again later while other users will have their requests forwarded to the JSP document of Figure 8.1. Assuming that visit_later is the name (as defined in the application deployment descriptor) of a component that generates the "please visit again later" HTML document, the Java servlet of Figure 8.8 accomplishes this. Notice that this servlet does not create any output itself, and therefore does not access the response object's PrintWriter at all.

The controller can pass data to a view component in several ways. First, it can store data in a persistent store that is accessible to the component, such as in a database or file. Second, it can call setAttribute() to assign values to attributes of the HttpServletRequest, HttpSession, or ServletContext objects, that is, to the objects corresponding to the EL implicit objects requestScope, sessionScope, and applicationScope, respectively. The forwarded-to JSP document can then access these attribute values as described earlier. The attribute values stored may be simple values (wrapped in appropriate classes, such as Integer); arrays; other JSP-accessible data structures such as Map objects; or JavaBeans objects.

Yet another approach is for the controller to add parameters to the HttpServletRequest object passed via forward() to the component, just as if these parameters were received as part of the HTTP request query string. However, adding a parameter to the forwarded HttpServletRequest object is not as simple as calling a method, since the Servlet API provides no method on HttpServletRequest for this purpose. Instead, one technique for adding a parameter is to wrap the original HttpServletRequest object within another object (a subclass of HttpServletRequestWrapper) that acts almost like the original object except when getParameter() (or a related method, such as getParameterNames()) is called. When getParameter() is called on the new object, it will return values for any parameters to be added as well as values for the original parameters. This new object rather than the original HttpServletRequest will then be passed as the first argument to forward().

To illustrate this procedure, consider the class of Figure 8.9. This class in effect adds a parameter special to an HttpServletRequest object. If an instance

```
import java.io.*;
import javax.servlet.*;
import javax.servlet.http.*;

/**
 * Servlet acting as MVC controller in a very simple application.
 */
public class Controller extends HttpServlet
{
    /**
     * If session is new then increment and display the application
     * visit counter.  Otherwise (this is the continuation of an
     * active session), display a message.
     */
    public void doGet (HttpServletRequest request,
                       HttpServletResponse response)
        throws ServletException, IOException
    {
        HttpSession session = request.getSession();
        if (session.isNew()) {
            RequestDispatcher visitDispatch =
                getServletContext().getNamedDispatcher("visit_count");
            visitDispatch.forward(request, response);
        }
        else {
            RequestDispatcher laterDispatch =
                getServletContext().getNamedDispatcher("visit_later");
            laterDispatch.forward(request, response);
        }
    }
}
```

FIGURE 8.8 Example MVC controller servlet.

myWrappedRequest of this class is created,

```
MyWrapper myWrappedRequest = new MyWrapper(request);
```

then evaluating myWrappedRequest.getParameter("special") will return the string You Win!, regardless of whether or not a parameter named special appears in the original HttpServletRequest object. In essence, we have added a parameter to the HttpServletRequest object (or we have overridden the value of the parameter if it was already present).

Notice that if getParameterNames() is called on an instance of MyWrapper, then special will not be one of the parameter names returned (unless it happens to be the name of a parameter in the original HttpServletRequest object). It is therefore good practice to also override methods related to getParameter(), such as getParameterNames() and getParameterValues(), so that their behavior is consistent with that of getParameter().

```
public class MyWrapper extends HttpServletRequestWrapper {

  /** Construct a ''wrapper'' of the given request that
   *  behaves exactly like the original request except
   *  for any methods this class overrides.
   */
  public MyWrapper(HttpServletRequest request) {
    super(request);
  }

  /** Override the original request's getParameter()
   *  method to simulate the addition of a parameter named
   *  "special".
   */
  public String getParameter(String paramName) {
    String paramValue = null;
    if (paramName.equals("special")) {
      paramValue = "You Win!";
    } else {
      paramValue = super.getParameter(paramName);
    }
    return paramValue;
  }


  /* Should also override getParameterNames() and
   * getParameterValues(); see text. */
}
```

FIGURE 8.9 Class used to simulate the addition of a parameter special to an HttpServletRequest object.

The javax.servlet.http package also supplies a HttpServletResponse Wrapper class, so that an HttpServletResponse may also be wrapped in order to modify its behavior.

Finally, you may be wondering how the controller determines where to forward a request in a large application. In the examples just given, the controller used tests on parameter values or the session object to make such decisions. Another common approach is to include information in the path portion of URLs. Recall that the HttpServletRequest object provides a getPathInfo() method that returns the trailing portion of the request URL path when a servlet-mapping path-prefix pattern matches the URL. For example, if the pattern /controller/* matches a URL ending in /controller/help?prod=324324, then getPathInfo() will return the string /help. Thus, a web application's components can provide direction to the controller by adding path information to the URLs they generate. In essence, the controller acts as an object supplying a number of methods that can be invoked by specifying the name of the method as path information. The controller might accomplish this by implementing a switch operation that chooses the correct case based on the path information provided, perhaps consulting session, parameter, and other information as well.

Now that we have seen how Java servlets can pass control to other components of a system, we turn to some MVC-related facilities within JSP.

8.7.3   JSP Actions Supporting MVC

Sometimes, one JSP view component may wish to call on other view components in order to generate portions of its output. For example, a JSP document might be responsible for generating a Web page that has a navigation bar along with the primary page content. We might like to design the original JSP document to call on two other JSP documents, one to generate HTML representing the navigation bar and the other to generate the primary content of the page. This design makes it easy to incorporate the navigation bar or content elements in other view components.

The JSP standard action `include` (not to be confused with the `include` directive covered earlier) causes the container to execute a component of a web application and to append the body of the response produced by the component to the `out` implicit object of the JSP document containing the `include` action. Other output actions performed by the component, such as setting header field values, will be ignored. The primary attribute of `include` is `page`, which specifies a URL (more on this in the next paragraph) of the component to be executed. Thus, if `/navbar.jspx` and `/mainContent.jspx` are the URLs for components generating a navigation bar and primary page content, respectively, then the following JSP markup will generate an HTML table containing both of these elements:

```
<table style="width:100%" border="0">
  <tbody>
    <tr>
      <td style="width:20%"
          ><jsp:include page="/navbar.jspx" /></td>
      <td style="width:80%"
          ><jsp:include page="/mainContent.jspx" /></td>
    </tr>
  </tbody>
</table>
```

Note that the template data for the `navbar.jspx` and `mainContent.jspx` documents will not begin with the `html` element, since these documents generate a portion of an HTML document rather than the entire document. For example, the `navbar.jspx` document might begin with a `table` element. Alternatively, the JSP `root` element described earlier might be used as the root of such a document.

The URL for the `page` attribute of an `include` action must be a relative URL, but it does not need to begin with a `/`. If it does, it will be interpreted as relative to the web application's context path, as with other URLs we have seen in this chapter. If it does not begin with a `/`, then it will be considered relative to the JSP document containing the `include`.

If desired, additional parameters can be added to the `request` object as if they were part of the original query string. These parameters are added only for the duration of the processing of the component specified by the `include` action and are effectively removed from the `request` when this processing completes. The syntax for defining these parameters is to include JSP `param` elements as content in the `include` element. Like the JSTL core `param` element discussed in the context of the `url` core action, a JSP `param` element has two attributes, name and value. These parameters represent the name and value, respectively, of the added parameter. So to pass a parameter named currentPage with value home to the navbar.jspx component, say, we could use the markup

```
<jsp:include page="/navbar.jspx">
  <jsp:param name="currentPage" value="home" />
</jsp:include>
```

This has essentially the same effect as the servlet HttpServletRequestWrapper mechanism described earlier: it creates a wrapped HTTP request that will be passed to the specified component and that conceptually adds a parameter to that request.

For completeness, I'll mention that while a controller normally performs forwarding and view components normally perform inclusion, JSP and the servlet API support other possibilities. In particular, RequestDispatcher objects have an include() method that takes two arguments, a request and a response, and performs the type of inclusion processing we have just described. Similarly, JSP supplies a standard action forward that is analogous to the RequestDispatcher object's forward() method described in the previous subsection. Like the include action, forward has a page attribute, and its content can optionally consist of param elements. In short, the JSP markup

```
<jsp:forward page="/somewhere.jspx" />
```

is essentially translated into the servlet code

```
RequestDispatcher dispatcher =
  getServletContext().getRequestDispatcher("/somewhere.jspx");
if (dispatcher != null) {
  dispatcher.forward(request, response);
} else {
  // throw run-time exception
}
```

8.8 Case Study

In this section, we'll transform the blogging application from a loose collection of various resource (servlets, HTML documents, etc.) to an integrated web application that follows the MVC paradigm. While we'll add no new features to the application, this implementation has many advantages over the approach based solely on servlets.

Recall that the servlet-based application consisted of three servlets, Login, AddOrPreview, and ViewBlog. The first two of these handled POST HTTP requests generated by the log-in and add-entry forms, respectively, while the third handled all GET requests. A support class, DisplayBlog, generated the actual HTML of the view-blog page. Also, if the blog entry sent to AddOrPreview contained a parse error, AddOrPreview would generate HTML for an error page (Figure 7.35).

We will restructure this somewhat in order to follow the MVC approach. First, we'll combine the three earlier servlets into a single controller servlet named MyOwnBlog. We will replace the DisplayBlog class with a JSP document named DisplayBlog.jspx.

And we will move the error-page HTML generation from the controller servlet to another JSP document, SAXException.jspx.

Another change will be that we will collect all of the files for the application under a single directory MyOwnBlog that will ultimately be deployed to the Tomcat server as a web application (so the context path for our application will be /MyOwnBlog). All of the static files for the application (HTML documents, JavaScript, etc.) will be placed in the MyOwnBlog directory itself, as will the two JSP documents. The controller class file as well as other support classes (TextCooker, Entry, DataStore, and WebTechUtil) will be placed in the MyOwnBlog/WEB-INF/classes directory. There will also be a web.xml deployment descriptor file in MyOwnBlog/WEB-INF.

Let's begin with the web.xml file, shown in Figure 8.10. Notice that names are defined for the DisplayBlog and SAXException JSP documents, even though there are no corresponding servlet-mapping elements. They are given names so that they can be referenced by name within the controller servlet. By using these names rather than actual file names, we can later change the file name for a JSP document without needing to change and recompile the controller code; we would only need to change the appropriate jsp-file element in web.xml. Accessing components via an intermediate name rather than directly is an example of *decoupling*, a concept that occurs frequently in modern software engineering practice. In essence, we would like components to know as little as possible about each other, thereby minimizing the impact of changes to one component on the other.

```
<web-app
  xmlns="http://java.sun.com/xml/ns/j2ee"
  xmlns:xsi="http://www.w3.org/2001/XMLSchema-instance"
  xsi:schemaLocation="http://java.sun.com/xml/ns/j2ee/web-app_2_4.xsd"
  version="2.4">
  <display-name>My Own Blog!</display-name>
  <description>
    Personal blogging tool.
  </description>
  <servlet>
    <servlet-name>DisplayBlog</servlet-name>
    <jsp-file>/DisplayBlog.jspx</jsp-file>
  </servlet>
  <servlet>
    <servlet-name>SAXException</servlet-name>
    <jsp-file>/SAXException.jspx</jsp-file>
  </servlet>
  <servlet>
    <servlet-name>controller</servlet-name>
    <servlet-class>MyOwnBlog</servlet-class>
  </servlet>
  <servlet-mapping>
    <servlet-name>controller</servlet-name>
    <url-pattern>/do/*</url-pattern>
  </servlet-mapping>
</web-app>
```

FIGURE 8.10 The deployment descriptor for the blogging application.

One other thing to notice about web.xml is that we are mapping all URLs having a postcontext path beginning with /do to the controller servlet MyOwnBlog. We will use path information following /do to determine whether a POST request directed to the controller is from the log-in or the add-entry form. For example, the start tag of the add-entry form is

```
<form id="addForm" action="do/AddOrPreview"
    method="post">
```

When this form is submitted, the relative URL do/AddOrPreview will be converted to an absolute URL and sent as part of the HTTP request to the controller servlet. When the servlet calls getPathInfo() on the HttpServletRequest object, the string /AddOrPreview will be returned. The log-in form contained in login.html, on the other hand, has an action value of do/Login, which will cause getPathInfo() to return /Login.

The controller servlet MyOwnBlog is primarily a combination of the init(), doGet(), and doPost() methods from the three earlier servlets. The two previous doPost() methods (one from AddOrPreview and one from Login) are merged into a single method that uses getPathInfo() to choose the appropriate code to execute.

A major difference between the controller servlet and the earlier servlets, of course, is that the controller will use JSP to generate the HTML responses. Consider, for example, the doGet() methods of ViewBlog and MyOwnBlog. The final lines of code in ViewBlog retrieved vectors of information from the data store and passed these as arguments to a Java method that then outputs the information as HTML:

```
Vector entries = DataStore.getEntries(month, year);
Vector months = DataStore.getAllMonths();
DisplayBlog.display(servletOut, entries, months);
```

In contrast, the MyOwnBlog controller servlet will add these vectors as attributes of the HttpServletRequest object and then forward the request to the DisplayBlog JSP document:

```
Vector entries = DataStore.getEntries(month, year);
request.setAttribute("entries", entries);
Vector months = DataStore.getAllMonths();
request.setAttribute("months", months);
RequestDispatcher viewBlog =
    getServletContext().getNamedDispatcher("DisplayBlog");
viewBlog.forward(request, response);
```

Similar changes are made in the doPost() method of the controller servlet.

Let's next consider the DisplayBlog JSP document. The html start tag declares a number of namespaces, including some that we haven't used before now:

```
<html
  xmlns="http://www.w3.org/1999/xhtml"
  xmlns:jsp="http://java.sun.com/JSP/Page"
```

```
xmlns:c="http://java.sun.com/jsp/jstl/core"
xmlns:fn="http://java.sun.com/jsp/jstl/functions"
xmlns:fmt="http://java.sun.com/jsp/jstl/fmt">
```

We will use a `toUpperCase()` function defined by the JSTL Functions area (associated with namespace `fn`) and a date/time formatting action `formatDate` from the Internationalization area (associated with namespace `fmt`), as described later in this section.

The next elements of `DisplayBlog.jspx` are the standard `jsp:directive.page` and `jsp:output` elements followed by HTML markup for several static components of the view-blog page: the `head` element and its content, the start tag for the `body`, and the banner image. Even this relatively simple markup had to be written carefully in order for JSP to handle it properly. First, if we include the markup

```
<script type='text/javascript' src='/MyOwnBlog/viewblog.js'>
</script>
```

in the file, the HTML document produced by `DisplayBlog.jspx` will contain an empty-element version of this markup:

```
<script type='text/javascript' src='/MyOwnBlog/viewblog.js' />
```

As discussed in Section 7.9.3, while to an XML parser the empty-element tag is functionally equivalent to a start and end tag with no content, many browsers (and in particular, IE6) will not properly process the empty-element form. As in Section 7.9.3, we can avoid this problem by forcing a space into the content of the `script` element:

```
<script type='text/javascript' src='/MyOwnBlog/viewblog.js'>
  <c:out value=" " />
</script>
```

A second small problem occurred with the markup for the `img` element used in our earlier versions of the view-blog page:

```
<img src='/MyOwnBlog/banner.gif' width='438' height='120'
     alt='"My Own Blog!" Banner' />
```

While this `img` element's `alt` attribute contains a legal XML value, JWSDP 1.3 had trouble translating `DisplayBlog.jspx` when this markup was included. I worked around this by removing the double quotes.

Next in `DisplayBlog.jspx` comes the markup that generates the HTML representation of the blog entries, which is shown in Figure 8.11. This markup begins with a `forEach` that iterates over the items in the object stored in the `entries` attribute of the `request` object. As we saw earlier, the controller servlet assigns to this attribute a `java.util.Vector` object before `DisplayBlog` begins execution. `Vector`, in turn, implements the `java.util.Collection` interface, so it can be used as the value of `items`.

```
<c:forEach var="entry" items="${requestScope.entries}">
  <div class='entry'>
    <fmt:formatDate var="dateTime" scope="page"
        value="${entry.createDateTime.time}"
        pattern="MMMMM d, yyyy, h:mm a z" />
    <div class='datetime'
      >${fn:toUpperCase(pageScope.dateTime)}</div>
    <div class='entrytitle'>${entry.title}</div>
    <div class='entrybody'>
      ${entry.text}
    </div>
  </div>
  <hr />
</c:forEach>
</div>
```

FIGURE 8.11 JSP markup for generating HTML representing blog entries.

The EL scoped variable entry will be assigned successive elements from the entries vector as the forEach action iterates through the vector. Recall (Section 6.12) that entries is a vector of Entry elements, and that Entry provides methods getCreateDateTime(), getTitle(), and getText() for retrieving a Calendar object representing the date and time at which the entry was created, the title of the entry, and its text, respectively. Since these methods all conform with the JavaBeans getter design pattern, the markup within the forEach uses EL expressions such as entry.title to (in effect) call these methods. There is one small point: our original Entry class was not declared to be public, while a class must be public in order to be used as a bean object. Declaring the class to public is the only change made to Entry.

The markup uses the JSTL fmt:formatDate action to format the entry's creation date and time into a string that is assigned to the dateTime EL scoped variable. Calendar supplies a getTime() method that returns a java.util.Date object, which is appropriate to use as the value of fmt:formatDate's value attribute. Given this, it should be clear that the EL expression entry.createDateTime.time evaluates to a Date value representing the creation date and time. The value of the pattern attribute conforms with the pattern conventions specified by the Java API for java.text.SimpleDateFormat, and in this case specifies that the month name should be spelled out (not abbreviated or represented as a number), that the date should not have a leading zero, and many similar properties. You might recall that the earlier DisplayBlog Java class (Section 6.12) used SimpleDateFormat to perform a similar task. So the pattern shown actually came directly from the earlier Java date-formatting code.

The markup for generating the view-blog page's navigation hyperlinks comes next. This markup also uses forEach, this time to iterate through the vector of Calendar items stored in the months attribute of the request object by the controller servlet before DisplayBlog began execution. As shown in Figure 8.12, the body of the forEach first uses fmt:formatDate actions to extract strings representing the month, year, and month number from a given Calendar object. It then generates a URL for the controller servlet

```
<ul>
 <c:forEach var="month" items="${requestScope.months}">
  <fmt:formatDate var="monthName" scope="page"
    value="${month.time}"
    pattern="MMMMM" />
  <fmt:formatDate var="monthNum" scope="page"
    value="${month.time}"
    pattern="M" />
  <fmt:formatDate var="yearNum" scope="page"
    value="${month.time}"
    pattern="yyyy" />
  <c:url var="doWithParams" value="/do">
    <c:param name="month" value="${monthNum}" />
    <c:param name="year" value="${yearNum}" />
  </c:url>
  <li><a href='${fn:escapeXml(doWithParams)}'
    >${monthName} ${yearNum}</a></li>
 </c:forEach>
</ul>
```

FIGURE 8.12 JSP markup for generating HTML representing navigation links.

and includes the month and year values as parameters. In particular, the generated URL will look something like this:

```
/MyOwnBlog/do?month=8&year=2005
```

This is because the c:url action adds the context path (/MyOwnBlog for our web application) to the beginning of the URL specified in value if that URL begins with a / character.

Before continuing to examine the rest of the markup in Figure 8.12, it will be valuable to pause for a moment and consider carefully the use of URLs within JSP documents. Since the file DisplayBlog.jspx is contained within the MyOwnBlog directory, couldn't we use markup such as

```
<a href="do">...</a>
```

to generate a hyperlink to the controller servlet? Perhaps, but it won't do exactly what we expect. Recall that when the blogger clicks on the "Add Entry" button of the add-entry form, the browser sends the form data in a request to a URL of the form http://localhost:8080/MyOwnBlog/do/AddOrPreview. This request is first processed by the controller servlet and then forwarded to DisplayBlog. Since forwarding (unlike redirection) is performed entirely on the server side, when the browser receives the HTML document generated by DisplayBlog, it will by default associate it with the base address http://localhost:8080/MyOwnBlog/do/AddOrPreview. Thus, the relative URL do in this document would correspond to the absolute URL http://localhost:8080/MyOwnBlog/do/do, which is not what we want. The URL generated by c:url, on the other hand, corresponds to the absolute URL http://localhost:8080/MyOwnBlog/do, as desired.

Hopefully it is now clear that the c:url feature of prefixing its argument URL with the context path is useful.

Now let's return to the DisplayBlog markup. Before being declared as the value of the href attribute on an anchor element, the URL generated by c:url is escaped by a call to the JSTL-supplied function escapeXml(), which escapes all five XML special characters (including both types of quote). We need to escape the URL because it contains an ampersand, which is not legal within an attribute value.

One last thing to notice is that, while our earlier HTML version of this markup looked like

```
<li><a href="index.html?month=8&amp;year=2005"
    >August 2005</a></li>
```

the corresponding markup in DisplayBlog.jspx escapes the leading ampersand in the   reference. The reason, of course, is that the markup in this file is going to first be read by an XML application and later output as HTML. Thus, in order to prevent the XML parser from interpreting   as an entity reference, we must escape the leading ampersand.

Finally, the content of the body of SAXException.jspx is shown in Figure 8.13. You should have little trouble seeing how this markup parallels the corresponding Java code at the end of Section 7.11. Notice especially that the JSP markup automatically handles casting the exceptions to strings and escaping XML special characters in these strings.

We now have all of the files needed for the web application. We can deploy the application to Tomcat by copying the MyOwnBlog folder and its contents to the webapps subdirectory of the JWSDP 1.3 installation directory and deploying the application through the JWSDP Web Application Manager. We can then begin to use the application by logging in at http://localhost:8080/MyOwnBlog/login.html or by visiting http://localhost:8080/myOwnBlog/do to view previous blog entries.

```
<h1>Error Parsing Blog Text</h1>
<p>
  An error occurred at line ${SAXException.lineNumber},
  column ${SAXException.columnNumber}:
  <c:choose>
    <c:when test="${!(empty SAXException.exception)}">
      <c:out value="${SAXException.exception}" />
    </c:when>
    <c:otherwise>
      <c:out value="${SAXException}" />
    </c:otherwise>
  </c:choose>
</p>
```

FIGURE 8.13 JSP markup for generating HTML displaying a SAX parse exception.

8.9   Related Technologies

We've now covered in some detail how JSP can be used to support the separation of data processing software from presentation software within a web application. In fact, JSP is by no means the only technology designed for this task. Here I will mention a few of these related technologies and briefly compare them with JSP documents.

If you understand the concepts presented in this chapter, adapting your skills to use any of these related technologies should not be especially difficult. In fact, the technologies tend to be similar enough that functionality is often not the deciding factor when choosing to use one of these technologies over the others for developing a web application. For example, I chose to present JSP document technology in this chapter not because I think that it is necessarily the best functionally, but because I think that it is particularly good for learning purposes within the context of this textbook: it is freely available, easy to run under all major operating systems, XML-based, and related to Java servlets (and therefore builds on and reinforces material in the previous two chapters). Some other factors that you might consider if faced with making a choice of one of these technologies over others include the technical backgrounds of the developers involved, the operating system that will host the application, the size of the project, the availability of integrated development environments (IDEs) supporting the technology, the level of vendor support desired, and whether or not access to the source code implementing the technology is required.

8.9.1   JSP Pages with Scriptlets

First, as has been noted, this chapter describes an XML version of JSP. Many existing JSP-based web applications use an older version of JSP that is not as compatible with XML; text written in this older version of JSP is referred to as a *JSP page* rather than a JSP document. A JSP page uses various special symbols as part of the string beginning a tag in order to indicate that the tag is not template data. For example, an `include` directive within a JSP page might look like

```
<%@ include file="aForm.html" %>
```

where the string `<%@` denotes the beginning of a directive.

Early versions of JSP also did not incorporate the EL language, and as a result early JSP pages tended to make extensive use of embedded Java scriptlet code (enclosed in `<%` and `%>` tag delimiters) for accessing and processing data. This approach produces JSP pages with a mixture of markup and Java, such as

```
<p>Hello
<%
   out.println(request.getRemoteHost());
%>
</p>
```

As we have seen, newer versions of JSP make it possible to implement MVC view components without the need for embedding scriptlets. As this makes the view components (a large part of many web applications) simpler to write and maintain, it would seem that over time most JSP pages will migrate toward the XML-based, nonscriptlet version of JSP documents covered in this chapter. In any case, [SUN-JSP-2.0] is the version 2.0 reference for both the JSP page and JSP document syntaxes, so you should not find it difficult to adapt to the JSP page syntax if necessary.

8.9.2 Active Server Pages and ASP.NET

Microsoft Active Server Pages (ASP) technology is supported by Microsoft's Internet Information Services (IIS) web server as well as by several other web servers. The syntax shown in the previous subsection for JSP pages is similar to that used in ASP (which is not surprising, since JSP was released after ASP had been in use for some time). Embedded code in ASP pages is written in either JScript (the Microsoft implementation of ECMAScript) or VBScript (a scripting language based on Microsoft's popular Visual Basic® development language). There is no analog to Java servlets in ASP, but if an MVC approach is used with ASP then the controller portion of the web application can be written as an ASP page consisting entirely of script. The model portion of an ASP application is typically written using some variant of Microsoft's COM technology rather than JavaBeans classes.

ASP.NET goes beyond ASP in a number of ways. First, in addition to JScript and VBScript, a wide variety of other languages—including the C# language, which is similar in many respects to Java—can be used for embedding code in an ASP.NET page. Also, ASP.NET pages are compiled to an intermediate form before being served, much as JSP pages are translated to servlets and compiled to Java byte code. Thus, an ASP.NET web application typically executes in much less time than a comparable ASP application, in which each page is interpreted each time it is accessed. In addition, the .NET framework provides a large number of COM objects designed to simplify the development of web applications by automating various common tasks, such as generating HTML and JScript code representing some form controls that are not directly supported by HTML forms. (Sun JavaServer™ Faces technology supplies some similar capabilities for Java-based web applications.) Full details on ASP.NET are available at `http://www.msdn.microsoft.com/asp.net/`.

8.9.3 PHP: Hypertext Preprocessor

PHP (an acronym with the infinitely recursive definition "PHP: Hypertext Preprocessor") is a Perl-like scripting language that can be embedded in HTML documents much as Java scriptlets can be embedded in JSP pages or scripting code in ASP. One nice difference is that the syntax

```
<?php ... ?>
```

can be used to embed PHP code, which means that an XML parser will interpret the tags as XML processing instructions with target php. Thus, PHP pages can be written so that they are fully compatible with XML tools.

Code implementing the PHP scripting language can be run on a variety of operating system platforms (Linux, Windows, Macintosh, etc.) as well as with a variety of web servers, including both Apache and IIS. Furthermore, there is a freely available, open source implementation of PHP available from `http://www.php.net`. In addition, a wide range of software based on or related to PHP is readily available; see the PHP Extension and Application Repository (`http://pear.php.net`) and the SourceForge PHP Foundry (`http://php.foundries.sourceforge.net/`), for example.

8.9.4 ColdFusion®

ColdFusion®, although one of the earliest of the technologies for embedding program logic in HTML documents, is a relatively clean approach to the task. All program logic is embedded as XML elements (with names beginning with the characters `cf`), so a ColdFusion document is XML compatible. A ColdFusion document may also contain expressions (e.g., function calls or variable references) enclosed in # characters, which are evaluated when a ColdFusion document is requested and replaced with the values obtained. This means that the author of a ColdFusion page must add the character # to the list of XML characters that must be treated in a special way.

Like JSP tag libraries, ColdFusion allows developers to create custom elements that can be used within ColdFusion documents. In fact, some versions of ColdFusion can use JSP tag libraries directly. In addition, MVC model software can be implemented in several ways, including as either COM or JavaBeans objects.

Much like PHP, ColdFusion software can be run on multiple operating system platforms and with multiple web servers, including Apache and IIS. In fact, much like Tomcat, ColdFusion software also comes bundled with its own web server, so ColdFusion does not require a separate front-end server as current versions of PHP do. Full details on ColdFusion are available at the `http://www.macromedia.com/devnet/mx/coldfusion`.

8.10   References

This chapter has focused on JavaServer Pages version 2.0, which is the version of JSP supported by JWSDP 1.3. The reference specification for JSP 2.0 is [SUN-JSP-2.0]. Version 1.1 of the JSP Standard Tag Library is included with JWSDP 1.3, and is documented at [SUN-JSTL-1.1]. Many of the elements of web application deployment descriptors are described in Chapter 13 of the Java Servlets specification [SUN-SERVLETS-2.4]. JavaBeans technology is described in detail in the JavaBeans Specification [SUN-JAVABEANS-1.01]. To understand some of the features of the JSP and Java Servlets technologies, we also discussed the model-view-controller paradigm, which is not a web technology per se but is instead an approach to building interactive applications. Sun's recommendations ("Blueprints") for developing web applications using MVC with JSP, Java servlets, and JavaBeans technologies can be found beginning at `http://java.sun.com/blueprints/patterns/MVC.html`.

Exercises

8.1. Consider the following JSP markup:

```
<jsp:set variable="hmm" value="&lt;&quot;&gt;" />
<c:out value="${hmm}" />
```

The XML parser that reads this markup will replace the three entity references in the value attribute (<, ", and >) with the three-character string <">. And we know that

```
<c:out value="<">" />
```

is not syntactically correct XML. So will the two lines of JSP markup lead to an error when the JSP document is translated or executed? Explain.

8.2. Assume that a deployment descriptor contains four servlet-mapping elements, each containing a url-pattern element with one of the following as its content:
   1. /jsp/*
   2. *.jspx
   3. /error.jspx
   4. /
   For each of the following post-context URL paths, which of these patterns will be the first to match the path? What value would getPathInfo() return in each case?
   (a) /trouble.txt
   (b) /trouble/in/river/city.jspx
   (c) /jsp
   (d) /jsp/trouble
   (e) /jsp/trouble/in/river/city.jspx
   (f) /error.jspx
   (g) /jsp/error.jspx
   (h) /error.jspx/jsp

8.3. Write an EL expression—suitable for embedding in a JSP document—that evaluates to true if the value of an EL variable someValue is between 1 and 5, inclusive.

8.4. Write an EL expression that returns the value of the Cookie with name JSESSIONID if it is defined within the request object, and returns the string no session cookie otherwise.

8.5. Write a complete JSP document that could be used as an error page. In particular, this document should call the getMessage() method of the exception represented by the implicit object exception and display the String returned by the method in an XHTML document. Do not use scriptlet code within your document.

8.6. Why is the following not a valid JSP segment? Suggest how you could make it valid while still providing essentially the same markup to the document importing this segment.

```
<p>Legal disclaimers go here.</p>
<p>Copyright notice goes here.</p>
```

8.7. Using core JSP actions, write markup to accomplish each of the following tasks.
   (a) If the variable flipper exists in session scope, then remove it; otherwise create it and assign it the value 2.
   (b) Output the start tag for an HTML a element that specifies for its href attribute the relative URL that begins with the web application context path followed by /test. The URL should also have a URL-encoded query string with two parameters: bool should have the (string) value a=b && c=d, while yee should have the value haw.

(c) If the value of the scoped variable questionable is negative, output No; if the value is 0, output Maybe; and if the value is positive, output Yes.

(d) Output a list of the parameter names contained in a request. Follow each name with all of the values associated with that parameter name, separated by spaces. Ensure that XML special characters are properly escaped in the list. (Hint: Use nested forEach actions.)

8.8. For each of the following method signatures, indicate whether or not it conforms with one of the JavaBeans simple property design patterns. If it does not, explain why. If it does, give the corresponding bean property name.

(a) `public void getBeanProp()`

(b) `public void setBeanProp()`

(c) `public String getBeanProp(String val)`

(d) `public String getbeanprop()`

(e) `public void setBeanProp(String val)`

(f) `public String getBProp()`

8.9. Write a JavaBeans class that defines a read-write bean property of type String named readWrite and a read-only boolean bean property named readOnly. Use the is syntax for the readOnly getter method.

8.10. Assuming that the JavaBeans class my.BeanTest exists and that the EL variable myBean has been defined, what is wrong with the following markup?

```
<jsp:useBean id="${myBean}" class="my.BeanTest" />
```

8.11. Write an EL expression that evaluates to the maximum age value of the cookie JSESSIONID if it is present in the request, and to null otherwise.

8.12. Write a tag file that performs temperature conversions. Specifically, implement a tag named tempConvert that has a required temp attribute and an optional scale attribute. The legal values for scale are F (for Fahrenheit) and C (for Celsius); F is the default. The tag file converts the value of temp from its current scale, as specified by scale, to the other scale and outputs the value. The formula for converting from Fahrenheit to Celsius is $C = (5/9)(F - 32)$. So, for example, assuming that the namespace prefix myTags has been declared properly, the markup

```
<myTags:tempConvert temp="212" />
```

should output 100.

8.13. Complete the implementation of MyWrapper (Figure 8.9) by overriding the getParameterNames() and getParameterValues() methods to simulate the presence of the special variable.

8.14. A request can be forwarded to a web application component (servlet or JSP document) by URL or by servlet name, if the component is named in a servlet element. Assume that a servlet name has been declared for a component. Which is more directly associated with the component's actual file-system or class name: the URL or the servlet name? Put another way, if someone makes a change to the deployment descriptor of a web application after the application has been developed, is the change more likely to cause a forward to be directed to the wrong servlet if the forwarding uses a URL, or a servlet name? Explain.

Research and Exploration

8.15. Study [SUN-SERVLETS-2.4] to learn more about the deployment descriptor elements listed in Table 8.2 that are not included in Figure 8.6. Chapter 13 gives an overview of the elements, although you'll probably want to refer to the DTD for version 2.3 of the deployment descriptor vocabulary (which is essentially identical to version 2.4 for purposes of this exercise) in Appendix B to understand details of the content model, unless you are already familiar with XML Schema. Then give deployment descriptor markup appropriate for each of the following tasks:

    (a) Return a MIME type of `application/xhtml+xml` if a file with extension `xhtml` is requested.

    (b) If the user browses to a URL mapped to a file directory, return the file `index.html` if present in the directory. Otherwise, if the file `index.jspx` is present, return it.

    (c) If the server has decided to return an HTTP response with status code 404, it should return the document at `/docs/error.html` relative to the document base directory.

    (d) If a request is made for a file having the extension `*.java`, the user should be required to log in (using BASIC authentication) in the `manager` role. (See Chapter 12 of [SUN-SERVLETS-2.4] for information about authentication.)

8.16. In addition to the JSP implicit objects accessible through the `pageContext` EL implicit object, within a JSP document that is an error page (as indicated by the `isErrorPage` page directive) `pageContext.errorData` evaluates to an instance of `javax.servlet.jsp.ErrorData`. This class, in turn, provides access to the status code of the response. Study the API for `ErrorData`, and write a complete JSP document that could be used to handle status code errors, that is, that could act as the target for the `error-page` deployment descriptor element when an error (4xx or 5xx) status code is generated (see Exercise 8.15(c)). The HTML document generated by the JSP document should inform the user that an error has occurred and give the status code.

8.17. Study the documentation of the internationalization area of JSTL in [SUN-JSTL-1.1], and write markup that will format a number contained in the EL variable `amount` as a currency in U.S. dollars. For example, if the value of `amount` is 14224.3, then your markup should output `$14,224.30`.

Projects

8.18. Implement one of the projects of Chapter 6, making appropriate use of the JSP, JavaBeans, and Java servlets technologies. Specifically, follow the MVC paradigm outlined in this chapter: use servlets for control, JavaBeans objects for data modeling, and JSP documents for presentation. Your web application should include a deployment descriptor (`web.xml`) file that gives your application a context name and appropriately maps HTTP requests for this context to your controller servlet.

8.19. Interleaved blogs.

    (a) Many web logs (blogs) can be accessed via RSS feeds. For two blog RSS feeds assigned by your instructor (presumably representing two different perspectives on some topic, such as politics), write a web application that interleaves posts from the two blogs. Specifically, write a JavaBeans class that will read the two RSS feeds and extract the `title` and `description` text from each `item` element (using the JAXP API, as discussed in Chapter 7). Note that the feeds might not use version 0.91 of RSS, so you will need to examine the XML structure of the feeds before writing your JavaBeans class. The class does not need to have any getter or setter methods, but should instead implement the java.util.Iterator interface. Specifically, the next() method of the class should return a String value each time it is called. On the first call, the return value should be the concatenation of the title and description from the first item of the first feed, on the second call the title and description from the first item of the second feed, then from the the second item of the first feed, and so on. The hasNext() method should return true as long as this interleaving process can continue and return false the first time a title and description are not available. This JavaBeans class should be instantiated on each request by a JSP document that iterates over the instantiated object to produce the result XHTML document showing interleaved title-description strings from the blogs. Write an appropriate deployment descriptor (web.xml file) for the application as well, and use a Java servlet as the controller (even though it may not do much).

(b) Modify your application so that the JavaBeans class also reads the link element of item's. For each item read, instead of concatenating the text from title and description to form a single String value, your bean should instantiate a second JavaBeans class having three String bean properties and store the title, description, and link text in these three properties. The next() method should be modified to return this second bean rather than a String. Also modify the JSP document to read data from this new bean and to represent each blog entry by its title, which will be hyperlinked to the URL contained in link element, followed by its description.

(c) Add a rating feature to the application. Specifically, the HTML document produced by the JSP document should now have two hyperlinks following each blog entry: "rate" and "view ratings." Both URL's should be created using the url Core action and should include a query string with a parameter uniquely identifying the entry (the link value can be used). When the controller receives such a URL, it should forward the request to the appropriate JSP document. The rating JSP document generates a form that allows the user to choose from seven ratings ranging from "entirely untrue" to "entirely true." In addition, the form should contain a textarea where a user can enter a comment. When the controller receives the POST from this form, it should update a JavaBeans object that tallies all user ratings of the entry and stores all of the comments entered. The controller should then forward the POST request to a JSP document that accesses this bean and displays the information that it contains. This JSP document should also be invoked if the user clicks the "view ratings" link.

(d) Modify your application to save the JavaBeans objects that contain the user ratings and to reload these objects if the web server is restarted.

(e) Modify your application to discourage users from rating a blog entry multiple times. Specifically, if a user attempts to rate an entry more than once during a single session, ignore any additional rating and display an error page. Also set the session timeout to one minute (to facilitate testing).

8.20. The following questions suggest extensions to the case study of Section 8.8.

(a) Modify the blogging application so that the blogger user name and password are input from the deployment descriptor rather than hardcoded.

(b) Implement one or more of the case study extensions of Exercise 6.17. Use appropriate technologies described in this chapter.

CHAPTER 9

Web Services
JAX-RPC, WSDL, XML Schema, and SOAP

We have learned about web applications, which are software systems that are designed to be accessed by end users through browsers or other web client software. In this chapter we turn to software systems that are also designed to be accessed using web protocols, but that are intended to be used by other software applications rather than directly by end users. That is, the technology studied in this chapter is used to provide services to software applications, much as a Java class might be viewed as providing services (instance variables and methods) for use by other software in a program. Because these services are intended to be accessed using web protocols and technologies, they are called *web services*.

At their lowest levels, web services are typically based on transmitting XML documents between clients and servers via HTTP. The vocabulary used for these documents is called SOAP (which once was an acronym, but now is merely a name). Among other features, SOAP provides conventions for representing structured data, such as arrays and objects. A separate XML vocabulary, the Web Services Definition Language (WDSL), is used to describe the operations provided by a web service. Describing an operation includes defining the data to be passed from the client to the operation (using SOAP) as well as the return value of the operation (also represented using SOAP). Data is usually defined within a WSDL using yet another XML vocabulary, XML Schema. Higher-level technologies, such as the Java API for XML-based Remote Procedure Call (JAX-RPC), can be used to automatically produce web service clients and servers from Java code that does not explicitly contain any data communication or XML processing commands.

This chapter will begin with an example illustrating how these various web services technologies interact. We'll then look at each of the technologies in more detail, moving from the high-level technology (JAX-RPC) toward the lowest level (SOAP). The chapter concludes with a brief look at related web services technologies, including the Microsoft .NET framework.

9.1 Web Service Concepts

We can think of a web service as a special type of web application. In fact, the Java Web Services Developer Pack (JWSDP 1.3) that you installed if you followed the directions in Appendix A implements a web service as a Java servlet. Like other servlets, a web service servlet accepts HTTP requests from clients and provides an HTTP response for each request received. However, unlike earlier servlets we studied, a web service servlet expects that each HTTP request it receives will contain a SOAP XML document in the body of the request (where a query string might appear in an HTTP request to a normal servlet). This SOAP document specifies an operation to be performed by the web service and supplies input data for that operation. For example, a weather-related web service might offer a forecast operation; a client requesting this operation would supply input data such as a location for which a forecast is desired. After processing a request for an operation, the web service servlet returns the processing results as a SOAP message in the body of the HTTP response. In the weather service example, this message might include data such as the current day's expected maximum temperature at the requested location.

As a concrete example, Figure 9.1 shows a portion of an HTTP request that I sent (using Telnet) to a weather-related web service supplied by the U.S. National Weather Service (NWS). Figure 9.2 shows a portion of the HTTP response I received. As shown in these figures, the body of both the request and the response is an XML document with root element having local name Envelope, which is the root element for SOAP documents (both the env and SOAP-ENV namespace prefixes are associated with the SOAP namespace, which is discussed later). The request asks the web service to perform the operation named NDFDgen; input data supplied in the request includes a latitude and a longitude. The SOAP message in the body of the HTTP response includes text representing the forecast maximum temperature. (The XML special characters < and > are escaped within the returned text because they represent character data, not markup, within the SOAP message itself.)

While low-level communication between web service clients and servers is normally carried out using HTTP and SOAP, and while tools exist for writing web service code at this level, other tools allow for writing client and server software at a high level that hides these implementation details. A key to making these tools possible is an XML vocabulary for describing web services, the *Web Service Definition Language (WSDL)*. A WSDL (pronounced "wiz'-dul") document for a web service identifies the operations provided by the web service, what the input data to each operation is, and what output data is produced by the operation. A portion of the WSDL for the NWS web service accessed by the request is shown in Figure 9.3.

You'll notice that the WSDL document not only supplies names for an operation and its input/output parameters but also data types for the parameters. The data types in

```
POST /forecasts/xml/SOAP_server/ndfdXMLserver.php HTTP/1.1
content-type: text/xml; charset="utf-8"
...

<?xml version="1.0" encoding="UTF-8"?>
<env:Envelope ...>
  <env:Body>
    <ns0:NDFDgen>
      <latitude xsi:type="xsd:decimal">40.28</latitude>
      <longitude xsi:type="xsd:decimal">-79.49</longitude>
  ...
  </env:Body>
</env:Envelope>
```

FIGURE 9.1 Portions of an HTTP request and embedded SOAP document sent to a weather-related web service.

```
HTTP/1.1 200 OK
Server: Apache/2.0.46 (Red Hat)
...

<?xml version="1.0" encoding="ISO-8859-1"?>
<SOAP-ENV:Envelope ...>
  <SOAP-ENV:Body>
    <NDFDgenResponse>
      <xmlOut xsi:type="xsd:string">
      ...
            &lt;name&gt;Daily Maximum Temperature&lt;/name&gt;
            &lt;value&gt;47&lt;/value&gt;
      ...
      </xmlOut>
    </NDFDgenResponse>
  </SOAP-ENV:Body>
</SOAP-ENV:Envelope>
```

FIGURE 9.2 Portions of the HTTP response with embedded SOAP document received in response to the request of Figure 9.1.

```
<?xml version="1.0"?>
<definitions ...>
  ...
  <message name="NDFDgenRequest">
    <part name="latitude" type="xsd:decimal" />
    <part name="longitude" type="xsd:decimal" />
    ...
  </message>

  <message name="NDFDgenResponse">
    <part name="xmlOut" type="xsd:string" />
  </message>

  <portType name="ndfdXMLPortType">
    <operation name="NDFDgen">
      <documentation>...</documentation>
      <input message="tns:NDFDgenRequest"/>
      <output message="tns:NDFDgenResponse"/>
    </operation>
    ...
  </portType>
  ...
</definitions>
```

FIGURE 9.3 Portions of a National Weather Service WSDL document defining an operation named NDFD-gen along with two of its inputs and its output (obtained from http://www.weather.gov/forecasts/xml/DWMLgen/wsdl/ndfdXML.wsdl).

a WSDL document are defined using yet another XML vocabulary, XML Schema. For example, XML Schema defines the syntax and semantics for the decimal data type, which is used to represent arbitrary-precision decimal numbers. So a WSDL document is, in essence, an API specification: it tells us what operations (methods) a web service has, the data types of an operation's input parameters, and the data type of its return value.

High-level tools exist that can read a WSDL document and produce code that implements the API specified. The implementation will handle all of the details of converting an API method call into the corresponding SOAP document, embedding this document in an HTTP request, sending the request to the appropriate operation of the web service, and then unpacking the data contained in the reply SOAP message into the appropriate return-value data type as specified by the API. Once the high-level tool has generated such an API implementation, the implementation can be called on by user-written code in order to access the web service.

For example, I ran the wscompile tool supplied as part of JWSDP 1.3 using a URL for the NWS WSDL document as input. This tool generated Java interfaces and classes that allowed me to access the NWS web service using code similar to the following:

```
// Create an object representing
// the NWS web service.
NdfdXMLPortType ndfdWS =
    new NdfdXML_Impl().getNdfdXMLPort();

// Request a forecast from the web service
BigDecimal latitude = new BigDecimal(40.28);
BigDecimal longitude = new BigDecimal(-79.49);
String forecast =
    ndfdWS.NDFDgen(latitude, longitude,
                    // other parameters ...
                    );
```

The NdfdXMLPortType interface and NdfdXML_Impl class were generated automatically by wscompile from the NWS WSDL document. The first line of the displayed code obtains an object named ndfdWS that implements the API described by the WSDL document. The last line accesses the NDFDgen operation of the NWS web service by simply calling the method of the same name on ndfdWS. This method takes care of all of the communication and data conversion tasks described earlier. As we will learn in more detail later, the BigDecimal class, in the java.math package, is the Java equivalent of the XML Schema decimal data type, and String is the Java equivalent of the string data type (not surprisingly). The bottom line here is that, while SOAP is a key technology underlying web services, tools exist that make it possible to write web service clients without dealing with SOAP documents directly.

In fact, there are also tools that make it possible to write a web service itself without directly processing SOAP documents. For instance, using tools in JWSDP 1.3, you can write a web service by creating two Java modules: an interface that defines (in Java) the methods (operations) of your web service, and a class that implements this interface. JWSDP 1.3 tools can then package your modules as a Java servlet representing a web service, and can even automatically produce a WSDL document for your web service. If an HTTP

```
public interface NdfdXMLPortType extends Remote {
    public String NDFDgen(BigDecimal latitude,
                          BigDecimal longitude,
                          // other parameters ...
                          )
        throws RemoteException;
}
```

FIGURE 9.4 Java interface for a web service.

request containing an appropriate SOAP document is sent to this servlet, code packaged in the servlet will automatically determine which operation is being requested, extract input parameter data from the SOAP document, convert this data to appropriate Java data types, and pass the result as parameter values in a call to the Java method—in the class that you wrote— that implements the requested operation. When your method returns, the packaged servlet code will convert the return value into an appropriate SOAP document and send this document back to the client in the body of an HTTP response.

To illustrate how simple your web service code can be, Figure 9.4 is a portion of a web service interface, and Figure 9.5 is a portion of a class implementing the interface. Using JWSDP 1.3 tools, these files can be converted into a web service with a WSDL similar to the one in Figure 9.3. In fact, a slight modification of the client Java code just shown can be used with wscompile-generated code to access this web service. However, unlike the actual NWS web service, our web service will always return the string specified as the value of retVal in Figure 9.5. So to build a useful web service would of course require more code than this. What you should note, though, is that this additional code will be application-oriented: there is no need to write any low-level code to deal with SOAP and HTTP communication, or even WSDL generation.

Now that you have had some introduction to key web service concepts, most of the rest of this chapter will be devoted to providing more detail on various technologies supporting web services. I'll follow a top-down approach, beginning with an explanation of how to use the high-level JWSDP 1.3 tools to build web service clients and servers, next moving to the WSDL–XML Schema level, and finally covering some SOAP specifics.

```
public class WeatherImpl implements NdfdXMLPortType {
    public String NDFDgen(BigDecimal latitude,
                          BigDecimal longitude,
                          // other parameters ...
                          )
        throws RemoteException
    {
        // Return dummy string, ignoring parameter values
        String retVal =
            "<?xml version='1.0' ?> <dwml version='1.0' ... >" +
            "..." + "</dwml>";
        return retVal;
    }
}
```

FIGURE 9.5 Java class implementing the interface of Figure 9.4.

9.2   Writing a Java Web Service

We'll begin by writing the server side of a web service. I'll first describe the web service to be written and then illustrate in detail the steps I followed to write a server for this service using JWSDP 1.3 tools.

9.2.1   Currency Conversion Service

We will write a simple web service to perform conversions between different currencies. Given an amount in one of the three currencies supported by the web service—dollars, euros, and yen—the web service will return the equivalent amount in the other two currencies. In a real web service, the exchange rates between currencies would be updated frequently; the service we write will have fixed rates.

Specifically, our web service will provide three operations: `fromDollars`, `fromEuros`, and `fromYen`. Each of these operations will take a single decimal number as its input parameter and will return an object containing three properties representing the input value and the equivalent amounts in the other two currencies.

9.2.2   Writing Server Software

I'll now describe how I built the web service using two tools from JWSDP 1.3, `wscompile` and `wsdeploy`. As outlined earlier, the code we write for a web service consists primarily of an interface and a class to implement this interface. Since our web service returns an object, we also need to write a class to define this object. After writing this code, we will run `wscompile` to convert these Java files into a WSDL document along with another intermediate output file. We'll then run `wsdeploy` to package our web service before finally deploying it as a web application.

Before beginning to write code, we need a place to store it. I created a working directory named `CurrencyConverter` (not under my JWSDP installation directory; we'll see why later), within this created a `WEB-INF` subdirectory, and within this created two subdirectories `src` and `classes`. Next, I created a `myCurCon` subdirectory of `src`. All source files mentioned in the rest of this subsection will be placed in the `src/myCurCon` subdirectory, and `myCurCon` will be used as the package name for these source files. The `WEB-INF` and `classes` directories must be named as shown, but the other directories could be given any legal names.

The starting point for writing a web service using the JWSDP 1.3 tools is writing a Java interface that specifies the operations that will be provided by the service (essentially an API for the service). This is known as the *service endpoint interface*. The basic rules for the service endpoint interface are:

- The interface must extend (directly or indirectly) the `java.rmi.Remote` interface.
- Every method in the interface must throw `java.rmi.RemoteException`.
- Every method parameter and every return value must conform to certain restrictions on the allowed data types (see the following paragraph).
- The interface must not contain any `public static final` declarations (global constants).

```
package myCurCon;

public class ExchangeValues {
    public double dollars;
    public double euros;
    public double yen;
}
```

FIGURE 9.6 Class ExchangeValues for representing the return values from operations of the Currency Converter web service.

The data types that can be used within a service endpoint interface include all of the Java primitive types (int, boolean, and so on), the corresponding wrapper classes (Integer, Boolean, and so on), and several other Java API classes and/or interfaces listed in Section 9.5.1. In addition, a class that only declares public instance variables for which the data types are Java primitive types can be used as a data type (the class must also have a public no-argument constructor and must not implement the java.rmi.Remote interface either directly or by inheritance). So, given the ExchangeValues class definition given in Figure 9.6, the interface shown in Figure 9.7 is a valid service endpoint interface for our web service.

Next, we need to implement this interface. For our example, this is straightforward. Figure 9.8 shows my implementation of the fromDollars() method contained in a class called CurConImpl that implements the service endpoint interface of Figure 9.7.

The three files ExchangeValues.java, CurCon.java, and CurConImpl.java are all the code that I needed to write for my web service. What remained was to run the JWSDP 1.3 tools on this code and install the result as a web service in my Tomcat server.

9.2.3 Packaging Server Software

In this section, I'll describe the steps I followed in order to package and install the currency conversion web service. First, I compiled my Java files created as described in Section 9.2.2. Recall that I placed them in a directory CurrencyConverter/WEB-INF/src. To compile the files, I opened a command prompt, changed to the WEB-INF directory, and issued the command

```
package myCurCon;

public interface CurCon extends java.rmi.Remote {
    public ExchangeValues fromDollars(double dollars)
        throws java.rmi.RemoteException;
    public ExchangeValues fromEuros(double euros)
        throws java.rmi.RemoteException;
    public ExchangeValues fromYen(double yen)
        throws java.rmi.RemoteException;
}
```

FIGURE 9.7 Service endpoint interface for the currency conversion web service.

```
public ExchangeValues fromDollars(double dollars)
    throws java.rmi.RemoteException
{
    ExchangeValues ev = new ExchangeValues();
    ev.dollars = dollars;
    ev.euros = dollars * dollar2euro;
    ev.yen = dollars * dollar2yen;
    return ev;
}
```

FIGURE 9.8 Method `fromDollars()` in class `CurConImpl` implementing service endpoint interface `CurCon`. Here `dollar2euro` and `dollar2yen` are constants defined elsewhere in the class.

```
javac -d classes src/myCurCon/*.java
```

This created class files in the `classes` directory (under the `myCurCon` directory, since the source files belong to the package of the same name).

Next, I used `wscompile` to create the WSDL document for my web service along with a so-called *model* XML document used by later processing. The inputs to `wscompile` are supplied via an XML document (what else would we expect?). The root of this document is a `configuration` element, which specifies a default namespace. The child of this element, when using `wscompile` to create a web service, is named `service`. The `service` element provides a name for the service, namespace names to be used in the WSDL that will be generated for the service, and identification of the package containing the Java class files as well as the name of the service endpoint interface. There are two namespace names: one for symbols that are associated with data types (such as `ExchangeValues` and its instance variables), and one for symbols associated with higher levels of the web service (such as the operation names `fromDollars`, `fromEuros`, and `fromYen` along with their parameters). We'll see how these namespace names are used when we analyze the generated WSDL document in detail in a later section. You can use any URIs you like for these names as long as they don't conflict with other namespace names used within the generated WSDL document. Normally, you should use a URI belonging to your own Web site (although it doesn't need to be the location of an actual resource). Alternatively, names beginning with `http://tempuri.org` are specially designated to be used for WSDL development purposes; I chose to use names of this form in my configuration file:

```
<?xml version="1.0" encoding="UTF-8"?>
<configuration
  xmlns="http://java.sun.com/xml/ns/jax-rpc/ri/config">
  <service
    name="HistoricCurrencyConverter"
    targetNamespace="http://tempuri.org/wsdl"
    typeNamespace="http://tempuri.org/types"
    packageName="myCurCon">
    <interface name="myCurCon.CurCon" />
  </service>
</configuration>
```

I saved this document in the file config.xml (any name could have been used) within the CurrencyConverter directory and then ran wscompile from the CurrencyConverter directory. This tool is installed as part of JWSDP 1.3 and should be accessible from a command prompt if you have followed the instructions in Section A.4.2. The following command (which is broken into two lines for readability, but which should be entered on a single line) is suitable for Windows systems; for other systems, such as Linux, use wscompile.sh as the command name instead:

```
wscompile -define -d WEB-INF -classpath WEB-INF/classes
          -model WEB-INF/model.xml.gz config.xml
```

The d option specifies the directory to receive the generated WSDL document, which will be named HistoricCurrencyConverter.wsdl because of the name attribute value given in the config.xml file. The classpath option was needed so that wscompile could find the class files created when I compiled my server software. A complete list of wscompile command-line options and defaults is provided by the jaxrpc/docs/jaxrpc-tools.html document within your JWSDP 1.3 installation directory. The model and configuration files may have any names; however, the model file is compressed, and its file name should have the gz type extension to indicate the form of compression used.

Next, I created another XML configuration file, this one in the file WEB-INF/jaxrpc-ri.xml. Unlike config.xml, the name jaxrpc-ri.xml must be used, and the file must be contained in WEB-INF. The file I used was

```
<?xml version="1.0" encoding="UTF-8"?>
<webServices
  xmlns="http://java.sun.com/xml/ns/jax-rpc/ri/dd"
  version="1.0"
  targetNamespaceBase="http://tempuri.org/wsdl"
  typeNamespaceBase="http://tempuri.org/types"
  urlPatternBase="/converter">

  <endpoint
    name="CurrConverter"
    displayName="Currency Converter"
    description=
      "Converts between dollars, euros, and yen."
    interface="myCurCon.CurCon"
    model="/WEB-INF/model.xml.gz"
    implementation="myCurCon.CurConImpl"/>

  <endpointMapping
    endpointName="CurrConverter"
    urlPattern="/currency" />

</webServices>
```

This document is similar in purpose to a web application deployment descriptor, with the endpoint and endpointMapping elements acting as analogs of the servlet and servlet-mapping elements in a deployment descriptor. endpoint provides information to a web server, including the names of the service endpoint interface and the class implementing this interface, as well as the location of the the model document generated by wscompile. The name specified for an endpoint is used to associate the endpoint with one or more endpointMapping elements (by matching the endpointName attribute's value). Like the url-pattern element of servlet-mapping in a deployment descriptor, the urlPattern in an endpointMapping element specifies the path for the web service relative to the context path of the web service. The same types of pattern—exact, path-prefix, etc.—are supported by urlPattern as are supported by url-pattern. The urlPatternBase attribute of webServices specifies the context path for the web service.

Although the jaxrpc-ri.xml file specifies much of the information that would normally be found in a deployment descriptor, we will also need to create a web.xml file in WEB-INF. This can in fact be simple. In particular, it does not need any servlet or servlet-mapping elements, because the jaxrpc-ri.xml file supplies any mappings needed. I used the following file as my web.xml:

```
<web-app
  xmlns="http://java.sun.com/xml/ns/j2ee"
  xmlns:xsi="http://www.w3.org/2001/XMLSchema-instance"
  xsi:schemaLocation="http://java.sun.com/xml/ns/j2ee/web-app_2_4.xsd"
  version="2.4">

  <display-name>Historic Currency Converter</display-name>
  <description>
    This web service converts between three currencies using their
    exchange rates as of a fixed date.
  </description>
</web-app>
```

We're nearly done. The WEB-INF directory and its descendants need to be placed in a JAR file, this file must be processed using the wsdeploy tool, and then the resulting WAR file must be deployed to a web server. First, I created the JAR (but we call it a WAR, which stands for "Web Archive") by executing the following command from the CurrencyConverter directory:

```
jar cf converter-temp.war WEB-INF
```

(You can learn more about the jar command at http://java.sun.com/j2se/1.4.2/docs/tooldocs/tools.html.) Any name could be used in place of converter-temp for the WAR file, but the .war extension should be used to correctly indicate the file type. Next, I ran wsdeploy as follows (again, use wsdeploy.sh in Linux):

```
wsdeploy -o converter.war converter-temp.war
```

Note that the portion of the file name before the extension of the WAR file generated by wsdeploy must match the urlPatternBase specified in jaxrpc-ri.xml.

Finally, I copied the converter.war file to my JWSDP webapps directory. That is, rather than creating a base document directory for the web service web application, as we have done with previous web applications, I simply placed a single WAR file in webapps to represent this application. This is why we created CurrencyConverter in a different directory.

Once you have successfully followed these steps, start your Tomcat server if it isn't already running, and browse to http://localhost:8080/converter/currency. If you see a page similar to the one shown in Figure 9.9, congratulations: you've created and installed your first web service! If not, you may need to use the Tomcat manager application to manually deploy your service (automatic deployment is an option that may or may not be enabled in your server). Manually deploying your web service is just like deploying a web application as described in Section 8.3.2, except that you type the name of the WAR file (converter.war) in the "War or Directory URL" text box rather than typing a base document directory name.

Before moving on to writing a client for this web service, a final note. Unlike standard Java methods, in which objects are passed by reference, if a method in the service endpoint interface has a parameter that is an object, this object is in effect passed by value from the client to the server. Thus, anything that your server software does with such an object, including setting the values of public instance variables, will have no impact on the copy of the object on the client machine. This makes sense when you consider that the client's parameter data is being converted to an XML document to be sent to the server. In any case, you should keep in mind when designing a web service that information can only be sent to the client via an operation's return value and not through any object-valued parameters it may have.

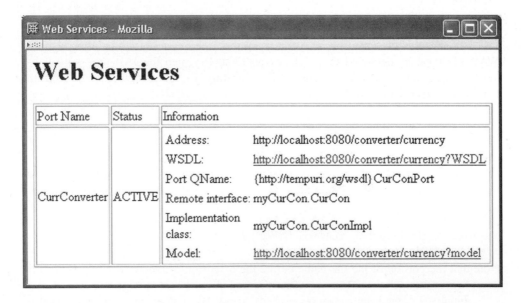

FIGURE 9.9 Status page for currency converter web service.

9.3   Writing a Java Web Service Client

In this section, I'll cover one way (there are several) to write Java client software to access the currency converter web service using the JWSDP 1.3 wscompile tool. At the end of this section, you should be able to use wscompile to develop clients for other web services.

To begin, we need to again create an input XML document for wscompile. This time, however, the child element of the root configuration element of this document will be a wsdl element that specifies the URL of a WSDL document to be read so that wscompile can generate a *proxy object*, that is, a Java object that can be called on by the client software in order to access the web service. The URL for our currency converter web service is shown in Figure 9.9. The input XML document also provides the name of a Java package in which the wscompile-generated code should be placed:

```
<?xml version="1.0" encoding="UTF-8"?>
<configuration
    xmlns="http://java.sun.com/xml/ns/jax-rpc/ri/config">
  <wsdl
    location=
    "http://localhost:8080/converter/currency?WSDL"
    packageName="myCurConClient" />
</configuration>
```

Both the location and packageName attributes of wsdl are required. I chose to use the package name myCurConClient, but of course you could use any package name you like.

I next created a web application subdirectory ConverterClient under the JWSDP webapps directory (creating this subdirectory in a separate location and copying it to webapps is a better idea, as discussed in Chapter 8, but I'm trying to keep the discussion simple). Then I placed the XML document just displayed in a file called config.xml within the WEB-INF subdirectory of ConverterClient. Next, I again created two subdirectories of WEB-INF, named classes and src, to contain the output of the wscompile tool. I made sure that Tomcat was running my web service, so that wscompile would be able to load the WSDL from the URL specified in the location attribute of config.xml. And finally, I opened a command prompt, changed to the WEB-INF directory, and ran wscompile as follows (again, for Linux, use wscompile.sh as the command name):

```
wscompile -gen -keep -d classes -s src config.xml
```

This command instructed wscompile to generate class files from the WSDL specified in config.xml, keep the Java source files generated, store the class files in the classes subdirectory, and store the Java source files in the src subdirectory.

My directory structure at this point looked like this:

```
webapps
  [[ other web application document base directories ]]
  ConverterClient
    WEB-INF
      classes
```

```
    myCurConClient
src
    myCurConClient
```

The myCurConClient directories were generated automatically by wscompile because I specified this in config.xml as the package name to be used. The generated .java and .class files are contained in these directories under src and classes, respectively. The names of the generated files are related to the values of various name attributes in the WSDL document. In particular, if we were to look at the currency converter WSDL document, we would find that the value specified for the name attribute of the service element was HistoricCurrencyConverter, which is the name we specified for our service in the config.xml document when running wscompile to generate our service's WSDL document. The corresponding HistoricCurrencyConverter.java file is the top-level file for the generated client code, so we'll start by looking at this file (Figure 9.10).

As shown in the figure, this file defines a Java interface, which defines just one method, getCurConPort(), which returns an object of type CurCon. By convention, wscompile creates a class implementing this interface with a name that is the same as the interface name suffixed with _Impl, and this class will have a public no-argument constructor. The object of type CurCon returned by the getCurConPort() method of an instance of this class is a proxy object representing the web service. Thus, we can obtain a proxy object for the currency converter web service with code such as

```
CurCon curCon =
  (new HistoricCurrencyConverter_Impl()).getCurConPort();
```

Next, we want to know how to call operations on the web service via methods on the proxy object. We can learn this by examining CurCon.java, which is shown in Figure 9.11. Notice that this code is functionally equivalent to the service endpoint interface of Figure 9.7. In essence, this interface is shared between the web service server and clients via the WSDL document, which contains all of the information needed to reconstruct the interface. On the server side, we wrote a class implementing this interface. On the client side, code

```
// This class was generated by the JAXRPC SI, do not edit.
// Contents subject to change without notice.
// JAX-RPC Standard Implementation (1.1, build R59)

package myCurConClient;

import javax.xml.rpc.*;

public interface HistoricCurrencyConverter
        extends javax.xml.rpc.Service {
    public myCurConClient.CurCon getCurConPort();
}
```

FIGURE 9.10 File HistoricCurrencyConverter.java generated by wscompile.

```
// This class was generated by the JAXRPC SI, do not edit.
// Contents subject to change without notice.
// JAX-RPC Standard Implementation (1.1, build R59)

package myCurConClient;

public interface CurCon extends java.rmi.Remote {
    public myCurConClient.ExchangeValues fromDollars(double double_1)
      throws java.rmi.RemoteException;
    public myCurConClient.ExchangeValues fromEuros(double double_1)
      throws java.rmi.RemoteException;
    public myCurConClient.ExchangeValues fromYen(double double_1)
      throws java.rmi.RemoteException;
}
```

FIGURE 9.11 File CurCon.java generated by wscompile.

implementing the interface is automatically generated by wscompile. The client code we write simply calls on the implementing class in order to communicate with the server via the generated code.

Before writing code to call methods on the proxy object, we need to look at the ExchangeValues class generated by wscompile, shown in Figure 9.12. This is not as similar to the class we wrote for the server as we might expect. The key difference is that the server-side class contained three public instance variables, while the class generated on the client side contains code representing a JavaBeans class with three read-write bean properties, as illustrated by the getter-setter code shown for the dollars property. It turns out that if we had used this generated ExchangeValues on the server side instead of the file we wrote, then the same WSDL document would have been generated. That is, in a Java class defining a data type to be used in a service endpoint interface, replacing a public instance variable with a public setter-getter pair representing a bean property of the same name has no effect on the WSDL document produced by running wscompile. (In fact, the class can also contain nonpublic instance variables and nonbean methods, which

```
public class ExchangeValues {
    protected double dollars;
    protected double euros;
    protected double yen;
    ...
    public double getDollars() {
        return dollars;
    }

    public void setDollars(double dollars) {
        this.dollars = dollars;
    }
    ...
```

FIGURE 9.12 Portion of the file ExchangeValues.java generated by wscompile.

will be ignored by wscompile.) So when wscompile is run on the client side, it has no way of knowing how a given element in the WSDL was originally represented, and follows the convention that all of the elements for a data type class will be represented as bean properties. The net effect is that our client code will access ExchangeValues instances somewhat differently than our server code did.

Now that we've examined the pertinent files generated by wscompile, we're ready to write our client code. Figure 9.13 shows a JavaBeans class that allows a currency and value to be specified and that returns an ExchangeValues object representing the exchange values corresponding to the specified currency and value. The getExValues() method of this class creates the proxy object for the web service and calls a method on this class to access the corresponding web service operation. I placed the Java file for this class

```java
package myCurConClient;

public class CurConBean {

    private double value = 1.0;
    private String currency = "dollars";

    public void setValue(double value) {
        this.value = value;
        return;
    }
    public void setCurrency(String currency) {
        this.currency = currency;
        return;
    }
    public ExchangeValues getExValues() {
        ExchangeValues ev = null;
        CurCon curCon =
            (new HistoricCurrencyConverter_Impl()).getCurConPort();
        try {
            if (currency.equals("euros")) {
                ev = curCon.fromEuros(value);
            }
            else if (currency.equals("yen")) {
                ev = curCon.fromYen(value);
            }
            else {
                ev = curCon.fromDollars(value);
            }
        }
        catch (Exception e) {
            e.printStackTrace();
        }
        return ev;
    }
}
```

FIGURE 9.13 Java class CurConBean for accessing the currency converter web service.

in the `WEB-INF/classes/myCurConClient` directory, opened a command prompt, and compiled the file after changing to the `classes` directory with the command

```
javac myCurConClient/CurConBean.java
```

Figure 9.14 shows portions of a JSP document `convert.jspx` that calls on the `CurConBean` JavaBeans class to perform a currency conversion and display the results in an HTML table. The document recognizes two query-string parameters, `cur` and `val`. If specified, they are used to assign values to the `currency` and `value` bean properties, respectively, of the JavaBeans object referenced by the `client` variable. The currency conversion is then performed by getting the value of the `exValues` bean property of `client`, and the resulting object (which—recall—is a JavaBeans instance with three bean properties) is stored in a page-scope EL variable named `exvals`. The value of each of the three bean properties of `exvals` is then output to an element of the HTML table after being formatted appropriately by the JSTL `formatNumber` action (part of the internationalization functional area of JSTL). Markup for outputting the euro value is shown in the figure; markup for the other two values is similar. After placing `convert.jspx` in the `ConverterClient` directory and browsing to `http://localhost:8080/ConverterClient/convert.jspx?val=59034.34`, the table shown in Figure 9.15 was produced.

```
<html ...>
  ...
  <jsp:useBean id="client" class="myCurConClient.CurConBean" />
  ...
    <c:if test="${!(empty param.cur)}">
      <c:set target="${client}" property="currency"
        value="${param.cur}" />
    </c:if>
    <c:if test="${!(empty param.val)}">
      <c:set target="${client}" property="value"
        value="${param.val}" />
    </c:if>
    <c:set var="exvals" value="${client.exValues}" />
  ...
      <tr>
        <td>Euros</td>
        <td style="text-align:right">
          <fmt:formatNumber
            type="currency" currencySymbol="&#8364;">
            ${exvals.euros}
          </fmt:formatNumber>
        </td>
      </tr>
  ...
</html>
```

FIGURE 9.14 Portions of JSP document `convert.jspx` that accesses the currency converter web service via the CurConBean JavaBeans class.

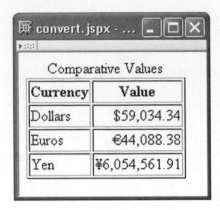

FIGURE 9.15 Table produced by accessing `convert.jspx`.

As a final note, if you were to write, say, a text-based Java application to execute the `CurConBean` class, you would need to add a number of Java Archive (JAR) files to the Java classpath before compiling your application (the files are added to the classpath automatically for servlets produced using JSP). These JAR files are included as part of JWSDP 1.3 and are located in various subdirectories of the JWSDP installation directory. You can determine the locations of these JAR files from the XML document located within your JWSDP installation directory at `jaxrpc/samples/HelloWorld/build.properties`. Even better, if you are familiar with the Apache Foundation's Ant build tool (details of which are beyond the scope of our discussion), then the file `build.xml` located in the same directory as `build.properties` provides an example of an Apache Ant build document that can be used to automatically add the JWSDP JAR files to the classpath before compiling a web service client application.

As you have now seen, it is possible to write web service clients and servers without the need to deal with SOAP at all. In fact, we also did not need to look at a WSDL document, except to learn the name of the web service when writing a client. However, for a number of reasons, it's still good to understand the lower-level technologies that make web services possible: you may need to develop in an environment in which high-level tools like `wscompile` are not available; even if high-level tools are available, you might at times need to tweak their low-level output in order to achieve a specific outcome; and understanding the lower levels can help you to better understand how to effectively use higher-level tools. In addition, XML Schema is used for a variety of applications, not just in support of web services. So, we'll spend the next several sections covering the lower-level technologies that support web services.

9.4 Describing Web Services: WSDL

Although I've used the term "web service" frequently in this chapter, I haven't yet attempted to formally define it. Let's do so now: a *web service* is a server application that uses HTTP to accept and return SOAP documents, where the content of the documents is specified by a WSDL document that uses embedded XML Schema markup to define data types. Thus, while we may be able to develop web service clients and services without having much knowledge of the WSDL vocabulary, in order to understand the implementation details of web services it is necessary to have some familiarity with WSDL.

WSDL version 1.1 is the de facto WSDL standard at the time of this writing, although technically it is not a standard at all but only a W3C Note (technical report posted for discussion purposes but not endorsed by the W3C). A W3C recommendation (version 2.0) is under development at the time of this writing, but since it is not yet widely supported, I will cover WSDL version 1.1 here. I will also focus on the features of the WSDL vocabulary as used by WSDL documents generated by `wscompile` and ignore some other features. You should refer to the WSDL 1.1 technical report [W3C-WSDL-1.1] for complete details.

We have already seen portions of a WSDL document in Figure 9.3. We'll now look in detail at the WSDL for the example currency converter web service (which is available in the file `webapps/CurrencyConverter/WEB-INF/HistoricCurrencyConverter.wsdl` if you built the currency converter web service as outlined in Section 9.2). Figure 9.16 shows the start tag for this document, including all of the namespace declarations. The default namespace is the namespace for the WSDL 1.1 vocabulary itself, `http://schemas.xmlsoap.org/wsdl/`. Any names defined in WSDL elements (such as the name of an operation, defined in an `operation` element) are assumed to belong to the namespace specified as the value of the `targetNamespace` attribute. You may recognize that the URI specified for this attribute in Figure 9.16 is one of the namespace names we provided in the `config.xml` file input to `wscompile` in order to generate this WSDL document. Also notice that the namespace prefix `tns` (which in this context stands for "target namespace") is associated with the same namespace URI. We'll discuss the namespace with prefix `ns2` shortly. Finally, the prefixes `xsd` and `soap` are associated with the XML Schema namespace and a WSDL namespace for dealing with SOAP, respectively.

Technically, all of the elements in the content of `definitions` are optional. However, most WSDL documents will contain a single `types` element followed by at least one of each of the following elements, which must appear in this order and may each be repeated any number of times: `message`, `portType`, `binding`, and `service`. We'll discuss each of these elements in turn as they appear in the example currency converter WSDL document.

The `types` element defines data types that can be used as the types of input parameters or return values later in the WSDL document. The `types` element for our example WSDL document is shown in Figure 9.17. The content of `types` is normally XML Schema

```
<?xml version="1.0" encoding="UTF-8"?>

<definitions name="HistoricCurrencyConverter"
  targetNamespace="http://tempuri.org/wsdl"
  xmlns:tns="http://tempuri.org/wsdl"
  xmlns="http://schemas.xmlsoap.org/wsdl/"
  xmlns:ns2="http://tempuri.org/types"
  xmlns:xsd="http://www.w3.org/2001/XMLSchema"
  xmlns:soap="http://schemas.xmlsoap.org/wsdl/soap/">
```

FIGURE 9.16 First lines of the WSDL document generated by `wscompile` for the currency converter web service.

```
<types>
  <schema
    targetNamespace="http://tempuri.org/types"
    xmlns:tns="http://tempuri.org/types"
    xmlns:soap11-enc="http://schemas.xmlsoap.org/soap/encoding/"
    xmlns:xsi="http://www.w3.org/2001/XMLSchema-instance"
    xmlns:wsdl="http://schemas.xmlsoap.org/wsdl/"
    xmlns="http://www.w3.org/2001/XMLSchema">
    <import
      namespace="http://schemas.xmlsoap.org/soap/encoding/"/>
    <complexType name="ExchangeValues">
      <sequence>
        <element name="dollars" type="double"/>
        <element name="euros" type="double"/>
        <element name="yen" type="double"/>
      </sequence>
    </complexType>
  </schema>
</types>
```

FIGURE 9.17 Second set of lines from the WSDL document generated by `wscompile` for the currency converter web service.

markup, and our example is no exception. Therefore, I'll defer discussion of most of this part of the WSDL document until the next section. For now, let me just tell you that this portion of the document defines the symbol `ExchangeValues` in the namespace named `http://tempuri.org/types`, which was associated with the namespace prefix `ns2` in Figure 9.16 (and was one of the namespace names we provided in `config.xml`). So references to `ns2:ExchangeValues` later in the document are references to the symbol defined here.

We next come to the `message` elements (Figure 9.18). Although it is not apparent from each `message` element itself, generally speaking, when a WSDL document is written, each `message` is intended either to define an input parameter list for an operation or to define the data type of the value returned by the operation. In this example, as the names imply, the first message is intended to represent the input parameters to the `fromDollars` operation, the second the return value from that operation, the third the input parameters to `fromEuros`, and so on. This example also illustrates a commonly followed convention of defining a separate pair of messages for each operation, even if some of the `message` elements are identical except for their names (notice that in this example, except for their names, all of the input parameter list messages are identical, as are all of the output value messages). Following this convention ensures that later changes to a parameter list or return value for one operation do not unintentionally affect other operations.

In an input message defining a parameter list, there will be one `part` element for each parameter. This element associates a name (used for SOAP purposes) and a data type with each parameter. Similarly, there is normally a single `part` element in a message intended for output; this `part` associates a name and data type with the output value represented by the message. As you can see, names do not need to be unique between messages. However, names do need to be unique within a message. So, for instance, if there were two `part`

```
<message name="CurCon_fromDollars">
  <part name="double_1" type="xsd:double"/>
</message>
<message name="CurCon_fromDollarsResponse">
  <part name="result" type="ns2:ExchangeValues"/>
</message>
<message name="CurCon_fromEuros">
  <part name="double_1" type="xsd:double"/>
</message>
<message name="CurCon_fromEurosResponse">
  <part name="result" type="ns2:ExchangeValues"/>
</message>
<message name="CurCon_fromYen">
  <part name="double_1" type="xsd:double"/>
</message>
<message name="CurCon_fromYenResponse">
  <part name="result" type="ns2:ExchangeValues"/>
</message>
```

FIGURE 9.18 Third set of lines from the WSDL document generated by wscompile for the currency converter web service.

elements within a message, then double_1 could not be specified as the value of the name attribute for both.

You'll notice that two different namespace prefixes are used for the type values. The xsd prefix indicates that the type is a built-in type defined by XML Schema itself, while (as mentioned earlier) the ns2 prefix indicates that the specified type was defined in the types element earlier in the document. Again, we'll learn more about XML Schema in the next section.

We're now finally ready to examine the portType element, which defines—at an abstract level—the operations of a web service. Actually, as already mentioned, there can be several portType elements in a WSDL document. Often, however, there is a single such element, as shown in Figure 9.19. As shown, the content of this element consists of operation elements, one for each operation provided. While the names of these elements are not required to be unique, most WSDL documents do not overload operation names. Each of these elements in turn consists of an input and an output element, each of which is associated with one of the messages defined in a message element (recall that these names are added to the namespace associated with the tns prefix). Normally, the content of an operation will be one input and one output, in that order. This represents the so-called *request-response* form of an operation, which is the form typically used by web services and the only form we will consider. The parameterOrder attribute is not needed for web services implemented using SOAP, so we won't discuss it here.

Next, we come to the binding element. The purpose of this element is to specify a way in which the operations specified abstractly in portType can be accessed remotely by a client. The binding element allows for web services that go beyond the SOAP-over-HTTP communication style we described earlier in this chapter. That is, the WSDL vocabulary allows for the possibility of a web service being implemented with an XML vocabulary other than SOAP and a communication protocol other than HTTP. Furthermore,

```
<portType name="CurCon">
  <operation name="fromDollars" parameterOrder="double_1">
    <input message="tns:CurCon_fromDollars"/>
    <output message="tns:CurCon_fromDollarsResponse"/>
  </operation>
  <operation name="fromEuros" parameterOrder="double_1">
    <input message="tns:CurCon_fromEuros"/>
    <output message="tns:CurCon_fromEurosResponse"/>
  </operation>
  <operation name="fromYen" parameterOrder="double_1">
    <input message="tns:CurCon_fromYen"/>
    <output message="tns:CurCon_fromYenResponse"/>
  </operation>
</portType>
```

FIGURE 9.19 Fourth set of lines from the WSDL document generated by wscompile for the currency converter web service.

even if SOAP-over-HTTP is used, the binding element allows various SOAP options to be selected.

Figure 9.20 shows part of the binding element for the currency converter example. The type attribute of this element specifies the name of the portType element to which this binding applies. Although multiple bindings are allowed to a single portType (so that the same operations can potentially be performed using different communication schemes), there is often just one binding element per WSDL document. The content of a binding element parallels that of a portType: it primarily consists of operation elements, one for each of the operation elements in the corresponding portType and having the same name. If SOAP-over-HTTP is used for the binding, then there will normally also be a soap:binding element essentially identical to the one shown in the figure; we'll have more to say about the rpc value for the style parameter.

The content of each operation element in a binding is a pair of input and output elements, just as there was within each operation element of a portType. As shown, these elements normally have no attribute specifications (no names are needed, since there is just one of each) and contain a single soap:body element that provides communication details such as whether or not the associated message should be encoded and, if so, what form of encoding should be used. The values for use and encodingStyle shown in the figure are discussed later when we cover SOAP.

Each operation element also contains a soap:operation element. If a request for this operation is sent as an HTTP request to the web service defined by this WSDL document, then the value specified for the soapAction attribute of this element will be used as the value of an HTTP request header field named SOAPAction. This header field can be used for various purposes depending on the web service implementation. As shown here, the WSDL document generated by wscompile specifies an empty string as the value for this field, which essentially means that soapAction is not being used by the web service generated by our use of wscompile and wsdeploy.

At last we come to the service element (Figure 9.21). This provides a name for the overall web service (HistoricCurrencyConverter in this example) and contains

```
<binding name="CurConBinding" type="tns:CurCon">
  <operation name="fromDollars">
    <input>
      <soap:body
         encodingStyle="http://schemas.xmlsoap.org/soap/encoding/"
         use="encoded" namespace="http://tempuri.org/wsdl"/>
    </input>
    <output>
      <soap:body
         encodingStyle="http://schemas.xmlsoap.org/soap/encoding/"
         use="encoded" namespace="http://tempuri.org/wsdl"/>
    </output>
    <soap:operation soapAction=""/>
  </operation>
  <operation name="fromEuros">
    ...
  </operation>
  <operation name="fromYen">
    ...
  </operation>
  <soap:binding
    transport="http://schemas.xmlsoap.org/soap/http"
    style="rpc"/>
</binding>
```

FIGURE 9.20 The fifth set of lines from the WSDL document generated by wscompile for the currency converter web service. The contents of all of the operation elements are identical, so the contents of the second and third are not shown.

one or more port elements (normally just one), each of which associates a binding with an Internet address. In the case of SOAP-over-HTTP, this address is specified by including a soap:address element in the content of the port, as shown. While the WSDL document generated by wscompile contains the string shown as the value of the location attribute, this is replaced with an absolute URL by the server when you browse to the web service's WSDL URL. For example, if you browse to http://localhost:8080/converter/currency?WSDL, the WSDL document displayed in your browser will show the URL to which you browsed as the value of location. In general, any WSDL document that you publish for others to use must specify an actual URL for location.

```
<service name="HistoricCurrencyConverter">
  <port name="CurConPort" binding="tns:CurConBinding">
    <soap:address location="REPLACE_WITH_ACTUAL_URL"/>
  </port>
</service>

</definitions>
```

FIGURE 9.21 Final lines of the WSDL document generated by wscompile for the currency converter web service.

Finally, be aware that the names declared in a WSDL document may differ in small ways from the Java names produced when creating a proxy object by running wscompile on the WSDL document. For example, if the name of a data type defined in the types element of a WSDL begins with a lowercase letter, then the class generated by wscompile will begin with an uppercase letter, in keeping with the Java convention for class names. Similarly, if, say, the name of a parameter within a WSDL message element contains characters that are not allowed within a Java identifier, those characters will be removed from the message parameter name to form the corresponding Java identifier name. The transformations performed by the wscompile tool are defined as part of the specification of the Java API for XML-based RPC (JAX-RPC), which is the technology on which wscompile is based. See Chapter 20 (an appendix) of the JAX-RPC 1.1 specification [SUN-JAXRPC-1.1] for complete details of the name transformations performed between WSDL documents and Java identifiers.

9.5   Representing Data Types: XML Schema

A web service client or server written in Java must convert between its internal representation of data and character strings appropriate for representing that data in a SOAP document. For example, when the client for the currency converter example wishes to call the fromDollars operation of the web service, it needs to convert a Java double value representing a dollar amount into a string representation that can be sent to the server in a SOAP document. But what string representation is appropriate: are there limits on the number of digits the string can contain? Can scientific notation (such as 4.34e4) be used? Are negative values only represented using standard mathematical notation (by a leading minus sign, as in -23.43), or can an accounting format (such as (23.43)) be used? Obviously, web service clients and servers must agree on these and other formatting details if they are going to communicate effectively. Furthermore, how can more general data structures, such as arrays and objects (which may themselves have instance variables containing array or object values) be passed between clients and servers using SOAP?

These problems arise not only with respect to web services using SOAP, but any time XML is going to be used to communicate data between software applications. To address such issues, the W3C has developed an XML vocabulary known as XML Schema. A key contribution of XML Schema is its definition of a collection of standard data types. Each data type definition includes a specification of the range of values that can be represented by the data type (for example, integers ranging from −32,768 to 32,767) and details on how to represent those values as strings (for example, negative numbers are represented by a leading minus sign). In addition, the XML Schema vocabulary defines elements that can be used to describe data structures. The combination of these features effectively addresses the issues raised.

In fact, more generally, an XML Schema document can be used in place of an XML DTD to define an XML vocabulary, complete with element content and attribute declarations. For example, the formal definition of the Java servlet deployment descriptor document syntax is given as an XML Schema document (Chapter 13 of [SUN-SERVLETS-2.4]). However, since our main interest in this chapter is in web services, our focus here will be on those aspects of XML Schema that are commonly used within a WSDL document; this should be a good basis for further study of XML Schema later, if the need arises. I'll begin by briefly covering the standard data types XML Schema provides, and I'll then describe some of its mechanisms for defining data structures.

9.5.1 Built-In Data Types

The data types defined by the XML Schema specification itself are called its *built-in data types*. We have seen several examples of the use of XML Schema built-in data types in earlier documents. For example, in the markup

```
<latitude xsi:type="xsd:decimal">40.28</latitude>
```

from the SOAP document of Figure 9.1, `xsd:decimal` is a reference to the XML Schema built-in type named `decimal`, while

```
<part name="latitude" type="xsd:decimal" />
```

is corresponding markup in the WSDL document of Figure 9.3 that also refers to this built-in data type.

As already mentioned, the XML Schema definition of each built-in type provides two kinds of information: the character strings that may be used to represent a value of the given type, and the set of values that may be represented by such strings. XML Schema has a wide variety of data types in order to support various applications. First, it has data types that correspond to all of Java's primitive types. In fact, for each of Java's primitive types except `char`—that is, for `boolean`, `byte`, `short`, `int`, `long`, `float`, and `double`—XML Schema defines a data type with the same name. Each XML Schema type is similar to its corresponding Java type in terms of the set of values that can be represented by the type and the syntax of strings that can be used to represent these values. So, for example, a Java `double` value within a SOAP document follows essentially the same syntactic rules as a Java `double` literal: a minus sign is used to represent negative values, scientific notation is allowed, etc. One data type that does differ noticeably between XML Schema and Java is `boolean`: in XML Schema, the strings 0 and `false` can both be used to represent the boolean "false" value, and similarly both 1 and `true` represent the "true" value. A Java `char` value can be represented by the XML Schema `string` built-in type, as discussed in Section 9.5.3.

In addition to data types oriented toward programming languages, all of the XML DTD attribute-value data types (`CDATA`, `ID`, etc.) have counterpart XML Schema built-in types with the same names. This facilitates the use of XML Schema as a replacement for XML DTDs. Furthermore, XML Schema defines a variety of other data types for representing arbitrary-precision integer and decimal values (`integer` and `decimal`, respectively), dates and times (e.g., `dateTime`), URI's (`anyURI`), XML qualified names (`QName`), and binary data. In addition, it defines several data types that are restricted forms of other built-in types, such as `nonNegativeInteger`. We will see how a few of these types relate to Java classes later in this subsection. See Section 3 of the data types part of the XML Schema specification [W3C-XML-SCHEMA-DATA-1.0] for a complete list of the built-in types as well as their formal definitions.

Within a WSDL document, XML Schema built-in types generally appear within `types` and `message` elements. Within `types`, the built-in types are the building blocks from which user-defined types are constructed. In Figure 9.17, for example, the user-defined type `ExchangeValues` is defined in terms of elements of the built-in type `double` (details of user-defined types are given later). Within a `message` element, built-in types are often used to declare the data type for an operation parameter or return value. For example, we see `double` used to declare the types of three parameters in Figure 9.18.

You'll notice in these figures that a namespace prefix was added to `double` within the `message` elements but not within the `types` element. The namespace that defines the XML Schema built-in data types is called the XML Schema *document namespace* and is named `http://www.w3.org/2001/XMLSchema`. A namespace prefix was not needed within `types`, because this namespace was declared to be the default namespace within the `schema` child element of `types` (Figure 9.17). Since no other default namespace declaration appears at lower levels of the element tree, this default applied to the `element` elements of `types`. However, examining the WSDL document carefully, we can see that the default namespace for the `message` elements is the one declared for the overall document, which is the base WSDL namespace. Therefore, within the `message` elements, `double` must be qualified with the prefix corresponding to the XML Schema document namespace (declared to be `xsd` in Figure 9.16).

When `wscompile` is used to create a WSDL document from a Java service endpoint interface, relatively few of the XML Schema built-in types appear in the generated document. Table 9.1 shows the mappings from the Java API classes that every JAX-RPC implementation must allow in a service endpoint interface to the XML Schema types used to represent their values within a SOAP document. The XML Schema types shown in this table along with those corresponding to Java's primitive types are the only built-in types that will appear in a `wscompile`-generated WSDL document.

When `wscompile` generates an interface from a WSDL document, the XML Schema built-in types corresponding to Java primitive classes are mapped in the obvious way, and the types in Table 9.1 are mapped to the corresponding Java classes as shown in the table (`dateTime` is mapped to `Calendar`, as are the built-in `date` and `time` types). Most of

TABLE 9.1 JAX-RPC Mappings between Supported Java Classes and XML Schema built-in Data Types

Java Class	XML Schema Type
String	string
java.math.BigDecimal	decimal
java.math.BigInteger	integer
java.util.Calendar	dateTime
java.util.Date	dateTime
java.xml.namespace.QName	QName
java.net.URI	anyURI

the remaining built-in types are mapped to the Java `String` class. Code generated by `wscompile` will map any of these data types to a Java `String` that is simply a copy of the corresponding character data from the SOAP document. It is then the responsibility of user-written code to perform any parsing needed to interpret such strings.

9.5.2 XML Schemas

In addition to built-in types, XML Schema defines—in the same namespace `http://www.w3.org/2001/XMLSchema` that contains the built-in type names—elements that can be used to define new data types. There are two classes of XML Schema data types: simple and complex. A *simple type* is a data type whose values are represented in XML documents by character data, while a *complex type* is represented using markup. Generally speaking, simple types are used to represent individual values, and complex types are used to represent structured data.

Within a WSDL document, definitions for both simple and complex types are contained within the `types` element (Figure 9.17). These user-defined types are then used in `message` elements to specify the types of operation parameters and return values that do not belong to one of the built-in types. The return type of the three response messages in Figure 9.18, for example, is the `ExchangeValues` type defined in the `types` element of Figure 9.17. A user-defined type may also be referenced within the `types` element itself in order to define another user-defined type; an `Employee` type might be used as part of the definition of a `Department` type, for example.

XML markup such as that shown in the `types` element of Figure 9.17 is known as an *XML schema* (note the lowercase "s"). Specifically, an XML schema is markup that conforms with the W3C-defined XML Schema vocabulary, particularly the portion of the recommendation dealing with data structures [W3C-XML-SCHEMA-STRUCT-1.0]. An XML schema defines all or part of the vocabulary for another XML document. For example, as we will learn in more detail in Section 9.5.4, the markup defining the `ExchangeValues` type in Figure 9.17 specifies that an element conforming with this type will consist of a sequence of three elements of types `dollars`, `euros`, and `yen`, each containing a value conforming with the XML Schema `double` syntax. An XML document that is written in order to conform with an XML schema is called an *instance* of the schema. In addition to defining data types, an XML schema can specify the elements and attributes allowable within an instance document, element content, and so forth. However, our focus here will be on XML Schema's data type definition capabilities.

The `schema` element is the root element for any XML schema markup, whether the schema is embedded within another XML document (as shown in Figure 9.17) or is the root element of an XML *schema document* (a document consisting solely of XML schema markup). Child elements of `schema` can include XML Schema elements for defining data types. The `complexType` element in Figure 9.17 is an example of such an element; as you might guess, this element is used to define a complex data type. As you might also guess, the XML Schema element `simpleType` (not shown in this figure) is used to define simple data types. Each data type defined using one of these elements is given the name specified as the value of the `name` attribute of the element; in Figure 9.17, the `complexType` element defines a data type named `ExchangeValues`. This name is added to the namespace indicated by the `targetNamespace` attribute of `schema` (much as the names of operations, messages, and so on defined by elements in the WSDL namespace are added to the namespace indicated by the `targetNamespace` attribute of the WSDL `definitions` element). Referring to Figure 9.17, we see therefore that `ExchangeValues` is added to the `http://tempuri.org/types` namespace.

With that introduction to schemas, we'll now examine the `simpleType` and `complexType` elements in the next two sections.

9.5.3   User-Defined Simple Types

All of the XML Schema built-in types we have covered are simple. One way of defining a simple user-defined type is to specify one or more restrictions on the values of a simple built-in type. The built-in data type that is restricted is called the *base type* of the restricted type.

For example, the following XML Schema markup defines a simple data type named `memberType` that restricts the `string` built-in data type to just four possible values:

```
<simpleType name="memberType">
  <restriction base="string">
    <enumeration value="platinum" />
    <enumeration value="preferred" />
    <enumeration value="gold" />
    <enumeration value="member" />
  </restriction>
</simpleType>
```

If a SOAP (or other XML) document is parsed by software that checks for schema conformance and the content of an element is supposed to be of type `memberType` as thus defined, then an error will occur if the content of this element is anything other than one of the four strings shown.

All built-in data types have various *facets* that can be used within a `restriction` to form a simple user-defined type. The `enumeration` element, for example, represents a facet that applies to all built-in data types except `boolean`. I will briefly cover most XML Schema facets here; a complete list of the facets available in XML Schema and the built-in types to which each facet applies can be found in Appendix B of the XML Schema Primer [W3C-XML-SCHEMA-PRIMER-1.0].

In addition to `enumeration`, some other facets are `length`, `minLength`, and `maxLength`, which apply to string-oriented data types such as `string`, `QName`, `anyURI`, and `ID`; `minInclusive`, `maxInclusive`, `minExclusive`, and `maxExclusive`, which apply to numeric and time-oriented data types; and `totalDigits` and `fractionDigits`, which apply to most numeric data types. Multiple facets may be used to define a single restricted type. For example,

```
<simpleType name="priorityType">
  <restriction base="int">
    <minExclusive value="10" />
    <maxInclusive value="100" />
  </restriction>
</simpleType>
```

defines a simple type `priorityType` that is an `int` in the range from 11 to 100 (inclusive; the value 10 is excluded). The `length` facet is used to specify that string values must be of exactly a certain length, while `minLength` and `maxLength` are used to specify lower and upper bounds, respectively, on the acceptable lengths of string values. Thus, an analog to the Java `char` type can be defined using XML Schema markup such as

```
<simpleType name="char">
  <restriction base="string">
    <length value="1" />
  </restriction>
</simpleType>
```

The meanings of the other facets mentioned should be clear from their names.

Another facet, `pattern`, applies to almost every built-in type except a few of the XML DTD types. It takes a value that is a regular expression and specifies that all values belonging to the restricted type must conform with this expression. The XML Schema regular expression syntax is similar to that described for JavaScript in Section 4.12.5. For instance, the type

```
<simpleType name="phoneNumType">
  <restriction base="string">
    <pattern value="\d{3}-\d{3}-\d{4}" />
  </restriction>
</simpleType>
```

will match any input string consisting of exactly 10 digits with hyphens following the third and sixth digits. See Appendix F of [W3C-XML-SCHEMA-DATA-1.0] for complete details on XML Schema regular expression syntax.

In addition to restricting built-in types, simple data types can be defined in several other ways. First, the base type for a restriction can be any simple type, user-defined as well as built-in. Second, a simple type can be formed by taking the union of two or more existing simple types. As a rather odd example, if we wanted to create a data type `oddType` with values that are either the strings in the `memberType` enumeration described earlier or a phone number as defined by `phoneNumType`, we could use the XML Schema markup

```
<simpleType name="oddType">
  <union memberTypes="memberType phoneNumType" />
</simpleType>
```

The value of `memberTypes` is a white-space-separated list of simple type names.

Finally, a data type whose values are white-space-separated lists such as the value of `memberTypes` just given can be created using the XML Schema `list` element. For example,

```
<simpleType name="intList">
  <list itemType="int" />
</simpleType>
```

defines a data type with values that are white-space-separated lists of int values. This provides a simple way to represent an array of values.

9.5.4   User-Defined Complex Types

As mentioned earlier, complexType is the XML Schema element used to define a complex type, that is, a type whose values are represented in an XML document using markup. For example, Figure 9.17 contains a complexType element defining an XML Schema user-defined complex type named ExchangeValues. An instance document containing an element anExchangeValue conforming with this type definition might look like

```
<anExchangeValue xsi:type="ExchangeValues">
  <dollars>1.0</dollars>
  <euros>0.746826</euros>
  <yen>102.56</yen>
</anExchangeValue>
```

Notice that a data value of a complex type will be represented in an XML document by an element that (with certain exceptions, such as empty elements) has as its content other elements specified as part of the type definition. In the example just given, the element of type ExchangeValues contains three elements (dollars, euros, and yen) as content.

Although the syntax of complexType is different from that of the XML DTD ELEMENT tag, their purposes are similar: to define an XML content specification. In the case of complexType, the content is specified indirectly for elements belonging to the defined complex data type, while in the case of ELEMENT the content is specified directly for an element. The sequence element is the XML Schema analog of the sequence operator "," in an XML DTD content specification, so the markup

```
<complexType name="ExchangeValues">
  <sequence>
    <element name="dollars" type="double"/>
    <element name="euros" type="double"/>
    <element name="yen" type="double"/>
  </sequence>
</complexType>
```

is roughly equivalent to the XML DTD markup

```
<!ELEMENT anExchangeValue (dollars, euros, yen)>
```

That is, an instance document that contains an element conforming with the Exchange-Values data type must contain three child elements with element type names dollars, euros, and yen, in that order, as shown in the earlier example.

Each of the element elements within a complexType defines an element type that is part of the content of the complex type being defined. As shown, each of the element types has its own associated data type (double in this example), which may be simple or complex, built-in or user-defined. However, if a user-defined type is used, the namespace prefix associated with the schema target namespace must also be used (in the example of Figure 9.17, the appropriate prefix would be tns).

In addition to name and type, element has attributes minOccurs and maxOccurs that are used to specify the minimum number of times that the element must occur and the maximum number of times that it may occur, respectively. Both attribute values default to 1. Thus, markup such as

```
<complexType name="Arguments">
  <sequence>
    <element name="optArg" type="string"
             minOccurs="0" />
  </sequence>
</complexType>
```

means that optArg is optional within an element of type Arguments. Any nonnegative integer can be specified as the value for minOccurs and maxOccurs, but it is an error to specify a smaller value for maxOccurs than for minOccurs. Also, the special value unbounded can be specified for maxOccurs, indicating that the expression may by repeated an arbitrary number of times.

You might be wondering how a Java program will respond if it receives a SOAP message that leaves out an optional value: how will this be stored internally in the Java program? In the case of an optional string, as in the last example, it is simple enough to give the corresponding String variable the value null. But what if the optional element is of a type corresponding to a Java primitive type, such as double? The solution is that wscompile represents such variables using the corresponding wrapper class; for instance, it would use Double rather than double as the type of the variable corresponding to the element. Hence, the value null can still be stored in the Java variable corresponding to such an element.

On the other hand, how does a Java program represent an element for which the value of maxOccurs is greater than 1? This is also fairly easy to handle: it stores the data in an array.

An alternative to sequence that is often used in WSDL documents is all. Actually, anyOrder would probably be a better name for this element: the child elements of all may appear in any order within the declared element, but they all must appear exactly once. In fact, an element can be omitted if 0 is specified as the value of its minOccurs attribute (values greater than 1 are not allowed). For example,

```
<complexType name="ExchangeValues">
  <all>
    <element name="dollars" type="double"/>
    <element name="euros" type="double"/>
    <element name="yen" type="double"/>
  </all>
</complexType>
```

still requires that all three elements dollars, euros, and yen appear within an element of type ExchangeValues, but now they are allowed to appear in any order. It is an error to attempt to specify a value other than 1 for `maxOccurs` on an element within an `all` element.

The schemas that can be written using XML Schema go far beyond what we have covered here. First of all, the vocabulary for creating complex data types is much richer than we have covered: it includes an analog to the XML DTD choice operator (`|`) and a form of inheritance for complex types, among other features. Beyond this, as mentioned near the beginning of this section, XML Schema can be used to completely define an XML vocabulary, specifying not just data types but also the elements and attributes that must be present within a document conforming with the vocabulary. But what we have covered here should be sufficient for understanding XML Schema as it is used in many WSDL documents. For complete details on specifying data types, elements, and attributes with XML Schema, see [W3C-XML-SCHEMA-STRUCT-1.0].

9.5.5   XML Schema within Instance Documents

In a moment, we are going to look carefully at SOAP documents. A primary purpose of the XML schema within a WSDL document is to specify the form of some of the content of SOAP documents passed between a web service client and server. Portions of SOAP documents can therefore be viewed as XML schema instances. XML Schema defines a few attributes that can be used within instance documents; we'll look at three of these here.

Within an instance document, rather than leaving an optional element out entirely, an alternative is to specify `true` for the element's `nil` attribute. (Actually, since this attribute's data type is the built-in type `boolean`, it is equivalent to specify 1 as the value.) XML Schema uses the separate namespace named `http://www.w3.org/2001/XMLSchema-instance` for `nil` and its other attributes that may appear in instance documents. Thus, XML Schema has two namespaces: this *instance namespace*, and the *document namespace* `http://www.w3.org/2001/XMLSchema` that we saw used earlier within the `schema` element of a WSDL document (Figure 9.17). As illustrated by the examples in this chapter, the document namespace is usually associated with the namespace prefix `xsd`, and the instance space with `xsi`.

In short, returning to our earlier example of the optional element named `optArg`, if an instance document associates `xsi` with the XML Schema instance namespace, then that document might include the markup

```
<optArg xsi:nil="true"></optArg>
```

This is a way of explicitly stating that the element's value is effectively `null` rather than simply leaving the element out of the document (which might have been done mistakenly). If `nil` is specified as `true` (or 1) on an element, then that element must have no content.

Another oft-used attribute in the XML Schema instance namespace is `type`. This attribute can be used to explicitly state the type of an element within an instance document, rather than leaving it to an application to infer the element type by reference to a schema. We've seen examples of this in earlier documents, such as in the following markup from the SOAP document shown in Figure 9.1:

```
<latitude xsi:type="xsd:decimal">40.28</latitude>
<longitude xsi:type="xsd:decimal">-79.49</longitude>
```

Even though the WSDL document specified that within an instance document the content of `latitude` and `longitude` elements should be string representations of data belonging to the built-in type `decimal`, the SOAP instance document itself contains this information explicitly as well. Note that the `xsd` prefix must be associated with the XML Schema document namespace so that the reference to `decimal` can be resolved. Actually, the type specified in an instance document does not need to exactly match the type specified in the schema. For instance, a type that is a restriction of the associated schema type can be specified in the instance. You should refer to [W3C-XML-SCHEMA-STRUCT-1.0] for details on the `type` XML Schema instance attribute.

Finally, the `schemaLocation` attribute can be used within an instance document to specify a URL for the XML schema that defines the instance vocabulary. For instance, we have seen this attribute used in deployment descriptors (e.g., Figure 8.6) to specify a URL for the location of the XML Schema document that defines the Java servlet 2.4 deployment descriptor vocabulary. This is analogous to including a `DOCTYPE` element in an XML document for which a DTD is used to define the document vocabulary.

9.6   Communicating Object Data: SOAP

We are finally ready to look more closely at the lowest level of the hierarchy of technologies defining web services, SOAP. "SOAP" was originally an acronym standing for "Simple Object Access Protocol," but the current W3C Recommendation [W3C-SOAP-FRAMEWORK-1.2] treats it as a name rather than an acronym (because SOAP is now considered to be much more than a protocol for accessing objects). In any case, SOAP is an XML vocabulary that can be used to communicate data, and in particular was originally designed for communicating structured data that might typically be found in object-oriented programs.

9.6.1   SOAP Elements

The element structure defined by SOAP 1.1 (the version most widely used at the time of this writing and that is supported by JAX-RPC 1.1) is extremely simple. The document root element is `Envelope`, which has an optional `Header` element followed by a required `Body` element, which may contain an optional `Fault` element that in turn has several elements (such as `faultcode` and `faultstring`) defined as its content. Elements in other namespaces may appear anywhere within the `Header` and `Body` elements and may appear after the `Body` element within `Envelope`.

The primary data of a SOAP document—which for a web service would be the operation name and parameter values from the client and the return value from the server—are contained in the `Body` element. The `Header` element provides a mechanism for passing supporting information; for example, it could be used in place of the HTTP cookie mechanism to communicate a session ID. The `Fault` element can be used to communicate error or status information. We'll focus on the `Body` element in this section; details on all of the SOAP 1.1 elements are provided in a technical report published as a W3C Note [W3C-SOAP-1.1].

In addition to defining an XML vocabulary, the SOAP 1.1 technical report suggests a possible mechanism for encoding data values and structures within the Body element of a SOAP document, specifies how SOAP documents can be communicated via HTTP, and describes a means of using SOAP to implement a style of communication known as *remote procedure call* (RPC) processing; we'll describe this in more detail in the next subsection. The SOAP 1.1 report also makes clear that alternatives are allowed: other data encodings can be used in SOAP documents; SOAP documents can be communicated by non-HTTP protocols such as SMTP, FTP, or even proprietary protocols; and SOAP documents can be used for non-RPC communication. Despite this potential flexibility, many web services—including our example currency converter service—use the SOAP-defined options, so these are the options we'll focus on here. We'll first consider SOAP's RPC representation, then its data encoding, and finally its transport via HTTP.

9.6.2   RPC Representation

Let's begin by describing what a remote procedure call is. In essence, RPC is the generic term for the type of communication we have described for web service operations: the client makes a call to a method (or "procedure") that resides on another machine ("remotely"). This concept has been implemented in many ways by many programming languages and operating systems. All of the implementations share the concept of communicating parameter data to another machine that executes a procedure on that data and returns a response. What distinguishes web service operations is that they are defined in terms of open, widely supported, text-based standards, which potentially enables clients written in nearly any language and running on nearly any operating system to issue RPC-style communications to servers written in nearly any language and running on nearly any operating system.

The style attribute of the soap:binding element in the WSDL document of Figure 9.20 indicated that the web service defined by this WSDL expected to communicate with clients in an RPC style, and the soap:body elements indicated using an encoding specified by SOAP 1.1 to represent the RPC. In the SOAP-specified representation of RPC calls, the call is modeled as a form of data structure known as a struct. From a Java point of view, a *struct* can be thought of as an instance of a class that consists entirely of public instance variables: it is simply a container in which data can be stored in named variables. From an XML Schema point of view, the type of data structure defined by a complex type is a struct. The instance variables (Java point of view) or child elements (XML Schema point of view) are known as the *accessors* of the struct.

The specific struct used in a SOAP representation of an RPC call has a name that is the procedure name and has one accessor for each parameter to be passed to the procedure. In the context of calling a web service operation, the operation name is the name of the struct, and each parameter in the request message associated with the operation becomes an accessor (with the same name as the parameter) in the struct. This struct is then encoded as XML markup in some way (an example will be given shortly), and the resulting markup is made a child of the SOAP Body element.

Referring back to Figures 9.18 and 9.19 of the currency converter WSDL document, we see that the fromDollars operation has a single input parameter named double_1 of built-in type double. Thus, the struct representing an RPC call to this operation will be named `fromDollars` and will have one accessor named `double_1` representing a value of type `double`.

Figure 9.22 shows a SOAP request from the currency converter client to the server. The RPC request struct in this example is encoded using the SOAP data-encoding rules, as indicated by the values specified for the `use` and `encodingStyle` attributes of the appropriate `soap:body` in Figure 9.20. In this form of data encoding (discussed in more detail in the next subsection), the name of the struct/operation is qualified with a namespace prefix, but the accessor/parameter names are not qualified. So, in Figure 9.22, the operation name `fromDollars` is qualified (with a prefix associated with the `targetNamespace` specified within the `types` element of the WSDL document for this web service [Figure 9.17]) while the parameter name `double_1` is not qualified. In a SOAP data encoding, simple XML Schema data types are represented using the XML Schema representation rules; the string `1.0` is, of course, a valid XML Schema representation of a value of the simple type `double`.

As an aside, note that the SOAP-encoded markup uses namespaces in a nonstandard way. For example, if a standard XML parser read the document of Figure 9.22, it would assume that `double_1` is in no namespace, since `double_1` is not prefixed and a default namespace is not declared in this document, even though `double_1` is actully in the `ns0` namespace. For this reason and others, web services implementations are expected to increasingly favor a so-called *literal encoding*—that is, an encoding conforming with the XML schema contained in the web service's WSDL—over SOAP 1.1 encoding of data. A literal encoding is indicated within a WSDL by specifying `literal` for the `use` attribute of a `soap:body` element. You can learn more about literal encodings from the WSDL 1.1 technical report [W3C-WSDL-1.1], and about JAX-RPC (and therefore JWSDP) support for literal encoding in the JAX-RPC specification [SUN-JAXRPC-1.1].

The namespace defining the SOAP 1.1 elements in Figure 9.22 is `http://schemas.xmlsoap.org/soap/envelope/`. It is expected that no other version of SOAP will use this namespace name, so the namespace name can also be used to recognize that this is a SOAP 1.1 document (there is no SOAP 1.1 `version` attribute). The `encodingStyle`

```
<?xml version="1.0" encoding="UTF-8"?>
<env:Envelope
  xmlns:env="http://schemas.xmlsoap.org/soap/envelope/"
  xmlns:xsd="http://www.w3.org/2001/XMLSchema"
  xmlns:xsi="http://www.w3.org/2001/XMLSchema-instance"
  xmlns:enc="http://schemas.xmlsoap.org/soap/encoding/"
  xmlns:ns0="http://tempuri.org/wsdl"
  xmlns:ns1="http://tempuri.org/types"
  env:encodingStyle="http://schemas.xmlsoap.org/soap/encoding/">
  <env:Body>
    <ns0:fromDollars>
      <double_1 xsi:type="xsd:double">1.0</double_1>
    </ns0:fromDollars>
  </env:Body>
</env:Envelope>
```

FIGURE 9.22 SOAP document sent by client to currency converter web service.

attribute of Envelope specifies the same value as that specified for the encodingStyle attribute in the corresponding soap:body element of the WSDL. Note that the encodingStyle attribute of Envelope must always be prefixed, regardless of the namespace of the element specifying it.

The SOAP representation of a response to an RPC call is similarly represented by a struct. By convention, the struct's name is the operation name suffixed with the string Response. The struct contains a single accessor representing the value returned by the RPC. (Technically, SOAP RPC supports call-by-reference parameters as well, and such parameters could also be part of the response struct. However, it is never necessary to have such parameters in an RPC call, and this feature is not supported in JAX-RPC 1.1. So we will not consider such parameters further here.)

Before looking at the SOAP response document sent by the currency converter server in response to the SOAP request of Figure 9.22, let's recall some aspects of the WSDL document defining this web service. Referring to Figure 9.19, we see that the response from a fromDollars operation is a CurCon_fromDollarsResponse message, which according to Figure 9.18 has a single part named result of type ExchangeValues. Figure 9.17, in turn, shows us that a value of type ExchangeValues is an object with three double-valued instance variables named dollars, euros, and yen.

Given this background, Figure 9.23 shows the SOAP document generated in response to the earlier request. As we would expect from the discussion of the paragraph before last, the Body of this document contains an element named fromDollarsResponse, which in turn contains an element (named result) that encodes the value of the RPC response using the SOAP data encoding. Again, details of SOAP's data encoding are covered in the next subsection.

```
<?xml version="1.0" encoding="UTF-8"?>
<env:Envelope
  xmlns:env="http://schemas.xmlsoap.org/soap/envelope/"
  xmlns:xsd="http://www.w3.org/2001/XMLSchema"
  xmlns:xsi="http://www.w3.org/2001/XMLSchema-instance"
  xmlns:enc="http://schemas.xmlsoap.org/soap/encoding/"
  xmlns:ns0="http://tempuri.org/types"
  env:encodingStyle="http://schemas.xmlsoap.org/soap/encoding/">
  <env:Body>
    <ans1:fromDollarsResponse
      xmlns:ans1="http://tempuri.org/wsdl">
      <result href="#ID1"/>
    </ans1:fromDollarsResponse>
    <ns0:ExchangeValues id="ID1" xsi:type="ns0:ExchangeValues">
      <dollars xsi:type="xsd:double">1.0</dollars>
      <euros xsi:type="xsd:double">0.746826</euros>
      <yen xsi:type="xsd:double">102.56</yen>
    </ns0:ExchangeValues>
  </env:Body>
</env:Envelope>
```

FIGURE 9.23 SOAP document sent by currency converter web service server to client.

Before turning to SOAP data encoding, you should know that WSDL 1.1 defines two *operation styles*: RPC and document. The RPC style has been described. Specifying document for the style attribute of soap:binding selects the document operation style. In *document style*, parameter and return value elements are direct children of the SOAP Body element rather than being wrapped under another element. In the case of a request to a web service represented in document style, the operation name must be passed to the web service by some means other than as the name of a child element of the Body; for example, the SOAPAction HTTP header field might be used. As with literal encoding, more information on the document operation style is available from the WSDL and JAX-RPC references [W3C-WSDL-1.1] and [SUN-JAXRPC-1.1]. Be advised that JAX-RPC 1.1 does not require support for the combination of document style with SOAP encoding (the document/encoded *operation mode*). The other three operation modes—rpc/encoded, rpc/literal, and document/literal—are supported.

9.6.3   SOAP Encoding of Struct Data

SOAP defines a simple but effective mechanism for representing struct data, whether it be a struct representing an RPC call or response or a struct representing a parameter or return value. We have already learned that in a SOAP data encoding, a struct can be represented as an element with a type name the same as the struct name and with child elements having the same names as the struct's accessors; also, the child element names are not prefixed. As you might guess, if one of these accessors has a value that is a struct, then this can be represented by adding children (with unprefixed names) to the original accessor element. But what if two different structs have accessors that both reference another struct? Worse yet, what if two structs recursively reference one another?

Figure 9.23 illustrates the SOAP data encoding for representing references to structs. Any struct that is to be referenced by other structs contains a specification for its id attribute. The value specified for id must be unique with respect to all of the values specified for id attributes within the document (because SOAP defines the value of this attribute to be of the XML DTD type ID). An accessor within another struct encodes a reference to this struct by specifying for the href attribute of the accessor a URI fragment identifier for the id of the referenced struct. Thus, in Figure 9.23, the value of the result accessor of the fromDollarsResponse struct is a reference to the ExchangeValues struct, which contains the actual response data.

If SOAP RPC encoding is used, the XML elements representing the RPC request and response structs are not considered data elements and do not have associated type information. In fact, if you look carefully at Figures 9.22 and 9.23, you'll notice that the elements having RPC struct names—fromDollars and fromDollarsResponse—are in the http://tempuri.org/wsdl namespace, not the http://tempuri.org/types namespace that contains the user-defined data types. (One of the features of the document operation style is that it eliminates these nondata elements from the Body of a SOAP message.) Along the same lines, the result element in Figure 9.23 does not have an xsi:type attribute, because the element itself is empty in this document and therefore doesn't actually represent the ExchangeValues data type.

Another noteworthy aspect of the SOAP data encoding is that it allows some flexibility in how struct data will be represented. For instance, the `result` accessor of Figure 9.23 could have instead been written as

```
<ans1:fromDollarsResponse
  xmlns:ans1="http://tempuri.org/wsdl">
  <result xsi:type="ns0:ExchangeValues">
    <dollars xsi:type="xsd:double">1.0</dollars>
    <euros xsi:type="xsd:double">0.746826</euros>
    <yen xsi:type="xsd:double">102.56</yen>
  </result>
</ans1:fromDollarsResponse>
```

This flexibility in converting from an internal form of data to a SOAP representation—a process known as *serialization*—comes at the price of forcing the software that deserializes a SOAP representation to be prepared to accept SOAP documents in a variety of forms.

9.6.4   SOAP Encoding of Arrays

In addition to specifying encodings for structs, SOAP specifies how arrays can be encoded. For example, suppose that we changed the currency converter so that it returned an array of three `double` values rather than an `ExchangeValues` object. Before seeing how this would be represented using a SOAP encoding, let's consider the impact on the web service's WSDL document. The `types` element of the WSDL document generated by `wscompile` would now include one `complexType` element in addition to the one defining `ExchangeValues` shown in Figure 9.17. (I've also repeated the `import` element from before, because I'm going to have something to say about it):

```
<import
  namespace="http://schemas.xmlsoap.org/soap/encoding/" />
<complexType name="ArrayOfdouble">
  <complexContent>
    <restriction base="soap11-enc:Array">
      <attribute ref="soap11-enc:arrayType"
        wsdl:arrayType="double[]"/>
    </restriction>
  </complexContent>
</complexType>
```

The WSDL `message` representing the response from `fromDollar` would become

```
<message name="CurCon_fromDollarsResponse">
  <part name="result" type="ns2:ArrayOfdouble"/></message>
```

The XML Schema markup defining the `ArrayOfdouble` complex type illustrates one of the XML Schema mechanisms for complex type inheritance. In particular, `ArrayOfdouble` inherits from a complex type named `Array`. The XML Schema markup defining this type is located at `http://schemas.xmlsoap.org/soap/encoding/` and is incorporated into the WSDL document's `schema` element via the `import` element shown. This URI is also the namespace name for the SOAP encoding namespace, which is associated with namespace prefix `soap11-enc` in this WSDL document. I'm not going to go further into the details of this markup here, other than to say that the type name specified as the value of the `wsdl:arrayType` attribute can be any XML Schema built-in type as well as the qualified name of any type declared elsewhere in the `schema` element. So, for example, recalling that the `schema` element also defined the complex type `ExchangeValues` in the namespace associated with prefix `tns`, we could create a type representing an array of objects by specifying the value `tns:ExchangeValues[]` for the value of `wsdl:arrayType` within a similar `complexType` element.

Now that we see how SOAP-encoded array types can be represented in a WSDL document, we're ready to consider the SOAP encoding of such an array value within an instance document. As with objects, the SOAP encoding of arrays is straightforward. For example, Figure 9.24 shows the `Body` of a SOAP response from the currency converter modified to return an array of three values rather than an object of type `ExchangeValues`. As shown, an array can be referenced by other markup just as an object is referenced, via the `href-id` mechanism. The array itself is represented by defining an element having a name that is the array type name and by specifying a value for the `arrayType` attribute (in the SOAP encoding namespace) that indicates the number of elements in the array and their data type. In this case, the value `xsd:double[3]` indicates that the array consists of three values conforming to the XML Schema `double` built-in data type. The elements themselves are then represented as elements all with the same (arbitrary) name, each representing its value using SOAP data encoding.

9.6.5 SOAP and HTTP

Finally, the currency converter web service specified (via the `transport` attribute of `soap:binding` in Figure 9.20) that it would send and receive SOAP documents via HTTP. As mentioned earlier in this chapter, SOAP 1.1 specifies that this is implemented by placing the SOAP request and response documents in the bodies of the HTTP request and response

```
<env:Body>
  <ans1:fromDollarsResponse
      xmlns:ans1-"http://tempuri.org/wsdl">
    <result href="#ID1"/>
  </ans1:fromDollarsResponse>
  <ns0:ArrayOfdouble id="ID1"
    xsi:type="enc:Array"
    enc:arrayType="xsd:double[3]">
    <item xsi:type="xsd:double">1.0</item>
    <item xsi:type="xsd:double">0.746826</item>
    <item xsi:type="xsd:double">102.56</item>
  </ns0:ArrayOfdouble>
</env:Body>
```

FIGURE 9.24 Body element of SOAP response document sent by modified currency converter web service that returns an array rather than an `ExchangeValues` struct.

messages, respectively (SOAP documents embedded within HTTP messages are sometimes referred to as *SOAP messages*). SOAP 1.1 also specifies that a SOAPAction HTTP header field (described in Section 9.4) must be present in any HTTP request message carrying a SOAP document, although it is not required that a value be specified in this header field. If a value is specified, it must be either a syntactically valid URI or the empty string.

9.6.6   Java Support for SOAP

Java provides support for creating and manipulating SOAP documents through SAAJ, the SOAP with Attachments API for Java™ technology. This API is included with JWSDP 1.3; you can browse the Javadoc documentation of the API by browsing to the docs/api folder of your JWSDP 1.3 installation directory. The javax.xml.soap package is a good starting point for learning about these capabilities. Given the description of the SOAP vocabulary and usage contained in this section, you should not have much difficulty in learning to use SAAJ if needed. But given how much can be done with higher-level technologies, it's quite possible that you'll never need to write code at the SOAP level. So I won't go into the details of SAAJ here.

9.7   Related Technologies

There are many other technologies related to web services in addition to those discussed in this chapter. I'll briefly mention a few of them here.

First, I have chosen to cover web services as provided by JWSDP 1.3, because the focus of JWSDP is on web technologies. However, versions of the Sun J2EE™ platform can also be used to develop web services and include many features that would be useful in large-scale web-oriented systems. Another alternative for building Java web services is Apache Axis (http://ws.apache.org/axis/), an open-source implementation of JAX-RPC, which has its own collection of high-level web service creation tools. In addition, there are several commercial systems available for developing Java-based web applications and services. The IBM® WebSphere® and BEA® WebLogic® development platforms are two of the more popular such products at the time of this writing.

Like JWSDP and the other Java-oriented technologies, Microsoft .NET allows developers to construct web services code using either high-level tools or lower-level APIs (or some combination). At a low level, APIs in the System.Web and System.Xml .NET namespaces provide the necessary communication and data manipulation facilities to create and read SOAP messages as well as communicate them via HTTP. At a higher level, the ASP.NET WebMethods framework provides tools for automatically generating a WSDL document and server-side SOAP serialization classes from, say, a C# class definition. On the client side, the .NET command-line tool wsdl.exe can be used much like wscompile to generate a proxy object and supporting data-related objects from a WSDL document.

Web services can also be created using PHP as the underlying development platform. The PHP Extension and Application Repository (PEAR) (http://pear.php.net/) contains a SOAP package that provides both high-level web services tools—such as a method for parsing a WSDL and creating a proxy object—and a low-level SOAP API for PHP scripts.

All of the technologies mentioned thus far are alternative implementations of concepts covered in this chapter. A concept not covered previously is that of a *registry* for web services. A primary example of a web services registry technology is Universal Discovery, Description, and Integration (UDDI), which allows a web service to be described in a registry so that other developers can discover the service and potentially integrate their web service clients with it. In particular, UDDI provides the specification for a web service that can be used to register other web services and that can be queried to learn about web services that have previously been registered. UDDI also specifies identifier and categorization systems ("tModels") that can be used to formally describe registered web services. The Java API for XML Registries (JAXR) is distributed as part of JWSDP 1.3 and supports the interaction of Java programs with UDDI servers as well as with other XML-oriented registry systems. The other web-services platforms mentioned earlier also provide UDDI support.

The Web Services-Interoperability Organization (WS-I) Basic Profile is not a technology, but is instead a specification of how web service developers should use various web services technologies. For example, the WSDL 1.1 report does not require that XML Schema should be used to specify user-defined data types; WS-I Basic Profile version 1.0 makes the use of XML Schema a requirement. This requirement, of course, is consistent with our usage of WSDL. However, some WS-I Basic Profile requirements differ markedly from the usage of WSDL and SOAP illustrated in this chapter. In particular, SOAP encodings of objects and arrays are not allowed. Instead, the literal operational encoding must be used. That is, the value `literal` must be specified for the use attribute of `soap:body` elements in the WSDL document for a web service conforming with the WS-I Basic Profile. The `wscompile` tool can be instructed to run in a WS-I-compliant mode by adding the option `-f:wsi` to the command line. I have covered the SOAP encodings because, at the time of this writing, many web services still use them.

9.8   References

While there is currently no formal standard for WSDL, WSDL 1.1 is a de facto standard and is documented as a W3C Note at [W3C-WSDL-1.1]. The formal references for version 1.0 of the XML Schema language are [W3C-XML-SCHEMA-STRUCT-1.0] and [W3C-XML-SCHEMA-DATA-1.0]. The first of these describes the XML Schema elements and attributes that can be used in schema and instance documents, while the second gives complete details on all of the simple data types defined by XML Schema. The W3C also provides an introductory tutorial [W3C-XML-SCHEMA-PRIMER-1.0] that combines detailed explanations and examples of key XML Schema features with links into the reference documents. Similarly, the W3C has published three recommendations for SOAP 1.2: a primer [W3C-SOAP-PRIMER-1.2], a part covering SOAP elements and other fundamental aspects of the SOAP framework [W3C-SOAP-FRAMEWORK-1.2], and a part covering SOAP encoding, RPC representation, transport via HTTP, and related "adjunct" topics [W3C-SOAP-ADJUNCT-1.2]. However, SOAP 1.1 is currently the version most widely used, and is documented as a W3C Note [W3C-SOAP-1.1].

The UDDI specifications are available at `http://www.uddi.org/specification.html`, and the JAXR API for accessing UDDI and other XML registries is described in the JWSDP documentation (located in the `docs/api` subdirectory of your JWSDP installation directory) of the `javax.xml.registry` package and its subpackages. The WS-I Basic

Profile and related documentation can be found at `http://www.ws-i.org/deliverables/` `workinggroup.aspx?wg=basicprofile`.

Exercises

9.1. Writing a web service (with JWSDP).

  (a) Write a complete service endpoint interface named `CreditCheck` in a package named `com.example`. The interface should define an operation `check` that has a single `String` parameter (representing an identification number) and returns a `float` representing a credit score for the identified individual (with a negative number used to flag an error).

  (b) Write an XML file that would be used as input to `wscompile` in order to create a service implementing the interface in part (a). The service name should be `CreditCheckService`.

  (c) Write specifications for the `jaxrpc-ri.xml` file's `urlPatternBase` and `url-Pattern` elements that would be appropriate for accessing the `CreditCheck Service` web service with the URL `http://localhost:8080/credit/check` (assuming that the client is on the same machine as the server and the server listens to port 8080).

9.2. Based on the information displayed in Figure 9.9, what are two request query-string parameters recognized by the servlet implementing a Java web service built using the JWSDP tools? Do you think that the servlet returns a SOAP document in the HTTP response to a request containing one of these parameters? Explain.

9.3. Writing a web service client (with JWSDP).

  (a) Assume that a WSDL document for the web service for which you want to write a client has URL `http://www.example.com/credit/WSDL`. Also assume that you want to use the package name `creditClient` for your client. Write an XML file that could be used as input to `wscompile` in order to generate a service endpoint interface and associated Java files from this WSDL document.

  (b) Assume that `CreditCheckService` is specified as the value of the `name` attribute of the `service` element in a WSDL document. What will you find in the `wscompile`-generated file `CreditCheckService.java`? What is the name of the Java class that can be used to obtain a proxy object implementing the service endpoint interface?

  (c) Assuming that the proxy object is referenced by a variable named `proxy`, write Java code to call the web service operation `check` defined in Exercise 9.1(a) from your client, passing the identifier `123456789` and storing the result in a `float` variable named `score`.

9.4. Write a WSDL `message` element representing a parameter list consisting of an `xsd:double` value named `amount` and an `xsd:string` value named `type`. Name the `message` element `convertParams`.

9.5. In which child element(s) of the root element of a WSDL 1.1 document should you look for the names of the operations of the associated web service?

9.6. Are the elements `soap:body`, `soap:operation`, and `soap:binding` in Figure 9.20 defined by the SOAP or the WSDL vocabulary? How do you know?

9.7. Based on the way in which a web service is created and deployed using JWSDP 1.3, why do you think that the WSDL generated by `wscompile` specifies the string

REPLACE_WITH_ACTUAL_URL as the value of `location` in a `soap:address` element rather than simply specifying a URL?

9.8. In Java, the character literal '\n' represents the newline character (0x0a). The XML Schema `string` built-in data type does not recognize such character strings as escaped character values. Why do you think this is the case? How can you represent a newline character within the content of an XML element that contains `xsd:string` data?

9.9. XML Schema simple data types.

  (a) Write XML Schema markup defining a simple type named `money` that restricts `double` values to two digits following the decimal point.

  (b) Using the `union` element, write XML Schema markup defining a simple type named `userID` that is either seven or nine characters long.

  (c) Repeat part (b) using an XML Schema regular expression instead of `union`.

  (d) Write XML Schema markup defining a simple type named `idList` representing a white-space-separated list of values of type `userID`.

9.10. XML Schema complex data types.

  (a) Write XML Schema markup that could be used to add a definition for a complex type named `DatedExchangeValue` to the `types` element of Figure 9.17. Elements of this type should contain two required elements in the following order: a `date` element of built-in type `dateTime`, and a `values` element of user-defined type `ExchangeValues`.

  (b) Modify the markup in part (a) so that `date` is optional.

  (c) Further modify the markup so that the two elements contained within an element of type `DatedExchangeValue` may appear in either order.

  For the following exercises, you may assume that the prefixes `xsd` **and** `xsi` **are associated with the XML document and instance namespaces, respectively.**

  (d) Assuming that `DatedExchangeValue` is as defined in the previous part of this exercise, write instance document markup for a `dev` element of type `Dated-ExchangeValue` that explicitly assigns a null value to its `date` element. You may assume that the default namespace is the target namespace of the schema defining `DatedExchangeValue`, `ExchangeValues`, and `dev`.

9.11. Write (assuming the rpc/encoded operation mode covered in this chapter) the Body of a SOAP request representing a call to a web service operation named `translate` that takes three `string` parameters: the name of a language from which to translate, the name of a language to which to translate, and text to be translated. Assume that these parameters are named `string_1` through `string_3` in the WSDL and that `translate` is in the namespace associated with namespace prefix `ns0`. Your call should represent an RPC to translate the string `Hello world!` from English to French.

9.12. Give a SOAP data encoding of a struct `msgBuffer` of complex type `circBuffer`. The data type has three elements: a `string` named `data`, and two elements of type `msgBuffer` named `prev` and `next`. The value of `msgBuffer`'s `data` accessor is `funny`, and the `prev` and `next` values are both references to the `msgBuffer` struct itself. Assume that `msgBuffer` and `circBuffer` are both defined in the namespace associated with prefix `ns1`.

9.13. Give a SOAP data encoding of an array `valArray` of user-defined type `arrayOf-ExcVals` consisting of two items of type `ExchangeValues`. Both of these items should be references to the same `ExchangeValues` object having the values shown in Figure 9.23. Assume that `valArray`, `arrayOfExcVals`, and `ExchangeValues` are all defined in the namespace associated with prefix ns1, and assume that enc represents the SOAP encoding namespace.

Research and Exploration

9.14. Use wscompile to build a client to access one of the following web services:

(a) Amazon's E-Commerce Service (ECS) is a web service that allows programs to request product information available at Amazon's Web site as well as to access some services at the site, such as shopping carts. Learn about ECS and sign up for a free developer subscription ID at http://www.amazon.com/gp/aws/landing.html (be sure to read the license agreement and understand that there are limitations on the frequency of access to the web service). Then create a JSP client that accepts a book ISBN as a parameter and displays the the book author and title if the ECS has information for the ISBN.

(b) At the time of this writing, Google Inc. has a beta web service that allows programs to perform Web searches as well as to call some other operations, such as spell checking. Learn about the Google Web APIs and sign up for a free Google account at http://www.google.com/apis/ (be sure to read the license agreement and understand that there are limitations on the frequency of access to the web service). Then create a JSP client that accepts a search phrase and returns the estimated total results count and the summary from the first search result returned (if any).

(c) At the time of this writing, the U.S. National Weather Service operates an experimental web service that provides weather forecasts for locations in the United States. Information about the service is currently available at http://www.nws.noaa.gov/forecasts/xml/. The service is freely available, but see the service documentation on requested limitations on access frequency. Write a JSP client that accepts latitude and longitude parameters and returns the XML document (with MIME type text/xml) representing the "glance" product.

9.15. Compare the definition of the Java double primitive data type in the Java Language Specification [SUN-JLS-2] with the definition of the XML Schema double built-in type in the XML Schema specification for data type [W3C-XML-SCHEMA-DATA-1.0]. Give at least one difference between the values represented by these data types.

9.16. A web service client generated by wscompile sends its SOAP request messages by default to the URL specified in the WSDL document's soap:address element. However, this default can be overridden. For example, the following code could be used to cause the currency converter client of Section 9.3 to send its SOAP request message to the URL http://localhost:8080/servlet/LogHttpRequest:

```
Stub stub = (Stub)
    (new HistoricCurrencyConverter_Impl()).getCurConPort();
stub._setProperty
      (Stub.ENDPOINT_ADDRESS_PROPERTY,
       "http://localhost:8080/servlet/LogHttpRequest");
CurCon curCon = (CurCon)stub;
```

Modify one of the web service clients you have written (as directed by your instructor) to override its default server URL as shown. Then write a servlet LogHttpRequest that will input the body of the HTTP request it receives (you can use the object returned by the getReader() method of HttpServletRequest for this purpose) and output it using System.out (this will be written in the logs/launcher.server.log file under your JWSDP 1.3 directory). Use Telnet and the SOAP request message you have captured to obtain the SOAP response message that is generated by the web service if this message is sent to it.

Projects

9.17. Implement Exercise 6.15 as a web service. Specifically, the book data should be stored on a server and made available to clients through a web service. Implement a client in Java (either text-based or with a GUI, as directed by your instructor).

9.18. Implement either Exercise 6.16 or Exercise 8.19 as a web service. Specifically, the application data should be stored on a server and made available to clients through a web service. Implement a client using Java servlet, JSP, and JavaBeans technologies appropriately.

APPENDIX A

Software Installation

All of the examples discussed in this textbook can be run on a variety of systems using freely available software. This appendix provides instructions for obtaining and installing this software. If you have any difficulties obtaining or installing software as described here, updated Web addresses and instructions may be available at the textbook Web site listed in the preface.

Instructions are given in this appendix for Windows XP and Linux operating systems. They should be adaptable to related systems, such as Mac OS® X, with little or no change.

A.1 System Basics

There are a few basic concepts you should be familiar with before attempting to install software on your system.

A.1.1 Command Prompt

Several of the instructions here and elsewhere in the textbook ask you to type a command "at a command prompt." This subsection explains how to obtain a command prompt.

Windows XP
In Windows XP, you can obtain a window with a command prompt as follows:

- Click the Start button.
- Select Run.
- Type cmd in the Run window.

The command prompt in Windows is normally a directory path followed by a greater-than sign (>), such as `C:\Documents and Settings\SomeUser>`.

Linux
In many Linux systems a "shell," "console," or "terminal" window will appear on the screen when you log in. The prompt in a Linux terminal window often begins with your machine and/or user name followed by either a dollar sign ($) or a percent sign (%). If a terminal window is not displayed when you log in and your window system has a menu similar to the Start menu in Windows, try searching the menu for an application with one of the three terms mentioned. If this fails, try left- or right-clicking on the desktop, and search in any pop-up menu that appears for an item containing one of the three terms. If none of these suggestions works, consult your system's documentation or administrator.

A.1.2   Environment Variables

Environment variables are used to tell applications where to look for certain files. For example, the CLASSPATH environment variable can be used to tell the Java compiler and virtual machine where to look for user-defined Java class files.

Windows

In Windows XP, select the System item from the Control Panel (under Performance and Maintenance if you view the Control Panel with the Category View). Under the Advanced tab, click the Environment Variables button near the bottom of the System Properties window. You can then add or edit environment variables in the Environment Variables pop-up window. You normally will set user variables (top panel) rather than system variables.

Some environment variable values may have multiple parts. For example, several directories may be included in the value of CLASSPATH. For environment variable values that may have multiple parts, use semicolon (;) characters to separate the parts.

Linux

Setting environment variables depends on the shell program used. If using bash, sh, or similar shells (which normally have a prompt ending in a dollar sign ($)), the following is an example of the syntax that can be used either at a command prompt or within a start-up file such as .bashrc:

```
PATH=/usr/java/jwsdp/bin:${PATH};export PATH
```

This adds a directory before any existing list of directories contained in the PATH environment variable. Notice that colon (:) is used as the separator character for multipart environment variable values in Linux.

In shells such as csh or tcsh (which normally have a prompt ending in a percent sign (%)), the syntax used to set an environment variable is illustrated by the following:

```
setenv PATH /usr/java/jwsdp/apache-ant/bin:${PATH}
```

Again, this can be entered either at a command prompt or as part of a start-up file such as .cshrc.

A.1.3   File Paths

In Linux, directories in a file path are separated by the forward slash character (/); in Windows they are separated by the backslash character (\). However, when invoking the javac compiler or java run time from a Windows command prompt, either separator character can be used. For example, from a Windows prompt, either of the following commands is valid and produces the same effect:

```
javac myCurConClient\CurCon.java
javac myCurConClient/CurCon.java
```

Since the forward slash works in Java command lines for both Linux and Windows systems, I will show all Java commands in this format. I will also sometimes show file paths in this format even when I'm talking about something other than a Java command line. For example, I might say "place this file in the `WEB-INF/src` directory." If you are using a Windows system, you should replace forward slashes with backslashes in contexts such as this.

A.2   Browser Software

The examples in this textbook were tested using Mozilla 1.4; later versions of Mozilla should work similarly (preliminary testing with Mozilla 1.7 showed no obvious differences). Because versions of Netscape 7 are closely related to the Mozilla products, the examples should work with these browsers as well. Firefox 1.0 is also closely related and intended to be standards-compliant, although it does not automatically include some of the components (such as the JavaScript debugger) that are bundled with Mozilla. Finally, most examples will work with IE6, except as noted in the text.

At the time of this writing, Mozilla 1.x browsers can be obtained from `http://www.mozilla.org/releases/`. From this page, select the version of the browser you wish to install, click on the Release Notes link, then click on the Installation Instructions link appropriate to your system. Follow these instructions to install Mozilla. I recommend using the Full installer to ensure that you obtain all of the components mentioned in this textbook.

It is important to note that if you choose to use an older browser (such as Mozilla 1.4) for development and testing of Web software, you should avoid using the browser to surf the Web. Security holes discovered in older browsers are often only patched in later versions of the browser software, so using an older version of a browser leaves you vulnerable to known software attacks. At the time of this writing, the SeaMonkey™ project (`http://www.mozilla.org/projects/seamonkey/`) is releasing software based on the Mozilla suite and is patching security flaws as they are discovered.

A.3   Java

The web server software described in this textbook requires Java 1.4.1 or a later version of Java 1.4. The server software does *not* work properly with servlets compiled with versions of Java following 1.4, such as J2SE 5.0 (JDK 1.5). This section explains how to check your Java version and install an appropriate version if needed.

A.3.1   Determining Your Java Version

You can verify the version of Java running on your machine by entering the command `java -version` at a command prompt. If the version is 1.4.0 or earlier, you will need to install a newer version of Java as outlined in the next section. If the version is 1.5 or newer and you do not also have an appropriate 1.4 version installed, you will also need to install another version as described.

Your machine should also have a Java SDK installed, which includes the compiler and other tools, and not merely a JRE (Java Runtime Environment). Type `javac -help` at a command prompt to verify that you have a compiler. You should see a list of compiler options. If not, follow the instructions in the next section to install a Java SDK.

A.3.2 Installing the Java SDK

I used the Java 2 SDK version 1.4.2 (J2SE 1.4.2) platform for the examples in this text-book; J2SE 1.4.1 should also work. These instructions specifically apply to the J2SE 1.4.2 version.

After you have completed installing the J2SE software as outlined in the following, use the test in the previous section to ensure that the correct version of Java is being accessed. If not, modify the PATH environment variable appropriately to ensure that the `bin` subdirectory of your new Java installation directory appears before any other Java installation directories.

Windows XP

- Navigate to `http://java.sun.com`, and download the version of J2SDK 1.4.2 without the NetBeans^{TM} development environment. Save this file to your desktop. (You can use either the standard installer or the offline installer.)
- Double-click the `j2sdk_1_4_2*-windows-i586-p*.exe` icon (the first star (*) will be a revision number such as _05, and the second will be the string `-iftw` if you downloaded the online installer).
- Click the "I accept the terms in the license agreement" radio button.
- Click Next.
- The default installation directory is `C:\j2sdk1.4.2*\`. To change this, click Change and select a different directory. You can also modify the features to be downloaded (I recommend obtaining all subfeatures for both the development tools and the run-time environment). Click next to continue.
- Select only the Mozilla browser, unless you also want this SDK to be used with other browsers. Click Next to continue.
- Click Install, and wait while J2SDK is installed onto the computer.
- Click Finish to exit the installer.

Linux

- Navigate to `http://java.sun.com`, and download a version of J2SDK 1.4.2 without the NetBeans^{TM} development environment.
- Open a terminal window.
- In the terminal window, `cd` to the directory where you downloaded the installer.
- In the terminal window, type

```
chmod 755 j2sdk_1_4_2_*-linux-i586.bin
```

in order to make the downloaded file executable (replace the * with the appropriate version number for the file you downloaded).
- In the terminal window, type

```
./j2sdk_1_4_2_02-linux-i586.bin
```

- Click "I accept the terms of the license agreement."
- Click Next.
- The default installation directory is /usr/java/j2sdk1.4.2_02/. To change this, click Change.
- Click Next to continue.
- Click Install, and wait while J2SDK is installed onto the computer.
- Click Finish to exit the installer.

A.4 Web Server and XML Processing Tools

This section describes how to obtain and install the Java Web Services Developer Pack 1.3 (JWSDP 1.3) from Sun Microsystems; the examples in many chapters assume that you have installed either JWSDP 1.3 or a sufficiently similar product. The JWSDP includes a version of the Tomcat web server along with a number of Java packages that facilitate the processing and transmission of XML documents.

I have chosen to use JWSDP 1.3 as the server-side example software in part because a single download will provide you with a web server as well as APIs and other tools supporting web services. However, be advised that the Tomcat server included in JWSDP 1.3 may have unpatched security weaknesses. I strongly suggest running the server behind a firewall that blocks access to the server ports (primarily port 8080 in the default installation). In addition, you may want to configure the server itself to accept connections only from your machine, as outlined in Section 1.7.6. It is also prudent to stop your server each time you are finished using it, which will reduce the amount of time that your server is exposed to potential software attacks.

A.4.1 Installing JWSDP 1.3

- Download the appropriate JWSDP file from http://java.sun.com/webservices/ downloads/1.3/index.html for your operating system: jwsdp-1_3-windows-i586. exe for Windows, or jwsdp-1_3-unix.sh for Linux (or Mac OS X). (These files are approximately 27 Mbyte each, so you will need a high-speed Internet connection for this download.)
- Execute the file:
  Windows: Double-click the jwsdp-1_3-windows-i586.exe application icon.
  Linux: Open a terminal window, change to the directory where you downloaded the installer, type chmod 755 jwsdp-1_3-unix.sh to make the file executable, and type ./jwsdp-1_3-unix.sh to execute it.
- Click the Next button to continue from the Introduction screen.
- Click the APPROVE radio button to accept the license agreement, and click "Next."
- If the installer now displays a directory for an appropriate version of Java, click the Next button to continue. Otherwise, click Browse to locate the directory containing your J2SE installation (you must use version 1.4.1 or later version of 1.4), or follow the instructions of the previous section to install an appropriate version of the JDK before continuing.
- Click the Next button to accept the default installation directory.
  Windows: This will normally be C:\jwsdp-1.3.

Linux: The installation directory will normally be something like /home/username/ jwsdp-1.3, where username is your log-in name.

- If your connection requires proxy information (as provided by your instructor or systems administrator), specify it in this window. If not, leave this screen blank. Click the Next button to continue.
- Select the "Typical—with bundled Tomcat" radio button and click the Next button to continue.
- You must create a Tomcat user. It is not advisable to use your user account password, as it is human readable in a file in the installation directory. It is acceptable to use the same username. Type in a username in the upper box. Enter a password in the middle, and confirm the password in the bottom. Click the Next button to continue.
- Click the Next button to continue past the confirmation screen, and wait while JWSDP installs.
- Click the Next button to continue past the successful installation screen.
- If you have write access to the directory where Java is installed, follow the instructions on this screen beginning with "Alternatively" to create a directory named endorsed in the specified location (within your Java installation directory), and then to copy files from the directory named at the bottom of the screen to this new directory. (If you do not have write access to the Java directory, see the instructions in the next subsection.) Click the "Next" button to continue.
- Click the Finish button to exit the installer.

A.4.2   Postinstallation Tasks

You should carefully follow the instructions in this section before attempting to run any of the textbook examples that use the JWSDP-installed software. I'll first give a quick summary of the tasks and then provide details on how and why to perform each task.

First, a word on notation. Many of the instructions include the string $JWSDP_HOME. This should be replaced with the path to the directory in which you installed JWSDP 1.3, which is typically something like C:\jwsdp-1.3 on Windows or /home/username/jwsdp-1. 3 on Linux. Or, in Linux, if you define an environment variable named JWSDP_HOME with the appropriate directory as its value, then you should be able to follow these instructions exactly as they appear.

In a nutshell, the tasks are:

- Ensure that the following are included in your CLASSPATH environment variable (as noted earlier, change forward slashes to backslashes for Windows):

  . (the current-directory symbol)
  $JWSDP_HOME/common/lib/servlet-api.jar
  $JWSDP_HOME/jaxrpc/lib/jaxrpc-impl.jar

- Ensure that $JWSDP_HOME/jaxrpc/bin (or its Windows equivalent) is included in your PATH environment variable.

- Add a line to the file $JWSDP_HOME/jwsdp-shared/bin/launcher.xml (only needed if using secure communication with the Tomcat web server).
- Add a line to the file $JWSDP_HOME/jwsdp-shared/bin/setenv.sh (only needed on certain Linux systems).
- Include an option on the java command line (only needed if you do not have write access to the Java installation directory and are running certain programs).

Now for the detailed instructions. Before compiling or running any Java programs, if your CLASSPATH environment variable does not already contain . (the current-directory symbol), add this symbol to the CLASSPATH variable, separating it from other entries in CLASSPATH with the separating character appropriate for your system, as described in Section A.1.2. This is important because many of the textbook's example Java classes rely on other classes located in the same directory as the examples.

Chapter 1 explains how to access the Tomcat web server distributed with JWSDP 1.3 using encrypted (secure) communication. There is a small bug in the so-called "launcher" for JWSDP 1.3, which is the software that sets up the CLASSPATH environment variable and system properties before actually starting Tomcat 5.0. If this bug is not patched, then Mozilla 1.4 (and possibly other browsers) will be not able to access Tomcat 5.0 securely. This bug can be patched as follows. You must add one line to the file launcher.xml, which is located in the jwsdp-shared/bin subdirectory under $JWSDP_HOME (which again is shorthand for the name of the directory in which you installed JWSDP). Specifically, following the line

```
<pathelement location="${JAVA_HOME}/jre/lib/ext/jaccess.jar" />
```

add the lines

```
<pathelement
   location="${JAVA_HOME}/jre/lib/ext/sunjce_provider.jar" />
```

In addition, I noticed intermittent problems when securely accessing Tomcat running on a Linux system: sometimes pages load, sometimes they do not (and exceptions are then thrown). This problem, which only seems to affect certain Linux versions (such as Red Hat 9.0), can be avoided by setting the LD_KERNEL_ASSUME environment variable to a value of 2.2.5 before starting Tomcat. You can either do this at the command line each time before you run Tomcat, or you can add the line

```
LD_KERNEL_ASSUME="2.2.5"
```

to the end of the file $JWSDP_HOME/jwsdp-shared/bin/setenv.sh. This will cause the environment variable to be set automatically before Tomcat is started. It may also clear up similar problems with other software running on your Linux system.

In order to compile Java servlets from the command line (as we do in Chapter 6), you will need to add the JWSDP's servlet-api.jar file to the CLASSPATH environment variable. This JAR file is found in the common/lib subdirectory under your JWSDP installation directory. For example, if you installed JWSDP in the typical default location on a Windows system, then you should add `c:\jwsdp-1.3\common\lib\servlet-api.jar` to your CLASSPATH variable.

If you do not have write access to the Java directory, then when you run Java programs from the command line that use the Java API for XML Processing (JAXP)—such as several of the examples in Chapter 7—you need to include the following argument to the `java` command:

```
-Djava.endorsed.dirs=$JWSDP_HOME/jaxp/lib/endorsed
```

where again $JWSDP_HOME must be replaced with the name of the directory in which you installed JWSDP (and you would normally replace the forward slashes with backslashes on a Windows system).

In order to compile Java programs using JAX-RPC (Chapter 9), you also need to add the `jaxrpc-impl.jar` file from the `jaxrpc/lib` subdirectory of your JWSDP installation to CLASSPATH. You should also add the `jaxrpc/bin` subdirectory of the JWSDP installation directory to your PATH environment variable. This facilitates running some of the command-line utilities used in Chapter 9.

A.4.3   Running the Tomcat Server

The JWSDP installs both Java APIs that can be invoked by Java software you write and a web server called Tomcat. You must start the Tomcat web server before you can access it from a web browser, and it is good practice to stop the server when you are not using it. This section explains how to start and stop Tomcat and how to access it from a browser.

Windows XP

Starting Tomcat: Click on **Start|All Programs|Java(TM) Web Services Developer Pack 1.3|Start Tomcat**.

Stopping Tomcat: As with starting, but select **Stop Tomcat** from the final menu. Wait several seconds before restarting the server.

Linux

Assuming you have installed JWSDP 1.3 in the default location, at a command prompt enter

```
~/jwsdp-1.3/bin/catalina.sh start
```

If you add $JWSDP_HOME/bin to your PATH environment variable, then this command can be shortened to

```
catalina.sh start
```

The server can be stopped with the command

```
~/jwsdp-1.3/bin/catalina.sh stop
```

or the equivalent shortened version if the JWSDP `bin` directory is added to your PATH variable.

Testing Your Tomcat Server

The Tomcat server can take well over a minute to start, depending on the speed of your computer and the number of sample web applications (see below). The file `launcher.server.log` in the `logs` subdirectory of your JWSDP installation directory will include a line such as

```
INFO: Server startup in 41594 ms
```

when the server initialization is complete.

You can then browse to your server to verify that it is operating. By default, the Tomcat server accepts connections from browsers at port 8080 rather than the standard port 80. This means that you need to include a port number when you browse to your server. For example, if you are running a browser on the same machine running the Tomcat server, you can browse to

```
http://localhost:8080
```

and you should see a JWSDP welcome page. If you are browsing from a machine other than the one running the server, enter the machine name or IP address in place of `localhost`.

By default, JWSDP includes many sample web applications which are loaded when you start Tomcat. The server will start faster if you undeploy these applications following the instructions in Section 8.3.2. You should not undeploy the applications with paths `/`, `/admin`, and `/manager`; all other applications can be undeployed.

APPENDIX B

Storing Java Objects as Files

The Java interface `java.io.Serializable` makes it relatively easy to store most Java objects as files. For small classroom projects, this mechanism for object storage may provide a simple and reasonable alternative to setting up and maintaining a database management system. This appendix discusses several aspects of Java object storage that are often not covered in introductory Java programming courses. This material is only intended as an overview sufficient for standard small-project usage scenarios; see the Java Object Serialization Specification `http://java.sun.com/j2se/1.4.2/docs/guide/serialization/` for a comprehensive discussion of serialization within the J2SE 1.4 platform.

B.1 Serializable Objects

When an object is serialized, the data contained within the object is transformed into a stream of bytes representing the data. This object data stream can then be stored in a file, transmitted over a communications network, or otherwise treated like any other stream of data. In the other direction, a stream of data representing the serialization of an object can be used to reconstruct an internal, nonserial representation of the object.

If a Java object contains only member variables of primitive types, such as `char` and `int`, then serialization is straightforward: the member variable names and values are streamed. However, Java objects often contain references to other Java objects, which may in turn contain references to other objects or even references back to objects that reference them. In Java, serialization of an object involves not only serializing the object itself but serializing all structures referenced by the object in such a way that the entire network of structures can later be reconstructed (we call this *deserializing* the object).

Not all Java objects can be serialized. The objects belonging to a class can be serialized if the class implements the `java.io.Serializable` interface—either directly, or indirectly by extending a superclass that is serializable or by implementing an interface that is a subinterface of `Serializable`. The `Serializable` interface defines no methods; it is simply used to indicate to the Java run-time system that the class author intends that objects belonging to the class can be serialized. So, for example, if a definition for a class named `SerializableClass` begins

```
public class SerializableClass implements java.io.Serializable {
```

and has a public no-argument constructor, then an instance of this class created as follows will be serializable:

```
SerializableClass serializableObject =
  new SerializableClass();
```

Many classes in the Java API are serializable, including the classes that wrap primitive types (such as `Integer`) and many classes that implement data structures (such as `java.util.Hashtable`). Arrays are also serializable.

B.2   Reading and Writing Serializable Objects in Java

Assuming that an object and all of the member variables of the object are serializable, it is simple to serialize and deserialize the object. For example, suppose that we would like to write the serializable object `serializableObject` declared in the preceding section to a file named `myObject.ser` (`ser` is often used as the extension for a file containing a serialized object). Code such as the following could be used (the buffering is not necessary, but in general will improve performance):

```
import java.io.*;
// ...
ObjectOutputStream outobj =
   new ObjectOutputStream(
     new BufferedOutputStream(
       new FileOutputStream("myObject.ser")));
outobj.writeObject(serializableObject);
outobj.close();
```

Again, this writes all member variables (except transient variables) of `serializableObject` to the file, including variables of primitive data types as well as arrays and referenced objects. A run-time error will occur if any of the objects referenced by `serializableObject` are not themselves serializable. Note that only member variables are written to the file; class variables (those declared as `static` in the class definition) are not.

Reconstructing a serialized object is also straightforward:

```
import java.io.*;
// ...
File aFile = new File("myObject.ser");
if (aFile.exists()) {
  ObjectInputStream inobj =
    new ObjectInputStream(
      new BufferedInputStream(
        new FileInputStream(aFile));
  serializableObject =
    (SerializableClass)inobj.readObject();
  inobj.close();
}
```

To write multiple objects to a stream, simply call `writeObject()` multiple times on the `ObjectOutputStream` object. On the input side, you need to make sure that the calls to `readObject()` appear in the same order. That is, if on output you call `writeObject()` with an argument of type `serClassOne` followed by an argument of type `serClassTwo`, then on input the first call to `readObject()` will return an object of type `serClassOne`, and the second call an object of type `serClassTwo`.

It is good practice to test an object after it has been deserialized to ensure that its member variables are valid. For example, if a variable is supposed to contain only positive integer values, then you would test to ensure that the value after deserialization is positive. This can protect your program from odd behaviors caused by corrupted serialized objects.

B.3   Supporting Object Evolution

What happens if you write a serialized object to a file, then modify the class to which the object belongs, and finally attempt to read the object back from the file? This can cause an error, because the Java run time creates an identifier for a class based on the names and types of its members and includes this identifier with the other information produced when an object is serialized. Specifically, if the identifier in a serialized object does not match the identifier that would be produced for the class into which the object is being deserialized, then an error occurs.

In order to allow an object to be deserialized into a newer version of its class, a static variable named `serialVersionUID` can be added to the class to override the identifier that would otherwise be computed for the class by the Java run time. You can determine an appropriate value for this variable by running the `serialver` command line tool (documented at `http://java.sun.com/j2se/1.4.2/docs/tooldocs/tools.html#rmi`). For example, if `SerializableClass` in the preceding section is part of the `test` package, and if the directory for this package is part of the CLASSPATH environment variable, then typing

```
serialver test.SerializableClass
```

at a command prompt will produce output such as

```
test.SerializableClass:
    static final long serialVersionUID = 8844961462849771830L;
```

Including the second line of this output in `SerializableClass` causes the Java runtime to use the specified value (`88449...L`) as the value of the identifier for `SerializableClass`, even if the class is changed.

However, to maintain compatibility between the original version of a class and modified versions, certain modifications should not be performed. One of the primary restrictions is that you should not delete any member variables from the class. If you do, and if the original version of the class software reads a serialized object generated by your later version of the class having the deleted field, then the original version will not find a value for this field in the serialized object. This will likely cause an error when the original software attempts to use the object.

Some other changes that should not be made to a serializable class containing a `serialVersionUID` declaration are:

- Nonstatic member variables should not be changed to static (class) variables, and non-transient variables should not be changed to transient (the effect on the serialized object is similar to that of deleting the variable)
- If a variable has a primitive variable type, the type should not be changed.

- Classes should not be moved in relation to other classes in the type hierarchy; for example, if ClassA is a superclass of ClassB, which in turn is a superclass of ClassC, then you should not change this so that, for example, ClassC becomes a direct subclass of ClassA.

A complete list of restrictions that should be observed when modifying a serializable class can be found in Chapter 5 of the Java Object Serialization Specification (available at http://java.sun.com/j2se/1.4.2/docs/guide/serialization/).

B.4 Case Study

We'll now see how to implement the DataStore class for the blogging application using object serialization. The class has three class (static) variables, declared as follows:

```
/** Flag indicating whether or not initialization has
 *  occurred. */
private static boolean initialized = false;

/** Data store file. */
private static File dataStore = new File("MyOwnBlog.ser");

/** Vector of all blog entries, most recent first. */
private static Vector entries = null;
```

(Obviously, you could change the location of the data store file to anything you like.) The variable dataStore represents a file named MyOwnBlog.ser located in the user's home directory (in Windows XP, this is the folder within Documents and Settings that has your user name).

We'll begin with the code for adding an entry, which is split between two methods (Figure B.1). The public addEntry() method first adds a unique ID to its argument entry. Since our application only adds elements, never removes them, we can simply use the current size of the vector of entries as the ID. Next, the method adds the entry to the beginning of the entries vector (so that the most recent addition is always first) and then calls on the second method, writeBlog(), to output the vector of blog entries to the file system using writeObject(). We can do this because both the java.util.Vector class and our implementation of Entry implement the Serializable interface. Entry also defines a serialVersionUID variable to facilitate later modifications to the class.

There is a potentially serious problem with this implementation: if the program halts in the middle of writing to the file system, the resulting file will be corrupted and the last uncorrupted file will be overwritten and lost. A fuller implementation might first rename the existing file before writing a new file, thus at least saving a backup. A more sophisticated implementation might include an automatic restore from the backup file.

The initialize() method, shown in Figure B.2, is the only method that inputs from the file system. Every other method assumes that, at the time the method is executed, entries contains all entries that have ever been added to the blog. This assumption will be valid if there is only one copy of the application running at any one time and if the methods

```
/**
 * Add an entry to the blog.  This also assigns a
 * unique ID to the entry.
 */
synchronized public static void addEntry(Entry entry)
    throws IOException
{
    entry.setID(entries.size());
// Add to beginning (latest entry first)
    entries.add(0, entry);
    DataStore.writeBlog();
}


/**
 * Output the blog entries to data store.
 */
synchronized private static void writeBlog()
    throws IOException
{
    ObjectOutputStream outobj =
        new ObjectOutputStream(
            new BufferedOutputStream(
                new FileOutputStream(dataStore)));
    outobj.writeObject(entries);
    outobj.close();
    return;
}
```

FIGURE B.1 Methods for adding an entry to a blog's internal data structure and to the copy of the blog stored on the file system.

```
/**
 * Open the data store file and input the blog entries.
 */
synchronized public static void initialize()
    throws IOException, ClassNotFoundException
{
    if (!initialized) {
        if (dataStore.exists()) {
            ObjectInputStream inobj =
                new ObjectInputStream(
                    new BufferedInputStream(
                        new FileInputStream(dataStore)));
            entries = (Vector)inobj.readObject();
            inobj.close();
        }
        else {
            entries = new Vector();
        }
        initialized = true;
    }
}
```

FIGURE B.2 Method for reading a blog's entries from the file system.

are properly synchronized. Again, a fuller implementation of this class would probably avoid this assumption.

The remaining two methods, `getEntries()` and `getAllMonths()`, simply search through the internal representation of the blog and create a vector of the information found. As already mentioned, these methods assume that the internal blog is consistent with the one stored in the file system, so they do not read the blog in before performing their searches. Since our focus in this appendix is on data storage and these methods perform no input/output operations, I won't cover them any further here.

All methods are synchronized, so if one thread is reading or modifying the blog, no other thread can access the blog until the first thread has completed. Also, there is only one blogger, so there should only be, at most, one thread adding to the blog at any given time. Based on these observations and considering the possible execution paths through the application, it seems that there should not be any unexpected behavior due to threading.

APPENDIX C

Databases and Java Servlets

This appendix assumes that you are already familiar with database concepts, including the Structured Query Language (SQL). Our purpose here is to briefly explain how to obtain database management system (DBMS) software if needed, as well as how to connect a Java servlet—or other software run in a web application environment, such as a JavaBeans object—to a DBMS.

The J2SE 1.4 platform supports Java database access with the Java Database Connectivity (JDBC^TM) API, which in turn is defined by the packages `java.sql` and `javax.sql` (also see `http://java.sun.com/products/jdbc/reference/` for additional documentation). In order to connect a Java program to a database, *JDBC driver software* must be installed on the machine running the Java program. The driver implements the communication layer of the API, in effect converting calls to the JDBC API into communications to a particular DBMS and converting the results received from the DBMS into appropriate Java return values.

Once a JDBC driver has been installed on a machine, a servlet running on the machine must load the driver software before using other JDBC methods to access the database. Once the driver has been loaded, use of JDBC is largely independent of the DBMS or driver used. Therefore, if you want to change the database used by a web application, you should normally only need to install a new driver and change a limited amount of JDBC initialization code. Other JDBC code should remain unchanged.

In this appendix, we'll first discuss installing and loading drivers. Then we'll consider basic JDBC methods for accessing a database.

C.1 JDBC Drivers

JDBC drivers can be obtained from a variety of sources, provide different levels of functionality, and vary in their use of supporting software. Sources for JDBC drivers include the J2SE SDK itself, database vendors, and third-party developers; see `http://servlet.java.sun.com/products/jdbc/drivers/` for an extensive source list. Functionality is defined by the version of JDBC supported by the driver: at the time of this writing, JDBC 3.0 is the most recent release, but many drivers fully support only earlier versions such as JDBC 2.0 or even 1.0.

The supporting software required by a driver depends mainly on the driver's type. One type, called a Type 4 driver, is Java software that is loaded onto the client machine and supports direct communication with a DBMS. Type 4 drivers need no supporting software other than the DBMS itself; all of the other types rely on additional software to complete their functionality. A Type 3 driver is Java client software that communicates with intermediary server software, which in turn communicates with one or more actual database systems. A Type 2 driver allows JDBC software on a client machine to communicate with non-Java DBMS communication software also loaded on the client, which in turn communicates with the DBMS itself. Finally, a Type 1 driver connects JDBC software on the client to Open Database Connectivity (ODBC) software also residing on the client; the ODBC software can then be used to access any of the many ODBC-compliant DBMSs. A Type 1 driver is also referred to as a *JDBC-ODBC bridge*. See `http://java.sun.com/products/jdbc/driverdesc.html` for a fuller description of the four JDBC driver types.

To illustrate common JDBC driver setup and usage, I'll cover two typical scenarios here: connecting to a local Microsoft Access database using a JDBC-ODBC bridge, and connecting to an open-source MySQL® database using a Type 4 driver. In both cases, the connection will be made from a Java servlet.

Before moving to driver specifics, let me mention a few points about the DBMSs themselves. First, if you have a Windows XP (Home or Professional) system, then, whether or not you have Access itself installed on your system, you should be able to follow the instructions in the following subsection to create and manipulate an Access database on your system. That is, even without Access itself installed, your system should contain drivers that allow software you write to perform Access database functions. So if you have a Windows XP system, there is no need to install a DBMS in order to experiment with JDBC. Also, by installing a Type 3 intermediary server (such as RmiJdbc (`http://rmijdbc.objectweb.org/`)), your Access database can be accessed from other machines running the appropriate Type 3 driver.

Second, if you do not already have some other DBMS installed, MySQL (`http://www.mysql.com/`) runs on both Linux and Windows systems, is widely used in web-based systems, and is freely available. One note of caution under Windows: when I installed MySQL 4.1 as a Windows service on my system running the Windows Firewall provided by the Windows Security Center, the firewall blocked connections from machines other than my own without any warning. So, if you have installed and configured MySQL carefully but cannot connect to your MySQL database from other machines, I suggest checking your firewall settings. For the Windows Firewall, select **Security Center** from the Control Panel, click on the **Windows Firewall** link, click on the Exceptions tab, click the Add Program . . . button, and navigate to the `mysqld-nt.exe` file in the `bin` subdirectory of your MySQL installation directory (typically found under `C:\Program Files\MySQL`).

C.1.1   Connecting Locally to MS Access

In this scenario, we wish to connect to a Microsoft Access database running on the same Windows XP machine that hosts our Java servlet. Since Access is ODBC-compliant, we can do this with a Type 1 driver. There is no JDBC driver software to install in this case, because a Type 1 driver is included in the J2SE 1.4 SDK (although it is not recommended for production use). We also do not need to install any ODBC client software, because this is installed by default on Windows XP. But we do need to tell the Windows ODBC client software about our database.

For the moment, let's assume that you have already created an Access database named `People` and stored it in a file named `People.mdb`. Next, you associate an ODBC driver with this database as follows. From the Windows Control Panel, choose **Administrative Tools** and then **Data Sources (ODBC)**. In the ODBC Data Source Administrator window, select the **User DSN** tab and click the Add . . . button. In the Create New Data Source window, select **Microsoft Access Driver (*.mdb)** and click the Finish button. In the ODBC Microsoft Access Setup window, enter `PeopleDB` in the Data Source Name text box, click the Select . . . button in the Database area, and browse to your `People.mdb` file. After selecting your file and clicking OK in the Select Database window, click OK in the ODBC Microsoft Access Setup window. You should now see `PeopleDB` in the list of User Data Sources in the ODBC Data Source Administrator window. Finally, click OK in this window.

If you don't have an Access database already, you can create one via the ODBC tool as follows. Follow the instructions in the preceding paragraph, but in the ODBC Microsoft Access Setup window, after entering the Data Source Name click the Create . . . button instead of the Select . . . button. Then give your database a file name, such as `People.mdb`, and click OK. You should see a pop-up message telling you that your database was successfully created (whether or not you have Access installed). As in the preceding paragraph, click OK several times to complete the ODBC setup.

Once the ODBC association has been made, you can connect to the `People` database from a Java servlet (or in fact from any Java program) as follows:

```
String dataSourceName = "PeopleDB";
String dbURI = "jdbc:odbc:" + dataSourceName;
try {
    Class.forName("sun.jdbc.odbc.JdbcOdbcDriver");
    java.sql.Connection con =
        java.sql.DriverManager.getConnection(dbURI, "", "");
    // JDBC calls to con methods go here ...
    con.close();  // close connection when done
}
catch (Exception e) {
    e.printStackTrace();
}
```

The static `forName()` method of `Class` causes the Java virtual machine to load the specified class, which is the name of the SDK-supplied Type 1 JBDC driver. When `getConnection()` is subsequently called on the JDBC `DriverManager` class, it uses this driver to establish a connection with the database indicated by its first argument, a URI. When connecting to a database via the JDBC-ODBC bridge, the URI is a URN consisting of the prefix `jdbc:odbc:` followed by an ODBC data source name. In this example, we use the data source name `PeopleDB` that we associated with the `People` database using the Data Sources administrative tool. The other two arguments to `getConnection()` are the log-in name and password associated with the ODBC `PeopleDB` data source, which by default are both the empty string. (These defaults can be changed from the ODBC Data Source Administrator window by double-clicking PeopleDB, clicking the Advanced . . . button in the ODBC Microsoft Access Setup window, and entering values in the Login Name and Password fields.) The `Connection` object returned by `getConnection()` will also use the driver loaded by `forName()` for all database communication needed to support JDBC methods called on this object.

C.1.2   Connecting to MySQL

In this scenario, we wish to connect to a MySQL DBMS running on a server machine from a Java servlet running on a client machine (a client in relation to the MySQL DBMS, but a server in relation to web browsers). We will accomplish this using a Type 4 (Java) driver provided by MySQL.

We assume that you have already created a MySQL database named People on a machine with host name db.example.net. We'll also assume that the MySQL DBMS accepts TCP/IP connections (local or remote) on its default port 3306 and that the user someuser with password mypassword has been granted full access to the People database from the client machine. You will need to download the MySQL Connector/J driver JAR file to the client machine. The following instructions are for version 3.0 of Connector/J, which I downloaded by following a link at http://dev.mysql.com/downloads/connector/j/3.0.html; but similar instructions should apply to later versions.

After uncompressing the download file, you should see two directories, one beginning with mysql-connector. In this directory you will find the driver JAR file, which also has a name beginning with mysql-connector. Copy this file to the shared/lib subdirectory under your JWSDP installation directory. The next time you start or restart Tomcat, this JAR file will automatically be added to the CLASSPATH for any servlets run by the server.

Once the Connector/J JAR file has been installed, the following code can be used to access the People database from a servlet, or from any Java code that has the Connector/J JAR file on its CLASSPATH:

```
// change the following four String's as appropriate
String host = "db.example.net:3306";
String dbname = "People";
String username = "someuser";
String password = "mypassword";
String dbURI = "jdbc:mysql:" +
    "//" + host +
    "/" + dbname +
    "?user=" + username +
    "&password=" + password;
try {
    // The newInstance() call is a work around for some
    // broken Java implementations
    Class.forName("com.mysql.jdbc.Driver").newInstance();
    Connection con =
        DriverManager.getConnection(dbURI);
    // JDBC calls to con methods go here ...

    con.close();
}
catch (Exception e) {
    servletOut.print(e);
}
```

The code here is similar to that used earlier to access an MS Access database using a Type 1 driver. One key difference is that the name of the Connector/J class is passed to the static `forName()` method of `Class`, causing this Type 4 driver to be loaded and used by the subsequent call to `getConnection()` as well as calls on the `Connection` object returned by `getConnection()`. Another difference is the form of the URI passed to `getConnection()`: it begins with the prefix `jdbc:mysql:` followed by a string that syntactically is similar to a URL, complete with query string. Notice also that the user name and password are embedded in the connection URI rather than passed as arguments to `getConnection()`. Obviously, if the communication between your database client and server machines is not trusted (for example, is carried over the Internet), then you should configure your MySQL database to use secure communication to avoid divulging passwords and other sensitive information.

C.2 JDBC Database Access

A `Connection` object can be used to obtain information about the database, such as the tables it contains, as well as to set parameters of the interaction with the database, such as whether or not changes to the database will be committed automatically (autocommit is the default). For simple database access, however, the only method called on `Connection` is often `createStatement()`. This method returns an object of type `Statement` that can be used to send SQL statements to the database and to retrieve results produced by the statements. In particular, if a `String` representing a SQL statement is passed to the `execute()` method of a `Statement` object, then the database will execute that statement. The result of executing a SQL statement may be nothing (if creating a table, for example), a row count (if performing an INSERT, UPDATE, or DELETE), or a result set (if performing a SELECT). The methods `getUpdateCount()` and `getResultSet()` can be used to retrieve the row count and result set, respectively, after executing a SQL statement.

For example, assuming that a `Connection` object named `con` has been created as described, the following statements will create a table, insert a row in the table, and output a message (to a Tomcat file, if run as part of a servlet) indicating that one row was inserted:

```
Statement stmt = con.createStatement();
stmt.execute("CREATE TABLE PersonalInterests " +
            "(Name VARCHAR(50), Interests VARCHAR(50))");
stmt.execute("INSERT INTO PersonalInterests VALUES " +
            "('Ben', 'drawing, Legos, writing')");
System.out.println("Row count is " + stmt.getUpdateCount());
```

The `getResultSet()` method returns an object of type `ResultSet`, or `null` if a result set was not produced by the most recent call to `execute()`. The `ResultSet` object provides methods for positioning to a certain row within the result set and for obtaining data from the fields in a row. Continuing the example, the following code could be used to iterate through all of the rows in the `PersonalInterests` table created by the preceding code and to output both fields of each row:

```
stmt.execute("SELECT * FROM PersonalInterests");
ResultSet rs = stmt.getResultSet();
if (rs != null) {
    while (rs.next()) {
```

```
        System.out.println(rs.getString("Name"));
        System.out.println(rs.getString("Interests"));
    }
}
```

The next() method positions the result set cursor at the next row each time it is called. Initially, the cursor is positioned just before the first row, so the first call to next() positions the cursor at the first row. The calls to getString() access fields in the row pointed to by the cursor. Fields can also be accessed by ordinal (1, 2, etc.) rather than name, which is generally faster than access by name but not as resilient to database structural modifications.

Each data getter method, such as getString(), will attempt to convert from the specified field's SQL data type to the Java data type specified by the name of the getter method. The getString() method, for example, converts from the SQL VARCHAR data type to the Java String type. A large number of other getter methods are provided by ResultSet objects. Full details of the supported data type conversions are contained in the JDBC Specification [SUN-JDBC-3.0].

Bibliography

APACHE-TOMCAT-5-CONFIG. *Tomcat 5 Server Configuration Reference*. Apache Software Foundation. `http://jakarta.apache.org/tomcat/tomcat-5.0-doc/config/`.

APACHE-TOMCAT-5-UG. *The Tomcat 5 User Guide*. Apache Software Foundation. `http://jakarta.apache.org/tomcat/tomcat-5.0-doc/introduction.html` (this retrieves Chapter 1; click links under User Guide heading at left to navigate to other chapters).

ECMA-262. *ECMAScript Language Specification, 3rd Edition*, ECMA. December 1999. Available from `http://www.ecma-international.org/publications/standards/Ecma-262.htm`.

IANA-CHARSETS. *Character Sets*. Internet Assigned Numbers Authority. `http://www.iana.org/assignments/character-sets`.

IANA-MIME. *MIME Media Types*. Internet Assigned Numbers Authority. `http://www.iana.org/assignments/media-types`.

IANA-PORTS. *Port Numbers*. Internet Assigned Numbers Authority. `http://www.iana.org/assignments/port-numbers`.

IANA-SCHEMES. *Uniform Resource Identifier (URI) Schemes*. Internet Assigned Numbers Authority. `http://www.iana.org/assignments/uri-schemes.html`.

IANA-URNS. *Uniform Resource Names (URN) Namespaces*. Internet Assigned Numbers Authority. `http://www.iana.org/assignments/urn-namespaces`.

ISO-639-2. *Codes for the Representation of Names of Languages Part 2: Alpha-3 Code*. International Organization for Standards. `http://www.loc.gov/standards/iso639-2/langhome.html`.

MOZ-DOM. *Gecko DOM Reference*. The Mozilla Foundation. `http://www.mozilla.org/docs/dom/domref`.

MOZ-DOM-WINDOW. *DOM window Reference*. The Mozilla Foundation. `http://www.mozilla.org/docs/dom/domref/dom_window_ref.html`.

MS-DHTML. *HTML and DHTML Reference*. Microsoft Corporation. `http://msdn.microsoft.com/workshop/author/dhtml/reference/dhtml_reference_entry.asp`.

MS-DHTML-WINDOW. `Window` *Object*. Microsoft Corporation. `http://msdn.microsoft.com/workshop/author/dhtml/reference/objects/obj_window.asp`.

NCSA-MOSAIC. *NCSA Mosaic Technical Summary (Rev. 2.1)*, Marc Andreessen. National Center for Supercomputing Applications, May 1993. `ftp://ftp.ncsa.uiuc.edu/Web/Mosaic/Papers/mosaic.ps.Z` (PostScript® file compressed with Unix compress command).

RFC-1345. *Character Mnemonics & Character Sets*, K. Simonsen. June 1992. `ftp://ftp.rfc-editor.org/in-notes/rfc1345.txt`.

RFC-2045. *Multipurpose Internet Mail Extensions (MIME) Part One: Format of Internet Message Bodies*, N. Freed and N. Borenstein. November 1996. `ftp://ftp.rfc-editor.org/in-notes/rfc2045.txt`.

RFC-2046. *Multipurpose Internet Mail Extensions (MIME) Part Two: Media Types*, N. Freed and N. Borenstein. November 1996. `ftp://ftp.rfc-editor.org/in-notes/rfc2046.txt`.

RFC-2047. *Multipurpose Internet Mail Extensions (MIME) Part Three: Message Header Extensions for Non-ASCII Text*, K. Moore. November 1996. `ftp://ftp.rfc-editor.org/in-notes/rfc2047.txt`.

RFC-2049. *Multipurpose Internet Mail Extensions (MIME) Part Five: Conformance Criteria and Examples*, N. Freed and N. Borenstein. November 1996. `ftp://ftp.rfc-editor.org/in-notes/rfc2049.txt`.

RFC-2077. *The Model Primary Content Type for Multipurpose Internet Mail Extensions*, S. Nelson and C. Parks. January 1997. `ftp://ftp.rfc-editor.org/in-notes/rfc2077.txt`.

RFC-2109. *HTTP State Management Mechanism*, D. Kristol and L. Montulli. February 1997. `ftp://ftp.rfc-editor.org/in-notes/rfc2109.txt`.

RFC-2141. *URN Syntax*, R. Moats. May 1997. `ftp://ftp.rfc-editor.org/in-notes/rfc2141.txt`.

RFC-2246. *The TLS Protocol Version 1.0*, T. Dierks and C. Allen. January 1999. `ftp://ftp.rfc-editor.org/in-notes/rfc2246.txt`.

RFC-2616. *Hypertext Transfer Protocol—HTTP/1.1*, R. Fielding, J. Gettys, J. Mogul, H. Frystyk, L. Masinter, P. Leach, and T. Berners-Lee. June 1999. `ftp://ftp.rfc-editor.org/in-notes/rfc2616.txt`. Errata at `http://purl.org/NET/http-errata`.

RFC-2818. *HTTP Over TLS*, E. Rescorla. May 2000. `ftp://ftp.rfc-editor.org/in-notes/rfc2818.txt`.

RFC-3066. *Tags for the Identification of Languages*, H. Alvestrand. January 2001. `ftp://ftp.rfc-editor.org/in-notes/rfc3066.txt`.

RFC-3151. *A URN Namespace for Public Identifiers*, N. Walsh, J. Cowan, and P. Grosso. August 2001. `ftp://ftp.rfc-editor.org/in-notes/rfc3151.txt`.

RFC-4288. *Media Type Specifications and Registration Procedures*, N. Freed and J. Klensin. December 2005. `ftp://ftp.rfc-editor.org/in-notes/rfc4288.txt`.

RFC-4289. *Multipurpose Internet Mail Extensions (MIME) Part Four: Registration Procedures*, N. Freed and J. Klensin. December 2005. `ftp://ftp.rfc-editor.org/in-notes/rfc4289.txt`.

SAX-2.0.1. *SAX2 API*. `http://www.saxproject.org/apidoc/overview-summary.html` (this URL is not version-specific and may return a newer version of the API).

STD-1. *Internet Official Protocol Standards*. Internet Engineering Task Force. `ftp://ftp.rfc-editor.org/in-notes/std/std1.txt`.

STD-5. *Internet Protocol*. Internet Engineering Task Force. `ftp://ftp.rfc-editor.org/in-notes/std/std5.txt`.

STD-6. *User Datagram Protocol*. Internet Engineering Task Force. `ftp://ftp.rfc-editor.org/in-notes/std/std6.txt`.

STD-7. *Transmission Control Protocol*. `ftp://ftp.rfc-editor.org/in-notes/std/std7.txt`.

STD-13. *Domain Names*. Internet Engineering Task Force. `ftp://ftp.rfc-editor.org/in-notes/std/std13.txt`.

STD-63. *UTF-8, a Transformation Format of ISO 10646*. Internet Engineering Task Force. `ftp://ftp.rfc-editor.org/in-notes/std/std63.txt`.

STD-66. *Uniform Resource Identifiers (URI): Generic Syntax*, `ftp://ftp.rfc-editor.org/in-notes/std/std66.txt`.

SUN-JAVA-API-1.4.2. *Java 2 Platform, Standard Edition, Version 1.4.2 API Specification.* Sun Microsystems, Inc. `http://java.sun.com/j2se/1.4.2/docs/api/index.html`.

SUN-JAVABEANS-1.01. *JavaBeans Specification, Version 1.01*, Graham Hamilton. Sun Microsystems, Inc., August 1997. `http://java.sun.com/products/javabeans/docs/spec.html`.

SUN-JAXP-1.2. *Java API for XML Processing, Version 1.2*, Rajiv Mordani and Scott Boag. Sun Microsystems, Inc., September 2002. `http://java.sun.com/xml/downloads/jaxp.html`.

SUN-JAXRPC-1.1. *Java API for XML-based RPC, JAX-RPC 1.1*, Roberto Chinnici. Sun Microsystems, Inc., October 2003. `http://java.sun.com/xml/downloads/jaxrpc.html`.

SUN-JDBC-3.0. *Java JDBC Data Access API Specification, Version 3.0*, Jon Ellis and Linda Ho with Maydene Fisher. Sun Microsystems, Inc., October 2001. Available from `http://java.sun.com/products/jdbc/download.html`.

SUN-JLS-2. *The Java Language Specification, Second Edition*, James Gosling, Bill Joy, Guy Steele, and Gilad Bracha. Sun Microsystems, Inc., June 2000. `http://java.sun.com/docs/books/jls/second_edition/html/j.title.doc.html`.

SUN-JSP-2.0. *JavaServer Pages Specification Version 2.0*, Mark Roth and Eduardo Pelegri-Llopart. Sun Microsystems, Inc., November 2003. Available from `http://jcp.org/aboutJava/communityprocess/final/jsr152/index.html`.

SUN-JSTL-1.1. *JavaServer Pages Standard Tag Library Version 1.1*, Pierre Delisle (editor). Sun Microsystems, Inc., November 2003. Available from `http://jcp.org/aboutJava/communityprocess/final/jsr052/index2.html`.

SUN-JWS-TUTORIAL-1.3. *The Java Web Services Tutorial*, Eric Armstrong, Jennifer Ball, Stephanie Bodoff, Debbie Bode Carson, Ian Evans, Maydene Fisher, Scott Fordin, Dale Green, Kim Haase, and Eric Jendrock. Sun Microsystems, Inc., December, 2003. `http://java.sun.com/webservices/docs/1.3/tutorial/doc/index.html`.

SUN-SERVLETS-2.4. *Java Servlet Specification Version 2.4*, Danny Coward and Yutaka Yoshida. Sun Microsystems, Inc., November 2003. Available from `http://jcp.org/aboutJava/communityprocess/final/jsr154/index.html`.

UNICODE. *The Unicode Standard. Version 4.0.* The Unicode Consortium, August 2003. Available from `http://www.unicode.org/versions/`.

W3C-CGI. *CGI: Common Gateway Interface.* World Wide Web Consortium. `http://www.w3.org/CGI/`.

W3C-CSS-1.0. *Cascading Style Sheets, Level 1*, Hkon Wium Lie and Bert Bos. World Wide Web Consortium, January 1999. `http://www.w3.org/TR/1999/REC-CSS1-19990111`.

W3C-CSS-2.0. *Cascading Style Sheets, Level 2. CSS2 Specification*, Bert Bos, Hkon Wium Lie, Chris Lilley, and Ian Jacobs (editors). World Wide Web Consortium, May 1998. `http://www.w3.org/TR/1998/REC-CSS2-19980512`.

W3C-CSS-2.1. *Cascading Style Sheets, Level 2 Revision 1. CSS 2.1 Specification (W3C Candidate Recommendation)*, Bert Bos, Tantek Çelik, Ian Hickson, and Hkon Wium Lie (editors). World Wide Web Consortium, February 2004. `http://www.w3.org/TR/2004/CR-CSS21-20040225` (work in progress).

W3C-DOM-1. *Document Object Model (DOM) Level 1 Specification, Version 1.0*, Vidur Apparao, Steve Byrne, Mike Champion, Scott Isaacs, Ian Jacobs, Arnaud Le Hors, Gavin Nicol, Jonathan

Robie, Robert Sutor, Chris Wilson, and Lauren Wood. World Wide Web Consortium, October 1998. `http://www.w3.org/TR/1998/REC-DOM-Level-1-19981001`.

W3C-DOM-2-CORE. *Document Object Model (DOM) Level 2 Core Specification, Version 1.0*, Arnaud Le Hors, Philippe Le Hgaret, Lauren Wood, Gavin Nicol, Jonathan Robie, Mike Champion, and Steve Byrne. World Wide Web Consortium, November 2000. `http://www.w3.org/TR/2000/REC-DOM-Level-2-Core-20001113`.

W3C-DOM-2-EVENTS. *Document Object Model (DOM) Level 2 Events Specification, Version 1.0*, Tom Pixley. World Wide Web Consortium, November 2000. `http://www.w3.org/TR/2000/REC-DOM-Level-2-Events-20001113`.

W3C-DOM-2-HTML. *Document Object Model (DOM) Level 2 HTML Specification, Version 1.0*, Johnny Stenback, Philippe Le Hgaret, and Arnaud Le Hors (editors). World Wide Web Consortium, January 2003. `http://www.w3.org/TR/2003/REC-DOM-Level-2-HTML-20030109`.

W3C-DOM-2-STYLE. *Document Object Model (DOM) Level 2 Style Specification, Version 1.0*, Chris Wilson, Philippe Le Hgaret, and Vidur Apparao. World Wide Web Consortium, November 2000. `http://www.w3.org/TR/2000/REC-DOM-Level-2-Style-20001113`.

W3C-HTML-3.2. *HTML 3.2 Reference Specification*, Dave Raggett. World Wide Web Consortium, January 1997. `http://www.w3.org/TR/REC-html32`.

W3C-HTML-4.01. *HTML 4.01 Specification*, Dave Raggett, Arnaud Le Hors, and Ian Jacobs (editors). World Wide Web Consortium, December 1999. `http://www.w3.org/TR/1999/REC-html401-19991224`.

W3C-HTML-HIST. *Tags used in HTML*. World Wide Web Consortium. `http://www.w3.org/History/19921103-hypertext/hypertext/WWW/MarkUp/Tags.html`.

W3C-P3P. *The Platform for Privacy Preferences 1.0 (P3P1.0) Specification*, Lorrie Cranor, Marc Langheinrich, Massimo Marchiori (author and editor), Martin Presler-Marshall, and Joseph Reagle. World Wide Web Consortium, April 2002. `http://www.w3.org/TR/2002/REC-P3P-20020416/`.

W3C-SOAP-1.1. *Simple Object Access Protocol (SOAP) 1.1 (W3C Note)*, Don Box, David Ehnebuske, Gopal Kakivaya, Andrew Layman, Noah Mendelsohn, Henrik Frystyk Nielsen, Satish Thatte, and Dave Winer. World Wide Web Consortium, May 2000. `http://www.w3.org/TR/2000/NOTE-SOAP-20000508` (made available for discussion purposes).

W3C-SOAP-ADJUNCT-1.2. *SOAP Version 1.2 Part 2: Adjuncts*, Martin Gudgin, Marc Hadley, Noah Mendelsohn, Jean-Jacques Moreau, and Henrik Frystyk Nielsen (editors). World Wide Web Consortium, June 2003. `http://www.w3.org/TR/2003/REC-soap12-part2-20030624/`.

W3C-SOAP-FRAMEWORK-1.2. *SOAP Version 1.2 Part 1: Messaging Framework*, Martin Gudgin, Marc Hadley, Noah Mendelsohn, Jean-Jacques Moreau, and Henrik Frystyk Nielsen (editors). World Wide Web Consortium, June 2003. `http://www.w3.org/TR/2003/REC-soap12-part1-20030624/`.

W3C-SOAP-PRIMER-1.2. *SOAP Version 1.2 Part 0: Primer*, Nilo Mitra (editor). World Wide Web Consortium, June 2003. `http://www.w3.org/TR/2003/REC-soap12-part0-20030624/`.

W3C-SVG-1.1. *Scalable Vector Graphics (SVG) 1.1 Specification*, Jon Ferrailolo, FUJISAWA Jun, and Dean Jackson (editors). World Wide Web Consortium, January 2003. `http://www.w3.org/TR/2003/REC-SVG11-20030114/`.

W3C-VAL. *W3C MarkUp Validation Service*. World Wide Web Consortium. `http://validator.w3.org/`.

W3C-WSDL-1.1. *Web Services Description Language (WSDL) 1.1 (W3C Note)*, World Wide Web Consortium, March 2001. `http://www.w3.org/TR/2001/NOTE-wsdl-20010315` (made available for discussion purposes).

W3C-WAI. *Web Content Accessibility Guidelines 1.0*, Wendy Chisholm, Gregg Vanderheiden, and Ian Jacobs (editors). World Wide Web Consortium, May 1999. `http://www.w3.org/TR/1999/WAI-WEBCONTENT-19990505/`.

W3C-XHTML-1.0. *XHTML. 1.0 The Extensible HyperText Markup Language (Second Edition)*. World Wide Web Consortium, August 2002. `http://www.w3.org/TR/2002/REC-xhtml1-20020801/`.

W3C-XHTML-DTDS. *Extensible HTML Version 1.0 DTDs*. World Wide Web Consortium, August 2002. `http://www.w3.org/TR/2002/REC-xhtml1-20020801/dtds.html`.

W3C-XML-1.0. *Extensible Markup Language (XML) 1.0 (Third Edition)*, Tim Bray, Jean Paoli, C. M. Sperberg-McQueen, Eve Maler, and Franois Yergeau (editors). World Wide Web Consortium, February 2004. `http://www.w3.org/TR/2004/REC-xml-20040204/`.

W3C-XML-NAMESPACE-1.1. *Namespaces in XML 1.1*, Tim Bray, Dave Hollander, Andrew Layman, and Richard Tobin (editors). World Wide Web Consortium, February 2004. `http://www.w3.org/TR/2004/REC-xml-names11-20040204/`.

W3C-XML-SCHEMA-DATA-1.0. *XML Schema Part 2: Datatypes (Second Edition)*, Paul V. Biron and Ashok Malhotra (editors). World Wide Web Consortium, October 2004. `http://www.w3.org/TR/2004/REC-xmlschema-2-20041028/`.

W3C-XML-SCHEMA-PRIMER-1.0. *XML Schema Part 0: Primer (Second Edition)*, David C. Fallside and Priscilla Walmsley (editors). World Wide Web Consortium, October 2004. `http://www.w3.org/TR/2004/REC-xmlschema-0-20041028/`.

W3C-XML-SCHEMA-STRUCT-1.0. *XML Schema Part 1: Structures (Second Edition)*, Henry S. Thompson, David Beech, Murray Maloney, and Noah Mendelsohn (editors). World Wide Web Consortium, October 2004. `http://www.w3.org/TR/2004/REC-xmlschema-1-20041028/`.

W3C-XML-STYLE-1.0. *Associating Style Sheets with XML Documents Version 1.0*, James Clark (editor). World Wide Web Consortium, June 1999. `http://www.w3.org/1999/06/REC-xml-stylesheet-19990629/`.

W3C-XPATH-1.0. *XML Path Language (XPath) Version 1.0*, James Clark and Steve DeRose (editors). World Wide Web Consortium, November 1999. `http://www.w3.org/TR/1999/REC-xpath-19991116`.

W3C-XSLT-1.0. *XSL Transformations (XSLT) Version 1.0*, James Clark (editor). World Wide Web Consortium, November 1999. `http://www.w3.org/TR/1999/REC-xslt-19991116`.

Index